POPULAR MECHANICS DO-IT-YOURSELF ENCYCLOPEDIA

POPULAR MECHANICS DO-IT-YOURSELF ENCYCLOPEDIA

FOR

HOME OWNER, CRAFTSMAN

AND HOBBYIST

IN TWELVE VOLUMES

Volume VIII

Complete Index in Volume XII

J. J. LITTLE & IVES Co., Inc. • NEW YORK

DESIGNED AND PRODUCED BY
BOOKSERVICE AMERICA, NEW YORK

FIRST PRINTING 1955
PRINTED IN THE UNITED STATES OF AMERICA

PAINTING
Interior and Exterior

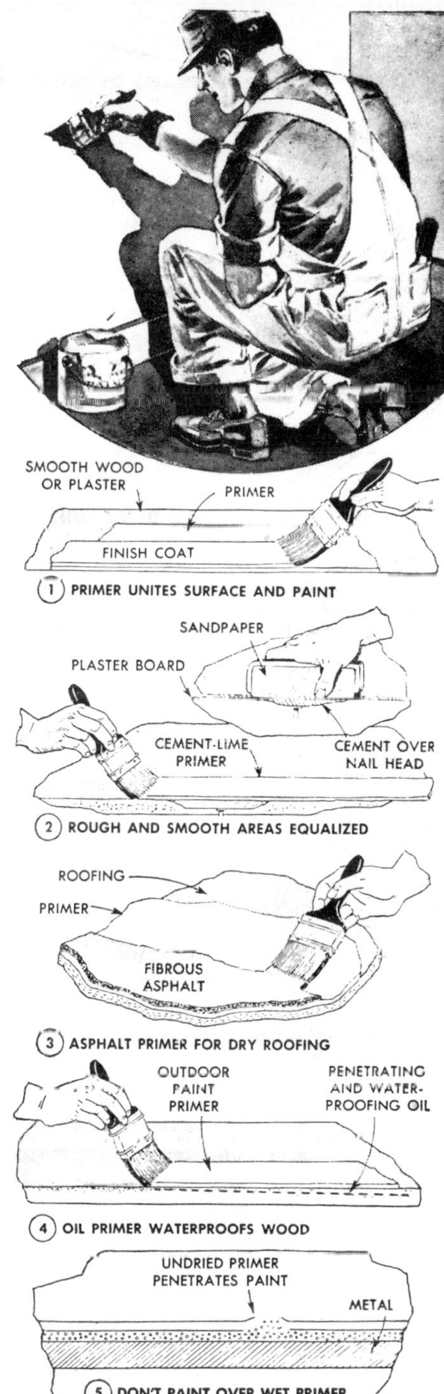

(1) PRIMER UNITES SURFACE AND PAINT

(2) ROUGH AND SMOOTH AREAS EQUALIZED

(3) ASPHALT PRIMER FOR DRY ROOFING

(4) OIL PRIMER WATERPROOFS WOOD

(5) DON'T PAINT OVER WET PRIMER

UNDERCOATING

SELECTING the right primer for any paint job depends upon the kind of paint you intend to use and the surface to be covered. As shown in Fig. 1, on a smooth, indoor wood or plaster surface, the primer acts as a seal over the work surface, and combines readily with the paint to form a uniform, even finish coat. If, however, the surface is made up of both hard, compact areas and rough, soft spots, such as are produced on plaster board when cemented areas over joints or countersunk nail heads are sanded smooth, Fig. 2, the primer must equalize the surface texture so that when painted the hard areas will not show as slick spots and the rough areas will not absorb the paint and appear as dull blotches. Where oil paint having a lustrous finish is used on such a surface, it is best to apply two primers, one consisting of a cement-lime ingredient to produce a toothy layer that will equalize the surface, and another made up of the proper base ingredients to unite with the paint. It is more economical to use two primer coats than to try to cover an imperfectly prepared surface with several coats of finish paint.

A primer used on dried-out composition roofs should be some nonfibrous asphalt liquid capable of resaturating the felt, after which a coat of heavy fibrous asphalt is applied, Fig. 3. Under heavy-bodied outdoor paints, primers having greater bonding strength than those applied on indoor work should be used. To gain this additional bonding strength, a primer must be able to penetrate the surface of wood or other porous material, Fig. 4. Therefore, it should contain penetrating and waterproofing oil. A satisfactory primer for metal surfaces must adhere firmly, be waterproof, and provide a suitable base for the finish paint. Also, it must have full drying time. Red lead and outdoor aluminum paint are commonly used over metals. If paint is applied before the primer has dried, the unevaporated, volatile content, sealed underneath by the nonporous metal, will be forced to penetrate the paint layer over it, Fig. 5.

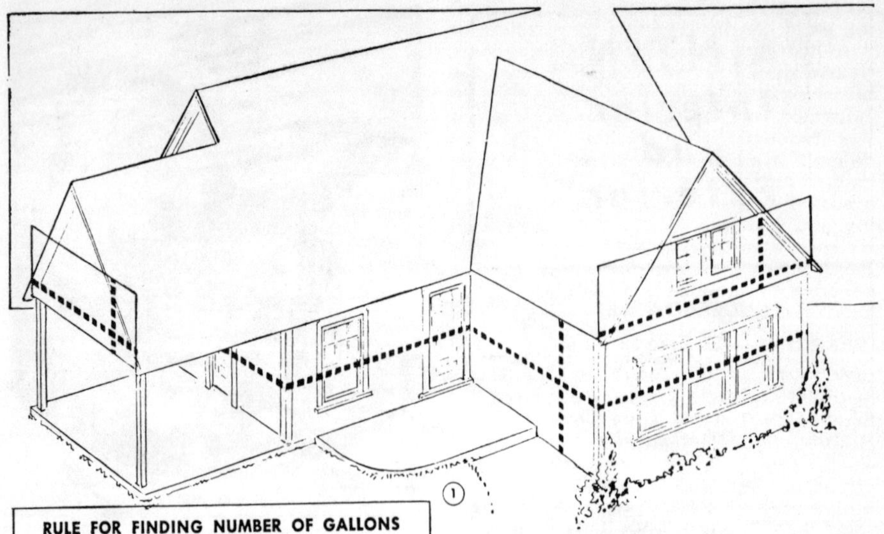

RULE FOR FINDING NUMBER OF GALLONS REQUIRED

Measure distance around house in lineal feet. Multiply by height to eaves. Divide by 600 where surface is in good condition—by 400 if surface is in poor condition. Measure width of gables and multiply by half the height

PRIMER
UNDERCOAT
2nd COAT
FINISH COAT
3rd COAT

(2) TWO ACCEPTED METHODS OF PAINTING THE AVERAGE FRAME HOME

The result is a breakdown of the entire paint surface and a spoiled job.

Good paint will stick to almost any surface—for a while. How long it stays on is something else, for in the matter of durability it's what's under the paint film that counts. In general, the appearance of a house is not always a reliable guide to the condition of the surface over which paint is to be applied. Rather, adhesion of the paint film, original quality and formula of the paint and the condition of the building structurally are usually the factors determining the amount of work it will take to get the surfaces in proper condition for repainting.

Old paint worn thin by slow chalking and weathering—both normal processes—may appear to be in poor condition. But because of tight adherence to the wood and a solid bond between what remains of previous coating, it still will provide a good painting surface, Fig. 3. However, if the surface presents one or more of the defects shown in Figs. 4, 5, 10 and 11, which have been somewhat exaggerated for purposes of illustration, then the job of preparation

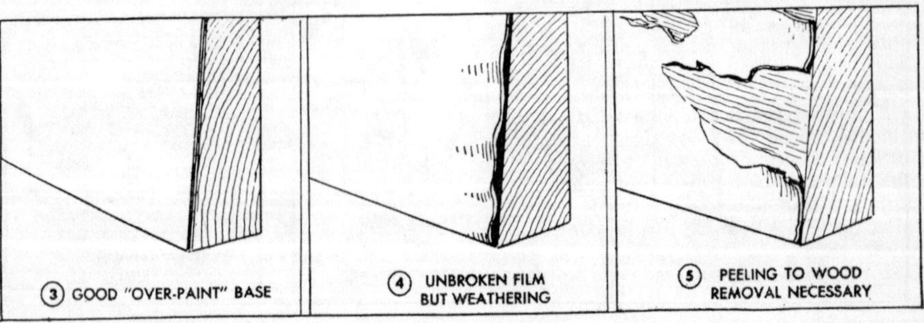

(3) GOOD "OVER-PAINT" BASE

(4) UNBROKEN FILM BUT WEATHERING

(5) PEELING TO WOOD REMOVAL NECESSARY

for repainting will be more extended. Scaling paint can be removed by scraping or wire-brushing, after which the surfaces are treated similar to new wood. But extensive blistering of the paint film and the peculiar "alligator," or "crackled lacquer," surfaces less frequently seen are among the most difficult of all defects to remedy. In most cases complete removal is necessary, but if a blistered area is small a thorough scraping and sanding to level the paint film which still adheres sometimes will suffice. Paint remover in the paste form also is effective on small areas. Likewise, the prepared remover may be used in cleaning off small spaces presenting cracked, chipped or alligator surfaces. It also is especially effective in cleaning up turnings, newels and ornamental work which frequently adorns porches and cornices of very old houses. However, where the area is large, such as a side or gable end of the building, burning off the defective paint film to the wood with a blowtorch, Fig. 6, is considered the best practice. Unless you are accustomed to the work it's best to get experienced help for this job. In any case, it's essential that the siding be tight, that the flame be directed against the surface at an angle and slightly downward, and that the torch be moved continually to prevent charring the wood. Follow the flame with a scraper to remove the softened paint immediately. And always work with the torch on a quiet day—never when it's windy.

The first coat of paint applied to any surface to fill the pores and form a hard surface is the primer. Priming must always be freshly made from pigments ground in refined linseed oil, paste driers and pure turpentine or mineral spirit. The priming solution is sold ready for use. The use of old flat paint (smudge), the aggregate of leavings from other jobs, as priming is unsatisfactory. The partially oxidized oil content prevents penetration of the surface and creates a film that is too elastic to withstand the surface strain developed by the aging of the superimposed paint.

Fig. 2 illustrates two accepted methods

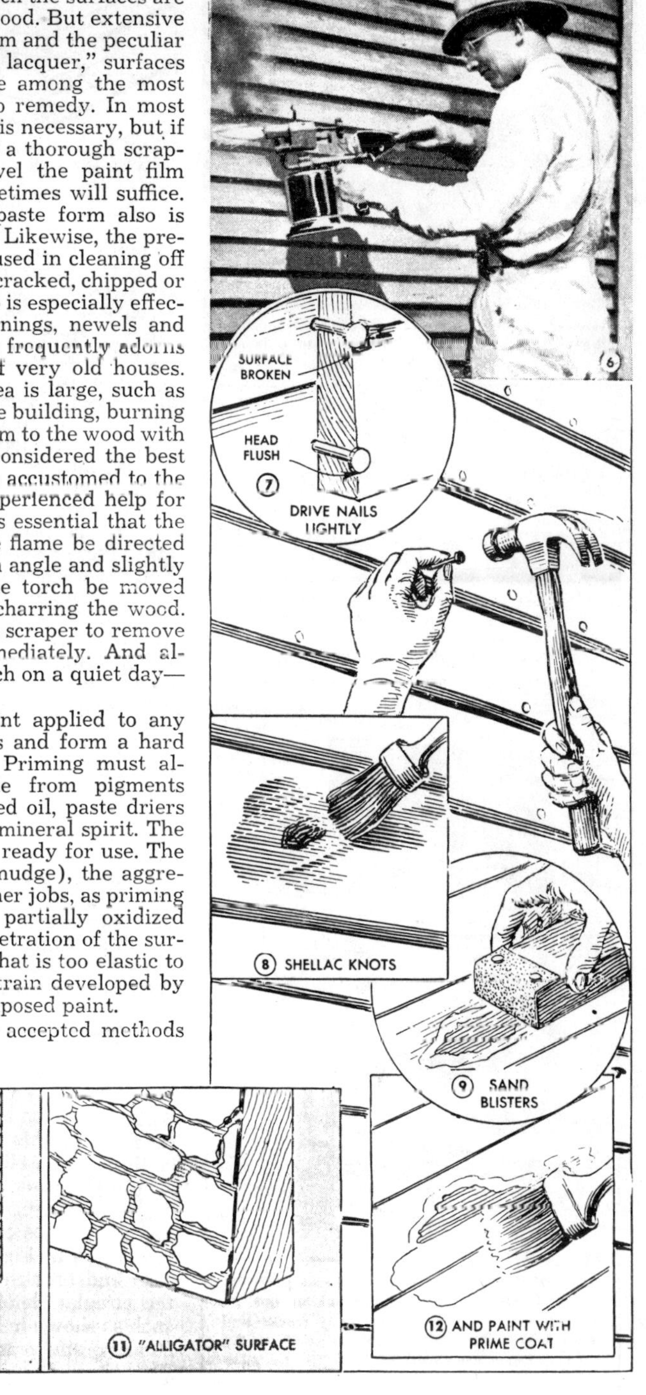

(13) Siding should be thoroughly wire-brushed to remove all loose pigment. Follow wire-brushing with a light dusting immediately before applying fresh paint to the surface

(15) End checks and cracks in trim boards, door stiles and rails, sash and window frames should be cleaned and coated with primer before filling with white-lead putty

(16) Reconditioning old sash and frames preparatory to painting involves breaking out all loose putty, priming and filling cracks and checks, and in some cases tightening up the sash frames by nailing loose rails to stiles

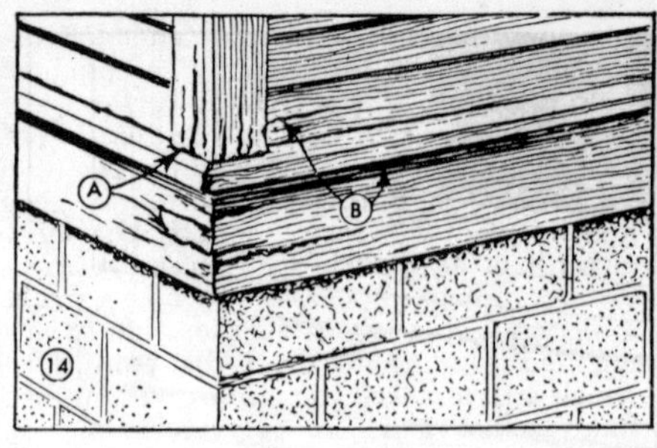

of painting the average frame home—two coats over a primer, or one finish coat over a prepared undercoater. If you paint at intervals of less than four or five years the latter method is sufficient. But if the painting schedule calls for renewal only once in five years or longer, the three-coat job usually is recommended. Preparation begins with an estimate of the amount of paint required for the job. Unless the surfaces are in unusually poor condition this can be calculated with fair accuracy by means of the simple procedure and formula shown in Fig. 1. Of course, in using the formula other factors should be taken into account. For example, where there are more than the ordinary number of windows or glass-paneled doors, it is safe to deduct the area of the glass. "Cut-up" gable construction and varying heights to the eaves also will affect the accuracy of the calculation.

Next, where the house is of frame construction, the siding comes in for a thorough going over. Often it will be necessary to renail the siding, especially where it is exposed to weathering. Siding "cupped" outward between the studding calls for care in renailing. Use short, galvanized nails as these hold better when driven into the sheathing boards, and drill undersized pilot holes through the siding. Usually it's better to use two nails for each space between studs as in Fig. 7. Drive the heads flush, but do not sink them below the surface. After renailing go over all the siding, window frames, trim and cornices with a wire brush as in Fig. 13. This will remove any loose material that might flake off under the new coats of paint. It's a good idea to wear an approved respirator if you do much of this work. If any knots show through, sand off the paint and shellac as in Fig. 8. Some painters use spar varnish for this purpose. Any blistered spots where the paint chips off to the wood should be treated as in Figs. 9 and 12. Go over all sash and break out the loose putty as in the circular detail of Fig. 16. Conditions such as shown in Figs. 14, 15, 16, 17, 19 and 20 are quite common on the older houses. First clean the dirt out of all cracks and

All spaces bared by removal of loose putty from sash should be coated with primer

openings of the kind shown, then apply the first coat of primer as it comes from the container, without thinning. Brush at right angles to the cracks as in Fig. 15 to work the paint well into them. At the same time coat all bared spots on the sash where old putty has been removed as in Fig. 18. After this paint coating is thoroughly dry fill the cracks with a paste white-lead putty, using a regular glazier's putty only on the sash. Paste white lead as it comes in the container usually will serve, but if it should be too soft it may be brought to proper consistency by adding a small quantity of whiting. It's important to fill the cracks completely, otherwise the putty soon will loosen and drop out. At this stage some master painters remove all outside doors and prime-coat the bottom edges, first making sure that the doors close easily without sticking. When applying paint in the manner described it's essential to brush out all excess to a thin film so that it does not show through succeeding coats. Siding boards which are lapped at the corners frequently warp and split and the end grain weathers badly in time. No amount of paint will hide this unsightly defect. Treat these corners as shown in Fig. 20, first renailing if necessary. Siding boards mitered at the corners sometimes warp slightly and pull apart, opening the joint. Master painters often gently pry these joints open far enough to fill the space with white-lead putty. Then renailing will tighten the joints once more to a neat fit. In any of these preparatory jobs where white-lead or glazier's putty is used it is of the greatest importance that the putty be allowed to dry thoroughly before paint is applied over it.

Fig. 16, details A to G inclusive, show the common defects one finds on old sash and window frames, particularly where intervals between paintings are longer than average. Frequently the lower rail will be loose, perhaps dropped partially at one or both ends due to opening of the joints and weight of the glass, as at D. In many cases this defect can be repaired by wedging the rail back into place and nailing through into the stile, using a single large finishing nail. Paint the cracks in the trim boards and fill with the lead putty as already described. Do the same with the sash frame where necessary, Fig. 17, A and B. Also, you may find small openings where the siding boards butt against the

(19) Cracks in old porch columns must be filled with white-lead putty before painting

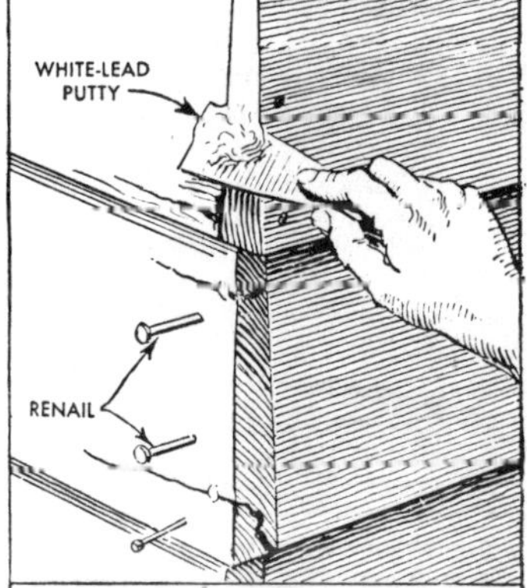

(20) Coat the end grain of corner-lapped wide siding boards with white-lead putty and renail the corners if it is necessary to close wide cracks

Usually it's best to remove sash for puttying as only small breaks can be repaired effectively with the sash in the frames

frames of brick buildings is a regular practice and usually the caulking should run all around the frame, including sills and thresholds, Fig. 24. Frequently, rather fine, irregular cracks following the mortar joints will be seen in brick walls. Those shown in Fig. 22 are quite common and are generally due to settling. Usually caulking compound gunned into such cracks makes a suitable repair as it will remain semiplastic after drying and will not break out even though there be slight movement between the edges. It also effectively keeps out water and frost. However, if the crack is wider than 1/4 in. the repair generally should be made by pointing up with mortar. Likewise, brick walls in rather bad condition, Fig. 23, with brick faces eroded and mortar crumbled out of the joints, should be pointed before painting. Buildings and homes of ornamental brick seldom are painted, but homes of all other types of brick—common, soft, pressed and de-aired—often are made more attractive architecturally and more durable by painting. Either the so-called white-lead-and-oil paints or the water-soluble paints made especially for outside masonry can be used satisfactorily on brick. The oil paint dries with a slight gloss on brick in good condition while the water paints dry with a flat, nongloss surface. Either paint is especially effective in "dressing up" old homes of brick. Except for the hard-pressed and de-aired

Caulking will effectively seal small cracks in both brick and stonework

Brick walls in badly eroded condition should be pointed with mortar before painting

window frames or the corner boards, B in Fig. 14. Here's where the caulking gun comes in handy. Run a line of caulking compound into corner board and siding cracks and all around the window frames, also into the crack under the sill, as at A in Fig. 17. If the stops, G in Fig. 16, are loose, gently pry out the strip, prime-coat it and tap it back into place. Finally, putty the sash in the manner described, Fig. 21. In most cases, it is better to remove the sash from the frame for puttying, as it is easier to do the job properly with the sash flat and on a solid support. Smooth the putty into place with considerable pressure of the knife so that it will bond properly to both the wood and glass without any open spaces beneath. Open cracks usually will be found underneath boxed cornices, Fig. 27, and, although the wood is not subjected to weathering, the open cracks allow passage of cold air in winter and insects in summer. Fill with a caulking gun as indicated. If you find it necessary to seal the joint between a porch roof and the siding with roofing compound, Fig. 28, this should be done before painting. Such roofs should be flashed to the siding, of course, but in some instances it is easier to maintain the seal with roofing compound where flashing was not originally used.

Figs. 22 and 23 show two common defects, due largely to natural causes, which must be remedied before painting brick walls. Caulking around window and door

Window frames in old brick homes must be recaulked before painting. Be sure that the cracks are filled flush with the surface

types, brick is porous and absorbs paint faster than most kinds of unpainted wood. For this reason the coverage per gallon on brick painted for the first time generally is considerably less than on any bare wood.

If the brick is in good condition and all common defects have been repaired as previously described, there need be little other preparatory work, except that on very old brick homes a light wire-brushing is helpful in removing dirt and loose sand. Sometimes there are discolorations beneath windows due to rusty screens, soot or dirt. Usually a thorough brushing with a handled wire brush will suffice. Discolorations due to other causes, such as mildew or "sweating" chimneys, should be treated with a zinc-sulphate solution or white asphaltum before painting. Follow the manufacturer's directions when applying any of these preparations.

Before painting brick with a water-soluble paint it generally is recommended that the wall be kept moist just ahead of the paint application. This can be done with a wheelbarrow sprayer, wetting only a small area at a time. A damp wall retards drying, making it possible to apply these fast-setting paints without brush marks or laps showing. On the other hand, when applying a lead-and-oil paint it is essential that the brick be thoroughly dry.

Two more points to think of before you paint are (1) the formula of the paint applied previously, and (2) how the paint you are to apply may change the appearance of the building. Using the lighter colors and white over a surface previously coated with a paint containing a tinting pigment of any of the so-called "earth" colors may under certain conditions cause "bleeding," that is, the darker color underneath may bleed through to the surface of the new paint, resulting in spotty discolorations. However, on old work in reasonably good condition where the previous paintings have been oxidized thoroughly, a good wire-brushing to remove all loose material down to the hard surface underneath and the use of a prepared undercoater is sufficient precaution against the possibility of bleeding.

"Before" and "after" views show how painting changes appearance

Cracks around cornices usually are best filled with a caulking gun. Be sure to force sufficient compound into the opening so that the soft material will bond to the wood

Joints between siding and roofs should be resealed with paste roofing compound before painting, or better, flashed to the siding if this was not done on the original work

Figs. 25 and 26 are an example of how painting sometimes changes the appearance of an old house, of either brick or frame construction. Note in this instance how certain constructional details have been almost completely hidden by the paint job, while other features, particularly the size of the house, have been emphasized. Generally the lighter colors, including white especially, will tend to make the house appear larger in its setting. It's always well to bear in mind that painting can be used to accentuate or minimize certain details of a structure as well as to preserve its surface.

PAINTING THE OUTSIDE

Painting the outside of the house provides the surface with both protection and decoration. As explained previously, the outside surface must be thoroughly cleansed of rust, dirt and grease. Old paint should be removed by burning off or by means of a liquid paint remover. Knots and resin spots in wood should be coated with knotting. After following the directions in applying the primer and treating the wood with filler, you are ready to apply the first coat of paint to the outside of the house. If followed through properly, there is no reason why the paint job shouldn't last for a few years.

Repainting the exterior of your home regularly every three to five years is the cheapest home repair. An unbroken film of paint protects the surface against weathering and against changes in temperature and variations in moisture content which cause swelling and checking of wood. Paint also discourages various fungus growths that flourish in the presence of moisture and cause rapid decay of siding and framing. A good paint job increases the appraisal value of the property as much as 10 percent by adding the beauty of durable harmonious color to both new and old homes. A little time spent in learning the proper painting procedures and how to wield a paintbrush with professional skill pays off in substantial savings to the homeowner who will tackle the job himself.

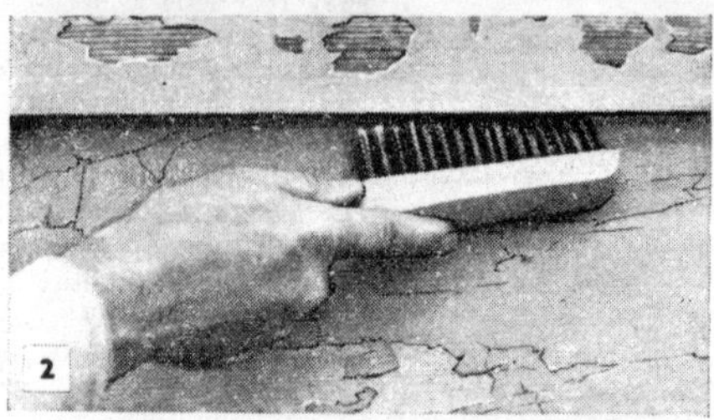

Remove all loose, flaking and blistered paint with wire brush and scraper. Exposed wood is then primed

When to paint: Just when to paint depends on the local weather conditions but, in general, paint can be applied any time when the surface is dry and the temperature is fairly certain to remain above 50 deg. F. until the paint is dry. Avoid painting on hot, humid days or any time when a high wind is blowing as the freshly painted surface may become coated with dust and, in the summer, with small insects. The best time to paint a house is during a period of clear, cool weather, as the humidity usually is low and the drying conditions are ideal.

Above, before painting, dust is brushed from corners and horizontal surfaces where it always accumulates. Below, after loose putty has been removed and the bare wood primed, new glazier's putty is applied

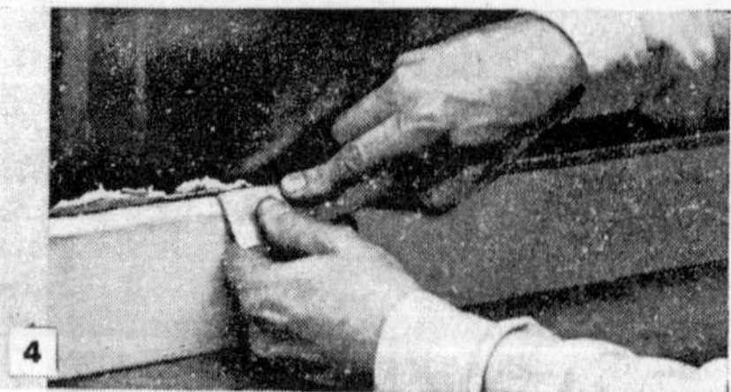

Selecting the paint: This depends to some extent on whether the building needs a one, two or three-coat job, and whether the first requirement is a full priming or only a spot priming after cleaning and dusting thoroughly. Manufacturers of paints now supply special primers, or undercoaters, for both new and old work which are especially compounded to "build" a suitable surface over which to apply a finishing coat. When preparing ready-mixed paints for use, pay close attention to the manufacturer's recommendations for reducing them to a brushing consistency. When undercoaters are used on old work on which the paint is in fair to good condition, one coat of undercoater and one finishing coat usually will produce a first-class job. Master painters seldom use three coats except in some cases where it is necessary to remove all the old paint down to the bare wood or, in rare instances, where the color used makes a three-coat job necessary to build a paint film of sufficient body to hide discolorations or other surface defects. Very often one coat will be sufficient to produce a crisp, neat job over old paint of the same color.

How much paint: Although there are many factors which will determine the actual amount required for the job, it's easy to get a rough estimate of the number of gallons needed by figuring the number of square feet to be painted. Just multiply the width in feet by the height on rectangular areas. On the gables, multiply the width by one-half the height. Add the results and do not deduct for windows or doors. On a fair to good surface, a gallon of outside paint, or undercoater, will cover with one coat about 600 sq. ft. However, the coverage will vary from 450 to 750 sq. ft. depending on the condition of the surface. On a good surface, the coverage per gallon of the finish coat over an undercoater will probably average 750, and possibly 800 sq. ft. The undercoaters greatly extend the coverage of the finish coat even on surfaces which are in relatively poor condition for a finishing coat.

The undercoat is the layer of paint between the primer and the finishing coats. The function of the undercoat is to build up a substantial film to obscure the ground and provide a firm surface for the final coatings. In color, these coatings should be about the shade of the final covering. The undercoat must be applied with care, because careless brushwork cannot be covered later.

Preparing the surface: Chalking of paint is a normal weathering process unless, of course, the chalking is excessive. On a surface that is chalking normally, a slight rubbing on a small spot will produce a dull luster. If this condition is uniform all over the building a light dusting will prepare the surfaces for painting. On

Calking seals open joints where doors and windows join masonry. A gun applies it easily and quickly

FIRST BRUSH DUST FROM CRACKS

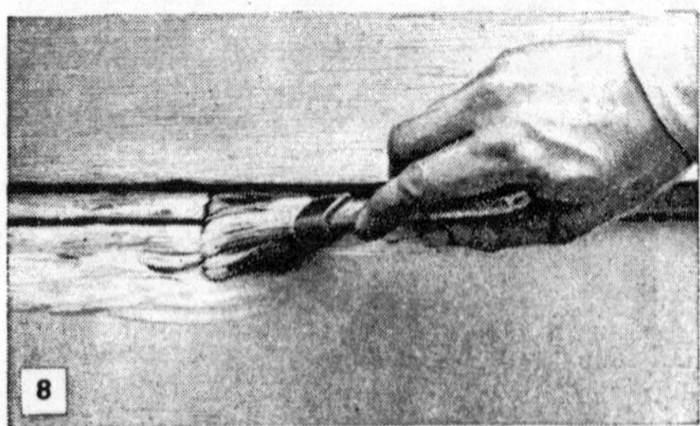

NEXT, APPLY PRIMING COAT

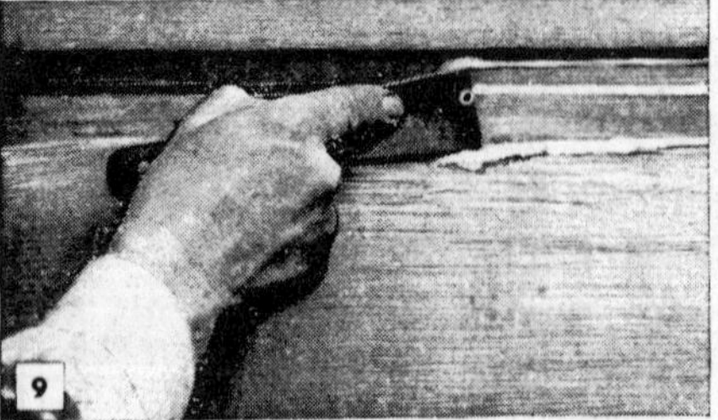

THEN FILL WITH "WHITE LEAD" PUTTY

the other hand, if bare patches of wood show here and there and if rubbing the surface fails to produce even a dull luster, wire-brushing will be necessary to clean the surfaces of fine, loose particles and flakes of paint pigment. Two coats will be needed to finish such a surface. If the old paint is broken by fine checks or has blistered and peeled rather badly, then more labor will be required to prepare the building for repainting. All the loose material must be removed by scraping and wire-brushing, Fig. 2. The rough edges of the paint film around the bare spots where blisters have occurred must be leveled by sanding and building up a new film by spot-priming. (Caution: It is advisable to wear a respirator when sanding, scraping or wire-brushing a painted surface.) Areas which are deeply checked by horizontal and vertical cracks—painters refer to this condition as an "alligator" surface—may either be sanded smooth or the paint removed entirely with a paint remover and the paint film rebuilt by prime-coating, followed by the regular undercoater and finish coats applied in the course of painting the whole structure. When preparing the building for repainting, examine the surface closely for the light-brownish discolorations caused by paint mildew. This is more likely to be found on old structures just above the foundation and under a wide cornice, and also on the siding back of large shrubs. The fungi, or molds, which are responsible thrive only in the presence of moisture and the cause should be removed before repainting. The dry mold can be removed by washing with household ammonia or with a solution of trisodium phosphate. Rinse with clear water after washing. All minor structural repairs, such as nailing loose siding, filling cracks and replacing gutters and downspouts which are no longer serviceable, should be made before repainting. Dust window sills as in Fig. 3 and prime and reputty old sash as in Fig. 4. Remove all the loose putty first, then prime the open rabbet before applying new putty. Fill cracks and nail holes, using the procedure pictured in Figs. 7, 8 and 9, with special white-lead putty consisting of 1 part white lead in oil and 2 parts of whiting by volume. This is softened to a working consistency with japan oil. Calk around door and window frames as in Fig. 6, using a gun and calking compound of gun grade. Spot-prime all areas where the old paint has been removed down to bare wood. Seal any exposed knots and resinous areas with orange shellac.

Brushes and equipment: For the average job you'll need a 1-in. sash brush, a 3-in. brush for doors and trim, and a 4 or 5-in. brush for painting the siding. Carry a dusting brush, a putty knife, a wire brush and a scraper. Ladders needed will depend on the size of the house, of course, but a stepladder is essential and an extension ladder will be needed to reach the high gables. Usually, painting of the walls can be done faster and safer from a scaffold rigged with heavy planks and ladder jacks. The two sections of the extension ladder can be used for this purpose.

Mixing the paint: Both the undercoater and the finishing paint must be thoroughly mixed before using. Pour the paint from the pail into a larger container and stir with a flat paddle, adding reducer in small quantities as the stirring proceeds. To check the consistency, lift the paddle from time to time. When the mixture has been thinned to the proper brushing consistency, the paint on the paddle will run back into the container in a thin, steady stream which finally breaks into a series of drops. If the paint drips slowly into the container, it is too thick and will drag under the brush.

Where to start: As a rule, one should begin painting at the peak of the highest gable and work down as in Fig. 5. When working from a ladder, it usually is more convenient to bring the trim down on the high gables at the same time the siding is painted. Otherwise avoid working with two colors at the same time. When painting siding, begin at the corner board or, on gables, at the frieze board, and paint the lower edges first as in Fig. 10. Then lay the paint on the flat surfaces and brush it out by using the procedure detailed in Fig. 11, A to D inclusive. When painting siding, do not attempt to cover a panel more than five to eight boards in width. Finish this panel across the wall to a corner, or to a door or window before stopping. If you stop anywhere on the wall for more than a few minutes, the paint will set partially, making it impossible to brush out the lap when you begin again. This lap will show under several coats of any light-colored paint. It's a rule always to finish the panel to a corner or other suitable stopping place before you end work for the day or for other reasons.

Handling the brush: When working from a ladder at the higher levels, it's usually handier to paint above the ladder, as you can reach both ways and thus avoid the labor of moving a heavy ladder frequently. In handling the brush on long strokes, use a free and easy motion of the arm and wrist. The trick in lifting the brush off the painted surface without leaving a mark at the end of the stroke is to turn the brush slightly as it is lifted. This movement lifts the bristles with a wiping motion which does not leave a mark on the fresh paint film. Leveling and finishing strokes should overlap, details C and D in Fig. 11. Finishing

10

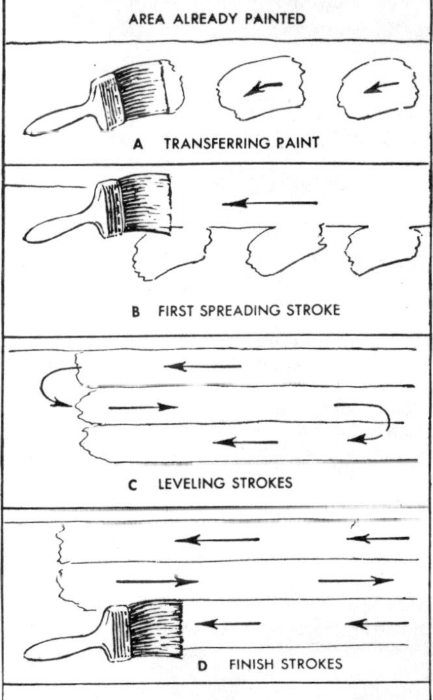

For uniform distribution of paint and the least spattering, first transfer the load from brush to surface with a few daubs, A. Then spread by right and left strokes, B and C. Finish with sweeping strokes as at D

11

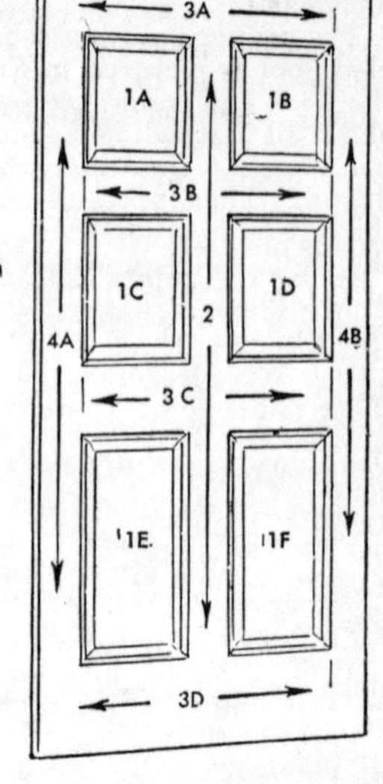

12

On paneled doors, prevent laps and brush marks by using proper painting sequence. Paint molds and beveled edges first as on the panel above. Finish each in the order indicated. Then finish crossrails and stiles in the sequence shown

13 PAINTING SEQUENCE FOR PANELED DOORS

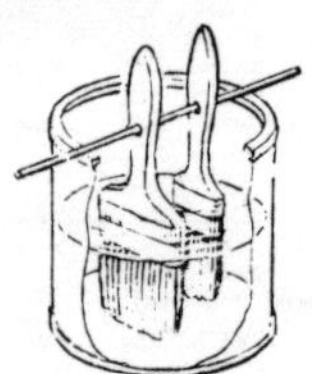

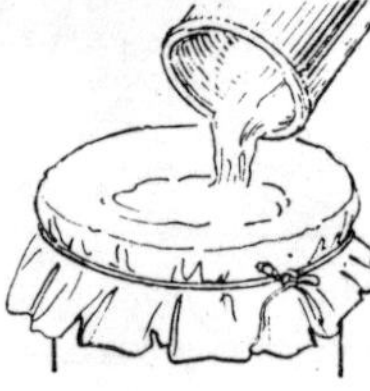

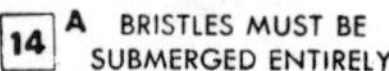

14 A BRISTLES MUST BE SUBMERGED ENTIRELY B PAINT CLEANED BY STRAINING

strokes should be light to avoid carrying the paint from one area to another, resulting in an uneven coverage. Each time the brush is dipped in the paint, slap the bristles against the side of the pail to remove the excess which may otherwise drip onto the siding below or onto the ground and be wasted. The first coat will require more brushing than the second, or finish, coat. Care must be taken to brush each coat to a uniform thickness. On buildings which have not been painted for a number of years the surface will absorb the oils in the first coat more quickly than will a surface which has been painted recently. Here, special care must be taken to prevent the undercoater from building too fast as it is applied, resulting in a heavy, uneven coating which may wrinkle or break up on drying. One way to avoid trouble under this condition is to cut down on the amount of paint picked up at each dip of the brush. Dust off the surface thoroughly just before applying the undercoat. On a good drying day, the paint in the pail may tend to thicken somewhat owing to evaporation of a small quantity of its volatile oils, especially toward the end of the day. Add a little reducer and stir occasionally to prevent this. Drying time allowed between coats should never be less than 48 hours. A week to 10 days is better.

Sash, trim and doors: Cutting-in sash, Fig. 1, with a paint either lighter or darker than the trim color requires skillful handling of the sash brush to produce a neat, workmanlike job. It is, of course, much simpler to paint the sash with the trim color, particularly on double-hung wooden sash where otherwise it is essential to cut a sharp color line at the point where the sash stiles and the upper rail meet the stops. When trim color is used this is not necessary. In either case, the first thing to do is lower the upper sash so that you can reach the outer side of the lower-sash check rail. On double-hung sash, this is always painted the outside color as it is exposed to view from the outside when the lower sash is raised. In painting divided-pane sash, cut in the muntins first on both the top and bottom edges. (The muntins are the vertical and horizontal bars which join the stiles and rails of divided, or multiple-pane, sash.) Keep the sash brush well loaded with paint so that it will stroke, or cut, a full-bodied line to an unpainted edge. Paint the sash stiles and rails and the window frames and casings last. If the sash have been scraped and sanded in preparation for repainting, it will pay to apply an undercoater. This will build a good base over which to apply the finish coat.

The proper painting sequence on a paneled door is pictured in Figs. 12 and 13. If the door and frame are in good condition, about all that will be needed to prepare for painting is a thorough wire-brushing and dusting. Then proceed as in Fig. 12 and the left-hand detail in Fig. 13, by painting the ovolo molds and the rabbeted portion of the raised panel. The proper sequence is shown in the right-hand detail, Fig. 13. Begin with panel 1A and continue in the order indicated until panel 1F has been finished. Cut-in the molds and rabbets first, then finish the entire panel. Next, take the center stile 2 and follow by painting top rail 3A first, then 3B, 3C and 3D. Finish with the outside stiles 4A and 4B. On an outside door, paint the top and bottom edges. If the door swings out, the edge on the lock side also takes the outside color. The outside color line comes to the outside corner of the doorstop all the way around the frame on doors that swing out. On doors that swing in, only the edge to which the hinges are attached takes the outside color. The outside color comes to the inner corner of the stops. To get a neat, sharply cut line around the hinges and lock plate requires careful work. Often it will save time to remove the hinges and lock plates before painting.

Painting metal: Gutters, downspouts and metal porch rails should be carefully wire-brushed to remove scale and rust. If the gutters have been previously primed and painted and the coating is still in good condition, repriming will not be necessary. New galvanized gutters and downspouts should weather six months before priming and painting. However, iron grillwork and railings should be primed with special primers before painting in the color desired.

Paint and brush care: Keep all paint containers closed tightly when not in use. The paint in the container you use regularly becomes contaminated with dust and particles of dirt. Strain frequently into a clean container through a piece of cheesecloth or silk hosiery as in Fig. 14, B. To prevent paint on brushes from hardening overnight hang them in water with the bristles submerged as in Fig. 14, A. If the brushes are out of use for a longer period, hang them in a solution of turpentine and linseed oil, equal parts. When the painting is finished for the season, clean brushes in two or three changes of turpentine, wash in a trisodium-phosphate solution and then in warm, soapy water. Before storing the brushes, rinse them thoroughly and, after drying, wrap them in oiled paper to protect the bristles from dust.

Selecting a brush: For wall painting, inside and outside, a flat wall brush is used. The professional painter usually prefers a long-bristle brush for the reason that it holds more paint, therefore requiring fewer dips to the paint pot, and enabling one to cover more square feet of surface per day.

The real value of a paintbrush is not in the kind of ferrule or the size and shape of the handle but in the bristles. Of course, a quality brush will have a handle designed to make the whole thing balance to a nicety and it will be shaped to fit the hand comfortably. The ferrule will be made to assure rigidity of the handle, but after all, the bristles do the work. A long-bristle brush will also last longer under steady, continuous service. For the amateur, however, a short-bristle brush is better, as one must be experienced in order to use the long-bristle brush. The former, if made of high-quality bristles properly balanced, will do good work and costs considerably less. Wall brushes are made in various widths from 3 in. to 5 in., the most popular being 3½ and 4-in. sizes.

For varnishing, enameling and lacquering, a flat varnish brush is ordinarily used. Most of the high-grade varnish brushes are made with a chisel or tapered edge, being so shaped to permit easier flowing of the varnish, enamel or lacquer. Flat varnish brushes come in different widths from 1 in. to 3 in., the width used depending upon the size and nature of the surface to be finished. For window sash, spindles, scrollwork, etc., the painter uses a sash brush—a small-size tool from 1 to 2 in. wide for working in close places, and a wider one for larger trim work. Sash and trim brushes are made with a long handle. Another type that should be mentioned here is the calcimine brush which is usually about 7 or 8 in. wide, with a sturdy handle. The important thing about calcimine brushes is their care. They should be washed in clean water immediately after using, the bristles straightened out, and the brush hung up by the handle to dry. The calcimine brush should never be used in oil paints. Careful painters always use a dusting brush for cleaning dust, cobwebs and soot off the surface before painting. Dusting brushes are made in the same general way as the ordinary paintbrush, but with finer bristles, and are available in both flat and round styles. You'll find it's good economy to keep several brushes on hand and use separate ones for painting, varnishing, lacquering and enameling. If, for example, you use a varnish brush for paint, it will be impossible to clean it satisfactorily for use in varnish again, no matter how carefully it is done.

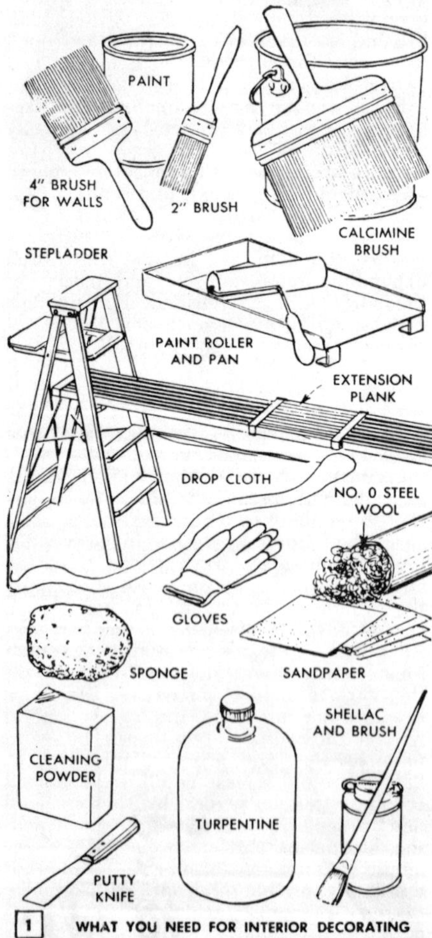

1 WHAT YOU NEED FOR INTERIOR DECORATING

PAINTING THE INSIDE

It's easy for any homeowner to do good interior painting by following the simple but important steps of correct procedure in both preparatory work and painting.

Kinds of paint: Paint selection for interior work depends largely on the effect desired—on whether you want a gloss, semigloss or flat finish. Today most oil paints and enamels for interior use are relatively fast drying. Gloss finishes, often used in kitchens and bathrooms, dry to a hard finish, shed dust and wash easily. Semigloss or eggshell finishes produce less glare and, therefore, are preferred generally for living, dining and bedrooms. The latest type of semigloss enamels have excellent wearability and are easy to apply. Flat paints eliminate glare almost completely but soil easily and show fingermarks. As they set within a few minutes, they are somewhat difficult for the average layman to apply.

Enamels are made in grades to suit internal or external surfaces and the best results can be obtained only if an enamel is used on the surface for which it was made. Full-gloss, semigloss and flat finishes are supplied in an almost unlimited color range. A surface to be enameled must be prepared so that it is nonabsorbent and perfectly even, with very fine granulation to assist grip. The enamel is applied with fairly compact brushes, well brushed-out and finished with heavy strokes.

Water-soluble paints come in powder or paste form. They include calcimine and casein as well as the more complex resin-emulsion paints. Most water-soluble paints have excellent hiding power and cover in one coat, although many oil paints of similar consistency will cover equally well. It is possible to clean water-soluble paints fairly well by rubbing lightly with a sponge, clean rag or soft brush moistened with soapy water. The resin-emulsion paints will withstand ordinary cleaning. Calcimine cannot be washed to clean it but must be removed entirely and replaced. Repainting over some types of water-soluble paints with oil paints is possible if a special sealer is first applied. However, in the case of casein paints, the best practice is to remove the old coat with the aid of paint remover. This is neutralized with turpentine which is allowed to dry before oil paint is applied.

Plastic texture paints, available in either water-soluble or oil-base types, are used to improve the appearance of old walls which are in such poor condition that the surface defects and irregularities cannot be concealed by ordinary paints. This type of paint produces rough-textured finishes.

The characteristics of any particular brand of paint and the amount required for

How to get professional results and make big savings by doing the work yourself. Includes important preparatory steps and many little tricks of painting

a job should be taken up with the paint dealer. A one-coat repaint job is often sufficient to cover a previously painted wall of the same or nearly the same color. Two coats generally are required if there is a change in color. When applying two coats, the first should be allowed to dry for 12 to 18 hours before the second is applied.

Often enamel undercoater is applied to a surface prior to enameling it. The purpose is to produce the best possible bond between the two, thereby lessening the tendency of the enamel to chip and also providing a base on which a substantial amount of enamel can be applied with minimum trouble from runs and sags.

Tools and equipment: Fig. 1 shows what you need. For fast, uniform coverage of large surfaces, use a 4-in. brush; the 2-in. size is handy for sash and door work. Excellent results on walls and ceilings are possible with a paint roller, supplementing this with a brush to cut in the paint neatly at the woodwork and in corners and to reach into small spaces. For calcimining, use a calcimine brush to get quick, uniform coverage. You can work from a single stepladder, but two 4 or 5-ft. stepladders (or two wooden boxes of the right height) and an extension plank are much more convenient. A drop cloth protects floors and built-in furniture from paint drops, but newspapers can be used. You also need a putty knife, sponge, some 1/0 sandpaper and No. 0 steel wool, a trisodium-phosphate cleaning powder, a box of patching plaster, and either the non-shrinking, plaster-of-paris type of crack filler, or the type that remains somewhat flexible for use where there is movement and vibration of adjoining surfaces. Also get a gallon of turpentine, a bottle of shellac and a small brush. Don't forget a cheap pair of canvas gloves to prevent painful blisters if you're not accustomed to handling brushes, and rubber gloves for protection against strong cleaning solutions.

Preparations for painting: Expert results in painting depend largely on the thoroughness of preparatory work, especially cleaning, crack filling and sealing. Remove all loose furniture, drapes, curtains, Venetian blinds, pictures and other fixtures nailed

Lower the light-fixture canopy so that you can paint under it easily

Plates on flush wall switches and outlets must always be removed

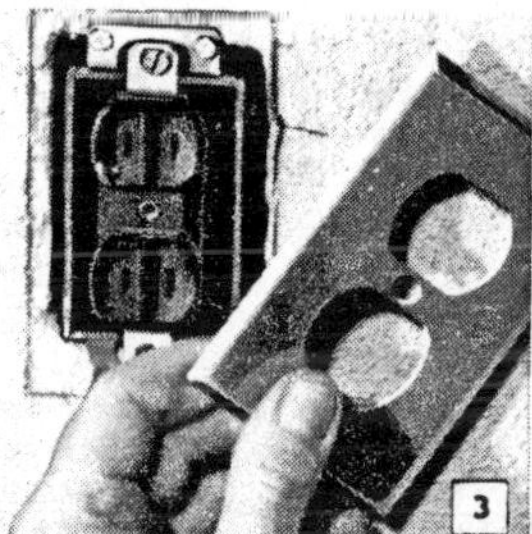

All hardware is removed from doors and windows and kitchen cabinets

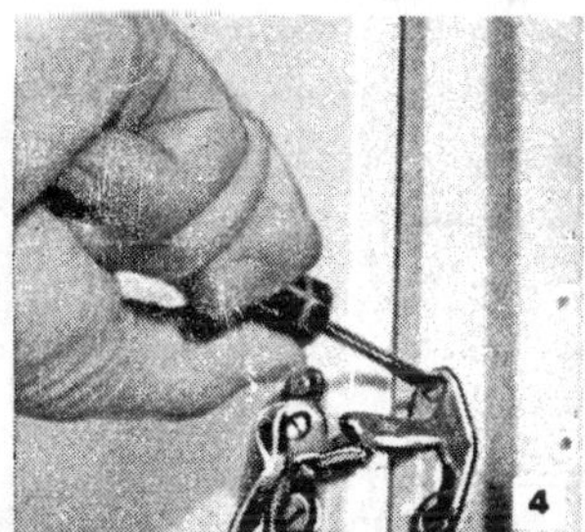

Reposition the base shoe molds at the floor level if there are wide gaps as shown in details at right

A thorough washing with cleaning solution assures surfaces that are entirely free from dirt and grease

or screwed to the walls, and extract nails and screws. Loosen the canopies of lighting fixtures and remove plates from wall switches and outlets, Figs. 2 and 3. For a professional appearing job, remove hardware from doors, windows and cabinets, Fig. 4. Chromium hardware can be immersed in a strong solution of cleaning powder until ready to replace it, at which time it is rinsed and dried. Lacquer-coated brass hardware is not subjected to this cleaning treatment. Kitchen-cabinet doors can be taken to the basement for painting. To get behind the kitchen stove when cleaning and painting, turn off the gas supply at the meter, disconnect the stove and move it. Put a cap on the end of the gas pipe.

Repositioning the shoe mold: Owing to

BASEBOARD
SHOE MOLD
A
B
GAP
FLOOR
SUBFLOOR
6

shrinkage of wood and settling of a house, gaps often develop between the shoe mold and floor or baseboard, details A and B of Fig. 6. To correct this, pry off the shoe mold carefully with a wide chisel. If it breaks, replacement is not expensive. Scrape away dirt stuck to the floor or baseboard and replace the shoe at floor level, Fig. 5. Then sandpaper down the rough edge of paint where the mold joined the baseboard.

Thorough cleaning procedure: Paint should never be applied to a dirty or greasy surface, nor to one covered with wax. Dirt and grease are washed off with a strong solution of cleaning powder. This also dulls glossy surfaces and puts them in better condition for paint adhesion. Wax is removed with a turpentine-saturated cloth followed by a thorough washing with cleaning solution. When washing a room, do the ceiling first, as in painting. Use a sponge, Fig. 7, on smooth walls; a soft brush is better for rough surfaces. Wring out surplus solution from the sponge to prevent dripping, apply to the surface and let the chemical work. Then rub the surface and wipe up with a sponge wrung out in clean water. Such a washing also removes starch coatings and calcimine. Besides the wall surfaces, all the woodwork is washed thoroughly, scraping away dirt from baseboard corners and the tops of door frames with a putty knife.

Crack filling: Cracks, scratches, gouges, as well as nail and screw holes that will not be used again are closed with a crack filler. The kind that remains slightly flexible is used where there is any vibration, expansion or contraction, which would loosen a hard crack filler. Very small cracks can be filled with "spackling" compound. Cracks 1/4 in. wide or more, are undercut to inverted V-shape with a putty knife as in detail A of Fig. 8. As the plaster on each edge of large cracks often is raised, dress the raised portions down flush with the rest of the plaster surface, using sandpaper as in detail B. Edges of a crack are wet with water before applying plaster-of-paris type crack fillers or patching plaster. Cracks larger than 1/4 in. as well as spots from which loose plaster has been removed, are filled with patching plaster. Smoothing plaster

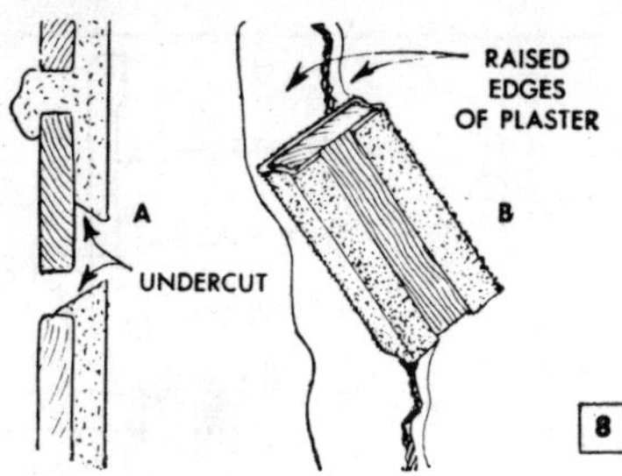

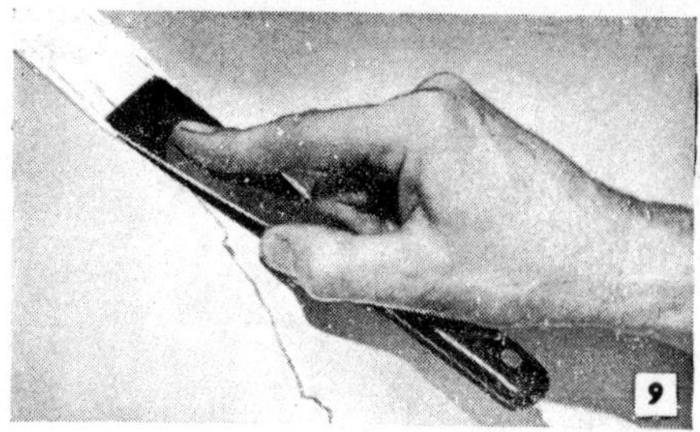

Use a stiff putty knife to press the crack filler into holes, dents and cracks in the plastered walls

on large patches is done with a trowel. As there may be shrinkage in patching plaster, a second application is sometimes necessary. When using crack filler which sets quickly, mix only enough for ten minutes' use. Setting of the plaster can be retarded by the addition of a little vinegar.

Press the filler into cracks on flat surfaces with a putty knife as in Fig. 9. In corners, this is done more easily with the finger, wearing a finger tip as in Fig. 10, or just putting some adhesive tape over the finger. A water-moistened sponge or rag is drawn over the filler to smooth it immediately after it is applied. When the filler is dry, sandpaper it smooth. Also sand down rough spots, trowel marks left from plastering and spots of dirt and brush bristles stuck to the previous coats of paint. Remove flaky or loose paint and feather the sharp paint edge with sandpaper as in Fig. 11, so it will not show through succeeding coats of paint.

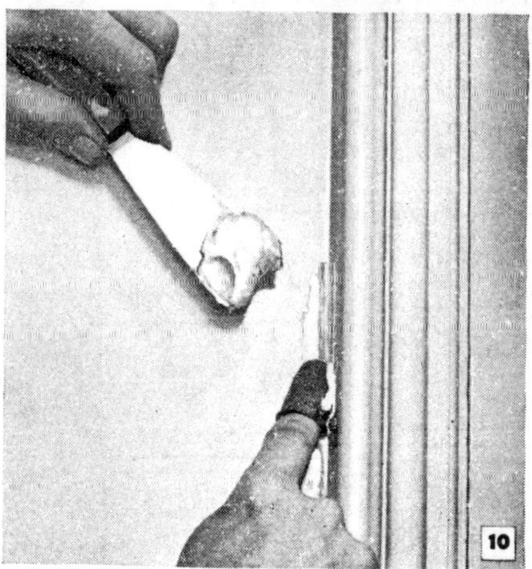

One easy way to apply crack filler in corners is to press it in place with the index finger as shown

Sealing the crack filler: It is necessary to seal the pores of plaster filling and old plaster bared by sandpapering, to prevent excessive paint absorption, which causes dull spots under the finish coat. This is best done with two or three applications of paint, Fig. 12, allowing each coat to dry before applying the next. Before sealing, wipe away all dust and brush the paint to a feather edge around the spot.

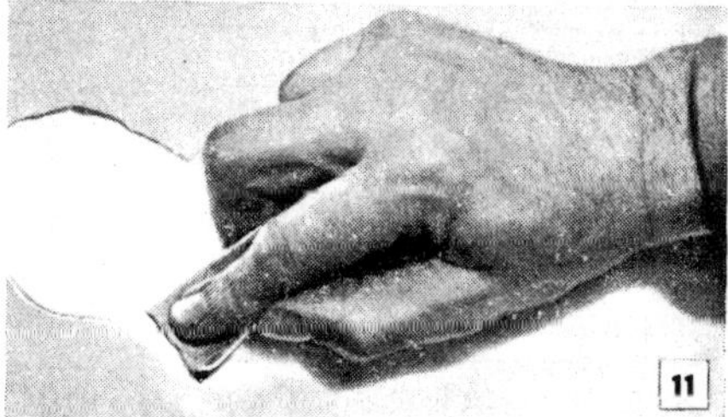

Above, sand off paint blisters and feather the edges. Below, seal the exposed plaster with sealer or paint

Preparing to paint: Before applying paint, read the manufacturer's directions, which will vary somewhat with different products. Stir the paint thoroughly. All the pigment which has settled to the bottom of the container must be dissolved completely in the liquid in order to bring the mixture to a uniform consistency. Thin the mixed paint with the recommended thinner or reducer. The container from which you paint should be about half full. Cover the floor and any built-in furniture with a drop cloth or newspapers and arrange the stepladder or ladders and the extension plank. Where possible, it is preferable to work away from a window so that you can see the wet edge of the paint. This position will help you to avoid brush marks, laps and "holidays" (skipped places). Have clean cloths handy

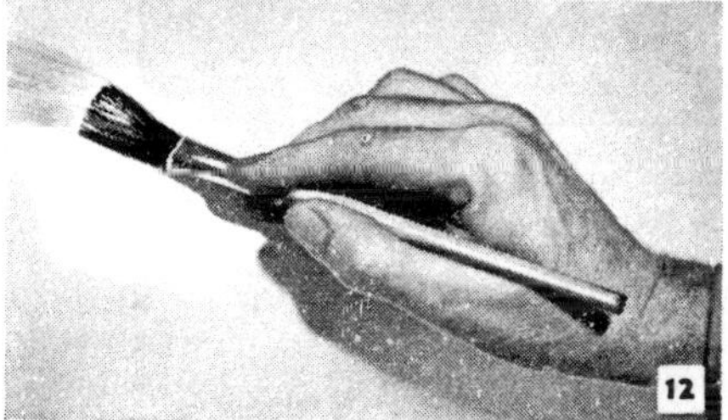

REFLECTED LIGHT FROM WINDOW SHOWS UP PAINT COVERAGE

13

14

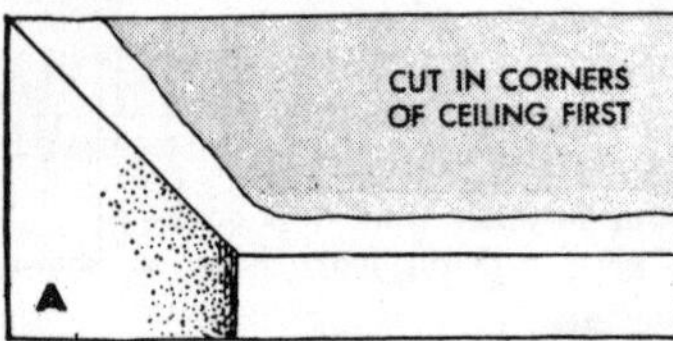

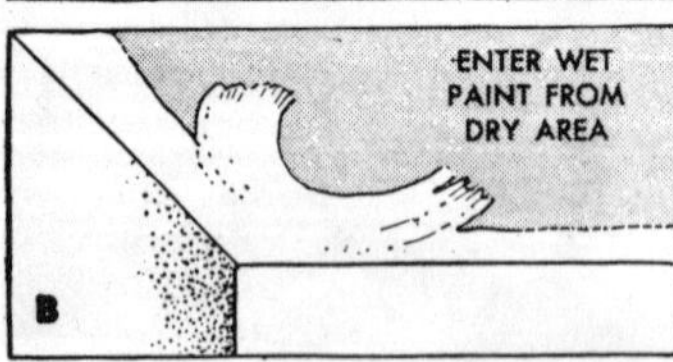

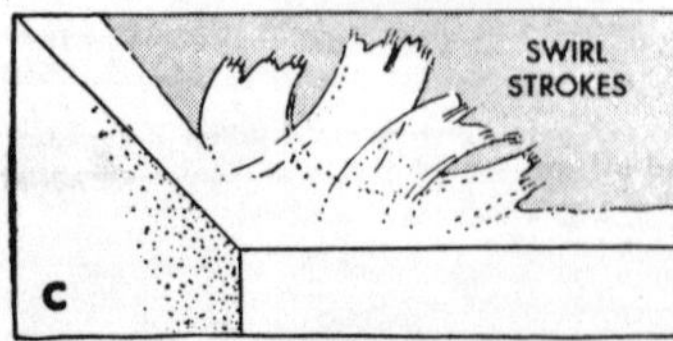

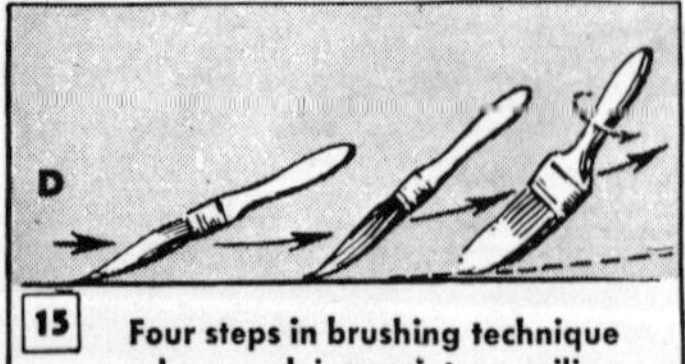

15 Four steps in brushing technique when applying paint on ceiling

to wipe up drips and unwanted smears immediately before the paint sets. In interior work, the paint is flowed on with a minimum of brushing. However, too heavy an application on vertical surfaces may sag or run before it sets. Avoid applying paint in daubs; rather, dip the brush about 1 in. in the paint and apply to the surface with light strokes until the brush is "empty." Do not brush out the paint as in exterior work. Stroke each separate application just enough to spread it uniformly.

Paint the ceiling first: When painting a room, take the ceiling first, setting up ladders and extension plank as in Fig. 13. Usually it's more convenient to work a ceiling in strips from left to right, each painted strip being about as wide as you can reach easily. Remember that in order to get back to a wet edge at the starting point you'll have to work fast. Try to complete each strip across the ceiling before the paint sets at the starting point. If the paint sets, it will be difficult to brush out the lap, as the fresh paint will build on that already applied.

Cut in the corner where the ceiling meets the wall with a single flat stroke of full brush width as in detail A, Fig. 15. A little pressure will be required to "fan out" the bristles when cutting the paint to the corner. Then lay paint on the ceiling with overlapping swirl strokes of the brush as in details B and C, Fig. 15. Once you acquire the knack, you'll find this method of laying on interior paint simple and very fast. Another trick with the brush that's worth learning is shown in detail D. By turning the brush slightly at the end of the stroke the bristles will come off clean without leaving a mark on the fresh

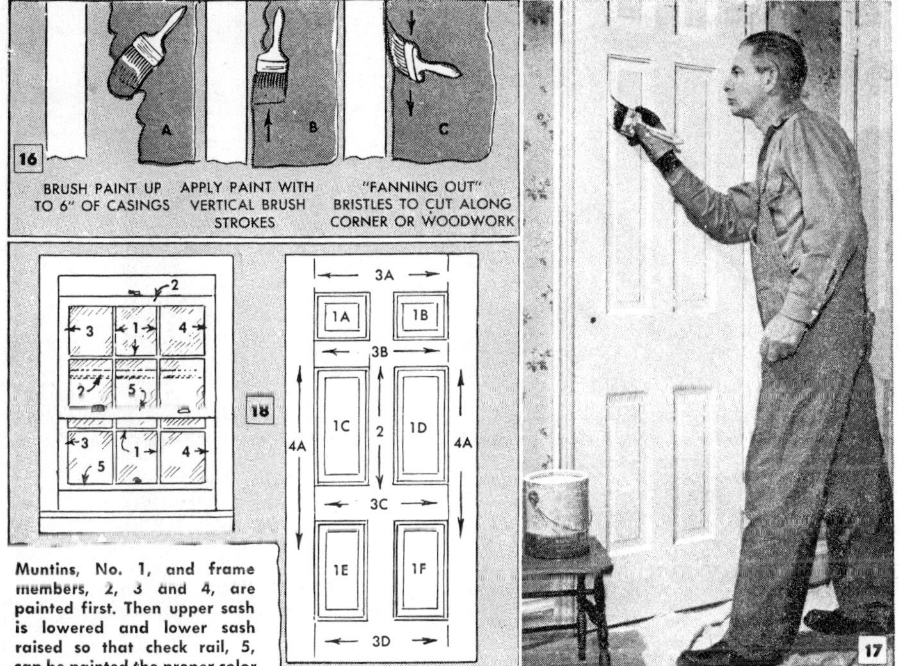

Muntins, No. 1, and frame members, 2, 3 and 4, are painted first. Then upper sash is lowered and lower sash raised so that check rail, 5, can be painted the proper color

paint. If you are applying flat paint to a large ceiling measuring more than 12 ft. either way, it will be necessary to apply the paint in narrow strips, not more than 18 or 20 in. wide, if you are working alone. On large ceilings the job is best handled by two persons, one beginning in a corner, the other halfway across the ceiling. After this first strip has been painted next to the ceiling edge, you perhaps can work a somewhat wider strip. Do not stop work until the entire ceiling has been finished.

Walls are next: Proceed in similar fashion on the walls, starting at your left, and working from the ceiling to the baseboard in 2 or 3-ft. strips, Fig. 14. Use the same overlapping swirl stroke as on the ceiling. Brush bristles are fanned out to cut along woodwork and corners as in detail C, Fig. 16. Work up to the woodwork as in details A and B. Don't stop painting in the middle of a wall as this will cause a conspicuous lap; stop only at a corner or cabinet edge that extends from ceiling to floor, Fig. 14.

Painting woodwork: Sand rough spots and gouges, using 1/0 sandpaper on flat surfaces and No. 0 steel wool on curved surfaces. After brushing or wiping off dust, start painting at the top of cabinets, door and windows, and work downwards. Finish doors and windows first, then the frames, Figs. 17 and 18, following the painting sequence outlined in Fig. 18. Paint the top, bottom and sides of a door while it is open and let it remain open until the paint has dried. The baseboard is painted last, a cardboard or plastic guard being used as in Fig. 21, to prevent getting paint on the floor or dirt on the brush. The guard also is handy when painting windows. When the frame of a room door is a different color on each side, the meeting line of the two colors is made at the stop strip as in Fig. 20. On swinging doors such joints are made midway on the jambs. Use masking tape as in Fig. 19 to assure getting a straight line.

Preparing varnished woodwork: Paint applied to varnished or enameled surfaces often chips off in spots. To prevent or minimize this trouble, apply a coat of specially prepared undercoater which combines with the varnish and forms a better base for subsequent coats of paint or enamel. The undercoater also acts as a sealer to prevent bleeding of stain. If woodwork is stained but not varnished—or if the varnish has been removed, exposing the stain—apply a coat of prepared stain sealer. This will prove more dependable than shellac or aluminum paint formerly used for this purpose. When woodwork has prominent grain that cannot be concealed by brushing on paint, the last coat should be stippled. To prepare oil paint for stippling, mix in some white lead. A long-bristled brush is used for stippling. As the ordinary painter's

19

Masking tape is used to get straight meeting line on swinging-door frame where two colors are used

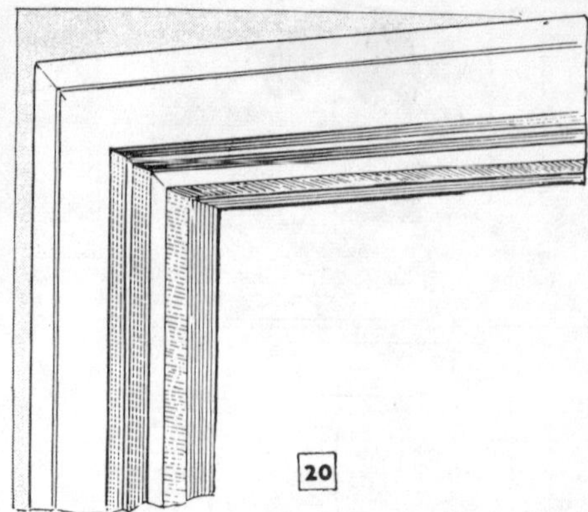

20

On hinged doors that swing in one direction the dividing line between colors is made at edge of stop

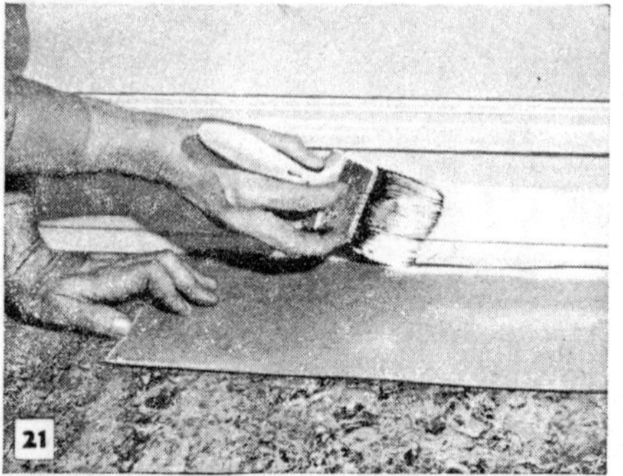

21

When painting the baseboard and shoe mold, a cardboard guard prevents getting paint on the floor

stippling brush is expensive, use a Dutch type of calcimine brush for this job.

Removing paint accumulations: In many older homes, numerous coats of paint and enamel applied throughout the years form thick layers which become badly chipped, scarred and roughened by paint runs and brush marks. To make such surfaces flat and presentable, you can cover them with canvas. Or, they can be given a rough texture by applying plastic texture paint. The only other alternative for improving such walls is to remove the paint with paste paint remover, which is slow, tedious and messy, but effective. The accumulation of paint can be removed from woodwork in the same way, but in some cases it is simpler to replace the woodwork. Always neutralize paint remover with turpentine and allow to dry before painting.

Brush and paint cleanliness: Scrupulously clean brushes are essential to good work. Wash them thoroughly in turpentine before using them for a different color. Paint can be kept from hardening on brushes overnight by immersing them in water. Wipe off the water on dry newspapers before using the brushes the next day. As soon as a paint job is finished, brushes should be cleaned thoroughly. When not in actual use, paint containers should be kept covered tightly. In case skin forms on paint and cannot be removed completely, stir the paint and strain it through a coarse cloth before beginning to use it.

Small holes may appear in the paint surface, but they should not extend all the way through to the ground surface. These holes are mainly found in varnish and enamel finishes. They are usually caused by the addition of turpentine or mineral spirit. Varnish and enamel are made ready for use and should not be diluted. Another cause for this condition may be that the work was done in a damp close atmosphere.

Calcimine on ceilings: Calcimine is used on ceilings, except in the kitchen and bathroom which are painted. Old calcimine is washed off before new is applied and one fresh coat is sufficient. Use a calcimine brush to apply it uniformly in narrow strips and work as rapidly as possible until the entire ceiling is covered. Calcimine can be applied over a previously painted surface but paint should not be applied over calcimine as this will result in peeling.

Starch-coating over paint: To protect painted surfaces, particularly in kitchens, you can starch-coat them. Use laundry starch and follow directions for mixing as given on the starch package. However, use a standard measuring cup full of starch to a quart of water. Apply the cool solution with a calcimine brush or paint roller and stipple with a fine-grain sponge or stippling brush before it dries. The coating is transparent and is easy to replace when soiled, as it is simply sponged off with warm water.

PAPER CUTOUTS

LIFELIKE paper cutouts are always popular with a youngster, especially when they can be folded to stand by themselves. The six animals included in the representative group shown below will get a child off to a good start on a real circus menagerie and will serve to suggest others. Made of gold, silver or colored paper, the animal cutouts will also make novel party place favors.

Each animal is fashioned in one piece from construction paper. Actual-size half patterns are given on the opposite page for tracing directly from the magazine page. If you have no objection to cutting the magazine, the page can be pasted to a sheet of cardboard and each pattern cut out with a razor blade to provide accurate master patterns that can be used over and over again. The complete pattern is made by flipping over the half pattern along a center line on your paper. Folding is done on the heavy dotted lines, and the photo below can be followed in shaping each particular animal. Note that the bodies are rounded out to give contour and that the legs are creased to add stiffness. A simple method to use in rounding the bodies is to hold the paper animal between the thumb and a knife or scissors blade and pull the blade across the paper. This will make the paper curl nicely and is especially helpful in producing the right curl for tail feathers of the rooster and wings of the swan.

By cutting each particular animal from paper of an appropriate color, such as yellow for the giraffe, white for the swan, tan for the kangaroo, etc., the coloring can be completed quickly with water-color paints.

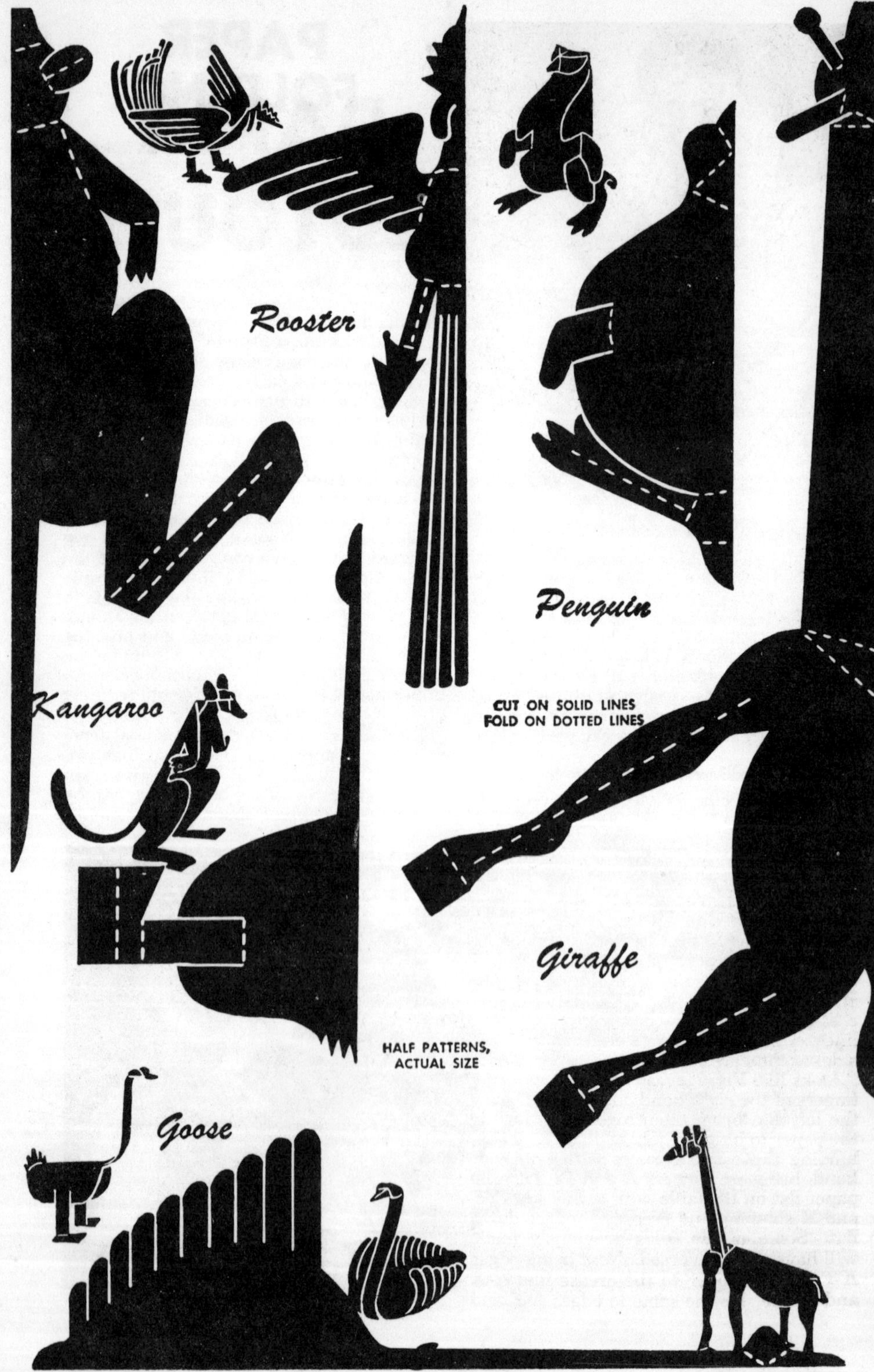
Rooster
Penguin
Kangaroo
CUT ON SOLID LINES
FOLD ON DOTTED LINES
Giraffe
HALF PATTERNS,
ACTUAL SIZE
Goose

PAPER FOLDING

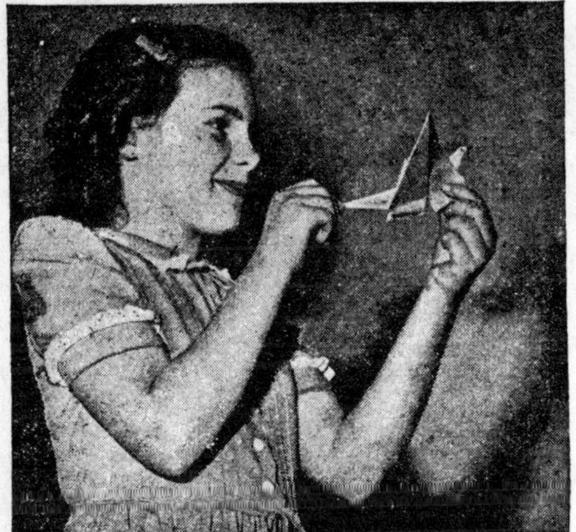

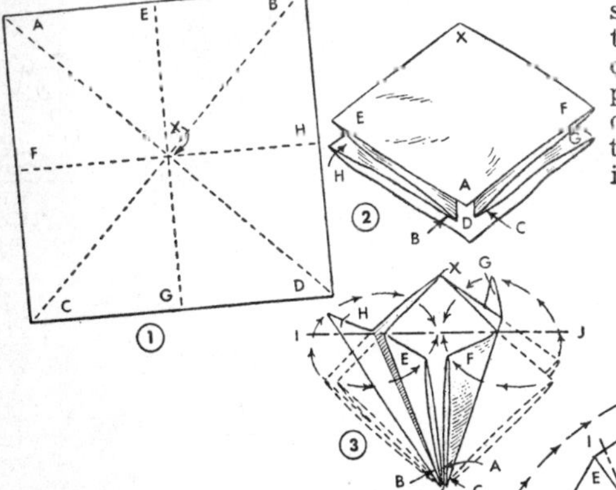

THERE is real fascination for children and grown-ups alike in taking nothing more than a square piece of paper and, by a few folds, producing a bird that flaps its wings or a frog that hops.

For the bird, use a piece of heavy paper about 8 or 9 in. square. First the square is creased by folding it according to the dotted lines in Fig. 1, then it is lettered on both sides as indicated. To fold the paper so that it looks like Fig. 2, grasp corner B with the fingers of the right hand and corner C with the left and bring them together, allowing the paper to hinge or fold at point X. Then, holding these two corners with your left hand, bring up corners A and D. Lay the paper flat on the table with corners A, E, F and X showing and crease all edges down flat. Some of the folds previously made will have to be reversed. Next bring edges A-F and C-F over to the crease line A-X and crease. Do the same to edges A-E and B-E. Now turn the whole thing over and make similar folds by bringing corners H and G to crease line D-X. It now should look like Fig. 3, the arrows showing the direction of the folds. Next place the paper flat on the table with corners E and F showing and mark the pencil line I-J. Place the fingers of the right hand along the edge of the pencil line so that the palm covers point X and with the left hand fold corners E and F outward. Grasp corner A with the left fingers and fold and crease it at line I-J as shown by the arrows in Fig. 4. After this fold corner A flat over corner X. Corners E and F will open up by first swinging out and then back again so that E and F will come together in the center as shown in Fig. 5. Turn the paper over and do the same thing with corner D. Now place the paper on the table with E and F showing and following the dotted lines and arrows in Fig. 6 fold tips C and B upward and outward to form crease N at approximately the

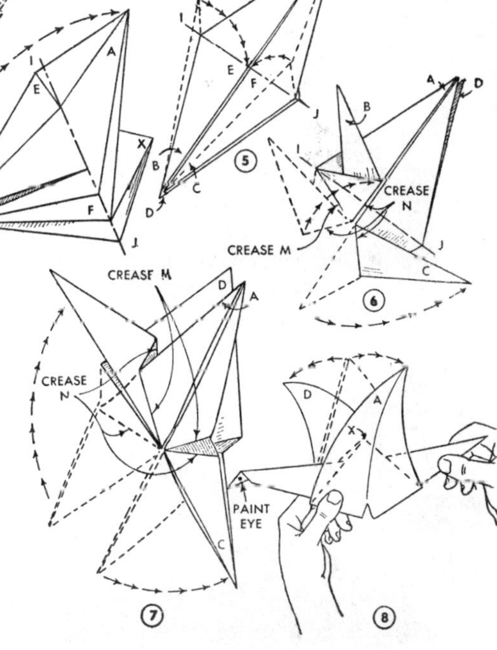

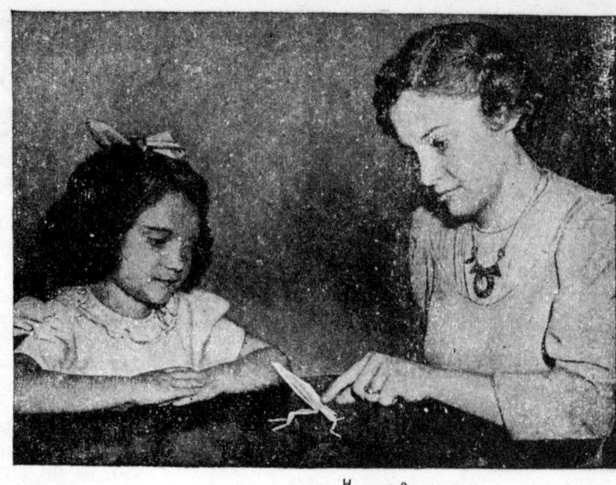

same position and angle as indicated in Fig. 6. Crease M, extending from the inside corner formed by crease N to the outside corner of I-J line, is folded in a similar manner, except that the paper is folded upward and inward. Return tips C and B to their original positions, as the creases merely serve as guide lines. Now, holding the paper in the left hand with G and H showing, you will find a small triangle between points A and D. Open the right-hand side of the triangle and with the right hand grasp the two edges of tip C just below crease N and move them upward as shown by the arrows in Fig. 7. You will notice that creases N and M on one side of tip C will

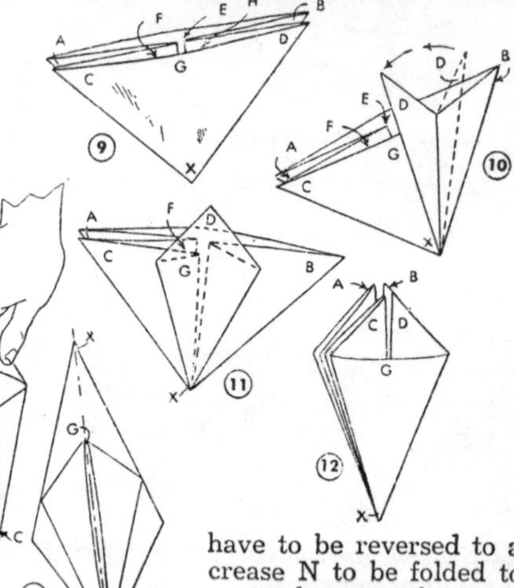

have to be reversed to allow crease N to be folded to the center between the two sides of the small triangle. Turn the paper around and do the same to tip B. Points A and D are curved downward to represent wings, while the protruding points form the neck and tail. Fold one of the extending tips to form the head and paint eyes on both sides. Holding the bird as shown in Fig. 8, the wings are made to flap realistically by pulling the tail.

A square folded and labeled as in Fig. 1 also is used to make the hopping frog detailed in Figs. 9 to 18 inclusive. To fold the paper as in Fig. 9, grasp the creased line H with the right fingers and creased line F with the left fingers and bring them together, allowing the paper to fold at point X. Then, holding these corners with the left hand, bring up the crease lines E-G. Lay the paper flat with corners C, D and X showing, and crease all edges down flat. Notice that some of the folds will have to

PAPER FOLDING

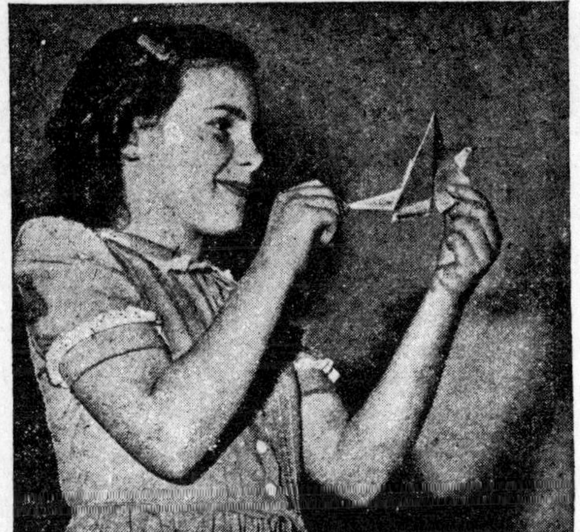

THERE is real fascination for children and grown-ups alike in taking nothing more than a square piece of paper and, by a few folds, producing a bird that flaps its wings or a frog that hops.

For the bird, use a piece of heavy paper about 8 or 9 in. square. First the square is creased by folding it according to the dotted lines in Fig. 1, then it is lettered on both sides as indicated. To fold the paper so that it looks like Fig. 2, grasp corner B with the fingers of the right hand and corner C with the left and bring them together, allowing the paper to hinge or fold at point X. Then, holding these two corners with your left hand, bring up corners A and D. Lay the paper flat on the table with corners A, E, F and X showing and crease all edges down flat. Some of the folds previously made will have to be reversed. Next bring edges A-F and C-F over to the crease line A-X and crease. Do the same to edges A-E and B-E. Now turn the whole thing over and make similar folds by bringing corners H and G to crease line D-X. It now should look like Fig. 3, the arrows showing the direction of the folds. Next place the paper flat on the table with corners E and F showing and mark the pencil line I-J. Place the fingers of the right hand along the edge of the pencil line so that the palm covers point X and with the left hand fold corners E and F outward. Grasp corner A with the left fingers and fold and crease it at line I-J as shown by the arrows in Fig. 4. After this fold corner A flat over corner X. Corners E and F will open up by first swinging out and then back again so that E and F will come together in the center as shown in Fig. 5. Turn the paper over and do the same thing with corner D. Now place the paper on the table with E and F showing and following the dotted lines and arrows in Fig. 6 fold tips C and B upward and outward to form crease N at approximately the

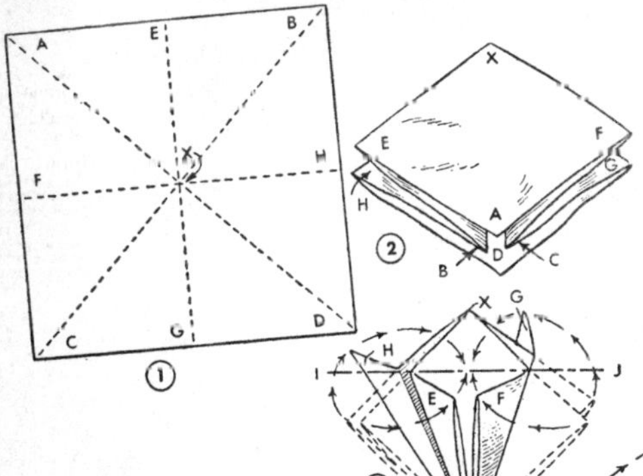

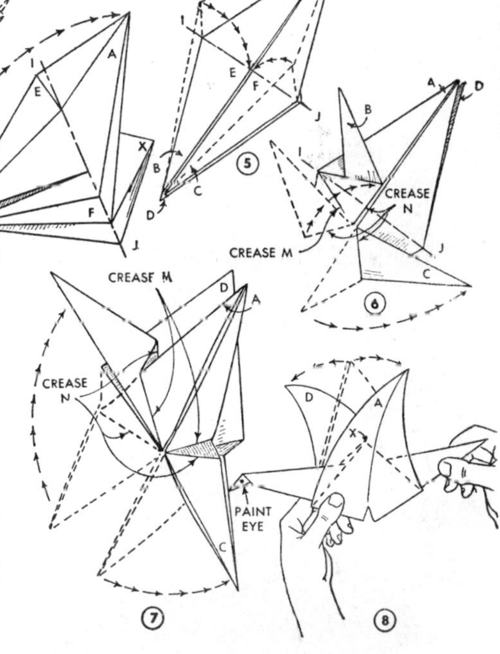

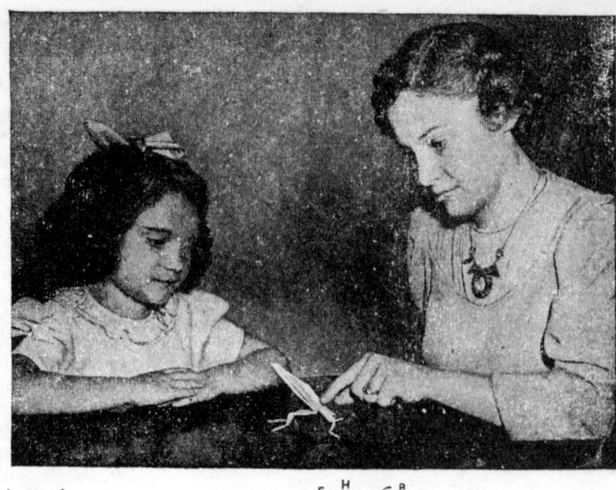

same position and angle as indicated in Fig. 6. Crease M, extending from the inside corner formed by crease N to the outside corner of I-J line, is folded in a similar manner, except that the paper is folded upward and inward. Return tips C and B to their original positions, as the creases merely serve as guide lines. Now, holding the paper in the left hand with G and H showing, you will find a small triangle between points A and D. Open the right-hand side of the triangle and with the right hand grasp the two edges of tip C just below crease N and move them upward as shown by the arrows in Fig. 7. You will notice that creases N and M on one side of tip C will have to be reversed to allow crease N to be folded to the center between the two sides of the small triangle. Turn the paper around and do the same to tip B. Points A and D are curved downward to represent wings, while the protruding points form the neck and tail. Fold one of the extending tips to form the head and paint eyes on both sides. Holding the bird as shown in Fig. 8, the wings are made to flap realistically by pulling the tail.

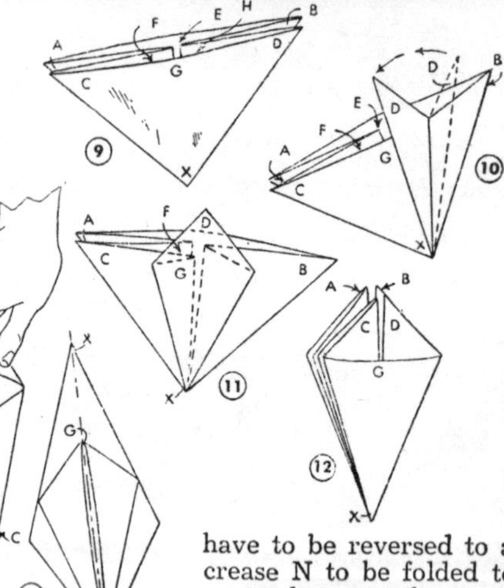

A square folded and labeled as in Fig. 1 also is used to make the hopping frog detailed in Figs. 9 to 18 inclusive. To fold the paper as in Fig. 9, grasp the creased line H with the right fingers and creased line F with the left fingers and bring them together, allowing the paper to fold at point X. Then, holding these corners with the left hand, bring up the crease lines E-G. Lay the paper flat with corners C, D and X showing, and crease all edges down flat. Notice that some of the folds will have to

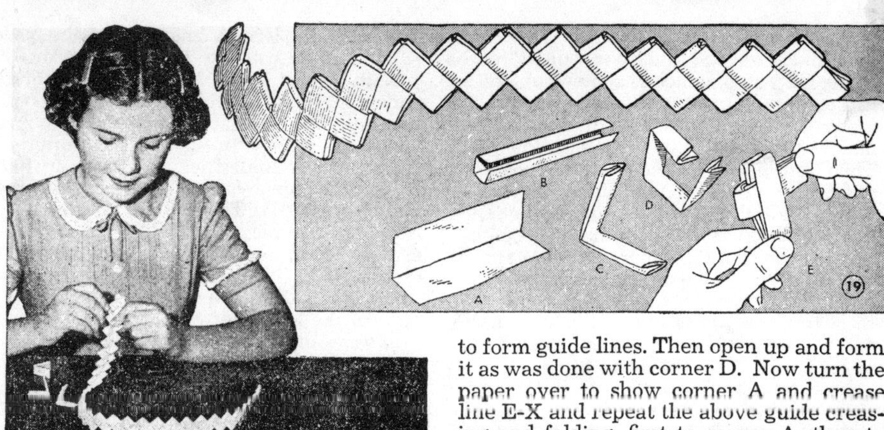

be reversed. Be sure the labeled crease lines are positioned as in Fig. 9. Edge D-X then is folded over to align with crease line G-X, Fig. 10. Crease this new fold which is to serve as a guide crease when folding as in Fig. 11. This is done by unfolding corner D to its original position. Then, holding the paper at corner X with the left hand, spread the two guide creases apart with the right hand, starting at corner D. Note that the left-hand guide crease has to be reversed. Now flatten the folded edge D-X directly over the folded edge G-X, shown as a dotted line in Fig. 11. Place the paper flat, Fig. 11, and lift up the right-hand guide-line crease so it hinges on the D-X line and fold it over, placing it on top of the left-hand guide-line crease. This exposes crease line H-X. Edge B-X is then folded over so it aligns with crease line H-X and is creased to form guide lines. Then open up and form it as was done with corner D. Now turn the paper over to show corner A and crease line E-X and repeat the above guide creasing and folding, first to corner A, then to corner C. Grasp the paper with the left hand at point X and fold over the right-hand guide-crease edge from right to left, exposing crease line G-X and corners C and and D, Fig. 12. Turn the paper over and repeat, exposing crease line E-X and corners A and B.

The paper then is laid flat with point X away from you and corners C and D showing. Now fold in the top right and left-hand unmarked corners to the center crease line

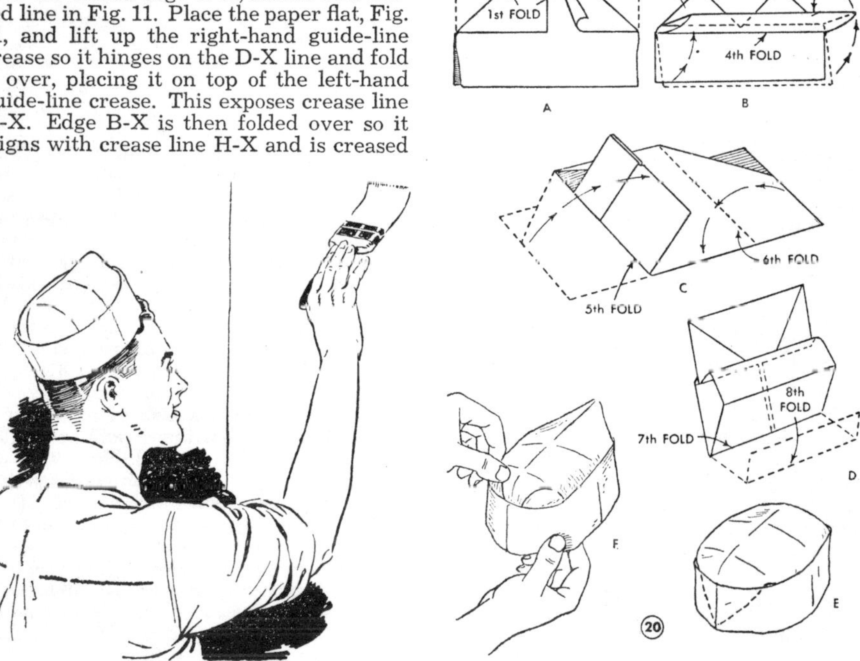

G-X and crease as in Fig. 13. These two new folded edges are used as guide creases in the next step, which is somewhat similar to a process in making the bird. Draw a line across the newly formed right and left corners at right angles to the crease line G-X. Then unfold them to their original positions and with your right hand lift up edge G as in Fig. 14 and fold it back along the pencil line, which is creased as in making the bird. The cut edges of the paper will fold in to the center, after which the small kite-shaped folds are pressed flat against the paper, Fig. 15. Turn the paper over to show edge E and repeat the above process. Then locate edges F-H and do the same thing.

Now hold the paper in your left hand with point X at the top and arrange the eight unmarked corners so that the small kite-shaped folds marked G are facing you and the ones marked E are at the back. The two lower tips facing you will be labeled C and D, the back two A and B. Lay the paper flat with G showing and fold the two upper right-hand unmarked corners to the center and crease the fold to taper to a point at tip C. Do the same to the two upper left-hand unmarked corners and crease to tip D, Fig. 16. Turn the paper over, showing corner E, and repeat the above, folding and creasing to tips A and B. Then turn the paper over again and fold tips C and A as in Fig. 17. Fold tips D and B so they project out to the left. A smart tap on the back will make the frog, Fig. 18, jump vigorously.

With heavy wrapping or colored craft paper, any youngster can make a decorative belt. Sixty or seventy pieces of paper about 4½ by 2¼ in. in size are required. Each piece is folded lengthwise as in Fig. 19, A, after which each edge is folded to the center crease, B. The ends of this strip are brought together, C, to make the center crease. Then the ends are folded to this crease, as at D. This piece is joined to another, made the same way, by inserting the ends of the latter between the folds, E, and pulling both together firmly. Other pieces are added similarly to produce a belt of the required length.

The cap shown in Fig. 20 is made from a double newspaper sheet. The size can be varied by increasing the size of the paper proportionally. To start, fold down the corners of the paper so that the edges meet, as at A. Then the second, third and fourth folds are made as at B, and the paper turned over before making the fifth fold at C. The latter is really two separate folds. After the sixth and seventh folds are made, C and D, the remaining flap is tucked into a pocket formed by the third, fourth and fifth folds, detail E. Finally, the peaks are tucked under the band at both ends, as in Fig. 20, detail F.

PAPER MASKS

Masks for Wall Plaques Molded On Modeled Clay Base

Molding paper-mask wall decorations, such as those shown on the opposite page, is a fascinating hobby that even children can enjoy, as it is easy to do and costs very little. Materials needed are potters' modeling clay, a few wooden blocks, some crinoline or sheeting, casein glue, shellac and paper toweling or newspapers.

Fig. 1 shows various suggestions for masks. Other styles can be made as desired. First, wooden blocks are set on a base to provide a form over which the clay is pressed at least an inch thick to prevent its cracking, Fig. 3. The blocks can be removed easily when the clay has dried. Next, features are molded with the fingers or with any handy small tool such as a skewer or awl, Fig. 2, after which the model is left for about 24 hrs. When the clay is dry, vegetable oil or grease is applied all over, Fig. 4, and cloth is pressed into all the contours, Fig. 5. Paper towels now are torn into small pieces and dropped into a pan of casein glue, Fig. 6, then are laid on the cloth in three overlapping layers, Fig. 7, and allowed to dry. The moisture in the glue breaks down the fibers in the paper, leaving a skin-smooth papier-mache mask. The model is removed from the block form and the clay is picked out with an ice pick or other pointed tool, Fig. 8, without, of course, piercing the paper, after which the mask is coated with shellac, Fig. 9, and painted to suit. Gold or silver paint can be applied, or green poster color in a water-base gold paint will give a bronze finish. Other effects can be obtained with either water colors or oil paints.

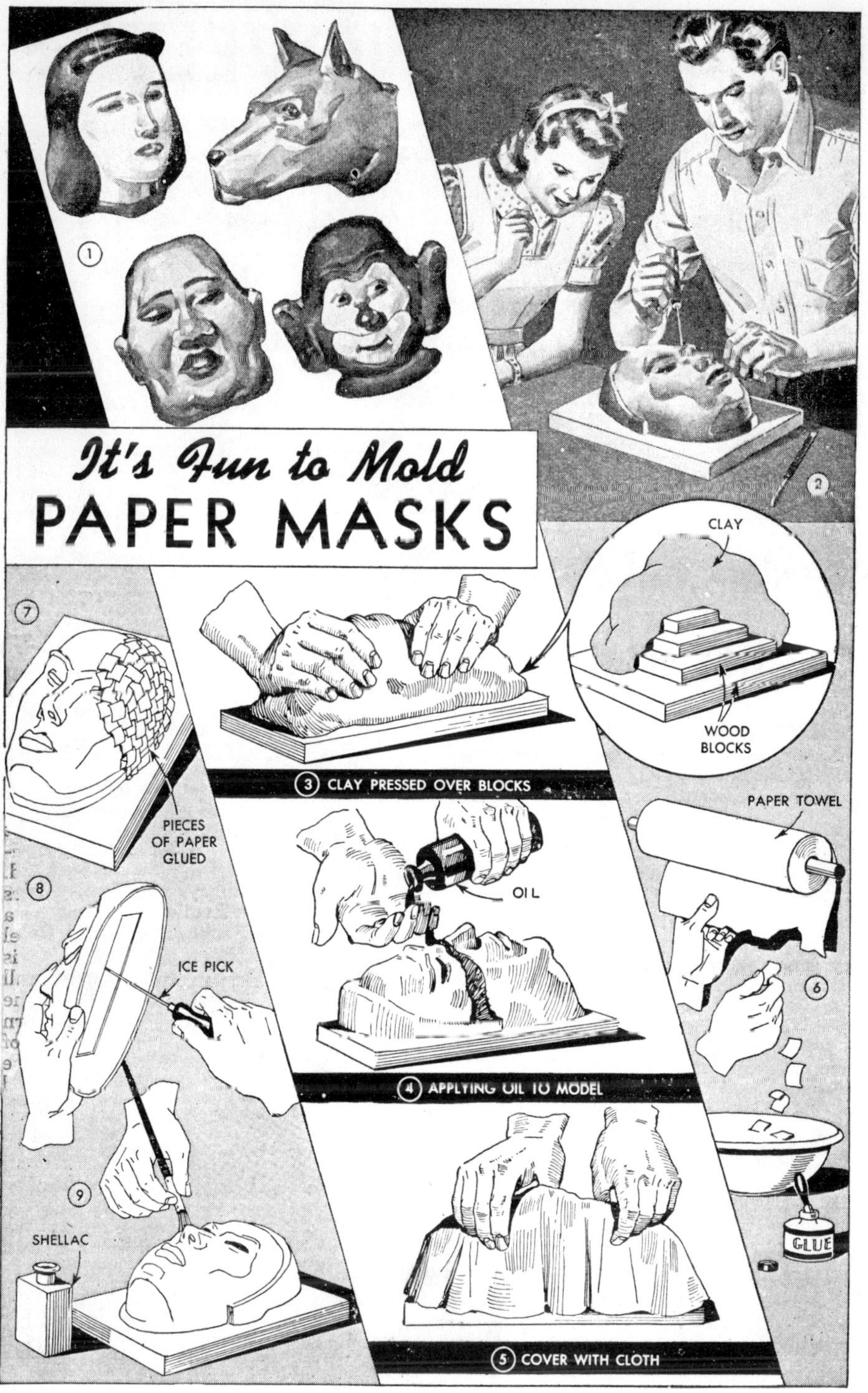
It's Fun to Mold
PAPER MASKS
1
2
CLAY
WOOD BLOCKS
3 CLAY PRESSED OVER BLOCKS
OIL
4 APPLYING OIL TO MODEL
5 COVER WITH CLOTH
PAPER TOWEL
6
GLUE
7
PIECES OF PAPER GLUED
8
ICE PICK
9
SHELLAC

PAPER NOVELTIES

Sturdiness of Paper Will Surprise You!

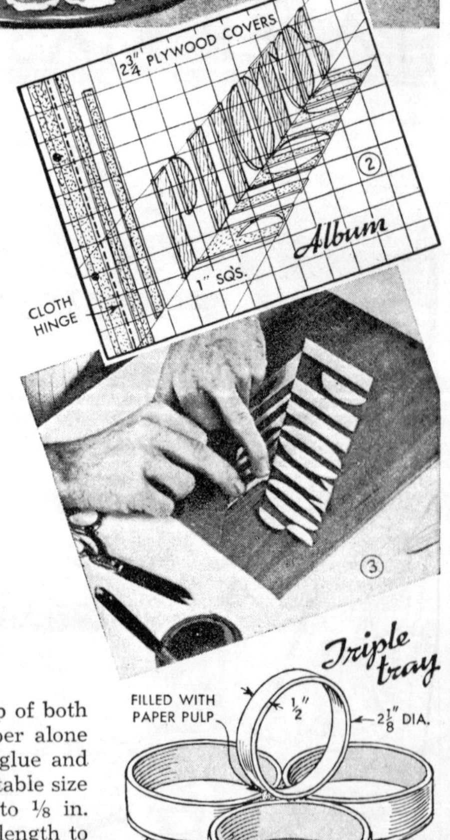

PAPER and cardboard glued up in layers to form sheets or tubes can be used as a substitute for wood and metal in making many useful articles such as those shown in Fig. 1. Material formed in this way can be sanded, cut with a saw and, when sized with glue, it can be painted, enameled, etc.

The photo album in Figs. 2 and 3 shows the sheet material cut into strips and letters and used as overlays. These are coated on one side with glue, which is allowed to become tacky before pressing them into place. This saves time as the paper adheres more quickly so that the work can progress without the usual long waiting period. When attached, the overlays are sanded, sized and finished as desired. Round tubes such as were used in making the triple tray shown in Fig. 4, are built up of both paper and cardboard. For small tubes, paper alone is sufficient. It is coated on one side with glue and then wound on a dowel or other form of suitable size to produce a tube having walls from 1/16 to 1/8 in. thick. A strip at the starting end equal in length to the periphery of the form must be left uncoated so that the finished tube will not stick to the form. Cans may be used as forms for making large tubes. First

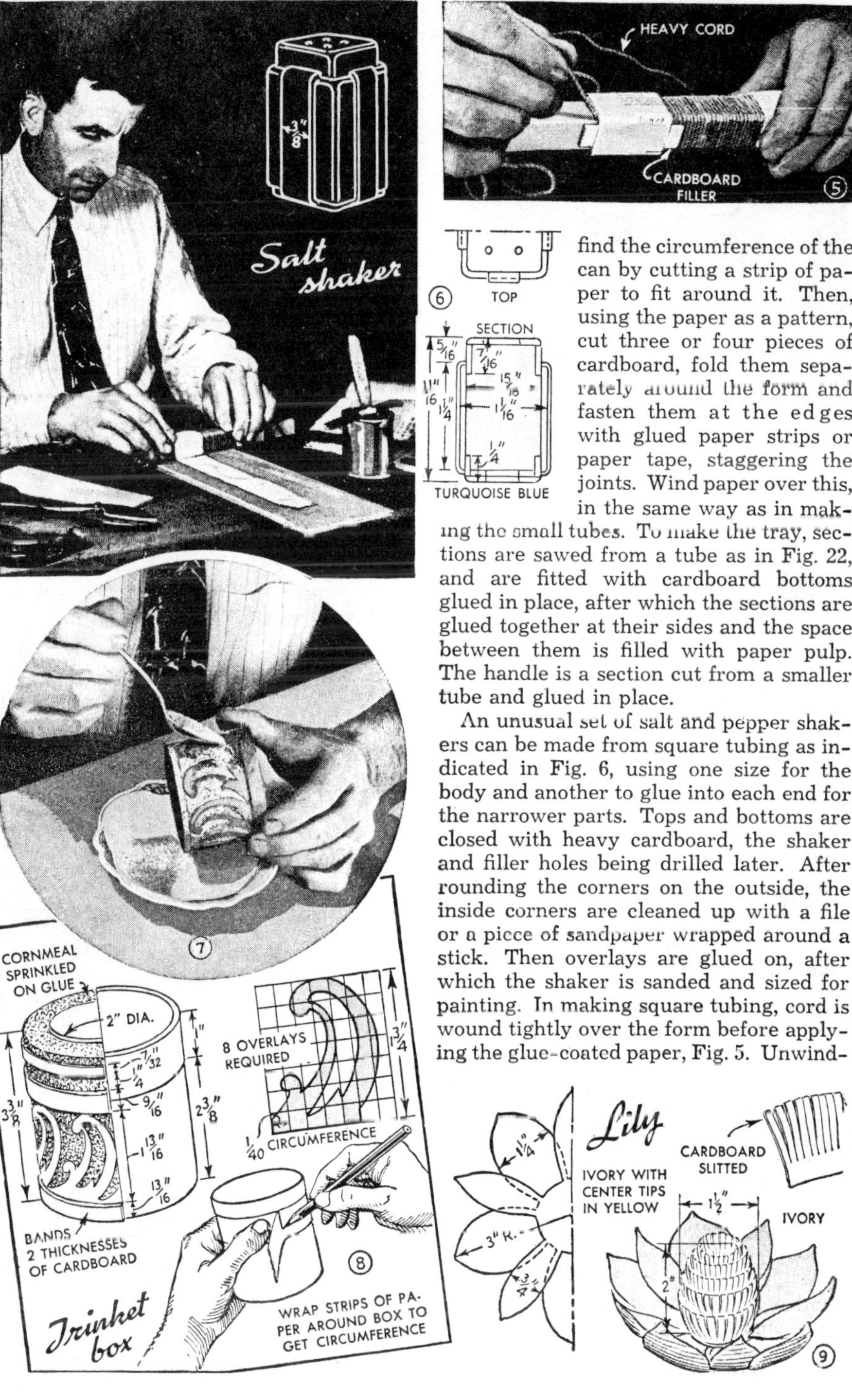

find the circumference of the can by cutting a strip of paper to fit around it. Then, using the paper as a pattern, cut three or four pieces of cardboard, fold them separately around the form and fasten them at the edges with glued paper strips or paper tape, staggering the joints. Wind paper over this, in the same way as in making the small tubes. To make the tray, sections are sawed from a tube as in Fig. 22, and are fitted with cardboard bottoms glued in place, after which the sections are glued together at their sides and the space between them is filled with paper pulp. The handle is a section cut from a smaller tube and glued in place.

An unusual set of salt and pepper shakers can be made from square tubing as indicated in Fig. 6, using one size for the body and another to glue into each end for the narrower parts. Tops and bottoms are closed with heavy cardboard, the shaker and filler holes being drilled later. After rounding the corners on the outside, the inside corners are cleaned up with a file or a piece of sandpaper wrapped around a stick. Then overlays are glued on, after which the shaker is sanded and sized for painting. In making square tubing, cord is wound tightly over the form before applying the glue-coated paper, Fig. 5. Unwind-

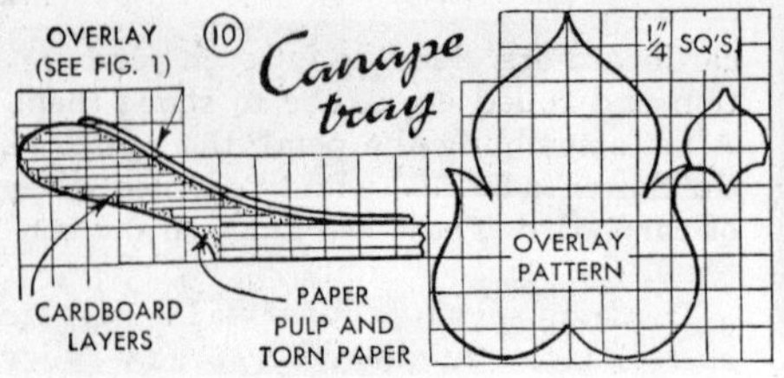

ing the string after building up the tube aids in removing it from the form. As in round tubing, the first turn of paper or cardboard must be left uncoated so the finished tube can be slipped off the form. Possibly the tube will shrink at the ends as it dries. If this is objectionable, use cardboard strips to enlarge the form so that the ends will be slightly oversize. After shrinking, the tube will be uniform in size throughout its length. The corners can be made sharp by adding two or three thicknesses of paper at these points. They are sanded to shape after drying. Large tubing also can be made by using square or rectangular cans as forms. When this is done, it is unnecessary to wind string on them as the tubes will slip off easily. Both cardboard and paper are used also for large square tubing.

The trinket box in Figs. 7 and 8 shows the combined use of round tubing and overlays ornamented with cornmeal to produce a stippled background. After gluing on a disk bottom, apply the overlays as indicated. Then coat the box between them with thin glue, and run a pointed instrument along the edges of each overlay to make narrow scores in the glue. When the overlays are painted

2 1/4" · 3/4" · 1/2" · 2 3/8" · WOOD PLUG · 2 3/8" R. · BALL · 4 3/4" · 7 3/4" · CARDBOARD BULKHEADS · 1 1/4" · 2 1/2" · 1 3/8" · 1 1/4" · BASE · 4 1/4" · LEAD SHOT IN PARAFFIN · 14

FOR LOWER COVE · 12 REQ'D. · 1/2" SQ'S. · 1" MAILING TUBE CUT OFF FLUSH · 1/4 PATTERN FOR ONE-HALF OF BALL · 1/4 PATTERN FOR BASE · 15 · GORE PATTERN FOR UPPER COVE 12 REQ'D.

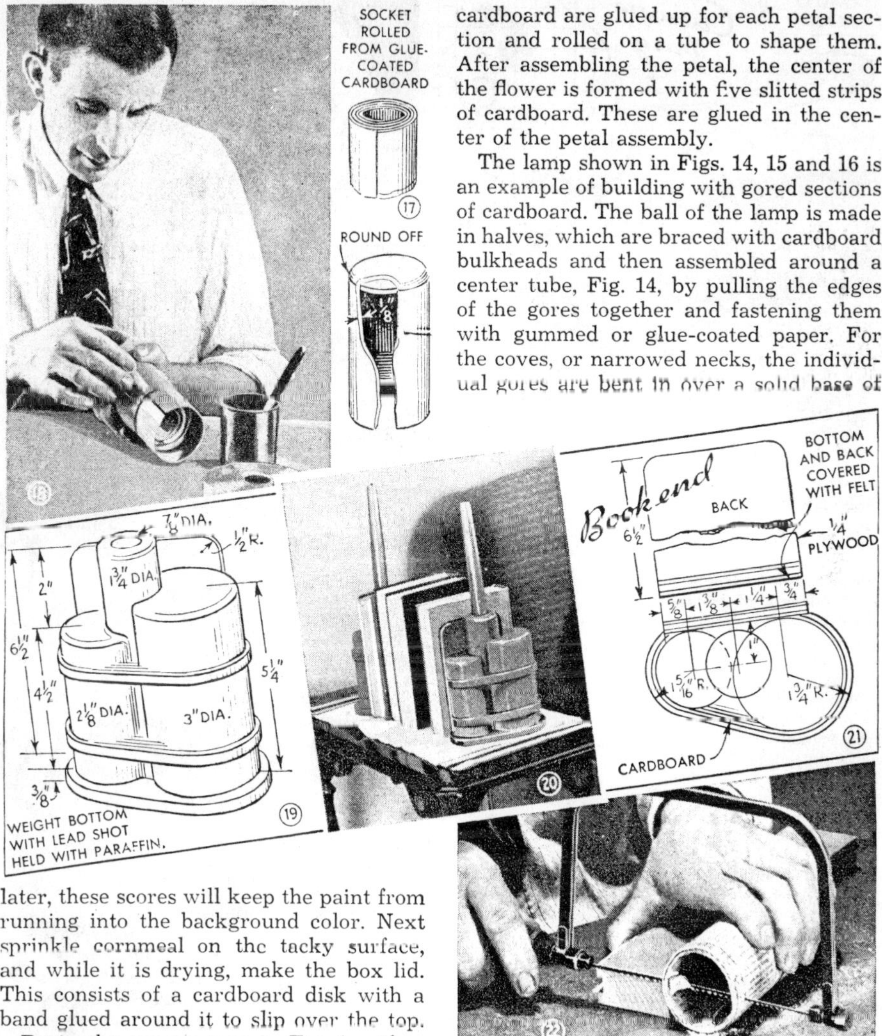

later, these scores will keep the paint from running into the background color. Next sprinkle cornmeal on the tacky surface, and while it is drying, make the box lid. This consists of a cardboard disk with a band glued around it to slip over the top.

Begin the canape tray in Fig. 1 with a plywood disk as indicated in Fig. 11, and build up a rim on it with layers of cardboard arranged step fashion as shown in the left-hand detail of Fig. 10. Then smooth up the stepped surface with paper pulp pressed into place firmly with a spatula, Fig. 12. When partly set, smooth the pulp with a clean spatula dipped in glue. Complete the rim with torn pieces of paper picked up with the glue brush and pressed to the glue-coated surface as in Fig. 13. Cardboard overlays like the ones in the right-hand detail of Fig. 10 are applied inside the tray. A flower to decorate the tray is shown in Fig. 9. Three thicknesses of cardboard are glued up for each petal section and rolled on a tube to shape them. After assembling the petal, the center of the flower is formed with five slitted strips of cardboard. These are glued in the center of the petal assembly.

The lamp shown in Figs. 14, 15 and 16 is an example of building with gored sections of cardboard. The ball of the lamp is made in halves, which are braced with cardboard bulkheads and then assembled around a center tube, Fig. 14, by pulling the edges of the gores together and fastening them with gummed or glue-coated paper. For the coves, or narrowed necks, the individual gores are bent in over a solid base of cardboard strips and wet-pulp filler. Cardboard washers are slipped over the tube and the gores are bent in between them. Then, a wooden plug is placed in the upper end of the tube for attaching a lamp socket. The base is weighted with lead shot held in paraffin to keep it from rattling.

In Fig. 20, large cylinders fit around the candlesticks, which are mounted on bases and backs of plywood as shown in Figs. 19 and 21. The bands are three-ply cardboard, widened between cylinders to four or more plies. Candlesticks are made as shown in Figs. 17 and 18.

PAPER NOVELTIES

CANDY AND NUT TRAY

Candy by the wheelbarrow—or you may put this little novelty to work as a cigarette holder. A length of mailing tube, cut as shown and fitted with wooden ends, forms the hopper. The rest of the cart is made of scraps of ¼ and ½-in. pine. The wheel can be made to turn or it can be simply glued in the slotted end. Draw in the flower designs with yellow and red crayons and give the rest of the work a coat of yellow water-color paint

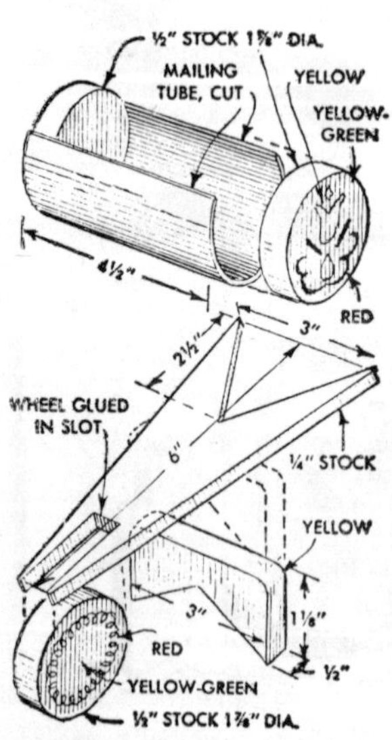

WITH a few paper mailing tubes, some scrap wood and a little ingenuity you'll be surprised at the number of unusual and attractive novelties that can be made at practically no cost. And with a ready market for such novelties here's your chance to cash in. Wax crayons and water colors are used to decorate the novelties, after which they are finished with clear shellac to seal the colors. The four examples presented here show what can be done and will give you a start. Notice in each case that the novelty is built around a piece of mailing tube. Bases are of scrap wood and, if desired, you could perhaps incorporate plastic. If you have a lathe, you'll be able to turn out perfect disks for the bases in a jiffy, or you may find that you can do better by cutting them on a scrollsaw, sawing several at a time, and then smoothing the edges with sandpaper or a file. Choice pieces of scrap wood, such as walnut, maple or cherry, could be used and finished in their natural color with a coat of shellac or varnish. Quick-drying lacquers can be used to speed the painting. If you size the paper tubes first with a thin wash coat of clear lacquer or shellac, the paint will not be absorbed as readily. Another finishing method is flocking. Flock can be had in a variety of colors and is simply sifted onto the work after it is coated with glue. The excess flock is shaken off and re-used. The finish obtained is a velvety texture resembling cloth and gives a professional looking job. Natural or dyed sawdust sprinkled on a tacky surface and pressed with your fingers will also give the work a novel finish.

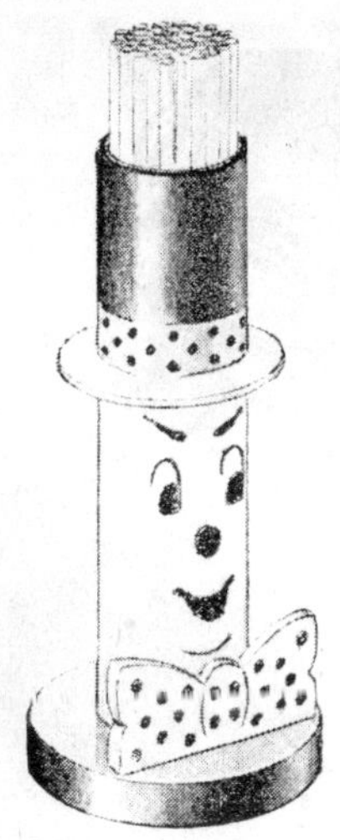

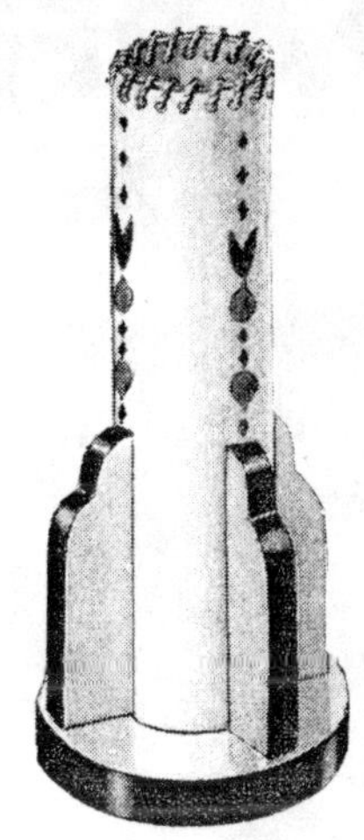

STRAW SERVER

Dapper Dan purposely "blew his top" to let you put soda straws in his stovepipe hat. Make him from a tube 8 in. long and see that the brim of his hat fits snugly around the tube, 3 in. from the top. He's attached to a circular base by a disk nailed to the top, and then dolled up with a sporty polka-dot tie. His features can be applied with a wax crayon and the rest done in water colors as suggested below. Finish with clear shellac and let dry

CIGARETTE BOX

Treat your friends to a smoke from this novel cigarette box. The lower end of the tube is capped with a two-part base the same as Dapper Dan. The lid is built up of 4 disks, the topmost one being drilled for a cord and set on edge. A screw driven up from the bottom fastens all 4 disks together. The design and cross-hatching are drawn with wax crayons and then the background is done in water colors. Seal the colors with a coat of shellac

ARTIFICIAL FLOWER VASE

Just the thing to hold paper flowers. You start by making a two-piece base like you did for the others. The tube sets over the top disk of the base and is glued or nailed to it. Four side supports are spaced equidistantly around the tube and fastened to the base with brads. Then holes are punched around the upper edge of the tube and laced with a cord to give a finish. Wax crayons color the side pieces; the tube is painted with water colors

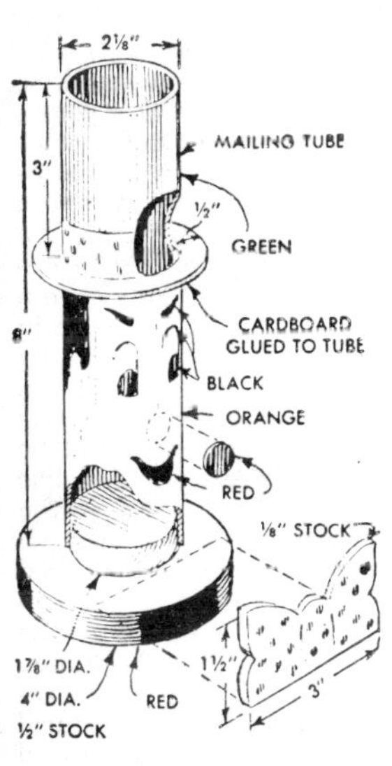

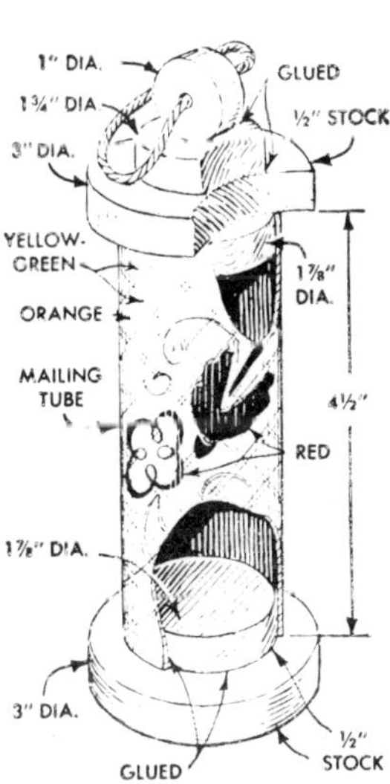

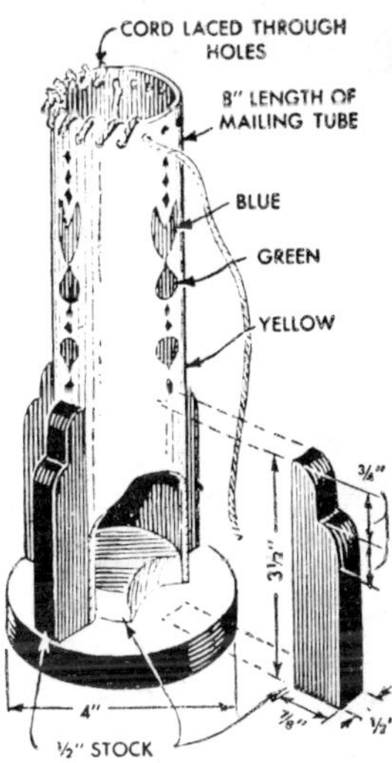

PAPERBOARD TOYS

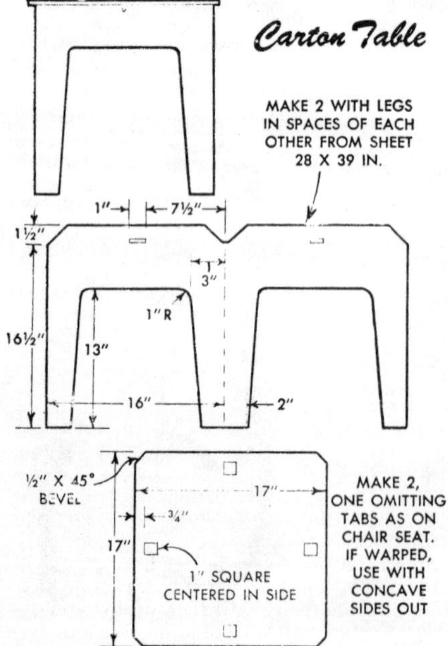

Carton Table

DO YOU save paperboard cartons in hopes that they will come in handy sometime? If you have children for whom to make toys, you'll be glad you saved those cardboard containers. Unbelievable as it may seem, all of the attractive toys shown in this article were made from paperboard cartons.

Stronger than they look, paperboard flat surfaces are excellent for making vehicles, doll houses, play furniture and toy boats. Cars, boats and other toys which are to be sat in should be more than 12 in. wide and 10 in. high, depending upon the age of the occupant for whom they are made. A vehicle 13 x 10½ in. is suitable for children up to 5 years old. An 8-year-old child would require a car or boat measuring at least 14 x 12 in. A minimum length of 28 in. should be used. A length of 30 in. is average while 33 in. will fit almost any child who will be interested in these toys. The toy house should be more than 25 in. long, 14 in. wide and 25 in. high. If you use especially heavy paperboard, the house may be as large as

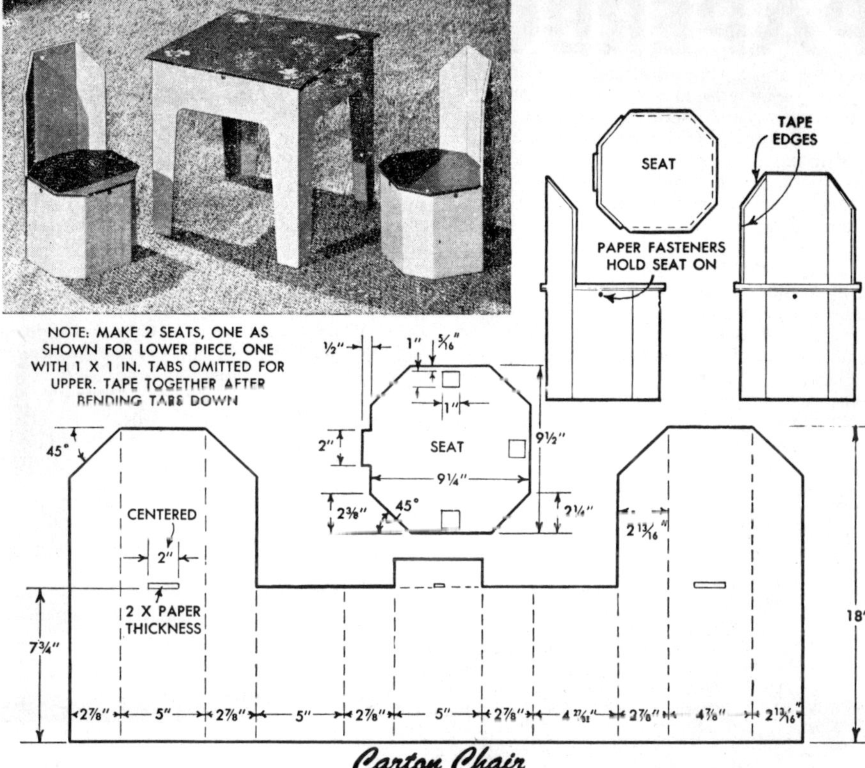

Carton Chair

30 in. long, 16 in. wide and 28 in. high without getting too floppy. This will fit over two 5-year-old girls who don't mind somewhat crowded conditions. Don't skimp on the length of the house, as active youngsters can easily kick out the sides. The height of the table should measure at least 16½ in., and the top 17 x 17 in. As for the chairs, the distance from the floor to the seat should be at least 7¾ in., and the seating surface 9¼ in. wide and 9½ in. long. These are minimum requirements, and a larger table and chairs should be made for older children.

Flatten the cartons, using the utmost care in taking out the staples or tearing off gummed paper or labels. Start construction on any of the toys shown here by drawing the outlines to be cut full size directly on the piece of board to be used. The dimensions and patterns for a table-and-chairs set, a truck, a trailer, a play house and a boat are given in this article. Study the diagrams carefully before the toy is laid out, as you will want to make sure that the piece of paperboard chosen is large enough. You will note that some of the toys, such as the chairs, truck, trailer and boat, require large pieces of material. It is important that the parts indicated in the diagram be cut in one piece, as piecing together takes away from the over-all sturdiness of the toy.

Have the board supported on a table or any other large, flat surface at a convenient working height. If the paper is warped, draw the layout on the concave side (the lines come on the outside of the finished toy) as these designs will tolerate a surprising amount of warpage in this direction. Do not use the edges of the board as part of the layout, as they are almost bound to become damaged during work and because most paperboard is not cut straight or square enough for this work. Start by laying down two straight lines at right angles, all the way across the sheet. One of these should accurately parallel the corrugations and they should be placed so as to become part of the layout. All measurements are made from these lines so be sure they are straight and at right angles. A conveniently long straightedge can be made from a 6-ft. length of ½ x 4-in. clear yellow pine, which a lumber company will true up for you.

Draw the outline of the toy on the paperboard with a soft pencil, sharpened often, to make clean, dark lines without cutting into the material. Use solid lines where the paperboard is to be out; dotted lines for bends. Put all the lines on at this stage, including outlines for painting and decorating. It is not important in which direction the corrugations go in relation to the toy, but if you have a choice remember that cutting and bending go best when across the grain (the wiggly edge of the interliner showing). A cut across the grain also gives a better appearing edge.

Next, cut along the solid lines. Use a sharp knife as a dull one will catch and tear the interliner. Use a heavy straightedge to guide the knife for cuts over 1 in. long. Make all cuts from one side of the paper all the way through, the paper being supported behind with wood, paperboard or Masonite which you don't mind scratching. Be sure your cuts go through so the pieces will lift off easily without tearing.

Now crease all the bends, using a wooden creaser. The crease goes on the side which will form the inside after bending. Creases must be as accurately placed as cuts, so for those which go on the back of the paper mark the position by pushing a pin through at several places along each line. Put the crease in well by running over it several times. Bend the paper at each crease part way. Then with the sheet upside down (pencil lines under) lift the sides and fold them on the main creases until they come together at the middle and fasten them together with 3-in. lengths of gummed tape. The house is cemented at two places instead of taped at one for a stronger joint. Now push on the sides to erect the toy and complete all the folds and tucks.

Tape over the short lengths of tape with one continuous length of 2-in. tape. Use gummed (not masking) tape for greatest strength and permanence. Crease the tape before sticking it down. Try on the loose pieces such as windshield and fenders at this point and make necessary corrections.

Paint all the toys except the house after they are assembled, as the paint may crack upon bending. The house should be painted in the flat so you can ink in the trimmings. Colors will be brighter if a light coat of white is put on first. For a glossy finish, apply a coat of clear lacquer on the dried, painted surface. If the toy is to be folded often, apply tape over the ends of the tabs.

Two types of paperboard can be used,

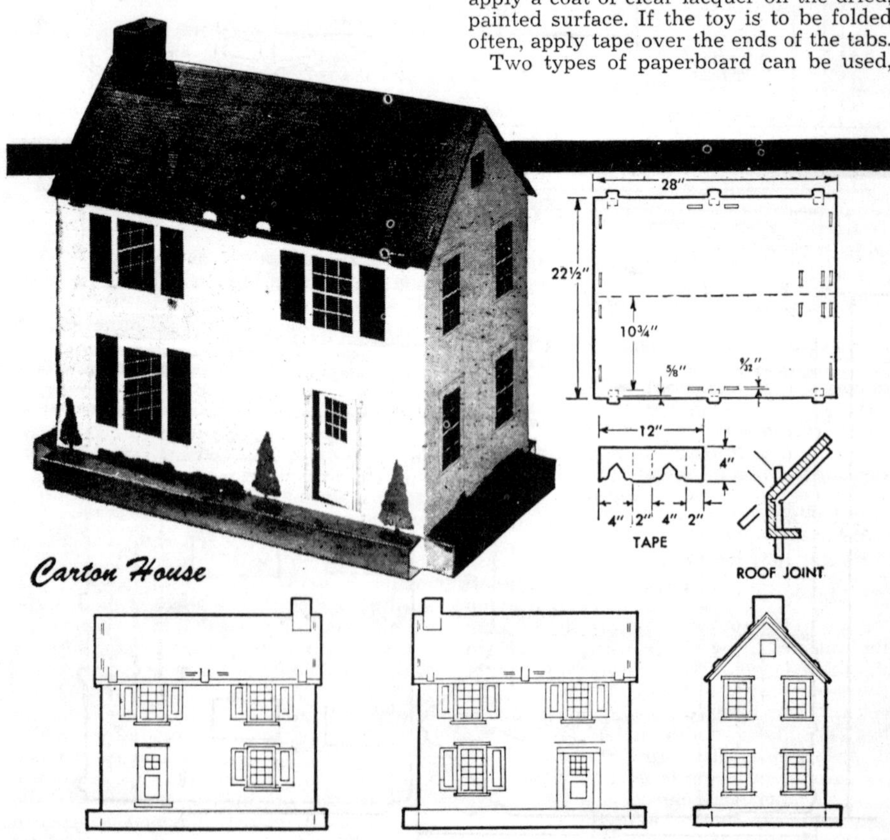

Carton House

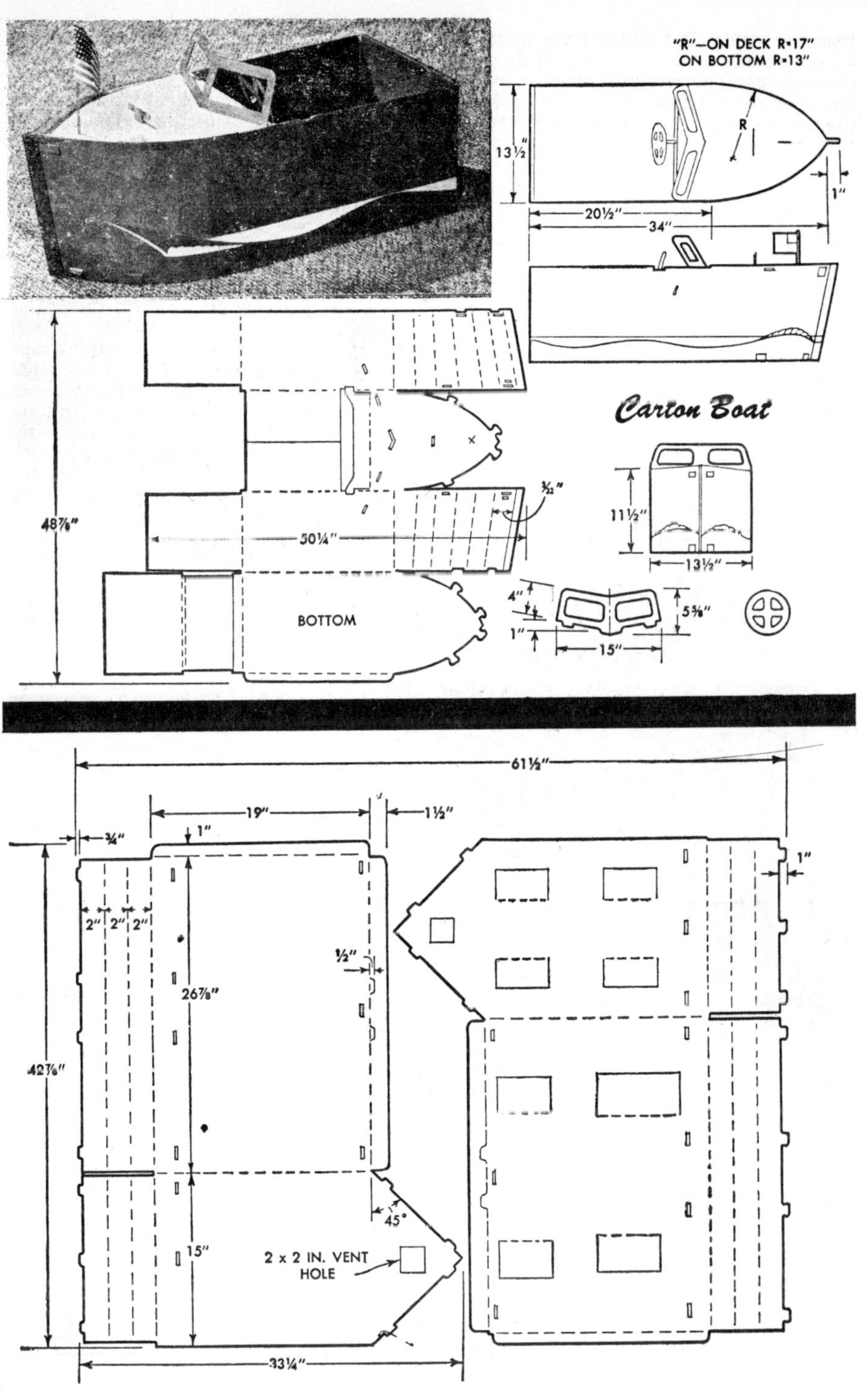

"R"—ON DECK R=17"
ON BOTTOM R=13"
R
13½"
20½"
34"
1"
1"
Carton Boat
48⅞"
50¼"
3/32"
11½"
13½"
BOTTOM
4"
1"
5⅝"
15"
61½"
19"
1½"
¾"
1"
2"
2"
2"
26⅞"
½"
42⅞"
1"
45°
15"
2 x 2 IN. VENT
HOLE
33¼"

both being of 200-lb. weight and either sisal or kraft paper. The 3/16-in. "A" flute paper looks better and is easier to handle but not stiff enough for larger toys. The "B" flute paperboard is 1/8 in. thick with closer-spaced corrugations and is suitable for larger toys like the truck.

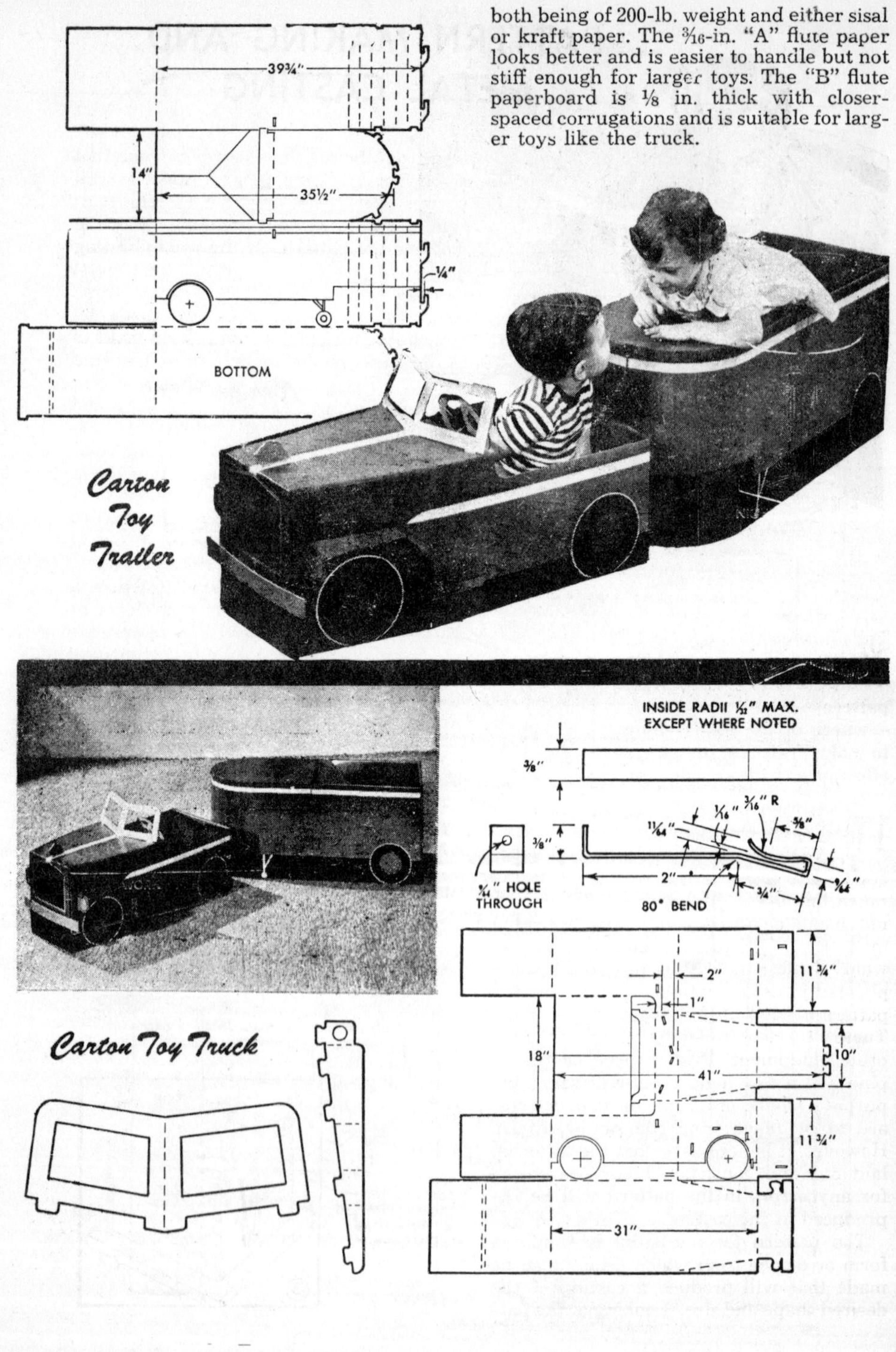

PATTERN MAKING AND METAL CASTING

Tells how castings are made in the foundry in sand molds —how to make your own patterns—what woods to use —where to use fillets—how to make draft and shrinkage allowances with 'shrink' rule

HOW often have you attempted to make up some metal part of stock materials and finally found that a casting would be much better for the purpose? Then, why not make a pattern and have a casting made from it that will be just what you want? Unless the casting required is complicated in detail or unusual in shape, the pattern needed will be a very simple affair. There's no need for fancy woods or elaborate equipment. Just a piece or two of pine and a few hand tools will serve the purpose where only one or two castings are to be made from the same pattern. However, it is necessary that the latter be laid out and constructed very carefully, for any errors in the pattern will be reproduced in the casting.

The pattern for a casting is simply a form or device from which a mold can be made that will produce a casting of the desired shape and size. Looking at the pattern from the molder's viewpoint, one that is perfect in every other respect is still useless if it is not possible to remove it from the mold without breaking either the mold or the pattern. If the rough casting made from the mold has insufficient metal to allow for machining you will have trouble finishing it. Castings are made by pouring molten metal into a sand mold of the desired size and shape, Fig. 4. The sand is retained in a box open at the top and bottom which is called the "flask." The latter is made in two sections, the lower of which is called the "drag" and the upper the "cope." These are fitted with guides and cleats or dowels to permit accurate realignment of the two sections. The first steps required in making a mold from a one-piece pattern are shown in Figs. 1

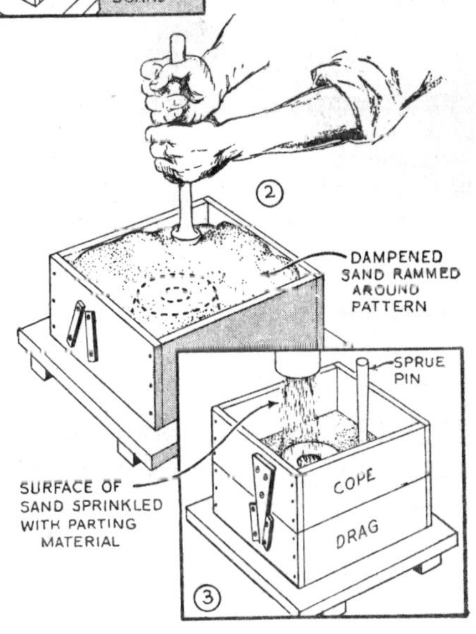

to 3. First the pattern is laid face down on the molding board, with the drag inverted around it. The sand, properly dampened, is rammed around the pattern until the drag is filled to the top and struck off level with a straight edge. The drag is then turned right side up on the bottom board and the surface is sprinkled with a parting material to prevent sticking. At the same time the second half of the pattern, if it is in two pieces, is set in place. The cope is set on the drag, a sprue pin is placed to form a pouring hole in the cope, and the latter is rammed with sand. It is then lifted off and the pattern is removed from both halves of the mold. After a pouring hole and gate for the metal are cut in the sand as in Fig. 5, the cope is replaced as in Fig. 6. This, in brief, is the common procedure. The pattern is invariably larger than the finished casting, and in all cases it is necessary that it be made with tapered sides, or "draft" as it is commonly called. This provision on the pattern makes it easy to remove from the mold without breaking up the print as in Fig. 7. Fig. 8 shows the same pattern constructed with the proper draft. The amount of draft that must be provided depends on the type of the mold and the location. Where possible, the pattern is made with the draft all running in one direction from the parting line, as at A in Fig. 9. In this case, and for the outside of the pattern, the amount of draft is generally ⅛ in. to the foot, as in Fig. 10. Note also in this illustration that on the side of a casting, where a hollow pattern is used, considerably greater draft is required. Generally a draft of $\frac{1}{16}$ in. to the inch is specified. If the opening is less than 1 in. in diameter, draft of ⅛ in. to the inch must be allowed. Where this amount of draft cannot be tolerated on an inside surface, it is necessary to use a solid pattern and form the hole with a core. This will be explained in the second article of this series.

SPRUE
SAND
GATE
(5) PATTERN LIFTED OUT AND GATE CUT

COPE REPLACED ON DRAG,-READY FOR POURING (6)

Another important provision with regard to draft applies to those cases where a pattern cannot be made in one piece, but is made in two pieces with

be made is that for finish. The surface of a casting is naturally rough and somewhat irregular, and if two castings must be fitted together accurately, or if extreme accuracy is necessary for any other reason, the surface will have to be machined down to the finished size. Generally an allowance of 1/16 in. is made for each finished surface on small castings, although for larger castings in which irregularities may be greater, a larger allowance for finish is needed. One more thing and you're ready to lay out the pattern. Wherever wood parts of a pattern join at right angles a fillet is necessary, Figs. 12, 13, and 14. Triangular leather fillets are obtainable ready-made in a variety of sizes and are easy to apply with glue. On small patterns such as those used for model parts, beeswax is usually better. It is simply pressed into place then worked to a true radius with a spherical-ended tool as in Fig. 14. The tool must be heated slightly at intervals.

The best way to lay out the pattern is to make a mechanical drawing of the part to be made as in Fig. 15. Locate the surfaces to be finished and use the symbol "f" to

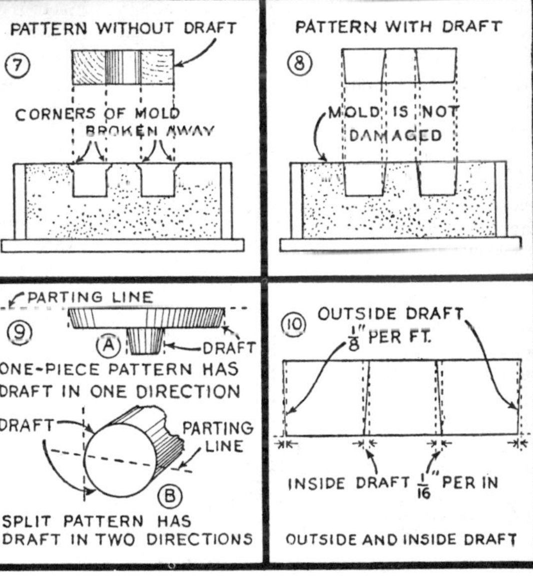

draft running in both directions from the parting surface, as shown in Fig. 9, B. Here it is necessary to double the draft on the section of the pattern that extends into the cope or upper section of the mold. This provision is made to assure easy parting of the pattern from the mold when the cope is lifted off the drag and the pattern is removed.

The second important characteristic that affects the pattern size is shrinkage. All castings shrink after solidification, the amount of shrinkage depending on the metal from which they are made. It is, therefore, necessary to make the pattern and mold somewhat larger so that the casting will shrink to the desired dimensions. Table I gives the approximate shrinkage for various common metals. To get this shrinkage accurately you simply lay out the pattern with a shrink rule instead of an ordinary rule. A shrink rule has each foot increased by 1/8 in., if for iron, and by 3/16 in., if for brass, and all subdivisions elongated proportionately. This saves the time necessary to calculate the shrinkage allowance on each dimension.

A third allowance which must frequently

denote them on the drawing. This will help in remembering to make the proper finish allowances. Patternmaking woods should be well dried and seasoned. Redwood is sometimes used, also cherry, mahogany, or maple when the pattern will be subject to repeated use. For ordinary work, clear white pine will do very well. Where gluing is necessary use a hide glue applied hot, as in Fig. 11. If possible the layout should be made directly on the wood that is to be used for the pattern. The pattern should be planned in advance so that, if possible, the draft is all in one direction from the parting line. With this

TABLE I
Approximate Shrinkage of Castings

Metal	Shrinkage
Cast iron	1/8 in.
Brass	3/16 in.
Aluminum	1/4 in.
Zinc	5/16 in.
Copper	3/16 in.
Lead	5/16 in.
Malleable iron	1/8 in.
Steel	1/4 in.

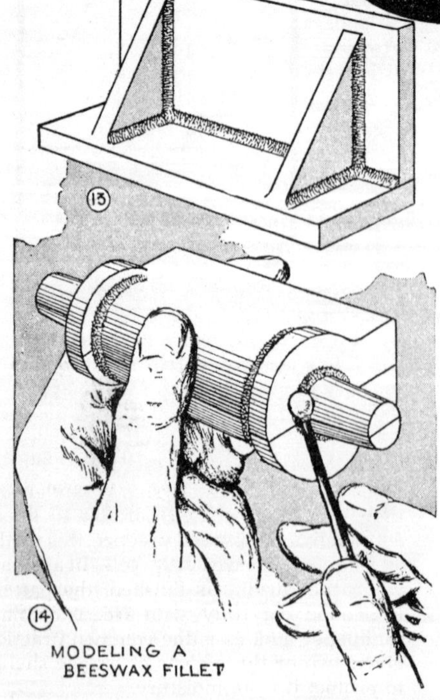

MODELING A BEESWAX FILLET

in mind, the layout is made, using a shrink rule for all dimensions and marking all lines with a sharp knife. It is best to start all measurements from the center line of the pattern, rather than from an edge; and to lay out any holes first before laying out edges. The steps in laying out a pattern for a simple bracket are shown in Figs. 16, 17, and 18.

When the layout is completed, the excess wood can be removed by sawing and the pattern finished with chisels and gouges. Cylindrical or other round sections, of course, may be turned in a lathe. The work should be finished to exact size very carefully. The quality of the finish, especially on small wood patterns, is very important. All surfaces of the wood which come in contact with the sand must be glass-smooth before applying shellac. Where hand tools are used to cut away waste it is necessary to use care when you approach the finish dimensions or you may cut too deep and spoil the pattern. It is essential that surfaces worked down with edge tools be left as smooth as possible so that sanding will be reduced to the minimum. Slight cavities or shallow cuts made inadvertently under the finish dimensions can be filled with woodturner's cement or wood putty. Have your tools razor-sharp so that you can cut with or across the grain without

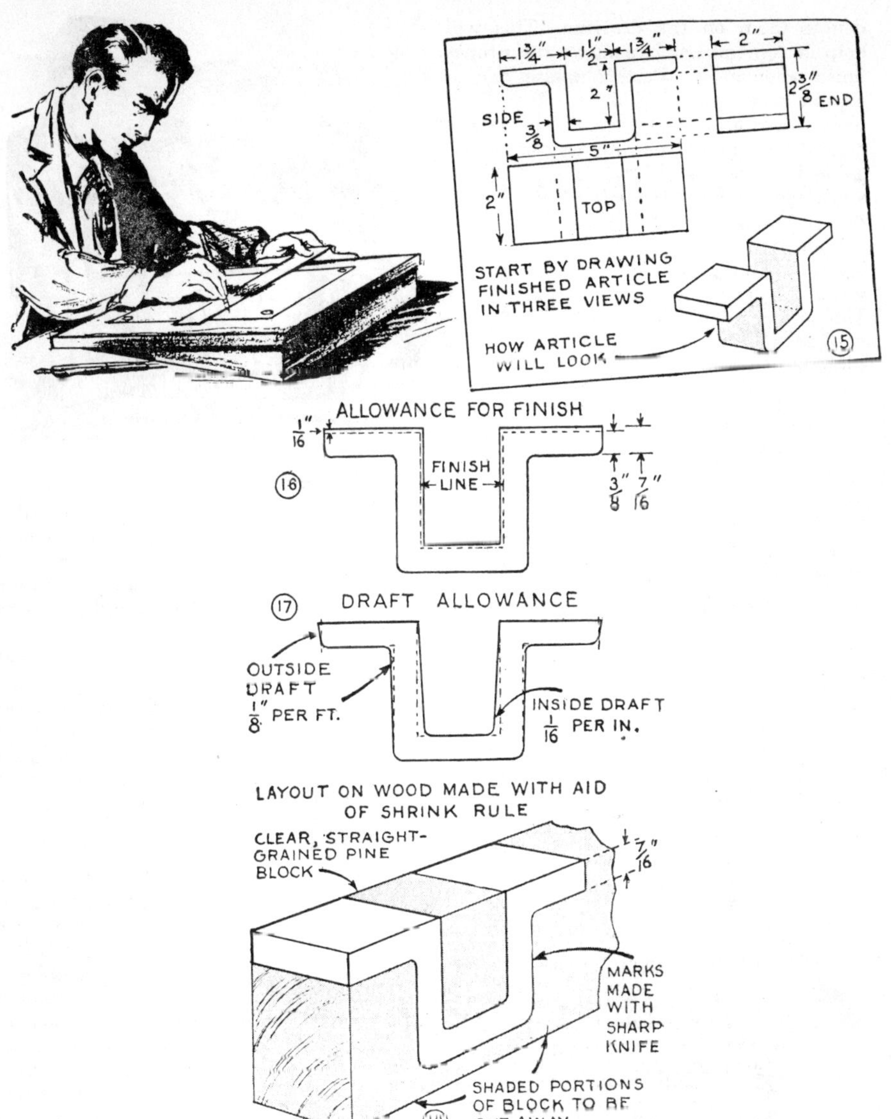

raising deep splinters. Sometimes a fine rasp is better than a chisel or gouge on the cross grain. The disadvantage of the rasp for general work is that it raises the fibers of the wood and leaves a rather rough surface which requires considerable sanding to smooth up. Lathe-turned patterns can be finished ready for shellacking with a minimum of hand work, of course. Sometimes small patterns are simply sanded and then dipped in melted paraffin to finish. Although not approved practice, this method frequently serves very well. In any case when the carving is finished, the pattern is sanded carefully with No. 0 or finer sandpaper and, as is the common practice, given two or three coats of orange shellac to protect it from moisture.

Two-Piece Patterns and Cores

WHERE the pattern must be of such shape that it cannot be made with the draft running in one direction from the parting line, it is necessary to resort to a split pattern of two or more pieces. As an example of this type of pattern, take the small V-pulley shown in Fig. 19. As you will see this pulley has no recessed web or spokes, so it can be cast in the vertical position as in Fig. 20. The parting line in this case will be on the diameter of the pulley. The curvature of the wheel and the V-shape of the belt groove will provide sufficient draft on these surfaces. However, the flat outside surfaces will require draft. Keep in mind that the amount of draft will be not less than ⅛ in. to the foot for that part of the pattern below the parting line, while on the half of the pattern above the parting line (the cope section) the draft should be twice as great, or not less than ¼ in. per foot. This permits easy parting of the cope and drag when the mold has been completed.

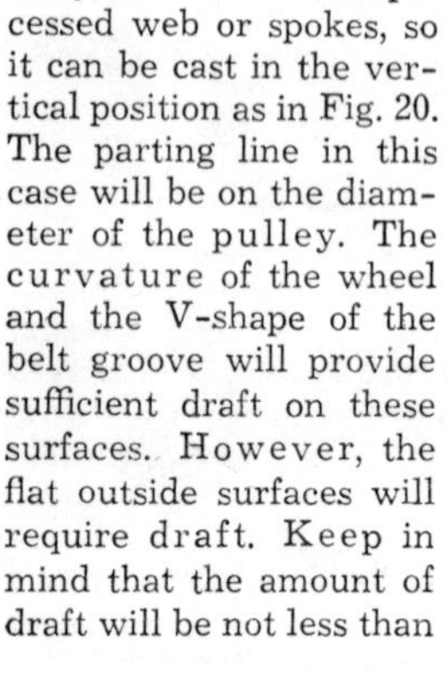

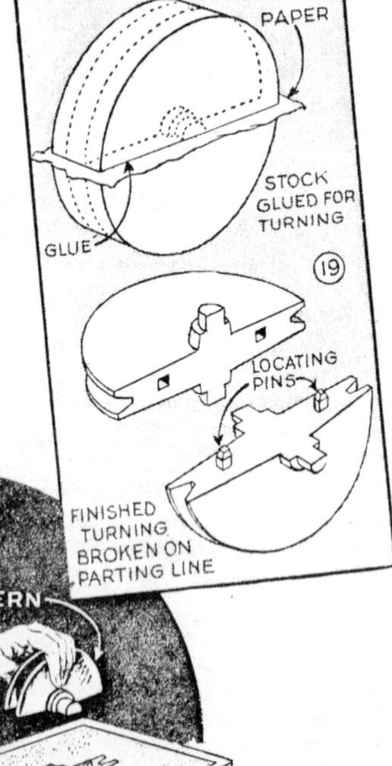

The layout of this pattern is made as shown in Fig. 22, and the method of turning it complete in the lathe is detailed in Figs. 23 to 26 inclusive. Irregular-shaped patterns are usually made with ordinary hand tools and carving chisels. In almost all cases of split patterns, it is best to make the pattern out of two pieces of clear white pine, the joint between the two parts corresponding to the parting line. If these two pieces are joined together with staples, corrugated fasteners or screws in Fig. 21 A, B and C, the pattern can be turned or

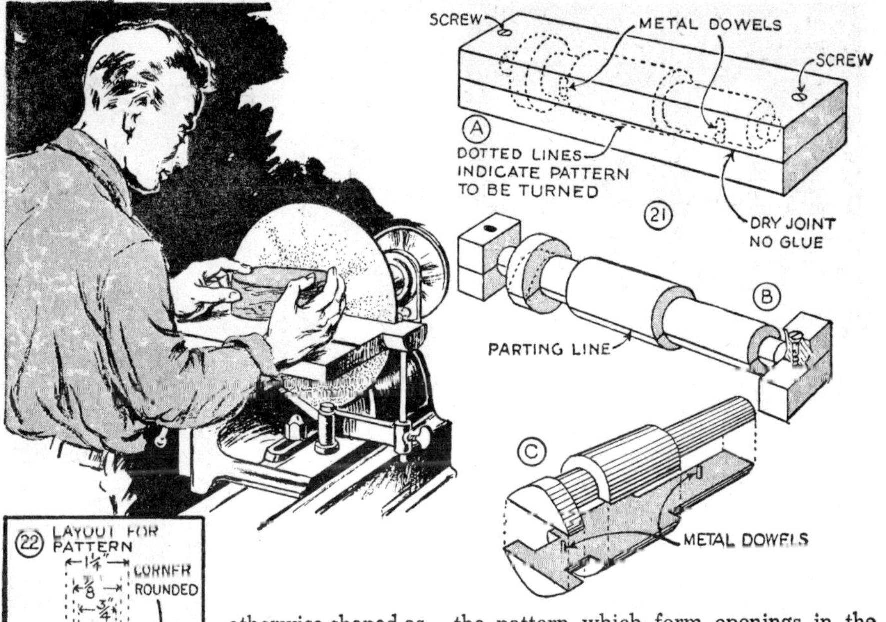

otherwise shaped as though it were in one piece. In those cases where it is not possible to locate staples or screws so that they will hold the parts together, the blocks can be joined by gluing with a sheet of newspaper between as in Fig. 19. This will give a good bond which can be broken easily when the job is completed without damage to the parts.

Before completing the V-pulley pattern you come to the matter of cores. Where a hole through the casting is required to have straight sides (without draft), or where it must be in such a position that it cannot be formed as a part of the pattern, the hole must be made by coring. In the case of this pulley the hole required for the shaft not only must be cylindrical, but it also would be impossible to form it with the pattern alone. For this reason it must be cored. Note the core prints in Figs. 19 and 22. These are simply projections from the pattern which form openings in the mold by which the core is supported as in Fig. 30. In regular practice core prints are usually tapered slightly, but in individual work where pattern and core are used only once or at most, a few times, this is seldom necessary. In small work especially, they can be the same diameter as the core and, of course, should be in direct line with the core. Usually the combined length of the core prints should equal at least half the length of the cored hole for proper support. The core prints can be either integral parts of the pattern, or separate turned pieces fastened to the main pattern with screws or dowel pins. In this particular case it will be easier to make them as part of the pattern.

Dry-sand cores are usually made in a core box of the proper shape and then baked dry. A simple core box can be made by inserting locating dowels in two pieces of white pine as in Fig. 27. Cut the pieces to such length as you want the core, then staple them together and drill the blank lengthwise, as in Fig. 28. The two halves are then separated as in Fig. 29, and the surfaces lightly sandpapered and shellacked all over. If the core is not cylindrical or if its cross-section is not constant throughout the length, hand work will be

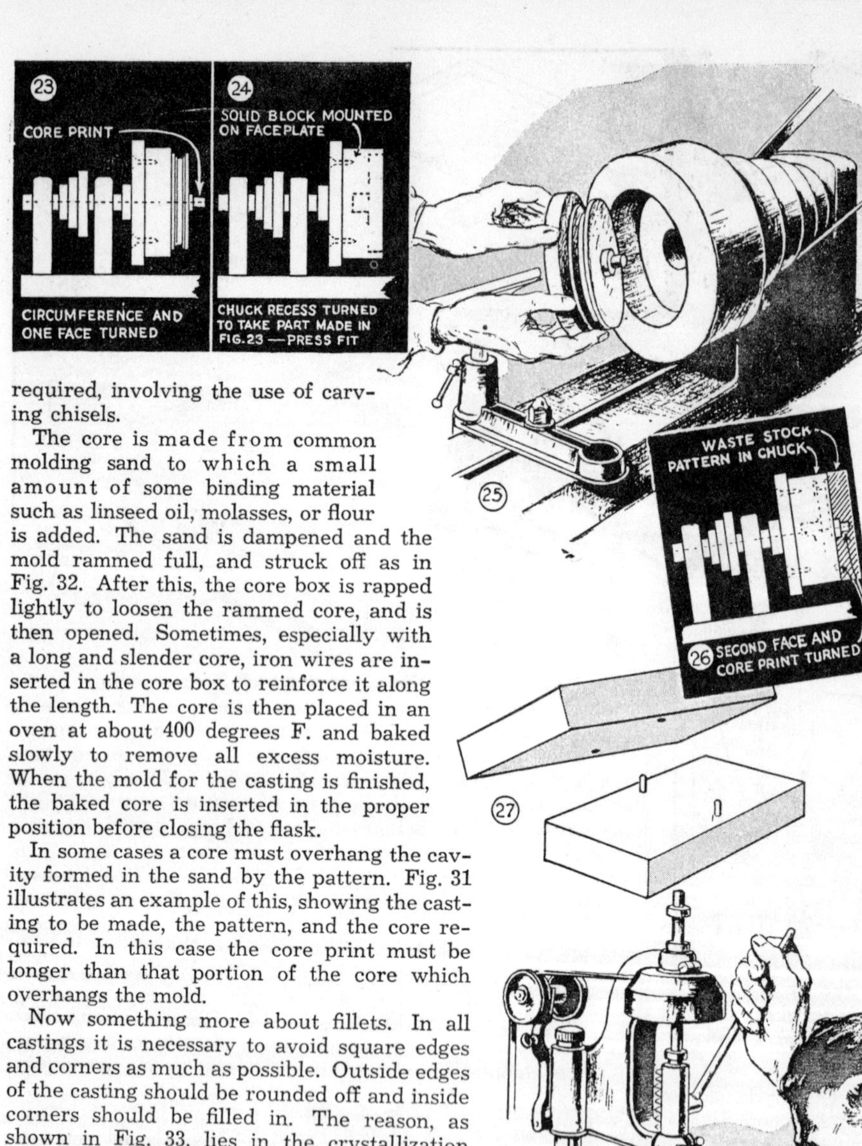

required, involving the use of carving chisels.

The core is made from common molding sand to which a small amount of some binding material such as linseed oil, molasses, or flour is added. The sand is dampened and the mold rammed full, and struck off as in Fig. 32. After this, the core box is rapped lightly to loosen the rammed core, and is then opened. Sometimes, especially with a long and slender core, iron wires are inserted in the core box to reinforce it along the length. The core is then placed in an oven at about 400 degrees F. and baked slowly to remove all excess moisture. When the mold for the casting is finished, the baked core is inserted in the proper position before closing the flask.

In some cases a core must overhang the cavity formed in the sand by the pattern. Fig. 31 illustrates an example of this, showing the casting to be made, the pattern, and the core required. In this case the core print must be longer than that portion of the core which overhangs the mold.

Now something more about fillets. In all castings it is necessary to avoid square edges and corners as much as possible. Outside edges of the casting should be rounded off and inside corners should be filled in. The reason, as shown in Fig. 33, lies in the crystallization characteristics of the metal. Crystals form perpendicular to the surface. The result is that the crystals fail to cohere at sharp corners. Shrinkage at the corner is in two directions, and the crystals are likely to pull apart and leave a crack or cavity, called a shrink hole. If the corners are rounded

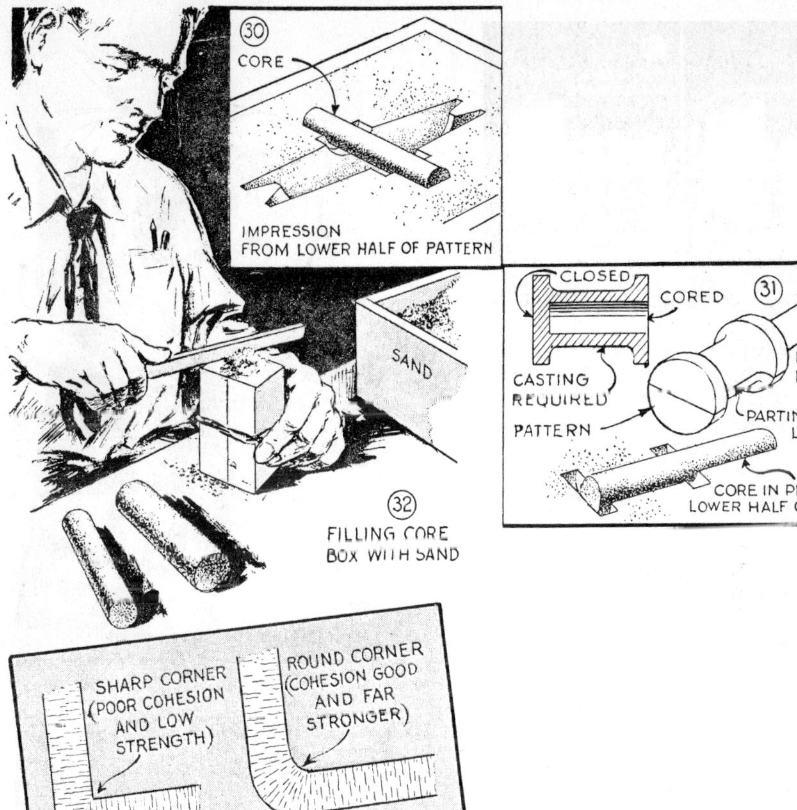

there is a gradual change in the direction of the crystal axis, and the strain is far less, resulting in a stronger casting. This is a matter which should be considered in designing an article for casting. In making the pattern, the outside corners are simply rounded off. Inside corners can be made sharp if more convenient, and then filled back with fillets.

Another point to remember in designing articles to be cast is to have as few changes in thickness as possible. Whenever a change in thickness is necessary the change should be made as gradual as possible. Thick and thin sections of the casting will not cool at the same rate and consequently distortion is likely. Moreover, where the difference in thickness is considerable, there actually will be a difference in the shrinkage, which makes warping inevitable. For these reasons castings should be designed as much as possible with constant thickness.

When the pattern is finished, dowels are inserted to hold the two halves in place. For small patterns it often helps to use a square dowel, as shown in Fig. 20. The dowels are always glued in the cope half of the pattern, never in the drag section. Holes for the dowels in the drag half should be large enough so that the two halves of the pattern will pull apart, yet sufficiently tight to prevent any play between the two parts. When the pattern has been completed it should be sanded lightly with fine sandpaper and then shellacked. Where your patterns are to be sent to the foundry, core prints should be coated with black shellac. The latter can be made by adding lamp black to ordinary shellac.

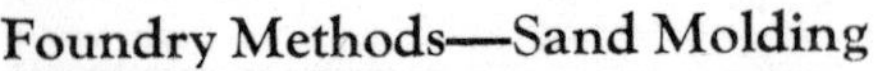

Foundry Methods—Sand Molding

MAKING castings successfully involves the use of a carefully made pattern for the construction of a sand mold, melting of the metal, and finally the pouring of the mold. Once the pattern has been completed, it is not a difficult task to prepare the mold and cast the metal. By following through with details carefully, anyone can make small castings readily out of such metals as aluminum, brass, pewter and other low-melting alloys. Although essentially the same methods apply, the higher temperatures involved render casting from iron and steel impractical for the small home shop.

Castings are ordinarily made in a sand mold. The mold is prepared from the pattern in a box, generally of wood, which is called the flask. The latter is constructed according to the general plan outlined in Fig. 30, which gives dimensions suitable for small castings. Large flasks or smaller ones also can be prepared according to the same general plan. The two parts of the flask, called the cope and drag, are con-

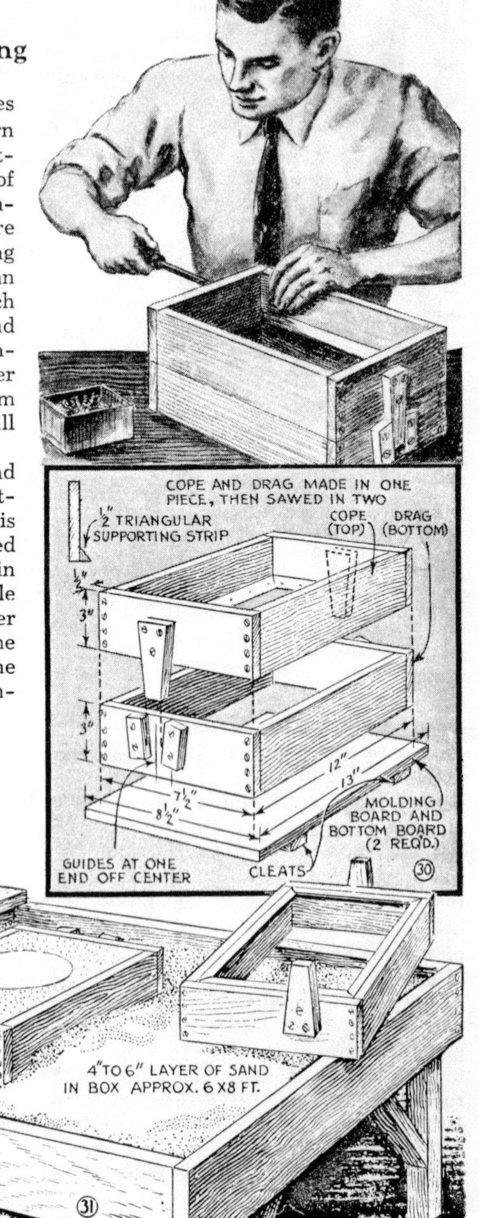

structed as one piece, then the wedges and cleats which make it possible to align the cope and drag are fastened in place with flat-head wood screws. The guides at one end should be off center so that it will be easy to realign the parts. The long wedge is then removed, the flask is sawed in half to form the cope and drag, and the wedges are replaced. A triangular strip is nailed on the inside of the cope to help retain the sand. When two flat boards (molding board and bottom board) of the size shown in Fig. 30 are prepared, the flask is complete. Fig. 31 gives you a suggestion for a handy molding bench, entirely practical for the home foundry or the small shop. It's just a roughly built affair of 1⅛-in. boards, the latter for the bottom and sides and 4 by 4-in. stock for the legs. Height to the top of the bench sides should be about 28 in., a trifle lower than standard table height. This is an aid in handling the heavy sand-filled flask and the ladles or crucibles of molten metal.

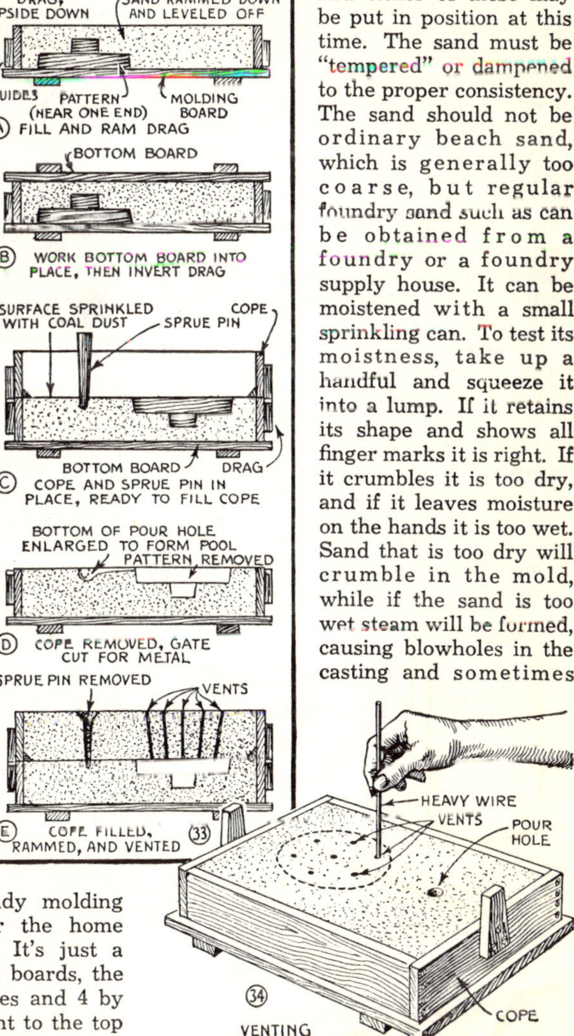

(32) RAMMER

(33)

(34) VENTING

Preparation of the mold is begun by placing the drag upside down on the molding board, A, Fig. 33, and placing the pattern in position, with parting surface down and near one end of the flask, as shown. If the draft of the pattern runs both ways from the parting line, the pattern will have been made in two pieces and either of these may be put in position at this time. The sand must be "tempered" or dampened to the proper consistency. The sand should not be ordinary beach sand, which is generally too coarse, but regular foundry sand such as can be obtained from a foundry or a foundry supply house. It can be moistened with a small sprinkling can. To test its moistness, take up a handful and squeeze it into a lump. If it retains its shape and shows all finger marks it is right. If it crumbles it is too dry, and if it leaves moisture on the hands it is too wet. Sand that is too dry will crumble in the mold, while if the sand is too wet steam will be formed, causing blowholes in the casting and sometimes dangerous blowing out of the molten metal.

The sand is spread over the pattern and rammed down firmly with a rammer, such as is shown in Fig. 32. The wedge-shaped end is convenient for ramming close to the edges of the flask. When the drag is filled and rammed, level off the top with a straightedge, sprinkle a little dry sand over the top, and place the bottom board on top, as at B in Fig. 33. Rub the board around until it rests firm without rocking, then grasp the drag and the two boards firmly between your hands, and turn the drag over. Slip the molding board off and sprinkle fine coal dust or parting sand from a cloth bag over the surface to aid in parting. Excess coal dust or parting sand should be blown off. For this operation a hand-operated bellows is very useful.

The cope is now put in place and a tapered pin set into the sand a few inches from the pattern as shown at C in Fig. 33. This is called the sprue pin and forms the sprue or pour hole. If preferred, the sprue pin can be omitted and the pour hole cut with a sharpened length of ½-in. pipe, or preferably tubing, after the cope is filled. If the pattern is in two pieces, the upper half is put in place at this time. When these preparations are finished the cope is filled with sand and rammed down in the same manner as the drag was. The top should be struck off carefully with a straightedge.

A straight length of heavy iron wire is used to punch the vents, E, Fig. 33, in the manner shown in Fig. 34. These are to permit the escape of gases evolved when the hot metal is poured, and should be about an inch apart over the entire face of the pattern. After the vents are finished, the sprue pin is removed and the mouth of the pour hole enlarged to funnel shape, so that the mold appears as in D, Fig. 33.

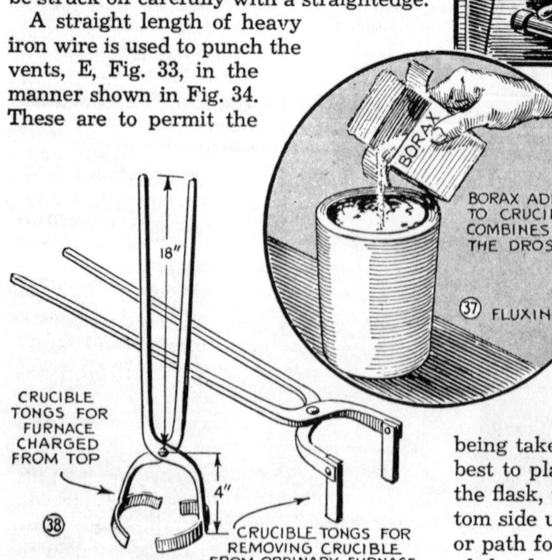

The cope is now temporarily removed and set aside, care being taken not to damage the mold. It is best to place the molding board on top of the flask, then lift the cope and set it bottom side up on the molding board. A gate or path for the metal is cut in the surface of the drag, from the bottom of the pour

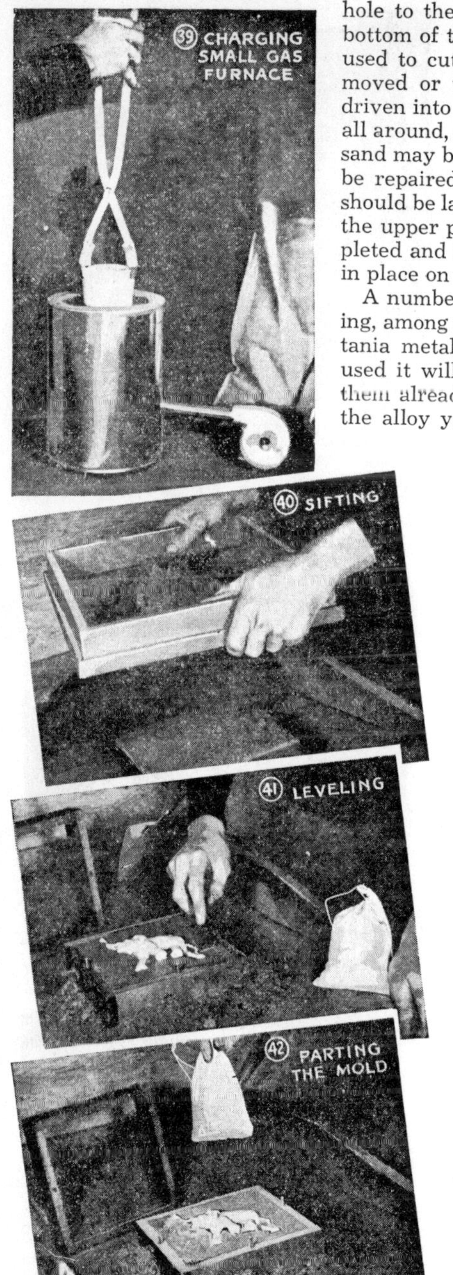

hole to the pattern. A small pool can be dug at the bottom of the pour hole. A spoon or trowel should be used to cut the gate, and all loose sand must be removed or tamped down carefully. A draw spike is driven into the pattern, the pattern is carefully rapped all around, and then is lifted from the mold. Any loose sand may be removed, and all breaks in the mold must be repaired. If the pattern is in two parts, the cope should be laid upside down on the molding board while the upper pattern is removed. The mold is now completed and it is only necessary to place the cope back in place on the drag.

A number of metals will be found suitable for casting, among them brass, aluminum, lead, tin, zinc, Brittania metal, pewter, and the like. Where alloys are used it will be just as satisfactory and cheap to buy them already alloyed, rather than attempt to prepare the alloy yourself. The metal should be melted in a crucible, either of clay or graphite or of iron. A cheap substitute for a crucible can be made from a pipe nipple and a malleable iron pipe cap. The cap must be of malleable iron to stand heating. For small quantities of soft metal an iron ladle with a long handle will be found convenient. The melting preferably should be carried out in a special gas furnace, such as the one shown in Figs. 31 and 39. This one is gas fired and is fitted with an electric blower. The softer metal also can be melted in the basement furnace, as shown in Fig. 35. The crucible should be covered, and the live coals banked around it. Low melting-point metals such as lead and pewter can be melted on an ordinary gas plate or stove, Fig. 36. In all cases a small amount of borax should be added to combine with the dross that is formed. This is called fluxing, Fig. 37. Crucibles should be handled with a pair of crucible tongs. Blacksmith's tongs to which iron jaws have been riveted as shown in Fig. 38 will be found most convenient for handling the crucible and pouring the hot metal.

Because of the high temperatures involved, it is most important to be sure that no molten metal strikes wood, paper, or anything else inflammable. In all cases, a clear gangway should be left open between the molding bench and the furnace. It is also wise to work over a bed of dry sand, especially if the shop floor is of wood. It is necessary to make sure before you lift the hot crucible from the furnace that you have a firm hold on it with the tongs. Special precautions always must be taken to offset any chance that the crucible might slip from the tongs and spill metal on the floor or on your hands or clothing.

The two halves of the flask must be held together as there will be a tendency for the cope to float when the metal is poured. One method is to lay a heavy slab of stone or metal on top of the mold.

When the mold is prepared and the metal is molten, it should be poured against the side of the sprue hole so that it flows gently into the mold. The crucible should not be held so high that the liquid will fall with excessive force. When the mold is filled it should be set aside until the metal has solidified. The excess metal in the crucible should be poured into a cavity in the sand, and allowed to cool. The "pig" thus formed can be remelted when needed. The metal never should be allowed to freeze in the crucible. Finished castings can be ground and polished as required. The molding sand can be used again but about 20 to 25 per cent of new sand should be mixed in at frequent intervals. Figs. 39 to 46 inclusive picture a variation of methods already described. Here any number of castings can be made from the same pattern, but it is necessary to ram up the mold for each separate casting. Frequently this is easier to do than making up a parted pattern, especially if the pattern is of irregular shape or is composed almost wholly of rounded or curved surfaces. In this method the drag is rammed right side up before the pattern is placed in position. The sand should be a trifle less moist than that used in the conventional procedure. After the drag has been rammed and struck off, the one-piece pattern is bedded one-half its thickness in the sand and the latter is leveled and parted as shown in Figs. 41 and 42. Then the cope is placed in position and rammed to complete the upper half of the mold. The remaining steps will be self-evident from examination of the illustrations. The cone of sand built up around the sprue pin as shown in Fig. 43 is sometimes a help when you are casting from a small pattern which has a projection extending well up into the cope. Frequently, in making small castings, the mold is not gated in the manner described, but instead the sprue pin is inclined slightly to form a slanting hole down which the molten metal runs directly into the mold.

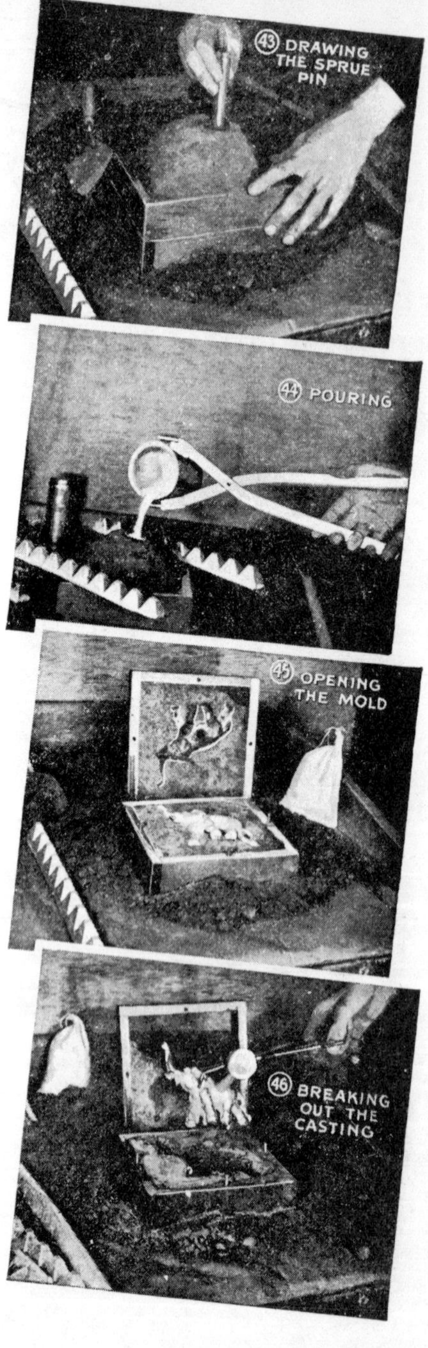
(43) DRAWING THE SPRUE PIN

(44) POURING

(45) OPENING THE MOLD

(46) BREAKING OUT THE CASTING

PERIMETER HEATING

These forced-air systems mean warm floors and more comfort for one-story basementless homes built over concrete slabs or crawl spaces

WARM-AIR perimeter heating not only improves living comfort in basementless homes but also has the advantages of simplicity and comparably low cost. Perimeter heating differs from ordinary forced warm-air heating in three ways: (1) Warm-air ducts are installed in or under the floor, keeping it warm and providing radiant heat for the rooms above. (2) Warm-air outlets with diffusing-type registers are located along outside walls at floor level and preferably under windows. This placement of the registers provides a curtain, or blanket, of warm air where it is needed most, thus eliminating the usual temperature differential in rooms. (3) Return air is taken back to the furnace through high grilles in partitions instead of through grilles located at floor level.

Four common arrangements: Perimeter-heating systems are applied in different ways. The loop system, Fig. 1, is used in basementless homes having slab-type floors of concrete. The warm-air ducts, which are embedded in the concrete, extend from the furnace to, and entirely along, the perimeter of the slab. The radial system, Fig. 2, can be used in homes built over either slabs or crawl spaces. This system does not assure an entirely warm border in slab floors, and usually is not used where the floor area exceeds 1000 sq. ft. The radial system is better suited to homes built over crawl

Certain photos and data courtesy of National Warm Air Heating and Air Conditioning Association

LOOP SYSTEM 1

RADIAL SYSTEM 2

EXTENDED-PLENUM SYSTEM 3

CRAWL-SPACE-PLENUM SYSTEM 4

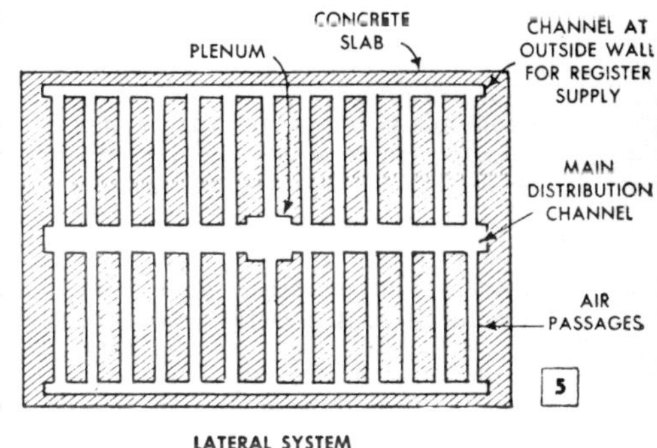

LATERAL SYSTEM

spaces, and in such installations the floor area may be over 1000 sq. ft. In long, narrow homes or where the furnace cannot be located centrally, the extended-plenum system, adaptable for crawl spaces, Fig. 3, has definite advantages in obtaining better heat distribution. The plenum is the chamber in or adjacent to a furnace from which warm air enters the distribution ducts. Fig. 4 shows a crawl-space-plenum system which is adaptable to small homes. It has stub ducts about 6 ft. long extending from the plenum. A fifth system, called the lateral system, Fig. 5, is used for large slab-floored buildings. It must be designed especially for the building to provide uniform space heating and to avoid excessively warm floors.

Dry location essential: Standing water and damp earth under a heated crawl space or a concrete slab are the cause of more unsatisfactory heating installations in basementless homes than any other single factor except possibly inadequate insulation. *Where such conditions cannot be corrected a heating system that introduces heat under or into the floor should not be used.*

You can minimize the collection of surface water under a slab or crawl space simply by installing drainage tile around the footings as in Fig. 7, A. The tile lines should have a slope of 1/4 in. per ft. They should connect to a combination sewer or a storm sewer, or to some other point of disposal such as a dry well, Fig. 7, B. The outside of the foundation walls also should be covered with a 1/2-in. layer of portland-cement plaster. After this has cured, apply a coat of damp-proofing compound or hot tar. Diversion of surface water is particularly necessary on the side of a house facing a rise of ground. In locations where the water table is apt to rise during spring months or after prolonged rainfall, it may be advisable to provide drainage lines under the house as in Fig. 7, C. The tile is covered with a substantial layer of coarse gravel or crushed stone. A moisture barrier over the gravel, Fig. 8, also is required.

Under-slab fill: Never use cinders as fill under a slab floor. Only coarse gravel with the fines removed is suitable. The layer should be at least 4 in. thick and must be

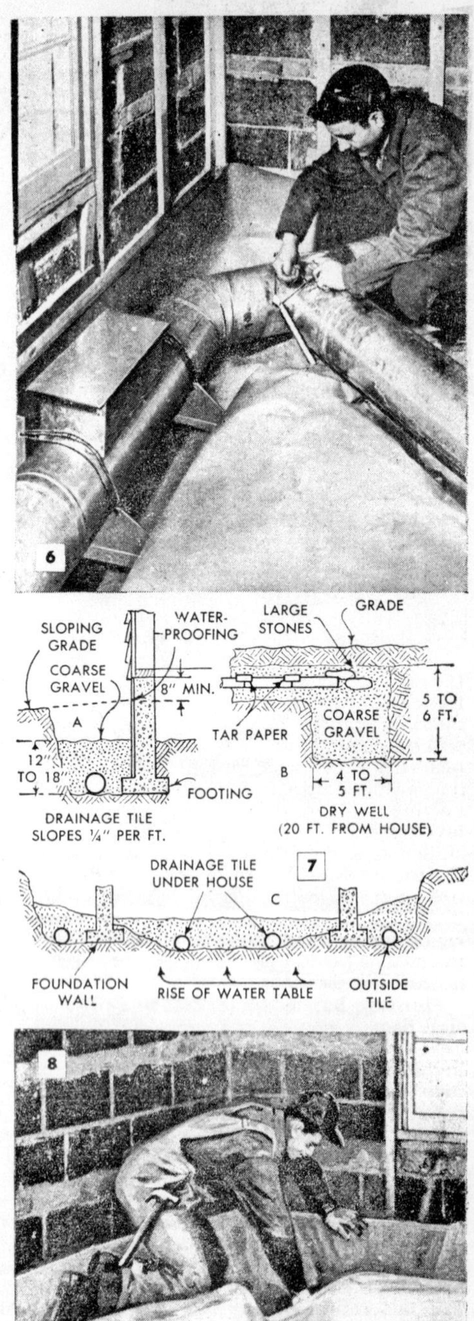

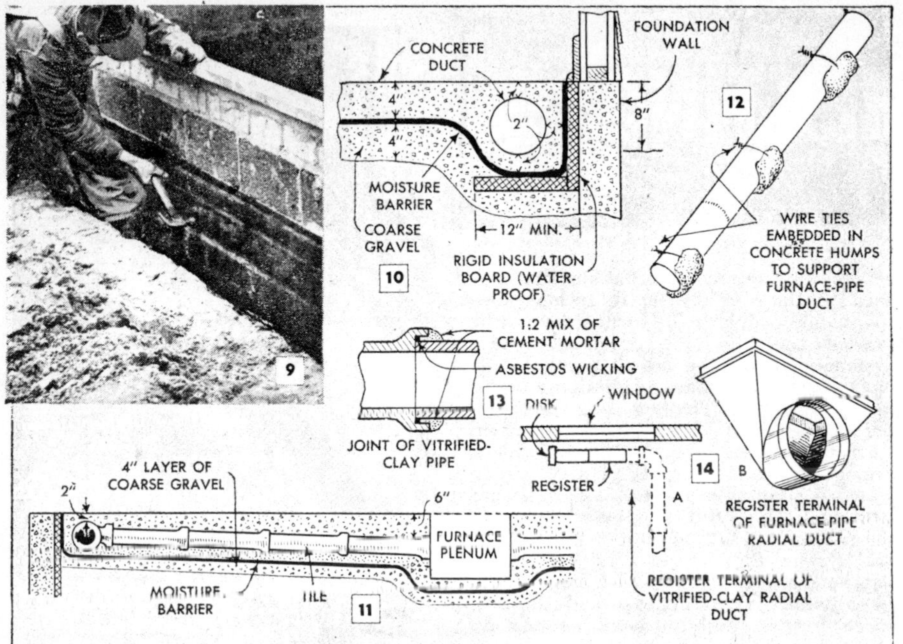

thoroughly tamped. Before placing the fill, trenches are dug at the locations of the ducts so that the gravel layer under them will be of equal thickness, Fig. 10. Trenches near the furnace plenum should be 6 in. deeper than those for perimeter ducts. Connecting ducts are sloped between the two levels as in Fig. 10. Edge insulation is installed as in Fig. 9 after leveling and tamping the gravel. This extends along the entire length of the foundation wall, between it and the slab, Fig. 10. It should be of the rigid, waterproof type, preferably 2 in. thick. The horizontal pieces should extend inward not less than 12 in.

Moisture barrier under slab: Before the slab floor is poured, the gravel fill is covered with a layer of 55-lb. asphalt roll roofing, Figs. 8, 10 and 11, which forms a moisture barrier. The edges are overlapped from 4 to 6 in. and sealed with roofing cement. The barrier should extend up along the foundation walls to the floor surface. Wherever it must be cut to fit around pipes, it should be sealed as in Fig. 19.

Placing ducts in trenches: Trenches should be deep enough to permit a 2-in. layer of concrete to be poured entirely around all the ducts as in Figs. 10 and 11. The concrete covering over ducts at the plenum should be about 6 in. thick, Fig. 11. The reason for this is to obtain uniform heat penetration through the floor—the air entering the ducts at the plenum being so much hotter than it is at the perimeter.

Installing sheet-metal ducts in slab: Furnace pipe of 28 ga. may be used for ducts. For small homes the 6, 7 or 8-in. sizes are sufficient. The size selected should be used throughout the system. Round ducts are recommended. Perimeter ducts are located so that the center of the registers will be from 7 to 9 in. inside the finished wall line to clear drapes and curtains, Figs. 16, B, and 25, B. Sheet-metal ducts must be held in place securely when the slab is being poured. This can be done by embedding wire in humps of concrete placed under the ducts to hold them at the correct height. Tie the wires around the ducts after the concrete humps have hardened, Fig. 12. Sheet-metal brackets, Fig. 6, often are used to support the pipe. Register fittings of sheet metal can be used at the ends of radial ducts as in Fig. 14, B, or rectangular forms as shown in Fig. 6 can be used.

Vitrified-clay ducts: Vitrified-clay pipe also may be used for ducts, Fig. 15. It is supported by gravel or sand, preferably fine gravel. The joints are calked with asbestos wicking, about one third their depth, then filled with a 1:2 mix of portland-cement mortar, Fig. 13. Both short and long radius fittings are used for changes of direction. The open ends of pipe at register locations of a radial system are closed with vitrified-clay disks, Fig. 14, A, which are held in place while pouring the slab.

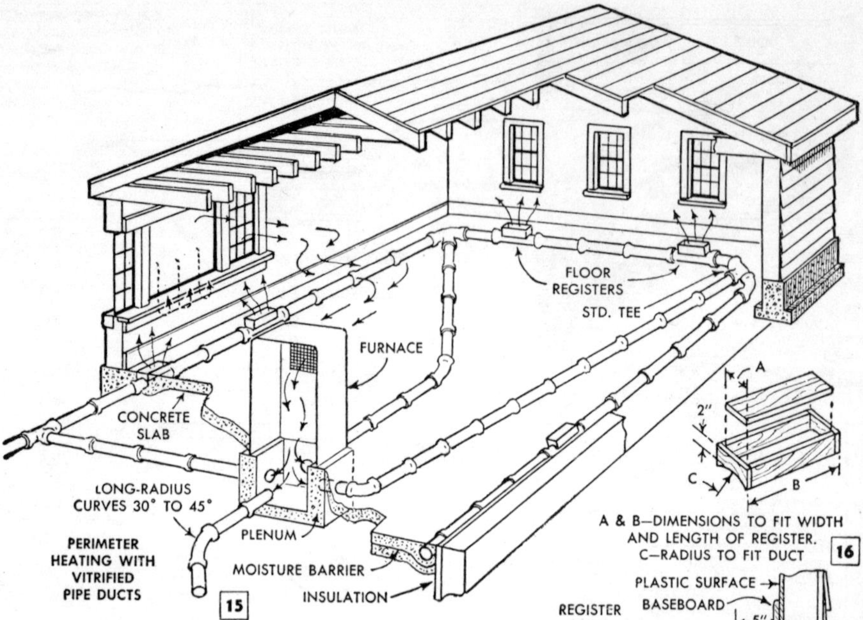

PERIMETER HEATING WITH VITRIFIED PIPE DUCTS 15

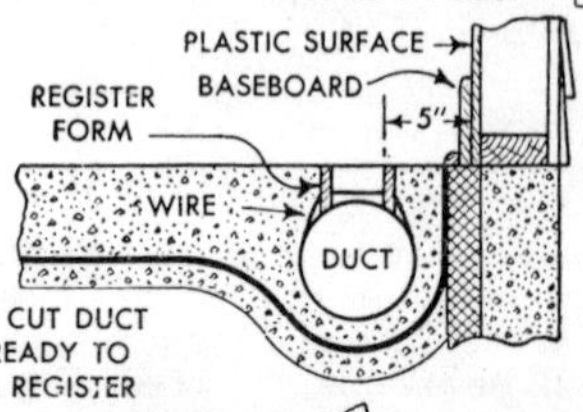

A & B—DIMENSIONS TO FIT WIDTH AND LENGTH OF REGISTER. C—RADIUS TO FIT DUCT 16

Register openings in slab floors: To form register openings in concrete over ducts, removable wooden forms fitted with covers as in Fig. 16, can be wired to the pipe or sheet-metal forms used, Fig. 6. However, the pipe is not cut until the registers are to be installed. If desired, the wooden forms can be left in place to provide a base to which registers may be fastened. Sometimes wall registers are installed just above floor level. In this case only the type designed for perimeter heating is used. Slotted baseboards may be used instead of registers, an installation particularly adaptable for crawl-space-plenum systems. Fig. 17 shows how a duct and register are placed under a kitchen cabinet that occupies the entire wall space. A wall-type register is used in bathrooms.

Concrete plenum cast with slab: In slab floors the plenum can be cast integral with the slab, using an inside form which is suitably braced. See Figs. 11 and 18, A. Sheet-metal ducts are allowed to extend through the form and are cut off flush with the wall of the plenum after the forms are removed. Vitrified-clay pipe is butted against the forms as shown in Fig. 18, B. The floor, laid after the forms are removed, should be not less than 2 in. thick, and should come from 1½ to 2 in. below the bottom of the ducts. If a metal plenum is used, it should be entirely enclosed in concrete. The plenum may be provided with

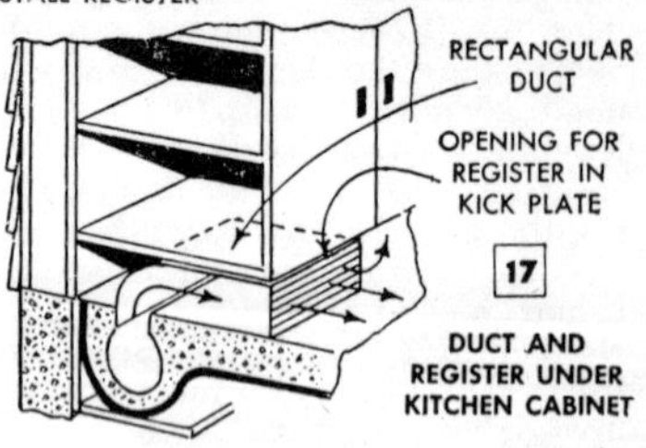

DO NOT CUT DUCT UNTIL READY TO INSTALL REGISTER

17 DUCT AND REGISTER UNDER KITCHEN CABINET

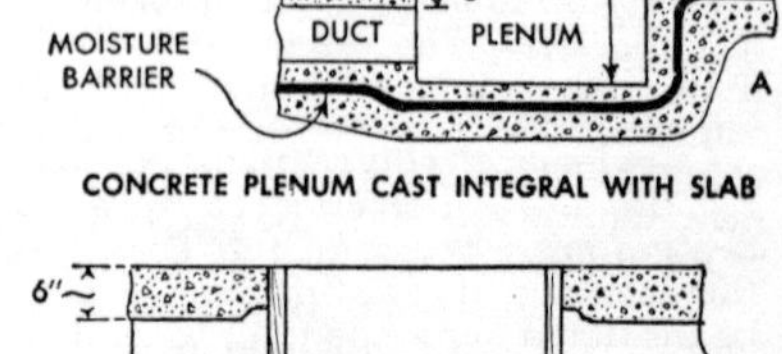

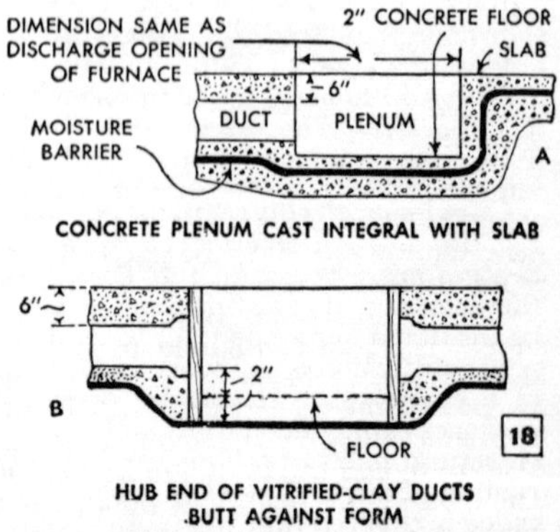

CONCRETE PLENUM CAST INTEGRAL WITH SLAB

18 HUB END OF VITRIFIED-CLAY DUCTS BUTT AGAINST FORM

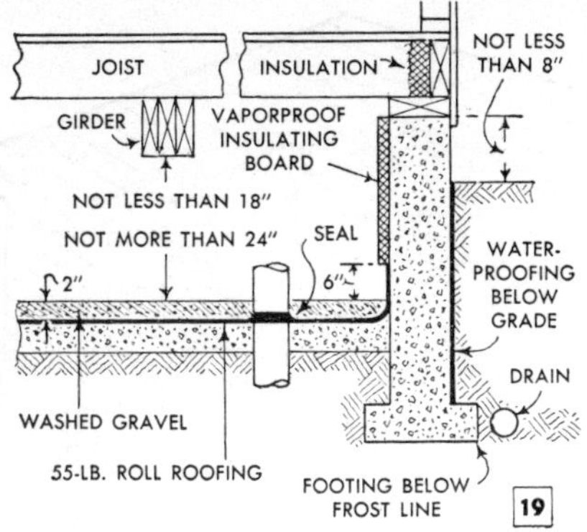

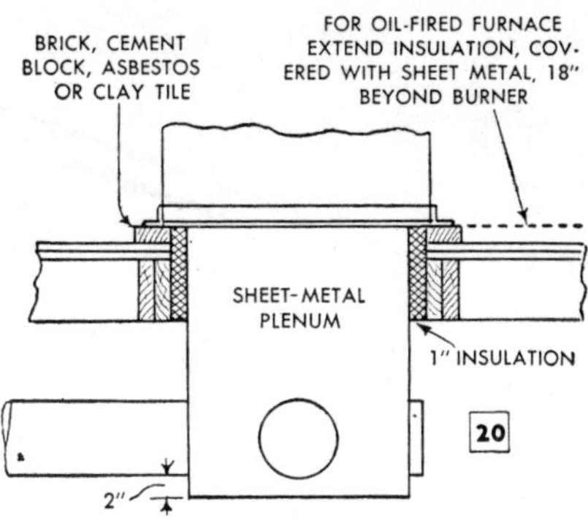

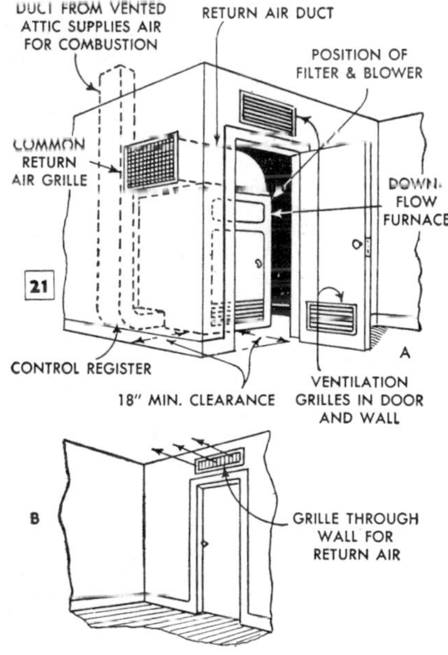

a floor drain over a small dry well as a precaution against the possibility of water collecting in the plenum due to an overflowing bathtub or water closet.

Crawl-space requirements: As shown in Fig. 19, a crawl space used for perimeter heating must be completely sealed against the entrance of moisture, and it also must be insulated and sealed at the walls to prevent infiltration of cold air. High humidity in a crawl space should be prevented as it causes rapid deterioration of the wooden structural parts of a house and also causes rusting of ducts. The earth floor of a crawl space is covered first with a layer of coarse gravel at least 4 in. thick. Over this is laid a continuous moisture barrier, the same as in slab floors. The moisture barrier is covered with a 2-in. protective layer of concrete or washed gravel. The space between the floor and the house girders should not be less than 18 in. nor more than 24 in. Foundation walls should extend below frost level and should be waterproofed on the outside. Drainage tile are provided where necessary. Cracks in the wall and those between it and the sill are calked. Rigid waterproof insulating board, 2 in. thick, is cemented to the inside of the walls with roofing cement. It should overlap the upturned moisture barrier of the floor.

Escape of air from a crawl space to an attic should be prevented by sealing all stud spaces in outside walls and partitions with insulating batts having vapor-barrier coverings. Vent openings as well as the entrance to a crawl space should be tightly sealed during the heating season. The floor of the house is not insulated, as heat transmission through it is one of the requirements of perimeter heating. Neither are the warm-air ducts insulated. The ducts may be either round or rectangular in shape and are suspended from joists, observing regulations as to clearance from combustible materials. Besides the warm-air outlets to the house, there should be one or more warm-air ducts opening into the crawl space; also a return-air duct, Fig. 22. The crawl space should never be used for storage.

Plenum for crawl spaces: The plenum for a crawl space is a square or rectangular sheet-metal chamber having the same size opening as the discharge opening of the furnace. A round plenum should not be used unless approved by the furnace manufacturer. The framed opening in the floor should be about 1 in. larger than the plenum, Fig. 20, and the space between the two should be packed with fireproof insulation. When connected to a down-flow furnace, both plenum and furnace should be supported on a base of noncombustible

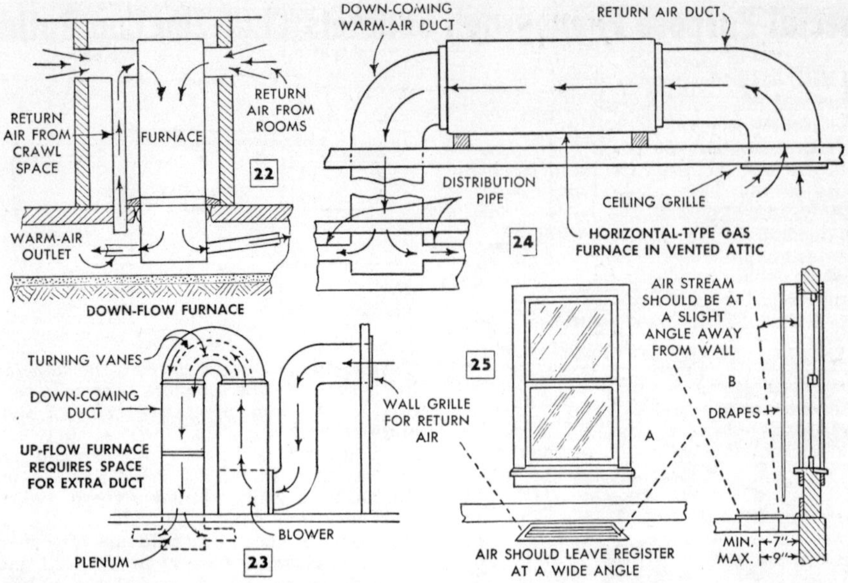

material such as brick, cement block, asbestos or clay tile. The joint between plenum and furnace must be tightly sealed with furnace cement or a suitable calking compound. The bottom of the plenum should be at least 1½ to 2 in. below the distribution pipes.

Return-air grilles: One or two return-air grilles in partitions next to the furnace, Fig. 21, A, generally are adequate for small homes. The grille, or grilles, should be of proper size and centrally located where air can flow to them unobstructed. A common return-air grille to the furnace should never be located in a kitchen, bathroom or bedroom. Fig. 21, B, shows how grilles are located over doors that are left closed most of the time. Those placed over bedroom doors should be the type that can be closed manually. When a furnace is installed in a confined space, the return-air grille in the wall of the enclosure should connect to a duct that is sealed to the furnace.

Furnace selection: Practically any automatic oil or gas-burning furnace designed for forced-air heating can be used. Although a down-flow furnace usually is the most adaptable type for perimeter heating, Fig. 22, the conventional up-flow furnace may be used if it is provided with two ducts as in Fig. 23. A horizontal gas-burning furnace can be placed in a vented attic as in Fig. 24.

If the building is so tightly constructed that a sufficient amount of air for combustion is not supplied by natural infiltration, a duct to provide combustion air can be run up to a vented attic as shown in Fig. 21, A. Clearance between the furnace and the closed door of the enclosure should not be less than 18 in. Similar clearance all around the furnace gives easy access for keeping the space clean and for servicing the furnace. A door providing access should have a grille at its bottom and another grille should be fitted in the partition above the door to provide for normal ventilation of the enclosure.

Automatic temperature controls: Automatic controls are furnished with the furnace. The room thermostat, which operates the burner, should be located at the recommended height on a partition well away from warm air coming from the registers, and also where temperatures are least likely to fluctuate from opening doors or using a fireplace. For perimeter heating, slow, continuous forced-air circulation is preferred, with the burner operating at frequent intervals, the room thermostat being adjusted to a differential of 1½ deg. In down-flow furnaces, failure of the blower to function will cause the filter motor and blower to become overheated. To prevent damage an additional limit-control switch is installed to turn off the burner when such trouble occurs. Registers should be of the type designed to discharge warm air in a fan-shaped spread and away from the walls as in Fig. 25, A and B. Registers should be fitted with adjustable dampers, or valves.

★ ★ ★

Special-Purpose Phonograph Cabinets That You Can Build

HERE ARE two phono cabinets that will meet the requirements of any music lover, or critical experimenter in high-quality recorded sound reproduction. Both cabinets are also attractive furniture pieces, whose simple design would fit in appropriately with practically any style of interior decor. The cabinet illustrated in photo A is designed for use with a separate loudspeaker; it houses the turntable and the amplifier and is placed some distance away from the loudspeaker enclosure, or exponential horn. Installed in a central location, it can be used with any multiple speaker for various rooms in the home or school. With a separate installation of this type, the loud bass notes are far enough away to prevent microphonic action of amplifier tubes, and feedback vibration on the delicate pickup required for present-day electric-cut records is eliminated. Another view of this cabinet appears in photo C and the detailed construction sketch, Fig. 2, on the following page. This cabinet is 38 in. high, 22 in. wide and 17¼ in. deep; the height given includes the hinged lid. Bins are provided for various sizes of record albums, so that you may accommodate the regular 10 and 12-in. disks as well as long-playing records.

Cabinet B is slightly smaller and is designed for those who prefer to use an 8-in

A

B

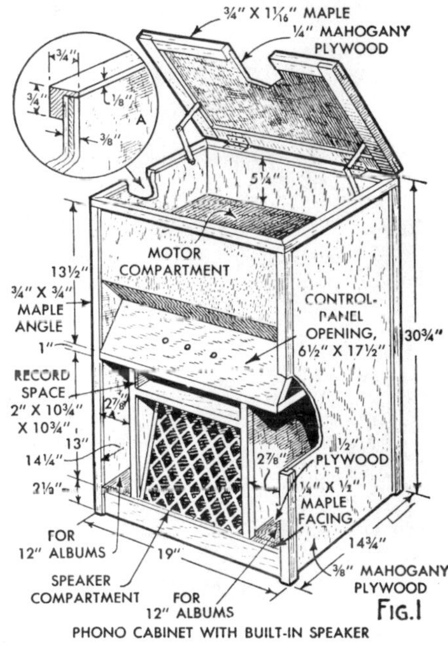

FIG. 1
PHONO CABINET WITH BUILT-IN SPEAKER

built-in PM speaker. Small bins on each side of the speaker take either 10 or 12-in. record albums. Above the speaker is a space for "loose" 10-in. records. The speaker panel is tilted to match the slope of the amplifier control panel. This slope in the speaker panel aids the hearing of treble notes which come from the speaker cone in a beam. All construction details are shown in Fig. 1. The case is made of ⅜-in. mahogany-faced plywood; the amplifier control panel and the center of the top are made of ¼-in. mahogany-faced plywood. All of the plywood edges of this cabinet are covered with solid maple "angles." Other front edges are faced with ¼ x ½-in. maple. The usual grille cloth and brass openwork outer cover for the speaker grille are held in place with ¼ x ¼-in. maple strips fastened with brads. Deep-red mahogany stain is used on the plywood sides, panel and top. This contrasts nicely with the natural blond color of the maple edges and facing as illustrated in the photo. The maple is finished with boiled linseed oil. The final finish for this cabinet, which is shown in photo B, is obtained with a clear varnish, rubbed down, and waxed.

The larger phono cabinet, photos A and C, detailed in Fig. 2, is also made of ⅜-in. mahogany-faced plywood bound with ¾ x 1-in. mahogany angles as shown, and using ⅜ x ⅜-in. mahogany facing for the storage bins. The amplifier space is 16 in. deep, and the control-panel opening is 4½ x 20½-in. The inner partitions are ⅜-in. fir plywood, painted a deep blue. The turntable motor board is ½-in. fir plywood and this is also painted a deep blue. All mahogany is stained dark red, given a coat of clear varnish, and then rubbed down and waxed.

For ordinary amplifier controls only three knobs and identifying plates are required (volume, treble and bass) and a toggle switch with an on-off plate. There is plenty of room on the panel for other controls if they are required. Two record changers were installed in the large cabinet, photos A and C. One was a combination for the long-playing 33⅓-r.p.m. and the regular 78-r.p.m. records, and the other was for playing the small 45-r.p.m. records. The motor compartment is 4⅝ in. deep and can be made deeper if necessary to house record changers of any type. Always check the dimensions of your equipment before starting construction.

The dimensions of these phono cabinets are not critical and can be easily changed by the builder to meet individual requirements. The record-album storage space can be modified in the one cabinet, photo C, to provide more depth room for any large amplifier or record changer. The other cabinet, photo B, may be used to house a radio-receiver chassis for a small phono-radio combination if the controls and dial can be shifted to the narrow control panel.

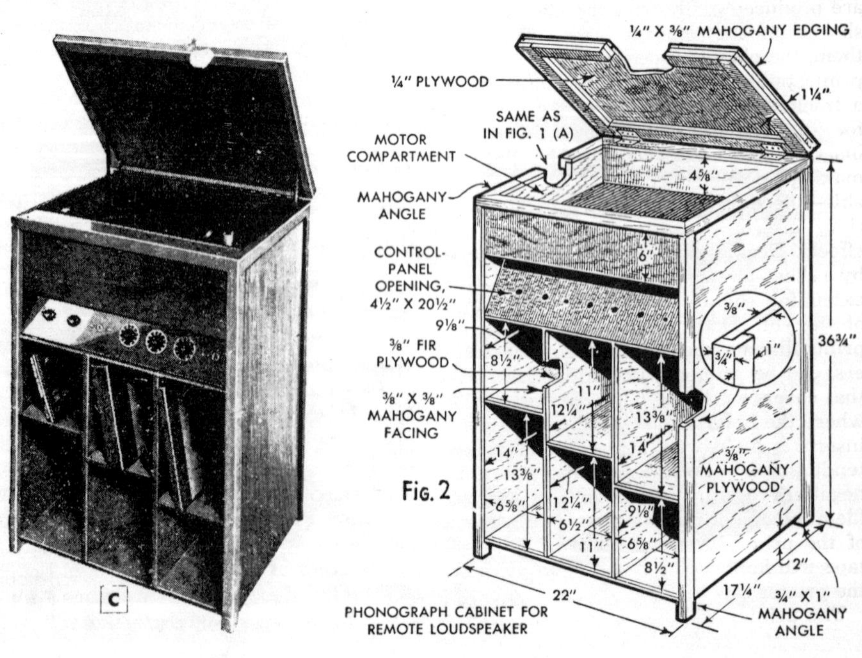

Cable Release Operated By Darkroom Timer

If your camera is not equipped with a built-in timer for taking self-portraits, you can use a darkroom timer of the windup type to trip the shutter remotely at a preset time. Just tape the end of the cable release to the timer's face in a position where the side of the pointer will contact and depress the plunger when it reaches the preset interval. Masking or adhesive tape can be used to fasten the cable to the timer.

Masking Arms of Photo Easel Squared on Ruled Card

To assure even borders on prints, the masking arms of a photographer's easel can be squared quickly by using a card ruled with crosslines at ¼-in. intervals as shown. When the arms have been lined up with adjacent lines, masking or adhesive tape may be used to secure them in position. The back of an 11 x 14 piece of double-weight print paper is satisfactory for this purpose.

PHOTO EDGE PRINTER

Photographer's Edge Printer

Plain or decorative borders on photos are produced easily with the edge printer shown on the opposite page. To make them, the photographer simply inserts the prints, pulls the handle of the platen down a fraction of an inch and closes a switch for the necessary exposure. Normally, black borders are satisfactory, but by making a portion of the printer top removable—piece A in Fig. 1—and providing various inserts, you can produce different effects. Deckle-edge borders are produced by a sheet-metal mask having a wavy edge extending slightly over the front portion of the slit. Dots to locate ring holes on prints that may be filed in loose-leaf binders, can be printed with an opaque mask that covers all of the light opening except where the holes are located. If one of the inserts is fitted with a piece of glass extending over the opening, you can use strip negatives to print your name and address, file numbers, or other matter on the edges of the prints. A small piece of cellulose tape will hold such a negative in place on the printer top.

The printer contains a 60-watt tubular lamp, the light passing through a slit in the top. Inside length of the box should not be less than 18¼ in. to provide enough space for the lamp and sockets, and the distance from the top surface of the lamp to the upper surface of the slit should be about 2 in. No danger exists from enclosing the lamp in such a small space as the lamp will be on intermittently only for a moment at a time. Paint the top surface a dull black—other parts may be any color. A wood stop is provided on the platen as detailed in Fig. 3. If desired, the stop can be made adjustable for various widths of borders. When no pressure is being exerted on the handle, the platen should rest so that its front edge is about ⅛ in. above the top surface of the box to permit insertion of the print. To keep the platen raised, a strip of springy sheet metal is mounted under the edge. Velvet or other soft cloth on the underside of the platen provides even pressure and assures a light seal. A red pilot window that indicates when the lamp is on, and a small switch are mounted on the front of the box as shown in Fig. 2. A diagram of electrical connections is given in Fig. 4.

EDGE PRINTER

Borders Your Photos

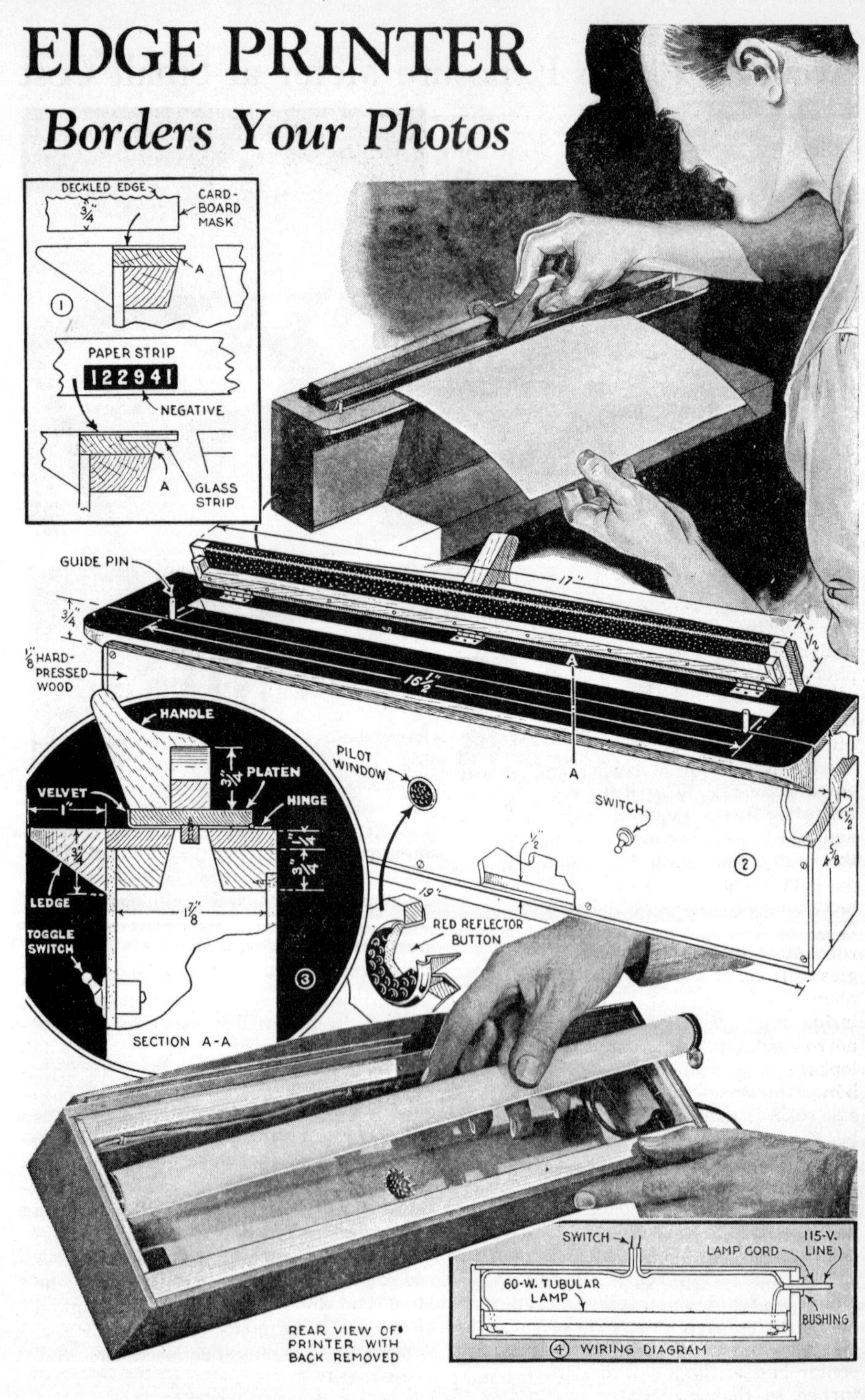

REAR VIEW OF PRINTER WITH BACK REMOVED

Accurate Photo Exposure Meter at Small Cost

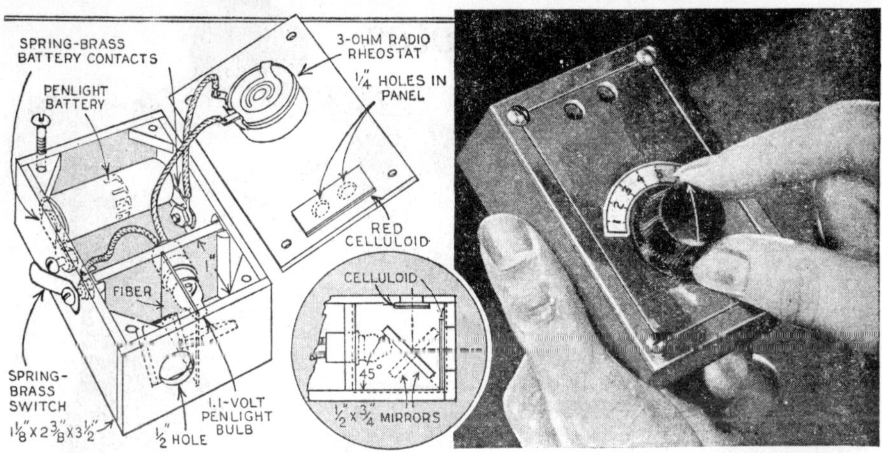

To use this exposure meter, you first look through two peepholes, one showing the illumination of the scene to be photographed, and the other showing illumination from a flashlight bulb. Then you turn a rheostat until both are of equal intensity. The illustration shows the parts and their arrangement, the bulb being mounted on a removable strip to facilitate replacement. Note the two small mirrors set at 45-degree angles in front of the peepholes. Red Cellophane is glued over both holes on the inside and a piece of black paper with a narrow slit across it is glued over the Cellophane so that you will see a narrow ribbon of red across the peepholes. The rheostat scale is marked off in seven divisions between points where the rheostat gives maximum and minimum illumination. A corresponding scale on the back, placed above two rotating, concentric dials, also has seven divisions. The dials are each divided into twenty divisions and marked as indicated. They rotate on a small bolt which has a pointer, this being set permanently to point toward the left, directly over the second division mark from the center line of the small dial when this is turned so that the center line points to

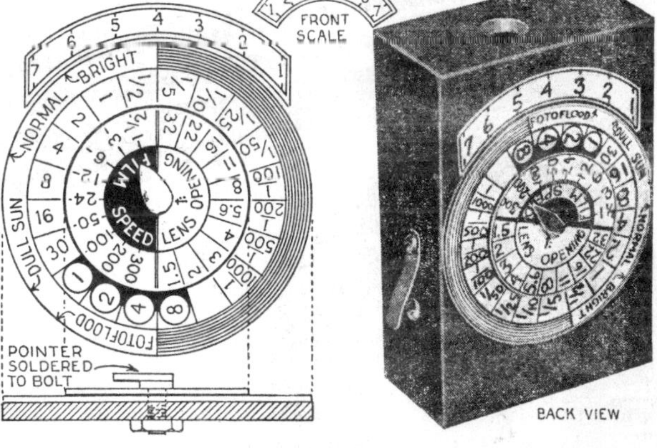

number 4 of the stationary scale. In use, hold the meter about 8 in. from the subject, adjust the rheostat to matching illumination and note reading. Set the large dial so the arrow from "bright" or other designation at edge of large dial points to rheostat reading on the stationary scale. Then turn the small dial so the number representing the Weston speed value of the film in your camera is directly under the pointer. Opposite portions of the two dials give the range of shutter speeds and corresponding lens openings that may be used to expose the photograph properly. Note that the arrowheads on the edge of the large dial are located over certain division marks just below the arrowheads. To assure accurate readings with the meter, replace the dry cell frequently.

Versatile FLASH-FLOOD LAMP UNITS

BUILT from common electrical parts at a nominal cost, the lamps of this lighting outfit can be used separately or in various combinations. Also, the unit can be packed into a flat carrying case no thicker than the diameter of a photoflood bulb. Parts needed to make it are sockets, shade holders, a 3-way plug, an extension cord, a flash gun and reflectors that can be flattened when unhooked at the seam. To use the outfit as a 2-lamp flash unit, screw the plug into the flash gun and insert the lamp leads as in Fig. 1. If desired, an extra lamp for overhead lighting can be connected into the third outlet of the plug. When using photoflood lamps, unscrew the 3-way plug from the flash gun and connect it to an extension cord, Fig. 2. A simple bracket, consisting of a short length of tubing fitted with a bolt and wing nut, permits the unit to be supported on a folding lamp or music stand, Fig. 3. To use the flash gun with a single reflector merely unscrew the parts required from the unit. Fig. 4 shows how the outfit can be used for an overhead bank of lights by suspending it from a support with cords or wire tied through holes in the ends.

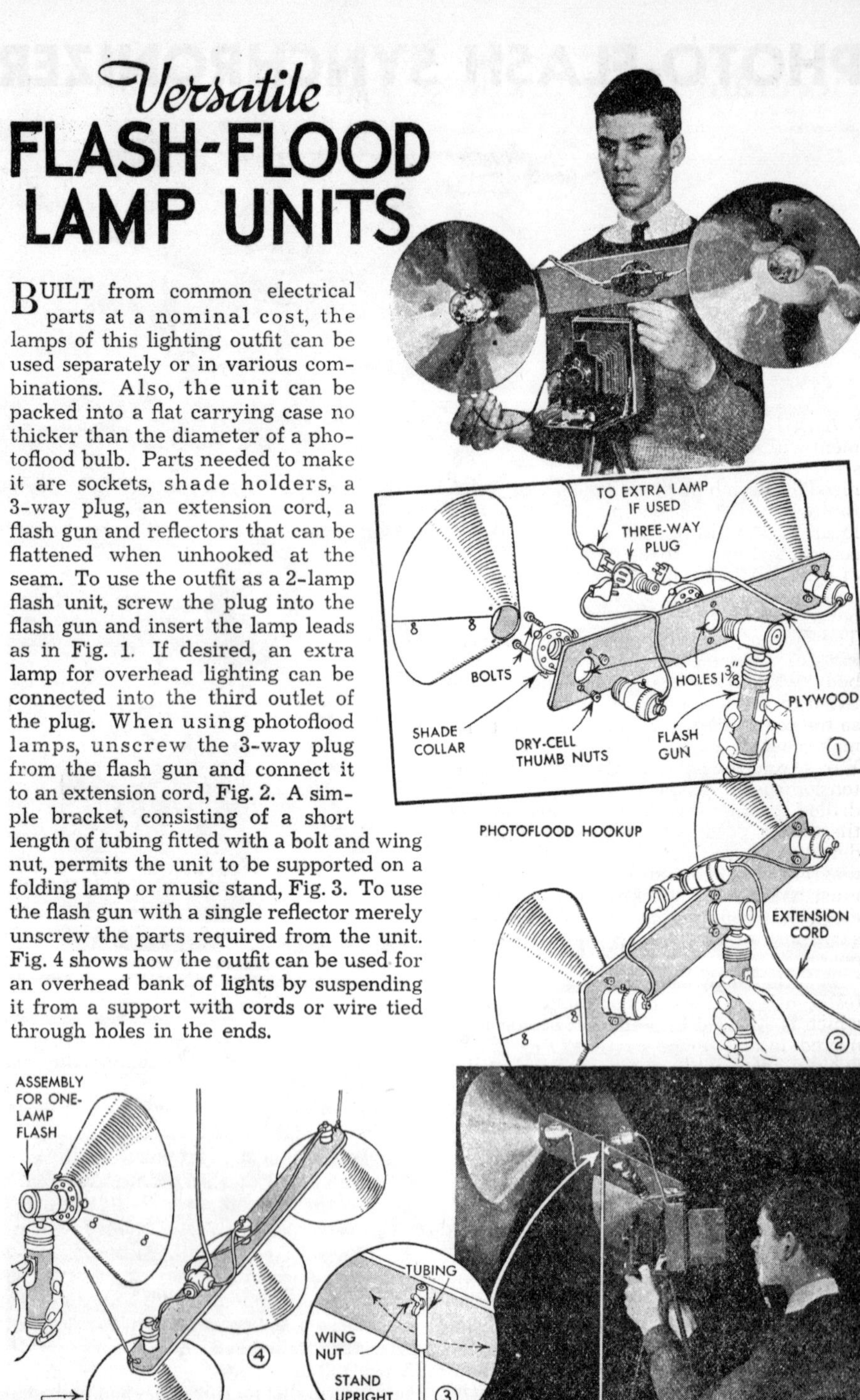

PHOTO-FLASH SYNCHRONIZER

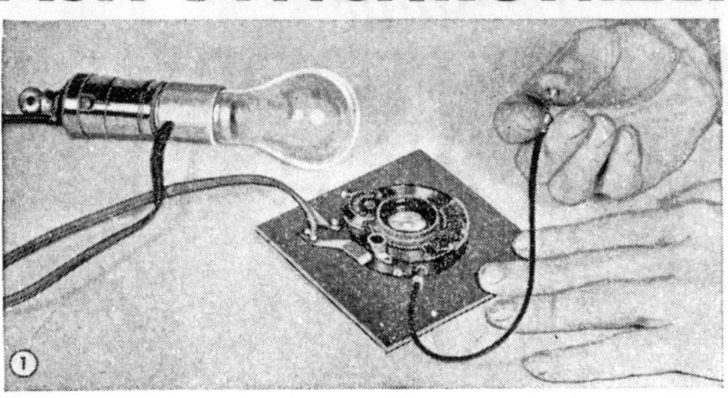

Auxiliary lens equipment with the cocking type shutter can be synchronized for flash bulb photography by using the cocking lever of the shutter as a contact switch. Two strips of brass about 5/16 in. wide make up the switch, as can be seen in Figs. 2 and 4. The shorter piece is clipped under the timing scale, or some other part of the shutter body, while the longer piece, which is fastened to the lens board, is bent and fitted so the cocking lever will brush over it and make contact when the shutter is operated. Wires from the switch terminate at an extension socket on the flash gun. A hole is drilled through the insulation and shell of the socket, permitting the wires to be soldered in place, as indicated in the wiring diagram, Fig. 2. Adjustment of the switch must be set so the cocking arm closes the electrical circuit and flashes the bulb at the same instant that the shutter diaphragm opens.

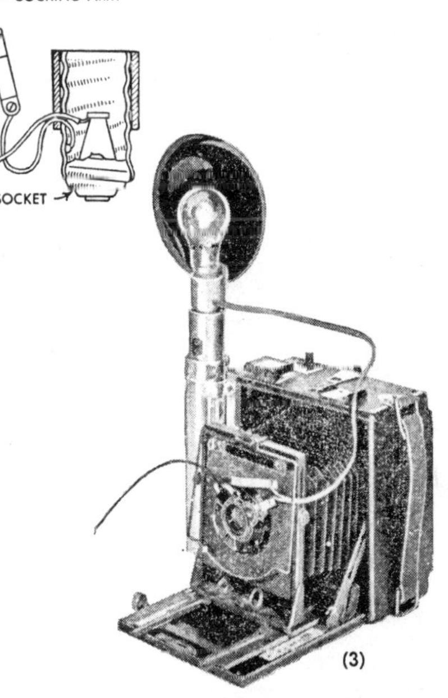

This is easily checked by making a tester using a 15-watt bulb in the socket which is screwed into another socket connected to the house current, Fig. 1. To avoid a shock when the lever brushes the spring during cocking, do not connect the socket to the outlet until this operation is complete. By watching the shutter, or by looking through the lens, it is easy to determine when the switch arm is properly located. The bulb should light when the shutter is open. The finished setup with a camera is shown in Fig. 3, the extension socket fitting into any standard type of flash gun. Good results are obtained with this switch up to a speed of 1/25 second. For this reason, fast-action pictures cannot be secured. At faster speeds, it is not wholly reliable since the contact is so momentary that the bulb sometimes fails to go off. Do not put the bulb in the socket until the shutter is cocked as the lever touches the switch arm during this operation and completes the circuit. This would flash the bulb when the shutter was closed.

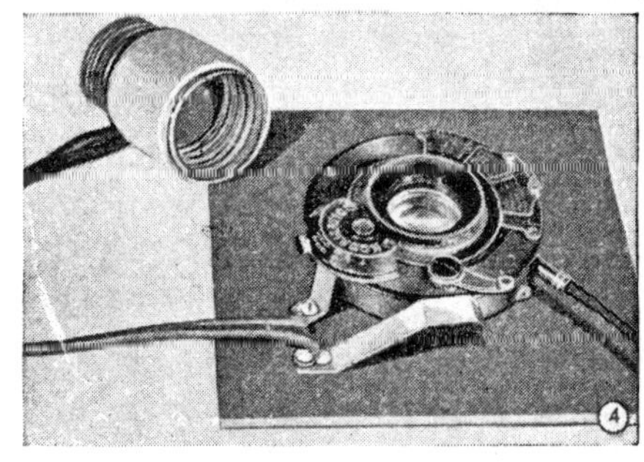

Saucer Used as Flash Reflector

When you wish to make flashbulb photographs and a regular reflector is not at hand, a white china saucer will serve as a substitute. The saucer is held against the bulb and socket as shown. This leaves one hand free to operate the camera. Care should be taken to hold the saucer and socket so the hand will be protected if the bulb breaks when it is flashed.

Flood Lamp Can Be Clamped Directly to Movie Camera

To keep the floodlight focused directly on a moving subject while filming movies, a unit such as the one shown can be clamped directly to the camera. This type of lighting is satisfactory for close-ups and especially suitable for photographing children because the photographer can follow the child about the home without stopping to move a separate lighting unit. Built-in reflector-type lamps can be used if the camera is loaded with extra fast film.

Clamp-On Photoflood Reflector

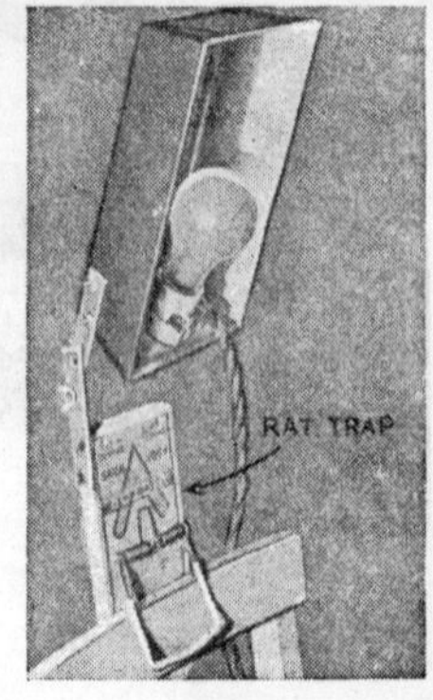

Using only a baking pan, a rattrap and a few odds and ends, this reflector for No. 1 floodlights can be made in a short time. The light socket is screwed to a piece of wood which in turn is fastened to one end of the pan. One part of the pivoted support is bolted to the side of the pan and the other to the side of the trap. Adjustment is provided by a wing nut which fastens the two parts of the brace together. Wrap the trap jaw with adhesive tape.

Flood Reflector Doubles as Spot

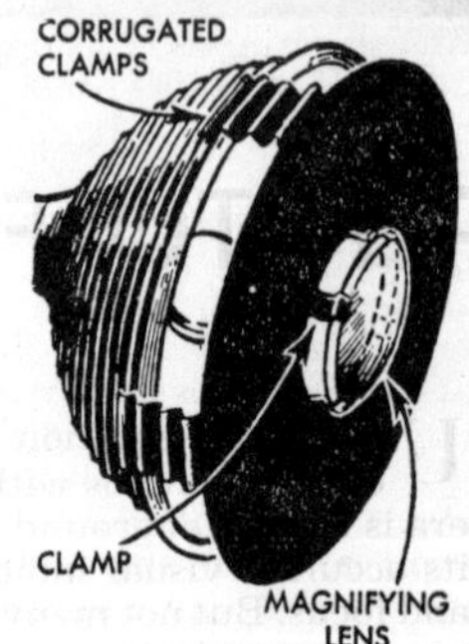

Photoflood lamps can be used as spotlights by attaching a metal shield fitted with an ordinary magnifying lens. The shield, of scrap sheet metal such as an empty oil container, is cut large enough to cover the reflector entirely, leaving four tabs about 2 in. by 4 in. which are bent as shown to clamp over the reflector rim, and are corrugated so as to be adjustable at various distances from the lamp. Four small tabs left when cutting the opening in the center, are bent to hold the lens in place.

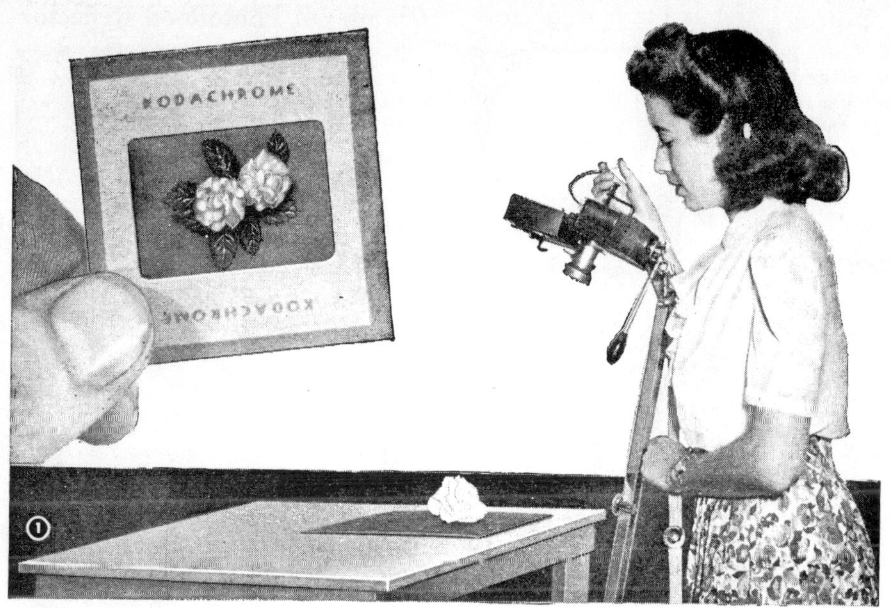

PHOTO FOCUSING ATTACHMENT

ULTIMATE solution to the problem of close-up photos with a miniature camera is the use of ground glass focusing with its accurate visual indication of both field and focus. But not many of the smaller cameras are regularly equipped with this convenience. Here is a copying attachment that makes needle-sharp focusing possible at very reasonable cost. With minor changes in the dimensions it can be made to suit several makes of miniature cameras of the type having a removable tube-mounted lens. The attachment consists of three units. One holds the lens and takes the tripod screws. Hinged to it at the bottom is a second unit which holds the camera box. Hinged at the top of the first unit is the third which carries the ground glass for focusing. This latter unit swings down into focusing position as in Fig. 2, while the second hinged unit holding the camera body swings out of the way as shown. Figs. 1 and 7 show the positions reversed with the camera box back in shooting position. Parts are shown in order of assembly in Fig. 3 and are detailed in Figs. 4, 5 and 6.

First get a lens mount or adapter ring to fit your camera lens. Then make up the lens-and-tripod unit as in Fig. 6. One member should be made of 3/8-in. plywood as in Fig. 3. Bore a hole of the size indicated, or vary it to suit the adapter ring you have, and screw the latter in place. Next come the swinging friction catches, which are bent to the shape shown in the lower view, Fig. 3. It will take a little careful measurement and then perhaps a trial bend or two in order to get these catches to perform properly. As you see in Fig. 7, these hold the camera-supporting unit when it is swung up into position. Notice especially how the camera unit is made. The hole through it is counterbored and this forms a light trap when the camera box is in position back of the lens. The camera box is held tightly against the opening by means of a bracket and clamp screw detailed in Fig. 5 and shown in the center view, Fig. 3. When hinging the camera unit to the lens unit be sure that the lens openings line up.

The ground-glass unit, Fig. 4, is made last. One dimension is quite important and will vary slightly with different makes of cameras. The dimension—1 29/64 in.—is, in this particular instance, equal to the distance from the front of the panel of the camera unit to the film-emulsion surface

in the camera box. A shift of 1/64 in. or so in a 2-in. lens changes its focus from 18 or 20 ft. to infinity. So it's important to make sure of this dimension by using a depth-gauge reading to 1/64 in. or less. Also, the front and back faces of this part should be parallel.

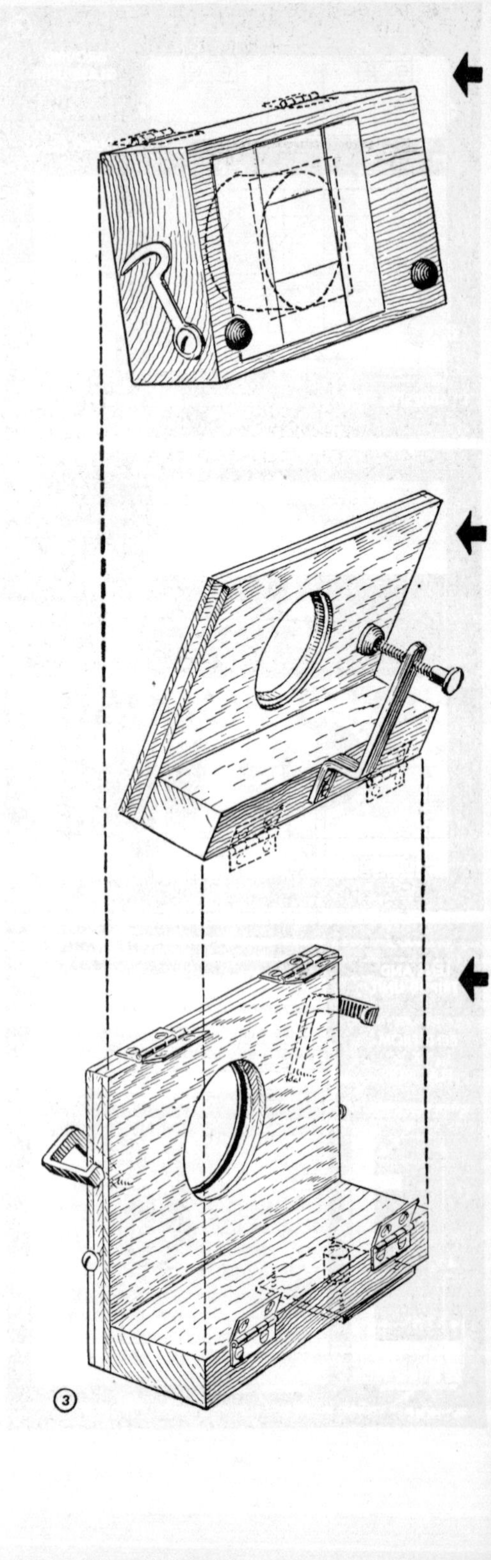

Next, bore a 1 7/8-in. hole through the block, locating it on the center indicated in Fig. 4. When the block is in position on the lens unit, the top edges of both units should be flush and the holes should register. Then attach hinges and hooks.

Two pieces of 2 by 2-in. lantern-slide glass are required for the ground glass although only one actually is used. The other serves as a grinding "tool." Mix abrasive powder of the grade known as "microscopic fine" with a few drops of oil and apply this to one side of one piece of glass. Then simply rub the two pieces together to produce a focusing surface. Draw diagonal lines from the corners of one glass and, with these as a guide, draw a rectangle 1 by 1½ in. to represent the picture or image area. Then center the glass over the lens opening with the ground side next to the block and with the top edge flush with the top edge of the unit. Fasten with adhesive tape. Two rubber-headed tacks, placed as in Fig. 5, protect the glass from breakage should the camera unit inadvertently be swung upward.

Now you are ready to check for correct focus and field. To check for focus, fit the camera lens on the adapter ring and, with the diaphragm wide open, set the focusing

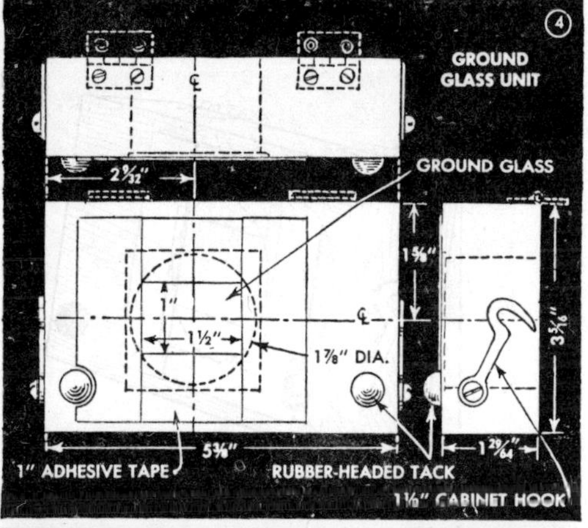

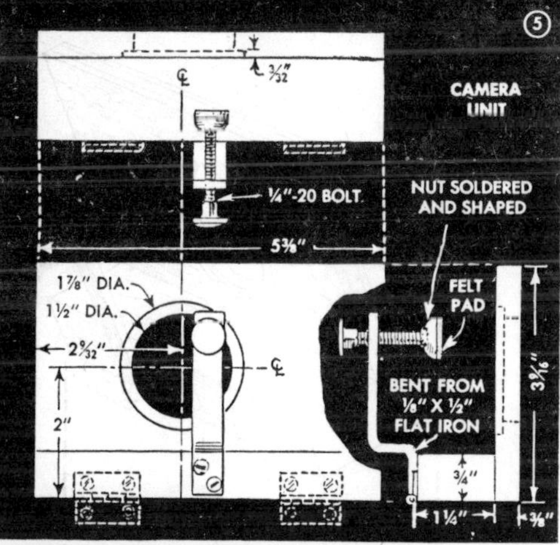

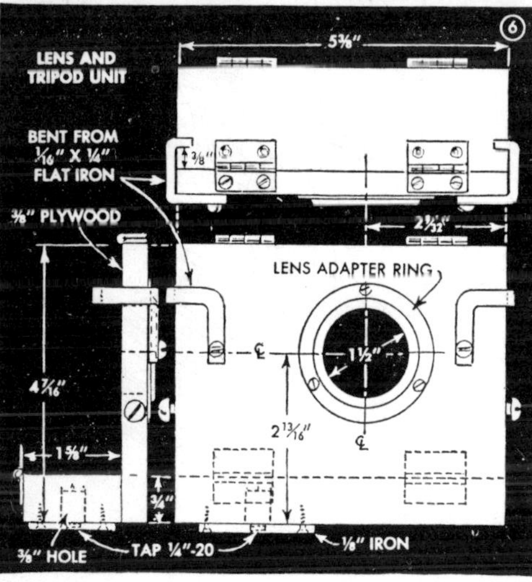

scale near the middle of its range, say about 12 ft. Load the camera and lock it in place on the camera-holder unit. Swing the ground glass unit into position as in Fig. 2. Place a magazine page about 12 in. directly in front of the lens and bring the camera into position as in Fig. 7. Make a test exposure. Then, without altering the lens setting, change the focus one division on the scale and make another exposure. Proceed in the same way until you have exposed film at four settings each way on the scale. Keep notes on each exposure.

Make 8 by 10-in. blowups from all negatives. The first should be the sharpest. But should a closer scale reading give the sharpest negative, then it's necessary to determine the amount of lens movement between the two settings. Usually this can be done by inserting a thickness gauge between the focusing scale ring and the depth of focus indicating collar. From this you can determine the difference in the two settings. Shim the ground glass back an equal distance and you have the focus corrected.

To check the field, use the same setup and mark on the magazine page the four points corresponding to the corners of the field on the ground-glass image. Enclose the rectangle with heavy ink lines and draw diagonals from the corners. Print a bold letter "T" near the top of the rectangle and then make a test exposure. With this point as a guide, it's easy to shift the ground glass slightly to correct any error in position.

Focusing Spotlight for Indoor Photography

A focusing spotlight, Fig. 2, ideal for table-top photography or similar projects where large areas need not be lighted, can be made using a standard 6 by 6 by 6-in. metal radio cabinet and a chipped condensing lens. Begin by removing the covers of the cabinet and draw diagonal lines on the top to locate the center. Cut a 3-in.-dia. vent in the top, Fig. 1, and fit a baffle to form a light trap. Then cut the slot in the bottom so the bulb can be moved for focusing. This slot also admits air for ventilation. A flange-type socket is fitted in the slot and slides back and forth in the light trap. A spice can, or a can of similar size, will serve the purpose, detail C of Fig. 1. Two 1/4-in. holes are drilled in the sides of the cabinet and 10-32 screws are inserted to hold the box in the cradle.

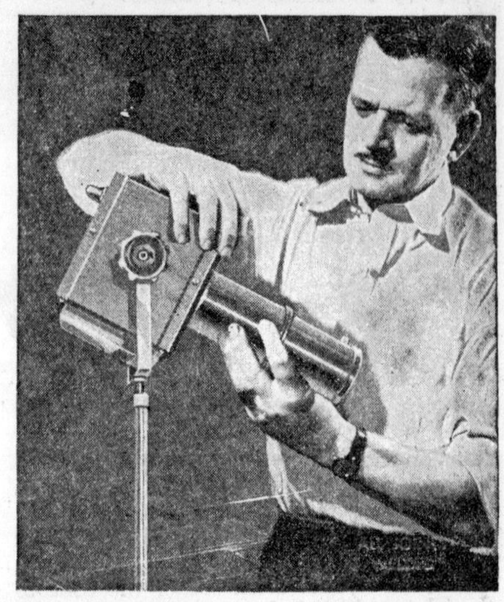

The opening in the front panel for the lens, detail B, Fig. 1, should be small enough so that it will cover any imperfec-

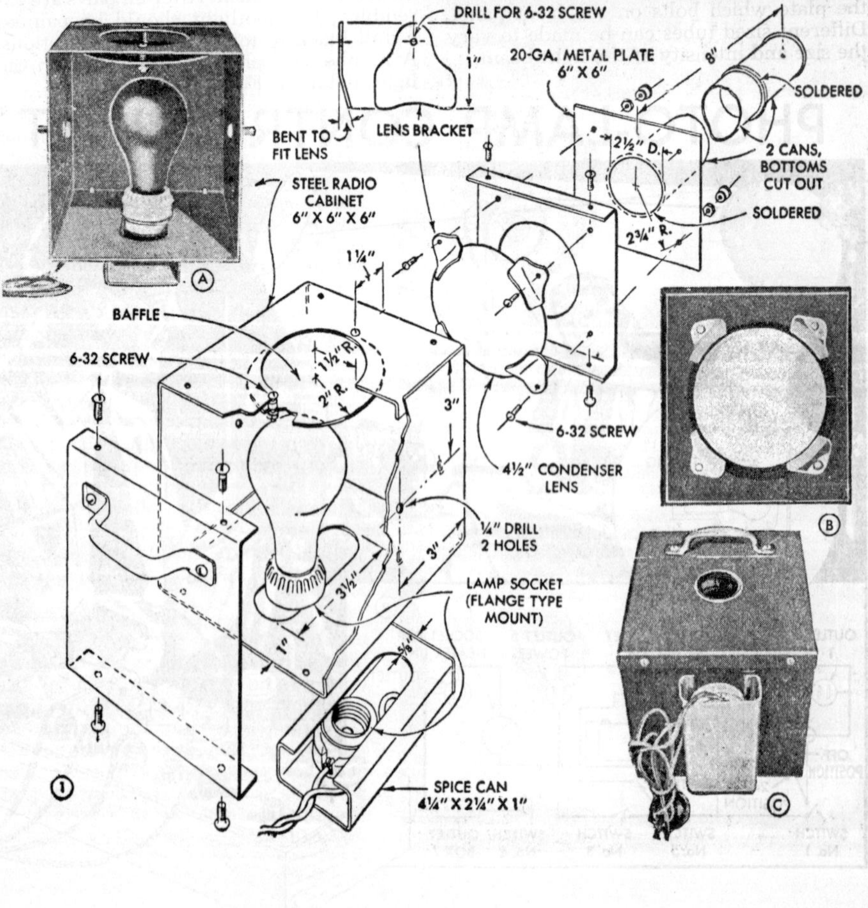

DRILL FOR 6-32 SCREW
1"
BENT TO FIT LENS
LENS BRACKET
20-GA. METAL PLATE 6" X 6"
8"
SOLDERED
2 1/2" D.
2 CANS, BOTTOMS CUT OUT
SOLDERED
2 3/4" R.
A
STEEL RADIO CABINET 6" X 6" X 6"
1 1/4"
BAFFLE
6-32 SCREW
1 1/2" R.
2" R.
3"
6-32 SCREW
4 1/2" CONDENSER LENS
B
1/4" DRILL 2 HOLES
3"
3 1/2"
LAMP SOCKET (FLANGE TYPE MOUNT)
1"
5/8"
SPICE CAN 4 1/4" X 2 1/4" X 1"
1
C

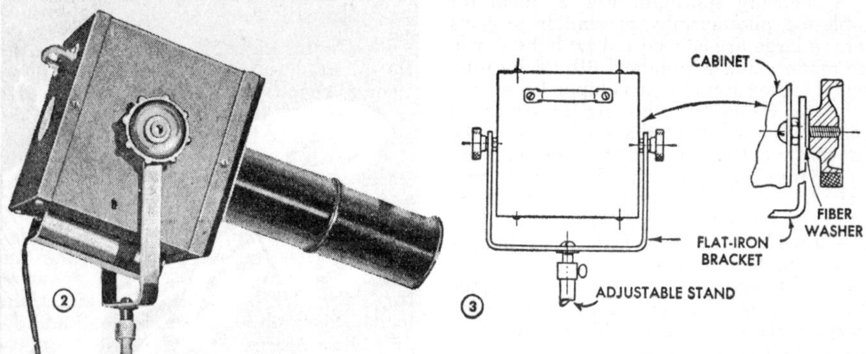

tions on the edges of the lens. The flat side of the lens is held against the panel with clips, as shown in Fig. 1. To make the light-control tube, cut the tops and bottoms out of two cans of the same diameter and solder them end to end. Then solder the tube to the plate which bolts on the front panel. Different sized tubes can be made to vary the size and intensity of the light beam.

For a diffusing device, organdy stretched over a sewing hoop will give just the right effect. The cradle, Fig. 3, is cut from a piece of flat iron and fastened to an adjustable stand so the light can be raised or lowered. As another aid to adjustment, a handle is fastened on the back. After all parts are assembled, the spotlight should be painted a dull black to minimize light reflections. A number one photoflood is shown in the light, detail A, Fig. 1.

PHOTO-LAMP CONTROL UNIT

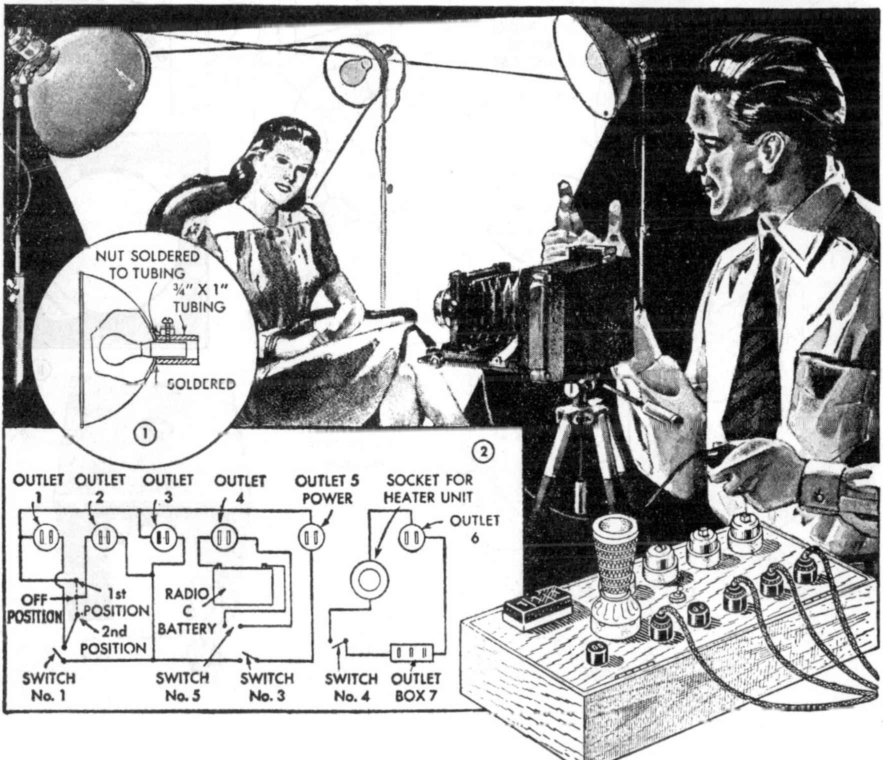

WITH this multiple-outlet unit you can control photo lamps for focusing, flash and flood lighting from one control panel. The unit consists of a battery of outlets and switches conveniently arranged on the cover or lid of a small wooden box of suitable size and depth to house the wiring and connections. The box lid serves as a panel on which the switches, plugs and a socket for a 600-watt porcelain heater unit are mounted. The box should be made from ½-in. hardwood.

Six-volt focusing and flash: Reflectors from 1937 Ford headlights are altered as in Fig. 1 by soldering a ¾-in. length of copper tubing to the back of the reflector in the position shown. A setscrew and nut hold the midget bulb adapter in place. By moving the adapter back and forth the light can be focused for both spot and flood. As many as six reflectors can be used. To operate, turn heater unit into the socket and plug the 110-volt line into outlet No. 6, Fig. 2. Plug reflectors, with 32-candle-power headlight bulbs, into outlet No. 7. Turn on switch No. 4 to focus and arrange lights. Turn off switch No. 4 and substitute midget flash bulbs. When switch No. 4 is turned on, bulbs will flash.

Floodlight: Plug 110-volt line into outlet No. 5 and plug floodlights into outlets Nos 1 and 2. Then turn off switch No. 1 and turn switch No. 2—designated by 1st, 2nd and off positions in Fig. 2—to the second position which dims the lights for focusing Turn on switch No. 1 and turn No. 2 to the first position for bright.

Flash on floodlight circuit: Turn off switches Nos. 1, 2 and 3 and plug the 110-volt line into outlet No. 5. Turn on switch No. 3 and plug lights into No. 3 outlet and focus. Then turn off switch No. 3 and remove flood lamps from outlet No. 3 and replace with flash bulbs. Turn on switch No. 3 and bulbs will flash.

Battery flash: Outlet No. 4 is connected to a 6½-volt radio C battery and by plugging into this outlet with flash bulbs and closing switch No. 5, the bulbs will flash. You can use any voltage C battery and flash any reasonable number of bulbs.

IF hot, bright photoflood lamps make your subjects uncomfortable while they are being photographed, this fluorescent portrait lighting unit will solve your problem. Its rays are intensely rich in actinic value and you should be able to click away at 1/10 second at f:16 on normal speed Panchromatic film. You will find that the negatives have a surprisingly long scale of tones and a welcome sparkle. The unit consists mainly of six 100-watt fluorescent tubes mounted on a piece of ¼-in. plywood and wired as indicated in Fig. 7. The unit is suspended from the studio ceiling and can be tilted to almost any desired angle.

Start construction with the combination reflector and mounting board, which is reinforced at the edges on the back side with wood cleats as in Fig. 1. This reinforcement is necessary to stiffen the board when it is suspended. After the cleats have been screwed in place, attach the tube-socket

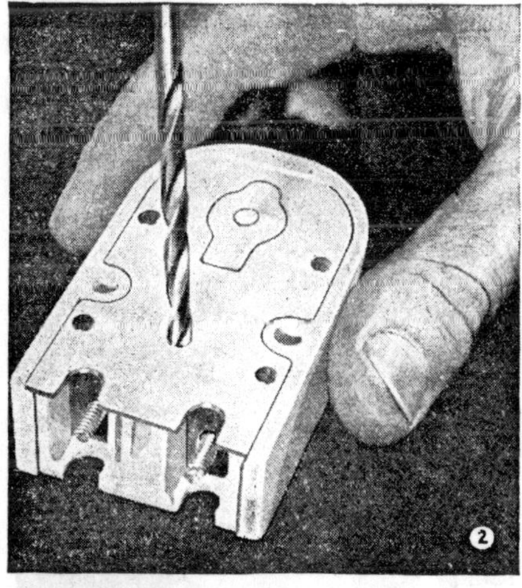

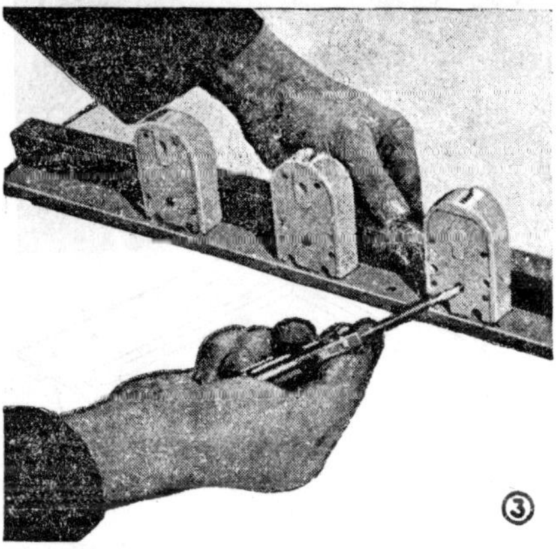

mounting cleats to the opposite side as indicated, and then paint this side with a washable, flat-white paint. You will need two sockets for each tube, or 12 in all. These usually are obtainable without mounting assemblies. Each socket should have a ³⁄₁₆-in. hole drilled in it as in Fig. 2 so that it can be screwed to the mounting cleats. Fig. 3 shows how the sockets are attached to the mounting cleats with a long wood screw through each one. In order that the unit be self-starting when the current is turned on, automatic tube starters are used. You will need six of these, one for each tube, and their sockets. The starters should be of the two-prong type and are mounted on the back side of the reflector close to the tube sockets, Fig. 5.

The unit now is ready for wiring. This may seem rather complicated at first glance, but upon closer examination of Fig. 7 you will see that the entire circuit is merely a repetition of the hookup of the first two tubes. At one corner on the back side of the reflector, attach a nine-contact terminal strip as in Fig. 4. All the wiring is done on the back of the reflector, as indicated in Fig. 7, and the wires connect at the terminal strip.

After completing the wiring on the reflector board to the terminal strip, you are ready to install the tube ballasts. Three of these are required, one for each pair of tubes. If there is any possibility that you may wish to transport the unit, it is best to mount the ballasts separately so that the unit can be taken apart. If all parts were installed on the reflector, the unit would be heavy to move about. Mount each ballast on a board about 1 by 7 by 21 in. in size, as indicated in Fig. 6, and wire the outlet end of each ballast to one 3-pole polarized receptacle and input end to one 2-pole polarized plug. Then connect the 110-volt line to three 2-pole receptacles, wiring the latter in parallel. There should be a switch in the line for turning the unit on and off.

You will need a cable consisting of three 3-wire smaller cables. The cable can be made up from ordinary lamp cord or other flexible insulated wire, and can be of any length required to reach from the terminal strip on the reflector board to the ballasts, usually about 20 ft. Each of the small cables terminates in a 3-pole polarized plug and is connected to the terminal strip. In Fig. 7, each wire is numbered so that you can easily trace it through the terminal strip, cables, ballasts and on to the 110-volt line. By following these numbers you should experience no difficulty in wiring the unit.

For example, wire No. 1 runs from a tube socket to the terminal strip, through one of the cables, then through the 3-pole plug and receptacle and into the outlet end of the ballast. Wire No. 2 is treated similarly. Wire No. 3 also is handled the same way except that it goes around the ballast directly to one side of the 2-pole plug, then to the 110-volt line. In Fig. No. 7 wire No. 3 is shown going into the cord leading from the current supply or input end of the ballast. Since there already are two wires coming out of this end of the ballast, wire No. 3 is merely connected to the one on the left-hand side as you face the ballast. Wires 6 and 9 are connected in a similar manner. In all cases, be sure that you connect the correct wires to the correct prongs in the plugs, and that the wires leading from the receptacle terminals correspond to those on the plug prongs.

This completes the unit except for installing the tubes, which should be of the 3500 Kelvin type as this color temperature is best suited to most portrait work. Before hanging the unit it is advisable to test it. To do this, first check the wiring, then put the tubes and starters in their sockets, plug in all ballast connections and close the switch in the 110-volt line. The tubes will flicker once or twice and then light up. Tubes or starters that fail to operate should be checked in other sockets.

A simple but strong ceiling support for the reflector can be made as indicated in Fig. 10. The support consists of three pieces of 1¾-in. square stock, the two vertical pieces being attached to the picture molding at the ceiling with small corner irons. Heavy angles are used at the joints between the horizontal and vertical members to reinforce them. A strong hook should be screwed into the bottom surface of the horizontal member and a small pulley hung from it for easily suspending the reflector board. A short length of clothesline rope is tied to two heavy screw eyes driven into the upper edge of the reflector near the ends. Another length of rope is tied to the center of the first, then run over the pulley in the support and down to a screw hook in the lower edge of the reflector at the center. The length of this latter rope will determine the height of the unit from the floor. Several loop knots

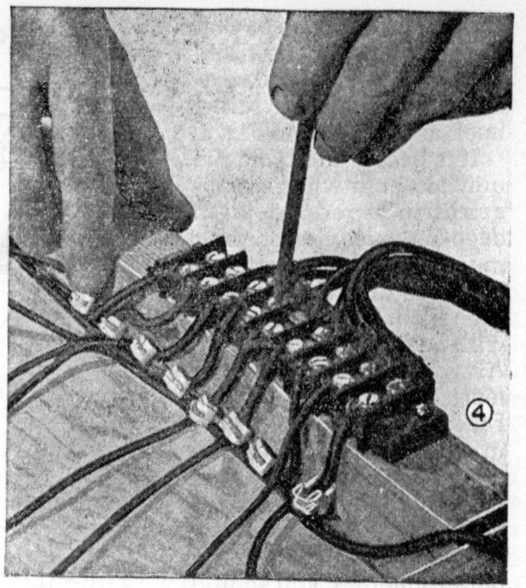

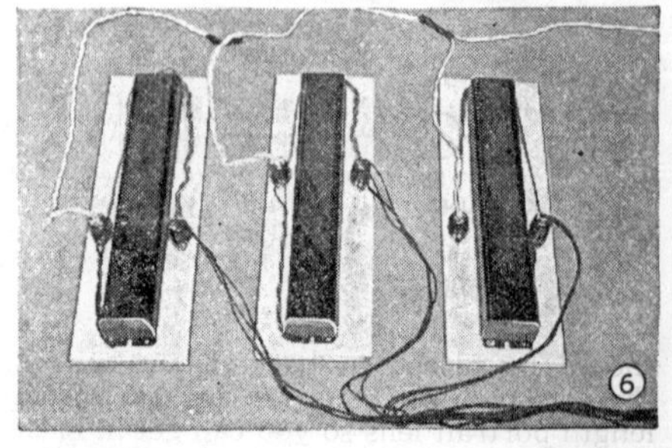

are tied in this rope so that the reflector can be tilted by hooking one of the various loops into the screw hook as indicated in Fig. 8.

It is best not to hang the unit too high when photographing people with deep-set eyes. A portrait must show high lights in the eyes and if you raise the unit too high, the eyes will be in subdued light. Always have the model at least 8 ft. from the unit. Fluorescent light is rich in violet rays and if the model is too close, the skin tones will appear chalky in the print. Although the unit does not cast sharp, harsh shadows, you should balance its light with a 100-watt lamp in a reflector on the side of the face opposite the fluorescent unit and close to the floor at a distance of 6 ft. from the model. Small spotlights or 150-watt mushroom lamps can be used to provide pickup lights in the hair. These lights

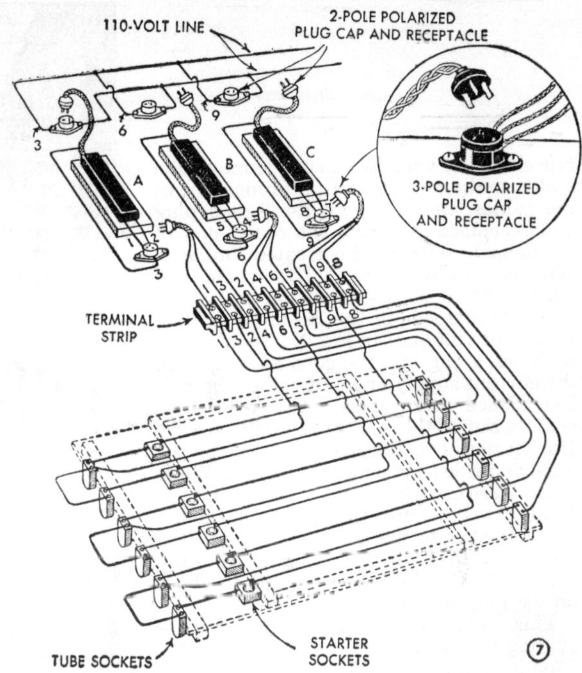

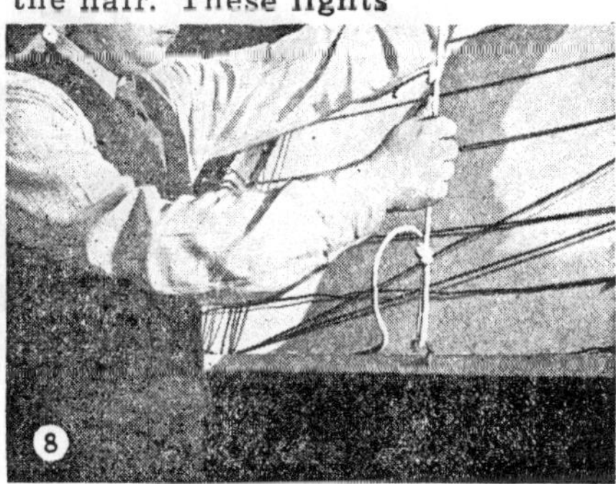

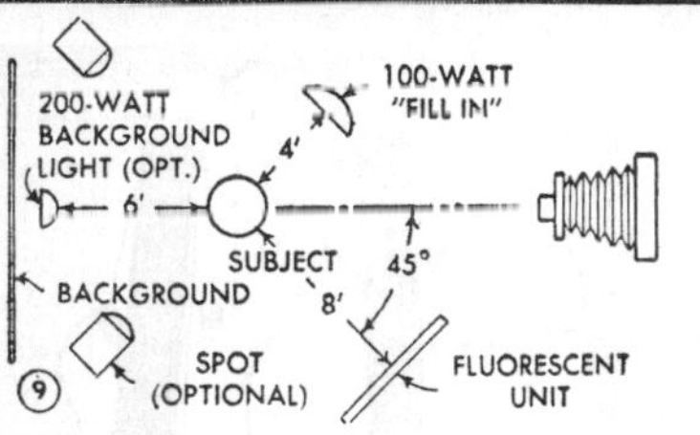

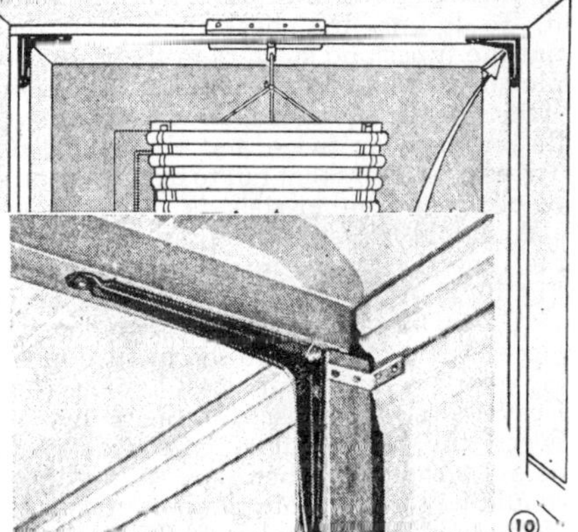

should be placed in back of the model. Fig. 9 shows the setup. Use a long focal length portrait lens so you can get in back of the unit and get a clearer image on the ground-glass screen.

Exposure is critical and you can overexpose easily. When correctly exposed the negatives made with this unit have what is called luminosity and "roundness." Retouching will be minimized because of the large area of the light coming from the unit. If you use an inexpensive color correcting filter over the camera lens, the unit can be used with color film. Information on the correct filter to use should be obtained from the manufacturer of the film. Also, when using a light meter take the reflection reading from the face of the model at a distance of 2 ft. For enlargements, best results are obtained by using a slow paper.

ℂIf for any reason regular lens-cleaning tissues are not available, the soft filter paper that is used in glass coffee makers provides a good substitute. This paper is sold in most grocery stores.

Show-Card Black for Lettering On Glossy Prints

For lettering captions or other notations on glossy prints, show-card black is better than waterproof ink, which eventually will crack off. Mix the show-card black with a little very soapy water which acts as a binder, and load the pen with a brush. This mixture will adhere also to china and glass, and may be wiped off with a damp swab.

PHOTO LIGHTING

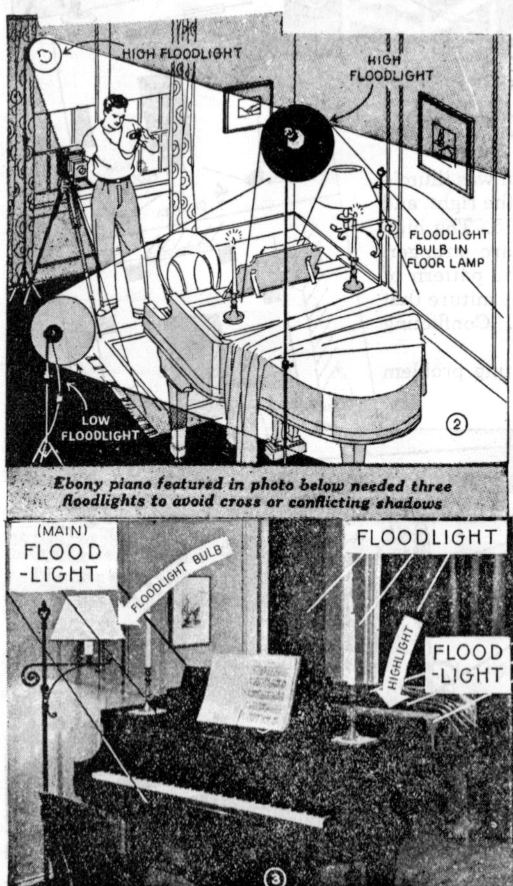

Ebony piano featured in photo below needed three floodlights to avoid cross or conflicting shadows

IN LIGHTING interiors for good photos, the main thing to keep in mind is that one source of light should dominate a scene, and that other light sources are to be subordinated. Fig. 1 illustrates the use of a single floodlight. The three table lamps were lighted to produce a natural effect and to add touches of life through the bright areas at the tops of the pottery bases. However, they supplied little light for the general scene.

Figs. 2 and 3 illustrate the lighting setup for a large dark piece of furniture, an ebony piano. In this case the basic lighting, again overhead and to the left, was so inadequate that it had to be assisted by a floodlight to the right, which was directed on the folds of the drapery on the piano, and another floodlight placed high and to the right, and directed against the further wall. Although three sources of light are used, note that conflicting shadows have been avoided. The subordinate lights have been placed so that they illuminate the immediate areas requiring it, and do not add much

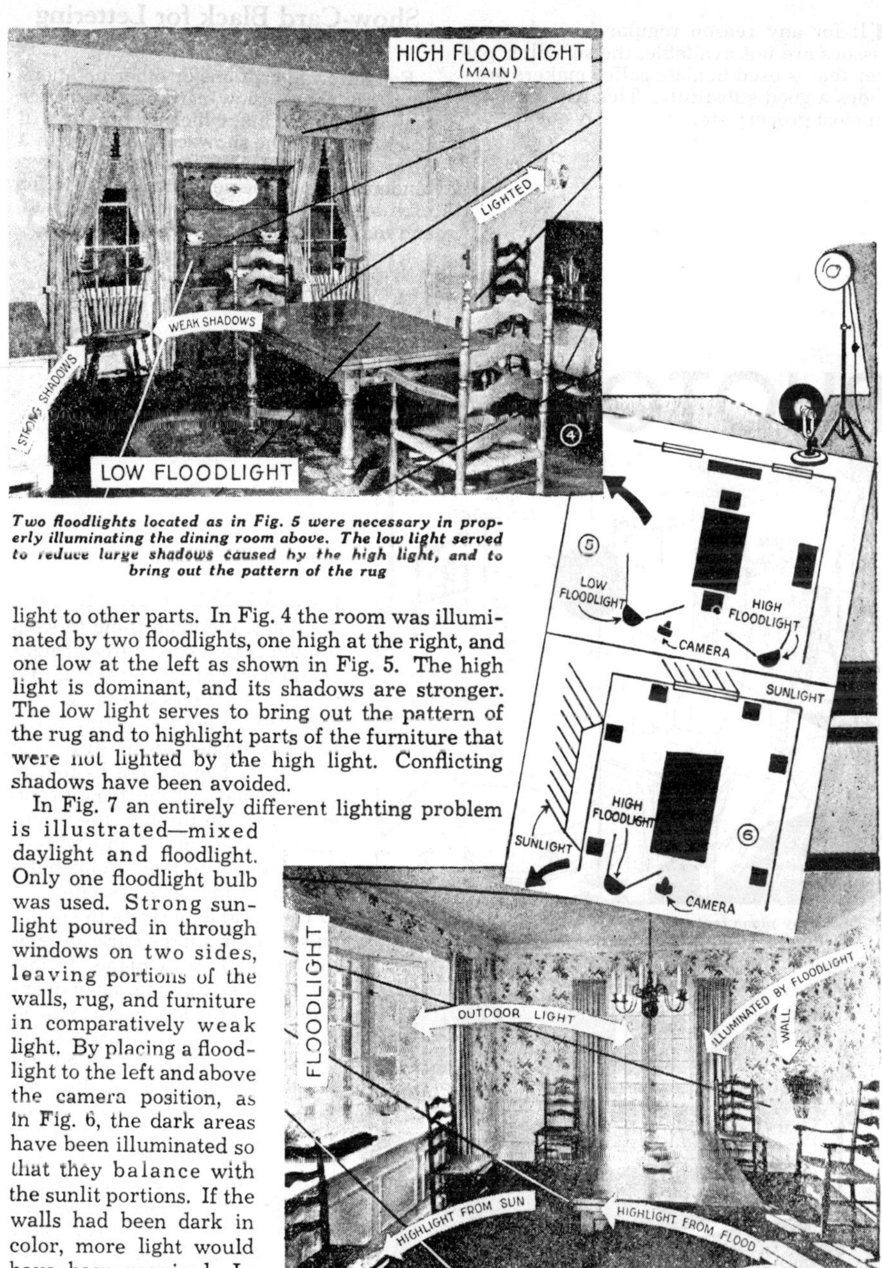

Two floodlights located as in Fig. 5 were necessary in properly illuminating the dining room above. The low light served to reduce large shadows caused by the high light, and to bring out the pattern of the rug

light to other parts. In Fig. 4 the room was illuminated by two floodlights, one high at the right, and one low at the left as shown in Fig. 5. The high light is dominant, and its shadows are stronger. The low light serves to bring out the pattern of the rug and to highlight parts of the furniture that were not lighted by the high light. Conflicting shadows have been avoided.

In Fig. 7 an entirely different lighting problem is illustrated—mixed daylight and floodlight. Only one floodlight bulb was used. Strong sunlight poured in through windows on two sides, leaving portions of the walls, rug, and furniture in comparatively weak light. By placing a floodlight to the left and above the camera position, as in Fig. 6, the dark areas have been illuminated so that they balance with the sunlit portions. If the walls had been dark in color, more light would have been required. In exposing for the interior, the bits of outdoors visible through the windows

With sunlight streaming into this room, the dark, unlighted areas had to be given sufficient artificial illumination to balance the sunlit portions. Fig. 6 shows the lighting arrangement

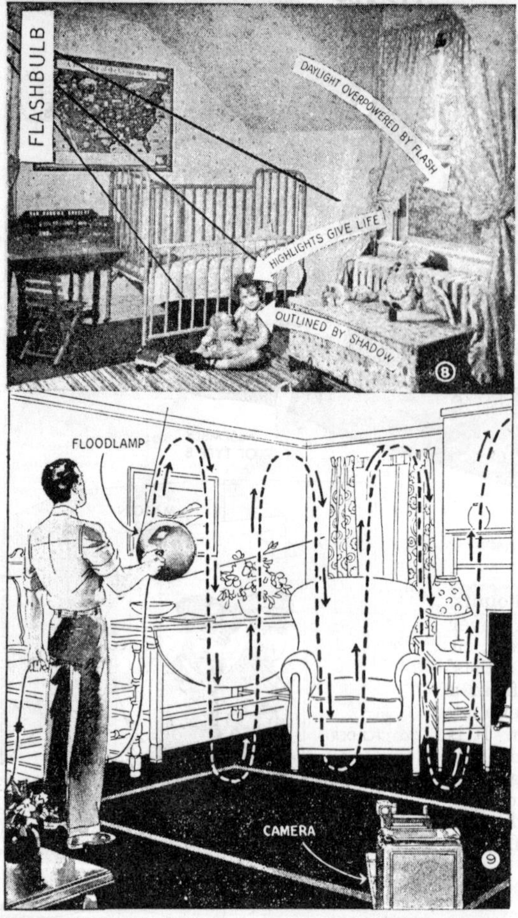

The nursery above, although open to daylight, was photographed practically by flashbulb alone. Fig. 9 shows how interiors can be illuminated by "washing" walls and furnishings with a floodlight while the camera is opened for a time exposure

are considerably overexposed. This is a fortunate circumstance, for it means that these portions print very light when pictures are made, and this aids the picture in two ways: It gives a realistic, bright atmosphere to the outside view that is similar to the visual effect of being in such a room, and it subordinates the outside detail, thereby concentrating attention on the inside. In Fig. 8 the outside light is comparatively weak, necessitating more artificial lighting. In this case, a large flashbulb was used. Shadows caused by daylight are completely missing. The only shadows are those caused by the flashbulb itself. The light was placed well forward of the camera position, but far enough to one side to be out of the field. The lens was well shielded by a hood.

Fig. 9 illustrates another method of interior lighting. It is a form of time exposure in which the operator "washes" the walls and furniture with a floodlight, gradually covering the complete scene and building up the exposure correctly. Due to the fact that the light source is constantly moving, this method produces a shadowless picture. Some difficult situations can be pictured easily by this method, especially when stationary floodlights introduce conflicting shadows that cannot be eliminated. To determine the exposure, take a reading of a moderately light portion of the room when the floodlight is playing on it from an average distance. Calculate the proper lens diaphragm setting for any convenient exposure interval, say 1 or 2 seconds, or even longer if the required depth of field necessitates a very small opening. Set the camera shutter for time, open it, and then methodically play the light over all portions of the scene. Keep the light moving constantly, but keep it in a given area long enough to give it the chosen exposure. Keep the light directed away from the camera, and stand so that your figure will not be silhouetted against light portions. When using this method it is easy to give darker objects longer exposure and to skip rapidly over light objects.

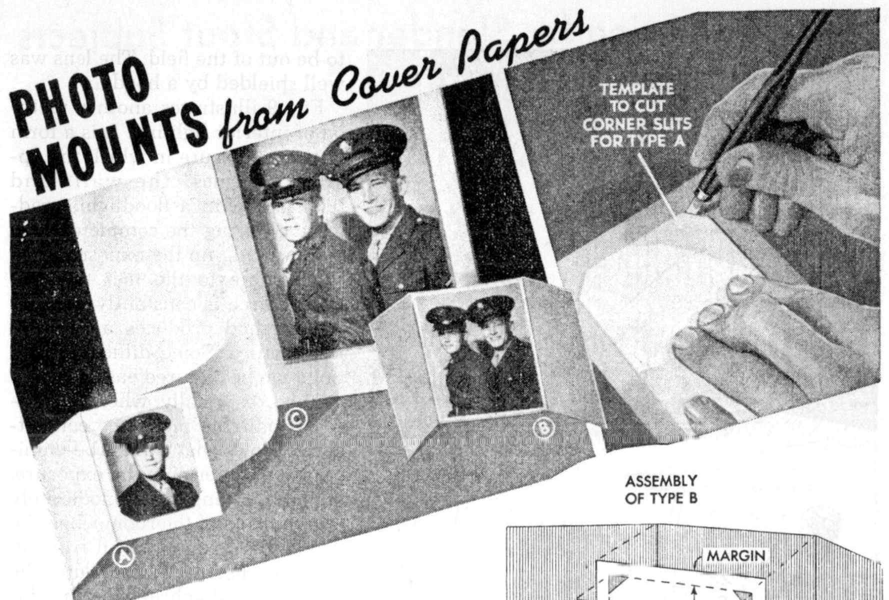

PHOTO MOUNTS from Cover Papers

IN THE absence of suitable photo mounts, you can make your own from cover paper, usually obtainable at printers, or other heavy paper purchased from artists' supply houses. Type A is made from a single sheet of stock which is stiff enough to support photos up to 4 by 5 in. It is scored at the center for folding and diagonal corner slits are cut to hold the photo in place. A cardboard template the same size as the photo facilitates making the cuts the right size in the correct position. Type B consists of a large sheet of cover paper folded twice to provide a back and two wings. Fold the left wing so it will overlap the other when closed. With this mount, art corners are used to hold the photo. They are pasted to a sheet of contrasting paper cut ¼ in. larger than the photo to form an underlay and to help stiffen the mount. For large photos, use a mount such as type C. Besides the folded back and a flyleaf, it has two masks over the photo, one of dark and the other of light paper. The opening in the dark mask is cut slightly smaller than the one in the light mask. The top mask should match the flyleaf. To assemble the mount, first glue in the flyleaf and then the photo, following with the masks, which first are glued together and then attached over the photo.

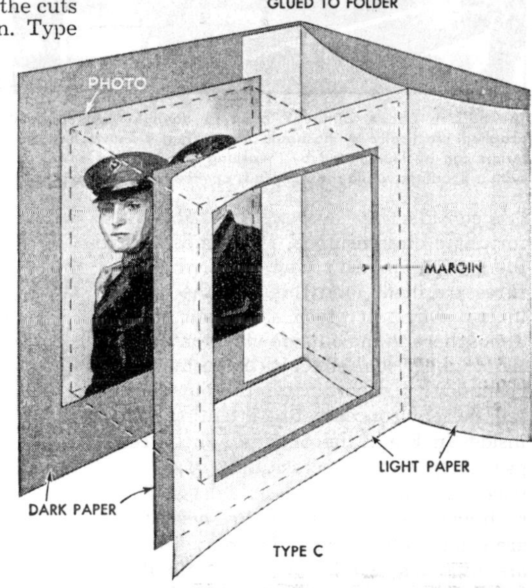

Portrait Lighting for Slender and Stout Subjects

Arrangement of lights, camera angles, composition — these and many other factors must be considered carefully by the portrait photographer in order to present his subjects in the most complimentary manner. To simplify taking portraits —and produce flattering results — here are two lighting setups, one for slender and one for stout subjects. Neither requires extensive equipment. The top detail suggests an arrangement for lights, camera and subject if the person you are photographing is slender. The bottom detail is for stout persons. When using the first setup, have the camera above eye level. Use a diffused main front light and have the subject face the camera. The head should be tilted down slightly and the body should be relaxed, sitting in a chair. Generally, a light background is better. To photograph stout persons, have the camera below eye level and use a sharp main side light. Take a three-quarter view with the subject leaning forward slightly. Here a dark background usually produces better results. To modify features, bear in mind the following suggestions: A long nose will photograph better if the head is tilted up and the reverse is true for a person having a short nose. Conspicuous ears are less noticeable if the head is turned slightly. Have the eyes looking in the same direction that the head is turned.

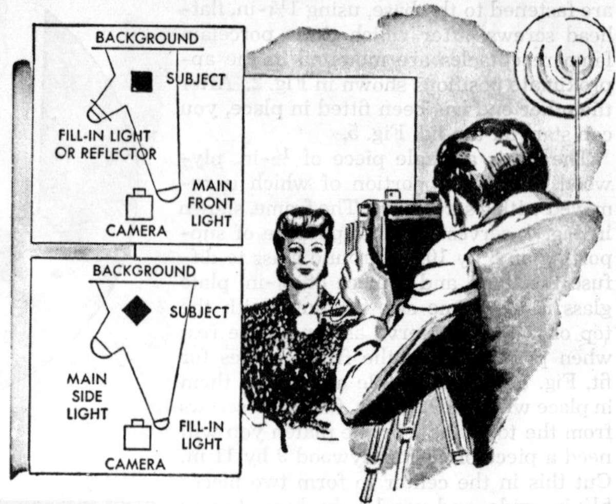

Photo PRINTER

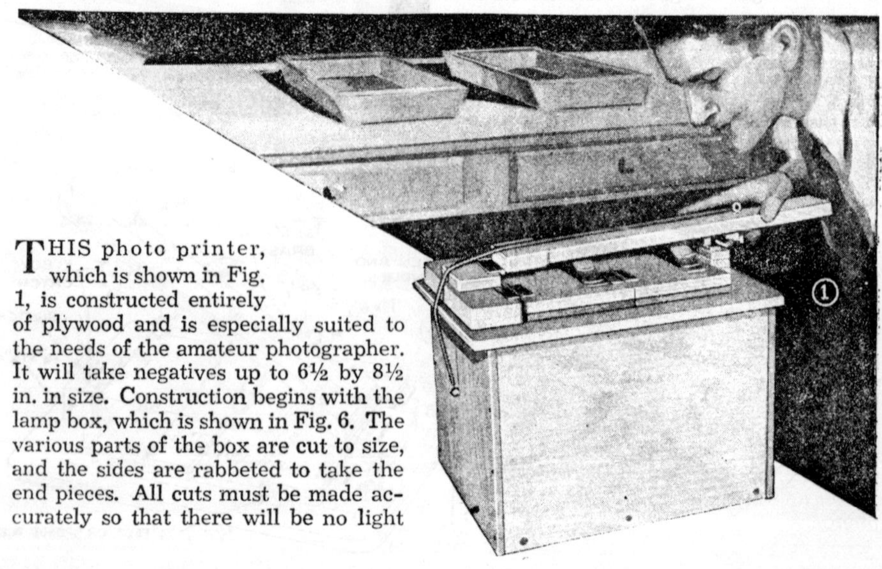

THIS photo printer, which is shown in Fig. 1, is constructed entirely of plywood and is especially suited to the needs of the amateur photographer. It will take negatives up to 6½ by 8½ in. in size. Construction begins with the lamp box, which is shown in Fig. 6. The various parts of the box are cut to size, and the sides are rabbeted to take the end pieces. All cuts must be made accurately so that there will be no light leaks at the joints. The sides and one end are fastened to the base, using 1¼-in. flat-head screws, after which three porcelain lamp receptacles are mounted in the approximate positions shown in Fig. 2. After the other end has been fitted in place, you can start on the lid, Fig. 5.

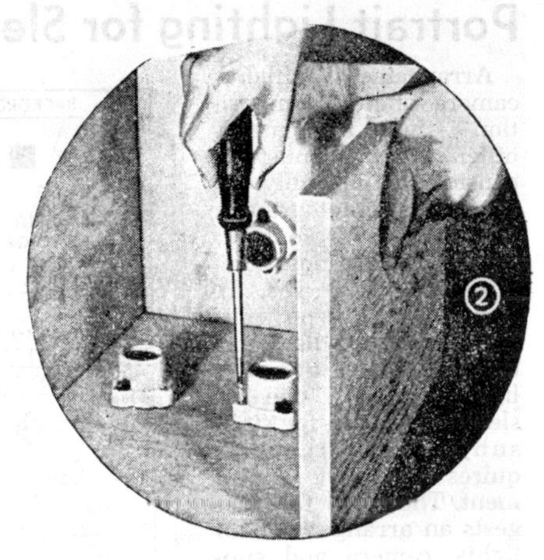

The lid is a single piece of ½-in. plywood, the center portion of which is removed with a scroll saw. The frame, shown in Fig. 4, serves the dual purpose of supporting an 8 by 10-in. ground glass to diffuse the light, and a piece of ¼-in. plate glass of the same size set flush with the top of the lid, to serve as a negative rest when printing. Try the frame pieces for fit, Fig. 3, then assemble and fasten them in place with No. 9, 1½-in. flat-head screws from the top side. For the platen you will need a piece of ½-in. plywood 9 by 11 in. Cut this in the center to form two pieces 5½ in. wide, and use 1½-in. brass hinges to fasten them together. Glue resilient felt or sponge rubber ¼ in. in thickness to the underside of the platen to assure even contact of the negative and printing paper. Then, hinge the platen to the 2½ by 9-in. piece at the back and proceed with the handle. Pressure bars are made of 1/32-in. spring brass and are screwed to the underside of the handle. A screen-door spring fastened to screw eyes in the handle and back of the lamp box, as shown in Fig. 1, keeps the handle in a raised position when adjusting the negative and printing paper. A 6-in. length of light chain connects the

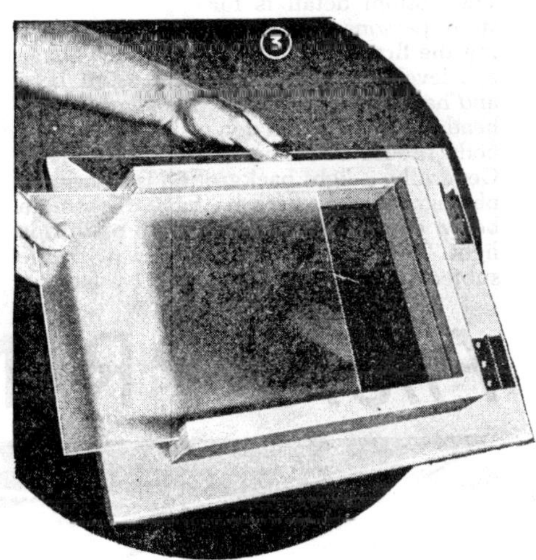

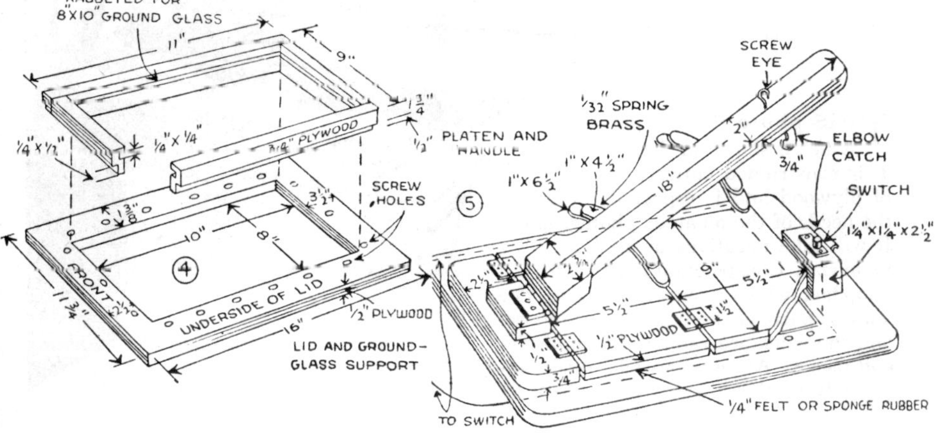

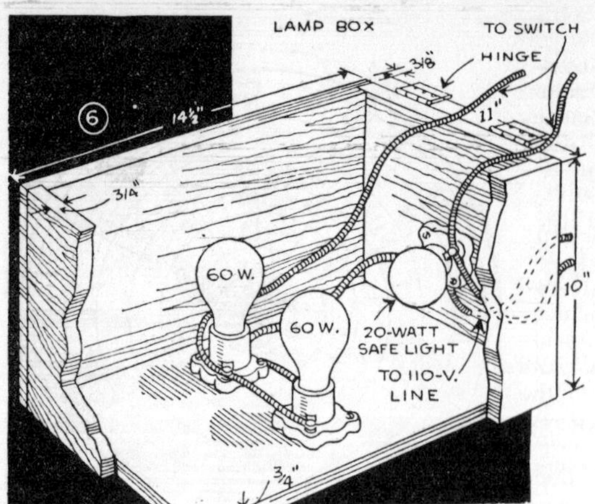

platen to the handle. The switch used is a regular make-and-break door switch altered so that two 60-watt lamps will light when the handle is depressed. An elbow catch automatically engages to hold the handle down for the required time, and the light turns off when the handle is raised. A 20-watt ruby lamp connected direct to the power line serves as a safe light. Giving the inside of the box a couple coats of white or aluminum paint, and staining the outside, completes the job.

PHOTO-PRINT TIMING

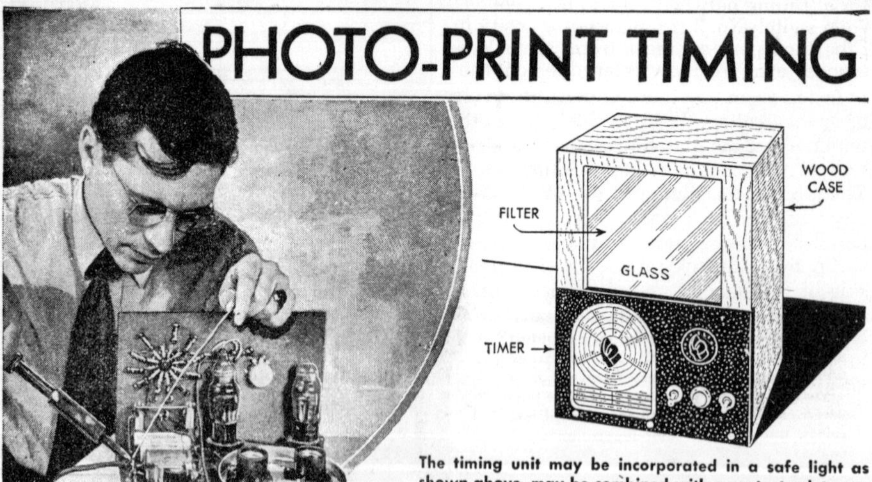

The timing unit may be incorporated in a safe light as shown above, may be combined with a contact printer, or housed in a cabinet and placed near a printer or enlarger

OF GREAT value to any photographer for controlling the time of exposing prints, when using either an enlarger or a contact printer, this automatic electronic timer gives accurate control between 1.5 and 61.5 seconds. Its greatest usefulness lies in exact timing of large numbers of duplicate prints, in which case printing time can be cut down to a minimum if the illumination in the enlarger or printer is increased proportionately. For color-separation work, the timer is also of special value, although any photographer will find it a great convenience in his daily work as it eliminates inaccurate counting and permits him to attend to other details in the darkroom while a print is being exposed. The timer is designed to operate on 115-volt, alternating current, and will control a lamp or electrical appliance that does not exceed a consumption of 250 watts. Being small in size, it may be housed in a cabinet or set on a shelf near the enlarger or printer, although it may be incorporated with a printer or with a safe lamp.

In use, the timer is plugged into a convenient outlet, and the enlarger or printer is connected to the timer. After these connections have been made, you can throw in switch No. 1, which lights the tubes and also the lamp of the enlarger or printer. As soon as the tubes have been warmed up, the lamp in the enlarger or printer will go off automatically provided it is not kept on by switch No. 2, which is used only to turn on the enlarger or printer lamp while focusing and arranging negatives or paper. Adjustment of the timing period is made by means of two variable controls, one centered on a paper dial and the other (switch No. 3) centered over a disk numbered from 1 to 12. These two controls work in conjunction with each other. When switch No. 3 is set in position 1, you get any variation of timing between 1.5 and 6.5 seconds. When switch No. 3 is advanced to position 2, the time period ranges from 6.5 to 11.5 seconds, etc. Position references on the

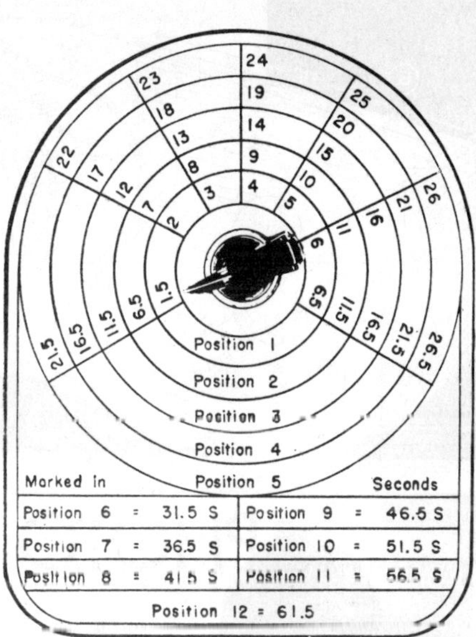

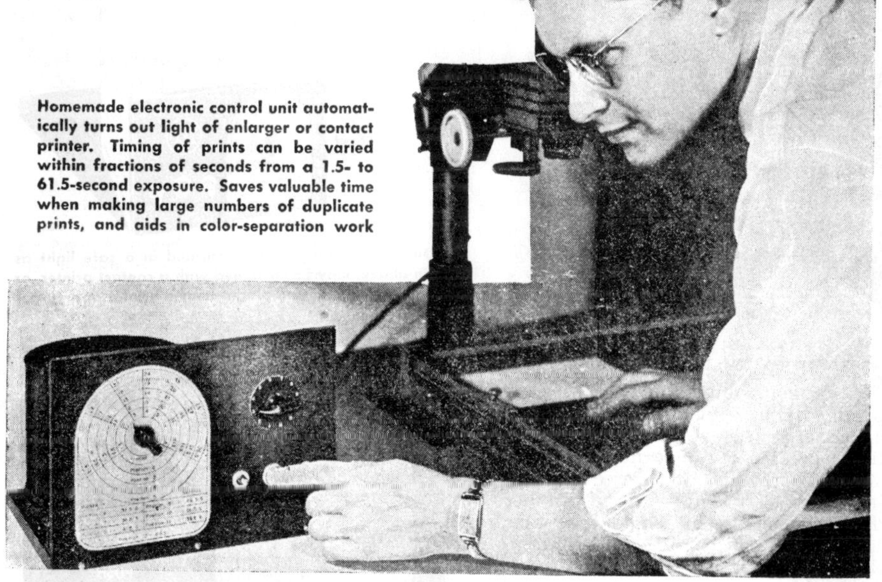

Homemade electronic control unit automatically turns out light of enlarger or contact printer. Timing of prints can be varied within fractions of seconds from a 1.5- to 61.5-second exposure. Saves valuable time when making large numbers of duplicate prints, and aids in color-separation work

dial refer to positions of switch No. 3. Assuming that you wish a timing period of 3.5 seconds, you put the pointer of the dial halfway between 3 and 4, and set switch No. 3 on position 1. Then you press the button, which turns on the enlarger or printer lamp for exactly 3.5 seconds. Similarly, suppose you wish a timing period of 22 seconds, you set the dial pointer toward 22, right on the line, and switch No. 3 in position 5, before pressing the push button. When finished using the timer, turn off

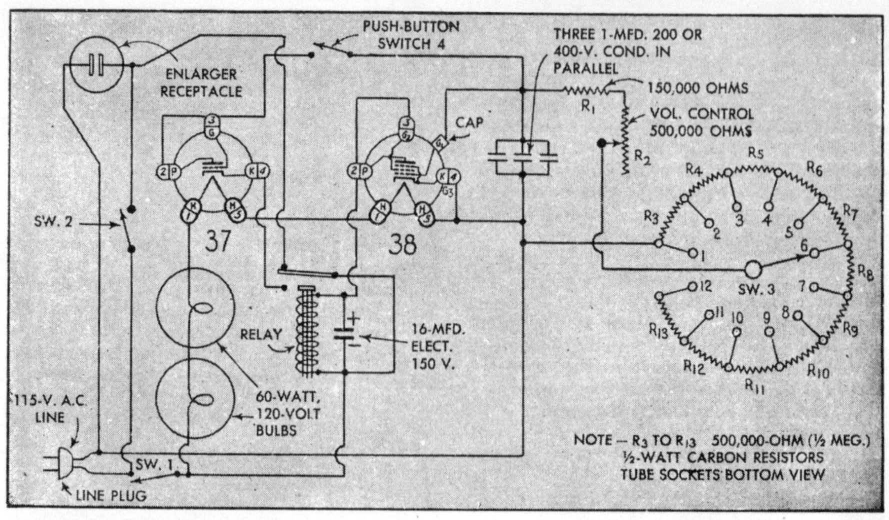

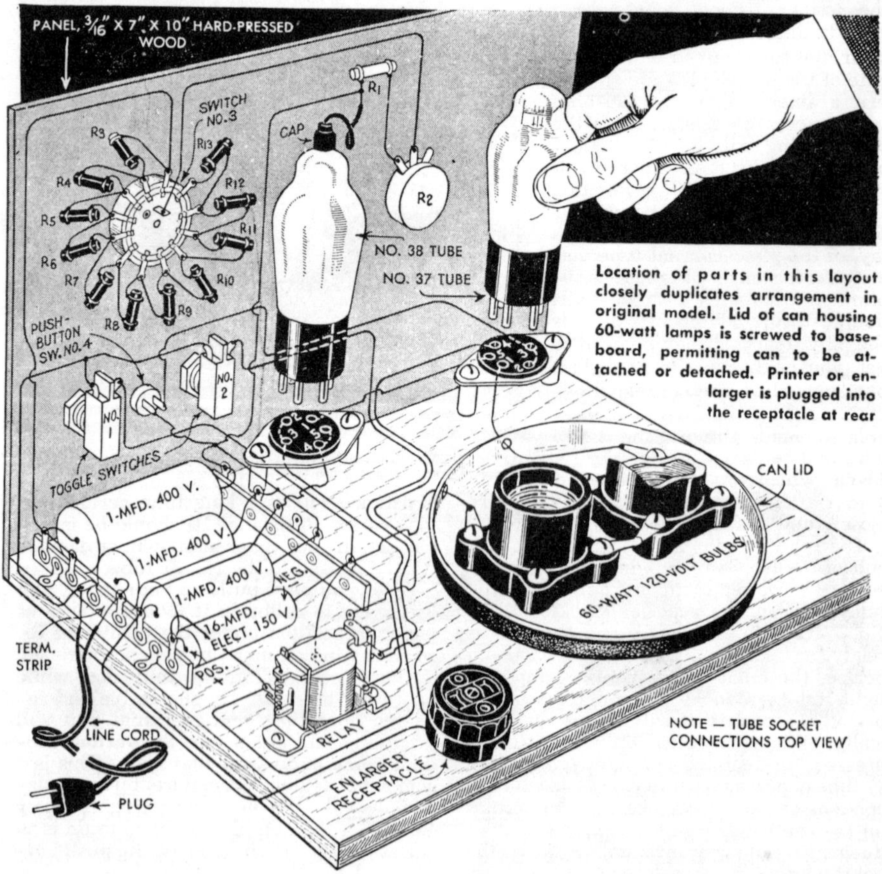

Location of parts in this layout closely duplicates arrangement in original model. Lid of can housing 60-watt lamps is screwed to baseboard, permitting can to be attached or detached. Printer or enlarger is plugged into the receptacle at rear

NOTE — TUBE SOCKET CONNECTIONS TOP VIEW

toggle switch No. 1, assuming that toggle switch No. 2 (used only for focusing, etc.), is off.

The two 60-watt Mazda lamps provide the necessary voltage drop to light the heaters of the No. 37 and No. 38 tubes. A large tin can houses the lamps so that the unit can be used safely in the darkroom. If the timer is incorporated with a safe light, the two lamps can be used for illumination in the safe light. If the timer is put in a cabinet, you may dispense with the tin-can light shield, but if it is incorporated in a printer, you use either the light shield or install a partition between the timer unit and the printer lamp to prevent accidental spoilage of paper. Three 1-mfd., 200 or 400-volt tubular paper condensers of good quality are used in conjunction with a resistance of 6 megohms to make up the timing discharge circuit of 61.5 seconds. If the eleven 500,000-ohm resistors, R_3 to R_{13} are of close tolerance, your dial will line up like the one of the writer; if not, your calibration may look slightly different. It will be only a coincidence if your dial turns out to be a duplicate of the one shown. Be sure to use a linear-taper, 500,000-ohm volume-control resistor, R_2, or the dial reading will be bunched at one end of the dial. To prevent relay chatter, a 10, 12 or 16-mfd., 150-volt electrolytic condenser is placed across the winding. The relay, of the plate-current type, has a coil resistance of about 2,500 ohms and actuates a single-pole, double-throw switch. As this is the only item that may be hard to get, you might have to improvise one from a low-voltage relay having a s.p.d.t. switch and a removable solenoid. Unwind the heavy wire and rewind with fine wire about No. 40-ga., which you can salvage from an old 3-to-1 audio transformer. Wind the wire closely and as full as possible.

The relay windings are in the plate circuit of the No. 38 tube, which, when heated up, draws plate current and closes the relays. Then the rectifier circuit of the No. 37 tube is completed, and the unit is ready for operation. During the warm-up period, the enlarger or printer lamp will light but as soon as the initial warm-up period is complete, it will go out automatically. When the push-button switch is pressed, the rectified voltage from the No. 37 tube charges the three paralleled 1-mfd. condensers. This puts a high negative bias on the control grid of the No. 38 tube, reducing its plate current immediately to the point where the relay drops out. The time required for the plate current to build up again to the point where the relay is actuated, is the timing period of printing, which varies according to the amount of resistance shorted across the condensers. A high resistance causes a long time period, and vice versa. Resistance R_1 should be incorporated in your timer as shown, or damage will be caused to the No. 37 tube.

After you have built up your timer, you are ready to calibrate it. Place a piece of paper in position under the pointer of R_2, so that you can mark in pencil where the various seconds fall on your dial while operating the unit. By successive and repeated operations and markings you will gradually find out where the various seconds come in on your dial scale. This is a somewhat tedious procedure, but once accomplished, it is very satisfying to know that from then on all you have to do is to select the time desired, press the push button, and the timing will be accurate. The writer used a large kitchen clock with a sweep second hand and had very little difficulty in calibrating.

MATERIAL LIST

1 Panel 7 by 10-in. black hard-pressed wood
1 Baseboard ½ by 7 by 10-in. plywood
1 Tin can to house two lamps
2 60-watt, 120-volt Mazda lamps
2 Cleat receptacles for lamps
1 Lampcord
1 Plug
1 Plug receptacle
3 1-mfd., 200 or 400-volt tubular condensers
1 16-mfd., 150-volt, elect. cond. (see text)
1 150,000-ohm, ½-watt resistor, (R_1)
1 500,000-ohm, linear taper variable control carbon resistor, (R_2)
11 500,000-ohm, ½-watt resistors, (R_3 to R_{13})
1 Relay, s.p.d.t., plate-current type
2 Toggle switches, s.p.s.t., panel type, (S_1 and S_2)
1 Pushbutton switch, push to close, (S_4)
1 12-point rotary selector switch, (S_3)
1 Switch plate marked 1 to 12
2 5-prong sockets
1 38 tube
1 37-tube
1 Grid cap for 38-tube
2 Tie-point terminal strips (6 Lug Type)
2 Knobs, 1¼ in.
4 Spacers for tube sockets, ¾ in. high
2 30-in. lengths spaghetti tubing
3 24-in. lengths No. 14 bus bar
12 1-in. No. 6 r.h. wood screws
6 ½-in. No. 5 r.h. wood screws

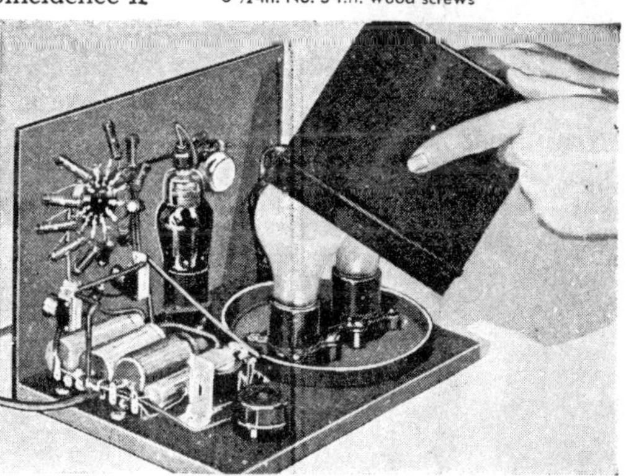

Flashlight "Writes" on Photoprint

When making photoprints, it's easy to write your name with light on the print so that the inscription is developed with the picture. To do this, fit a tapered piece of Lucite into the end of a fountain-pen flashlight and opaque the plastic with red nail polish. Then sand the color from the tip so that light will shine through, and use the flashlight as a pen. The writing should be done on a light portion of the print.

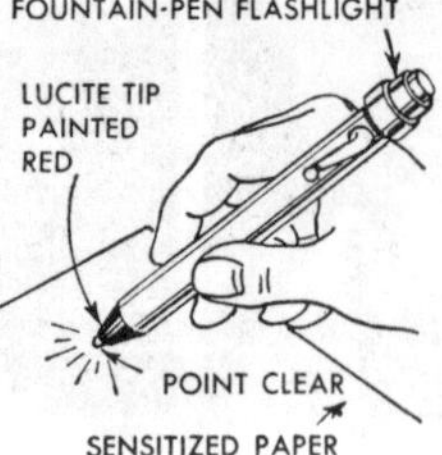

White Cardboard on the Camera Reflects Light on Subject

Certain subjects that require shadowless lighting can be illuminated with reflected light by turning the floodlights on a cardboard reflector in front of the camera. Place the lights so they shine on the reflector at an angle and use a large lens shade so the light will not strike the lens. It also may be necessary to cover part of the floodlights with black cardboard deflectors.

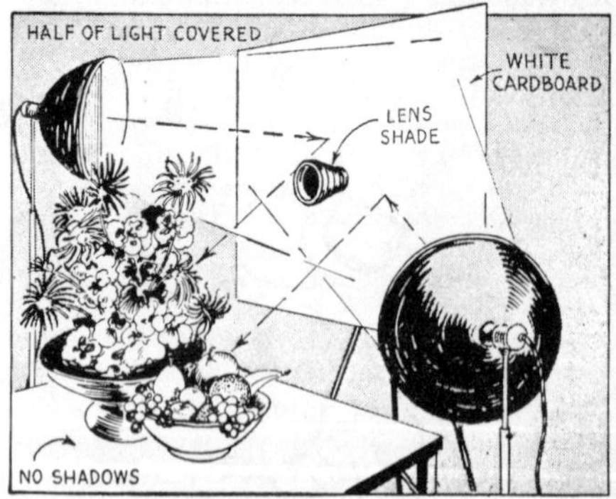

Side-and-Back Lighting Gives Portraits Depth

With this arrangement of side lighting you get just the opposite light-and-shadow effects from those obtained with the usual setup of lights directed at the subject from the front. Well rounded contours that result are especially pleasing for portrait work as they have a three-dimensional effect. Sides of the face receding farthest from the camera are lighted, the outline of the head and shoulders is brought out to separate the sub-

ject from the background and the parts of the face closest to the camera are slightly toned down in shadow. Also, the hair is highlighted, which gives it life and snap. Three photofloods of equal intensity are used. Two are set at equal distances from the subject, one on each side and slightly behind it so that the light is directed downward at about a 45-deg. angle. The third lamp is placed slightly on one side, ahead of and a little above the camera. Its distance from the subject should be about one-third greater than that of the other two lamps, or at a point where the face shadow is softened sufficiently. By moving it farther away you can deepen the "tone" or "mood" of the picture for special effect, but if you place it too far away the shadow on the face will be too dark. Moving it too close, however, will tend to "flatten" the picture by equalizing all three lights. Always use a lens shade, of course, to avoid direct glare into the lens. This arrangement of lamps can be used for home movies because no matter where the actors are, the light will reach all surfaces in about the same proportions.

Tripod Adjusted to Take Photos Close to Ground

Tripods that have sliding center camera supports are easily converted to take a photo with the camera close to the ground. All you have to do is to remove the support and insert it from the underside. Then attach the camera in the regular way. Be sure that it is turned so that one of the tripod legs is not in the way.

Photos taken with camera close to ground by inverting sliding support in tripod

Emergency Photo Stand of Wire

When you need a temporary stand to support a photo, one can be made quickly and inexpensively from a length of wire bent as shown. Such a stand also is handy for supporting small mirrors and similar items when a regular stand for the purpose is not at hand.

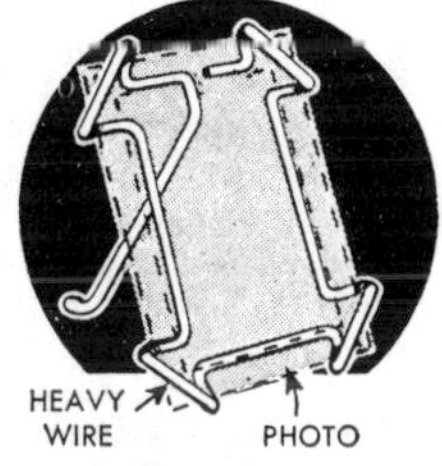

PHOTOS on METAL,

(1) METAL SURFACES THOROUGHLY CLEANED

(2) ACID DIP FOR BRASS AND COPPER

(3) DRYING UNDER COVER

FOR a lasting and novel display, your favorite photos can be printed on lamp bases, serving trays, beverage glasses, plates, mirrors, wastebaskets and many other items made of non-porous materials. The work can be a fascinating hobby and has possibilities as a profitable spare-time business. All you need is a good negative, preferably one having considerable contrast. This is held in contact with the surface of the material which you have previously cleaned and coated with a gelatin base and a sensitizing solution. Then the exposure is made and the exposed surface is fixed, washed, dried and coated with transparent lacquer. Doing the work is comparatively simple but it is highly important that you follow all details of the process carefully as described in this article. Photos can be applied to any flat surface and also to surfaces having a one-way curve, but not to surfaces having compound curves such as is the case with many vases and lamp bases, since the negative cannot be curved in two directions at the same time to contact the entire surface.

Cleaning the surface: The first step is to prepare the surface, making it perfectly clean and free from dirt, grease and corrosion. Metals should be scrubbed in hot soap water containing a few ounces of washing soda per gallon, as shown in Fig. 1. Fine steel wool or other abrasives can be used to aid in cleaning the work while washing it, but these too should be washed off the work with soap and water. The soap water is rinsed away in hot and cold running water. Following this, if there is any rust or corrosion, it must be removed. Brass and copper can be freed from tarnish by dipping in a solution of nitric acid, 1 lb., and hydrochloric acid, ½ oz., in water, 3 qts.,

GLASS *and* POTTERY

as shown in Fig. 2. The solution is prepared by slowly adding the acid to the water in a stoneware crock, stirring with a glass rod or a wooden paddle while mixing. Aluminum is dipped in a solution of 50 percent hydrofluoric acid, 1 part, and water, 9 parts. A lead or wax-lined container must be used for this solution as hydrofluoric acid attacks glass or stoneware. Or, aluminum can be dipped in a solution of sulphuric acid, 1 lb., and water, 1 qt., to which is added sodium dichromate, 1 oz.

The sulphuric acid is added slowly to the water in a stoneware crock, stirring while adding and, after mixing, the sodium dichromate is added. The metal is dipped in the solution for a few seconds and then rinsed in hot and cold running water. Then it is permitted to dry in air, protected against dust as shown in Fig. 3.

Mixing the gelatin: The surface on which the print is to be made is first coated with a gelatin mixture and later with the sensitizing solution. The gelatin mixture is prepared in two parts. First, put gelatin, 40 grains, in an enameled pan with water, 1 oz., allowing it to soak for about 15 min. While the gelatin is soaking, dissolve in a separate container chrome alum, 3 grains, in warm water, ½ oz. When the gelatin has soaked, place the pan on a stove and heat gently until the gelatin has dissolved. With the pan still on the burner, add the solution of chrome alum, a few drops at a time, as shown in Fig. 4, while stirring vigorously. When mixing is completed, add about 10 drops of a 10-percent solution of phenol (carbolic acid) and stir. To coat the work, place it face up on a level surface and pour a few drops of the gelatin-chrome-alum mixture on it as shown in Fig. 5. If the surface is not level, wedges should be used as in Fig. 3. The gelatin

(7) MASKING PICTURE BEFORE PRINTING

spots or exposed metal. Solution A is prepared, as shown in Fig. 8, by dissolving silver nitrate, 1 oz., in distilled water, about 12 oz., and adding to this solution part of the ammonium hydroxide, drop by drop, until the precipitate which forms at first has redissolved. Solution B is prepared as shown in Fig. 9, by dissolving in a separate container citric acid, 1 oz., and tartaric acid, ½ oz., in distilled water, about 12 fl. oz. When this has dissolved, ferric ammonium citrate (green scales) ½ oz., is added, and when that has been dissolved, the remainder of the ammonium hydroxide is added to this solution and mixed in.

The sensitizer is ready for use after solution A has been added to solution B, and stirred to mix well. This must be done in a subdued light. Enough distilled water is added to bring the total volume of sensitizer to 1 qt., and it should be stored in a brown bottle, tightly corked.

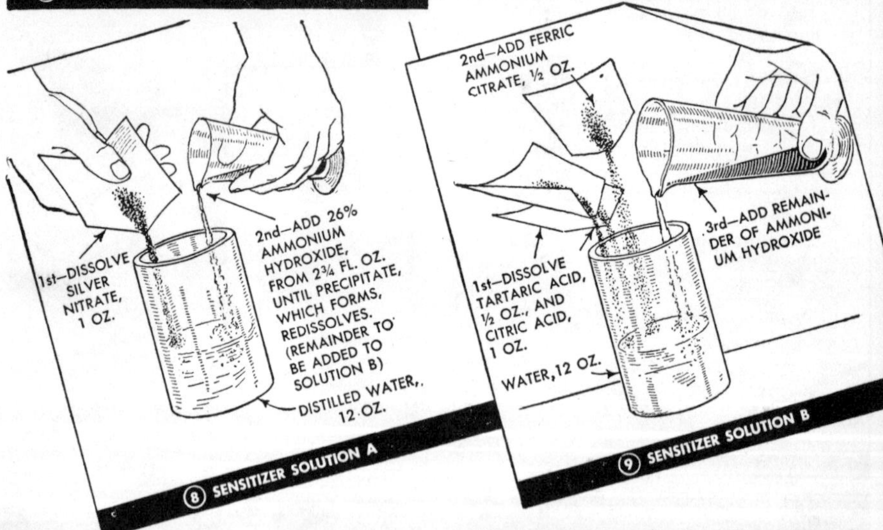

(8) SENSITIZER SOLUTION A

(9) SENSITIZER SOLUTION B

solution should be spread evenly over the surface, using a clean, soft brush as in Fig. 6. The layer of gelatin should be uniform and quite thin. It should be left for at least half an hour or until dry, protected from dust.

Preparing the sensitizer: While the gelatin is drying, the sensitizing solution is prepared in two parts, solution A and solution B. First measure out 2¾ fl. oz. of 26-percent ammonium hydroxide, which is the total amount required for both solutions A and B. Chemically pure (C.P.) chemicals and distilled water should be used in preparing the sensitizer. All mixing should be done in glass jars, beakers, or enameled vessels free from chipped

Sensitizing the gelatin: When the gelatin film on the work has hardened you are ready to sensitize it. Lay it, gelatin side up, on a level surface, or level it with wedges, and pour on a few drops of the sensitizing solution. Then brush the solution over the entire surface evenly with a soft camel's-hair brush. In working with the sensitizer avoid exposing it to sunlight or artificial light—keep it in subdued, reflected light although it is not necessary to use a photographic darkroom. The sensitized sheet should be set away, protected against dust and light, until it has had time to dry, which will take at least half an hour.

Exposure: Prints can be made from any good negative, although a contrasty negative will give the best results. The negative snould be placed with its dull or emulsion side in contact with the sensitized surface (working in subdued light) and a suitable mask placed around the part to be printed as shown in Fig. 7. All or any part of the negative can be used. Masks can be cut in any desired size and shape from lightproof paper or cardboard. A clean piece of glass or celluloid should be placed over the mask to hold the negative in contact with the sensitized surface, Fig. 12. On flexible material, the glass is clamped to it with paper clips or spring-type clothespins as in Fig. 11, a flat, rigid backing being provided. On curved surfaces, the mask and negative are placed under a piece of celluloid, or Cellophane, which is held on the work by rubber bands or cellulose tape as in Fig. 10.

The exposure can be made either by direct sunlight or a photoflood lamp. Usually exposure requires from 2 to 5 min., de-

(10) HOW TO PRINT ON CURVED SURFACES

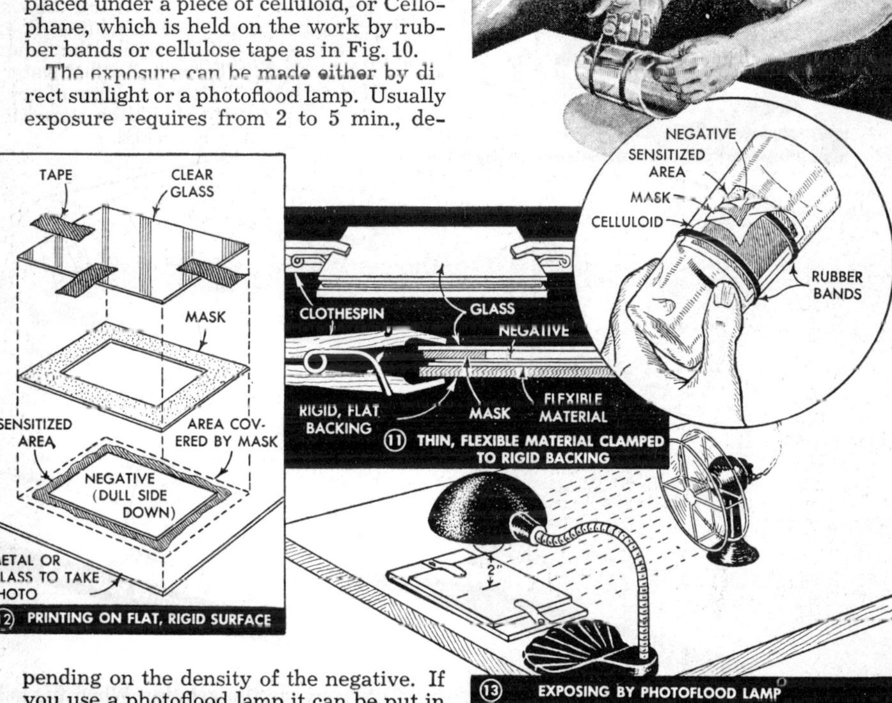

(11) THIN, FLEXIBLE MATERIAL CLAMPED TO RIGID BACKING

(12) PRINTING ON FLAT, RIGID SURFACE

(13) EXPOSING BY PHOTOFLOOD LAMP

pending on the density of the negative. If you use a photoflood lamp it can be put in a standard reflector or in a desk lamp as in Fig. 13. On small negatives, the lamp should be placed about 2 in. from the glass. For larger negatives the lamp should be raised so all parts of the negative are about the same distance from the lamp. A fan is placed as shown to prevent overheating.

Fixing and finishing: No development is required, but the print must be fixed for 30 sec. in a solution of sodium thiosulphate (hypo), 2 oz., in water, 1 qt., used at a temperature not over 65 deg. F. After fixing the print it is rinsed in cold water. Then the gelatin should be given a final hardening by immersing the print for 30 sec. in a solution of 40-percent formaldehyde, 1 part, and water, 10 parts, at a temperature not over 65 deg. F. The finished print is rinsed again in cold water and allowed to dry. Transparent lacquer applied on the finished work protects it from scratches.

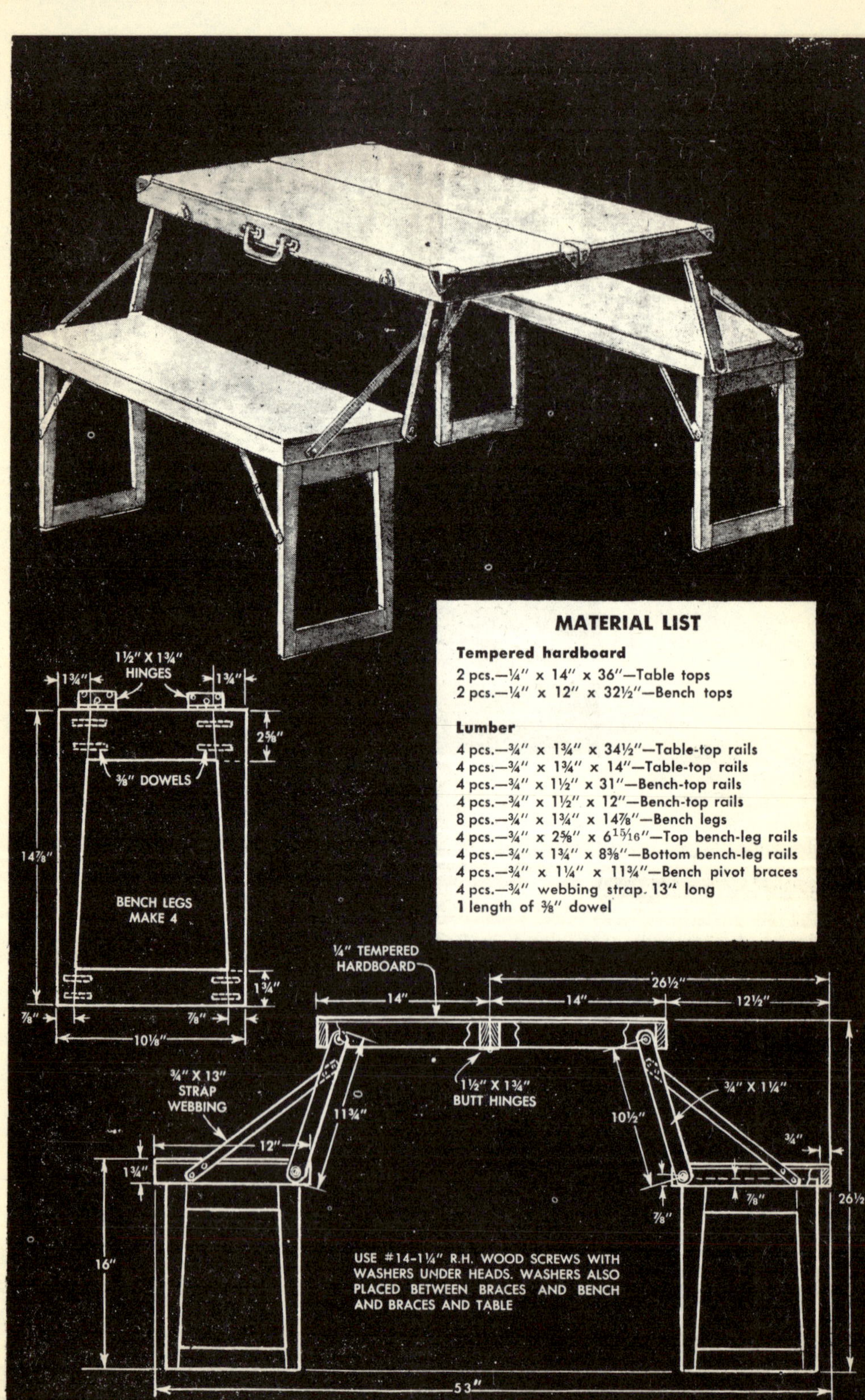
MATERIAL LIST
Tempered hardboard
2 pcs.—¼" x 14" x 36"—Table tops
2 pcs.—¼" x 12" x 32½"—Bench tops
Lumber
4 pcs.—¾" x 1¾" x 34½"—Table-top rails
4 pcs.—¾" x 1¾" x 14"—Table-top rails
4 pcs.—¾" x 1½" x 31"—Bench-top rails
4 pcs.—¾" x 1½" x 12"—Bench-top rails
8 pcs.—¾" x 1¾" x 14⅞"—Bench legs
4 pcs.—¾" x 2⅝" x 6 15/16"—Top bench-leg rails
4 pcs.—¾" x 1¾" x 8⅜"—Bottom bench-leg rails
4 pcs.—¾" x 1¼" x 11¾"—Bench pivot braces
4 pcs.—¾" webbing strap. 13" long
1 length of ⅜" dowel
1½" X 1¾" HINGES
1¾"
1¾"
2⅝"
⅜" DOWELS
14⅞"
BENCH LEGS MAKE 4
1¾"
⅞"
⅞"
10⅛"
¼" TEMPERED HARDBOARD
26½"
14"
14"
12½"
¾" X 13" STRAP WEBBING
1½" X 1¾" BUTT HINGES
11¾"
10½"
¾" X 1¼"
¾"
12"
1¾"
⅞"
⅞"
26½"
16"
USE #14-1¼" R.H. WOOD SCREWS WITH WASHERS UNDER HEADS. WASHERS ALSO PLACED BETWEEN BRACES AND BENCH AND BRACES AND TABLE
53"

Suitcase Picnic Bench

Have you ever packed a picnic basket and hurried off to the park only to find all the tables and benches taken? Such a situation will be of little concern when you have your own picnic table packed away in a compact "suitcase" measuring only 4½ x 14 x 36 in. It's small enough to fit nicely in the car and light enough to carry easily. Set up, the unit provides a 28 x 36-in. table flanked by two attached benches. The whole thing is designed so that the benches nest in the two halves of the table top. Regular card-table leg braces are used on the benches to permit the legs to fold flat inside the bench tops. Wooden links pivot the benches to the table, and strap webbing provides check straps to keep the bench tops level with table.—John Bergen, Chicago

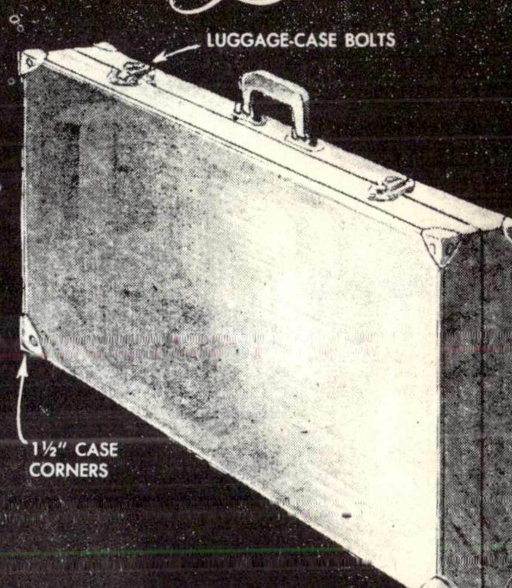

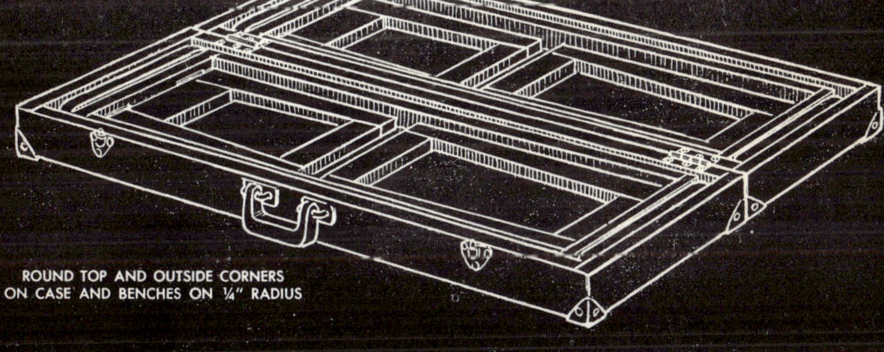

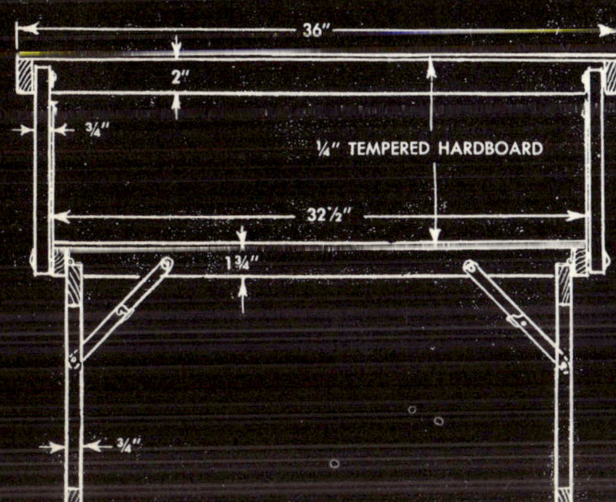

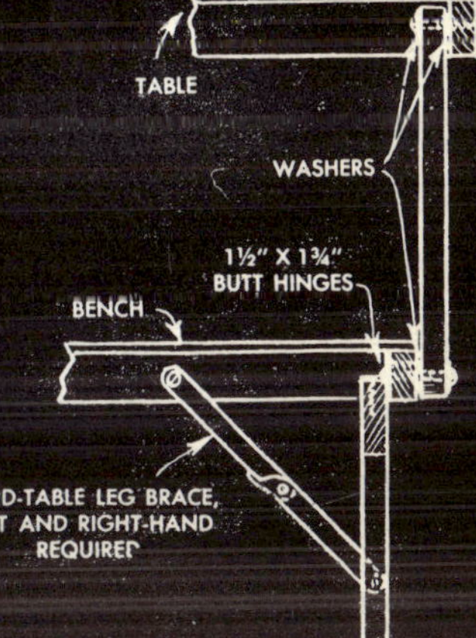

ROUTING BACK OF FRAME

Routing on drill press: First cut is on face side. Then back is routed with successive cuts to form picture rabbet. Note clearance holes as at right. Slots for cardboard tabs cut on shaper, using small saw and depth collar

Detail of Standard Frame

CORNER SLOTS ARE CUT ON SHAPER WITH SMALL SAW

Style 2 PLYWOOD PARTLY FRAMED WITH ½" DOWELS NO RECESS AND NO GLASS

Style 3 STANDARD STYLE SAME AS No. 1 BUT WITH TWO CELLULOID-COVERED OPENINGS

Assemble the picture, glass, cardboard backing and cardboard tabs. The tabs fit into grooved slots. Alternate simpler method is to brad the backing in place

Pictures with Plywood

Style 1 3/8" TO 3/4" PLYWOOD WITH CENTER CUT OUT AND RABBETED FOR PICTURE AND GLASS

These attractive plywood frames eliminate mitered corner joints, the center of a solid panel being cut out to take the picture. Frames can be round or square as desired. Best appearance is obtained by selecting a nicely figured face veneer and then giving the frame a liberal margin to show the wood. Style 1 showing basic construction is illustrated above and in photos at top of opposite page. Style 2 is a simple plywood plaque with picture mounted direct . . . a coat of clear lacquer over picture makes it dirtproof and washable. Style 3 shows how small pictures can be mounted in groups. Style 4 is handy for snapshots. Style 5 makes an attractive mount for small or large pictures. The molding at edges lends a decorative touch and conceals end grain. All frames are finished natural with clear lacquer except edges, which may be stained dark to conceal grain of wood

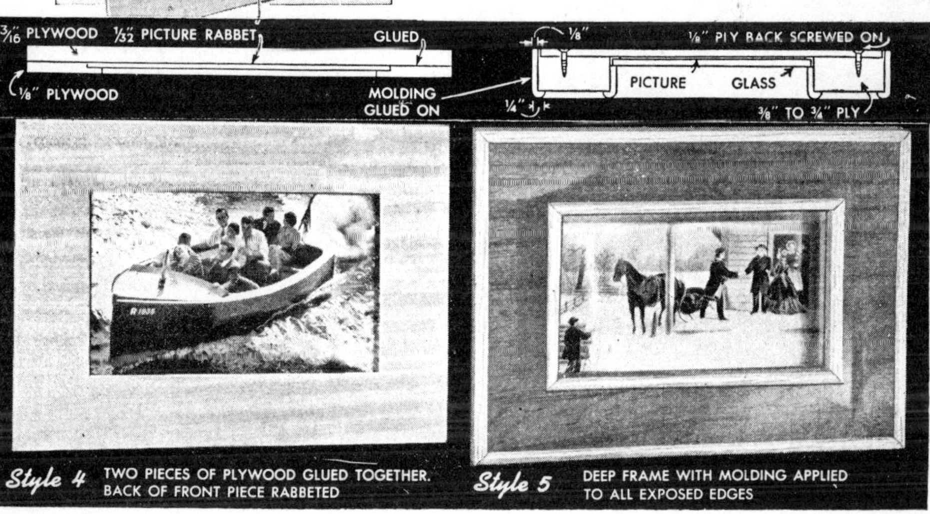

Style 4 TWO PIECES OF PLYWOOD GLUED TOGETHER. BACK OF FRONT PIECE RABBETED

Style 5 DEEP FRAME WITH MOLDING APPLIED TO ALL EXPOSED EDGES

Pictures are Pretty

9 Attractive Designs You Can Make

Frame No. 1
Courtesy Vargish & Co.

FOR A CLEAN, SHARP BEND, RUB THE HEATED PLASTIC WITH A CLOTH-COVERED BLOCK

HEAT PLASTIC AND THEN BEND BY PRESSING ON A CLEAN, SMOOTH SURFACE

All-Plastic Frames

SIMPLE in design, these plastic picture frames depend largely on the beauty and crystal clarity of the material for their effectiveness. Some of the frames, such as Photos 1, 2, 3 and 4 at the tops of these pages, use plastic for both frame and glass. Construction details are shown in the correspondingly numbered photo and line drawings at the side and bottom of this page. These frames are best worked on a strip heater, which confines the bending heat to the area required. Sharp bends are worked by heating the plastic along the bending line and then rubbing the joint gently with a cloth-covered block as the plastic cools. Large-radius bends are made by heating the required area and pressing the free end against any smooth, clean surface until the desired curvature is obtained. If the correct curve is not made on the first attempt, it's a simple matter to reheat the piece and repeat the bending process as often as is necessary.

Bent frames are illustrated by two simple designs, Photos 5 and 6. This type of construction always requires a form. The form for No. 6, illustrated by Fig. 6, is a simple arrangement of

pegs; the form for No. 5 is bandsawed to the shape shown in Fig. 5. The wood should be sanded until it is very smooth to prevent mark-off. Slots for the picture glass in design No. 5 are cut previous to bending. An over-all heat, commonly obtained by placing the strip in an oven, is used for all bent frames when smooth-flowing curves are required.

Straight frames, such as shown in Photo 7 and Fig. 7, are made from straight sections of plastic assembled with cemented butt joints. A solvent-type cement, such as methylene dichloride or vinyl trichloride, gives firm, clear joints on work of this kind and is easily and quickly applied. This type of frame has the edges sanded with 100-grit wet-or-dry paper used with water, which gives a frosty effect that combines nicely with the crystal plastic. Alternate designs for straight frames are suggested by Figs. 8 and 9. The same type of assembly and construction is used.

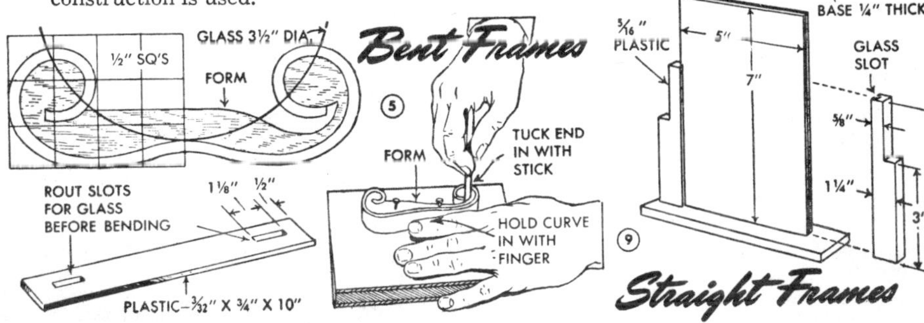

Walnut Picture Frame Has a Wood Spring Back and "Two-in-One" Inlay

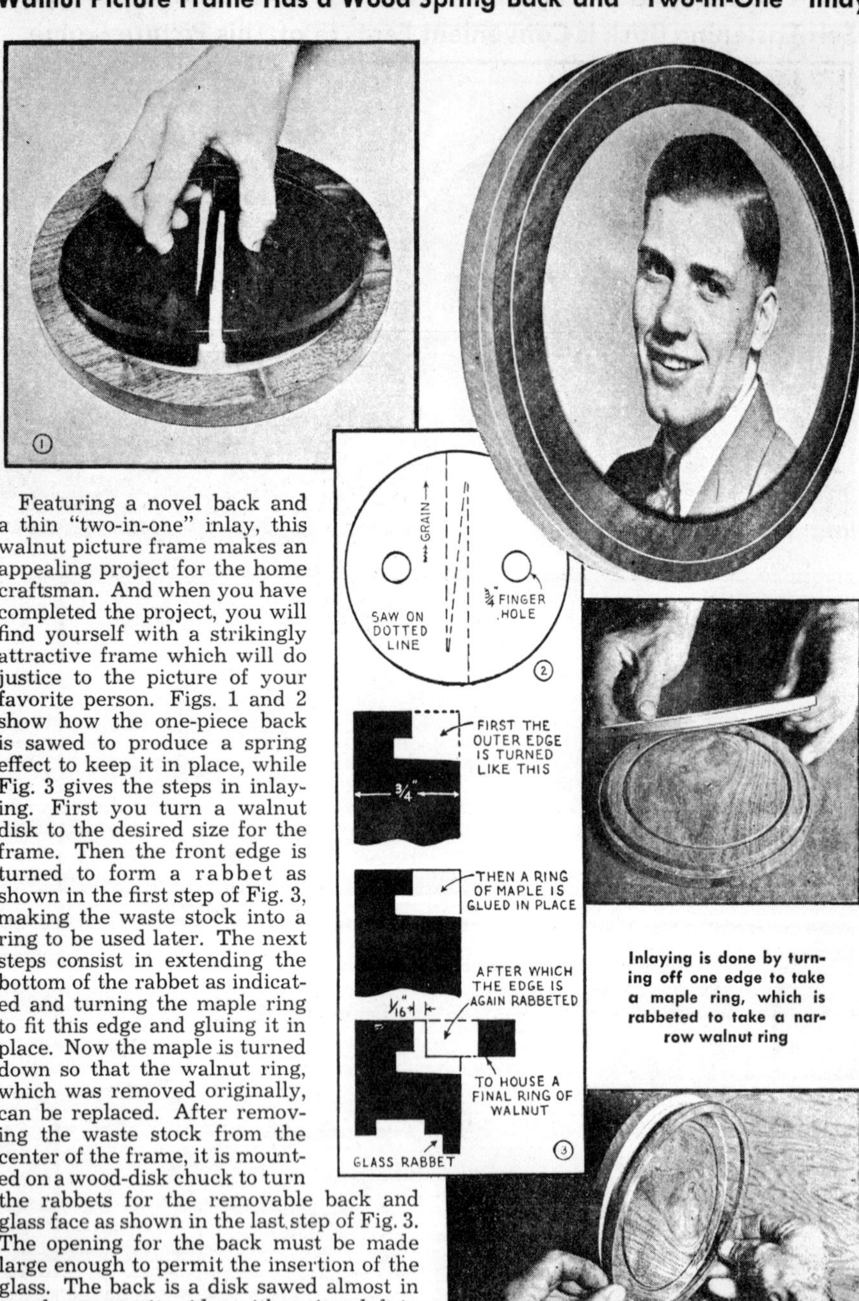

Inlaying is done by turning off one edge to take a maple ring, which is rabbeted to take a narrow walnut ring

Featuring a novel back and a thin "two-in-one" inlay, this walnut picture frame makes an appealing project for the home craftsman. And when you have completed the project, you will find yourself with a strikingly attractive frame which will do justice to the picture of your favorite person. Figs. 1 and 2 show how the one-piece back is sawed to produce a spring effect to keep it in place, while Fig. 3 gives the steps in inlaying. First you turn a walnut disk to the desired size for the frame. Then the front edge is turned to form a rabbet as shown in the first step of Fig. 3, making the waste stock into a ring to be used later. The next steps consist in extending the bottom of the rabbet as indicated and turning the maple ring to fit this edge and gluing it in place. Now the maple is turned down so that the walnut ring, which was removed originally, can be replaced. After removing the waste stock from the center of the frame, it is mounted on a wood-disk chuck to turn the rabbets for the removable back and glass face as shown in the last step of Fig. 3. The opening for the back must be made large enough to permit the insertion of the glass. The back is a disk sawed almost in two from opposite sides with a piece left in the center to serve as a spring. The two ¾-in. holes serve as finger grips for pressing the back together when inserting or removing it.

Self-Fastening Back Is Convenient Feature of This Picture Frame

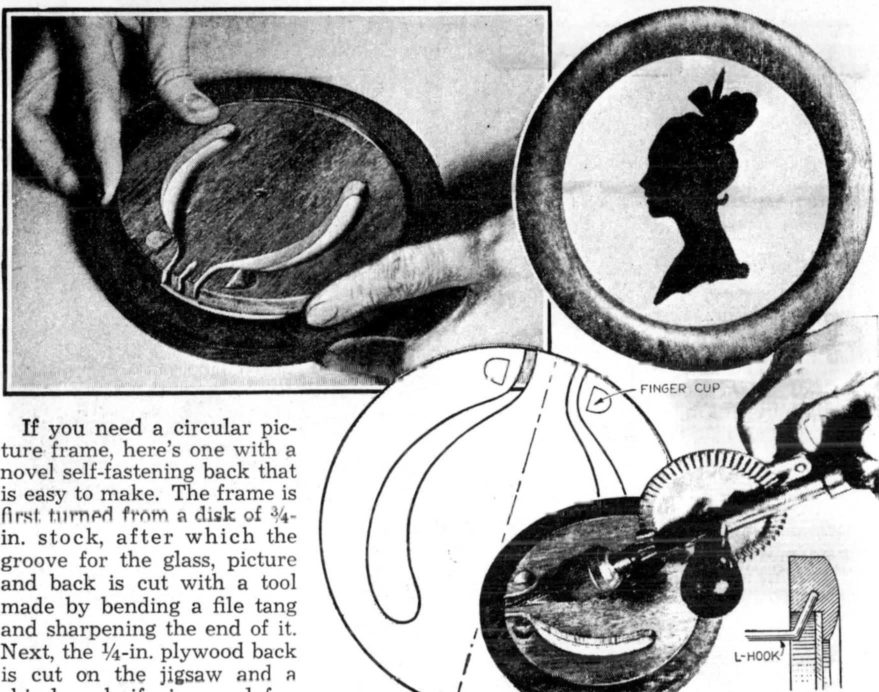

If you need a circular picture frame, here's one with a novel self-fastening back that is easy to make. The frame is first turned from a disk of ¾-in. stock, after which the groove for the glass, picture and back is cut with a tool made by bending a file tang and sharpening the end of it. Next, the ¼-in. plywood back is cut on the jigsaw and a chisel or knife is used for making the two finger cups. To insert the back in the frame, you merely press it in place as shown. The frame hangs on an L-hook which slips in hole drilled at an angle.

Horizontal Strips of Molding "Frame" Display of Pictures or Photos

One way to display a number of pictures or photographic prints is to mount them in rows, using horizontal strips of molding as racks. Suggested dimensions for the top and bottom pieces are given in the lower right hand detail. The distances between the two strips, 19½ in. for 20-in. pictures and 15½ in. for 16-in. pictures are for mounting 16 by 20-in. photographic prints either horizontally or vertically. Prints this size are about right for an ordinary-size room. Smaller pictures are pasted on mats to make them fit. Stock sizes of glass that fit the frame can be purchased. To change a picture, bend the pieces of molding out slightly—not enough to pry them loose—and removal and insertion will be easy.

Inexpensive, Easy-to-Make Frame Displays Photomounts Attractively

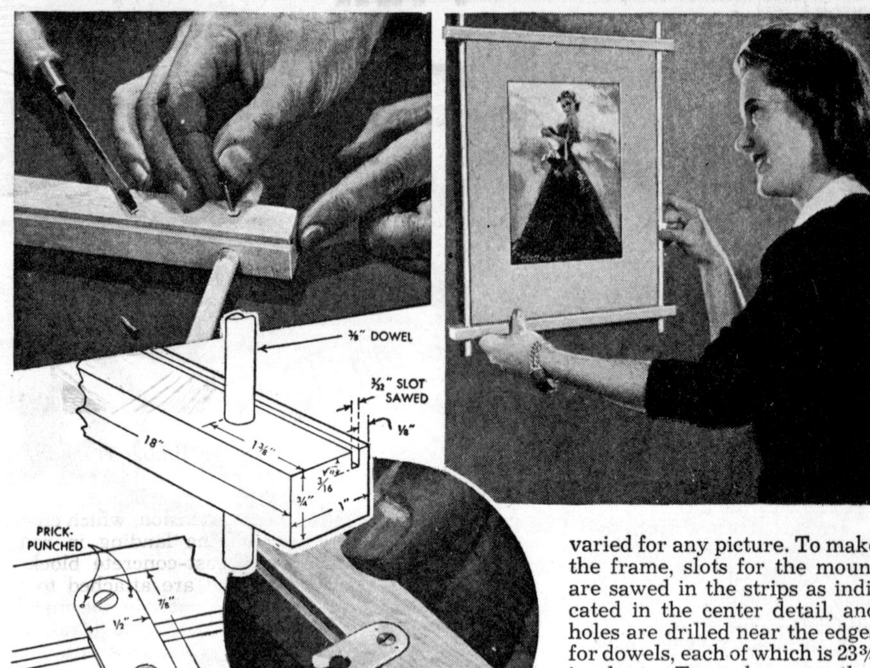

Emphasizing simplicity in design, this neat picture frame will set off your photographs and other pictures to good advantage. As it is made up merely of dowels and two strips of wood, the frame is as easy to make as it looks. The dimensions shown in the detail of the illustration are for a frame that will take a 16 x 20-in. photomount. However, the size can be easily varied for any picture. To make the frame, slots for the mount are sawed in the strips as indicated in the center detail, and holes are drilled near the edges for dowels, each of which is 23¾ in. long. To make sure that there is proper alignment of the holes, the strips are clamped together and each pair of holes is drilled at the same time. When they are in place, the dowels should project about 1½ in., and are held by screws driven into countersunk holes at the rear of the strips, as in the upper left-hand photo. For a hanger, a piece of flat metal, drilled and slotted as shown in the lower details, is attached with a screw to the rear surface of the upper strip, which is notched to receive the hanger. The frame can be finished to suit individual tastes.

Attractive Plastic Photo Bracelet Made From Lens and Letter Opener

Made from either a combination lens and letter opener or a plastic scale and lens, this photo bracelet is a novel bit of costume jewelry. Numbers or scale markings are removed with sandpaper and the scale is then formed to the desired shape by immersing it in hot water until it is soft enough to bend. The photo should be cut to fit inside the circular mounting and then glued to the lens with transparent glue. The plastic has sufficient spring so the bracelet can be put on and removed easily.

PIER

REQUIRING no pilings, this inexpensive boat landing which floats with the tide or water level is ideal for lake or river use. Designed to ride up and down on the posts of a fixed pier, one end of the landing is fitted with flat-iron yokes while the other end is anchored to a concrete block by means of a pantograph-type extension. Tarred telephone poles are excellent for the timbers of the landing. These are braced diagonally on the underside, after one end of each outer timber is shaped to take the flat-iron yokes, and then the surface is floored with narrow boards.

The pantograph extension, which checks side movement of the landing in rough weather, and the cast-concrete block to which it is anchored are attached to the outboard end of the poles in the manner shown. The whole assembly is floated into position, using the landing as a raft. Bolting the yokes in place and adding a small ramp complete the job. Metal parts should be copper-painted for salt-water use.

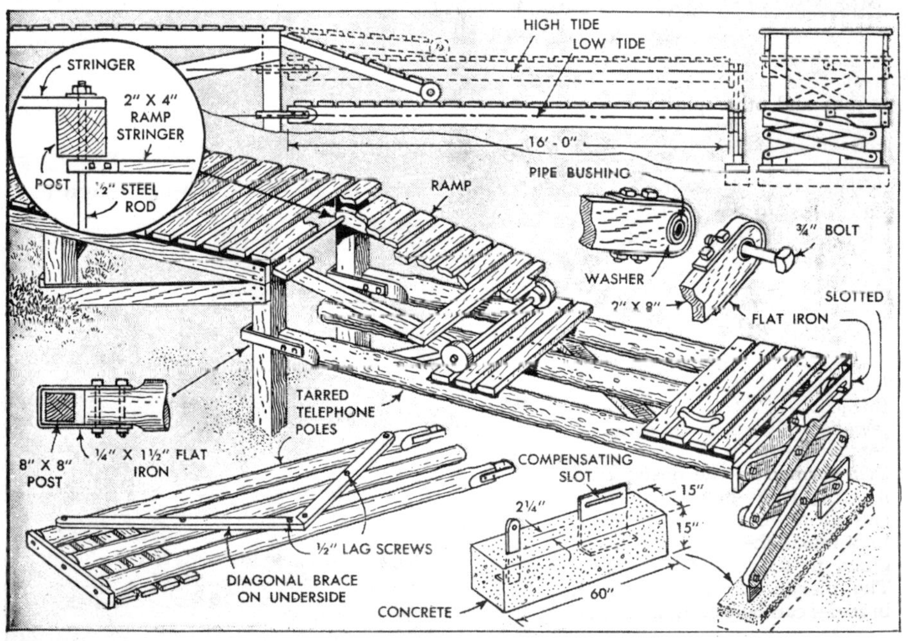

PIN-UP LAMP

Glass Brick Provides Shade for a Kitchen Pin-Up Lamp

You can have an unusually neat pin-up lamp that provides excellent illumination for your kitchen or dinette for the price of a glass brick, a bulb and a socket. The brick is of the type used as a vase, having an opening in one end as indicated in the large circular detail to the left. To assemble the lamp, mount the socket in the center of a wood block by means of a $\frac{1}{8}$-in. pipe nipple as shown in the small circular detail. The block, which serves as a base, should be just slightly larger than the brick and should have a short piece of spirally grooved molding attached to the underside near the outer edge to rest against the wall and serve as a brace. The lamp is supported on the wall by two screw hooks, which are fastened to the block to engage L-hooks or screw-eyes driven into the wall. The lamp is wired with an extension cord to a near-by wall outlet. It may be necessary to drive three or four short nails into the base to project into the opening of the brick and prevent vibration from working it off the base. The nails will be invisible from the outside. If you wish to avoid using nails, however, the base surface of the block can be grooved deeply to take and hold the glass brick.

Lamp Hung From Picture Molding Is Convenient to Move

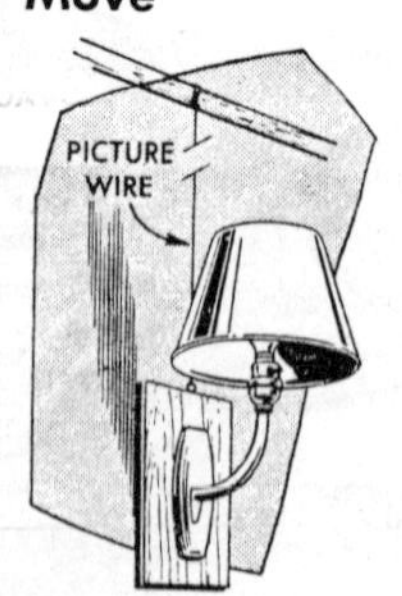

A pin-up lamp becomes a versatile lighting fixture when it is hung from the picture molding. In this way, it can be moved quickly to be used as a bed lamp or reading lamp and its location changed in a few minutes to illuminate a card table or other spot where extra light is needed. Mount the lamp on a wooden backboard and drive a screw eye into the top edge of the board to permit fastening.

Bracket Used as Lamp Support

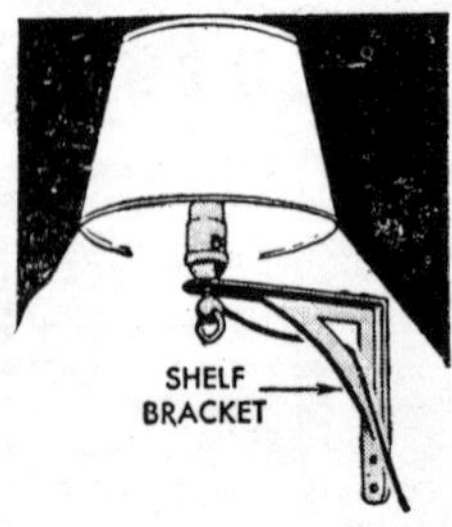

As a substitute for a side-wall lamp, use a shelf bracket and an ordinary drop-fixture socket. The end hole in one of the legs of the bracket will probably have to be enlarged to fit the threaded extension at the base of the socket. In the case of this particular lamp, an ornamental fitting from a chandelier was used to fasten the socket to the bracket, although any fitting with a male thread that fits will do. The cord is attached to a baseboard outlet.

PIPE FITTING

Do you want to replace a section of water pipe, change the location of a hot-water tank, or install a new plumbing fixture? Often you can save time and money by doing these simple plumbing jobs yourself. All you need are a few inexpensive tools and a knowledge of the essentials of pipe-fitting practice. It's easy when you know the right way to measure pipe and how to cut, thread and assemble it.

Correct measurements: Center-to-center measurements, which are necessary to lay out the job, are determined as shown in Fig. 1. The actual pipe lengths must be shorter than the center-to-center dimensions to allow for fittings and for the portion of the pipe that enters them. To determine exact lengths, subtract dimension A (center-to-face distance) of fittings from the center-to-center dimensions. Then add dimension C, Fig. 2.

The thread for a 1-in. pipe is not 1-in. outside diameter, as in other forms of thread. In piping, a 1-in. pipe has a nominal inside diameter of 1-in. with an outside diameter of 1.315 in. Another distinguishing difference between pipe threads and other forms of threads is that there is a ¾-in.-per-ft. taper in the diameter of the thread instead of a uniform diameter.

In modern pipe fitting, however, many materials are used, including copper, cast iron, wrought iron, etc. Copper piping has the advantage of a smooth bore and is easy to fit. The joints can be rapidly made, whether by compression, welding or soldering and the economy of labor costs thus achieved frequently outweighs the extra cost of copper as material. Wrought-iron piping properly protected from rust and corrosion with a coating of zinc is also much in favor, but should not be used in a district where soft water or water of an acid nature is apt to attack these metals.

If the handyman follows a few simple instructions, he should have no difficulty in making satisfactory pipe jointings.

Tools needed: Either of the vises shown in Fig. 6 will do, or you can use a machinists's vise fitted with detachable pipe jaws. You'll need two pipe wrenches for the average home plumbing jobs, an 8-in. and a 10-in. wrench. Using too large a wrench may result in buckling the pipe. The proper size wrenches for various pipe sizes are given in Fig. 6. You'll also need a pipe cutter, a reamer and a die stock with threading dies of the

Jointing and attachment of piping, in either water supply or drainage, depends on the size of the piping and material of which it is made. Small-diameter wrought-iron pipes are usually tapped and joined with a threaded sleeve. Center-to-center measurements, which are necessary to lay out the job, are determined in the diagram of dimensions, below. The thread data is given in Fig. 2

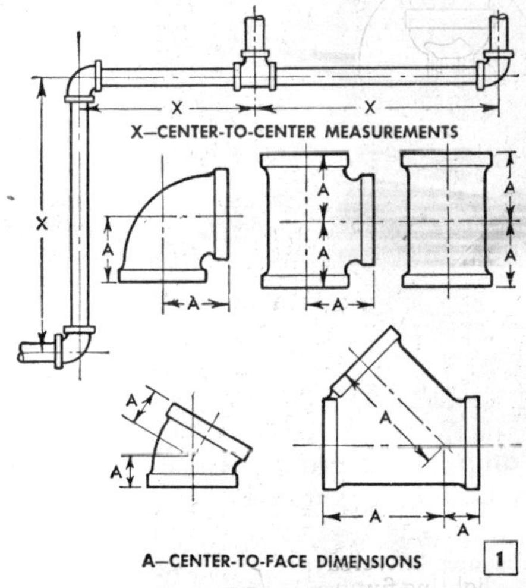

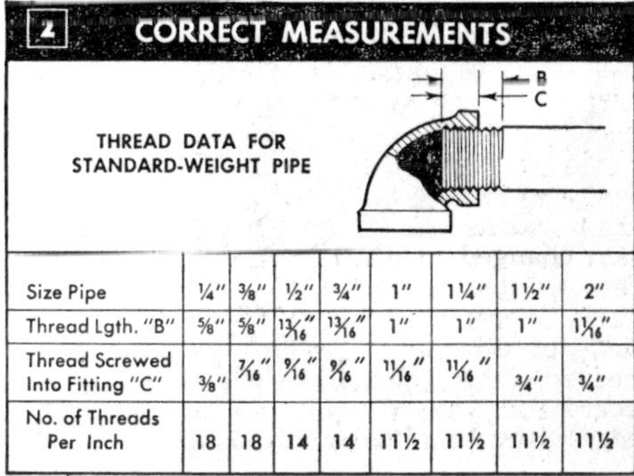

THREAD DATA FOR STANDARD-WEIGHT PIPE

Size Pipe	¼"	⅜"	½"	¾"	1"	1¼"	1½"	2"
Thread Lgth. "B"	⅝"	⅝"	13/16"	13/16"	1"	1"	1"	1 1/16"
Thread Screwed Into Fitting "C"	⅜"	7/16"	9/16"	9/16"	11/16"	11/16"	¾"	¾"
No. of Threads Per Inch	18	18	14	14	11½	11½	11½	11½

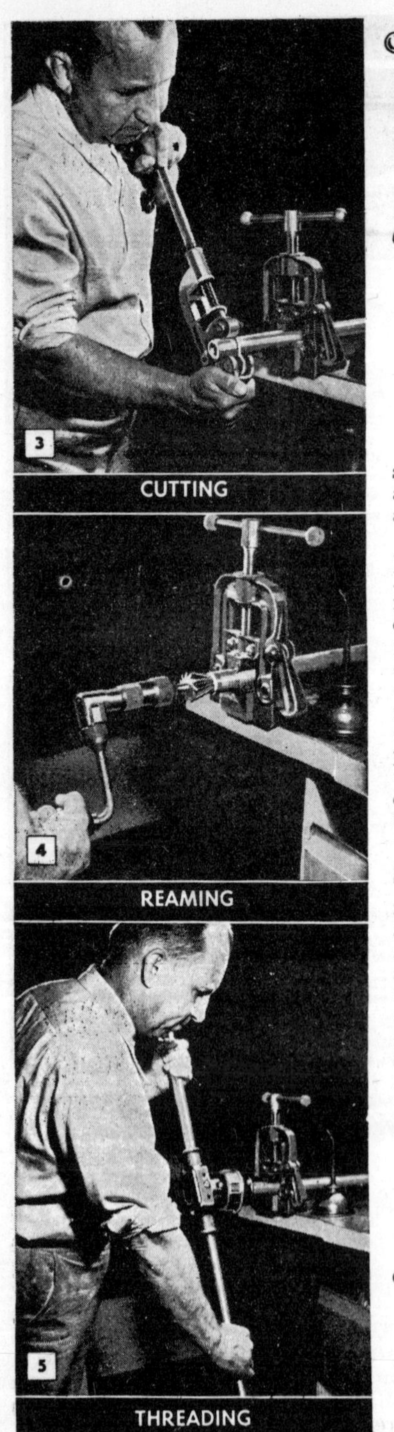

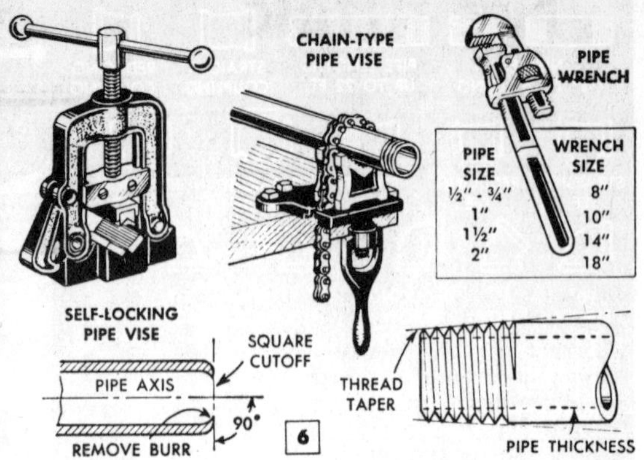

sizes required. Cutting oil is used for lubrication and also to dissipate heat caused by the cutting action of the die.

Cutting off and reaming: Good pipe joints have the ends of the pipe cut off at 90 deg. to the axis, Fig. 6. It's best to use a regular pipe cutter, Fig. 3, rather than a hacksaw. First mark the pipe for cutting, not less than 1 in. from the end. Then grip it in the vise so that the mark extends far enough to permit the cutter and threading tool to clear the bench. Set the cutting wheel on the mark and screw the handle down so that the rollers rest firmly on the pipe. Apply cutting oil and proceed, screwing down the handle a little each time the cutter is rotated. When cut, use a reamer chucked in a carpenter's brace, as in Fig. 4, to remove the burr formed inside the pipe.

Threading: Pipe dies, Figs. 5 and 7, are held in a stock, which is fitted with handles for turning. The ratchet-type stock has only one handle. Ordinary pipe stocks hold dies of several different sizes. There are two types of dies—the solid, nonadjustable type and the split die, which is adjustable for wear and cutting depth. A different die is required for each size of pipe. In a stock-and-die assembly there also is a guide bushing—one for each pipe size within the capacity of the die stock, or one that is adjustable for size. The bushing slips on the pipe first and lines up the die on the end of the pipe. Pipe dies cut tapered threads

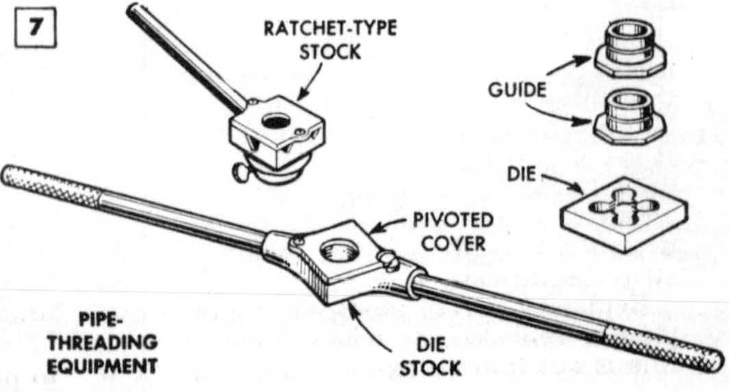

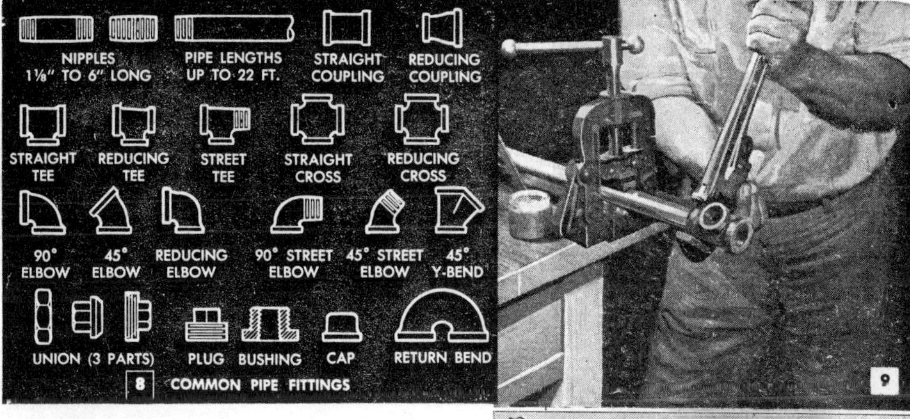

8 COMMON PIPE FITTINGS

9

as in Fig. 6, and for this reason it is necessary to make sure that the die is placed in the stock so that the largest diameter faces the guide.

After slipping the guide bushing over the pipe, press the die teeth on the pipe slightly while turning the stock slowly to the right. Keep the handle at right angles to the pipe and apply a steady pressure until the die engages. Apply cutting oil liberally. Then start the thread by turning the stock forward a half turn and then back a quarter turn to break the chips. Now turn the stock slowly to avoid excessive heating, and apply cutting oil every two or three turns. Stop threading when the end of the pipe projects slightly beyond the small end of the die. This distance indicates that a thread of approximately standard length (dimension B of Fig. 2) has been cut.

Assembling pipe and fittings: Fig. 8 shows common pipe fittings you will use in an ordinary pipe assembly. Before assembling pipe and fittings, clean the threads with a wire brush to clear them of chips. Then spread pipe-joint compound on the threads of the pipe—never apply it to the internal threads of a fitting as it will be forced inside the pipe and may start an obstruction or taint the drinking water. Turn on a fitting by hand for three or four threads, after which a few more turns with a pipe wrench will draw it up snugly. Tighten the fitting on the pipe while it is still held in the vise, Fig. 9, and before threading the opposite end. This prevents accidental damage to threads and keeps the dirt out. It is not necessary to draw the fitting unduly tight. A moderate pressure on the wrench is sufficient. Excessive wrench pressure may distort the fitting or even strip the threads.

Replacing part of pipe: When a defective pipe is replaced, or when a new branch line is cut into an existing one, Fig. 10, it

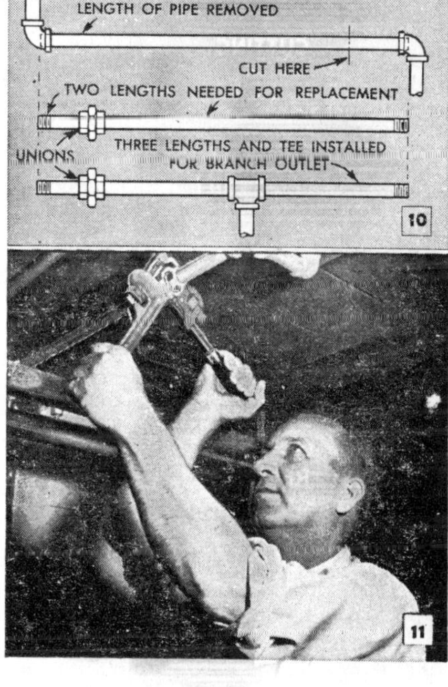

10

11

generally is necessary to saw the latter to permit unscrewing it except, of course, when there's a union to "break" the line. First shut off the water supply and drain the system by opening a faucet. Cut the pipe about 4 in. from a joint, never less if avoidable, and unscrew both pieces. The new section is made up of two lengths and a union, the total length of which should be equal to that of the old pipe. The same method is followed in installing a branch line, three lengths of pipe, a tee and a union being required. When tightening a union, Fig. 11, you'll need two wrenches to prevent the pipe from turning.

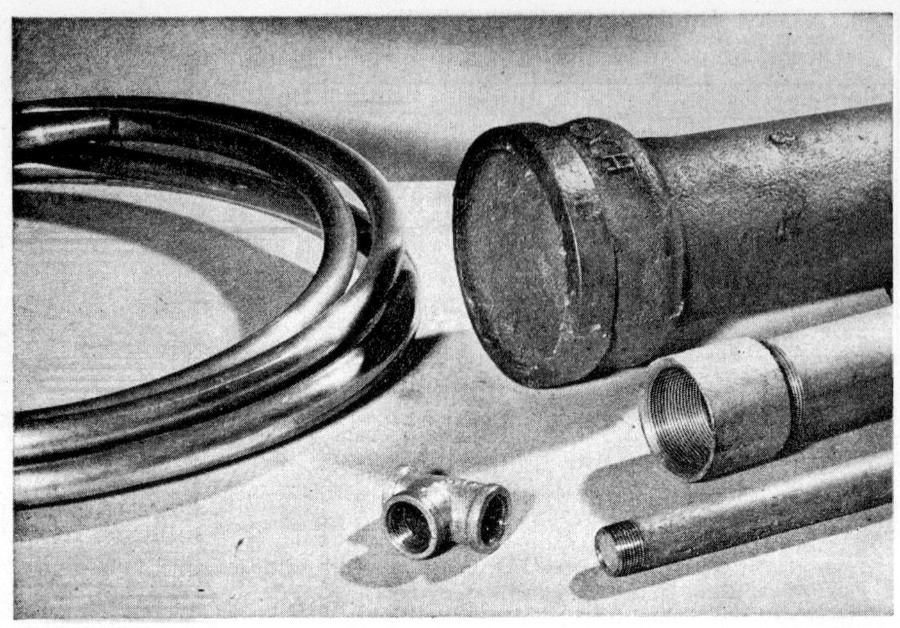

PIPE FOR ANY PLUMBING JOB

IT MAKES A BIG DIFFERENCE, generally, what kind of pipe and fittings you use for a plumbing job. Some kinds are developed for specific purposes while others have a variety of uses or may be more suitable for some jobs than others, besides varying in cost and durability. Therefore the reference data contained in this section concerning various kinds of pipe and fittings, their purposes, and also how pipe is prepared and installed will be of help in selecting and using pipe.

Kinds of pipe for plumbing: Pipe can be classified as to its use in home plumbing systems as follows: (1) Water-supply pipe, which may be galvanized wrought-iron and steel pipe, brass and copper pipe, copper tubing and also plastic pipe; (2) drain and vent pipe, which may be galvanized wrought-iron and steel pipe, cast-iron soil pipe, vitrified clay pipe, cement pipe, lead pipe, copper pipe and tubing, asbestos-cement pipe and bituminized-fiber pipe. Some of these are used for different purposes; others are restricted to certain specific applications and treatment.

Wrought-iron and steel pipe: Used for water distribution, for waste and vent lines, wrought-iron pipe is more resistant to rust than steel pipe but also is more expensive. Either kind is available in black or galvanized finish, but only the latter should be used for permanently installed lines because of the added protection it provides against rust. Life of galvanized steel pipe generally ranges from 15 to 30 years; that of wrought-iron pipe from 20 to 40 years. Identifying wrought-iron and steel pipe from appearance is difficult for the average person, and therefore he must rely for this on the manufacturer's markings put on first-grade pipe of either type. Reference here to steel pipe also includes steel-alloy pipe, such as copper-bearing pipe which contains about 0.2 percent of copper by weight and usually is galvanized.

Standard-weight wrought-iron or steel pipe comes in random lengths up to 22 ft., with both ends threaded and protected with couplings. Sizes range from ⅛ to 12-in. nominal inside diameters. Fig. 1 gives dimensions and other data on wrought-iron and steel pipe up to 2½-in. size. Besides the standard weight there is also an "extra strong" and a "double extra strong" weight. These, having thicker walls than standard-weight pipe, are used for higher pressures than usually found in most home plumbing

DATA ON STANDARD WEIGHT WROUGHT IRON AND STEEL PIPE FROM ⅛" TO 2½"; FURNISHED IN RANDOM LENGTHS UP TO 22 FT.
(All Dimensions in Inches)

Nominal Size	Outside Diameter	Inside Diameter	Wall Thickness	No. of Threads Per In.	Length of Effective Threads	Normal Engagement For Tight Fit (W)
⅛	0.405	0.269	0.068	27	.2639	¼
¼	0.540	0.364	0.088	18	.4018	5/16
⅜	0.675	0.493	0.091	18	.4078	⅜
½	0.840	0.622	0.109	14	.5337	7/16
¾	1.050	0.824	0.113	14	.5457	½
1	1.315	1.049	0.133	11½	.6828	9/16
1¼	1.660	1.380	0.140	11½	.7068	9/16
1½	1.900	1.610	0.145	11½	.7235	9/16
2	2.375	2.067	0.154	11½	.7565	⅝
2½	2.875	2.469	0.203	8	1.1375	⅞

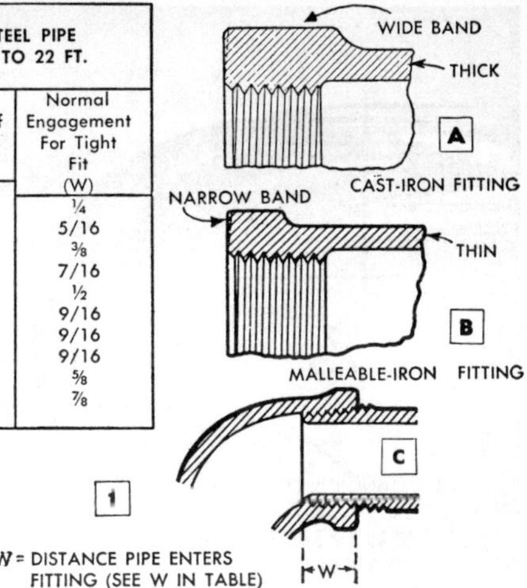

systems. The outside diameters of pipes having different wall thicknesses are the same, but the inside diameters vary. For example, the outside diameter of a 1-in. standard-weight pipe and that of a 1-in. double-extra-strong pipe are both 1.315 in., but the inside diameter of the former is 1.049 in., and that of the latter is only .599 in.

Water-pipe fittings: The only pipe fittings that are made of wrought iron and steel are nipples and couplings. Both are short lengths of pipe, nipples being threaded externally and couplings internally. Other fittings are made of cast iron or malleable iron. Malleable iron is preferable as it is tougher and not so brittle as cast iron. You can distinguish between cast-iron and malleable-iron fittings in that the latter have thinner and narrower bands as shown in Fig. 1A and B. Fittings in water lines should be galvanized to retard rusting.

A number of fittings in common use are shown in Fig. 3. Externally threaded ends are called "male" ends and internally threaded ends are referred to as "female." Nipples come in various lengths—17 lengths from 1⅜ to 12 in. in the ¾-in. size. Couplings connect two pipes end to end where they need not be disconnected later. A reducing coupling joins pipes of different sizes. Unions connect pipes end to end near meters, water heaters and other fixtures that may have to be disconnected; unions also are placed in a line where a branch line may be inserted later. Flange-type unions generally are used on pipes over 2 in. in size.

Regular and reducing elbows join pipe at 45 and 90 deg.; street elbows (45 and 90 deg.) differ in that they have one tapped and one threaded end, the latter end to join another pipe fitting or a matching tapped hole. Regular or reducing tees join three pipes at 90 deg.; a street tee has one outlet threaded like a street elbow. A Y-branch connects two pipes end to end, and a third pipe at a 45 deg. angle. There are also regular and reducing crosses.

Plugs are used to close one end of a fitting; caps to close the end of pipe. Bushings have a hexagon bearing surface to take a wrench; they are threaded internally and externally to make a connection from a pipe or fitting of one size to one of another size, where a reducing coupling cannot be used. Return bends connect the ends of two or more pipes running parallel to each other, as in a bank of pipes used for heating. Return bends are furnished in close, medium and open types for different spacing of pipes. On ¾-in. pipe, return bends have 1½, 1⅞ and 2½-in. center-to-center spacing respectively. Hose fittings have different threads and will not fit standard threaded pipe and fittings, except sill cocks and laundry faucets, which are threaded to permit hose connections.

Fittings for threaded drainage pipes: Fittings for threaded drainage pipes differ radically in design from ordinary pipe fittings. Those of larger sizes are usually cast iron. One essential difference between regular and drainage fittings is shown in Fig. 4. The internal diameter of the body section of a drainage fitting is the same as that of the pipe it fits. The tapped section of the fitting is recessed so that the end of the pipe butts against the shoulder, thus preventing a "ledge" against which waste can collect and start an obstruction. The second essential difference between regular and drainage fittings is that the latter have slightly slanted or pitched outlets (¼ in. per ft.) for connection to horizontal drainage and vent pipes that must be pitched. In Fig. 5, which shows a number of common drainage fittings. Pitch is indicated by the dotted lines. In drainage lines, fittings of long radii or a combination of fittings for gradual change of direction should be used

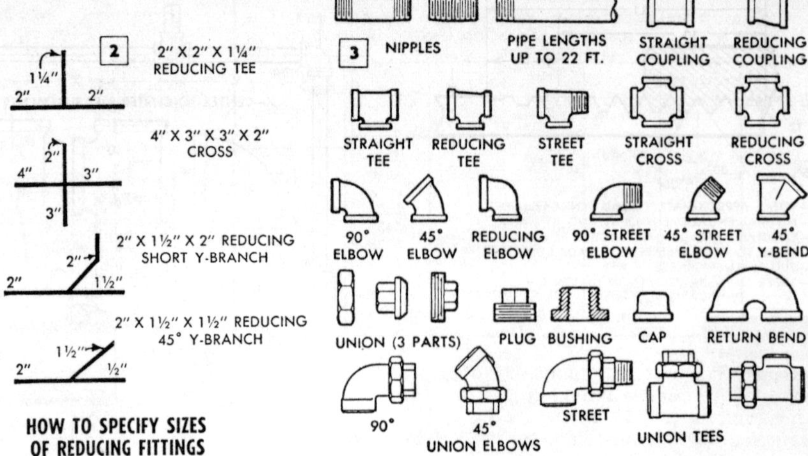

HOW TO SPECIFY SIZES
OF REDUCING FITTINGS

wherever possible as a preventive measure against stoppage.

Ordering pipe fittings: All fittings are referred to by the pipe size on which they are used, which precedes the name of the fitting. For example, a ¾-in. elbow has both outlets for ¾-in. pipe. In giving the sizes of reducing tees and Y-branches, the larger run is given first, then the smaller run followed by the inlet or branch, as indicated in Fig. 2. Reducing crosses should be specified similarly except that both outlets are given, the smaller one last. For crosses having both run openings of the same size and both outlets of one size, only the run and outlet sizes need be given. For bushings the external size comes first, then the internal size.

Brass and copper pipe: While the initial cost of brass and copper pipe is more than that of wrought-iron and steel pipe, it will last the life of a building. It is required in some localities where water is extremely corrosive. Besides the economy gained by avoiding replacement of steel pipe, of which a large percentage is labor cost, it is possible to use smaller sizes of brass and copper pipes, which means a saving. Smaller sizes can be used since brass and copper pipe has a smooth inside surface which causes less resistance to the flow of water than iron and steel pipe of similar size.

Brass and copper pipe is furnished in the same sizes and in practically the same wall thicknesses as iron and steel pipe, but in 12-ft. lengths. Threads are also the same size except for the fine thread used on thin-wall drainage fittings. When cutting and threading brass and copper pipe, a lubricant or cooling medium such as lard oil or soapy water reduces effort and helps to produce clean, sharp threads. Wrenches of

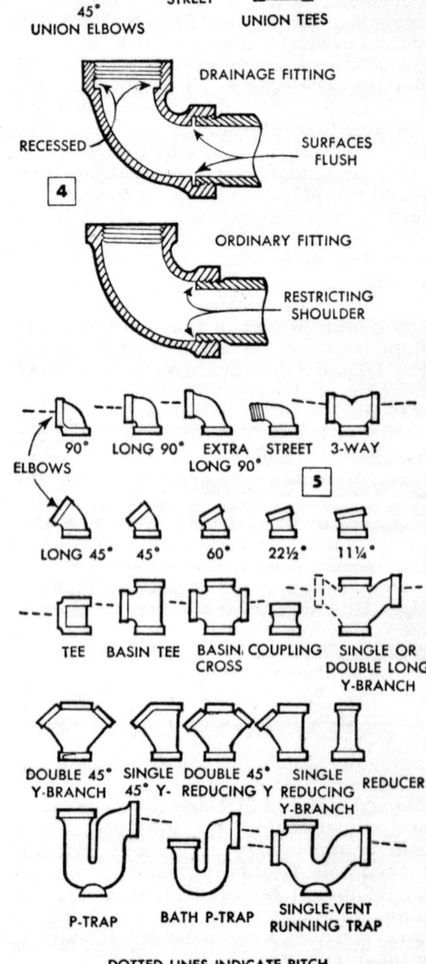

DOTTED LINES INDICATE PITCH

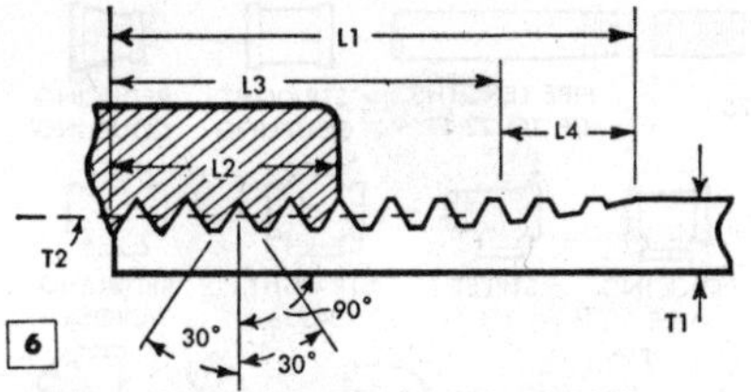

L1 — TOTAL APPROXIMATE THREAD LENGTH ON PIPE
L2 — NORMAL ENGAGEMENT OF FITTING BY HAND
L3 — EFFECTIVE THREADS THAT SHOULD BE SCREWED INTO FITTING
L4 — THREE TO FOUR IMPERFECT THREADS DUE TO DIE
T1 — FULL WALL THICKNESS OF PIPE
T2 — TAPER OF ¾ IN. PER FT. ON DIAMETER

8

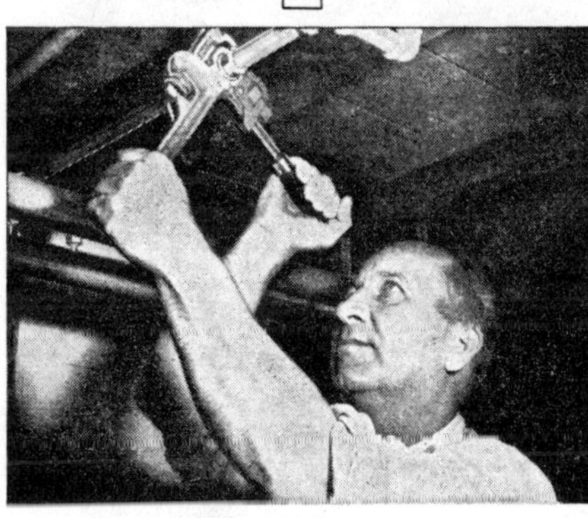

9

the friction or strap type should be used to avoid marring brass and copper wire. Also, the vises should be fitted with friction clamps instead of toothed jaws.

For brass pipe, the fittings used are the same type as those for iron and steel pipe. Special alloy fittings for either brass or copper pipe are used. Iron or steel fittings should not be used on brass and copper pipe as they will rust faster because of electrolytic action between dissimilar metals. Chrome-plated brass pipe generally is used for exposed portions of water-supply and

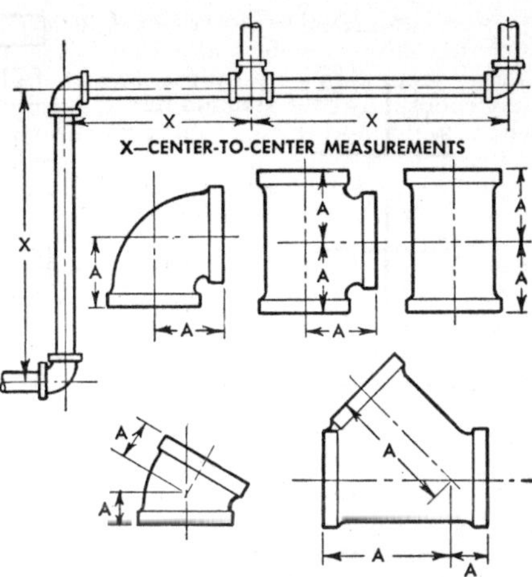

A—CENTER-TO-FACE DIMENSIONS

7

drainage lines that run from floors or walls to fixtures.

Standard pipe threads: To assure strong, well-fitting joints that are watertight, threads on pipe must be of correct length and depth and must be clean and sharp. Pipe threads have a taper of ¾ in. per foot. Fig. 6 shows the number of threads required on pipe for a good fit. Such correct thread length results when the die is brought flush with the end of the pipe or when the pipe projects only half a turn beyond the die. Table, Fig. 1, gives the correct distance that the threaded end of pipe should enter fittings as indicated in detail C.

How to measure pipe runs: When installing pipe, first take the actual center-to-center measurements of the pipe run, as indicated by letter X in Fig. 7. The lengths of pipe between the various fittings must be shorter than the X-dimensions to allow space for the fittings, yet must be greater than the distance between the fittings to allow for the portions of pipe entering them. Therefore you first subtract dimension A of the fittings from the X-dimensions, but then add the distances that the pipe enters the fittings as given in Table Fig. 1.

Making threaded pipe joints: Before screwing pipe into a fitting or vice versa, use a stiff bristle or wire brush to clean chips and dirt from the threads of each. Next, smear some pipe-thread compound or "dope" over the threads of the pipe only, but not on the inside threads of a fitting as this causes it to collect on the end of the pipe and to restrict pipe diameter at this point, besides imparting a disagreeable taste to water. Such a restriction interferes with the flow of water; also this forms a "drag" for building up a lime deposit that may eventually clog the pipe. Theoretically a watertight joint results from good threading and assembling, but there are slight variations that may result from threading, or there may be variations in the threads of fittings which can cause leakage at joints even though they appear tight. Therefore, it is general practice to use pipe-thread compound at all joints.

Defective fittings that are not tapped deep enough should not be used. Cutting a deeper thread on the pipe with an adjustable die in order to compensate for this only weakens the pipe by reducing its wall thickness, which may cause it to break later. It's better to replace the pipe, fitting or both. If threads fit properly a pipe can be screwed into a fitting, or vice versa, a distance of three or four threads by hand. A pipe wrench then is used to draw it up snugly. Often it is possible to attach or detach a fitting while the pipe is held in a vise as in Fig. 8. Generally, two wrenches are needed for assembling pipe, one on the pipe and the other on the fitting as illustrated in Fig. 9. Moderate pressure on wrenches should be sufficient. Excessive pressure may distort the fitting or squash the pipe. Exposed threads of iron or steel pipe joints should be coated with a suitable rust-resisting paint such as red lead or asphalt roofing paint.

Plastic pipe: Comparatively new but rapidly being accepted for many applications, strong, durable plastic pipe offers some specific advantages. It is extremely lightweight, from ⅛ to 1/13 the weight of metal pipe as evident from Fig. 10. It is rust, rot and corrosion proof; it can be cut with a saw or knife. Some kinds are especially designed to convey liquids intended for human consumption. Plastic pipe is entirely practical for jet wells and other cold-water plumbing installations, but it should not be used for hot-water lines or subjected to excessive heat.

The pipe comes in three forms — rigid, semirigid and flexible. Both the flexible and rigid kinds are shown in Fig. 11. The flexible pipe is ideal for installation in trenches as in Fig. 12. Available sizes range from ½ to 6-in. nominal inside diameters. The rigid pipe comes in 20-ft. lengths and is useful for well casings, septic-tank lines, field drainage, sprinkler and irrigation installations. The flexible pipe comes in coils from 100 to 400 ft. in length. It is especially suitable for jet wells and water-supply and distribution lines in locations free from rodent attack. Low temperature does not damage the pipe as it expands with freezing water.

Numerous fittings are available for both

10

11

Yardley Plastics Co. photos

12

Copper & Brass Research Assn. photo

13

Anaconda photo

14

types so that any kind of connection can be made. Varying with the composition of the pipe, connections are made by insert couplings and clamps and insert adapters. Connections are also made by cementing the pipe into a fitting, which within a few minutes results in a joint as strong as the pipe itself. You can use compression fittings and also threaded joints. Threaded joints are practical for low-pressure or gravity lines but not recommended for vertical runs. In threading the pipe, it is recommended that a mandrel be inserted for support. The same threading equipment as for standard metal pipe is used. Plain or soapy water is used as a cutting solution—not oil or lead. The threaded pipe is assembled with strap wrenches; pipe wrenches will damage the pipe. No pipe-joint compound is required at the threaded joint.

Copper tubing: Copper tubing has thinner walls than copper pipe and costs less yet is sufficiently strong to withstand all pressures normally encountered in water-supply lines and thus offers practically the same advantages for home plumbing. Copper tubing is also easy to install and it can be run through closed partitions, Fig. 13, when replacing rusted-out iron or steel pipe, or when installing plumbing in a house not previously piped.

Copper tubing is furnished in three wall thicknesses (types K, L and M) for assembly with either solder or compression-type fittings. Type K is the heaviest and most durable. Type L has a slightly thinner wall. Both are furnished either hard in 20-ft. straight lengths, or soft in 60 and 100-ft. coils. Type M is still thinner than the other types of tubing of the same size. It is furnished only hard in 1¼ to 12-in. sizes and only in 20-ft. straight lengths, and is generally installed with soldered fittings, not being intended for use with compres-

DIMENSIONS OF K, L AND M-TYPES COPPER TUBING FROM ⅜" TO 2"

Nominal Size	Outside Diameter	Inside Diameter			Wall Thickness		
	Types K-L-M	Type K	Type L	Type M	Type K	Type L	Type M
⅜	.500	.402	.430		.049	.035	
½	.625	.527	.545		.049	.040	
⅝	.750	.652	.666		.049	.042	
¾	.875	.745	.785		.065	.045	
1	1.125	.995	1.025		.065	.050	
1¼	1.375	1245	1265	1291	.065	.055	.042
1½	1.625	1481	1505	1527	.072	.060	.049
2	2.125	1959	1985	2009	.083	.070	.058

(All Dimensions in Inches)

15

TYPES OF COMPRESSION FITTINGS

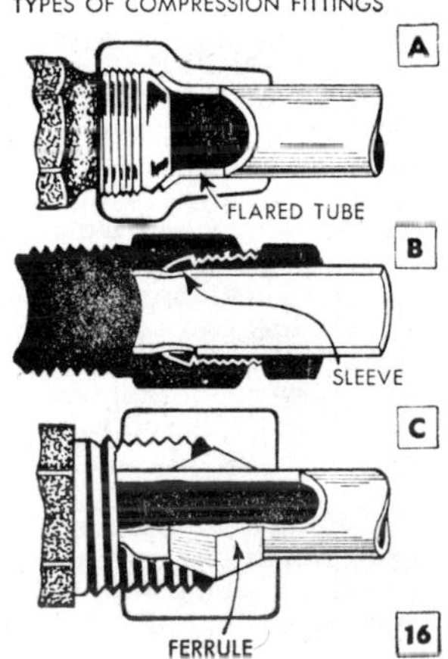

16

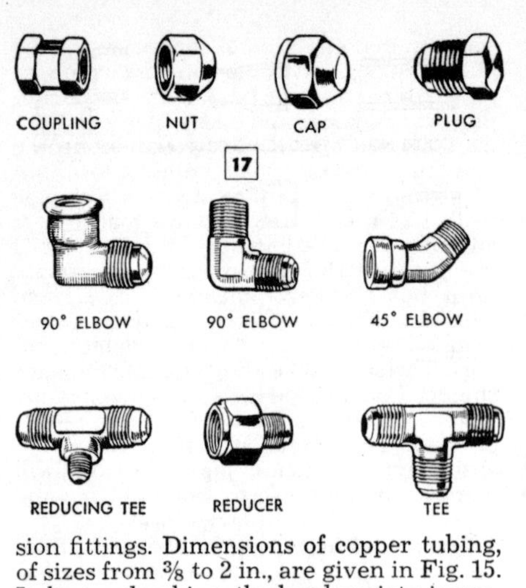

17

sion fittings. Dimensions of copper tubing, of sizes from ⅜ to 2 in., are given in Fig. 15. In home plumbing, the hard variety is preferred for horizontal lines; soft tubing is difficult to install without sag between supports, which prevents good drainage of the system. Soft tubing is satisfactory for vertical risers.

For underground water service, as in Fig. 14, soft tubing of type-K thickness is recommended. Compression-type fittings are better suited mechanically to resist the settling movement of earth. The fittings should be tack-soldered for added security. The tubing should not be laid directly on stones or rock, and when filling the trench, a 12-in. layer of soft dirt is thrown over the tubing before adding stones for fill. Where copper tubing is embedded in cinders, it should be protected from the acid that is formed, This is accomplished by means of a layer of sand mixed with lime that extends well above and below the pipe.

Compression fittings: Fig. 16 shows three kinds of compression fittings for connecting copper tubing. The kind in detail A requires flaring the tube ends. The kind shown in detail B is assembled by merely pushing the tube into the fitting and then tightening the nut. This shears the sleeve from the nut and also compresses it tightly on the tube to which it then becomes permanently attached. Detail C shows a somewhat similar compression fitting in which a ferrule is also compressed on the tube. The ferrule has two tapers, one seating in the nut and the other in the body of the fitting. Fig. 17 shows a number of generally used fittings of the flared-tube type. The process of connecting tubes to them consists of cutting a tube off squarely, Fig. 18, and reaming off the burr inside and out, with a reamer or round file, Fig. 19. You then flare the end of the tubing after a sleeve nut has been slipped on, Fig. 20. The final assembly is

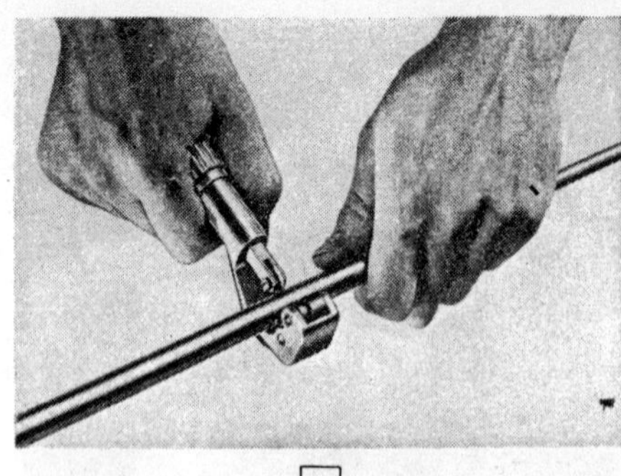
18

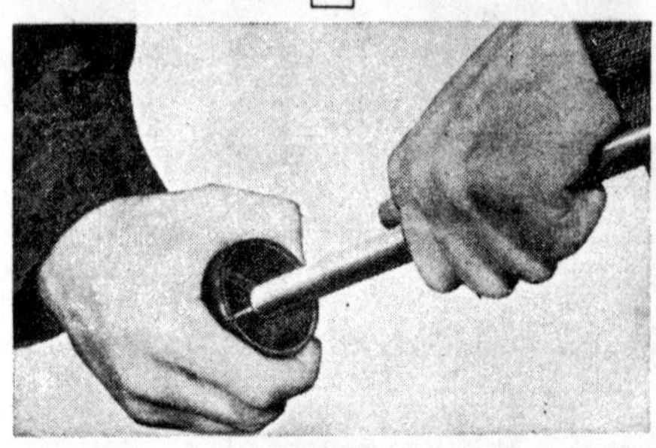
19

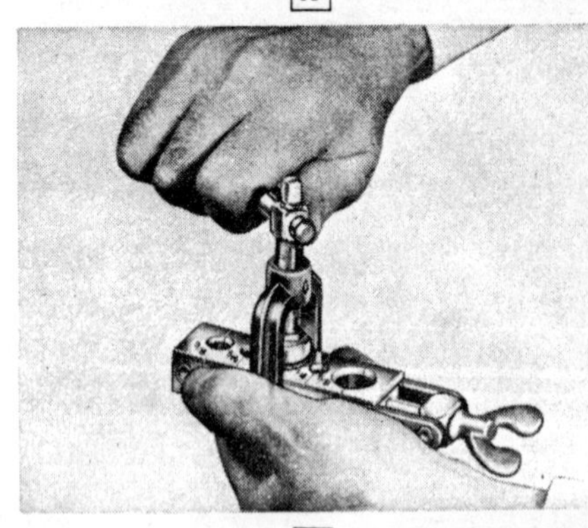
20

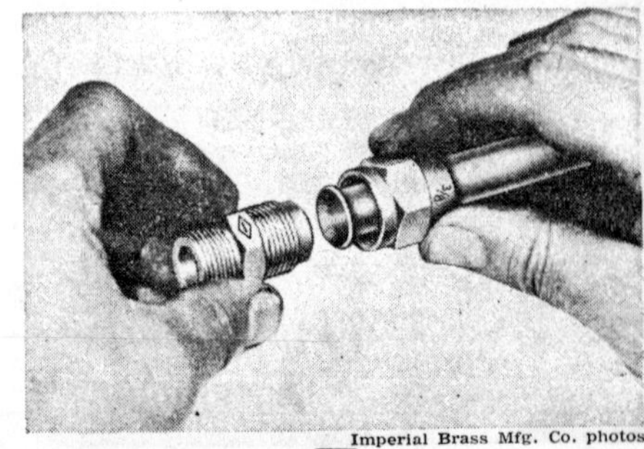
Imperial Brass Mfg. Co. photos

21

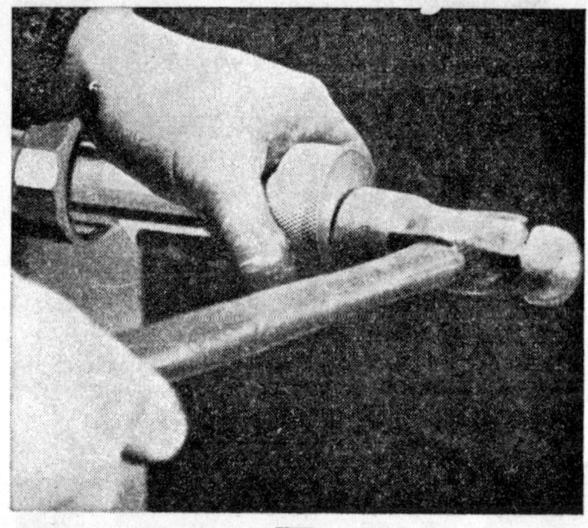

22

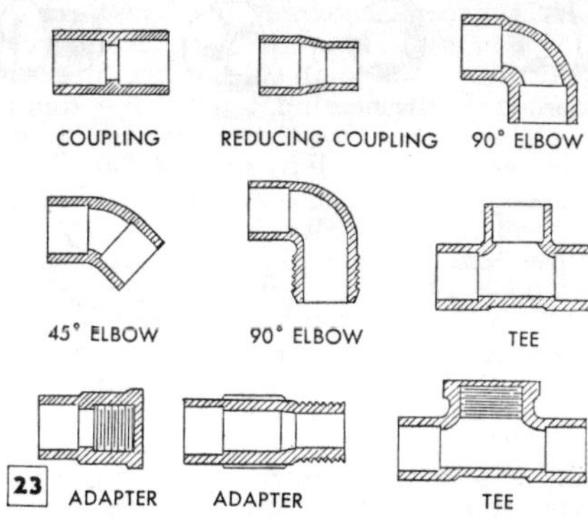

23

shown in Fig. 21. The tool section contains data on using these tools. Flaring can also be done with a punch and hammer as in Fig. 22, particularly on tubing of larger sizes.

Solder-type fittings: Fig. 23 shows some solder-type fittings; a large variety of others are furnished also. To install them, the ends of the tubing are first cut off squarely, either with a tube cutter or with a hacksaw as in Fig. 24. Then the cut ends are reamed to remove the burr. Often a sizing tool also is used to correct any possible distortion of the tube caused by handling—see section on "Plumbing Tools and Their Use." Next, the surfaces to be soldered together must be thoroughly cleaned, using emery cloth or steel wool, as demonstrated in Fig. 25, until the metal is bright. All traces of discoloration must be removed to assure uniform adhesion of solder. Wipe off all particles of dust and steel wool with a clean rag or brush, after which you apply a thin film of soldering flux completely covering both surfaces, Fig. 26. Paste flux is usually easier to handle for this purpose than liquid flux. Push the fitting over the tube as far as it will go and turn it back and forth a few times to assure getting the flux over the surfaces evenly.

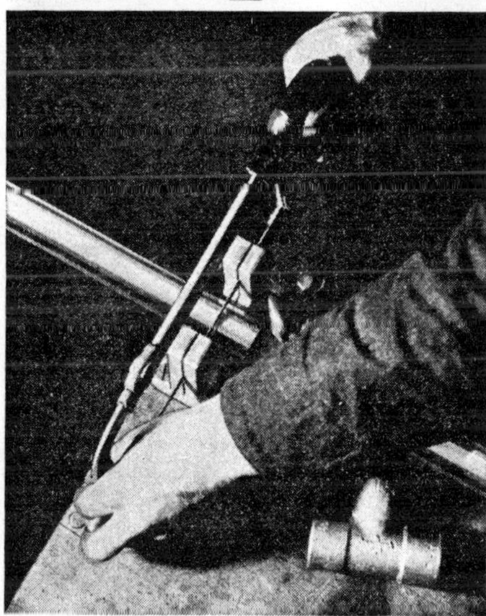

24

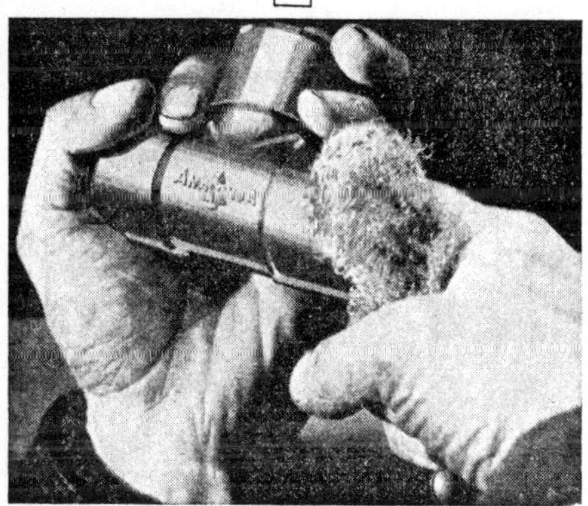

25

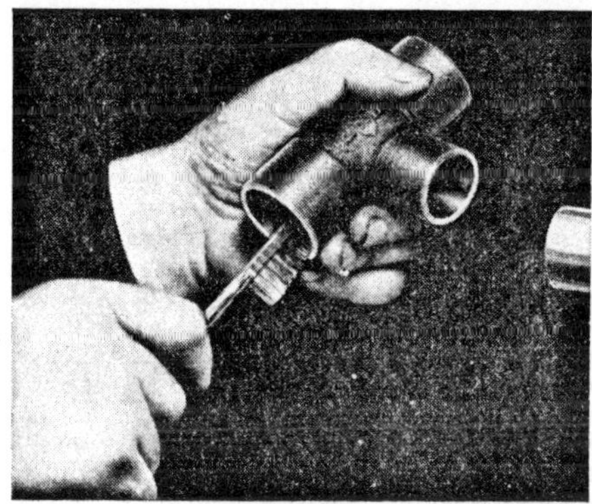

Anaconda photos

26

Heating comes next, using a blowtorch as shown in Fig. 27, or other type of torch. Direct the flame to all sides of the fitting if possible. While heating, touch the end of a length of wire solder to the edge of the fitting occasionally (outside the flame) to check for temperature. As soon as the solder liquefies instantly when touched to the fitting, the correct soldering temperature has been reached. Without waiting, feed solder between the tube and fitting by applying it all around the edge of the fitting, Fig. 28. The torch flame can be held on the fitting while solder is being applied to keep it hot. Generally the right amount of ⅛-in. solid-wire solder required is a length equal to the diameter of the tube. Kink the solder this distance from its end, and feed it up to this point. Solder applied at the edge of a fitting is drawn up between the contacting surfaces by capillary attraction, no matter at which angle the fitting is held. Solder even creeps up vertically this way for a greater distance than is required for making a good joint.

When applying solder, take care not to get it all over the tube or fitting. While solder is still liquid, you can use a rag or brush to wipe off any surplus, but leave it in the chamfer at the end of the fitting. Avoid movement of tube or fitting while the solder hardens; a disturbance at this time often causes weak joints. If the torch must be held near wood or other combustible material, protect the latter with a sheet of asbestos paper or asbestos board. An air-acetylene or liquefied-petroleum torch often is safer in such cases than a blowtorch as the flame is smaller.

To solder tubing into one or more outlets of a fitting already having a soldered joint, the solder in the existing joint is kept from melting by wrapping a wet rag around that portion of the fitting. Also, to disconnect a tube from a fitting without disturbing other soldered joints, use wet rags in the same way, as shown in Fig. 29. Large fittings require more care than small ones to heat them uniformly all around. This is particularly true with fittings of 2½ in. in diameter and larger, such as copper vent, waste tubes and soil tubes.

Kind of solder to use: A "soft" solder consisting of 95 percent tin and 5 percent antimony makes a considerably stronger joint than a 50-50 lead-and-tin solder. The former flows at temperatures in excess of 465 deg. F., and hardens at 450 deg., giving a plastic range of only 15 deg., which means quick hardening. This is desirable as it minimizes chances of poor adhesion caused by joint disturbance. Ordinary 50-50 lead-tin solder, customarily used by tinsmiths, melts at 250 deg. F., and has a 60-deg. plastic range. The best kind of solder for strong,

27

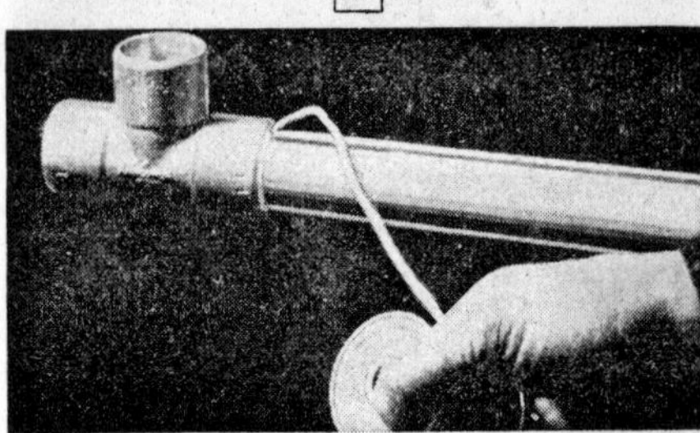

28

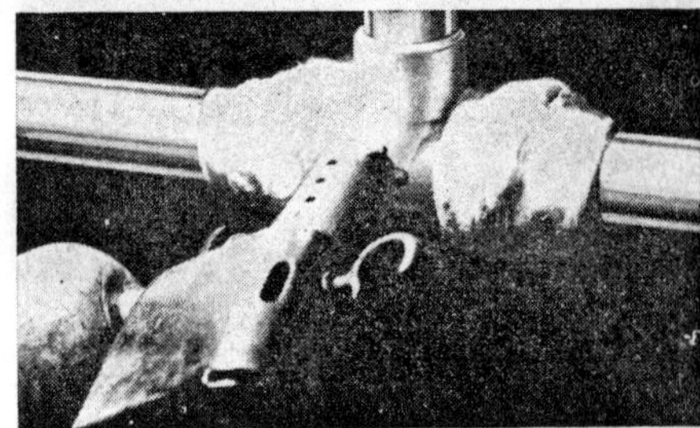

Anaconda photos

29

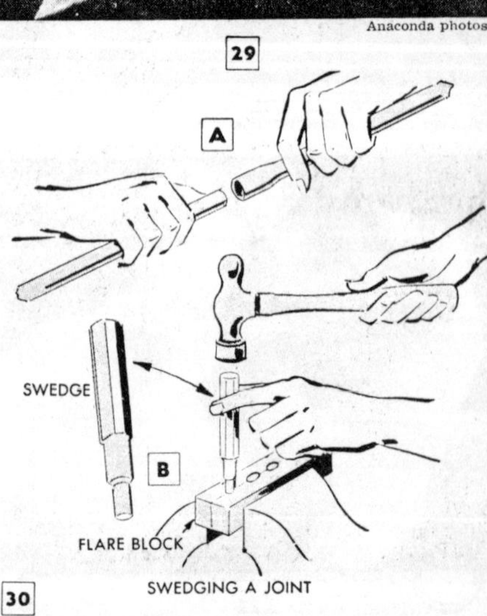

30 SWEDGING A JOINT

Lead Industries Assn. photos

31

32

33 LEAD PIPE FOR VENT AND DRAINAGE LINES

I.D. (In.)	Wall Thickness (In.)		
1¼	118	139	171
1½	.138	165	191
2	.142	177	205
2½, 3, 4, 5, 6	125		250

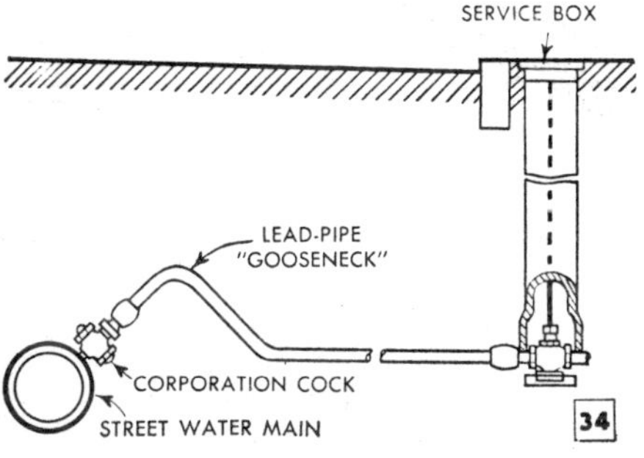

34

durable joints at fittings is "hard" solder consisting of copper and phosphorus, sometimes with silver added, which flows at temperatures from 1300 to 1400 deg. F.

Bending copper tubes: It is often necessary to bend tubing to pass ordinary obstructions in building construction. Soft tubing is generally used for this. Use a bending spring to prevent kinks. Hard tubing requires annealing (softening) the portions to be bent. This can be done by heating the portion of tubing to a dull red with a blowtorch. Applying cold, soaked rags to the heated portion helps annealing and cools the metal quickly.

Swedged copper-tube joints: Two lengths of soft copper tubing (or hard tubing annealed at the ends) of equal diameter can be joined by swedging instead of using a coupling. The end of one length is expanded to fit over the end of the other as in Fig. 30A. Then they are sweat-soldered together. To make such a joint the ends are first cut off squarely and reamed to remove burr. Then a swedging tool of proper size is driven into the end of one length while held in a flare block which is clamped in a vise, as in detail B. The tool is driven in up to its shoulder. After cleaning the surfaces to be soldered to a bright finish, using emery cloth or steel wool, flux is applied and sweat-soldering is done as previously described under "Solder-type fittings." A swedged joint should not be made where a bend is to be located, as the double wall thickness will make bending difficult. Also, a swedged joint should not be made within 4 in. from an end which is to be flared, as the joint will interfere with clamping the tube in the flare block.

Lead pipe: Lead is subject to less corrosion than other metals commonly used for drainage lines. The original lead plumbing of many early American homes is still in use today. Being flexible, lead pipe is particularly suited where building settlement, vibration, or expansion and contraction impose a strain on plumbing fixtures and rigid pipe connections: for example, bathtubs and water closets. Lead waste, vent and drum-trap connections remain watertight under normal conditions. Fig. 32 shows a lead bend installed between a water closet and rigid soil pipe. As lead pipe is easily bent for changes of direction, and can be installed without bulky joint connections and intricate pipe fitting, its use is especially desirable in restricted spaces.

Lead pipe that runs horizontally should be supported, its entire length if possible, by using wooden strips or metal troughs fastened to joists or hung from ceilings with hangers. Vertical runs should be supported at intervals of about 4 ft., using tabs sol-

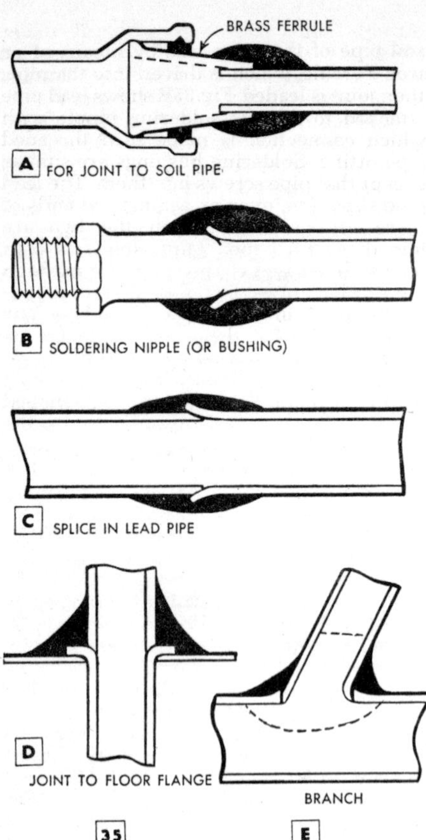

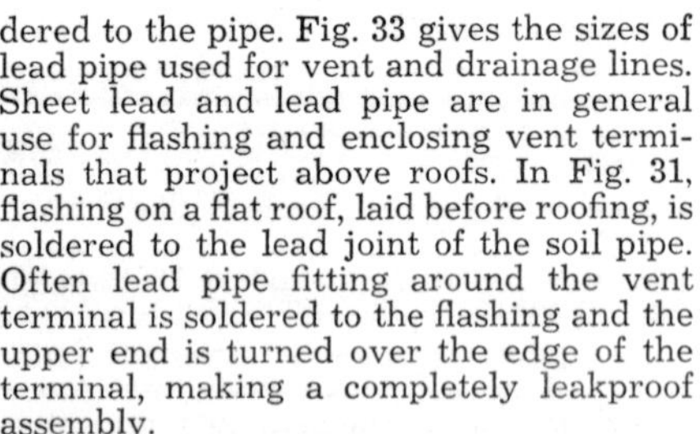

35

36

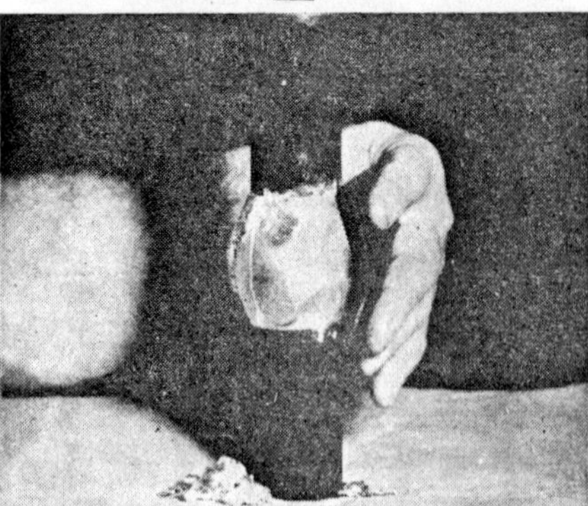

37

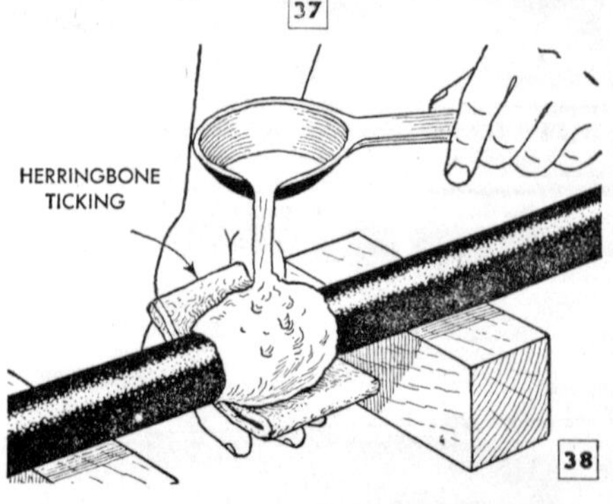

38

dered to the pipe. Fig. 33 gives the sizes of lead pipe used for vent and drainage lines. Sheet lead and lead pipe are in general use for flashing and enclosing vent terminals that project above roofs. In Fig. 31, flashing on a flat roof, laid before roofing, is soldered to the lead joint of the soil pipe. Often lead pipe fitting around the vent terminal is soldered to the flashing and the upper end is turned over the edge of the terminal, making a completely leakproof assembly.

Another common application of lead pipe in heavier wall thicknesses is for "gooseneck" connections between city water mains and house-service pipes as in Fig. 34. These connections are commonly used in many cities. Alkaline water in contact with lead produces a coating of insoluble lead carbonate, which prevents this water from dissolving lead and becoming toxic. The opposite is the case when lead pipe is used for soft water containing dissolved oxygen, carbon dioxide and organic acids. Therefore lead pipe is not recommended for use as water supply and distribution lines where the water is to be used for drinking and cooking purposes.

Connecting lead pipes to iron pipes: Fig. 35 shows a number of lead-pipe joints, all of which are made by wiping molten lead around the connection. Detail A shows how a lead pipe is attached to soil pipe by means of a brass calking ferrule. A lead closet sleeve or bend is connected to the hub of

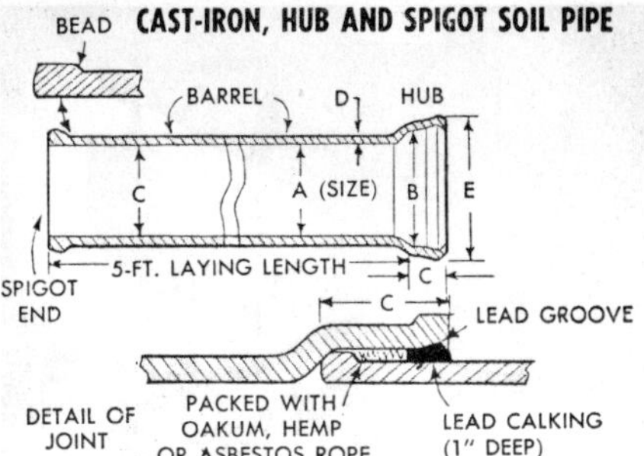

39

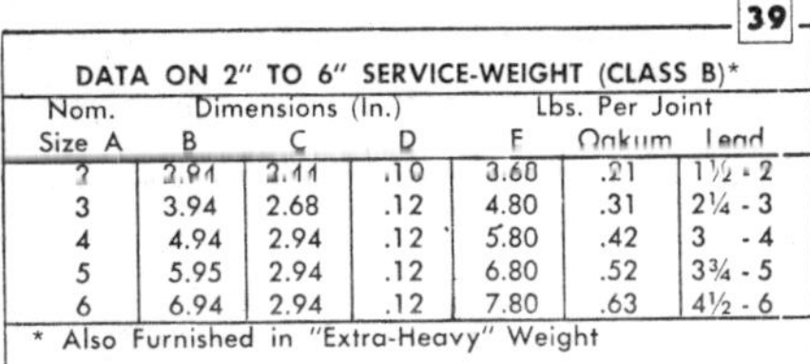

DATA ON 2" TO 6" SERVICE-WEIGHT (CLASS B)*						
Nom.	Dimensions (In.)			Lbs. Per Joint		
Size A	B	C	D	F	Oakum	Lead
2	2.94	2.44	.10	3.60	.21	1½ - 2
3	3.94	2.68	.12	4.80	.31	2¼ - 3
4	4.94	2.94	.12	5.80	.42	3 - 4
5	5.95	2.94	.12	6.80	.52	3¾ - 5
6	6.94	2.94	.12	7.80	.63	4½ - 6

* Also Furnished in "Extra-Heavy" Weight

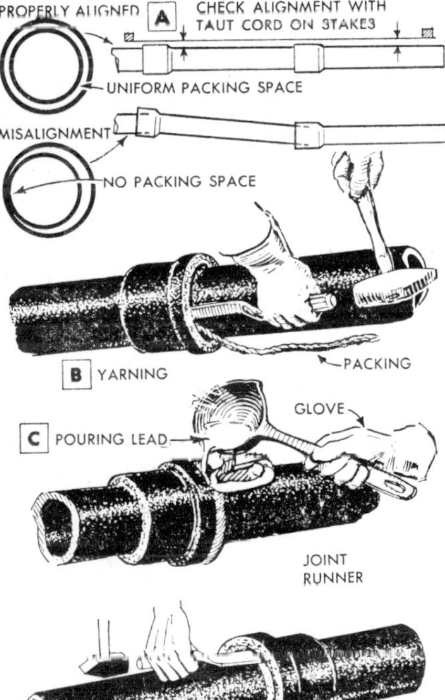

40

soil pipe of the same size by means of an iron Ferrule, which is driven into the pipe, then joint is leaded. Fig. 35B shows lead pipe attached to a brass soldering nipple with which connection is made to a threaded pipe fitting. Soldering bushings are similar except that pipe screws into them. The lead pipe slips into, over or against the ends of these fittings, after which the two are joined with a wiped joint. Joints of lead pipe to brass and copper pipe are made in the same manner. Detail C shows an end-to-end joint in lead pipe. Note how one edge is tapered on the outside so that it fits snugly into a flared and chamfered inside end of the joining length. Tapering is done with a rasp and flaring with a bell-shaped wooden plug of proper size driven into the end of the pipe with a hammer. Detail D shows a joint to a floor flange, and detail E shows a branch connection joined at an angle.

Wiped joints: A wiped joint must have an exposed surface extending not less than ¾ in. on either side of a joint, and the thickest portion should not be less than the thickness of the materials being joined. To make a good wiped joint requires skill and practice. It is done by thoroughly scraping the surfaces to be covered so that they are bright after a coating of plumber's soil (mixture of lampblack and glue) has been applied and allowed to dry. Then saltless mutton tallow is rubbed on the lead surface, and soldering flux on the brass or copper surface, these having been previously cleaned with emery cloth or steel wool. The tallow keeps the lead from oxidizing and also acts as a flux for molten solder, which is poured on slowly from a ladle as in Fig. 36. Although not shown, gloves should be worn. A wiping pad (herringbone ticking folded to several thicknesses) is held under the joint to catch the solder running down and at the same time to shape the joint. Grease on the wiping pad will prevent solder from adhering to it. After the solder joint has been built up, the surface is wiped smooth as in Fig. 37. It is easier to make a wiped point when the pipe is horizontal, in which case it can often be laid on blocks as shown in Fig. 38. A good solder for wiped joints consists of 37 percent tin and 63 percent lead. When melted for application, it should be just hot enough to scorch a piece of paper.

Cast-iron hub-and-spigot soil pipe: Coated with coal-tar pitch to make it acid-resisting, cast-iron soil pipe of the hub-and-spigot type, Fig. 39, is most commonly used for underground drainage lines within a building; also this type can be used for the soil stack and the drainage lines from water closets to the stack. Often this pipe is used also for house sewers. It is furnished in 5-ft. lengths (laying lengths), in sizes from 2 to 15 in. nominal inside diameter. The 3 to 6-in. sizes are most common. Lengths having a hub at each end are furnished also. These are convenient and economical since two short lengths of pipe can often be cut from one double-hub length instead of cutting these from two regular lengths.

Assembling soil pipe: When assembled, the spigot end of the soil pipe faces the direction of flow and fits into the hub end (also called "bell" end) of the next length. Before joining pipes, each length should be tested by striking it lightly with a hammer at the ends. A clear bell-like ring indicates that the pipe is not cracked. The spigot end has a bead which fits snugly into a hub so that packing material will not be forced inside the pipe. Joining ends should be thoroughly clean and dry, and the two joining lengths should be in perfect alignment, which can be checked with a taut cord tied to two stakes as in Fig. 40A. Misalignment in length causes misalignment at joints so that the space between pipe and hub (annular space) is not uniform in width.

The proper method of making a good joint starts with a packing of oakum, hemp or asbestos rope, which is wrapped around the pipe and is driven down with a yarning iron and hammer as in detail B. Work around the pipe evenly so that the packing is not forced tightly on one side while it is still loose on the other. This causes the pipe to shift off center. The packing should come to an inch from the rim of the hub to leave enough space for leading, which anchors in the hub groove. Strands of the packing should not project out of the hub as this may cause leakage. For pipe laid horizontally you need an asbestos joint runner to hold molten lead in the joint, detail C. Its use is explained in the tool section. A joint runner is not needed when pouring lead into a joint on vertical pipe.

Calking lead is used for this purpose, obtainable in 3 to 5-lb. cakes and in 90 to 100-lb. pigs. Amounts of lead and oakum required for filling soil-pipe joints are given in Fig. 39. The lead is melted in a fire pot. Correct temperature for pouring is indicated when the molt becomes cherry red. Then a ladle is used to pour the joint as in Fig. 40C. Before melting lead and using a ladle read instructions and precautions contained in the tool section. The entire joint should be filled at one pouring. When the lead hardens, the joint runner is removed. As lead shrinks slightly upon cooling, it must be tamped into firm contact with the pipe and hub, detail D. For this you use a light hammer and calking irons as shown in detail E. Avoid heavy blows which may

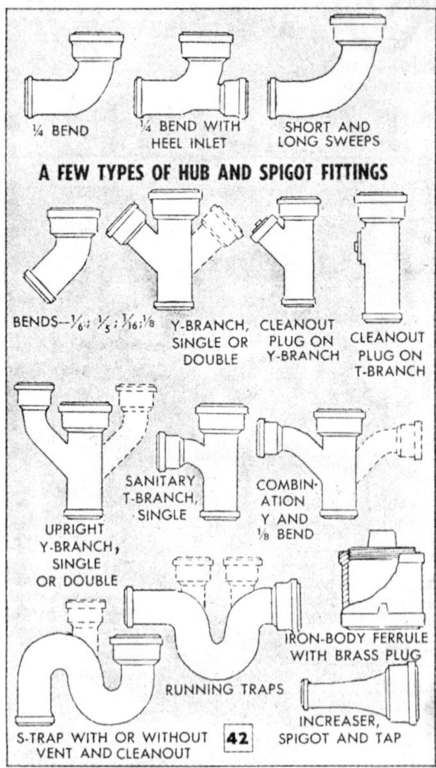

loosen rather than tighten the lead ring. Go around the joint with an "inside" calking iron to pack the lead against the pipe and an "outside" iron to pack it against the hub. When molten lead cannot be used, as for example under water or where the use of an open flame is dangerous, lead wool, which comes in ropelike form, is used. This is simply packed into a homogeneous ring, without the need of heat. Some codes, however, do not permit its use as a substitute for melted-lead joints in ordinary soil-pipe installations.

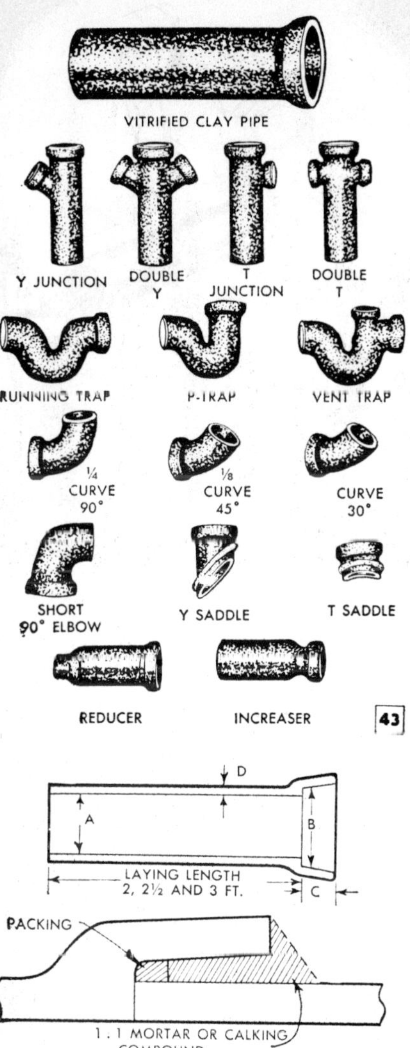

43

DATA ON STANDARD-STRENGTH VITRIFIED CLAY PIPE							
Size							
A	B	C	D	E	F	G	H
4	5¾	1¾	½	9	1430	.074	.44
6	8	2¼	⅝	15	1430	.234	.86
8	10½	2½	¾	24	1430	.365	1.13

E AVERAGE WEIGHT PER FT. OF LENGTH.
F CRUSHING STRENGTH PER LINEAL FT. ON SAND-BEARING PIPE.
G POUNDS OF JUTE (AT 25 LBS. PER CU. FT.) REQUIRED PER JOINT.
H POUNDS OF ASPHALT JOINT COMPOUND (AT 90 LBS. PER CU. FT.) REQUIRED PER JOINT.

44

Cutting soil pipe: A cold chisel and a hammer are used to cut soil pipe as shown in Fig. 41. First the pipe is marked with chalk so that the cut end will be square. Then the pipe is scored all around by tapping the chisel lightly. In doing so the chisel should be pointed toward the center of the pipe and moved forward in overlapping steps for successive blows. After scoring the pipe, it is placed on a support such as a wooden block or sandbag set directly under the point of cutting, and it is struck with increasingly heavier blows along the score. An even break usually occurs after circling the pipe a few times. Actually the pipe is not cut through but the narrow strip of metal along the score is weakened until it breaks. The same method is used also for vitrified-clay pipe.

Cast-iron soil-pipe fittings: Fig. 42 shows a variety of fittings for cast-iron soil pipe. These have ends to match the pipe and are joined in similar manner. For changes of direction, bends and sweeps are used. Their angle is not designated in degrees but by fractions of 360 deg. Thus a 90 deg. turn is called a ¼ bend; a 60 deg. turn a ⅙ bend; a 45 deg. turn is a ⅛ bend. Long-sweep turns offer least resistance to the drainage flow.

Vitrified-clay pipe: The smooth surface of vitrified-clay pipe does not wear or corrode, being inert to acids, alkalies and solvents. Other advantages of this pipe are its low cost, simplicity of installation, and its permanence when not subjected to abnormal strains that may crack or break it. It is furnished in 2, 2½ and 3-ft. laying lengths; in 4 to 36-in. nominal inside diameters; in two grades (standard and extra-strength); and in straight and curved lengths of various shapes, some of which are shown in Fig. 43. One end of each length is a hub or socket and fits over the spigot or plain end of an adjacent length as in Fig. 44, which also gives data on this kind of pipe as well as the amount of jute and calking compound required per joint.

Vitrified-clay pipe can be cut in the same way as cast-iron soil pipe. It can be connected to the latter of same size by using an increaser. Joints can be sealed with portland-cement mortar, or with asphalt-base jointing compounds. The ends should be thoroughly cleaned and free from grease or oil. After carefully aligning two adjoining lengths, the spigot end being inserted as far as possible in the hub, you lightly tamp in enough oakum or jute, about ½ in. thick, to seal the joint so that cement or melted compound will not seep through to the inside. The packing is done evenly from all sides to keep the joining sections in concentric alignment. Often packing is omitted, and only a rather stiff mortar is used, in which case the pipe is swabbed out.

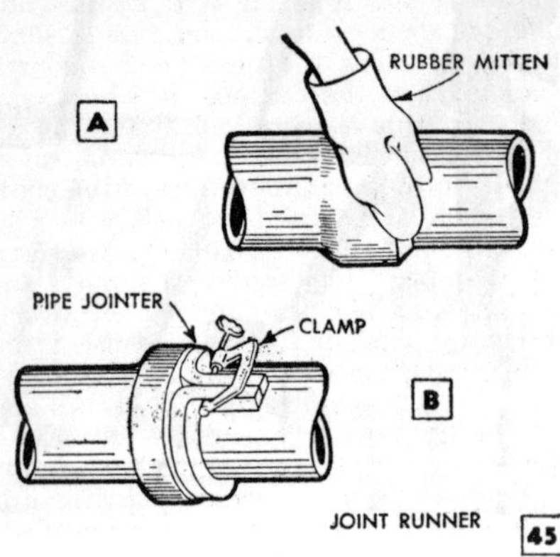

Mortar joints: After packing a joint with oakum, force into the joint a 1:1 mix of clean, sharp sand and portland cement, with just enough water added to make a rather stiff paste that will not run. A wooden calking tool will help to push the cement down solidly into the joint. The surplus is rounded off neatly with a trowel or a rubber mitten as in detail A of Fig. 45. Often two or three lengths of pipe are set up vertically, Fig. 46, for making joints with mortar that is plastic enough to be poured. This leaves fewer joints to be made in the trench. After letting the cement harden overnight, the pipe is carried by a stout pole slipped through it, after which it is lowered into the trench and joined to other similar lengths.

Other jointing compounds: A number of asphalt-base and other compounds are available for making good joints that remain slightly flexible and resist root penetration. Most of these compounds are poured while hot into thoroughly clean and dry joints after tamping in a seal of jute, oakum or asbestos rope. The melted compound can be poured into joints when several lengths are stacked vertically as in Fig. 46, but when joints on horizontal lengths are poured, a "joint runner," detail B, Fig. 45, or a clay dam is used. Compounds should be used in accordance with manufacturer's instructions. If they are overheated or kept hot too long they may become brittle. If not sufficiently heated, they may harden before the joint is completed. During cold weather they may not adhere effectively unless the pipe jointing is preheated.

Concrete pipe: Also shaped with hub and spigot ends, concrete pipe that is used for drainage purposes comes in 2, 2½, 3 and 4-ft. lengths, and in 4 to 24-in. nominal inside diameters. It is assembled in the same way as vitrified-clay pipe. Concrete pipe is subject to attack by acids and is

Clay Products Assn. photo

46

not as durable as vitrified-clay pipe for use as sewers, although its cost is approximately the same.

Asbestos-cement pipe: This pipe is hard, dense and strong, as the mixture from which it is made—asbestos fiber, portland cement and silica—is subjected to heavy pressure during manufacture. Being durable and highly resistant to corrosion, this pipe has been found successful as vent and sewer pipe. It is furnished in 5 and 10-ft. lengths, the advantage of the latter being that fewer joints are required. Although sizes range from 6 to 36 in. in diameter, the smaller sizes, from 2 to 6 in., are used for house sewers, Fig. 47, and vent pipes, Fig. 48.

Ends of the pipe are machined to take couplings of the same material. The use of special rubber rings between couplings and pipes, as shown in Figs. 49 and 50, gives a tight, flexible joint especially designed to overcome leakage and root penetration. Pipe and couplings are easily assembled by pressing them together as shown in Fig. 51, using the simple arrangement shown in Fig. 52.

A number of T and Y branches are furnished, as well as elbows, bends and special adapters to make connections to other pipes such as soil pipe. Where short lengths are required to make closures, the pipe can be sawed off with a carpenter's saw. Adapters are also furnished to join such a cut end to a machined end, or to join two cut ends together. In this case a seal is

47

Johns-Manville photos

48

49

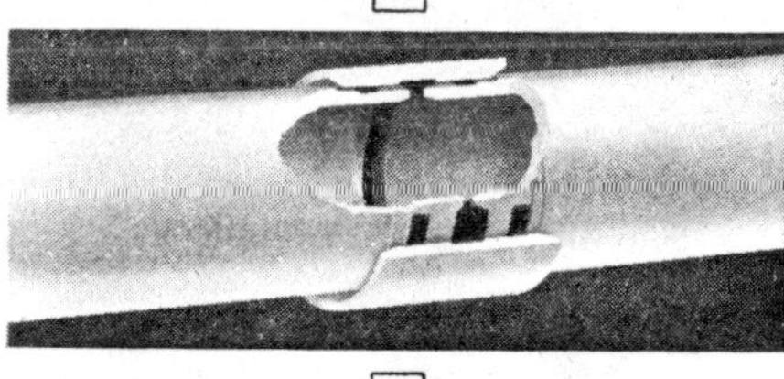

50

51

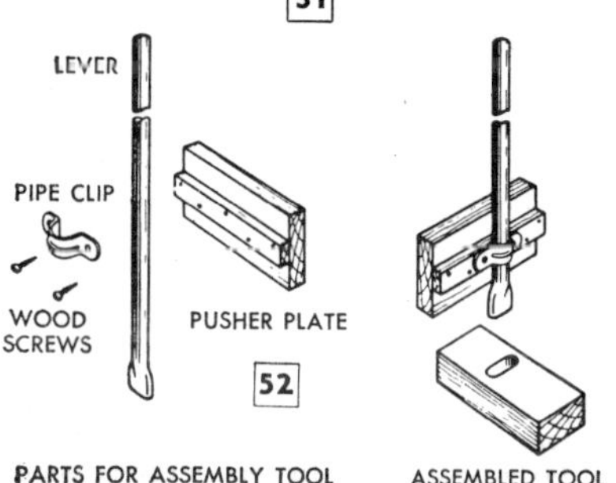

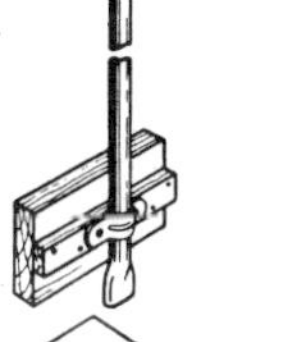

52

PARTS FOR ASSEMBLY TOOL

ASSEMBLED TOOL

made with cement, lead or other commercial jointing compound. Fig. 53 gives some data on dimensions and weight of house sewer and vent pipes made of asbestos cement.

Porous and perforated pipe: For disposal lines of septic tanks and for rapid drainage of ground water, porous drain tile is most extensively used. It comes in 1-ft. lengths and the 4 to 6-in. sizes are most common. The pipe is of uniform diameter and has no hub. The lengths are laid end-to-end, with tar-paper squares over the joints to prevent entrance of soil. Perforated pipe of vitrified clay and bituminized fiber is also made for this purpose.

53 ASBESTOS-CEMENT PIPE

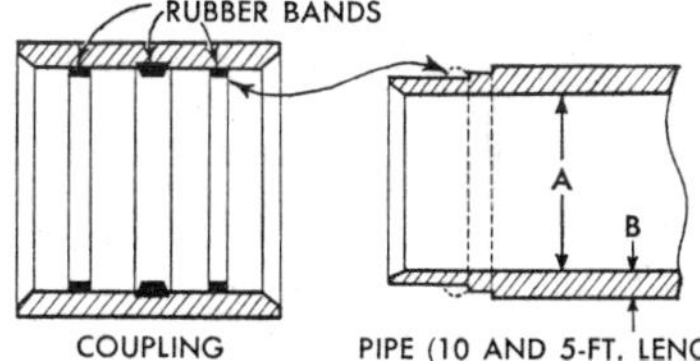

Nom. Size A		Thickness B	Weight C	Strength D
Sewer Pipe 1	Vent Pipe 2			
4		.27	4.7	1740
5		.30	6.3	1680
6		.30	7.5	1420
	2	.30	2.2	
	3	.32	3.2	
	4	.32	4.2	

1—PIPE FOR HOUSE-TO-SEWER CONNECTIONS; SIMILAR PIPE ALSO FURNISHED UP TO 36" DIA., IN TWO CLASSES AND IN 13-FT. LENGTHS
2—PIPE FOR VENTS IN HOUSE PLUMBING; HAS DIFFERENT STYLE JOINT THAN ONE ILLUSTRATED. OTHER PIPE FURNISHED FOR FLUES
C—WEIGHT IN LBS. PER FT. PER 10-FT. LENGTH WITH COUPLINGS
D—MINIMUM APPLIED LOADS (LBS. PER FT.) FOR CRUSHING TESTS

Orangeburg Mfg. Co. photos

54

55

56

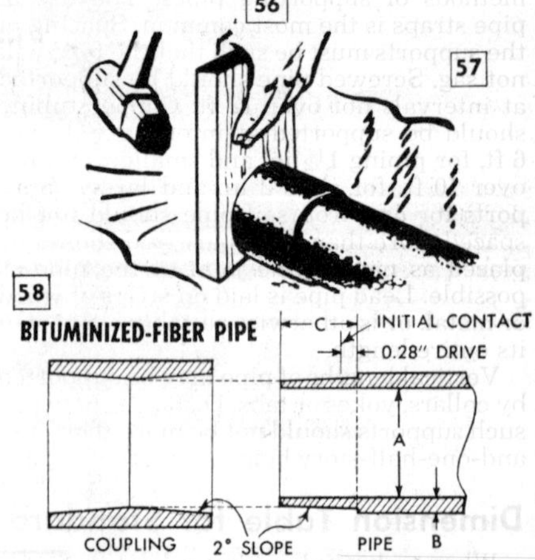

57

58

Bituminized-fiber pipe: Fiber pipe has been successfully used for many years for numerous purposes such as house sewers, outside downspouts, conductor pipe for irrigation and for farm and ranch gravity-type water supply and distribution lines. It is impregnated throughout with coal-tar pitch, is lightweight, non-corrosive and slightly flexible, which allows it to absorb shocks, earth tremors and normal soil movement without cracking, shearing off or pulling out at the joints. Sweeps of 45 and 90 deg., as well as numerous other fittings are furnished. Fig. 54 shows this pipe used in a house-sewer installation.

The pipes have tapered ends which are joined to couplings having slight inside tapers to match, Fig. 56. Driven together simply by using a block and hammer as in Fig. 57, the joints are so tight that tree roots cannot enter. Connections can be made to other pipes, either the threaded or the hub-and-spigot type, by means of special adapters. Joints to cast-iron soil pipe are sealed with flexible jointing compounds, molten lead or lead wool, as previously described under cast-iron and vitrified-clay pipe. Fig. 55 shows how an ordinary handsaw is used to cut fiber pipe to any length. A special cutter is required to taper ends cut in this manner, but where such a cutter is not available, these ends can be tightly sealed in a special coupling with the aid of jointing compound. Fig. 58 gives dimensional data on the smaller sizes of bituminized-fiber pipe.

Methods of supporting pipe: Pipes and tubing used in a plumbing system must be installed with adequate support to prevent undue strains and stresses on it. In a building, pipe is "hung" in pipe supports so that contraction, expansion and settling of the building will not break the pipe or place a strain on it. Pipe should not be attached rigidly to a building. Fig. 59 shows several

SIZE A (In.)	THICKN. B (Min.) (In.)	C (In.)	Length (Feet)	Weight D	Strength E
2	.23	1.43	5	1.24	1100
3	.28	1.69	8	1.71	1100
4	.32	1.94	8	2.66	1100
5	.41	1.94	5	4.44	1300
6	.46	1.94	5	5.78	1300
8	.57	2.48	5	9.81	1600

D—Weight Per Ft. Including Couplings
E—Crushing Strength Between Two Flat Plates

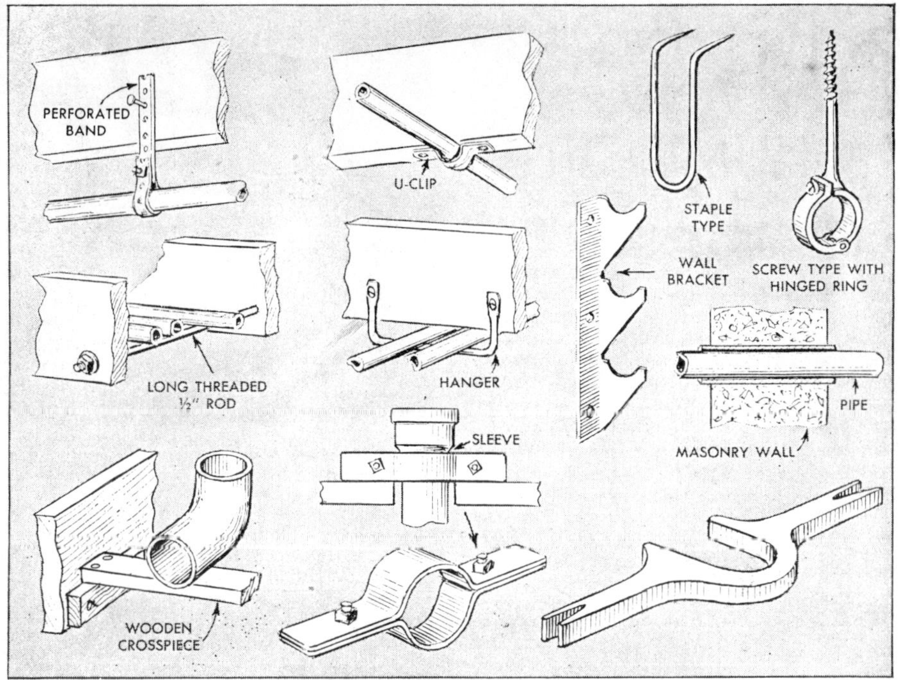

methods of supporting pipes. The use of pipe straps is the most common. Spacing of the supports must be such that the pipe will not sag. Screwed pipe should be supported at intervals not over 12 ft. Copper tubing should be supported at intervals not over 6 ft. for piping 1½ in. and smaller, and not over 10 ft. for sizes 2 in. and larger. Supports for cast-iron soil pipe should not be spaced more than 5 ft. apart, and should be placed as near to the joint of the pipe as possible. Lead pipe is laid on strips of wood or metal, or is otherwise suitably supported its entire length.

Vertical lengths of pipe may be supported by collars, yokes or tabs. Distances between such supports should not be more than one-and-one-half-story height for screwed pipe, one-story height for cast-iron soil pipe, one-story height for copper tubing 1½ in. and over in size. For copper tubing smaller than 1¼ in., and also for lead pipe, the spacing between supports should not exceed 4 ft.

Pipe hangers should be attached securely to the building construction, using nails, screws or bolts in wood, and screws or bolts driven into metal expansion sleeves for proper anchorage in masonry. Attachment of hangers to wooden plugs driven into holes drilled in masonry is not dependable as the plugs may shrink and loosen. Buried pipe should be laid on compact earth. In filled and other unstable earth, pipe other than cast-iron soil pipe should be supported on concrete pads suitably spaced to prevent settling.

Dimension Table for Standard Pipe Minimizes Measuring Errors

When making plumbing or heating repairs in the home, costly waste of pipe is likely to result from inaccurate measurements, such as, forgetting to allow for the threaded ends of the pipe inside the fittings. This table, which gives pipe diameters and thread lengths in fractions of an inch, will help you obtain correct measurements.

PIPE SIZE	⅛″	¼″	⅜″	½″	¾″	1″	1¼″	1½″	2″
INSIDE DIAMETER	9/32″	⅜″	½″	⅝″	13/16″	1 1/32″	1⅜″	1⅝″	2 1/16″
OUTSIDE DIAMETER	13/32″	17/32″	11/16″	27/32″	1 1/16″	1 5/16″	1 21/32″	1 29/32″	2⅜″
APPROXIMATE THREAD LENGTH ONE END	¼″	⅜″	⅜″	½″	9/16″	11/16″	11/16″	11/16″	¾″
APPROXIMATE THREAD LENGTH BOTH ENDS	½″	¾″	¾″	1″	1⅛″	1⅜″	1⅜″	1⅜″	1½″

PIPE RACK AND HUMIDOR

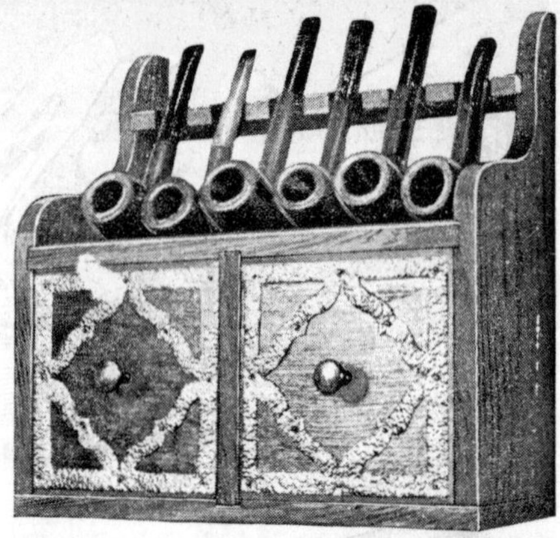

The back of each drawer compartment is drilled to permit attaching the rack to the wall with screws

THIS combination pipe rack and humidor solves the storage problem for pipe smokers. There's a glass humidor behind a false drawer front, a single drawer for accessories and a rack for six pipes combined in a small cabinet. The drawer fronts are ornamented with copper overlays having diamond-shaped cutouts and a hammered finish. The finish is applied with the point of a wood screw held by a twisted wire as in the lower right-hand detail. Either copper-foil stock or colonial (red) brass may be used. Lay out the pattern for each overlay on ¼-in. squares. Use a high-grade cabinet wood such as cherry, birch or mahogany for all wooden parts. The two members which, when assembled, form the pipe rack are notched to suit the individual stems and bowls of the pipes. The notches are cut on a jigsaw after which the side members are scrolled and grooved to take the top of the cabinet. The top is grooved at the center to take the divider between the drawers. Clamp the parts as in the upper right-hand detail until the glue is dry. Attach the lid of a large screw-top jar to the back of the right-hand drawer front.

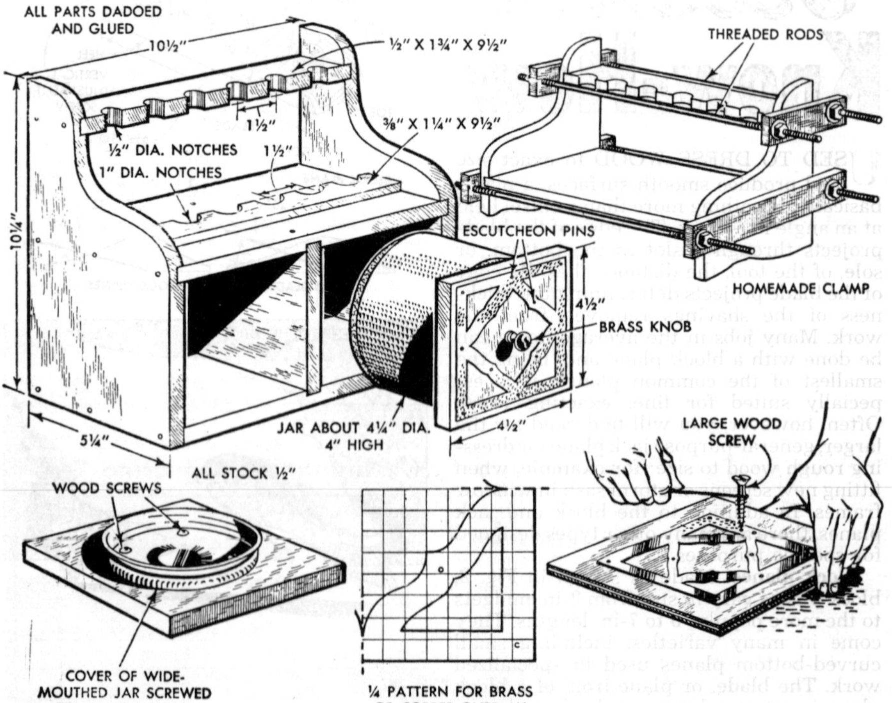

ALL PARTS DADOED AND GLUED
10½"
½" X 1¾" X 9½"
1½"
½" DIA. NOTCHES
1½"
1" DIA. NOTCHES
⅜" X 1¼" X 9½"
10¼"
5¼"
ALL STOCK ½"
JAR ABOUT 4¼" DIA. 4" HIGH
ESCUTCHEON PINS
4½"
BRASS KNOB
4½"
THREADED RODS
HOMEMADE CLAMP
LARGE WOOD SCREW
WOOD SCREWS
COVER OF WIDE-MOUTHED JAR SCREWED TO DRAWER FRONT
¼ PATTERN FOR BRASS OR COPPER OVERLAY

Plane Know-How

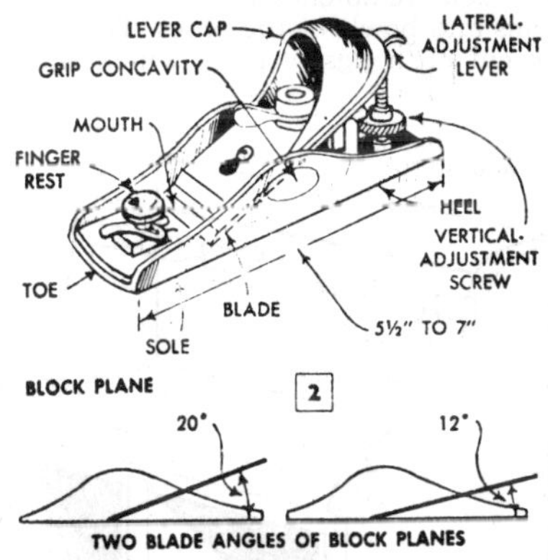

USED TO DRESS WOOD to exact size and produce smooth surfaces, a plane, basically, is nothing more than a chisel held at an angle in a block. The edge of the blade projects through a slot in the bottom, or sole, of the tool, the distance that the edge of the blade projects determining the thickness of the shavings removed from the work. Many jobs in the average home can be done with a block plane and, being the smallest of the common planes, it is especially suited for fine, exacting work. Often, however, you will find need for the larger, general-purpose jack plane for dressing rough wood to size; for example, when fitting new screens or storm sash in window frames. In addition to the block and jack planes, there are many other types designed for specific purposes.

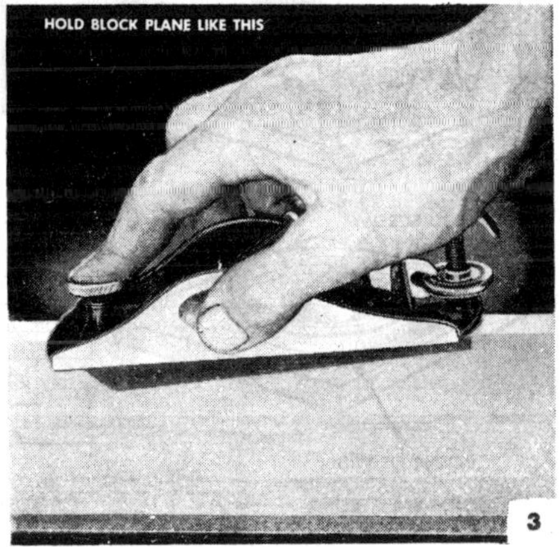

Block planes: Made as shown in Fig. 2, block planes vary in size from 2-in. midgets to the more popular 5 to 7-in. lengths. They come in many varieties, including small curved-bottom planes used in specialized work. The blade, or plane iron, of a block plane is set at a lower angle than that of larger planes. This low angle—usually 20 deg. and sometimes 12 deg.—permits cutting end grain and oblique hardwood grain more readily. The beveled edge of a block-plane blade, or iron, should always face upward instead of downward as on the larger planes. The blade is locked in position by means of a lever cap tightened with a small lever or thumbscrew and the upper end of the cap is usually rounded to fit the palm of the hand comfortably.

Block planes are held in one hand, as pictured in Fig. 3, with the index finger resting on the concave finger rest at the toe and the thumb and other fingers gripping both sides. The slot in the sole through which the blade projects is called the mouth, or throat. In some cases, its width is adjustable for fine or coarse work. A knurled nut at the heel provides for vertical adjustment, the movement that advances or retracts the blade through the mouth. On many block planes, lateral adjustment is obtained by means of a lever located at the heel of the plane. The lever tilts the blade toward either side and permits aligning the cutting edge parallel with the sole, so the shavings will be of equal thickness across the full width of the cut.

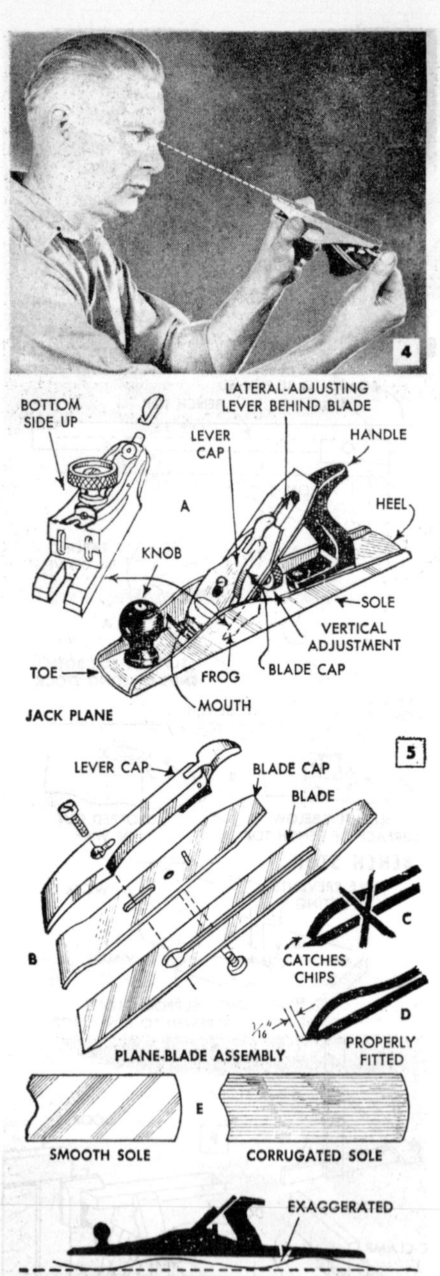

When making blade adjustments, a block plane, like other planes, is held as in Fig. 4. Sight across the sole to see how far the cutting edge projects and whether it is parallel to the sole. The usual error is to have the blade projecting too far. It should project only the thickness of a hair to produce thin shavings. Lateral blade adjustment on planes not equipped with a lever is made by loosening the lever cap and then pushing the blade toward one side or the other.

Jack planes: Made in lengths from 11½ to 15 in., jack planes are used for rough, heavy work in dressing stock to size. The parts and assembly are shown in Fig. 5, detail A. The frog is a steel block at the rear of the mouth to support the blade and, in some cases, it is adjustable to control the width of the mouth in proportion to the thickness of the shavings. The blade is fitted with a blade cap that prevents the blade from chattering and also acts as a chip breaker which diverts shavings so they will not break off ahead of the cutting edge. The blade and blade cap are held against the frog by means of a lever cap. Detail B shows the three parts separated. When the blade cap does not fit properly, as in detail C, wood shavings are likely to wedge under it, piling up and choking the plane. Detail D shows how the blade cap should fit, 1/16 in. behind the edge of the blade.

The thumb nut at the rear of the frog permits vertical adjustment of the blade to control shaving thickness. The lateral-adjustment lever is located between the blade and handle. As in detail E, the sole of the plane may be either smooth or corrugated, many users preferring the latter as there is less surface friction between the plane and the work. In use, a jack plane is held with both hands, as in Fig. 1, which gives control of pressure at both toe and heel.

Fore and jointer planes: Assembled in the same manner as a jack plane, jointer planes differ only in length, ranging from 18 to 24 in. long. A short jointer plane is called a fore plane. The length of a jointer plane allows it to dress the edges of long boards perfectly straight, as the plane bridges the concavities and dresses down the humps, Fig. 6, detail A. Shorter planes follow the surface contours as in detail B.

Smoothing planes: Ranging from 7 to 10 in. long, smoothing planes are used for fine finishing of surfaces that have been dressed down uniformly with a jack plane. The cutting edge of a smoothing plane must be kept razor sharp and the blade adjusted for extremely thin shavings. Equal pressure must be exerted at both ends to prevent forming hollows.

Work support: Work to be planed must be supported rigidly, which usually is done by holding it in a woodworking vise, Fig. 7 and Fig. 8, detail A. Other types of vises generally will mar the surface of the work unless wooden or hardboard pads are inserted between the jaws and the work. The best location for a vise is on the left end of a workbench, allowing plenty of clearance for long stock. To support long boards, two vises may be used or tapered dowels pressed into holes bored in the bench apron as in Fig. 8, A.

A bench stop, detail B, fitted near the left end of a bench also is convenient for holding stock being planed. When not in use, the stop is dropped below the surface of the bench top. Another type of bench stop, detail C, consists of a slotted wooden block which is screwed to the bench top. Short work also can be held by means of a bench hook, Fig. 9, detail J. Wide work, such as doors, screen frames and storm sash, is supported vertically on the floor by an improvised brace clamped to the work, or with an L-vise mounted on a sawhorse, as in detail E. Dressing the top edge of a door can be done without removing it from the hinges simply by inserting a wedge between the door and the floor to hold the door in position.

Consider the wood grain: Always examine stock to see which way the grain runs and then arrange the setup so you can plane with the grain instead of against it, Fig. 9, details A and B. Ordinarily, opposite edges of a board must be planed from opposite directions. When planing against the grain, the wood fibers are broken off, producing a rough surface. When the direction

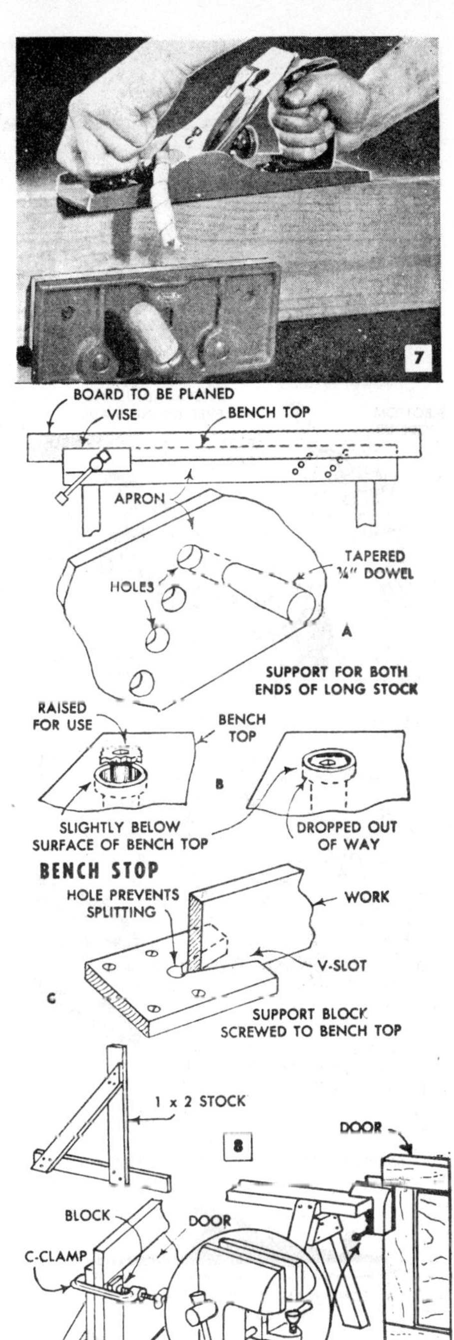

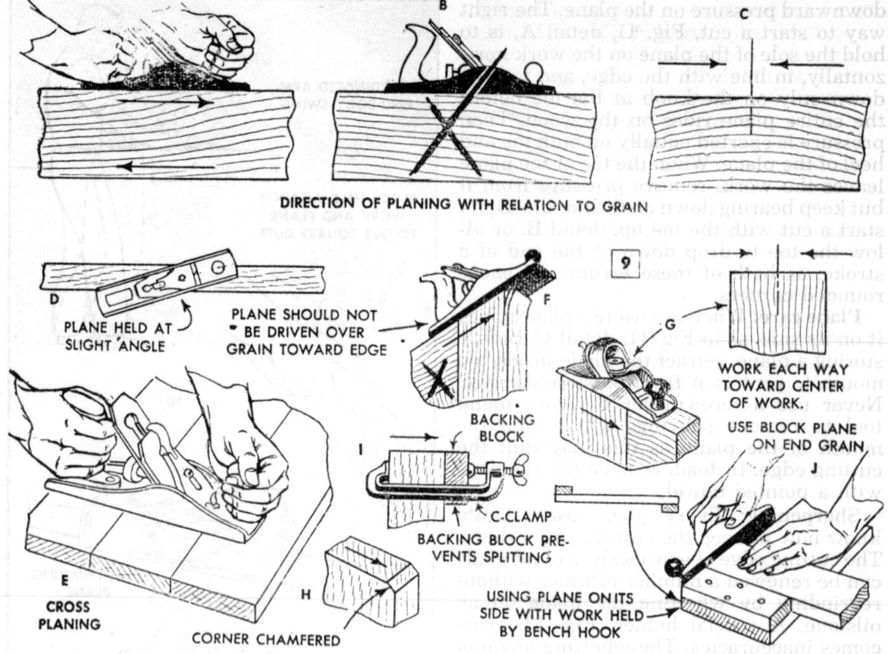

of grain changes somewhat along the edge, as in detail C, plane from both ends to the point where the grain direction changes.

Planing is easier if the plane is held at a slight angle, as in detail D, to produce a shearing action. Used in this way the blade will retain its cutting edge longer. Wide surfaces, consisting of several pieces of stock glued together, often are cross-planed as in detail E. A plane used for this purpose must be razor sharp and set to take a very shallow cut. When planing end grain, which is usually done with a block plane, the wood at the corner of the work is likely to break off, detail F, if the cutting edge of the plane is run off a corner. To prevent this, plane from the corners to the center as in detail G. Another method of avoiding chipping the corners is to chamfer the corner, as in detail H, or support the wood with a backing piece where it is likely to break off, details I and J.

Pointers on handling planes: An easy, coordinated swing of arms and body is used in planing. Plane toward the left, standing at one end of the work, with your left foot forward, as in Fig. 10, detail A. As you move the plane forward, keep your head approximately over the plane handle and rock your body forward, transferring the weight to the left foot toward the end of the stroke. When drawing the plane back on the return stroke, lift the blade above the work surface, as dragging the blade over the work will quickly dull the cutting edge.

Beginners often experience two troubles when planing: the planed edges of a board are not square with the sides, and more stock is removed from one or both ends of the work than at the center. To plane an edge square with the surfaces of a board, hold a wooden guide block under the plane and against the side of the board, as in detail B, hooking the thumb over the knob and grasping the front side of the plane and block at the same time. Still more accuracy in edge planing is assured by using an edge-trimming block plane, detail C, or by using a jointer gauge, D. The latter consists of an adjustable fence which is clamped on a plane and bears against the side of the work. Attached to either side of the plane, the fence can be adjusted for planing bevels and also fitted with a larger auxiliary fence for greater bearing surface. You can improvise a gauge by making interchangeable 45 and 90-deg. guides from hardwood, as in the lower detail. The bearing surfaces of the guides are sanded smooth and waxed to minimize friction and are screwed to tapped holes in the side of the plane.

The common tendency to remove more stock from the ends of a board than at the center results from incorrectly applying downward pressure on the plane. The right way to start a cut, Fig. 11, detail A, is to hold the sole of the plane on the work horizontally, in line with the edge, and to bear down only on the knob at the toe before the entire plane rides on the wood. Then pressure is exerted equally on both toe and heel of the plane. When the toe of the plane leaves the work, remove pressure from it but keep bearing down on the handle. Don't start a cut with the toe up, detail B, or allow the toe to drop down at the end of a stroke, as both of these errors will cause rounded corners.

Plane care: When not using a plane, place it on its side, as in Fig. 11, detail C. Before storing a plane, retract the blade inside the mouth to protect it from possible damage. Never use a screwdriver or other metal tool to remove shavings which clog the mouth of the plane as this may dull the cutting edge. Instead, remove the shavings with a pointed dowel.

Sharpening: Every plane user should know how to keep the cutting edges sharp. The cutting edge of a properly ground blade can be renewed a number of times without regrinding by whetting the blade on an oilstone. A special holder, Fig. 12, overcomes inaccuracies. The whetting angle of 30 to 35 deg., Fig. 13, detail A, is about 5 deg. greater than the grinding angle. After whetting, the fine burr or featheredge is removed by a few very light strokes on the other side of the blade while it is held flat on the stone, detail B. To avoid plane marks on the work, the corners of the blade should be rounded slightly. When reassembling the blade, attach the cap with its edge well away from the cutting edge of the blade, and then advance the cap to 1/16 in. from the edge as in Fig. 5, D.

Grinding is necessary when the cutting edge is nicked or worn by repeated whettings. In grinding, a plane blade must be passed squarely across the face of the grinding wheel, Fig. 13, detail C—not held against the side of the wheel. When grinding, don't

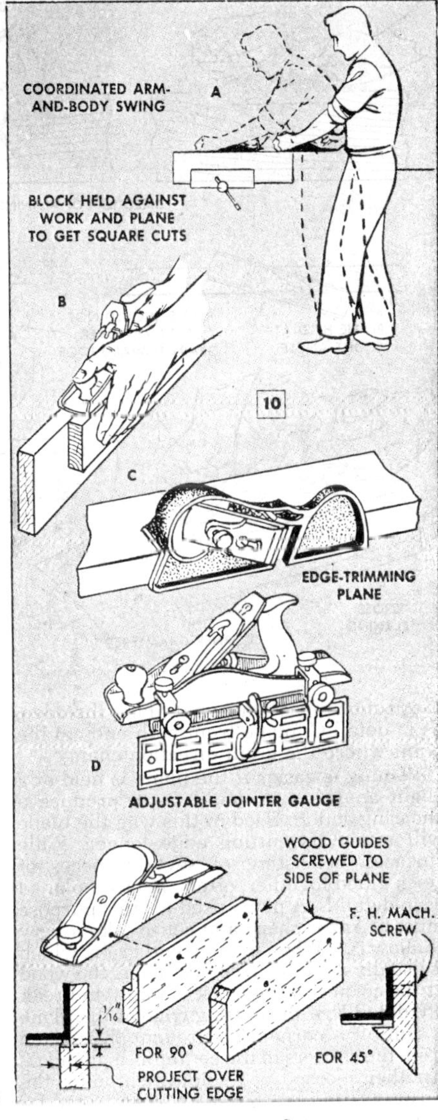

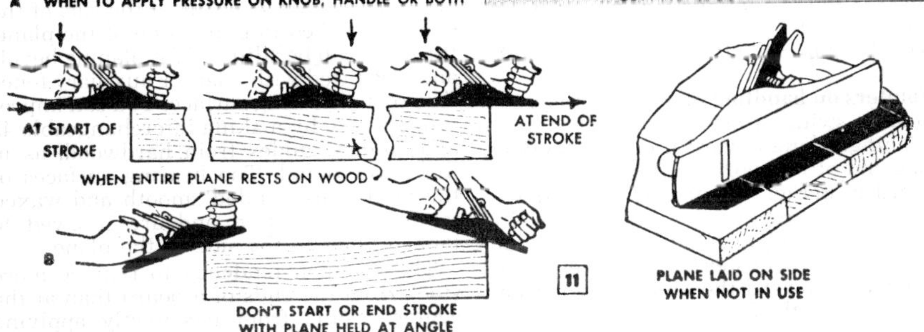

attempt to square the sides of the blade above the cutting edge, as many blades have slight clearance bevels on the sides. For grinding the bevel, hold the blade as in detail D, at a 25 to 30-deg. angle to a line running at right angles to the radial line of the wheel. The tool rest should be set to just clear the wheel in order to provide maximum support for the blade.

When properly aligned, the blade is advanced just far enough to barely touch the edge of the wheel when passed across it. Each advance feed should not be greater than the thickness of a piece of writing paper—sometimes less. The edge of the blade must be kept cool by dipping it in water after each pass, unless a grinding coolant can be used while the grinding proceeds. Overheating the blade to the point of color change removes the temper so that it will no longer hold a cutting edge. The blade is ground down until a fine burr or featheredge is visible. This is then removed on an oilstone.

Grinding plane blades is simplified considerably by using an adjustable tool rest similar to the one shown in Fig. 14. This gives accurate results that are hardly possible by hand grinding, due to the difficulty of grinding an edge straight and at 90 deg. to the blade axis. The features of the grinding fixture are a cross slide that gives straight-line accuracy and a threaded feed control for advancing the blade to the wheel. Although a satisfactory fixture can be made from hardwood, a better and more accurate job, of course, will result from using metal. ★ ★ ★

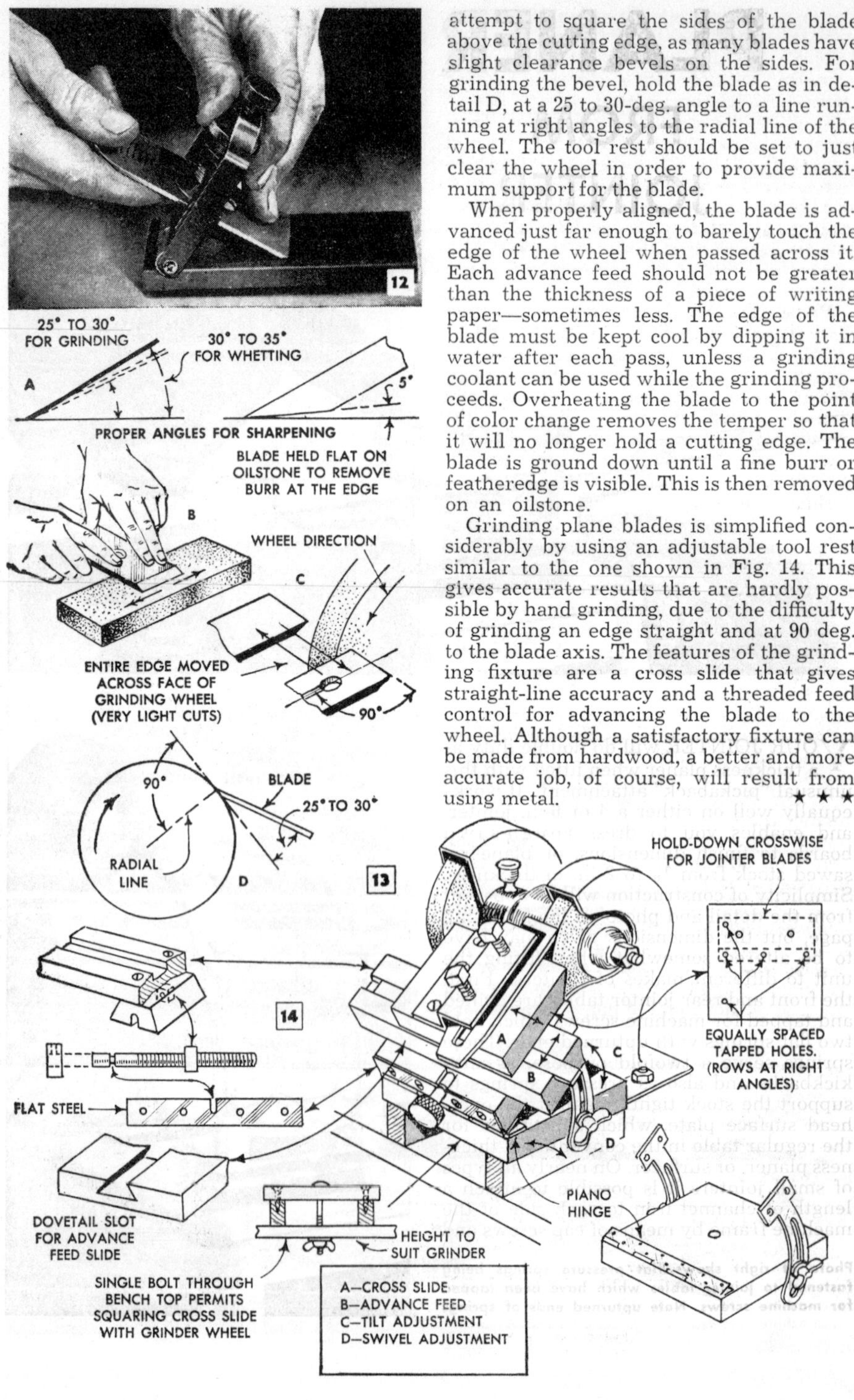

PLANER IMPROVISED FROM JOINTER

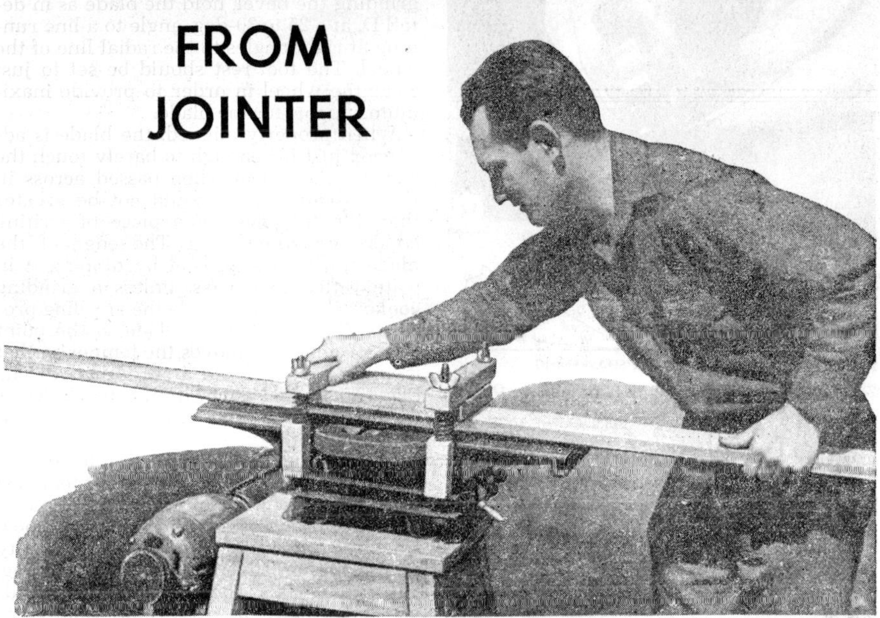

YOUR JOINTER will do double duty as a thickness planer when fitted with this unusual "pickaback" attachment. It works equally well on either a 4 or 6-in. jointer, and enables you to dress rough-sawn boards to finish dimensions, or plane resawed stock from 1/8 to 2 in. in thickness. Simplicity of construction will be apparent from the detail and photo on the following page, but the dimensions given may have to be altered somewhat when fitting the unit to different makes of jointers. First, the front and rear jointer tables are drilled and tapped for machine screws which hold two flat springs with upturned ends. These springs serve a twofold purpose, as antikickbacks and also as pressure springs to support the stock tightly against the overhead surface plate, which substitutes for the regular table in the conventional thickness planer, or surfacer. On nearly all types of small jointers it is possible to attach a length of channel iron to each side of the machine frame by means of cap screws and

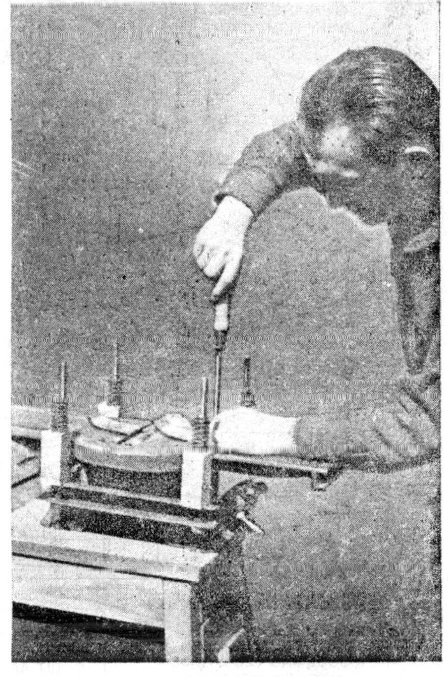

Photo at right shows flat pressure springs being fastened to jointer tables which have been tapped for machine screws. Note upturned ends of springs

Close-up pictures thickness-planer adapter mounted on jointer. Springs force surface plate against wing nuts

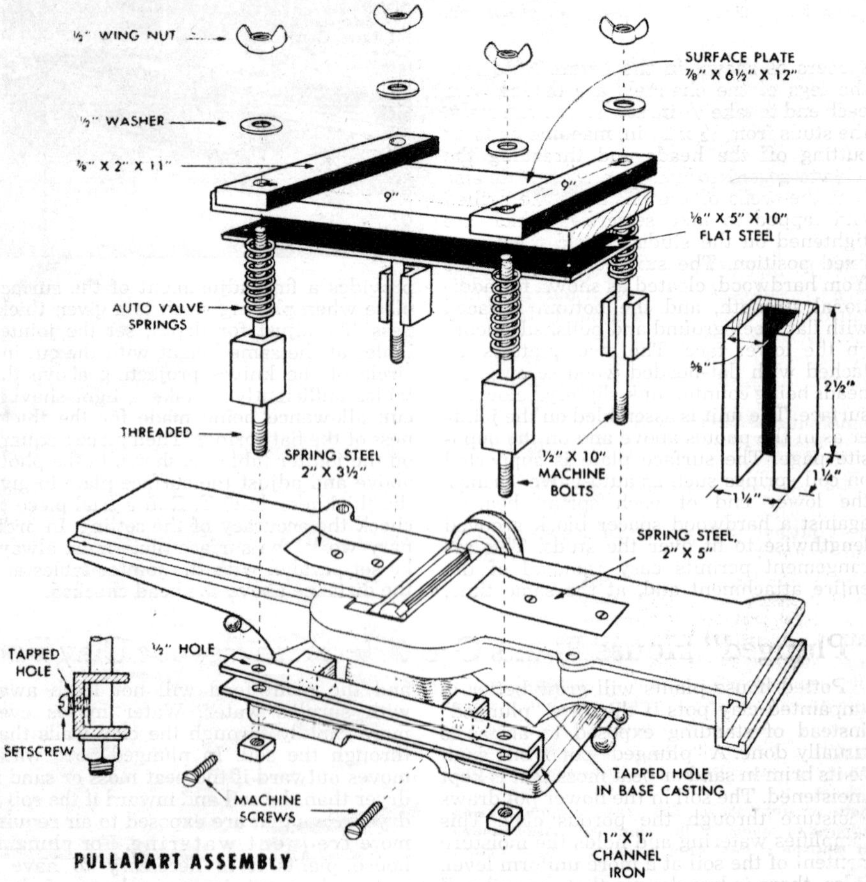

½" WING NUT

½" WASHER

⅞" X 2" X 11"

9"

9"

SURFACE PLATE
⅞" X 6½" X 12"

⅛" X 5" X 10"
FLAT STEEL

AUTO VALVE
SPRINGS

THREADED

SPRING STEEL
2" X 3½"

½" X 10"
MACHINE
BOLTS

⅝"

2½"

1¼"

1¼"

SPRING STEEL,
2" X 5"

½" HOLE

TAPPED
HOLE

SETSCREW

MACHINE
SCREWS

TAPPED HOLE
IN BASE CASTING

1" X 1"
CHANNEL
IRON

PULLAPART ASSEMBLY

Above, square is used to be sure surface plate is parallel with jointer table and to check distance above head. Right, jointer ready for planer unit

spacers as shown in the detail. Note that the legs of the channels are drilled near each end to take ½-in. studs. You can make the studs from ½ x 10-in. machine bolts by cutting off the heads and threading the ends to accommodate wing nuts. Note also that the webs of the channels are drilled and tapped to take setscrews which are tightened on the studs to hold them in a fixed position. The surface plate is made from hardwood, cleated as shown for additional strength, and the bottom is faced with flat steel, ground and polished smooth on the lower face. The steel plate is attached with flat-headed wood screws, the heads being countersunk slightly below the surface. The unit is assembled on the jointer as in the photos above and on the opposite page. The surface plate is supported on coil springs such as auto-valve springs, the lower end of each spring bearing against a hardwood spacer block grooved lengthwise to fit over the studs. This arrangement permits easy removal of the entire attachment and, at the same time, provides a fine adjustment of the surface plate when planing stock to a given thickness. To adjust for depth, set the jointer tables at the same height with the cutting circle of the knives projecting above the tables sufficiently to take a light shaving cut, allowance being made for the thickness of the flat springs. Then place a square on the jointer tables as shown in the photo above and adjust the surface plate to give the thickness desired. Run a trial piece to check the accuracy of the setting. In ordinary work, the surface plate must always be set parallel with the jointer tables and the distance above the head checked.

"Plunged" House Plants Grow Better in Porous Clay Pots

Potted house plants will grow better in unpainted clay pots if they are "plunged" instead of standing exposed to air as is usually done. A "plunged" pot is one sunk to its brim in sand or peat moss that is kept moistened. The soil in the flower pot draws moisture through the porous clay. This simplifies watering and holds the moisture content of the soil at a more uniform level. Also, there is less danger that the soil will pack too firmly for the good of the plant, and the plant food will not leach away with surplus water. Water moves even more rapidly through the clay walls than through the soil. In plunged pots, water moves outward if the peat moss or sand is dryer than the soil and inward if the soil is dryer. Pots that are exposed to air require more frequent watering. For plunging house plants it is necessary to have a watertight container, perhaps of sheet metal, in which to place the pots.

PLANT STAND

A GRACEFUL plant stand that gives the effect of fine ornamental ironwork can be made from square brass tubing. Use ¾-in. tubing for the base and standard, and ¼ or ⅜-in. tubing for the remaining parts. One way to form the tubing is to bend it around a wooden disk fastened to a bench top. Another way to bend the curved parts is to clamp an adjustable end wrench in a vise so that the jaws open in a vertical position. Then slide the tubing through the jaws, making a gradual bend. Always use a gentle, steady pressure. First, draw a full-size pattern as given in the squared drawing, and place the work on it occasionally to check the bending as you go along. After the parts are bent, assemble the stand as shown. If you prefer, the pot holders, C, and their supporting member, A, could be bent from a single length of tubing. Fasten all joints with small machine screws and high-strength alloy solder, and then file them smooth. The feet are jigsawed from pieces of hardwood and the tenon on each is cut to fit tightly into the tubing. Make a decorative wooden plug to fill the opening in each end of the base cross member. After the stand is assembled, enamel it white, or polish the brass with steel wool, apply a coat of clear lacquer, and stain and finish the wooden parts to harmonize with your other furnishings.

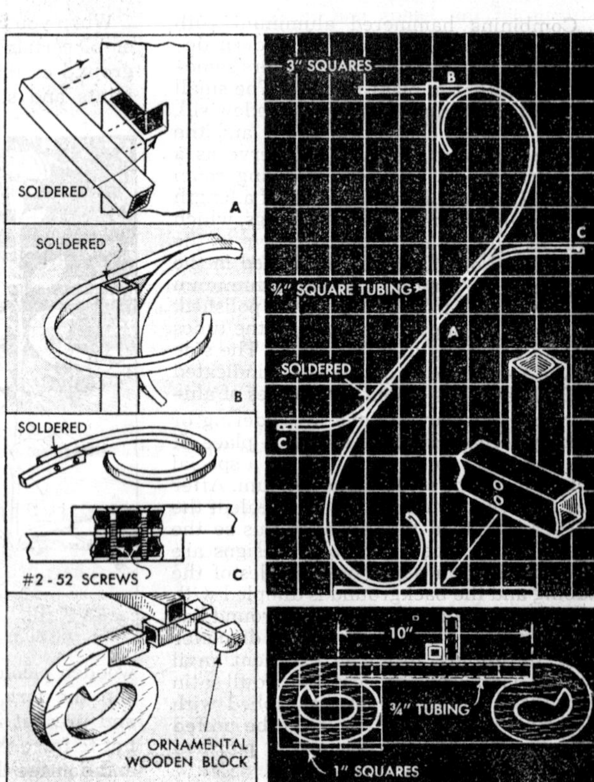

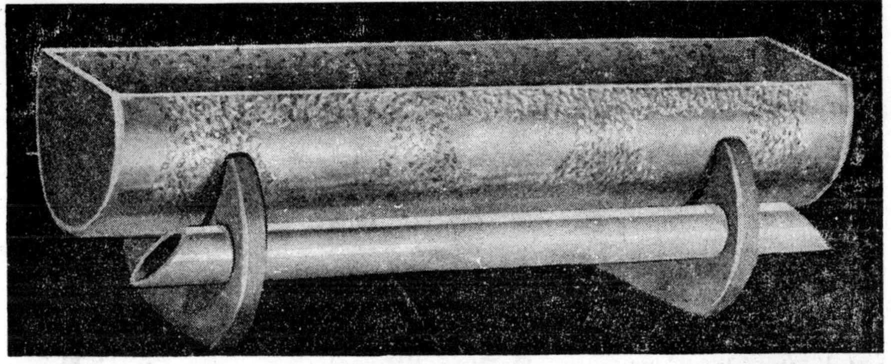

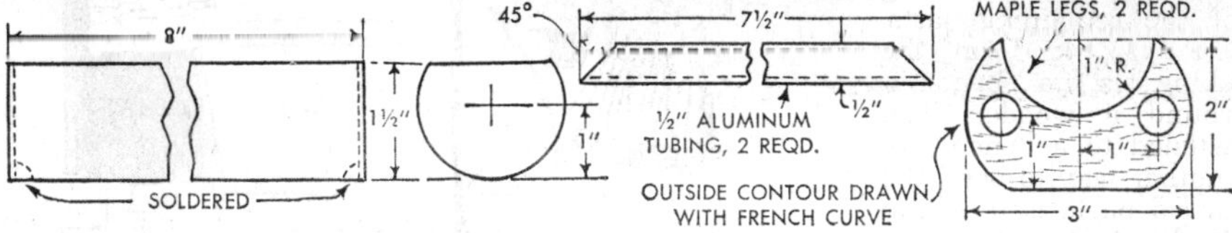

Modern Plant Holder in Hammered Aluminum

Combining hammered aluminum with polished maple in a pleasing modern design, this one-evening project offers something different in plant holders. The small size pictured is just right for a window sill, coffee table or chest of drawers, and the holder can be made larger to serve as a centerpiece on a buffet or dining-room table. The plant holder consists of a length of 2-in. aluminum tubing set on legs, which are cut from ¼-in. maple as shown in the right-hand detail. Holes are drilled in the legs for two lengths of ½-in. aluminum tubing and the legs are waxed and polished. To give rigid support to the legs, the tubes should be a snug fit in the holes. The side of the 2-in. tube is cut away as indicated and the ends are sealed with pieces of aluminum. This can be done by soldering or merely forcing oversize pieces in place. If the joints are to be soldered, use a special solder made for soldering aluminum. After the ends of the tube have been sealed, the corners are filed to a slight radius so the joints will not be noticeable. Designs are then outlined in pencil on the sides of the tubing and the background is dimpled with a ball-peen hammer. A piece of round bar stock or pipe, slightly smaller in diameter than the tubing, forms an excellent anvil for the hammering process. For a dull satin finish, the aluminum can be rubbed with fine steel wool and oil, or it can be buffed with jewelers' rouge if a highly polished finish is preferred.

Picnic Forks Pin Plant Branches To Ground to Start New Growth

When you want to hold a branch or trailer of certain kinds of plants close to the ground so that they will take root at the joints and start new growths, try using

wooden picnic forks for the purpose. Just slip the fork over the branch as shown and press it into the ground, taking care not to force the fork deep enough to pinch and damage the tender plant.

PLASTER

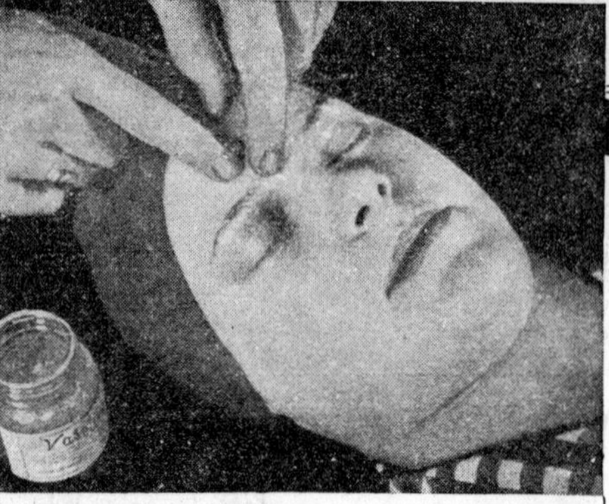

(2) See that hair is tucked in around edge of bathing cap and then cover eyes and eyebrows with small pieces of cigarette paper coated with vaseline

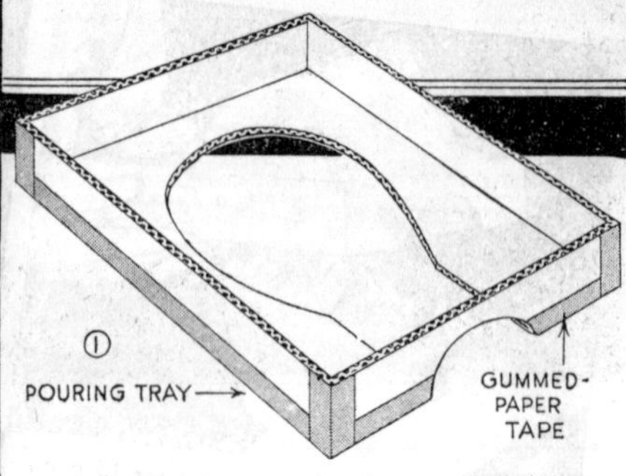

How the facial features of your friends or members of your family can be preserved indefinitely in a plaster-of-paris cast, which can be tinted or left white and used as a wall plaque

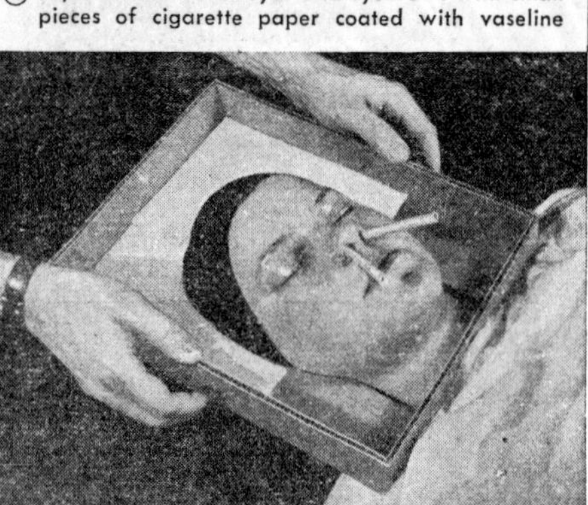

(3) Insert breathing tubes of paper or rubber in nostrils, packing cotton around the ends, and fasten pouring tray to cap with tabs of cellulose tape

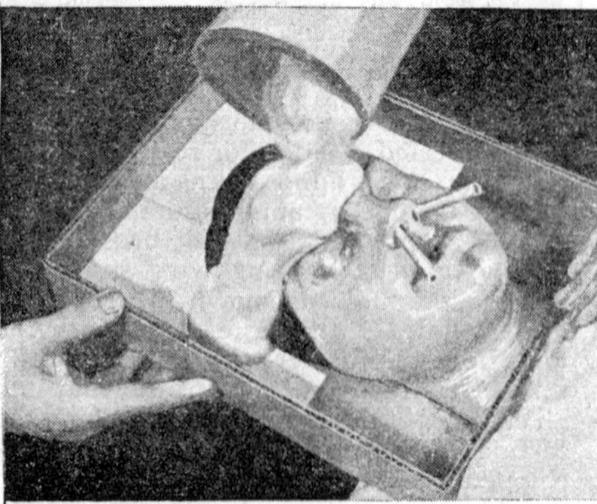

(4) After coating neck, face and bathing cap with cold cream to keep the mold from adhering, start pouring the plaster around the eyes, nose and mouth

THE first step in making a plaster cast of the face is to form a tray of corrugated cardboard like the one shown in Fig. 1, cutting the opening in it to frame the model's head and neck. This should fit the head rather snugly to retain the liquid plaster, although any error in cutting can be corrected later with fill-in pieces of cardboard held in place with tabs of tape. Now, with a bathing cap of the type shown pulled smoothly over the hair, and the model lying on a suitable table, begin covering the eyebrows and eyelashes with small pieces of cigarette paper coated with vaseline, smoothing them out carefully with the finger tips as shown in Fig. 2. If the model is a man, his face should be closely shaven, and if eyebrows are quite bushy, modeling clay can be applied and molded to the proper shape. A moustache can be treated in the same way. Next, place the tray in position over the head as in Fig. 3 and fasten it to the bathing cap with tabs of tape stuck here and there to the underside of the tray. Finally, breathing tubes of rubber tubing or large-size soda straws are placed in the nostrils and cotton is filled in around the ends to exclude the plaster. The diameter of the tubes should be of a size to prevent distorting the natural shape of the nostrils. Have the model get accustomed to breathing through the tubes with the mouth closed while you coat the face and neck lightly with cold cream.

Everything is now in readiness to pour the mold. Plaster of paris is used to make

CASTING

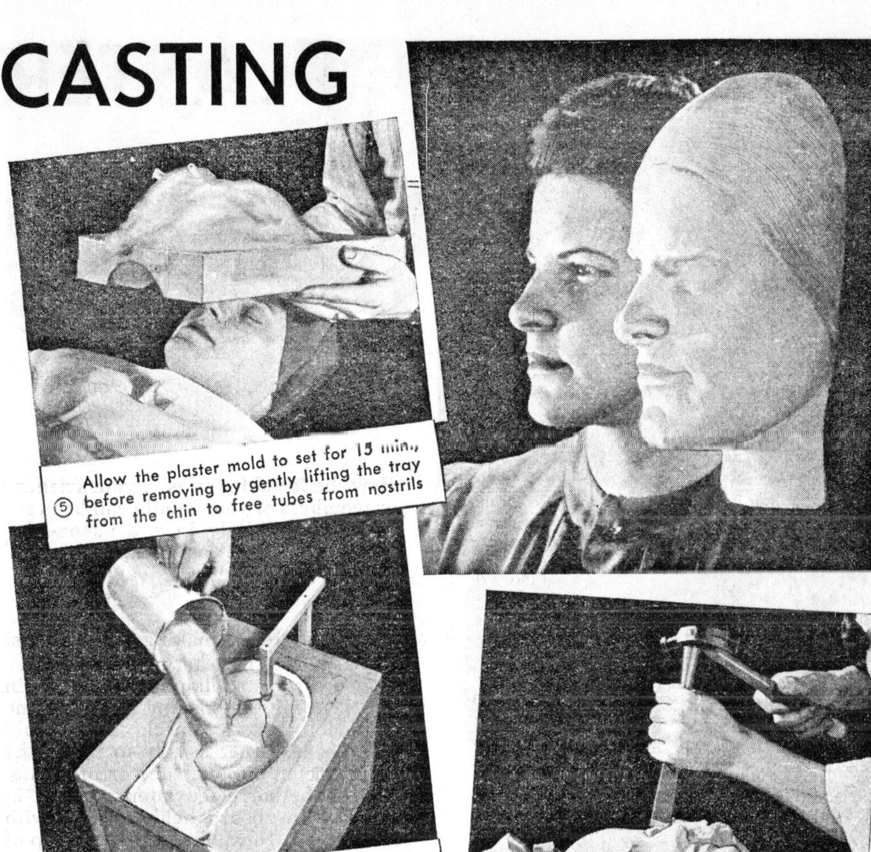

⑤ Allow the plaster mold to set for 15 min., before removing by gently lifting the tray from the chin to free tubes from nostrils

⑥ Provide the mold with a wire for hanging and then fill solid with plaster of paris after first painting the mold with soap

⑦ Let casting set overnight before chipping off mold with wood chisel. Work carefully to avoid cutting into the casting

both the mold and the casting. Prepare the mixture in a pail, adding the plaster a little at a time to cold water while stirring constantly, but slowly, to avoid air bubbles. As the mixture hardens very quickly upon reaching the consistency of thick cream, you will have to work fast in pouring. Cover the area around the nose first, being careful not to dislodge the breathing tubes, and then pour over the eyes. Flow the plaster thinly over all of the face at first to avoid flattening the features, and then gradually build up a thickness of about 1 in., Fig. 4. Just prior to pouring, the model should be instructed to "hold the pose" for 5 or 10 minutes to give the plaster time to set. After a total elapsed time of 15 minutes or so, the tray and mold can be lifted from the face as shown in Fig. 5. Any imperfections or cavities in the mold caused by air bubbles in the plaster should be filled in, after which cardboard sides are added to the sides of the tray to support the mold in an inverted position for soaping the inside and later filling with plaster. The soaping is done by applying lather from a cake of soap with a soft-hair brush.

Now, with a hanging wire suspended flush in the mold as shown in Fig. 6, the mold is filled with plaster level with the top. Here the plaster can be of a slightly thinner consistency to assure flowing into all crevices of the mold. After allowing the casting to harden overnight, the mold is chipped away as shown in Fig. 7. If you should accidentally cut into the casting with the chisel, the spots, if small, can be made practically unnoticeable by filling with freshly mixed plaster.

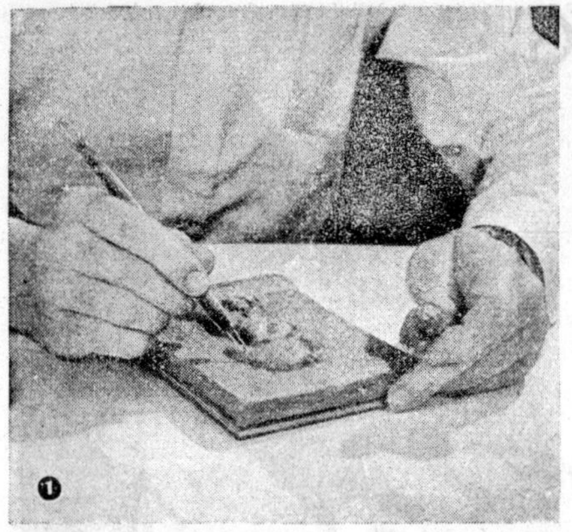

Outline the figure on a piece of clay and carefully pull away the material until the subject is in relief

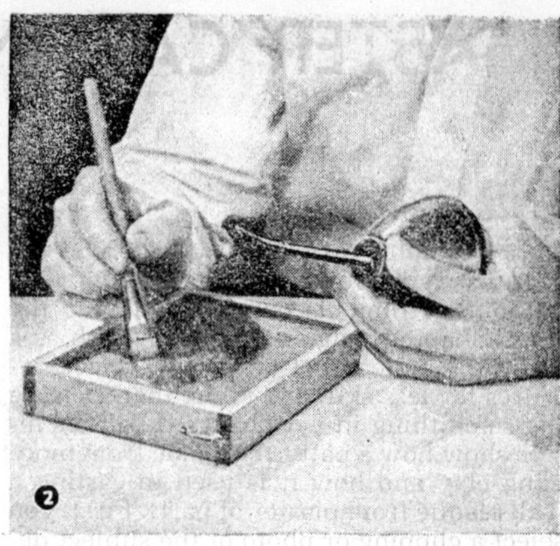

Place the clay in a wooden frame and paint the frame and surface of the clay with ordinary motor oil

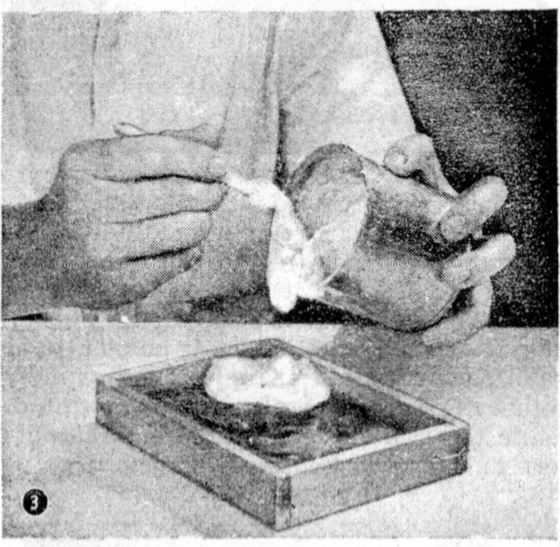

Mix a small quantity of plaster of paris to the consistency of pancake batter and pour the mold full

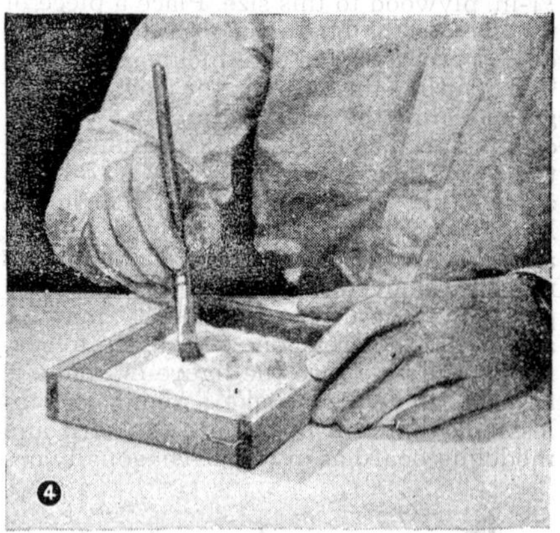

When thoroughly dry remove the clay model and give the surface of the plaster two coats of white shellac

Place the mold back in the frame, oil the surface and once again pour the mold full of plaster of paris

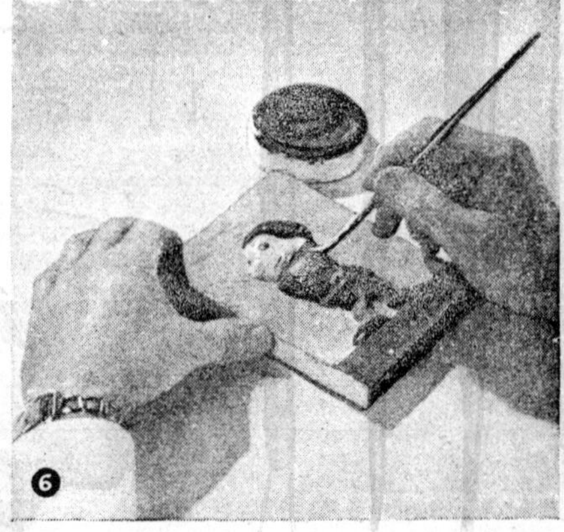

When the plaster cast has dried thoroughly, remove and shellac as before. Then paint with oil color

PLASTER CASTING

IF you begin with clay patterns it's easy to satisfy a desire to work in modeling clay without getting discouraged right at the start. Shaping a figure or object, such as a ship, in simple relief on a flat surface requires far less skill and effort than carving the same thing in wood. Figs. 1 to 6 inclusive show how a pattern is made from modeling clay and how it is used in casting a wall plaque from plaster of paris. First, you select a clipping or photo of the subject desired and from this determine the size of the plaque. Then cut a modeling board from ¼-in. plywood to this size. Place a piece of the clay on the board, smooth it out to the edges and square up to a thickness of about ⅝ in. Outline the figure in the clay, then begin modeling the relief by pulling away excess material as in Fig. 1. Professionals use the set of tools shown in Fig. 7, A to D inclusive, but for simple detail a hairpin, E, Fig. 7, does very well. You will see that the advantage of modeling clay is that if too much is removed or scraped away from any point on the surface, more clay may be added and the area gone over again to correct the error. Once the figure or shape is finished as desired, make a small bottomless box that will fit over the pattern and modeling board as in Fig. 2. Diagonally opposite corners are held with small hooks so that the box can be removed without damaging the pattern. After the plaster of paris mold has hardened it is placed in the box and shellacked. When pouring the plaster plaque as in Fig. 5, a small hanger bent from wire is placed at the top end as indicated. Fig. 6 shows a plaque being painted, while the two views in Fig. 8 show a pattern and the finished plaque made from it.

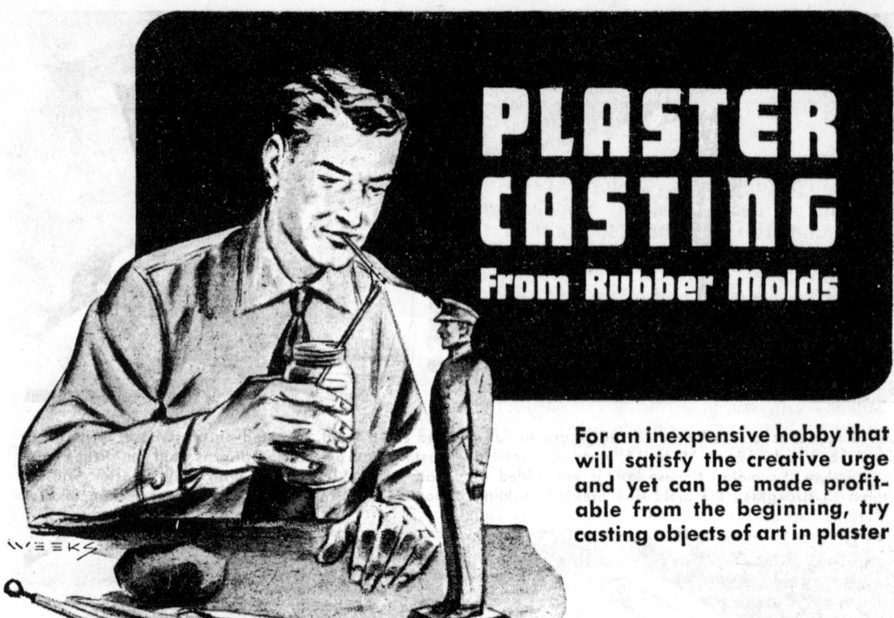

PLASTER CASTING

From Rubber Molds

For an inexpensive hobby that will satisfy the creative urge and yet can be made profitable from the beginning, try casting objects of art in plaster

THE ART OF CASTING in plaster is an interesting and exciting hobby that can be made profitable right from the start with an investment so small as to be no problem. Using rubber molds, you can duplicate objects of art or, for a more satisfying hobby, you can model your own carvings. Either has a ready sale through gift shops, ten-cent stores and other retail outlets.

Making the original model: The two common substances for carving original models are wet clay and plastaline. As wet clay has disadvantages, we will consider only plastaline, which can be purchased at any art-supply store. Lead or aluminum wire serves as an armature, or backbone, for an upright figure. Bend a length of wire about three times the height of the figure and twist it to form a small loop at the bend. When the distance from the top of the loop to the bottom of the twist is a little less than the figure height plus the thickness of the base, bend the ends outward to form a stand. A thin cake of plastaline is pressed onto a board which serves as a modeling stand and the end of the armature is embedded in it. Sufficient plastaline is then packed around the bottom to form the base and to anchor the armature. To finish the model, build up its general outline around the armature and then carve in the detail.

Making a "waste" mold: If you wish just one cast, the simplest method is to make a waste mold. To make a waste mold, mix enough plaster to cover the figure to a thickness of ⅛ in., coloring it with laundry bluing. Superfine statuary plaster, to which dextrine is added in the proportion of 35 grains to the pound for strength and hardness, will prove satisfactory. No. 1 casting plaster, which comes with the dextrine already added, is still more desirable. The proper mixture consists of plaster, 1⅔ lb. and water, 1 pt. Sprinkle the plaster into the water through the fingers. Do not use a sifter. Wait 1 min. and stir rapidly for 10 sec. Do not beat the mixture. Next, quickly spread it on the figure, using a fairly stiff brush.

When the blue plaster has set, make a larger quantity of white plaster and trowel it on over the blue to a thickness of about 1 in. Square off the top so that the mold can be set upright during casting. When this plaster has set, scrape out the plastaline model and armature from the mold with a spoon or modeling tool. Be sure that it is entirely removed, especially noting the eyes and ears. When the mold is clear, wash the inside with a heavy soap solution, working up a good lather. Tincture of green soap makes an excellent washing compound.

To make the casting, fill the mold with water, empty it in a mixing bowl, add plas-

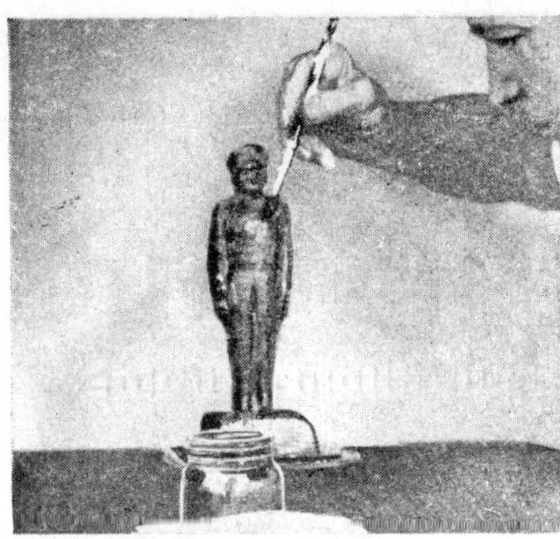

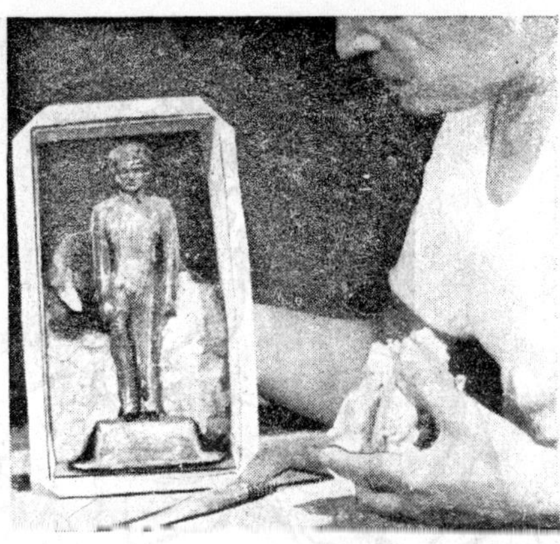

Liquid rubber is brushed over carved figure to form the rubber mold. From 10 to 15 coats are needed to complete the mold. Cheesecloth is embedded in rubber to strengthen the mold and prevent buckling

The cured mold, mounted on glass base, is shown in casting box as the clay dam is built up. When back half of mold is filled with clay, plaster will be poured into front half to make first section of shell

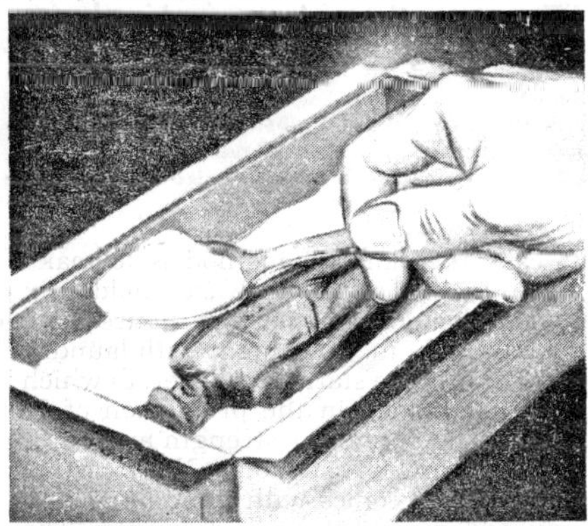

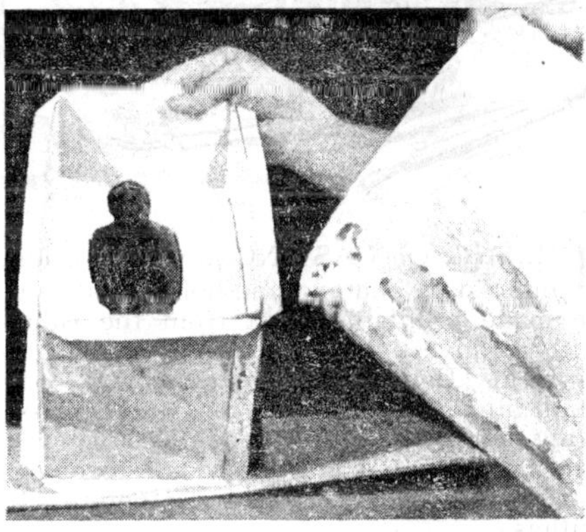

Above, spoon is used to make dimple on either side of figure in clay dam. Dimples will form keys to assure proper joining of mold sections. Below, the shell is taken out of the casting box and separated. The various parts of the casting box are at left

Above, after the first half of the casting shell has set and is coated with soap solution, the box is ready for pouring the second half of the shell. Below, the rubber mold has been cut from crown to base and the plastaline figure removed. Mold is now washed

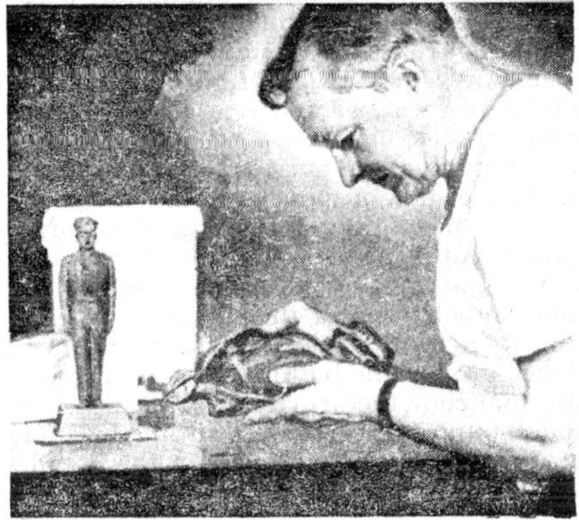

ter in the proportions already given and mix. Pour a small amount of the mixed plaster into the mold and shake. Pour the surplus back into the mixing bowl, give it one last stir, and pour the balance into the mold. Jar the mold while pouring and for a few minutes afterward to dislodge any air bubbles. Pour the mold a little over-full and then scrape the bottom flat with a spatula. Allow the cast to stand for an hour, then remove the waste mold by chiseling it away with a screwdriver and hammer. Begin at the base and work slowly and carefully. After the white plaster is removed, chip away the blue. Because of the soap film inside the mold, this job is easier than you might expect.

Multiple casts from rubber molds: Liquid-rubber compounds high in natural latex content are best for making rubber molds. You can use either a master cast taken from a waste mold or the original plastaline model for making the rubber mold. In both cases, the figure is first given two coats of shellac, thinned to about half strength. This is best applied with an oral spray, such as used by artists, but a brush can be used. Make certain that the shellac does not fill in the detail of the figure. Place a sheet of glass under the figure so it is 1 in. larger all around than the base of the model and use a small amount of liquid rubber to cement the figure to the glass. Usually 10 to 15 coats of rubber are required to complete the mold. Brush each coat on evenly and fairly thin. If, as in the model shown here, there are openings, such as between the arms and legs, incorporate pieces of shim brass in your model to prevent union of the rubber into a solid section impossible to remove. A coat of rubber dries in 20 min., and the succeeding coat may then be applied. After the second coat dries, begin laying on 1-in. strips of cheesecloth down the line along which the rubber mold is to be slit open. Brush on some rubber, lay the cloth on and brush it in place, using more rubber on the brush. The cheesecloth is applied every third or fourth coat and three layers may be applied down the outside of the arms and legs to prevent "shell pinching." In applying the rubber coats, carry each down to and out upon the glass for ½ in. When enough coats have been applied, set the mold in a cool, shaded place and cure for a week to 10 days.

The casting box: To act as a support for the rubber mold, a casting box must be made. Light-gauge galvanized sheet iron is best for this purpose. The accompanying sketch shows the construction. In calculating the dimensions for the box, be certain that when the mold is inserted it will face the opening, not the sidewalls.

Exercising extreme caution, craftsman replaces rubber mold in casting shell. Carelessness in this operation will result in "shell pinching," which will produce faulty castings. Below, construction diagram of casting box made of galvanized sheet iron. Dimensions will depend on the size of the figure

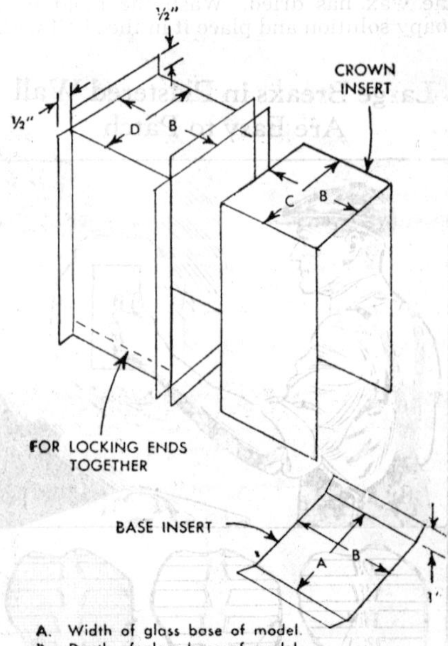

After the box is assembled, slide the rubber-covered model into it. With clay powder from the paint store, mix a stiff dough according to directions and pack it into the back of the casting box, fitting it to the sides of the box and to the contours of the figure. At this point, determine the median line of the figure and keep the clay from coming past this point. Otherwise it will be impossible to withdraw the model from the finished shell.

After the clay is packed, lay the casting box on its back and smooth out the clay around the figure. Scoop out a small dimple on either side of the figure to act as a key, so that the two halves of the mold will join properly. Fill the empty half of the casting box with plaster and allow to harden. Remove the clay and wash the half of the box that is now empty, to give it a coating of soap. Fill this portion of the casting box with plaster and allow to set before removing the casting box, parting the shell and taking out the rubber mold. With a sharp knife dipped in water, cut through the rubber mold to the model, extending the cut from the crown to the bottom of the base.

Before casting, prepare the shell by brushing it with a thin coating of floor wax and dusting it with talcum powder after the wax has dried. Wash the mold in a soapy solution and place it in the shell with the cut side up, adjusting to see that the fit is perfect. Then set the top half of the shell over the mold. Hold the two halves of the shell together with heavy rubber bands, set it upright and proceed with the mixing and pouring operation as before.

The bronze finish: To add a rich bronze finish to your casting, follow these directions: Varnish the cast and allow to dry. Give it a second coat and then blow on powdered statuary bronze. A small insect-powder blower is best for this job. Ten min. later a "craze" will appear on the surface of the cast. Spray on more powder until the craze disappears. The figure now has a modern-bronze finish. To give it an antique appearance, dissolve 1 teaspoonful of bluestone (copper vitriol) in ½ glassful of water and brush this solution on. In about one min., using another brush, cover the figure with an ammonium-chloride solution of the same proportions. The solutions will darken the figure, with the characteristic green showing in the hollows of the cast. When dry, polish the figure with a neutral-color shoe polish of the old-fashioned wax turpentine type. To complete the figure, glue on a felt pad using a glue without an acetone base. One last word of warning: If you reproduce art objects, be certain they are not copyrighted before you offer them for sale. ★ ★ ★

Large Breaks in Plastered Wall Are Easy to Patch

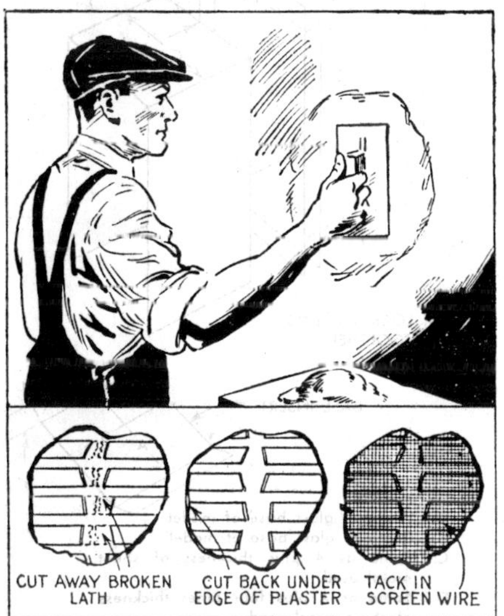

Always remove all cracked plaster, cut away damaged lath and then cover with piece of screen wire

Anyone can do a workmanlike job of patching breaks in plaster if a simple procedure is followed. If the break is a small crack, remove the crumbled material and undercut the edge of the firm plaster. But if the break is large and the laths are broken, remove the damaged plaster and cut away the broken parts of the lath. Then undercut the edges of the firm plaster and tack a piece of screen wire over the lath. Dampen the edges of the plaster so that the patching material will bond to it thoroughly. Regular patching plaster, which you can buy in any amount desired, is best, although a mixture of plaster of paris and water will do.

PLASTER PATCHING

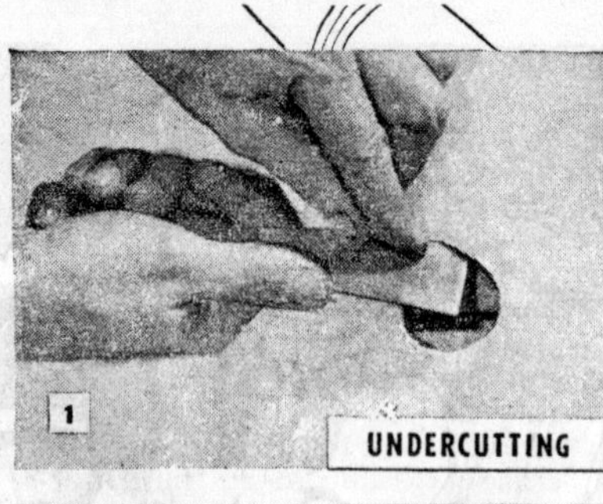
1 UNDERCUTTING

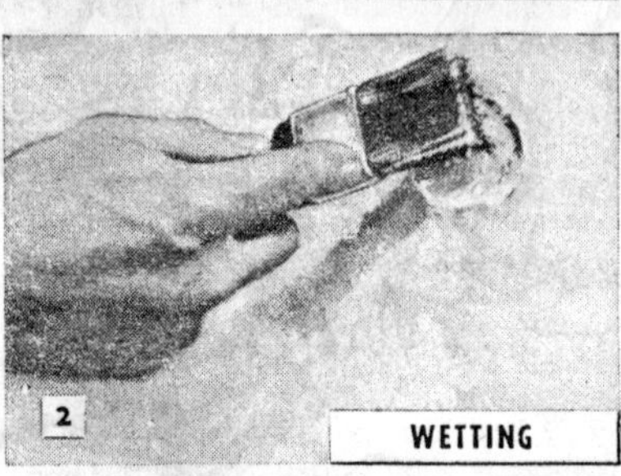
2 WETTING

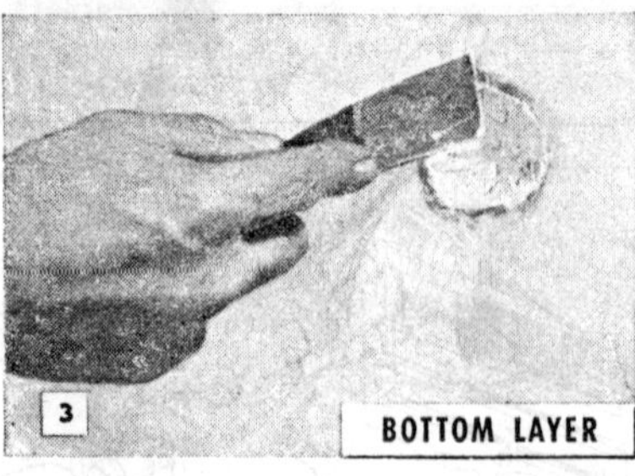
3 BOTTOM LAYER

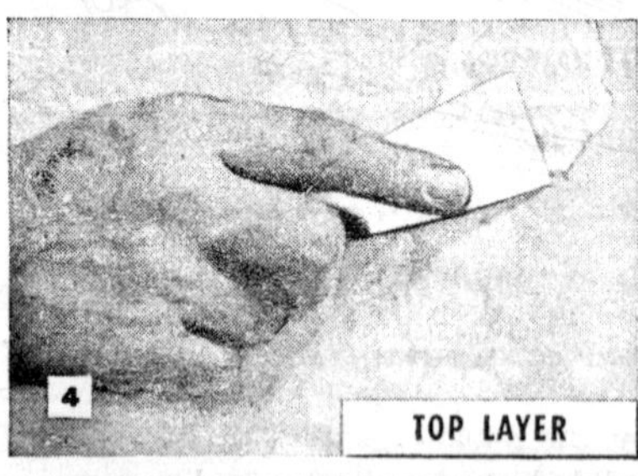
4 TOP LAYER

5 SAND HIGH SPOTS

IT'S NO JOB at all to make minor plaster repairs such as filling cracks, "spotting" nail holes and sealing spaces between wood trim and plaster. Equally important is the occasional job of replacing loose plaster, especially in older houses. The time to make these repairs is just before repainting or wallpapering. Many remodeling jobs also require some plastering, which the average homeowner can tackle. However, major replastering jobs such as entire walls and ceilings call for the skill and experience of a professional plasterer.

Where to use Spackling putty: You use Spackling putty to fill cracks in plaster, from hairline size up to about ⅛ in. wide; in nail and screw holes around which plaster has not broken away; for nicks and surface imperfections in plaster, and for cracks that have developed between wood trim and plaster. To use the putty, first remove grease with strong washing solution and clean off all loose paint and dirt particles. A putty knife or wide scraper is handy for applying it and to smooth it on flat surfaces. At corners you can use a spear-shaped window-glazing tool, or just your finger protected with a rubber finger cot. Wipe off excess putty and smooth down the filling with a wet sponge.

Patching plaster: For cracks over ⅛ in. wide, and for areas up to about a foot or so square, use patching plaster. The powder is prepared by adding water and mixing to a smooth paste. Don't mix more than you can use before it starts to set—from 10 to 30 minutes depending on the product. Setting can be retarded by adding an equal amount of vinegar to the water used for mixing. Undercut the edges of cracks and small patches to make them wider at the bottom than at the top as in Fig. 1. This anchors the plaster in place. Next, brush away all loose particles and soak the old plaster, and plaster base if exposed, with water, Fig. 2, using a brush. Try to avoid

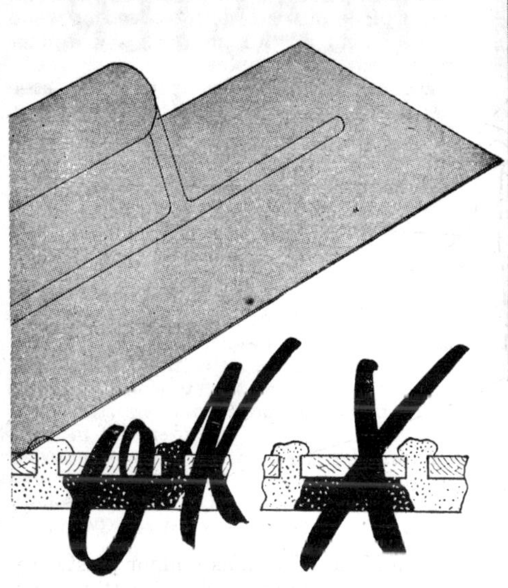

runs that may stain wallpaper. Wetting prevents rapid absorption of moisture from the patching plaster, which causes it to dry out too fast and crack away at the joints.

Press the plaster firmly against the under edges with the putty knife, Fig. 3. If the hole goes down to the lath, press the plaster down to key with the lath. Fill the hole, or wide crack, to ⅛ in. below the surrounding surface. If the hole is filled flush in one application, shrinkage of some kinds of patching plaster may cause a dish-shaped depression. Let the first application dry overnight, then wet the surface and complete the job, Fig. 4. If a nonshrinking type of plaster is used, fill the hole in one application. If the patch is too high when dry, dress it down with a coarse file (handle removed) or with sandpaper wrapped around a small block, Fig. 5. Seal the patch with thin shellac and allow this to dry before painting to prevent its showing up as a dull spot. If the adjoining wall surface has a sand-float finish, make the patch finish similar by adding an equal amount of clean, sharp sand to the last application, and pounce it with a piece of pile carpeting wrapped around a block.

Larger patches: When plaster bulges, particularly on ceilings where wood lath is used, and especially if it has been subjected to repeated soaking, chances are that it has loosened from the lath and is likely to fall off. Then the only remedy is removal of all loose plaster as in Fig. 6. Old plaster keys between the laths are pushed through, out of the way, so that the new plaster can key securely. Make the edges

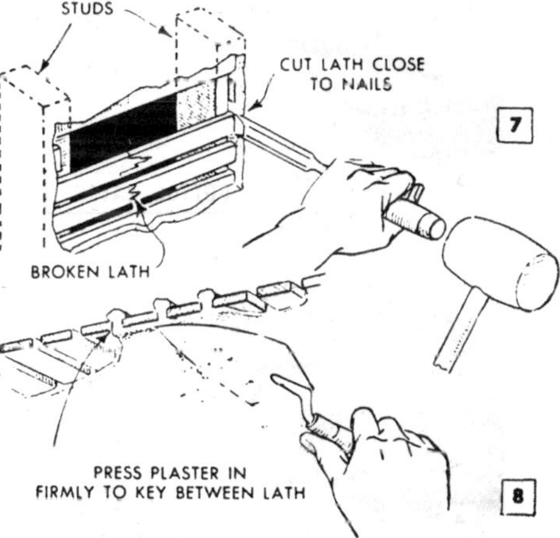

of solid plaster as regular in shape as possible—without jagged edges.

Sometimes the laths are loose; if so, nail them down solidly to joists or studs with lathing nails. If a lath has been pulled off, replace it. Broken laths are more likely to occur in walls crushed by heavy impact. In such cases the plaster is removed back to a stud on either side of the break and the broken pieces of lath are cut off midway on the studs with a chisel and mallet as in Fig. 7. This provides space to nail on new pieces of lath. Spacing between wood lath

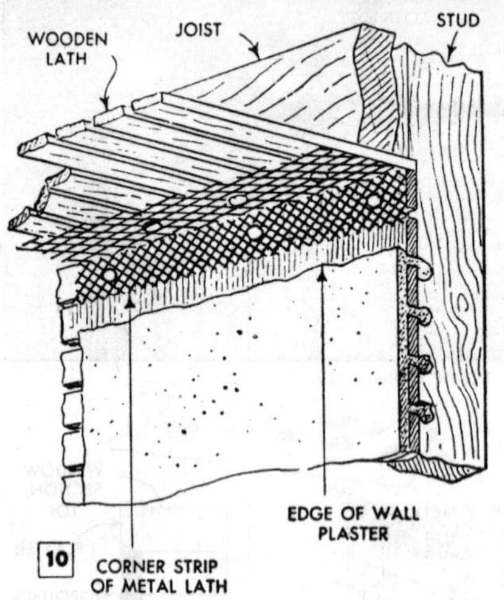

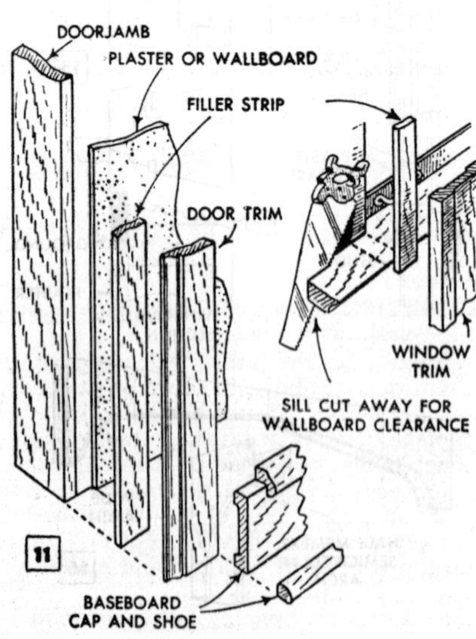

should be about ¼ in. If desired, you can use a piece of metal lath instead of wood lath, cutting it with tin snips and attaching it with ¾-in. staples.

Before patching, brush away all loose particles from the edges of the old plaster. Then wet the lath and plaster edges thoroughly. A pointing trowel or regular plasterer's trowel is more convenient to use in filling intermediate-size patches than a putty knife. A single, thick layer of patching plaster over lath, particularly on ceilings, often tends to sag. Therefore, after wetting the plaster edges and lath thoroughly, start by applying a layer to just cover the lath, pressing it down firmly to key it properly as in Figs. 8 and 9. After this has set, add more to build up the thickness until it comes ⅛ in. below adjoining plaster. Allow the plaster to dry overnight, then wet the surface and fill flush with a vinegar-retarded mixture so that you will have time to finish the surface properly. To match a smooth adjoining surface, use a trowel. To match a sand-float finish, add an equal amount of sand to the last batch of plaster and use a wooden float, Fig. 22, to even the surface. To get a surface level, check with a straightedge placed across the patch. While the filling is still soft, surplus plaster can be scraped off with the straightedge or with a wide metal scraper, moving it back and forth with a sawing motion while pushing it ahead. If adjoining surface is textured, allow the patch to dry, then apply texture paint as described under heading, "Covering unsightly walls."

For patches larger than a foot or so square, it's easier and more economical to use regular prepared plaster, application of which is covered under the headings, "Base-coat plaster" and "Finish coat."

Using trowel or float: When using a trowel or float for smoothing plaster, move it sideways, lifting the forward edge a trifle so it rides over the surface to avoid cutting into it. Keep the working surface of a trowel or float clean and smooth. When the finish surface starts to set, it can be troweled smooth and glossy by wetting the trowel a little, or running a wet brush ahead of the trowel as in Fig. 24. The float also should be dipped in water as necessary so that it won't adhere to and drag out soft plaster.

Covering unsightly walls: Old walls and ceilings that show many scars of previous patching jobs improperly done, may be restored to excellent appearance by covering with texture paint, provided the old plaster is securely attached to the lath. Texture paints, available in many tints, are of heavy consistency to permit filling low spots to produce a uniform surface. This may be pleasingly textured with brush marks, swirls, mottling with sponge or crumpled paper, or it can be stippled with a brush.

Replacing walls and ceilings: When loose plaster extends over large areas, it is probable that the entire wall or ceiling must be renewed for safety as well as for appearance. For a complete replastering job all old plaster must be removed; that between the laths is raked out or pushed back so spaces are open. If only a ceiling is replaced, a 2 or 3-in. strip of plaster is removed also from the top edge of walls as in Fig. 10. Strips of metal lath or ready-made corner strips are installed in corners to prevent cracks. The strips are fastened to studs and joists with large-head nails or long staples, spaced 6 in. where possible. You can do all this preparatory work and have a professional plasterer finish the job.

An unsightly ceiling, still tightly attached to the lath, can be covered with a new plastered ceiling if the supporting framework is strong enough to bear the added weight. Here, a plaster base of metal lath over furring strips, or self-furring metal lath, is installed, using washers and nails which are long enough to enter the joists about 1½ in. The nails should be spaced about 6 in. apart. Bend the lath to overlap walls where a narrow strip of plaster is removed, Fig. 10. Covering walls in this manner involves removing all trim and installing filler strips to bring door and window casings flush with the new plaster, Fig. 11. Considering this added work and expense, it may be better generally to remove the old plaster. In many cases, however, you can substitute ⅛-in. hardboard or ¼-in. wallboard for plaster, although this, too, requires the removal of trim and the addition of filler strips, Fig. 11.

Plaster bases: Either metal lath or gypsum lath is used for supporting plaster. Metal lath comes in sheets approximately 27 in. wide and 96 in. long. On large wall areas the sheets are run horizontally, the ends overlapped 1 in. and the edges about ½ in. Horizontal edges are held together with galvanized tie wire midway between studs. The sheets also are staggered so that the ends come on different studs or joists. Metal lath is nailed or stapled to these supports every 6 in., and is bent to fit inside and outside corners, running it past them to the next support to prevent corner cracks from developing.

Gypsum lath, Fig. 12, comes in 16 x 48-in. sheets, ⅜ and ½ in. thick. Some types are perforated to give a mechanical key besides the natural bond by suction. The sheets are nailed directly to studs and joists, or furring strips, with 1⅛-in. standard blued lath nails spaced 5 in. apart. For certain types of "floating" assembly, the lath is held by metal clips attached to studs and joists. Sheets are placed horizontally,

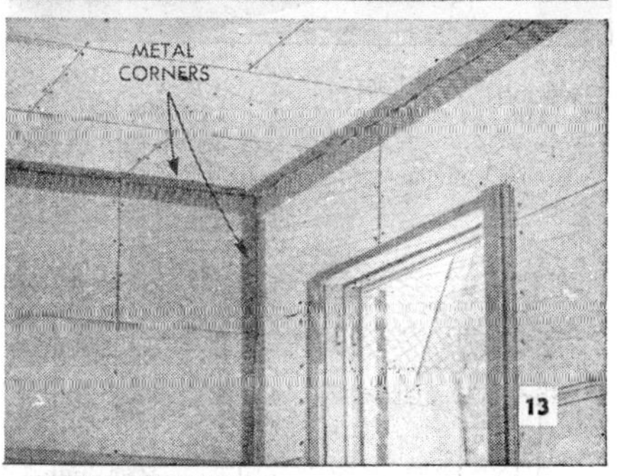

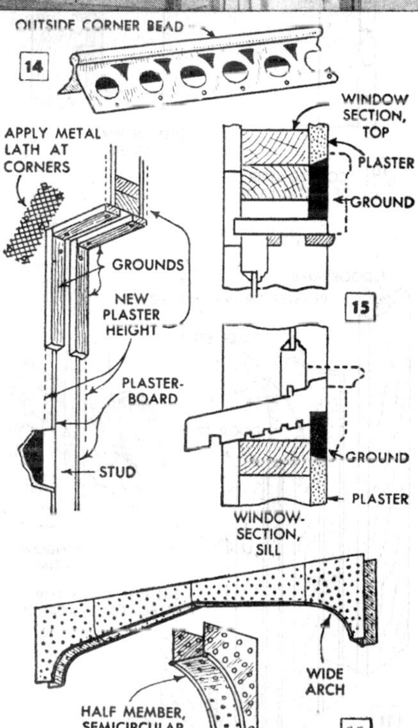

face side out, and are staggered so that the ends will come midway on different nailing supports. Use gypsum lath only as a base for gypsum plaster. Reinforce the corners where two walls meet, or those where walls and ceiling join, with special corner covering or prebent strips of metal lath, Fig. 13. Reinforcing strips are provided also over the upper corners of doors and windows (Fig. 15) to prevent cracks.

Corner bead, grounds, metal arches: For outside corners over any type of plaster base, you use corner bead, Fig. 14. This protects the plaster against blows and also provides a "ground" to which plaster comes flush. The corner should come exactly to plaster height of both adjoining walls.

Grounds at door openings which are cut through an existing wall or partition are installed as in Fig. 15 and later removed. Permanent grounds are placed along window casings or nailed across studs to come just below the top edge of baseboards. Sometimes an additional one is installed at floor level. In many remodeling jobs, the old wall to which plaster is joined serves as a ground, and the other grounds are adjusted to this height. The edges of old plaster should be cut off as smooth as possible to make the joint inconspicuous.

Ready-mixed plaster: Prepared plaster is available in which the right ingredients are exactly proportioned by manufacturers, requiring only the addition of water. Always follow carefully the manufacturer's directions. Gypsum plaster should not be used on outdoor walls, concrete or asphalt coatings, or on walls subjected to much moisture. But it can be applied to clean brick or building tile.

Base-coat plaster: The standard minimum thickness of plaster for new construction is ⅝ in. over metal lath and ½ in. over all other lath. In remodeling jobs, new plaster should come flush with the old plaster to which it is joined. Plaster is applied in separate coats—one coat of base plaster over gypsum lath, but two over metal lath, followed by a finish coat in each case. If the wall is to be painted or papered, the finish coat may be omitted.

Mix the plaster in a watertight box with sloping ends, Fig. 20. Mix only as much plaster as you can use in an

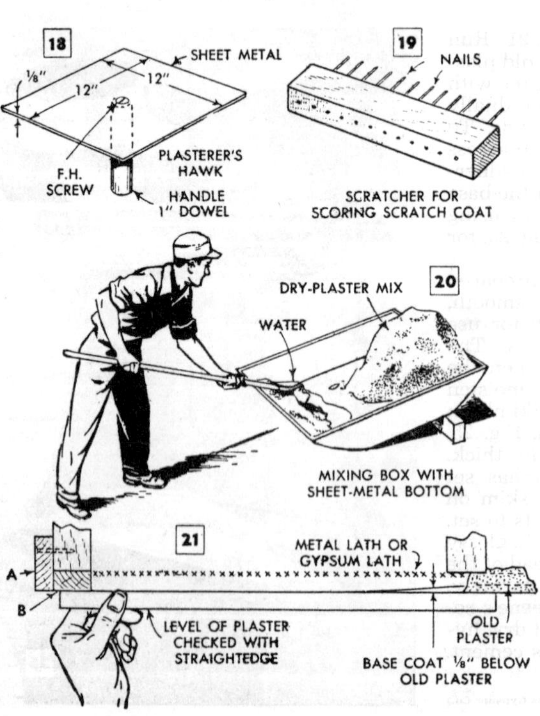

hour. Don't add water after the plaster has started to set, and don't mix plaster of a previous batch with a fresh batch. Put some on a hawk, Fig. 18, and apply it with a plasterer's trowel.

When applying plaster to lath, press the first coat down and work it through the spaces of the wood lath, or mesh of metal lath, to obtain good keying, or to form good bond to gypsum lath. Then, cover the lath about ¼ in. Score crisscross grooves about ⅛ in. deep while the plaster is soft, using an improvised scratcher, Fig. 19. After the first coat has set hard, apply a second coat as in Fig. 17, to come flush with the ground. Where the new plaster joins old plaster, soak edges with enough water to prevent rapid absorption of moisture from the new plaster. Soak the edges of the old plaster either with a sponge or a brush. The plaster and lath should be soaked just prior to patching.

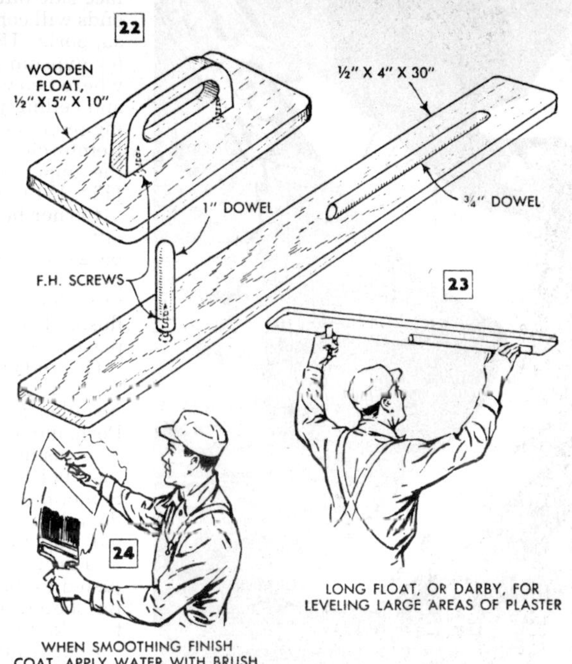

LONG FLOAT, OR DARBY, FOR LEVELING LARGE AREAS OF PLASTER

WHEN SMOOTHING FINISH COAT, APPLY WATER WITH BRUSH

It's best to keep the base coat ⅛ in. below the surface of old plaster, where it joints, Fig. 21. Run the corner of the trowel along the old plaster edge, and then "wipe" the plaster with a trowel back slightly, returning gradually to the plaster height of other grounds. To get plaster level, use a straightedge across the grounds as in Fig. 21. For good adherence of a finish coat, the surface of the base coat should be slightly roughened by using a float, Fig. 22. Use a long float, Fig. 23, for large areas.

Finish coat: You can also buy prepared finish plaster. There are two kinds: smooth, trowel finish and sand-float finish for use with steel trowel or float respectively. The base-coat plaster must be hard when the finish coat is applied. If dried out, moisten the surface but do not soak. "Skim" on finish plaster in two applications, Fig. 25, producing a coat from $\frac{1}{16}$ to ⅛ in. thick. As soon as the first application has set enough to prevent its wrinkling, skim on the second. When the plaster starts to set, give it a final troweling for a smooth, glossy finish, using a clean wet brush ahead of the trowel, Fig. 24, but use water sparingly. For an extra-hard surface, use Keene's cement in the proportion of 25 lbs. of dry, hydrated lime to 100 lbs. of Keene's cement.

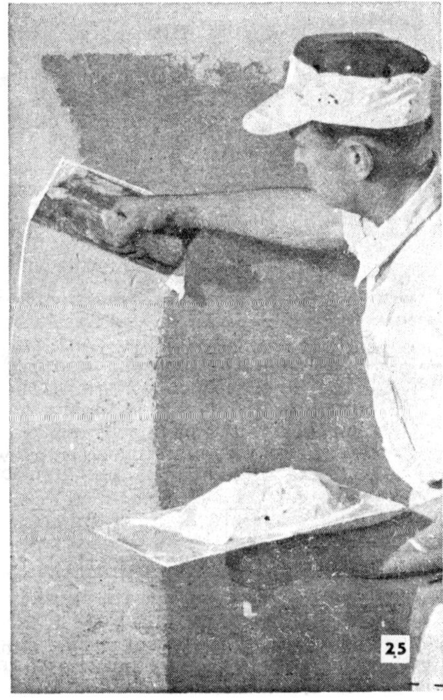

(Some photos courtesy United States Gypsum Co.)

PLASTIC

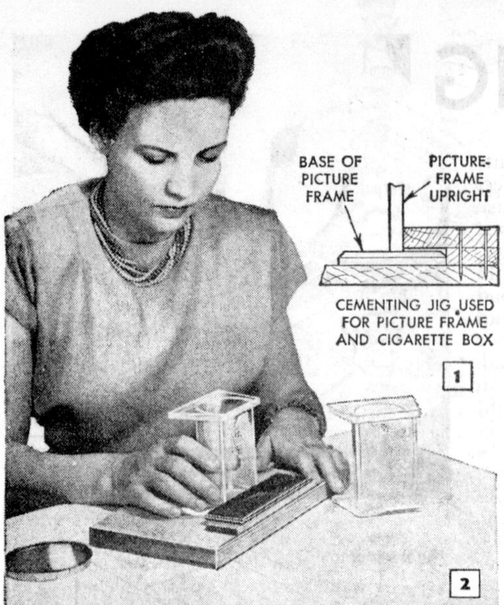

NO MATTER how much care is given to shaping and polishing the parts of plastic articles, such as those shown in Fig. 10, their entire appearance can be ruined by poorly cemented joints. Here is a simplified cementing technique along with two jigs to help produce the good joints upon which the beauty of plastic craftwork depends. This method applies only to the acrylic plastics (Plexiglas and Lucite).

All cements for acrylic plastics are solvents for the plastic, the bond being made by a softening and intermingling of the plastic at the joining surfaces. The best type of solvent for craftwork is vinyl trichloride, commercially known as Plexiglas

3 CEMENTS	NATURE OF CEMENT	SETTING TIME*	DRYING TIME	REMARKS
VINYL TRICHLORIDE	SOLVENT TYPE WATER-WHITE	30 SEC.	3 HRS.	BEST CEMENT FOR CRAFTWORK
ETHYLENE DICHLORIDE	SOLVENT TYPE WATER-WHITE		3 HRS.	FAST-SETTING. SECOND-BEST CHOICE FOR CRAFTING
METHYLENE DICHLORIDE	SOLVENT TYPE WATER-WHITE		3 HRS.	TOO FAST. JOINTS MAY DRY BEFORE ASSEMBLY
SOLVENT MIX	ANY OF ABOVE MIXED WITH PLASTIC SHAVINGS	1 MIN.	4 HRS.	SLOWER-SETTING THAN PURE SOLVENT. GOOD FOR BRUSH APPLICATION
MONOMER MIX	THE ORIGINAL PLASTIC IN LIQUID FORM	4 HRS.	24 HRS.	MAXIMUM STRENGTH. BEST BOND FOR SOAK CEMENTING

*NOT HARDENED, BUT WORK CAN BE REMOVED FROM JIG.

4 RESULTS

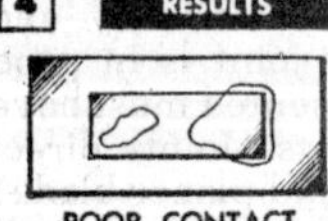
POOR CONTACT

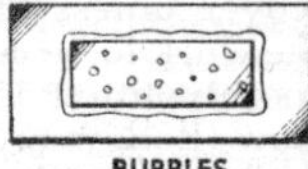
BUBBLES

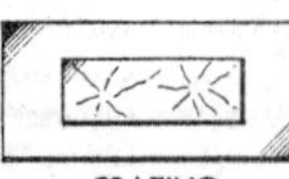
CRAZING

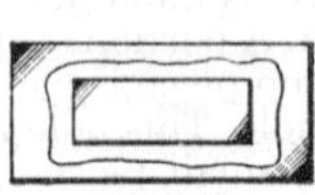
RUNOVER

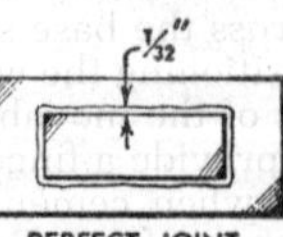

PERFECT JOINT

Above, poor contact indicates a badly fitted joint or insufficient cement. Bubbles are likely to occur with heavy cements. Crazing results from faulty cement or heavy clamping pressure. Runover happens most frequently when heavy cements are used. The perfect joint is crystal clear with just a slight runover

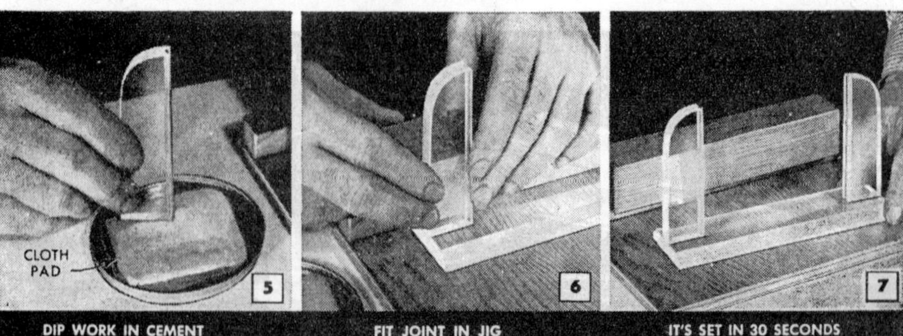

DIP WORK IN CEMENT — FIT JOINT IN JIG — IT'S SET IN 30 SECONDS

CEMENTING

1-C cement. Fig. 3 lists the five most suitable cements in their order of preference.

The best method of application to use with pure solvent-type cement is a fast dip. To do this, obtain a shallow container, such as the lid from a glass jar. Next fold a piece of soft cloth twice to form a pad and place the pad in the lid. Then, with an eye dropper, add solvent to the container until it is level with the top of the pad. The work to be cemented is pressed on the solvent pad, Fig. 5. Due to the slight give of the pad surface, the work actually is immersed to a depth of about 1/32 in. In order to distribute the cement evenly, the work is dipped three times in rapid succession and the joint is made immediately, Fig. 6. Cement is applied to one surface of the joint only. As quick and exact positioning of the cemented part is essential, a cementing jig should always be used. The joint is held in place with very light pressure of the fingers for about 20 to 30 sec. after which the work can be removed from the jig, Fig. 7. The joints are quite rigid within a minute and completely cured in about three hours.

Fig. 1 shows a simple jig for picture frames which also can be used for a cigarette box as in Fig. 2. As this type of T-joint is common in all plastic projects, it is worthwhile to make an adjustable jig like the one shown in Fig. 9. The dimensions are not critical and the sawcuts across the base serve as guide lines when positioning the work. A portion of the center of the movable top piece is routed out to provide a finger hole. This hole is helpful when cementing small pieces, as can be seen from Fig. 8. The corner jig, detailed in Fig. 12, is used as shown in Fig. 11. The rabbet in the guide strip prevents the cement from sticking to the wood.

ABOVE, CEMENTING HANDLE ON BOX LID WITH T-JOINT JIG DETAILED BELOW

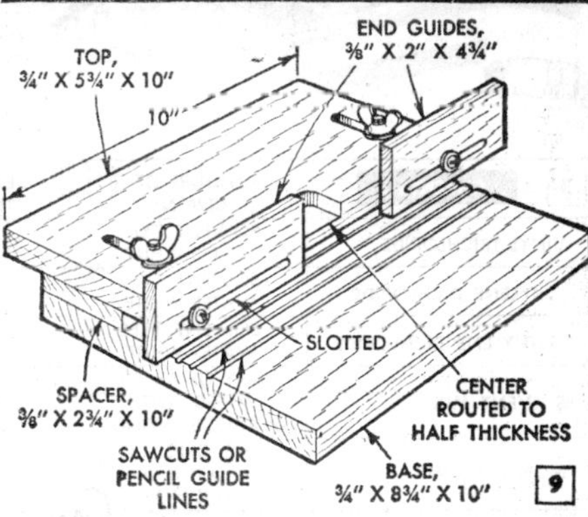

Because the cement has no body and will not cover unless the joint is in good contact, the work to be cemented must have close, smoothly fitted joints. Joints direct from the saw (hollow-ground planer blade) are satisfactory, as fine saw marks will vanish completely if the joint is perfectly cemented. Joints finished with 80 or 100 grit sandpaper also are satisfactory, but care

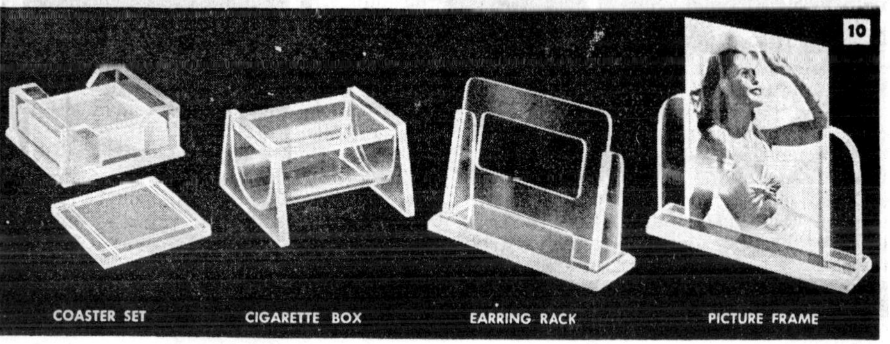

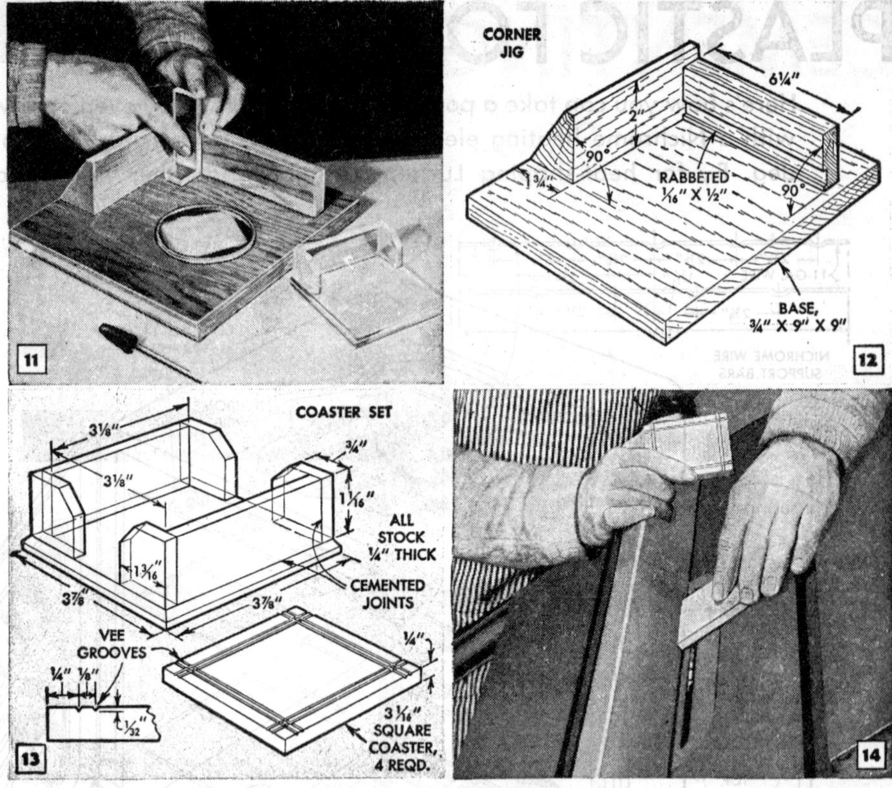

must be taken not to round off the corners.

Fig. 4 shows the usual faults of plastic joints, poor contact being the most common one when pure solvent is used. An accurate-fitting joint, and dipping the work three times and immediately fitting it, will eliminate this fault. It is important that the plastic edge carry all the cement possible. For this reason, all joints should be made with the cemented piece vertical and with the second piece flat and horizontal, as in Fig. 6, as more solvent can be carried on a horizontal joint without danger of runover. The bubble fault is common with heavy cements but rarely occurs with pure solvent. Crazing, which consists of hairline cracks at the joint, usually is caused by too much pressure at the joint or by use of certain solvents, such as acetone. Runovers are common if you use any type of thick cement made by dissolving a small quantity of plastic shavings in a solvent. The thicker the mixture, the more likely you are to apply too much of it to the joint, thus resulting in runover of the excess. Thick cements are not used with the dipping technique, but are handy for brush application on some types of joints. However, work of this kind should be clamped very tightly. The perfect joint is absolutely clear with a slight runover of cement all the way around.

In addition to the cements listed in Fig. 3, acetone and glacial acetic acid are solvent-type cements which can be purchased at almost any drugstore. Both do fairly good work except that acetone is somewhat too fast and liable to craze, while acetic acid is slow drying and tends to corrode and etch the polished surface around the joint, thus spoiling the appearance.

The coaster set, dimensioned in Fig. 13, makes an excellent project in plastic cementing. Use the dip application of solvent cement for all joints, assembling the ends first. The assembled sides can be dipped one end at a time. Remember to get the work thoroughly wet, shake it lightly to remove any excess cement and assemble immediately. If a drop of solvent should accidentally fall on the work, do not rub it. If rubbed it will smear, but if allowed to remain untouched, it will dry and disappear with little damage to the polished surface. Fig. 14 shows how the vee grooves in the coasters are cut on a circular saw.

PLASTIC FORMING OVEN

Here's how you can take a portable (on-the-stove type) oven and wire it with a Nichrome heating element to produce temperatures up to 800 deg. F., for heat-shaping Lucite, Plexiglas and other thermoplastics

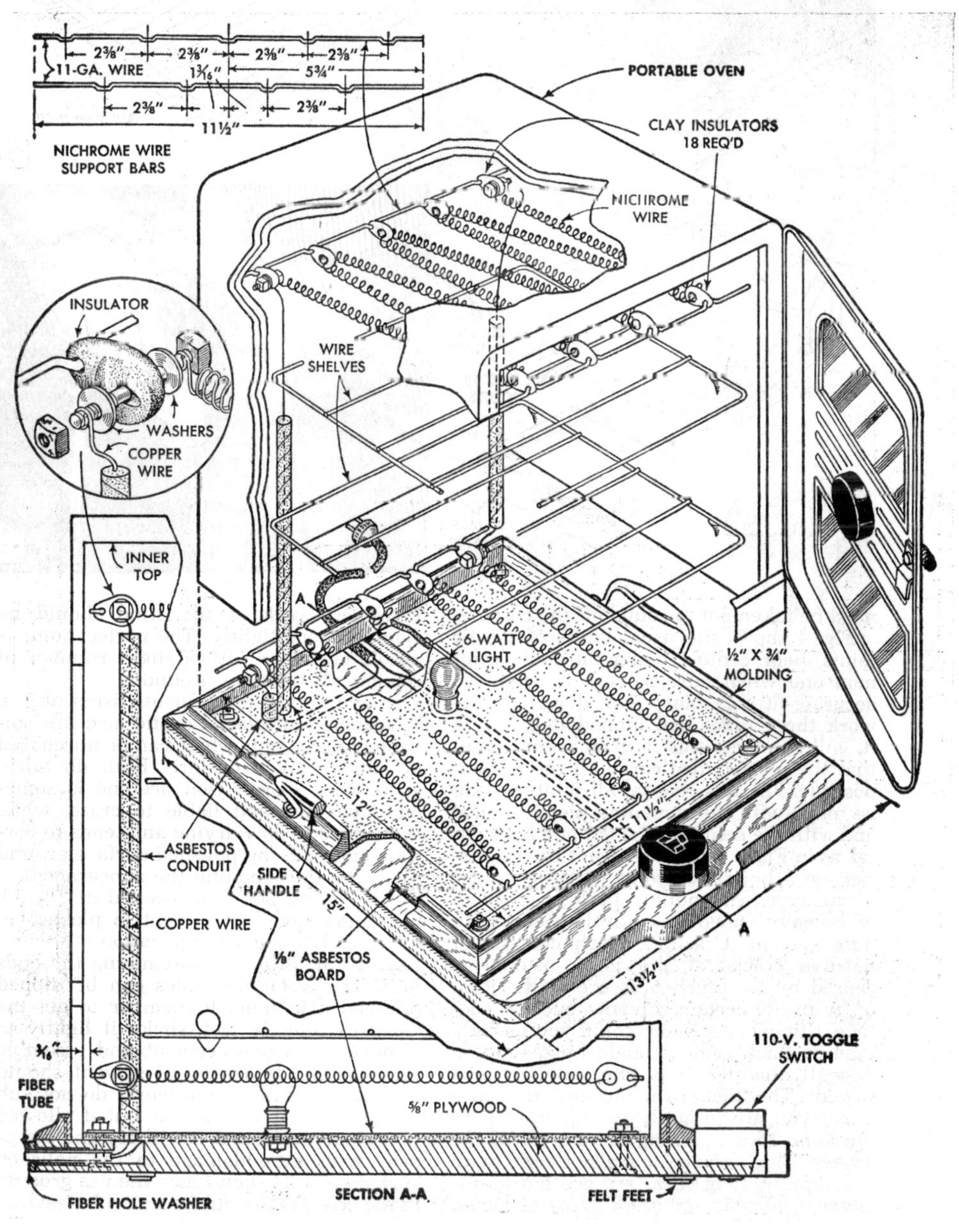

FORMING thermoplastic material into novelties, bracelets and other useful articles requires a suitable oven in which to heat the work to make it pliable. While an ordinary kitchen oven can be used for this purpose, you can furnish your shop with a neat little electric unit by purchasing a portable oven of the type used on top of a kerosene or heating stove and wiring it with an element as shown in the cutaway drawing in Fig 2.

The oven itself is not altered except for installing four element-support bars on the inside above and below the oven shelves. The bars are shaped of 11-ga. wire according to the detail at the top of Fig. 2, and are threaded with insulators before being installed. Suitable insulators can be molded of ceramic clay and fired, or you can buy aviation-type antenna insulators, sometimes called "egg" insulators. Note that the end insulators on the rear bars are fitted with small bolts for connecting the 110-volt line. The Nichrome heating element required is removed from the cone core of a regular heater element of 250-watt size and threaded through the insulators in the manner shown in Fig. 2.

The oven sets on an asbestos-covered base within a wood molding bordering the edge, but before the asbestos sheet is fastened to the base, the bulb-and-switch wiring is first installed as indicated by the dotted lines in Fig. 2. Use asbestos, heat-resistant fixture wire for this, and insulate the socket from the wood base. You have a choice of wiring the elements either in series or in parallel as shown in Fig. 1. In series, a temperature of approximately 285 deg. F. is had; in parallel, the temperature is increased to 800 deg. With the higher temperature the thickness of the asbestos board covering the wood base must be increased to provide adequate insulation. Conduit encasing the wires connecting the two elements is formed by wrapping strips of asbestos paper around the wires to build up a thick insulation as shown. Heating thermoplastic material requires 5 to 10 minutes, depending on the thickness of the plastic and the nature of the work. When heated, the material becomes almost as flexible as rubber and can be bent by hand.

1 CLAY INSULATORS

Plastic
PLANT TRELLISES

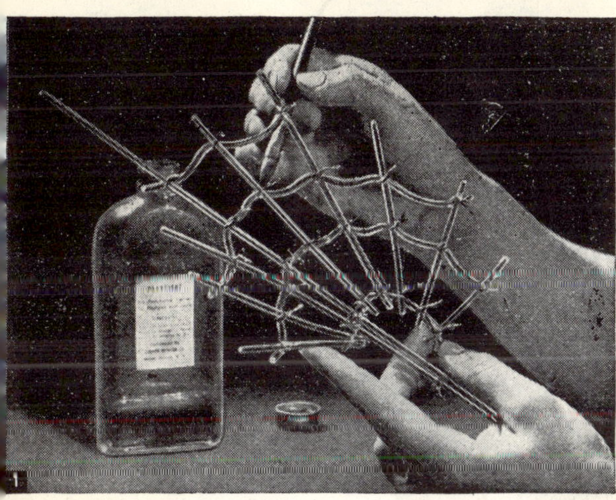
1

EASILY made in a short time, these plastic plant trellises are ideal for small house vines. One-eighth-inch thermoplastic rod is used and it can be formed in one of two ways. Fig. 2 shows how one section at a time is heated and then bent. However, for more intricate shapes, such as Fig. 3, a template is used. This is double corrugated cardboard with a design drawn and cut into the board. The lines should be about 3/16 in. wide. The heated rod is pressed into the pattern for forming. After the rods are formed, tie them together with light copper wire and place a drop of quick-setting cement at each point where there is an intersection, Fig. 1. With a little practice this can be done quite easily and the cemented joint will not show. Allow plenty of time, at least 30 minutes, for the cement to set before the wire is removed. By doing this, you will be sure of strong joints.

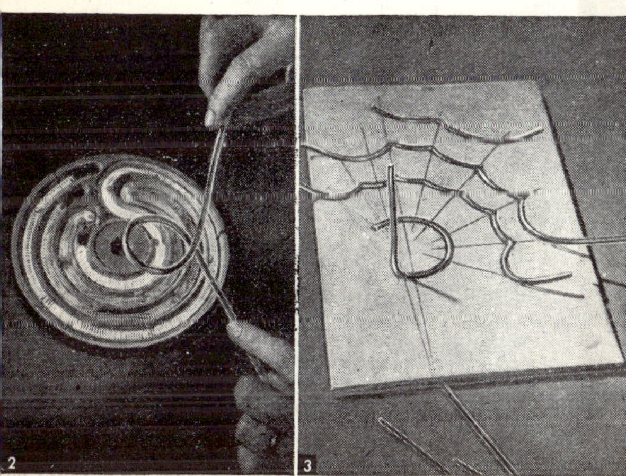
2 3

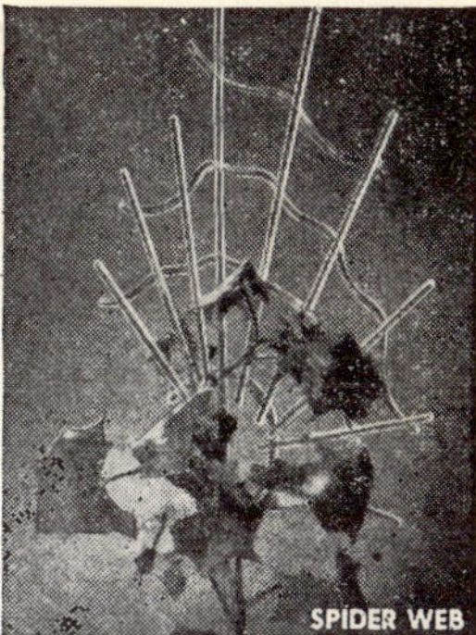
SPIDER WEB

CATTAIL

SCROLL

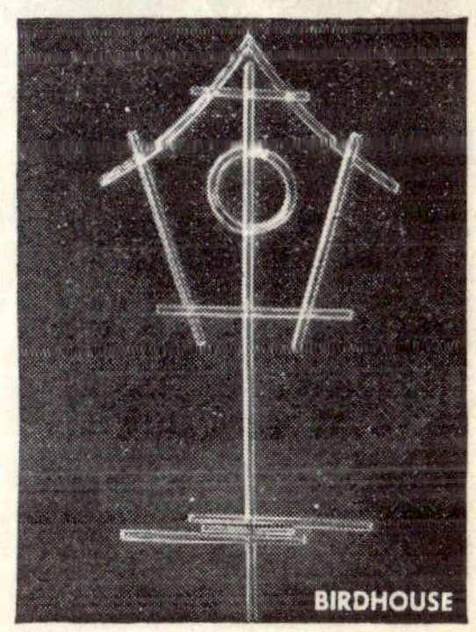
BIRDHOUSE

The plastic is made pliable by placing it in an oven set at 250 deg. F. When pliable, the plastic is handled carefully with gloves

PLASTIC

Humidor-and-pipe rack: The humidor, Fig. 2, is a cylinder formed from a sheet of heat-forming crystal plastic, $\frac{3}{16}$ x $4\frac{1}{2}$ x $13\frac{1}{4}$ in. Forming is done by heating the sheet until it is pliable, Fig. 1, and then rolling and placing it in a forming jig to cool. The jig consists of a piece of sheet metal held in cylindrical form by two pieces of plywood cut out to slip over each end, Fig. 3. When the plastic has cooled, it is removed from the jig, the two ends are coated with cement (ethylene dichloride) and held together a few moments until the cement sets. Then the plastic is again placed in the jig and wrapped with cord until thoroughly hardened.

The cylinder is cemented between two flat pieces of plastic. The top one is drilled for pipestems and an opening is turned in its center to suit the

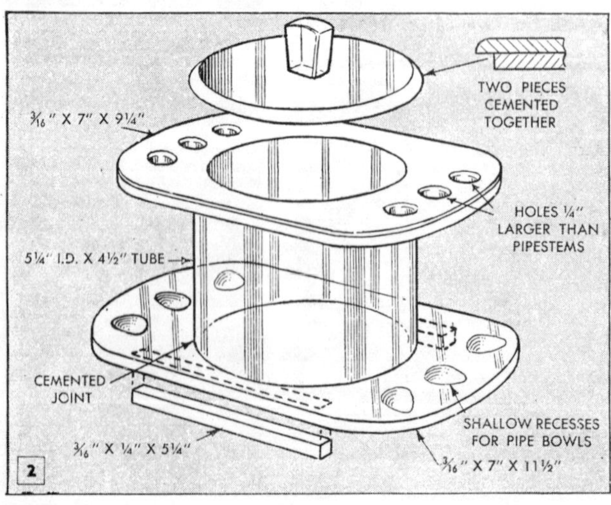

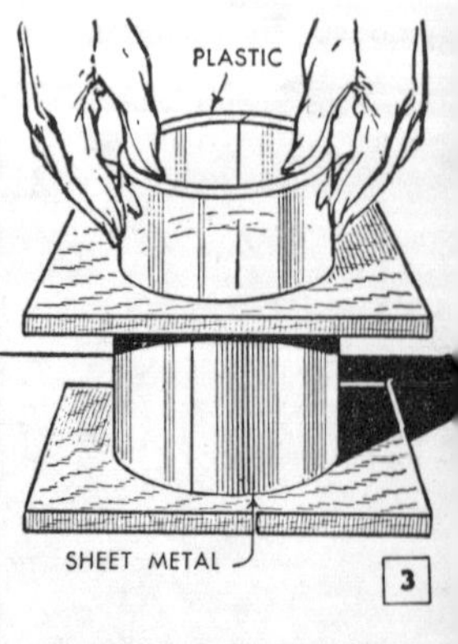

The pliable plastic is rolled to a cylindrical shape and placed in a sheet-metal mold to cool. As it cools, the plastic sheet will expand and conform to mold

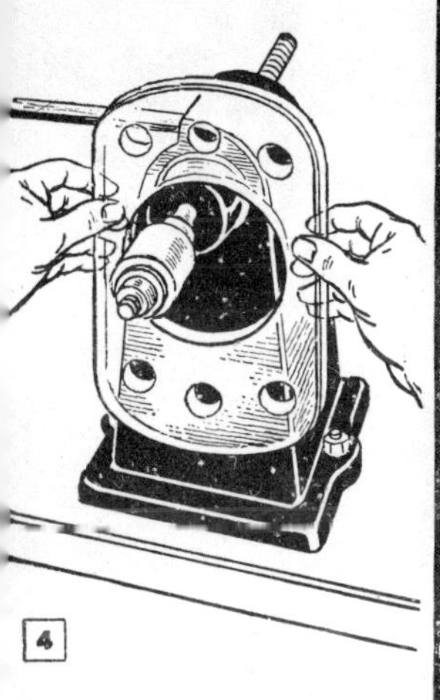

4

Internal edges of the plastic are polished with a felt spindle-type buffer attached to polishing head. The buffer is charged with rouge

PROJECTS

inside diameter of the humidor cylinder. The edges of the holes are polished as in Fig. 4, and shallow depressions for the pipe bowls are formed and polished in the top surface of the bottom piece with a hand grinder. Two strips are cemented to the bottom of the base to provide feet.

Chip-and-card holder: Wells for the chips are cut from standard tubular stock of the proper size. A groove is cut across the back of each tube near the top to receive the handle, and a finger slot is cut in the front of each tube. The wells are cemented to two separate pieces which are spaced apart and, in turn, cemented to a base piece to form a track for two playing-card containers. Note, Fig. 5, that shallow depressions are first filed in the edges of these pieces under the chip wells. These provide finger grips for removing the chips.

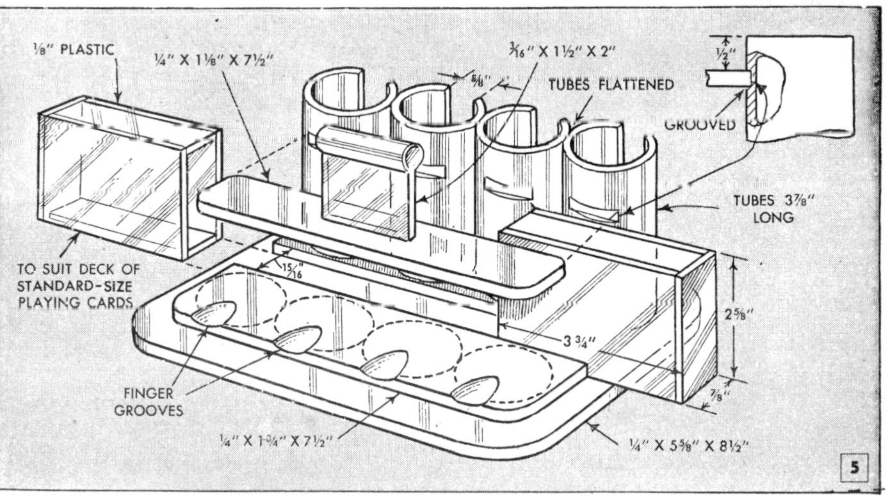

5

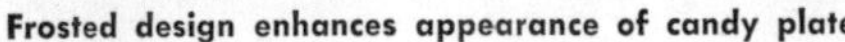

Frosted design enhances appearance of candy plate

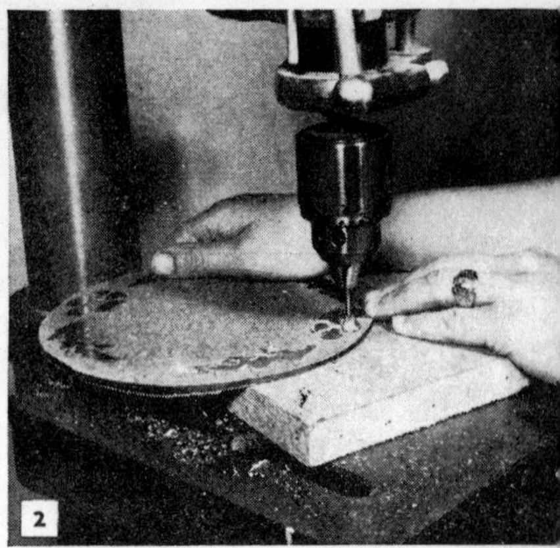

Routing plastic with small burr gives frosted effect

FROSTED CANDY PLATE AND JEWEL BOX

HERE ARE TWO quickie projects that utilize transparent plastic to the best advantage. The circular candy plate, Fig. 1, is entirely of plastic and features an unusual frosted design, while the jewel box, Fig. 6, is an attractive combination of clear plastic and pieces of select hardwood.

To make the candy plate, cut a 7-in. disk from 1/8-in. plastic, leaving the protective paper covering intact. Lay out the design on the paper covering according to the squared pattern, Fig. 3, and cut through the paper around the outline of the design with the point of a knife. Peel off the paper

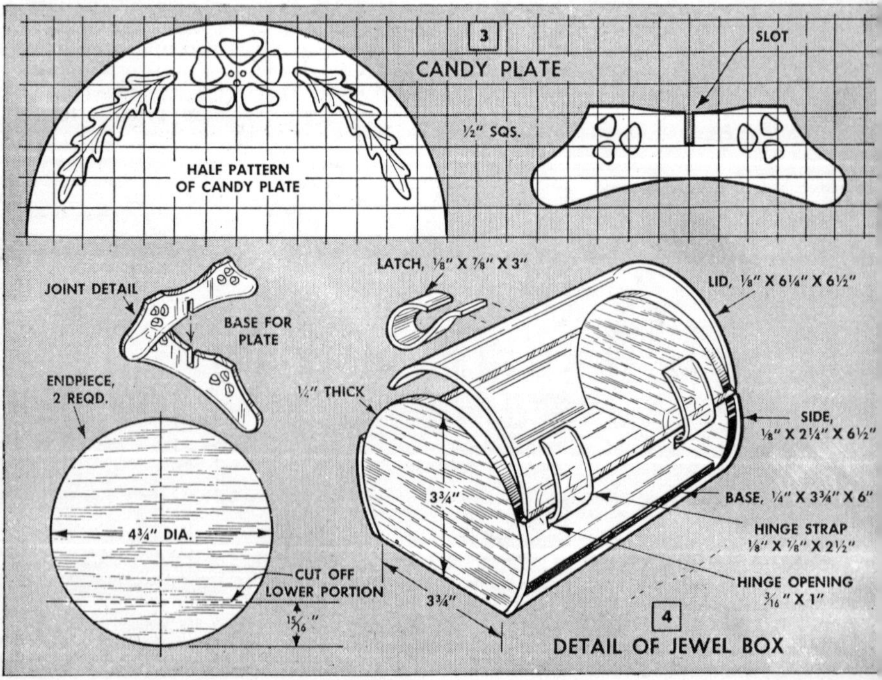

3
CANDY PLATE
1/2" SQS.
HALF PATTERN OF CANDY PLATE
SLOT

JOINT DETAIL
BASE FOR PLATE
ENDPIECE, 2 REQD.
4 3/4" DIA.
CUT OFF LOWER PORTION
15/16"
LATCH, 1/8" X 7/8" X 3"
LID, 1/8" X 6 1/4" X 6 1/2"
1/4" THICK
SIDE, 1/8" X 2 1/4" X 6 1/2"
3 3/4"
BASE, 1/4" X 3 3/4" X 6"
HINGE STRAP 1/8" X 7/8" X 2 1/2"
HINGE OPENING 3/16" X 1"
3 3/4"

4
DETAIL OF JEWEL BOX

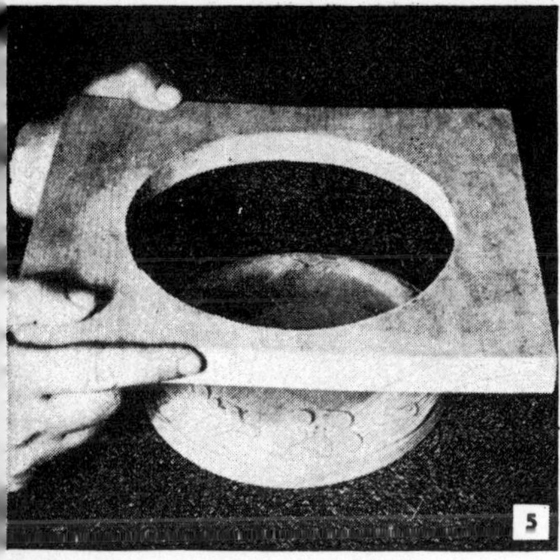

Left, plate curved by pressing plastic over wood form. Right, jewel-box lid is held closed with friction latch

to expose the areas to be frosted. Use a small flat-bottomed burr to frost the design, Fig. 2, and after frosting, vein the leaves with a fine grinding tool or a dentist's drill. The plastic is dished with the aid of a two-piece wooden form as in Fig. 5. The bottom of the form consists of a 6½-in. disk, one face of which has been rounded in the lathe. The top makes use of the waste stock from which the disk was jigsawed and is used to press the edges of the plastic over the form. To soften the plastic, remove the protective paper and heat the disk until pliable in an oven set at 250 deg. F. The two leg units are cut out as shown in Fig. 3. Be sure that the radius along the top edge of the legs matches the curvature of the plate. The legs are half-lapped and cemented to the underside of the plate.

Begin making the jewel box by cutting the ends and bottom from ¼-in. hardwood. The ends are disks with the lower portion cut off as in the left-hand detail, Fig. 4. The sides and the lid of the box are cut from ⅛-in. plastic and the lower edges of the sides are beveled so they are flush with the bottom of the box. One side of the box is slotted for plastic hinges. The parts are heated and shaped by bending around the box ends, Fig. 7. It is best to protect the hands with cotton gloves or cloth when doing this. After the sides have been cemented to the ends and bottom, the hinges are bent to fit through the slots, Fig. 8, and cemented to the lid. With the lid in the closed position, the latch is formed so it serves as a friction catch against the front side of the box, and it is then cemented to the center of the lid, the lower portion overhanging the front edge as in Fig. 6.

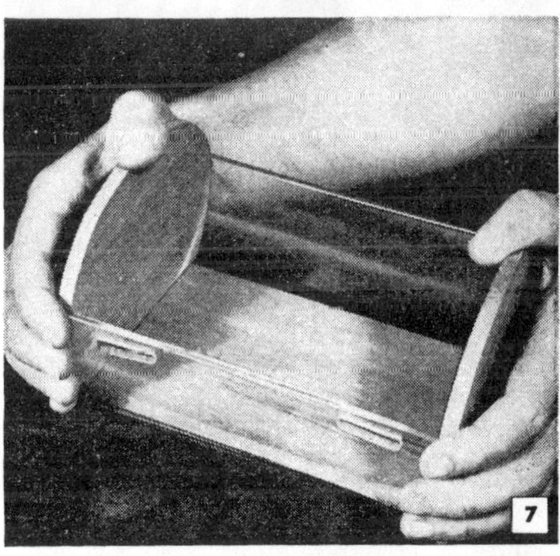

Above, plastic sides are heated, formed around ends of the jewel box and cemented to the edges of the wooden parts. Below, hinges are bent to engage slots cut in rear side of box and then cemented to lid

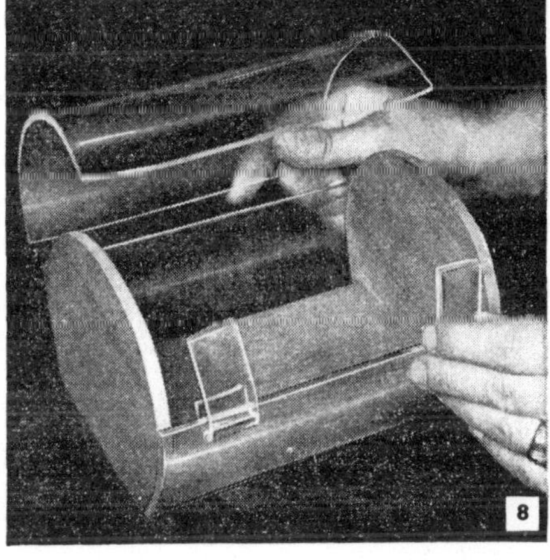

CHESSMEN IN PLASTIC

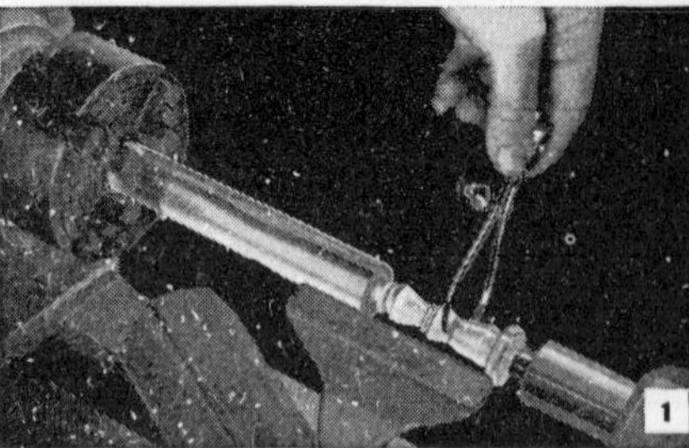

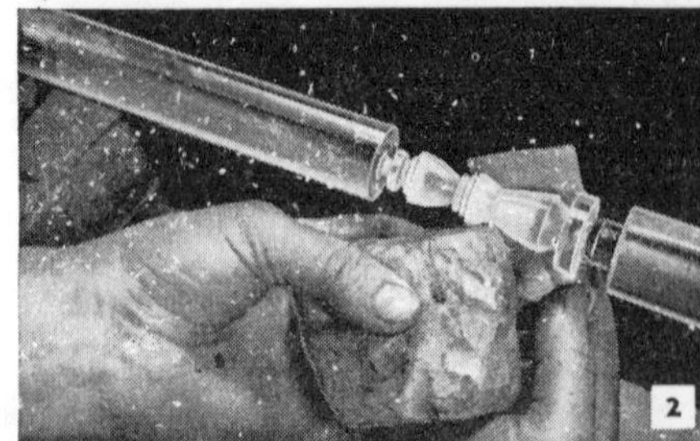

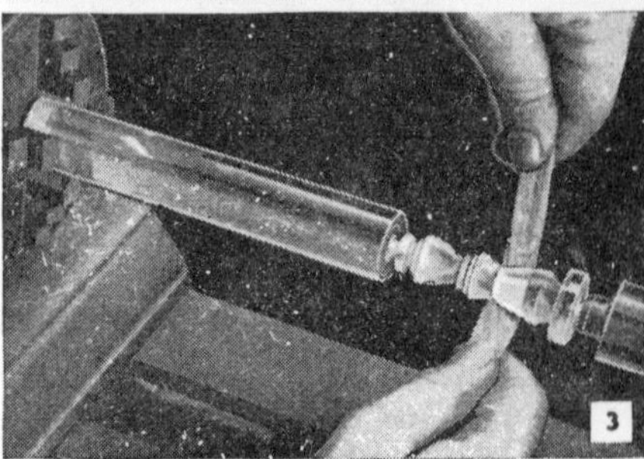

TURNED and carved from crystal-clear plastic, these distinctive chessmen are ideal for your own use or as a gift that will compliment the skill of any chess enthusiast. One set is left the natural color of the plastic and the other set is stained red. The chessmen generally follow the Staunton design, the kings, which are the largest pieces, being 3 in. high, and the pawns 1¾ in. high. All pieces are turned from 1-in. transparent plastic rod.

When turning the plastic, it is a good idea to form the base of the piece at the tailstock end of the rod. In this way, there is a minimum waste of plastic, as the hole made by the tailstock center is in the base of the piece and the entire length of the rod thus can be utilized. The work can be centered accurately by mounting one end of the rod lightly in the lathe chuck and bringing the tailstock against the other end. The chuck jaws are adjusted in or out so the tip of the tailstock center is in the exact center of the end of the rod. Cardboard templates for all pieces except the knights aid in turning the work to the correct proportions. These are made by using a half pattern of each design, following the squared pattern in Fig. 7. Calipers are employed to check the contours of each piece, Fig. 1, and, by the combined use of templates and calipers, the corresponding pieces can be turned to identical size.

After the turning is completed, each piece is polished in the lathe before it is cut from the rod. To do this, hold jewelers'

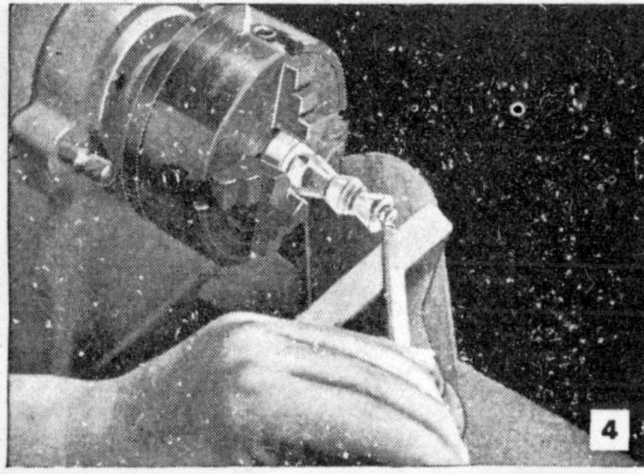

rouge against one side of the rotating piece and hold a dampened cloth pad against the other side, as shown in Fig. 2. This wet-polishing method will quickly produce a high luster on the surface of the plastic. With the piece still rotating in the lathe, it is given a final polish by holding a strip of soft cloth against it as illustrated in Fig. 3.

When the piece has been polished, it is cut free from the rod with a parting tool. Then, after removing the rod stock from the chuck, the base of the piece is chucked in the lathe and turning of the top portion is finished, Fig. 4. This is polished while the piece is still in the chuck. Then the work is reversed end for end in the chuck and the base is turned slightly concave, as in Fig. 5, so the piece will not tip easily. When chucking polished pieces, protect the surface in contact with the jaws by wrapping it with heavy paper. Give the pieces a final buffing or polishing by hand.

Now, square the crosses on the kings' crowns by sawing them flat on two sides and then polish. Carve the tops of the queens and castles (rooks), as shown in Fig. 7, and cut a slot in the top of each bishop. If available, use hand-grinder burrs for carving, chucking them in a drill press instead of a hand grinder to leave both hands free to manipulate the work.

When making the knights, turn the upper portions roughly to shape and finish-turn the bases. Then, saw away the surplus stock on the upper portions so the sides are flat and about ⅜ in. thick. Lay out the profile of the figure on one of the flat sides and saw it out. If a jigsaw is used for this purpose, a piece of wood must be laid between the saw table and the underside of the flat surface of the work to hold the piece level with the table, Fig. 6. When

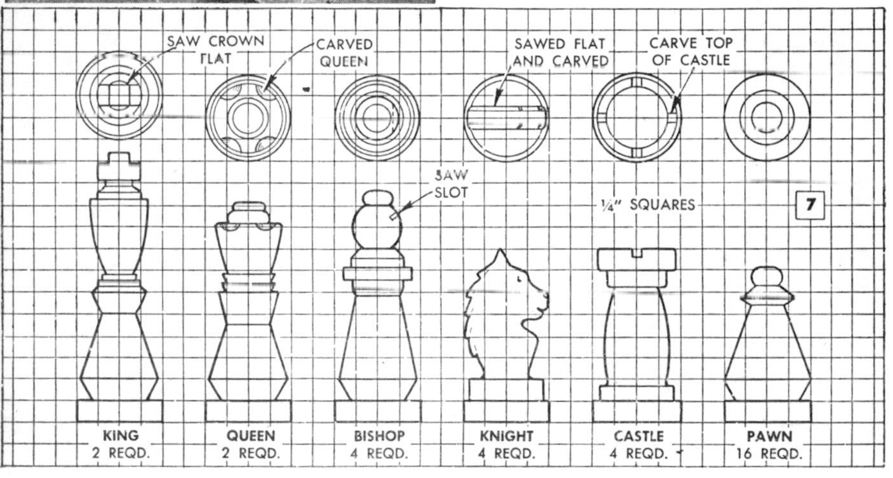

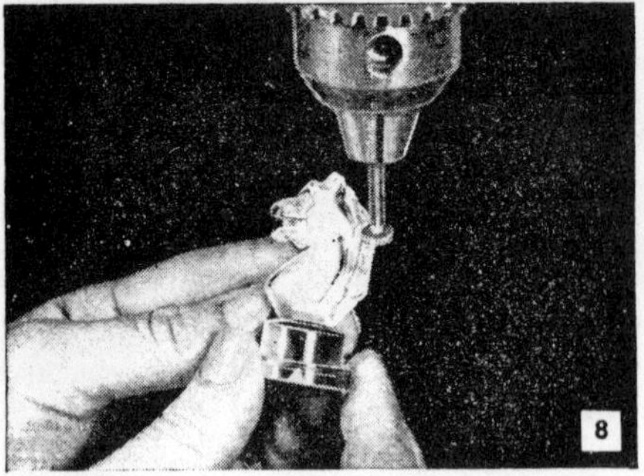

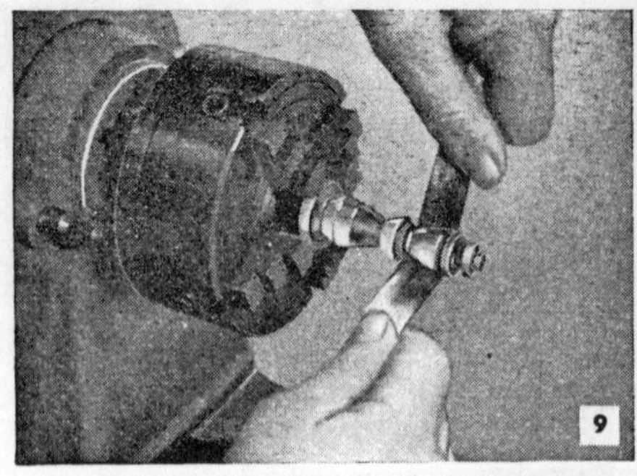

sawing the pieces, it is best to use a skip-tooth blade or a blade having widely spaced teeth. The saw should be run at slow speed to avoid overheating and possible melting and distortion of the plastic. The carving of the knights is also done with hand-grinder burrs chucked in a drill press, as in Fig. 8. As the knights cannot be chucked in the lathe for polishing, they are finished with a buffing wheel charged with buffing compound.

After all the pieces have been polished, one set must be stained to distinguish it from the other. An easy way to do this is to mount the pieces to be stained in a lathe chuck, remembering to protect the polished surface from being marred by the chuck jaws. Then the stain is applied to a soft cloth which is held against the piece as the latter turns in the lathe, Fig. 9. The pieces are reversed in the chuck to complete the staining. This method, of course, cannot be used for the knights, and the stain must be rubbed in them by hand. Applying the stain in this way does not produce a deep color, but rather a pale tint that is especially attractive in plastic. If deeper shades are preferred, the pieces may be stained by immersing them in a dye bath until a particular depth of color is attained. Although red stain was used for one of the original sets and the other was left clear, any desired color or color combinations may be used.

Plastic Cigarette-Package Holder Will Decorate Desk

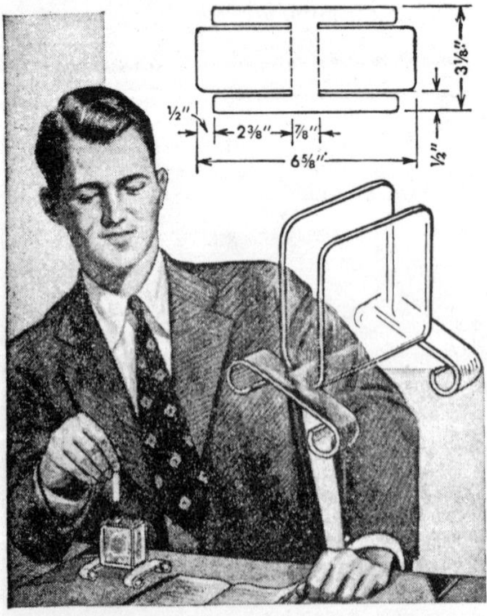

Made from ⅛-in. sheet plastic, this holder will keep cigarettes from spilling over the desk. Cut the material with a fine-tooth hacksaw and round off the corners with a file. Then smooth the edges with fine sandpaper until no cutting or filing marks are visible. Heat the plastic in an oven and bend to the shape illustrated. A ⅞-in. strip of wood is used as a form to bend the sides and the curved feet are bent around a dowel. Gloves should be used to handle this material after it is removed from the oven. After bending each strip, fasten with masking tape to hold it in place. It may be necessary to reheat the plastic and repeat the bending process.

Screws Held in Plastic With Cotton

If you find it difficult to assemble plastic parts with screws because they cause the material to chip or break around the holes, try this method of doing it. Drill holes in the plastic for the screws, then soak cotton in solvent and fill each hole with the cotton. When the screws are driven into this, they will form threads in the cotton which will harden and hold the screws securely.

PLASTIC SIGNS

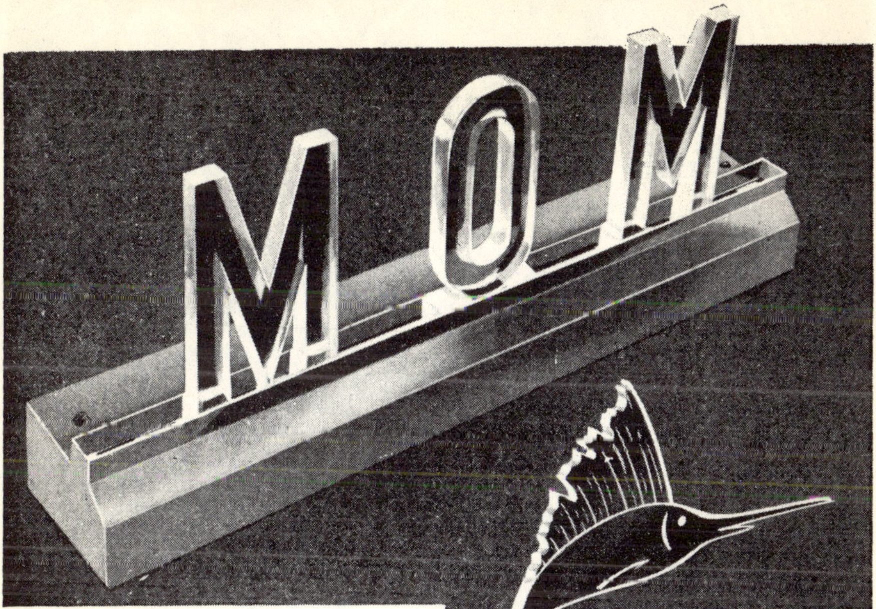

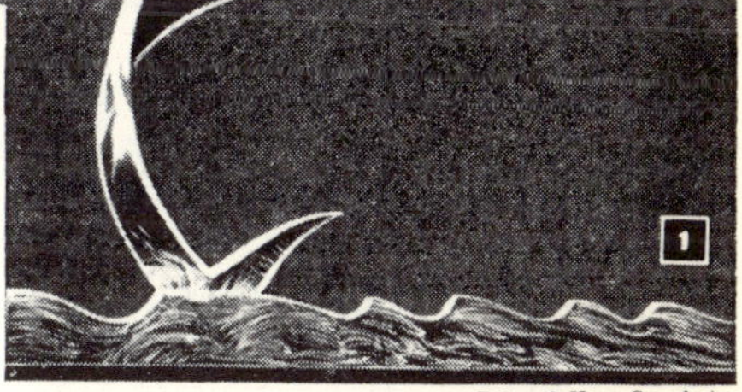

UNUSUAL and striking effects in lettered signs and displays are obtained by skillful use of the light-transmission and deflection properties of transparent plastics. These are both light and strong, and are good electrical insulators. They are readily formed by heating and can be engraved, etched, stained and painted. Properly finished, these plastics possess qualities of light-transmission, dispersion, reflection and refraction equal to those of fine-quality optical glass, Figs. 1, 2 and 3.

1

Rohm & Haas Co. photos

In the top sign a fluorescent bulb concealed in a slotted metal base gives the striking edge-lighting of the plastic block letters. In the lower design, light is "piped" through the curved body of the sailfish to the fin where it brilliantly outlines the edge

2

LIGHT-DIRECTING PROPERTIES OF PLASTICS

3

LIGHT TRANSMISSION AND REFLECTION

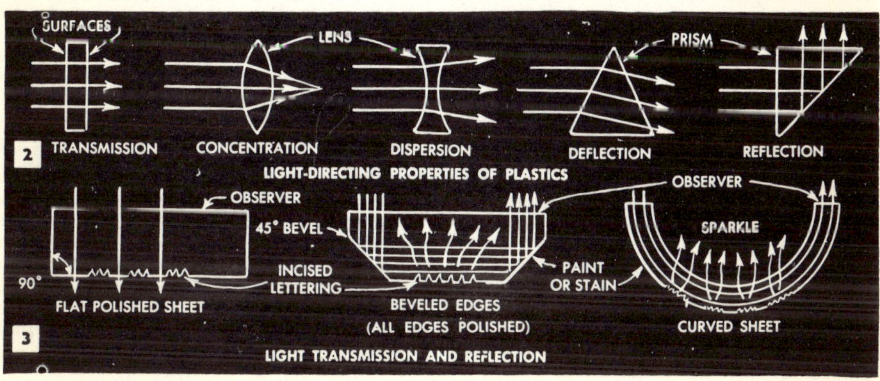

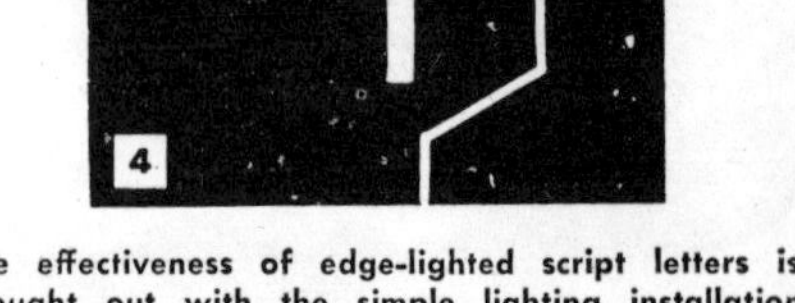

The effectiveness of edge-lighted script letters is brought out with the simple lighting installation shown in the detail above. The letters are inserted

SCRIBED, OUTLINE LETTER

BLOCKED IN BY CROSSHATCHING

ROUTED TO AN EVEN DEPTH

PAINTED, GILDED, LUMINOUS PIGMENTS, ETC.

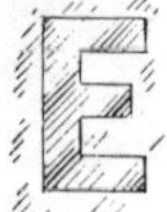

TRANSPARENT OVERLAY CEMENTED TO VENEERED BACKGROUND

FROSTED BY ETCHING OR SANDBLASTING

ENGRAVED OR CARVED

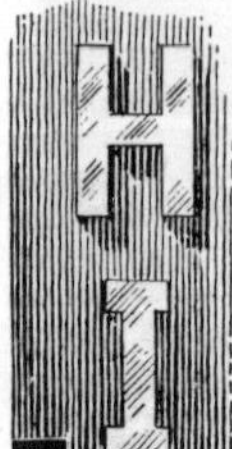

FORMED LETTERS INSERTED IN OPAQUE BACKGROUND AND LIGHTED FROM BACK

COLORED PLASTIC INLAID IN TRANSPARENT OR COLORED BACKGROUND

5

For signs which are to be viewed either by diffused artificial light or daylight, the most useful effects are those which result from internal reflection within the plastic itself. If the sign is made from a transparent plastic having parallel faces and square polished edges, and the design, or lettering, is applied to the side away from the observer, practically all of the incident light is transmitted directly through the plastic itself. If the back edges are beveled or the piece is curved, light entering from the front or the edge will, by a series of internal reflections, make the sign appear to have a brightly luminous border. Applied or incised lettering will stand out with greater brilliancy. If the reverse surface is either stained or painted, the color also will be picked up and transmitted to the eye. Light-directing effects are limited by conditions which must be carefully observed in order that the incident light will be internally reflected. Light cannot be successfully "piped" around a curve having a radius less than three times the thickness of the material or through angles greater than 48 deg. from the vertical without most of the light escaping from the surfaces of the plastic, Fig. 9. Light also will escape wherever the polished surfaces are scratched, abraded or painted. Such applications or incisions will appear brightly illuminated.

Sharper effects are obtained by the edge-lighting method shown in Fig. 1, where the letters are illuminated by a

Block letters cut from colored plastic can be inlaid in transparent plastic or inserted in openings cut through. Hard board or sheet metal can also be used

fluorescent bulb concealed in a metal base which is slotted for the letters. Fluorescent lights are preferred to incandescent bulbs for small, unventilated signs as they radiate less heat and provide continuous light for illuminating the edges of thin plastic sheets.

Signs employing this edge-lighting effect should have the top edges of letters or designs painted white and the sides and bottoms highly polished. In Fig. 4 the plastic script letters are inserted in slots cut in the background to a depth equal to the thickness of the plastic. The edges of the slot preferably should be lined with black felt or other light-absorbing material.

As it is only necessary to interrupt the passage of light through the polished surfaces of the plastic to make lettering stand out, sign-makers employ methods of etching, engraving and abrading suggested in Fig. 5. Another simple method of inlaying letters of colored plastic is detailed in Fig. 6. Colored block letters also can be inlaid or inserted in hard board or sheet metal. The letters are laid out and jigsawed in the same manner as the design shown in Fig. 7. In Fig. 8 letters are painted directly on the reverse side of the transparent plastic by using a stencil. The top coat is applied first and this is followed by one or more ground coats. The process is the reverse of normal painting procedure. Incised lettering and carving also can be stained and the cavities filled with plaster.

Using a simple stencil, block letters can be painted on the reverse side of a transparent panel or figure outline. Apply the top coat first, then ground coat

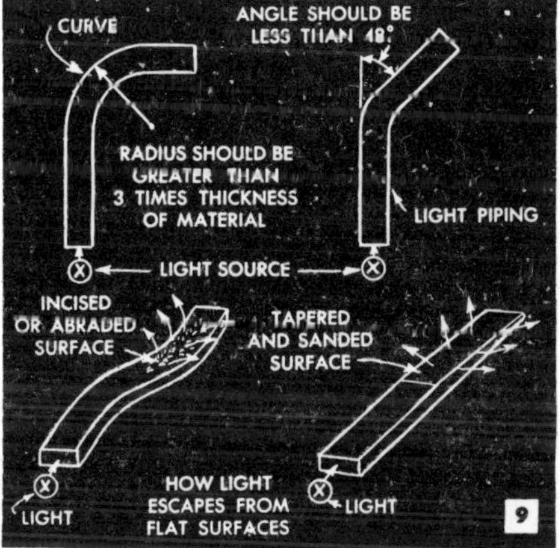

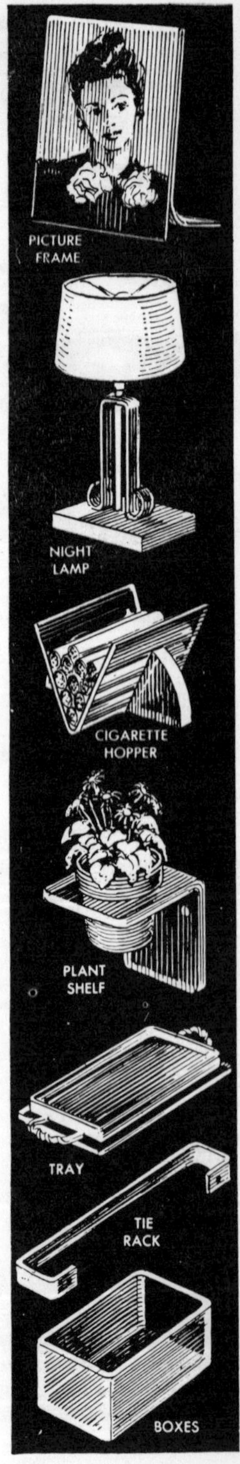

PLASTIC TECHNIQUE

AT a temperature slightly higher than boiling water, thermoplastic materials become almost as flexible as a sheet of rubber and can be bent or twisted by hand to almost any shape. After cooling for a few minutes, the plastic will retain its new shape. This pliability of thermoplastics permits them to be used in making many attractive articles which would be difficult or impossible to do otherwise.

Heating: The kitchen oven is an ideal heater. The temperature should be held to between 220 and 300 deg. F. Many stoves are equipped with thermostatic gas control, but it's not advisable to depend on this. Best practice is to turn the gas as low as it will go, which usually will give an oven temperature of about 250 deg. The plastic sheet or strip can be placed directly on the oven grid, as shown in Fig. 1. Very small pieces can be supported on a sheet of asbestos paper, wood or other material. The protective masking tape is removed from the plastic before placing it in the oven. The work should be kept clean—any dirt or an undried film of water will tend to bake into the plastic. Heating requires 5 to 10 minutes, depending on the thickness of the plastic and the nature of the work.

Peg forming: One of the simplest methods of forming is to bend the heated plastic over a suitable arrangement of wood pegs, as shown in Fig. 4. Soft cotton gloves should be worn for hand comfort and also to prevent finger marking the hot plastic. The hotter the plastic is, the more pliable it will be, but it also will pick up marks more readily from any rough surface. It is good practice to wave the hot plastic sheet in the air for a second or two after removal from the oven. This will give it a

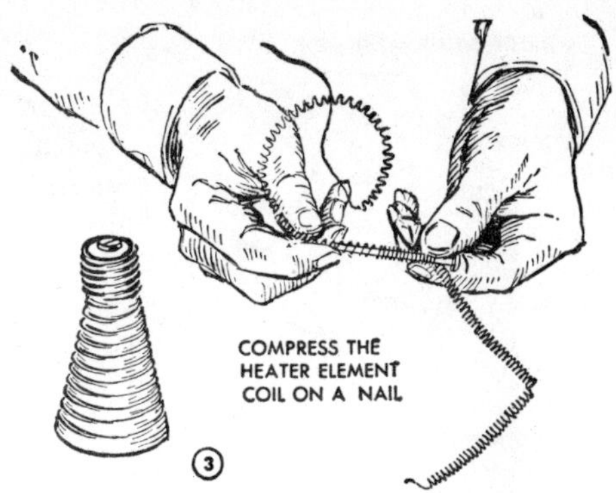

measure of surface hardness to withstand marring during handling but will not decrease its flexibility to any great extent. Whenever practical the pegs should be covered with felt or linoleum to provide smooth contact.

Strip heater: Some articles require heating only at certain points, the remainder of the plastic being retained in its original sheet form. For work of this kind, some type of strip heater is required. Fairly good results can be obtained with a heater element, as shown in Fig. 6. A better device, shown in Figs. 7 and 8, can be made from an asbestos shingle and a heater element. The heater element is unwound from its original core and then compressed on a nail, as shown in Fig. 3. It will be a bit long after compressing, making it necessary to jog two of the porcelain tubes through which it is fitted, as in Fig. 7. Of course, the heater could be made longer, but the one here is based on construction from a single 12 by 24-in. asbestos shingle. It is not practical to make the element shorter, as it will become too hot.

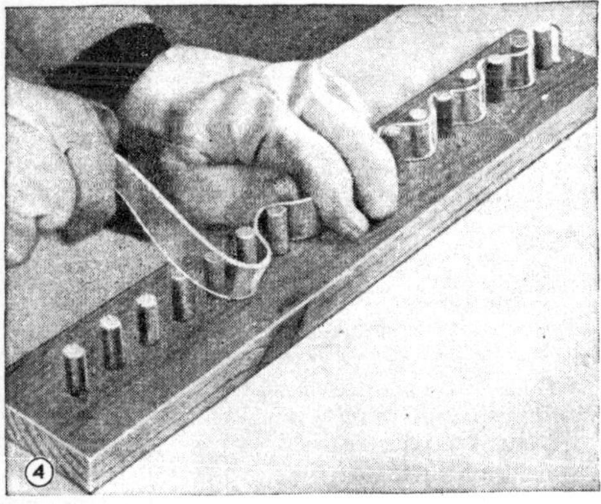

Soft cotton work gloves should be worn to protect hands and prevent finger marks when handling the hot plastic

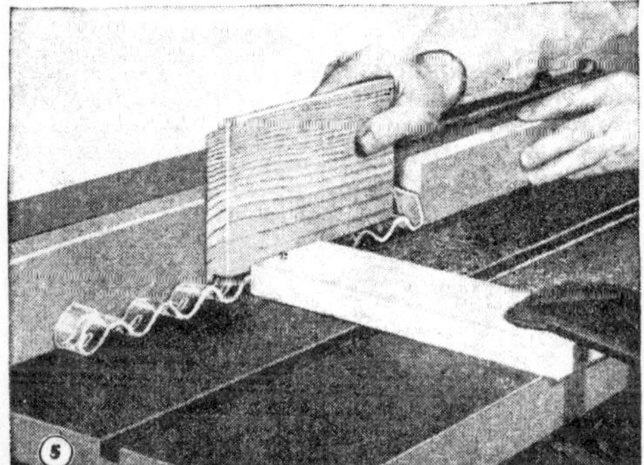

As a safety precaution, use a hold-down and pusher blocks when machine-sawing grooves in small pieces of plastic

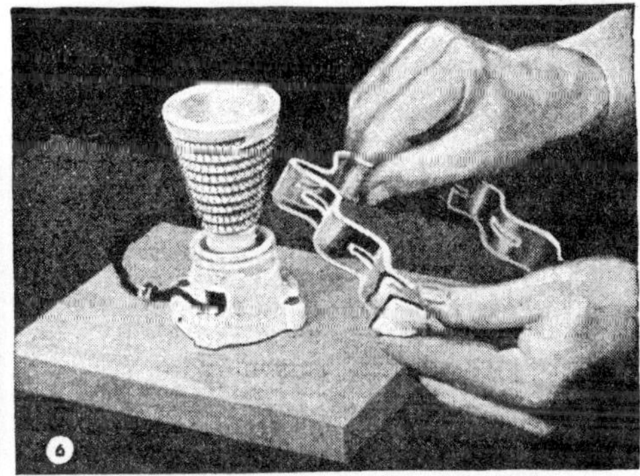

Localized heating for secondary bends can be provided by a heater element. Gloves need not be worn

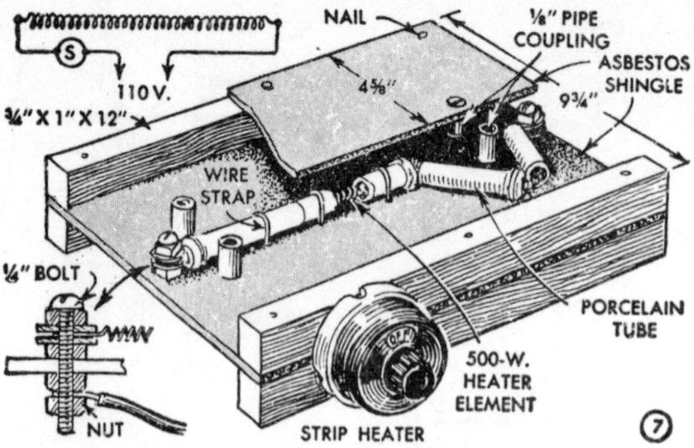

NAIL
1/8" PIPE COUPLING
ASBESTOS SHINGLE
110V.
4 5/8"
9 3/4"
3/4" X 1" X 12"
WIRE STRAP
1/4" BOLT
PORCELAIN TUBE
500-W. HEATER ELEMENT
NUT
STRIP HEATER
7

Many projects require only corner bends. The electric spot-heating device shown above concentrates heat only where the bend is to be made, permitting sharp corners to be formed as shown at the right

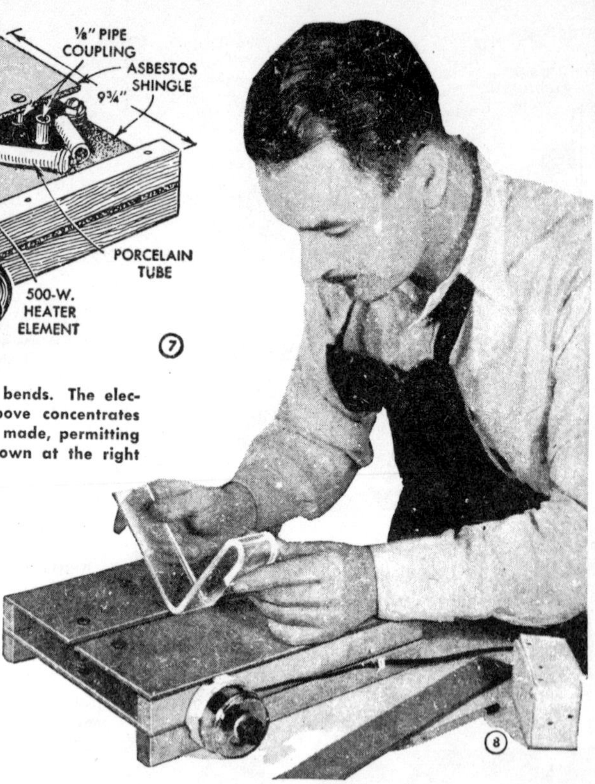

8

Twists: Ropelike twists are formed freehand after heating the plastic all over in an oven. A spring clothespin attached to each end facilitates bending, as shown in Fig. 10. The pins can be clipped to the plastic immediately after removal from the oven, or the clothespins can be attached before placing in the oven. In any case, the pins will mark the plastic slightly. The marks, being at the ends, can be cut off if objectionable.

Flat-strip forms: The flat-strip form is the most common jig for bending plastic strips. A typical example is the bud vase, Fig. 13, which is bent as in Fig. 12. Note that the end curve is pressed down with a cloth-padded wood block. Another example is the pin-up lamp shown in Fig. 15. The form for this, Fig. 14, has a groove to hold the starting curve and the balance of the work follows the line of the form with the final curve being held by a wood block. No pressure is required at any time in the bending of thermoplastics; the only purpose of the form is to supply the correct shape. Sanded wood forms are used.

Sometimes more complicated forms are cast in plaster. Complicated jigs are not

Attractive ropelike twists are formed easily by hand after the plastic has been heated in an oven

Simplified forming jigs can be made by driving nails into boards and padding them with bands of folded newspaper

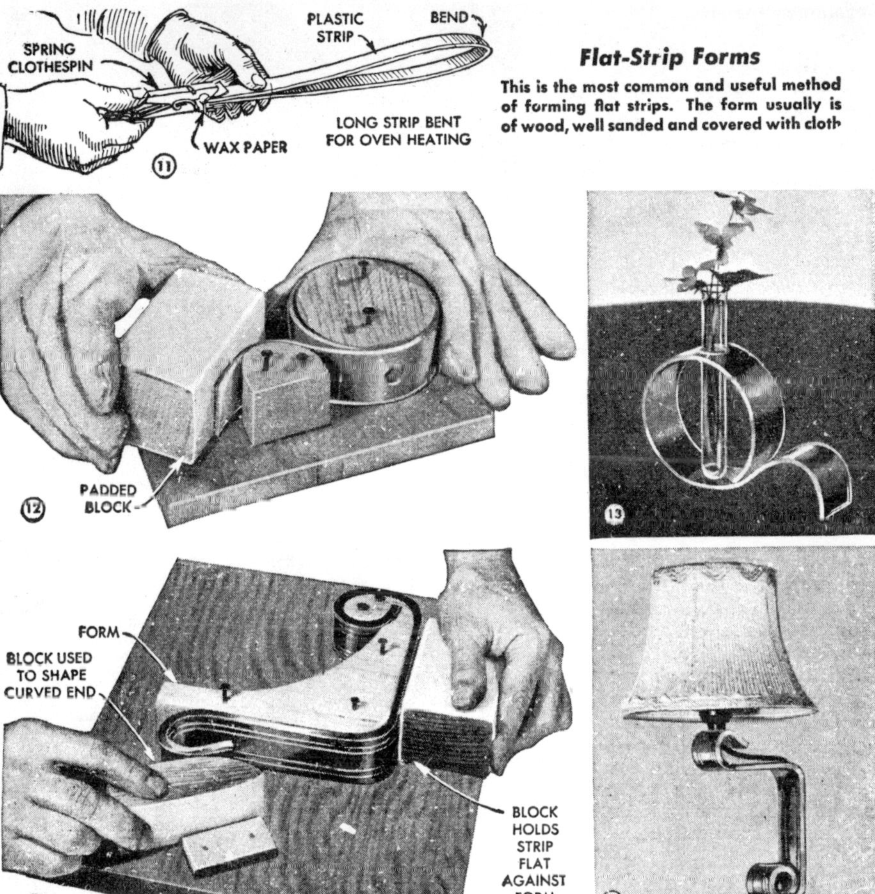

Flat-Strip Forms

This is the most common and useful method of forming flat strips. The form usually is of wood, well sanded and covered with cloth

shown here but it will be apparent that certain projects requiring long strips and many bends will demand some ingenuity in making a form which will provide the proper shape and permit rapid working. In some instances, the strip required will be longer than can be accommodated in the oven. In this case, apply heat locally at the center of the strip and then clip the ends together with a spring clothespin, using waxed paper at the joint to prevent sticking, as shown in Fig. 11.

Half-cylinder form: The best method of working this much-used bend is illustrated in Figs. 16 and 18. The form should be a bit deeper than the work requires and should be covered with soft cloth, such as outing flannel. The forming ring is made to fit snugly over the combined form and plastic, as can be seen in Fig. 17. This method is particularly suited for production work. When a single piece is being made, the form alone is sufficient, the plastic being formed by hand, as in Fig. 19, or by means of cloth-covered wood blocks which are pressed against the work. If the curve is not a complete half circle, the "sprung" method of forming, Fig. 20, is useful. All you do here is snap the hot plastic sheet in place between the retaining side pieces.

Machine operations: Bent plastics pose a problem as to whether machine operations should be done before or after bending. In some projects such as the bud vase, Fig. 13, and lamp, Fig. 15, the necessary holes can be drilled after the piece is formed. Craft workers favor this method because it permits exact placement of holes. The form itself can be used in most cases as a holding device and base block. Production workers favor doing machine work while the plastic is "in the flat." This

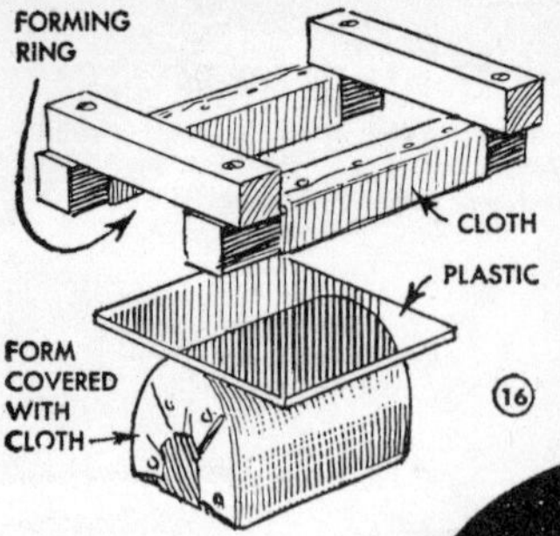

FORMING RING
CLOTH
PLASTIC
FORM COVERED WITH CLOTH
16

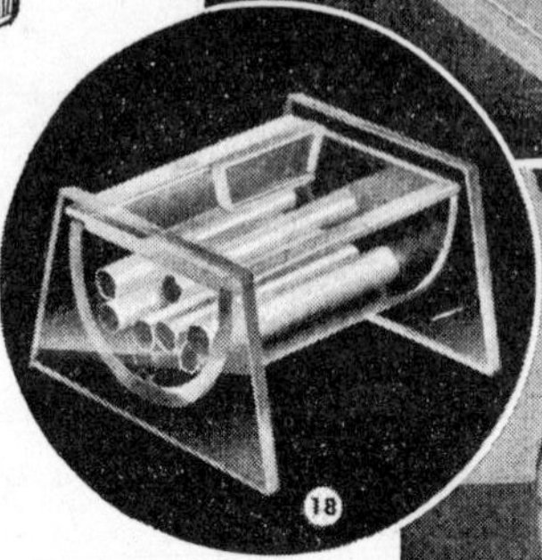

Half-Cylinder

This type bend is used for many projects. Cleanest method of working is with forming ring. Two other methods also are shown

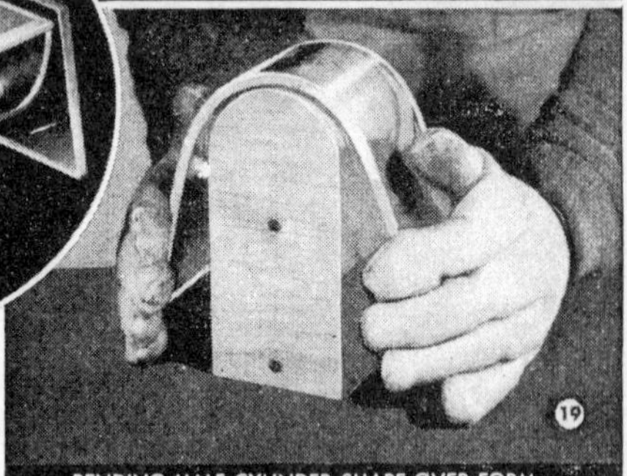

17 RING METHOD OF FORMING HALF CYLINDER

18

19 BENDING HALF CYLINDER SHAPE OVER FORM

20 "SPRUNG" METHOD GIVES GOOD RESULTS

method demands an initial bending of the piece to determine position of machine cuts. Once the right setup has been made, the work progresses quickly and accurately on repeat work. On pieces like the picture frame, Fig. 2, there is no choice but to machine the slot for the glass after the bends have been made. However, if the full frame shape is bent, it will be difficult to make the cut. Hence, the best practical solution is to bend the piece in a continuous strip, as in Fig. 4, after which it can be slotted, Fig. 5, and finally brought to the required shape by local heating and bending, as shown in Fig. 6.

Stretch forming shallow forms: Shallow three-dimensional forms such as curved crystals for clocks are best worked with

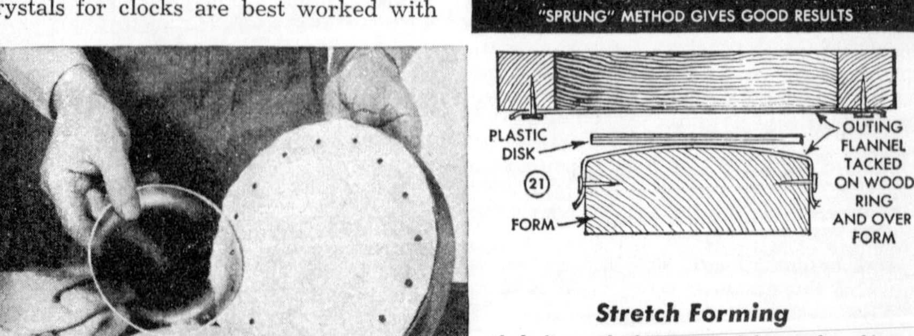

Stretch Forming

Cloth-ring method is most useful way of working and does perfect work on moderate curves. Form must be covered with cloth to prevent marring

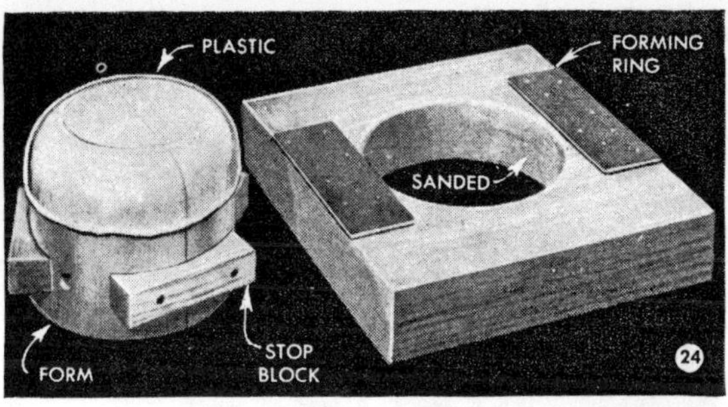

Stretch Forming Deep Forms

A close-fitting wooden ring permits drawing to about 1½ in. in a 5-in.-diameter dish. "Wrinkled" edge is later cut off by mounting form in lathe as shown below

the cloth-ring method shown in Figs. 21 and 22. This method does perfect work and can be used for a wide variety of shallow forming.

Stretch forming deep forms: Deep stretch forming requires a more positive shaping device than can be obtained with a cloth ring. A typical setup for forming a dish is shown in Fig. 24. The form preferably should be covered with cloth or flocked, the latter consisting of shredded cloth applied to the wood over a sticky binder coating. The forming ring should be the exact shape of the widest part of the form, plus the double thickness of the plastic, and the starting edge of the forming ring should be sanded round to prevent tearing the plastic which is heated to a temperature slightly higher than usual and then centered over the form. A single or double layer of soft cloth is placed over the disk, after which the forming ring is placed in position and pushed down to the limits of the stop blocks. Some deformity at the edges always results, but if an inch is allowed for trimming, very deep draws can be made easily by this method. Fig. 25 shows the dish being trimmed on the lathe.

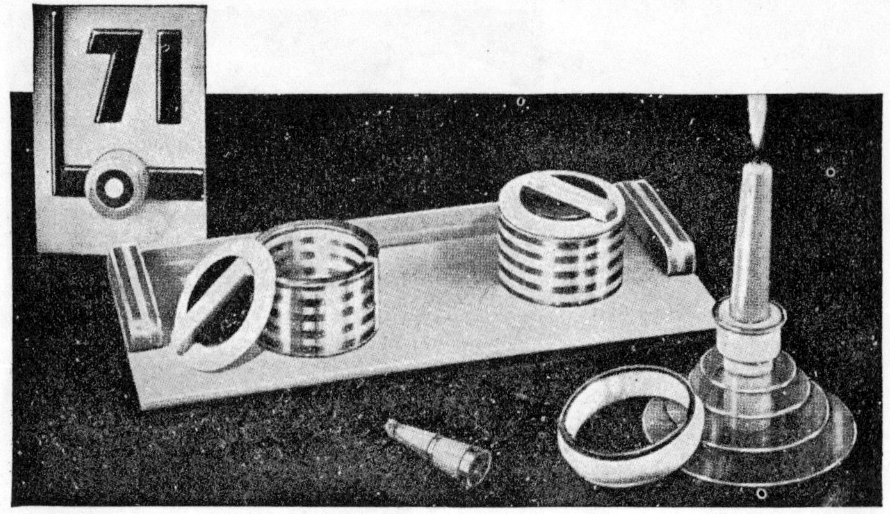

BRILLIANTLY colored plastic materials in sheet, rod and tube form can be utilized by the home shop worker in building many attractive novelties such as candlesticks, jewel boxes, clock cases, vanity powder sets, bracelets, desk sets, etc., and can also be used to good advantage by craftsmen in the construction of modern-type furniture. Plastics, which are hard, strong and have no grain, are different from either wood or metal so that the technique of working with them is also different in many ways. Yet they can be sawed, turned, carved, ground and polished with ordinary wood or metal-working tools. It is the technique of using plastics that the craftsman is primarily interested in knowing as this is, of course, the prerequisite of good workmanship. Therefore, in this article we will tell you how to handle this new material by going through the various steps in making a telephone note pad, Fig. 1, which was selected because it requires a number of different operations.

Sawing Sheet Plastic: After the telephone note pad has been planned carefully and all dimensions determined, templates are cut to the exact size of the various parts to be cut from sheet, and these transferred to the plastic stock, using a scriber. Straight, outside cuts in sheet material can be made on a circular saw. The saw blade should be well set, preferably swedge-set, and should have about 9 teeth per in. Wide setting is necessary as the material softens slightly when heated by sawing and then causes excessive friction. The saw is operated at normal speed as when cutting wood. Smooth cuts are produced if the saw is adjusted so that the teeth just barely cut through the material. Should there be any tendency for the work to heat excessively while cutting, water can be applied as a cooling medium. An inside cut is a job for the scroll saw—either hand or motor-driven. Such a cut is also needed on the telephone note pad. Holes are drilled near the corners to permit the insertion of the blade. When cutting with a scroll saw or with a band saw, select blades having about 14 or 15 teeth per inch. For all sawing operations, the work is fed slowly, cutting in the waste portion as closely to the scribed lines as possible.

Filing and Sanding: The stock is then dressed down to exact finish dimensions on the scribed lines, by using files, sandpaper, or by means of a disk or belt sander. If you use files and sandpaper on the work, it can be gripped conveniently in a vise, but in this case a piece of felt or cardboard is inserted between the vise jaws and the stock in order to avoid any mars on its surface. Ordinary files will be

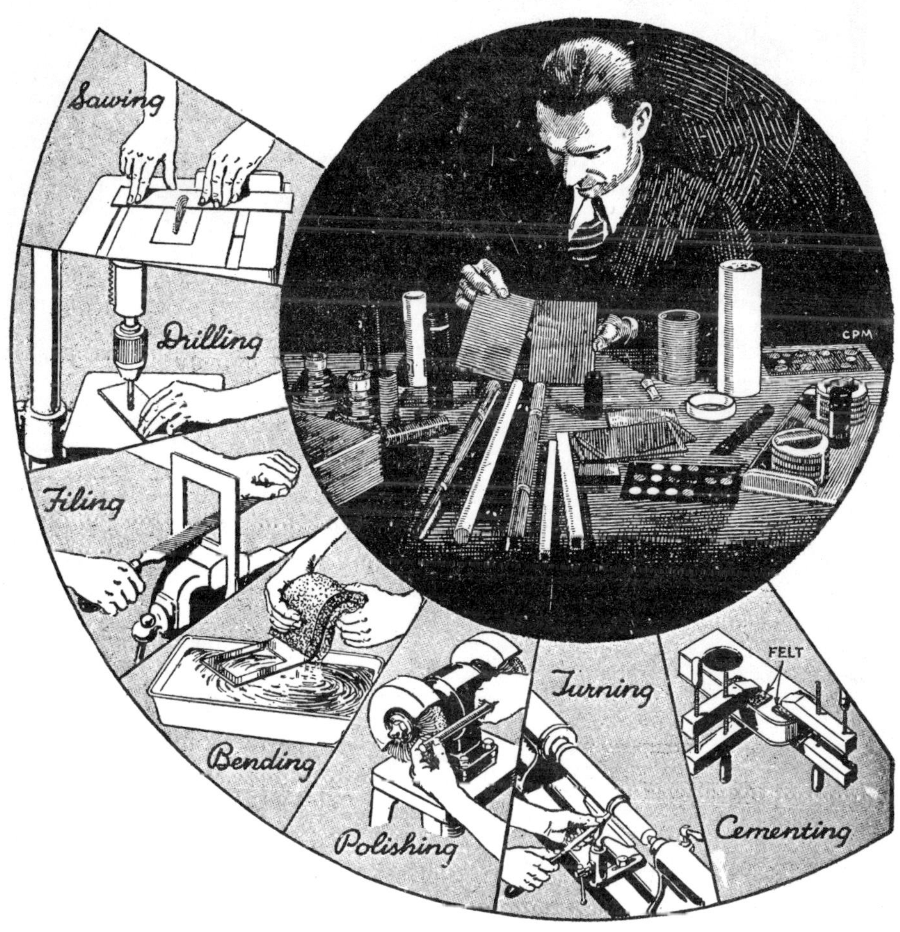

satisfactory for the purpose. The final finish to the filed edges is most readily produced with a strip of fine emery or sandpaper. It is advisable to bevel or round the sharp edges slightly to produce the best appearance and to facilitate lustrous polishing.

After the flat stock for the telephone pad has been cut and dressed to exact size, you are ready to make the pencil holder. For this purpose a 1-in. cylinder of black plastic material is cut to length as in Fig. 1. It is then sawed in half lengthwise, dressed down to a smooth finish and polished in the same manner as the sheet stock. Next, a portion of the curved surface is sanded down flat to provide sufficient area for cementing the piece in place. A disk sander will be found especially convenient for making true, flat surfaces and you can readily improvise one.

Simple Disk Sander: Figs. 3 and 4 show a simply designed disk sander which has been found efficient for dressing down small parts of plastic material. Get or make a couple of sanding disks to fit the

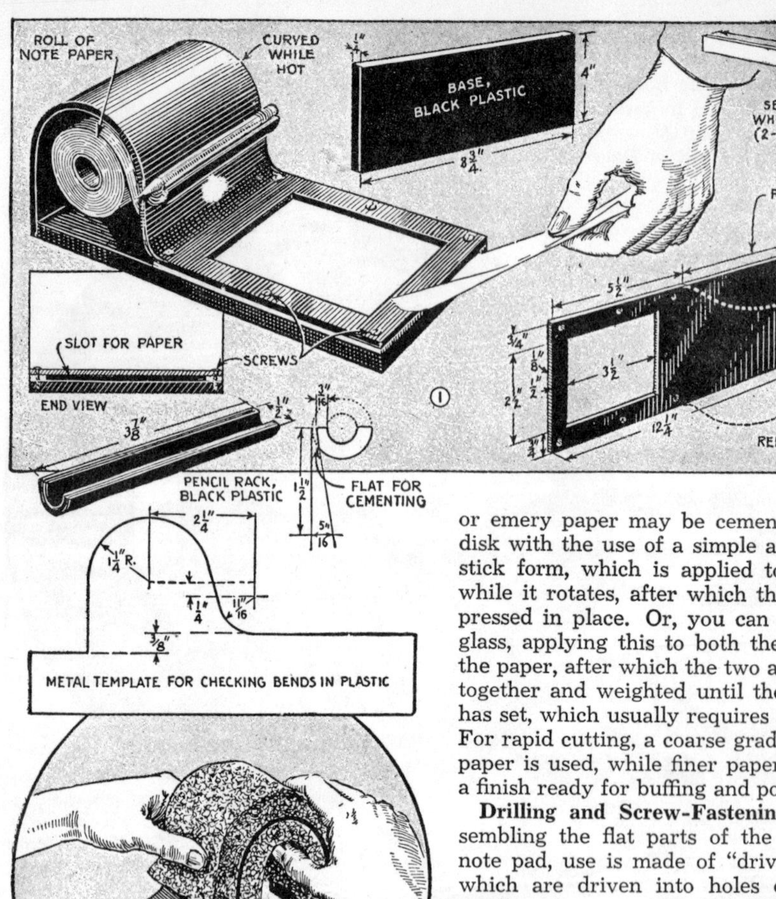

shaft of a small motor you may have on hand—a ¼-hp. motor being preferable for size. The motor is bolted to a hardwood base to which a vertical piece is attached to hold a steel thrust plate. The latter is drilled for a steel ball, which fits between it and the motor shaft, providing a simple but effective thrust-bearing arrangement. This is necessary where end pressure is brought against a motor shaft as is the case with this sander. Sandpaper or emery paper may be cemented to the disk with the use of a simple adhesive in stick form, which is applied to the disk while it rotates, after which the paper is pressed in place. Or, you can use water glass, applying this to both the disk and the paper, after which the two are pressed together and weighted until the adhesive has set, which usually requires 3 or 4 hrs. For rapid cutting, a coarse grade of sandpaper is used, while finer paper produces a finish ready for buffing and polishing.

Drilling and Screw-Fastening: In assembling the flat parts of the telephone note pad, use is made of "drive screws," which are driven into holes of slightly smaller diameter. These screws rotate while being tapped gently with a hammer and will cut their own threads. For this job it was found that suitable holes for the size drive screws used could be drilled with a No. 55 drill. The top piece, having the square cutout, is drilled at the points indicated in Fig. 1, and these holes serve as pilots to be used later for drilling the holes through the separators and base piece. Ordinary metal-working drills, preferably of the high-speed variety, should be used for drilling plastics. When deep holes are being drilled, the drill should be withdrawn from time to time to free the hole from chips, in order to prevent wedging, packing and heating. Besides the method of using drive screws, holes may be drilled for ordinary machine screws—slightly smaller than the screws.

In this case, also, the screws will cut their own threads and therefore it will not be necessary to tap the holes. Wood screws should not be used in assembling plastics as they tend to split the work.

Bending With Aid of Heat: Having all of the parts of the telephone note pad cut to dimensions, it now remains to bend the top section to conform with the curvature shown in the sketch. In order to assure accuracy in bending, it is advisable to make a sheet-metal template as in the upper detail of Fig. 2. Next, the top section of red material is placed in water heated almost to the boiling point. The entire portion to be bent is immersed. The rest of the section is kept out of the water, inasmuch as it is to remain straight. The time required to soften the plastic sufficient for bending is in this case about 5 min. For thicker sections, a longer period of immersion is required. After softening, the work is removed from the water and bent by hand while being held between two sheets of stiff sponge rubber as in Fig. 2. After the bend has been made as required to fit the template accurately, the work should be cooled by immersion in cold water. When bending plastics, it is important to remember that after the material has been immersed in hot water for a total period of approximately 30 min., the material cannot be softened again and bent by heating. When bending large sections, it therefore becomes important to plan the work in advance so that one heating only is required. For small parts where you heat them for a few minutes at a time, the work may be re-heated several times in order to produce bends which exactly meet the requirements of the project.

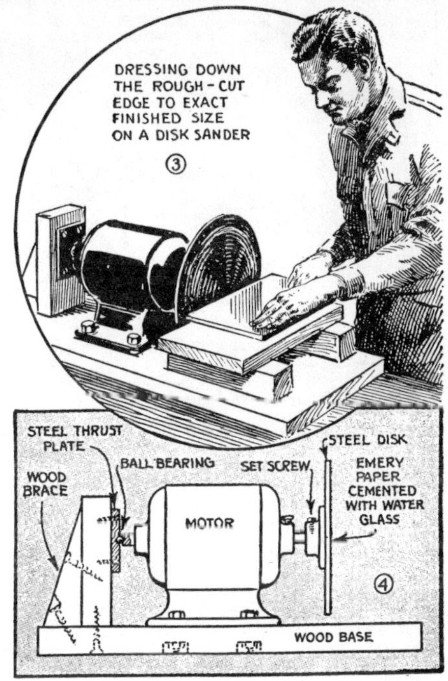

Buffing and Polishing: After the parts have been cut to shape, formed and dressed accurately to dimensions, the preliminary polish may be produced by using No. 1 buffing compound. This compound comes in stick form and is applied to a cloth buffing wheel while it rotates. Then the article is held against the wheel. The application of the first compound should continue until all of the surfaces

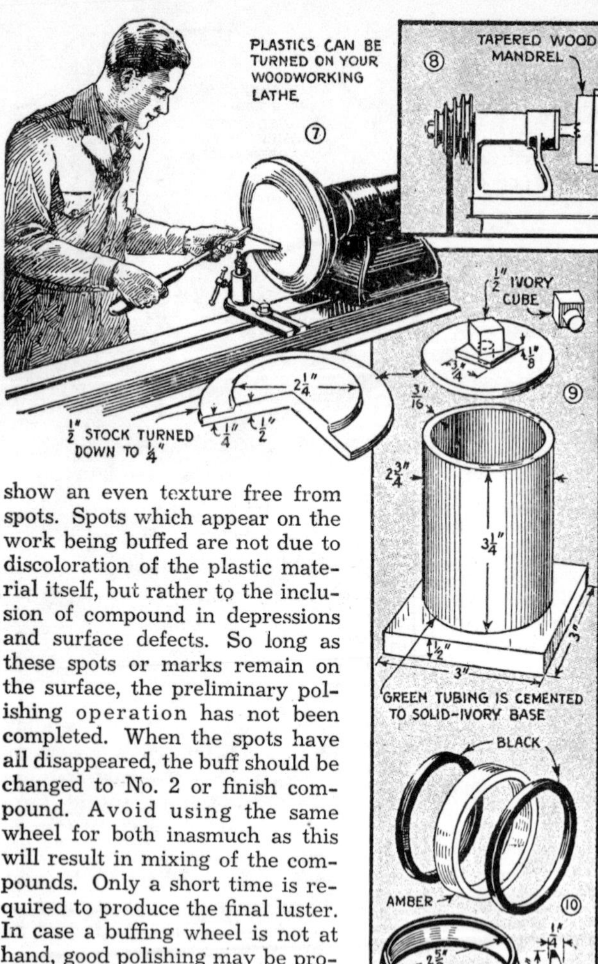

show an even texture free from spots. Spots which appear on the work being buffed are not due to discoloration of the plastic material itself, but rather to the inclusion of compound in depressions and surface defects. So long as these spots or marks remain on the surface, the preliminary polishing operation has not been completed. When the spots have all disappeared, the buff should be changed to No. 2 or finish compound. Avoid using the same wheel for both inasmuch as this will result in mixing of the compounds. Only a short time is required to produce the final luster. In case a buffing wheel is not at hand, good polishing may be produced by hand methods. For this purpose, wet abrasive paper is efficient. There are several grades available for this purpose. A coarse grade should be selected for the first operation. This is moistened with water and applied to the surface of the material. After all scratches and abrasions have been removed, the article is washed with water and the second polish produced by application of a finer grade of paper.

Cementing: After the parts to be screwed together have been assembled, it only remains to cement the pencil rack into position. For this purpose, a special type of plastic-to-plastic cement is available. This cement comes in small bottles and has a thick consistency. The best way to apply the cement, after making certain that the parts fit snugly, is to dip a small stick or the end of a match into the cement and pick up a small ball of it. The ball of cement is next dipped into ordinary muriatic acid. The cement will not harden properly unless it is treated with the acid as explained. After immersing the stick carrying the globule of cement in the acid, it is applied to the surface of the pencil holder to be cemented, spreading it over the entire surface of the holder and avoiding any excess which might be squeezed out later. Next, the pencil holder is pressed into the exact position where it is to remain. Clamps are then applied to hold it in position until set, which will require from 10 to 24 hours.

Turning: Plastic materials may be turned in any wood or metal-working lathe with ordinary wood-turning chisels. Although ordinary chisels work effectively, it has been found that chisels made from high-speed steel will last longer and are easier to keep in good condition than ordinary chisels. When a large flat section is to be turned, as would be required in the forming of a bowl, dish or lamp base, the plastic is cemented to a piece of wood, which in turn is fastened to the faceplate

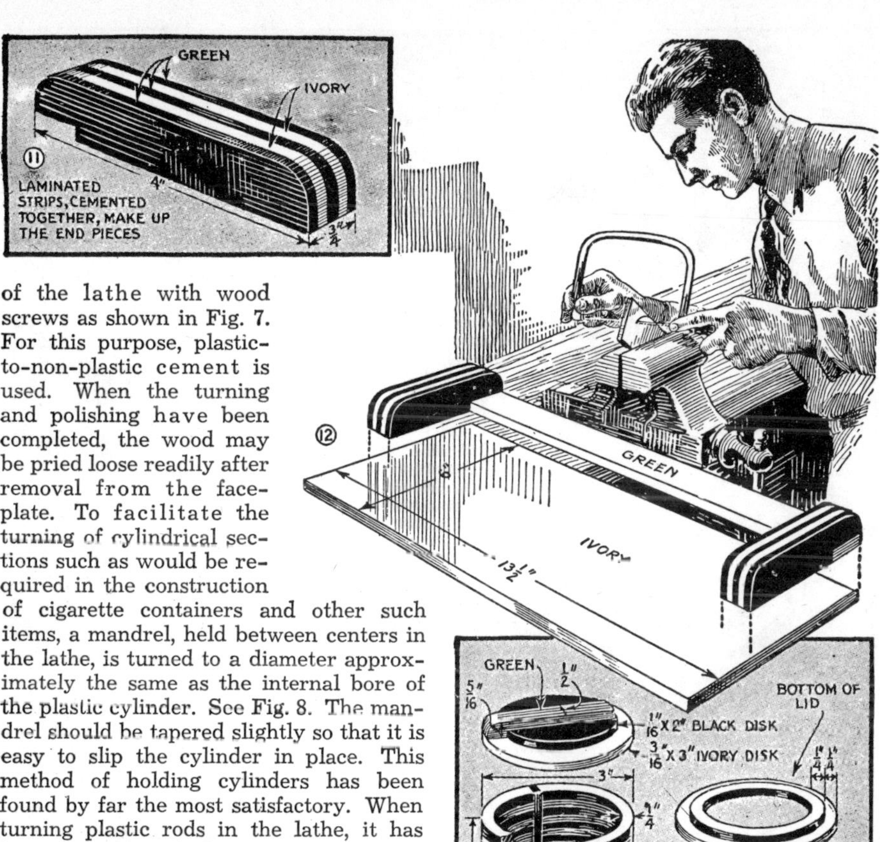

of the lathe with wood screws as shown in Fig. 7. For this purpose, plastic-to-non-plastic cement is used. When the turning and polishing have been completed, the wood may be pried loose readily after removal from the faceplate. To facilitate the turning of cylindrical sections such as would be required in the construction of cigarette containers and other such items, a mandrel, held between centers in the lathe, is turned to a diameter approximately the same as the internal bore of the plastic cylinder. See Fig. 8. The mandrel should be tapered slightly so that it is easy to slip the cylinder in place. This method of holding cylinders has been found by far the most satisfactory. When turning plastic rods in the lathe, it has been found that the best practice is to rotate them between centers in the ordinary way exactly as if they were made of wood. To prevent the tailstock center (a metal-turning center) from working too deeply into the plastic, which tends to soften under heat, it is advisable to make a small disk of sheet iron and center-punch it to correspond with the center, which is drilled in the rod to be turned. Turned plastics should be polished before removal from the lathe by applying the compound to the rotating work with a cloth.

In sharpening turning tools for plastic work, more efficient results will be had if the tools are slightly hollow ground as shown in Fig. 16. They should be roughly ground on a wheel about 2½ or 3 in. in diameter, and after the rough grind, they are finished on a wet wheel of the same diameter but made from very fine abrasive. In using wood-turning chisels, about the only difference that will be noted between working with plastics and with wood is that the speed of cutting must be reduced. The chisel should be held rigidly and applied cautiously until the proper pressure for best results has been found by the feel of the tool itself. In no case should the tool be forced nor should attempts be made to hurry beyond a reasonable working speed. If excess force is used or if the tool is dull, the material will become hot and the tool will be burned.

Grinding: Irregular slots, depressions, grooves and hard-to-form curves may be produced easily by the use of a small hand grinder, and this is also useful to remove any excess cement between corners as shown in Fig. 14. These units have a

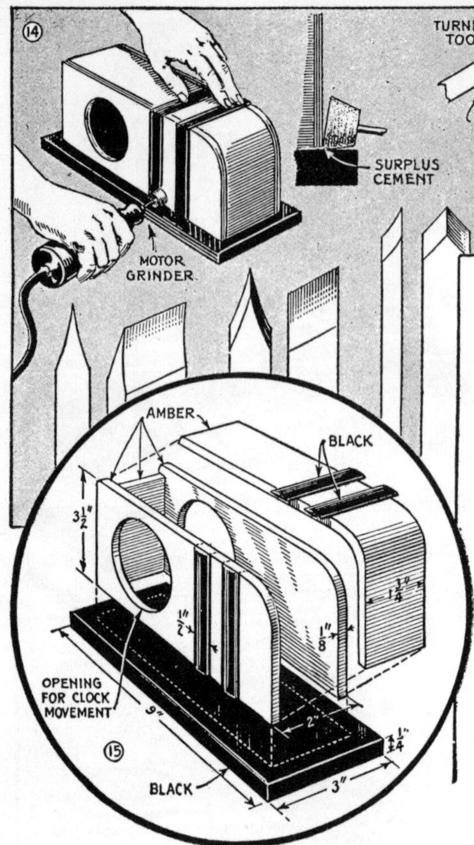

applications. A simple type of candlestick is shown in Fig. 6, while a flower vase as in Fig. 5 consists essentially of a tube and two disks. The vanity powder set shown in the photograph and detailed in Figs. 11 to 13, makes a worth-while item to tackle. Cigarette containers of many types are possible, an easy job being shown in Fig. 9. The bracelet in Fig. 10 has contrasting colors in alternate layers, cemented together and then turned. If you want a smart, modern case for a small clock try the one in Fig. 15.

Manufacturers of plastic materials will be glad to furnish you with a complete list of the stock sizes, shapes and colors they can furnish, which should be kept at hand for reference so that in designing things to make, you can keep within the limits of material that is readily available.

motor in the handle and come equipped with a large variety of hobs, grinders and cutters. By selecting the proper tools, almost any kind of engraving or carving may be done.

Inlaid Designs: Plastic materials can be ornamented in contrasting colors by scratching the design required into the surface of the material with a sharp-pointed, hard-steel scriber. After the design has been scratched into the work and the surface wiped clean, a contrasting color of quick-drying lacquer is applied with a cloth. The lacquer will fill the crevices and the surplus on the surfaces may be wiped away before it dries.

Variety of Applications: After experimenting with plastic materials on some simple project such as the telephone note pad described, you will find many other

Cutting Sheet Plastics Neatly On Milling Machine

On a job of cutting several thousand small squares of ⅛-in. plastic, and sawing left a ragged edge and too much clinging sawdust, a clean break was obtained in the work by running it between two sharp disks, which scored the material deeply on both sides so that it could be broken cleanly. The disks were mounted in a milling machine, one on the arbor and the other on an idler, which was mounted in a vise on the machine table. The latter was moved until the proper depth of mark was obtained. A guide similar to the rip fence on a circular saw was clamped to the vise, making it a simple matter to keep the marking parallel to the edge of the plastic.

PLASTIC TURNING

IT'S FUN to turn plastics in either a metal or wood-turning lathe. Common craft plastics turn beautifully, the chip comes off clean in a long, paper-thin ribbon and the surface left by a sharp tool requires a minimum of final finishing operations. Turnings that involve curves, such as candlesticks and lamp bases, are best handled on a wood-turning lathe as the tool must be worked freehand. Turning straight, true cylinders or tapers is best done on a metal lathe where the position of the tool is fixed and the feed uniform. Turning characteristics of common plastics are similar to nonferrous metals and ordinary metal-turning operations can be duplicated on plastics. Nearly all plastics will take a fairly sharp knurl; they face off and shoulder perfectly and can be worked successfully with shaped cutters. With care you can run a clean, sharp thread.

General turning data is given in the table, Fig. 1, while Fig. 5 lists suitable lathe speeds and converts feet - per - minute (f.p.m.) to revolutions-per-minute (r.p.m.) for specific diameters. As an example of how these tables work out, suppose you are turning down a 1-in. spindle of the thermoplastic Tenite II, Fig. 1 shows the correct speed to be 300 f.p.m. and referring to Fig. 5 you will see that a surface speed of 300 f.p.m. on a 1-in. spindle requires a lathe speed of 1150 r.p.m. However, surface speeds ranging from 100 to 400 f.p.m. will work satisfactorily. Note from the table Fig. 1 that the phenolics (cast resins) require a high spindle speed and a slow tool feed, and that the reverse is generally true of the thermoplastics. The speed recommendations apply quite closely to all work under 2 in. in diameter, but on work over 2 in. in diameter the turning speeds for thermoplastics can be increased considerably because of the longer cooling cycle.

A good indication of the correctness of procedure is the shape and nature of the chip. If it gums and adheres to the point of the lathe tool, the speed is too high; if the chip tends to shatter or powder, the tool is dull or the feed is too fast. But with the correct adjustments and the proper feed you get a long, ribbon chip that curls away from the tool point without breaking, Fig. 6.

Much of the technique of turning plastics requires a careful study of methods of

1 PLASTICS TURNING DATA

	TECHNICAL NAME OF PLASTIC	REPRESENTATIVE TRADE NAMES	FEET-PER-MIN. SPEED	FEED RATE (INCH PER REV.)	REMARKS
THERMO-SETTING	CAST PHENOLIC	CATALIN, MARBLETTE	400 OK 100 to 600	.004 or less	Slight odor. Turns easily with mild pressure. Cuts can be up to 1/8" deep. Heavy feed causes a powdery chip.
	LAMINATES	FORMICA, MICARTA	200 - 300	.004 or less	Very abrasive. Best turned with carbide tools. High-speed tool bits should have positive rake of about 15°.
THERMOPLASTIC	CELLULOSE ACETATE	LUMARITH, TENITE I	300 OK 100 to 400	.007 or less	Sourish odor. Turns very easily with light pressure. Cuts can be up to 3/16" deep. Heavy feed causes excessive tearing. Both plastics in this group are practically identical in physical properties. Excellent for hand turning.
	CELLULOSE ACETATE BUTYRATE	TENITE II	300 OK 100 to 400	.007 or less	
	ACRYLIC	LUCITE, PLEXIGLAS	200 or less	.010 or less	Sweetish odor. Use firm pressure when turning by hand. Slow spindle speed.
	POLYSTYRENE	PLAX, STYRON	120 or less	.015 or less	Mild odor. Requires firm pressure. Gums easily and must be worked at low speed.

METHODS OF CHUCKING SHEET PLASTIC

Chucking plastic disks with hardwood follow block

Plastic sheet is screw-fastened to block of hardwood

Plastic held by small bolt through the center hole

5 F.P.M. to R.P.M.

DIA. OF WORK	FEET PER MINUTE						
	100	120	200	300	400	500	600
		REVOLUTIONS PER MINUTE					
½"	764	917	1528	2290	3056	3820	4580
¾"	508	610	1016	1530	2032	2540	3060
1"	382	458	764	1150	1528	1910	2300
1½"	254	305	508	754	1016	1272	1508
2"	191	229	382	574	768	956	1148
3"	127	153	254	382	502	636	764
4"	96	115	191	286	384	476	572
6"	64	76	127	192	256	320	384
8"	48	57	96	144	192	238	288

Long, paper-thin chips indicate that turning setup is correct in all details. Negative rake is obtained by holding the tool handle slightly higher than point

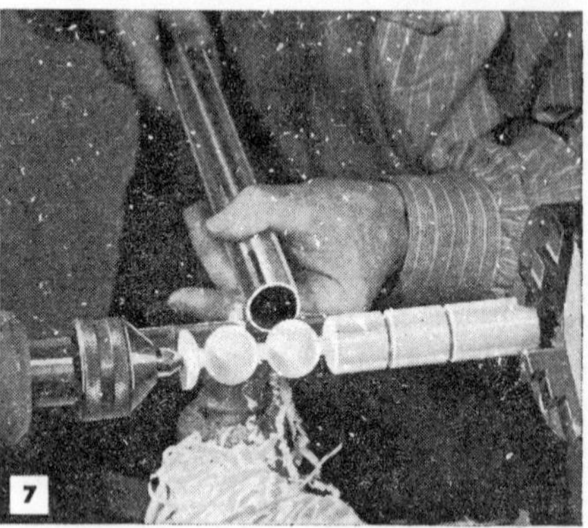

Above and below, it's easy to turn plastic balls by using a short length of steel tubing as the turning tool. End of tubing is ground to form cutting edge

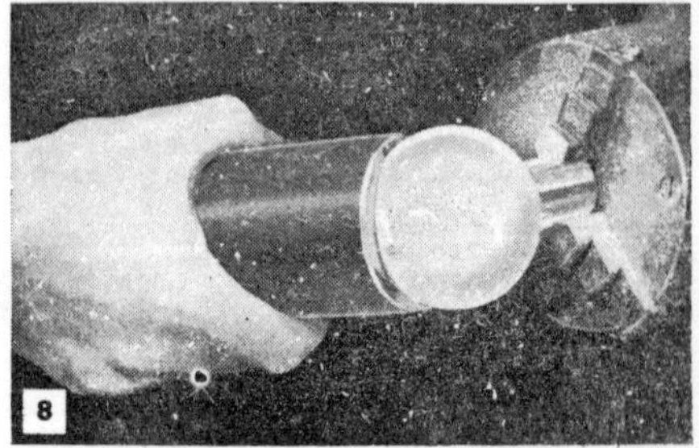

Beads and spirals are turned with a molding cutter mounted on a holder as in Figs. 10 and 12. Work longer than 4 in. should be supported on ball-bearing tailstock center as in Fig. 10. Short pieces are chucked as in Fig. 9

chucking the work. Figs. 2, 3 and 4 picture the fundamentals, and Fig. 9 shows the stock being held in a conventional 3-jaw chuck on a metal lathe. In Fig. 2 the plastic disk is clamped against a wooden backing plate with the tailstock center bearing against a hardwood follow block. In Fig. 3 a square of sheet plastic is simply screw-fastened to a block of hardwood attached to a faceplate. After the turning is completed it is cut free with a parting tool. Fig. 4 shows the simplest method of mounting thin sheet plastic where a center hole is permissible. A bolt passing through the center of a hardwood disk attached to the faceplate, holds the plastic disk firmly in place for turning. Figs. 7 and 8 show how to turn plastic balls to perfect spheres by means of a piece of steel tubing ground square across the end. The ball is rough turned with the regular turning tools and then finished with the tube tool, the inside diameter of which should be about three quarters of the finished diameter of the sphere.

Plastic rounds (spindles) are mounted between centers in the same manner as are wooden squares. With the center head of a combination square, score two lines at right angles to each other across the ends of the work to locate the centers. Then saw down the scored lines to a depth of about 1/16 in. on one end so that the lugs of the spur center will engage for a positive drive. Drill a small hole in the center of the opposite end of the piece so that the cup center will engage. In a metal lathe, the plastic also can be mounted between 60-deg. centers and driven with a dog just as in metal turning, or short rounds can be chucked as in Figs. 9 and 10. If the piece is more than 4 in. long, the outboard end should be supported by a ball-bearing tailstock center, Fig. 10. The latter illustration also shows how to utilize a molding cutter to form perfect beads by mounting the cutter on a short length of ¼-in. flat steel, Fig. 12. Then the unit is mounted in the toolholder of the metal lathe, Fig. 10. By connecting the carriage to the lead screw, the molding cutter will form a spiral as pictured at the left in Fig. 11. Of course, the thread feed must be equal to the width of the bead. While large beads, Fig. 10, can be spaced accurately enough with pencil marks, narrow beads are spaced by turning

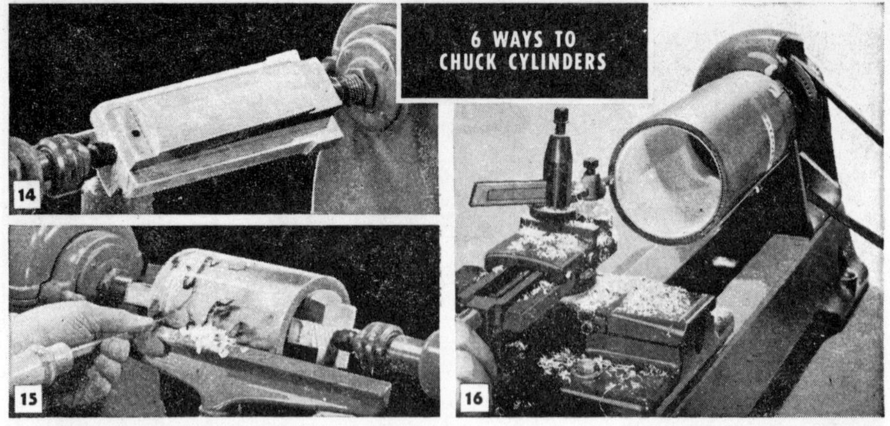

TAPERED HARDWOOD MANDRELS are used in chucking large hollow cylinders. The mandrel is tapered slightly to fit the taper of the cylinder. Mandrel can be solid or built up. For light turning operations, hollow cylinders up to 8 in. long can be gripped internally in the lathe universal chuck, without support at outer end

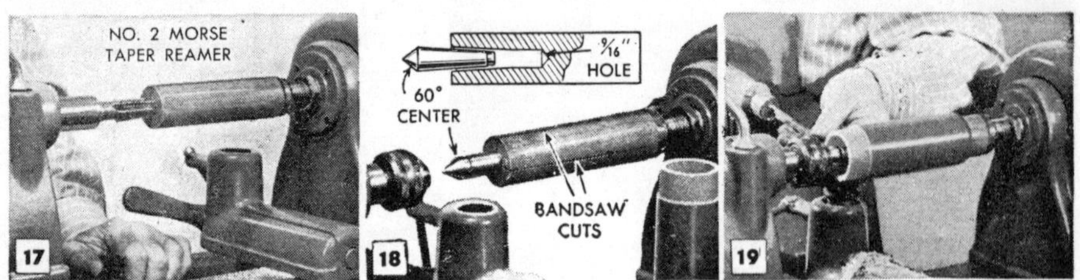

THE EXPANDING, OR WEDGE, CHUCK is ideal for holding small-diameter work. The chuck is drilled and slit lengthwise to take a standard Morse-taper center and chuck grips work by advancing the center into the hole

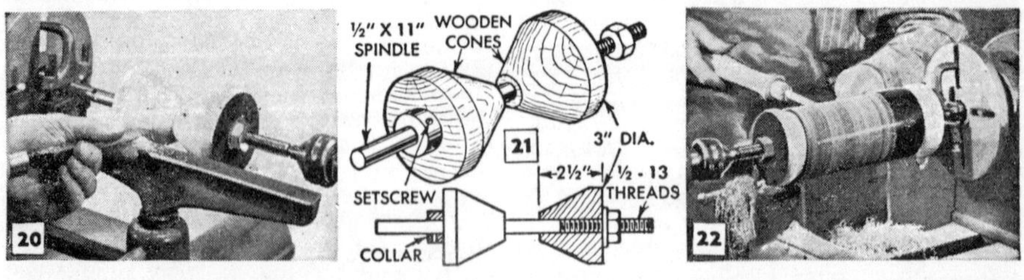

THE CONE CHUCK is especially useful for holding thin-wall cylinders. Two tapered turnings are placed on a threaded shaft and held between centers. Work is held securely between cones by tightening a nut on shaft

THE SPINDLE, OR FRICTION, CHUCK holds work by friction alone. For internal turning, the chuck is recessed to hold the work, the recess being slightly smaller than the diameter of the work. Work is limited to short lengths

27 FINISHING SCHEDULES FOR PLASTICS

TYPE OF PLASTIC	FIRST ROUGH	SECOND ROUGH	FIRST BUFF	SECOND BUFF	EXTRAS
PHENOLICS	Sand 150 Grit, Wet	Sand 240 Grit, Wet	"Learock" 155 or equal (Alum. Oxide)	"Learock" 304B or equal (Whiting)	
ANY	Sand 150 Grit, Wet	Sand 240 Grit, Wet	No. 2-0 or 3-0 steel wool		
ANY	No. 2-0 Pumice with water is equivalent to sanding operation		Any fine buffing compound, usually tripoli		Dry Buff
ACRYLICS	Sand 150 Grit, Wet	Sand 240 Grit, Wet	"Learock" 855 or equal (Sand 400 Grit)	"Learock" 884 or equal (Whiting)	Optional—low bake at 120° for 2 hrs.
ACETATES	Machine Smooth	Sand 220 Grit, Wet	"Learock" 855 or equal (Tripoli)	"Learock" 832 or equal (Lime)	

26

Wet sanding removes the tool marks and smoothes the surface ready for buffing and polishing operations

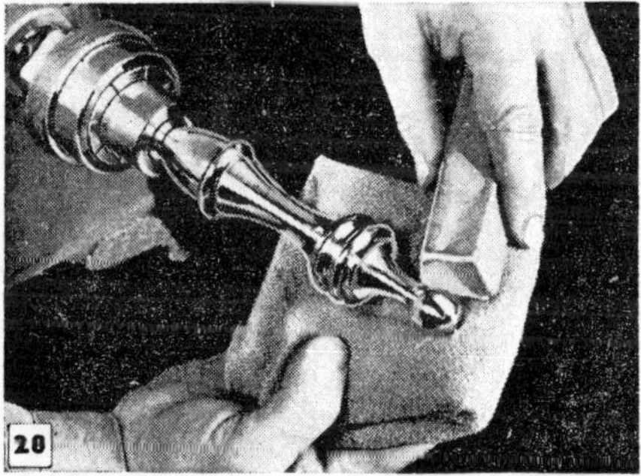

28

Above, high polish is easy to produce with buffing compounds. Below, use steel wool on wood-plastics

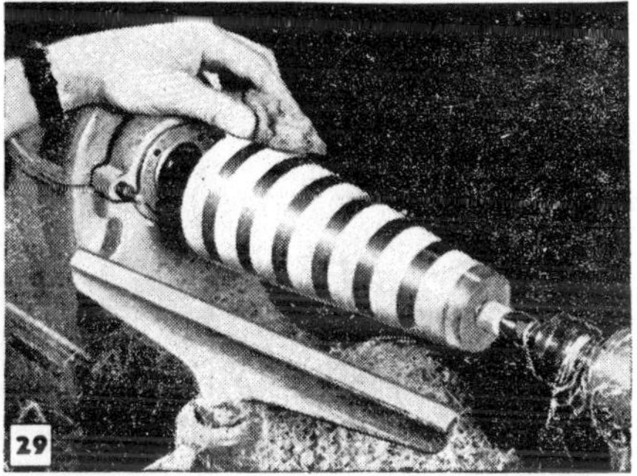

29

the compound parallel with the work and reading the spacing direct from the micrometer sleeve. For example, the 3/16-in. beading shown at the right in Fig. 11 is spaced 1/32 in. between the crowns, making each individual bead about 7/32 in. wide. In thousandths this is .218, or roughly, .200 in. which is just two full turns of the compound handle for each new spacing. In turning a spiral the width of the bead is .218 in., approximately equal to a 4½-pitch thread. Beads and spirals are worked at slow speeds, using light cuts.

The first rule in ordinary plastics turning is simply to grind the cutting tool with plenty of clearance and keep it sharp. Fig. 13 details the important points in grinding the tool, but this applies to the square tool bit held stationary in the toolholder. In working with hand tools on the wood lathe, the slight negative rake is obtained simply by holding the tool handle a little higher than the cutting point. Among the handheld lathe tools, the roundnose tool is most commonly used in turning plastics. Because of the radius of the edge, it offers the minimum area of contact and is less likely to leave chatter marks. Figs. 14 to 25 inclusive picture and detail methods of chucking and turning hollow plastic cylinders and tubes of varying length. Wedge chucks, various types of hardwood expanding chucks, or mandrels, and cones are commonly used. As a rule, the chucks are made in the lathe to suit the job in hand.

Fig. 26 shows a common setup on the wood lathe for polishing the plastics job after turning. Fig. 27 gives recommended finishing schedules. Speeds for wet sanding and buffing can be somewhat higher than for turning. When the job is composed of wood and plastic as in Fig. 29 the dry, rough sanding is followed by a rubbing with fine steel wool. After sanding has removed fine scratches and tool marks, a high luster is produced in a jiffy with a buffing compound applied as in Fig. 28. In sanding and buffing, care must be taken not to heat the work unduly.

PLUMBING *Installation* and *General Repair*

CHECKING LEAKY PIPES

AN ENTERPRISING homeowner can repair most leaky plumbing fixtures with only a few household tools and repair parts which are available anywhere. A single leaky faucet or flush tank may not appear to be so important, but in the course of a year's time, several dollars of needless waste can slip down the drain. Unnecessary delay and expense in repair costs can be eliminated if the homeowner tackles the job himself.

In the ordinary compression-type faucet, a rear opening leads to a chamber which is divided in two by a metal wall, with an opening through which the water can run. The handle of the faucet has a screw on the bottom which can be raised or lowered by turning the handle. A small metal disk is placed on the bottom of the screw. In turning the handle the metal disk is either pushed up against the chamber opening or away from it. Sometimes the metal disk is faced with a rubber or fiber washer to keep the water from leaking. When the faucet is turned on, the screw is raised and the water goes through the opening in the chamber and out the small curved outlet. The handle rod is packed with cotton twine to prevent leaking. When the faucet leaks, it is usually because the rubber or fiber washer is worn out, or because the cotton twine that is wrapped around the valve stem has become loose or has been mutilated in some way.

Repairing compression faucet: When any repair to the plumbing fixtures is to be

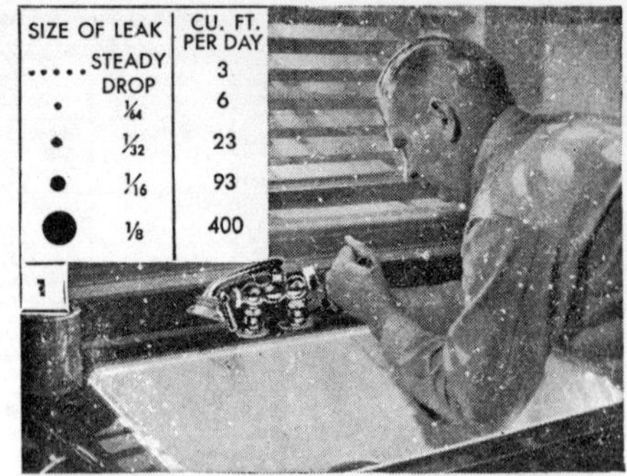

SIZE OF LEAK	CU. FT. PER DAY
..... STEADY DROP	3
• 1/64	6
• 1/32	23
• 1/16	93
● 1/8	400

1

2 First step is to unscrew cap nut from faucet

made, first shut off the water supply. There may be a shutoff valve near the fixture, such as the valve underneath the sink or flush tank, or it may be located in the basement. As a rule, it is best to shut off the main valve at the meter. Almost all faucets in modern homes are of the compression type. There are various styles of the compression faucet such as those having side handles and the two-faucet units having a common spout. Although the exterior characteristics may vary, the principle of operation is the same. The cutaway view of the faucet shown in Fig. 3 is typical. To replace the faucet washer, loosen the cap nut on the faucet. If the nut is hexagon shaped,

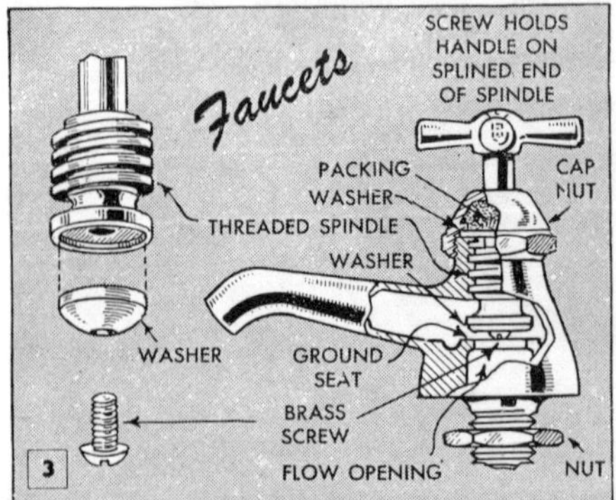

3

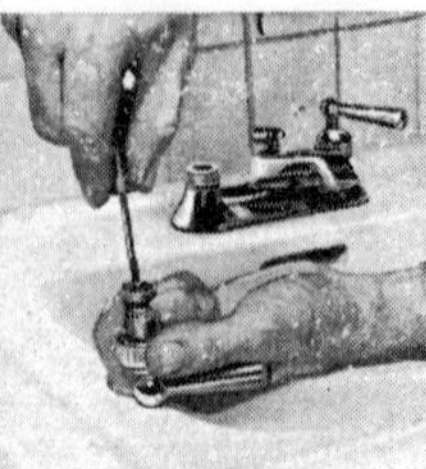

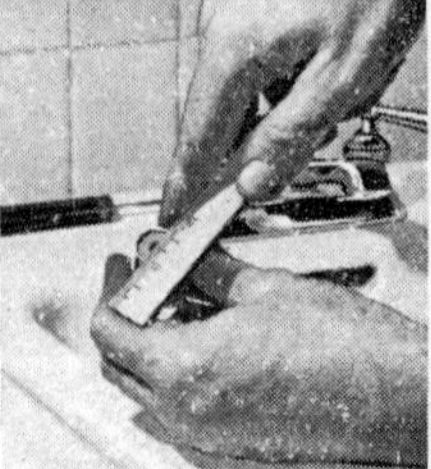

4 Lift out the spindle 5 Remove the washer 6 Measure washer size 7 Adjust faucet handle

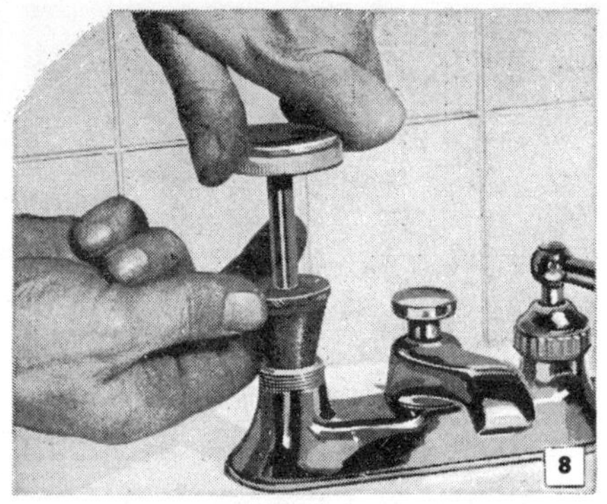

This hand tool quickly refaces faucet seats that are roughened by wear and corrosion. The tool has a tapered thread that screws into the faucet body

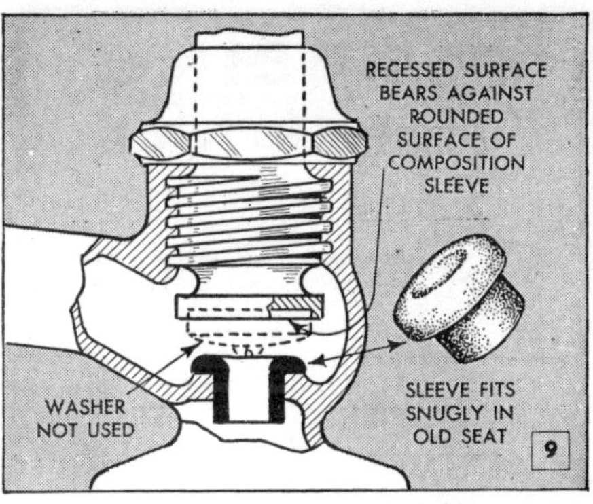

A special composition sleeve slipped into the faucet seat makes old faucets leakproof. Regular washer is not used as the washer seat bears on the sleeve

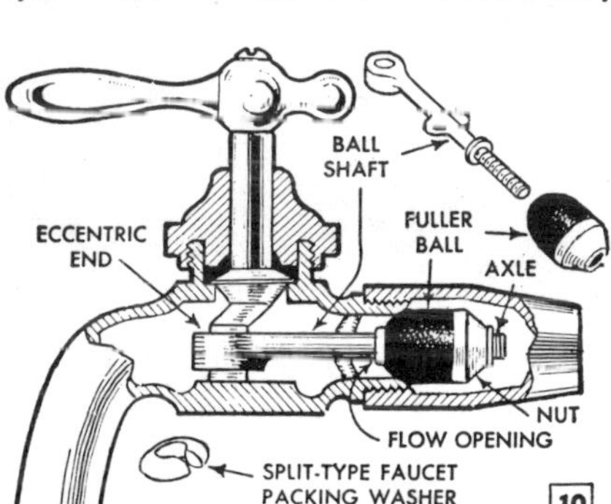

SECTION OF FULLER FAUCET

Leaks due to worn or frayed packing can be easily stopped with a packing washer or with a graphite-asbestos wicking especially made for this purpose

use an adjustable wrench, as in Fig. 2. Protect the chrome or nickel finish from being marred by inserting a strip of cardboard between the nut and the wrench jaws. If the cap nut is round and is serrated or knurled, a pipe wrench can be used, the nut being protected from damage by wrapping a cloth around it. After loosening the cap nut, turn the faucet handle in a counterclockwise direction so that the threaded spindle unscrews. Then you can lift out the spindle assembly as in Fig. 4. It may be necessary also to turn the faucet handle at the same time to provide clearance for the nut. Next, loosen the brass screw that holds the old washer on the end of the spindle, Fig. 5. Sometimes the screw is corroded and so tight that it will not loosen readily. An application of penetrating oil may help. If the screw breaks off, it usually can be removed by drilling a small hole in the remaining threaded portion, pushing the pointed tang of a small file into the hole and then turning the file. If necessary, scrape away all traces of the old washer. To determine the size of a new one, measure the diameter of the recess in which it goes, Fig. 6. It is sometimes necessary to dress the outside edge of a washer with a file to make it fit flat in the recess. With the new washer in place, turn the spindle into the faucet and then screw the cap nut down. When it is desired to shift the position of a faucet handle, the screw holding it is removed as in Fig. 7. Some faucets, however, have handles that cannot be removed from the spindles. For example, there is one in which the spindle works in a sleeve which is lifted out with the spindle. The spindle washer moves upward against the bottom of the sleeve when closing. Replacement of the washer is practically the same, except that a nut holds the washer instead of a screw.

Refacing faucet seat: If the flat surface of the faucet seat against which the washer compresses is rough, it will be impossible to prevent recurring leaks by merely installing new washers. Such roughness is caused by corrosion or by abrasion due to sand and rust particles becoming embedded in the washer. The roughened seat should be refaced by means of the tool shown in Fig. 8. After refacing the seat, see that all bits of metal are flushed away before replacing the faucet spindle. Another method

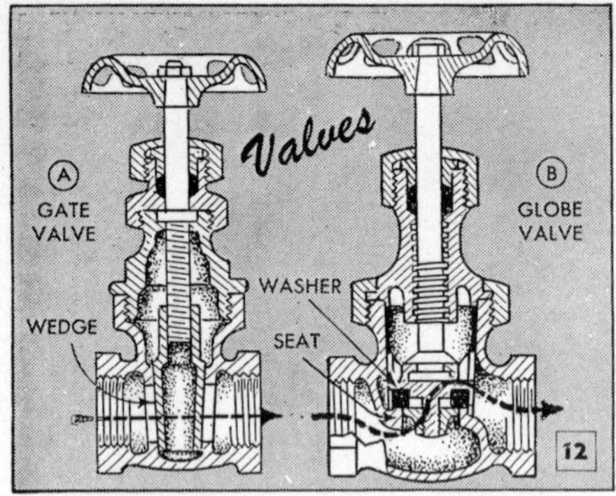

Two types of shutoff valves that are commonly used in water lines to shut off the supply to fixtures. The main shutoff valve usually is placed near meter

of providing a new seat, which eliminates the cost of a refacing tool, is to use a special hard-composition sleeve that is pressed inside the old seat, Fig. 9. The end of the spindle, from which the washer and screw are removed permanently, bears against the top rim of the sleeve when the faucet is closed.

Leaky stem: Leaks sometimes develop between the stem and the cap nut. If tightening of the cap nut does not stop the leak, loosen the nut, slip it up against the handle and replace the packing. You can use stranded graphite-asbestos wicking, which is wrapped around the stem as in Fig. 11. Or, you can use a ready-made packing washer available in either the slit or the solid type. The slit type, Fig. 10, is used on faucets from which the handles cannot be removed.

Repairing Fuller faucets: Although practically obsolete, there are still many Fuller faucets in older homes. On this type of faucet, Fig. 10, the handle can be swung in either direction to open or close the faucet. A horizontal spindle with an acorn-shaped rubber stopper or ball (known as a Fuller ball) at one end is moved back and forth by a crank-shaped vertical spindle to which the handle is attached. The entire faucet must be removed when the ball is adjusted or replaced. The sleeve enclosing the ball is unscrewed if the nut holding the ball cannot be reached with long-nosed pliers. Turning the nut to bring the ball closer to the seat may stop the leak, or a new ball, Fig. 10, may be required. A worn spindle or ball shaft can be replaced at small cost.

Sill cocks and shutoff valves: Sill cocks —outside faucets with threaded spouts to permit attachment of garden hose — are usually of the compression type and have washers just like indoor faucets. Repairs and replacements are made in the same way. Valves installed in water-supply

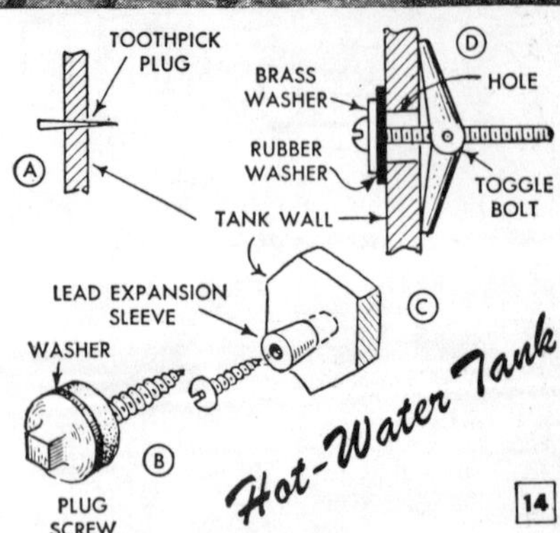

pipes are either of the gate or globe type, Fig. 12. The former, Fig. 12 A, has a sliding wedge to open and close it, while the latter, detail B, is similar to compression-type faucets. As shutoff valves generally remain open those of the globe type are apt to have warped washers and corroded seats from the constant flow of water, particularly hot water. Because of corrosion, they sometimes fail to completely shut off the water supply to permit repairing fixtures. Replacing the washer and perhaps refacing the seat of the valve is then necessary.

Leaky radiator valves: For hot-water and steam radiators, gate or globe valves of special construction are used. Escape of water or steam at the stem is stopped by

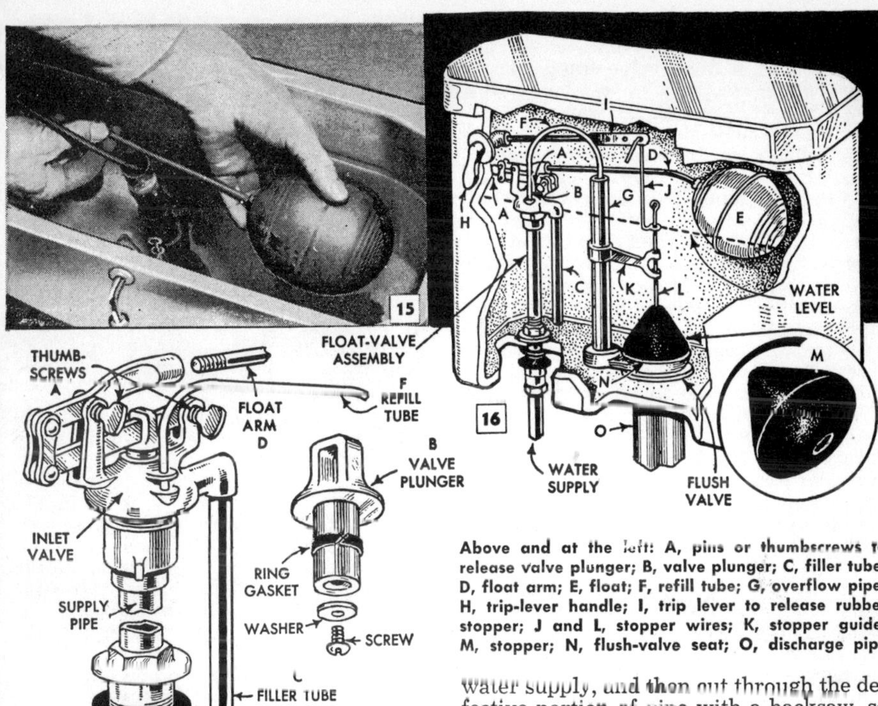

Above and at the left: A, pins or thumbscrews to release valve plunger; B, valve plunger; C, filler tube; D, float arm; E, float; F, refill tube; G, overflow pipe; H, trip-lever handle; I, trip lever to release rubber stopper; J and L, stopper wires; K, stopper guide; M, stopper; N, flush-valve seat; O, discharge pipe

tightening the packing nut slightly or by replacing the packing. When repacking is necessary, a hot-water system is drained until the water level is below the radiator; a steam boiler is kept at low heat so that no steam is formed. Then the valve to be repacked is closed, the handle is removed and the packing nut slipped off. Special metallic packing compound for this purpose can be had from plumbing shops, although asbestos wicking, the same as that used in faucets, will do. After removing the old packing, the new is pressed or wound in place tightly.

When a leak occurs at the union which connects to the radiator, and tightening the union does not stop the leak, there may be a little dirt between contacting surfaces. Take the union apart, clean it thoroughly and reassemble. It is best to use a large adjustable wrench for this purpose as in Fig. 13. A pipe wrench not only mars the fitting but may distort it.

Replacing leaky pipe: A temporary repair on a leaky water pipe requires just about as much time and effort as replacing a section of the pipe. First shut off the water supply, and then cut through the defective portion of pipe with a hacksaw, so that both ends can be unscrewed from the nearest fittings. Get two lengths of pipe of the same diameter as the old pipe and a union to connect them. The total length when connected should be equal to that of the pipe removed. Use pipe-thread compound on the threaded ends of the pipe to form a watertight joint.

Leaky hot-water tank: Leaks in a hot-water tank generally indicate that the tank is old and should be replaced. However, an old tank sometimes can be kept in service until a new one is installed if a temporary repair is made. On insulated tanks the outer jacket and the insulation must be removed first to get at the tank wall. Pin-sized leaks often can be plugged by driving in the ends of round toothpicks, Fig. 14 A. Swelling of the wood keeps these plugs tightly in place. Larger leaks may be stopped by driving in a plug screw as in Fig. 14 B. Another way is to drill or ream the hole to ¼-in. size to admit a tapered lead expansion plug as in detail C. Driving a screw into a small hole through the plug expands it. Still another method is to enlarge the hole enough to permit the insertion of a toggle bolt to hold a brass-and-rubber washer snugly against the outside as shown in detail D.

Water losses from flush tanks: Much more water can be lost through faulty valves of a lavatory flush tank than most homeowners realize. These tanks have an automatic float valve to admit water into the tank, and a flush valve fitted with a large rubber stopper to discharge the water, Fig. 16. Leakage of water from a flush tank nearly always is accompanied by a slight noise. In checking for a leak, first see if water constantly runs off through the overflow pipe. This indicates either that the float valve is not fully closed or that it leaks when closed. Next, find out whether any water leaks through the flush valve at the bottom of the tank.

To repair either valve, shut off the water supply and flush the water from the tank. If the trouble seems to be at the float valve, unscrew the float and the float rod, Fig. 15. Shake the float to see if it contains water as a result of pinhole leaks caused by corrosion. If so, replace it with a new one. Then release the two removable thumbscrews or pins in the linkage to the valve, detail A in Figs. 16 and 17. This releases the plunger B and permits replacing the washer. If the washer is held by a brass cap, remove the latter carefully to avoid breakage. When the washer is removed, examine the seat of the valve. If this is corroded, replace the entire valve assembly, Fig. 17. These assemblies come in either the long or the short size. To install one, turn off the water and disconnect the supply pipe at the underside of the tank. Then loosen the nut holding the float-valve assembly and lift out the latter. Reverse the procedure when installing a new valve.

When the leakage is traced to the flush valve, first see if the stopper seats properly, Fig. 16 M. The stopper guide K, which is clamped to the overflow pipe G, may not be centered over the valve seat. The wire L, which is screwed to the stopper, should project about an inch through the eye in the wire J, which connects to the trip lever I, or the stopper may not seat properly. If alignment and action of the stopper seem correct, remove the stopper by unscrewing it from the wire and clean the rounded surface. Also dry the valve seat N and clean it with fine emery cloth. If the valve still continues to leak, substitute a new stopper. Generally stoppers require replacement every few years. Occasionally the flush-valve seat is so badly corroded that it allows water to pass when the valve is closed, even after installing a new stopper. This requires replacement of the seat and overflow-pipe assembly, which is one unit.

Control for water temperature: The photo at the upper-right corner shows how a mixing faucet of pipe fittings controls water temperature. Utilizing either globe or gate-type valves, a convenient semiautomatic mixing faucet is quickly assembled for use in the laundry room or shop. Supply

valves are inserted in the hot and cold-water lines directly opposite each other and their handwheels are bolted together. When the valves are being assembled, one should be completely open while the other is fully closed. In this way, turning the handwheels closes one valve and opens the other at the same time. The two pipes are brought to a single outlet where the flow of water is controlled by a third valve.

Bench vise holds pipe securely: If the bench vise is not fitted with pipe jaws, pipes can be held, using a block of wood and a C-clamp to keep the pipe from twisting. The pipe is clamped in the vise near the end to be threaded and supported by the block which is placed near the edge of the bench. Then the free end of the pipe is drawn down and clamped to the far end of the bench with the C-clamp. The block of wood should be about the same height as the vise jaws and positioned as close to the center of the pipe as possible unless, of course, the pipe is longer than the bench.

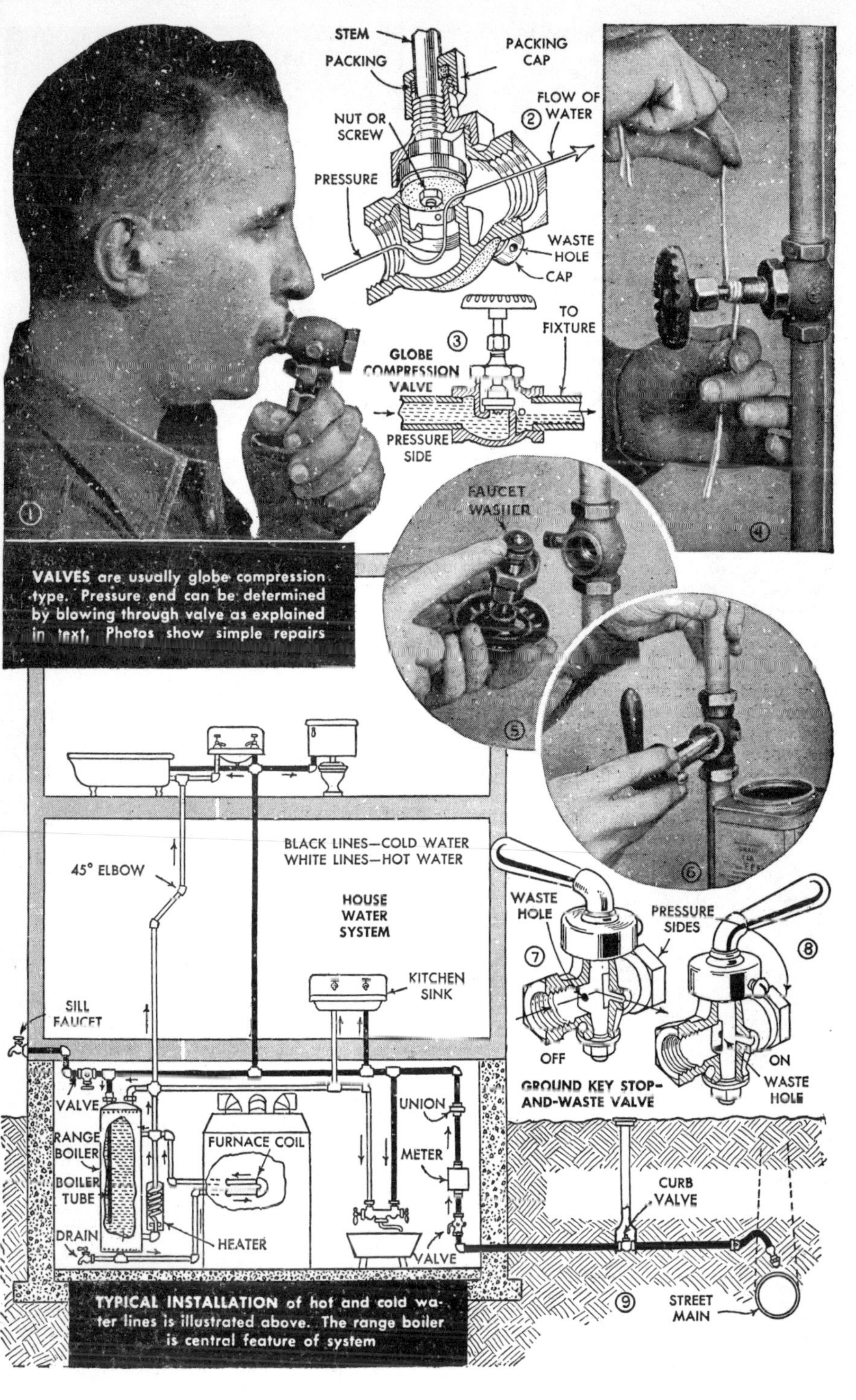

VALVES are usually globe compression type. Pressure end can be determined by blowing through valve as explained in text. Photos show simple repairs

TYPICAL INSTALLATION of hot and cold water lines is illustrated above. The range boiler is central feature of system

GENERAL REPAIRS

There are several small plumbing-repair jobs that need only a little "know how" plus a few minutes' work, and still another half dozen heavier repairs that are well within the capabilities of the average person.

To avoid the major repair jobs, it may be helpful to point out that one source of trouble comes from soap and grease. If the water in the locality is hard, that is, if it contains much lime in solution, this lime will readily unite with soapy water and grease in sewer water. It then forms a sticky and insoluble calcium slime. This calcium slime is very troublesome in drains, because there is no easy way to get it out.

Another is where there is a hot-water system as part of the plumbing of the house, and the clean water is hard. When hard water is heated, some of its lime settles on the inside of the pipes and eventually nearly closes them. The coil in the water heater should be removable for cleaning without tearing the whole heater down.

Faulty valve shut-offs cause no end of trouble, but the most common faults can be quickly corrected with the proper methods.

Valves: No. 1 rule in plumbing is "Know your valves." If a leak should develop anywhere in the system, muss is held to a minimum if you know exactly where the main shut-off valve is located. Take the family downstairs some evening and show every member just where and how water, gas and electricity can be shut off in case anything goes wrong. The main shut-off valve usually is a stop-and-waste valve, which stops the water when turned off, and also has a small opening in one side or the bottom to drain off waste water standing in the pipes on the house side. The most common style of stop-and-waste valve is made in the familiar globe pattern, as shown in the cutaway view Figs. 2 and 3. This valve is of the compression type—being worked by turning the handle, which compresses a composition or rubber washer against the seat of the valve. The most common repair to globe valves is replacement of the washer, Fig. 5. Ordinary faucet washers are used, and the size is determined by the size of recess into which the washer fits. Leakage around the stem can be cured by unscrewing the packing nut and wrapping four or five turns of candle wicking moistened with soap or oil around the stem, as in Fig. 4. Ordinary string will do in an emergency, but any temporary packing of this kind should be replaced with the permanent type soon.

The ground-key stop-and-waste valve, Figs. 7 and 8, is used in the same capacity as the globe valve, but works in an entirely different manner. This valve is a metal-to-metal contact, the tapered stem having a hole at its center which blocks or

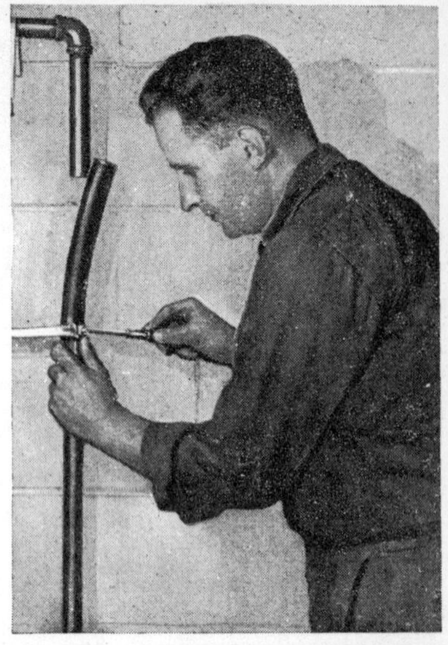

Pipe leaks can be repaired permanently with rubber hose, as shown above. Other temporary methods are shown below together with table for determining length of pipe replacements

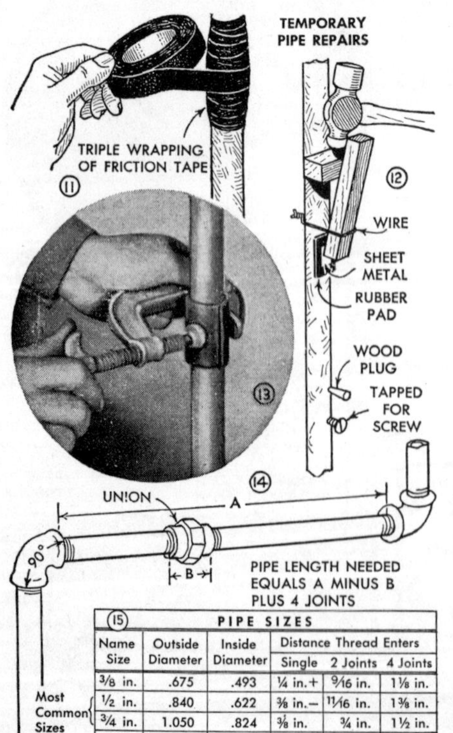

PIPE SIZES

	Name Size	Outside Diameter	Inside Diameter	Distance Thread Enters		
				Single	2 Joints	4 Joints
	3/8 in.	.675	.493	1/4 in.+	9/16 in.	1 1/8 in.
Most Common Sizes	1/2 in.	.840	.622	3/8 in.–	11/16 in.	1 3/8 in.
Most Common Sizes	3/4 in.	1.050	.824	3/8 in.	3/4 in.	1 1/2 in.
	1 in.	1.315	1.049	1/2 in.–	15/16 in.	1 7/8 in.
	1 1/4 in.	1.660	1.380	1/2 in.	1 in.	2 in.

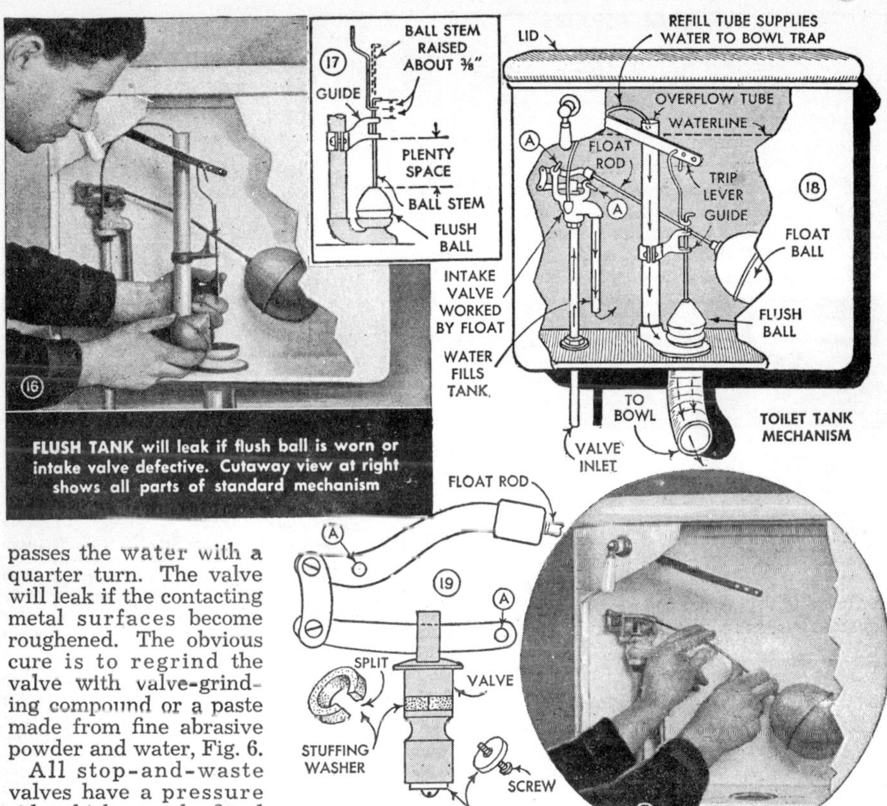

FLUSH TANK will leak if flush ball is worn or intake valve defective. Cutaway view at right shows all parts of standard mechanism

passes the water with a quarter turn. The valve will leak if the contacting metal surfaces become roughened. The obvious cure is to regrind the valve with valve-grinding compound or a paste made from fine abrasive powder and water, Fig. 6.

All stop-and-waste valves have a pressure side which must be fitted to the pressure side of the piping. If the valve is installed backward, it will leak water continually through the waste hole. Fig. 1 shows how a check can be made by blowing through the valve. If the valve is the globe type, open the cap that closes the waste hole. Now, with valve turned off and the waste hole open, you can blow through the house or fixture end, but you can't blow through the pressure end. On the ground-key valve, the waste hole is opened automatically when the valve is closed.

Pipe leaks: The best "fix-it" for a leaky pipe is to cut out the poor section and couple the pipe ends with rubber hose and hose clamps, as shown in Fig. 10. A repair of this kind will last for years. 1-in. automobile radiator hose is the right size for ¾-in. pipe; ¾-in. garden hose will fit ½-in. pipe. Other emergency ways to stop a leak are shown in Figs. 11, 12 and 13. Doping with white lead, varnish or anything of similar nature under the patch will assure a good job. Of course, the best way is to install a new pipe. When you do this you will need a union connection as in Fig. 14, since you can't screw both ends of a pipe in place at the same time. The last column of the table in Fig. 15 will help when calculating pipe lengths required.

Toilet flush tank: Likely about every 2 or 3 years the toilet flush-tank mechanism will need attention. Worst offender is the flush ball, Fig. 18, which becomes worn and permits water to escape continually into the bowl trap. Fix it by installing a new ball, observing the clearances required, as shown in Fig. 17. Fig. 16 shows the operation, but in actual practice you lift the ball stem and then turn the stem with one hand while you hold the ball in the other. Be sure that the guide is high enough. If it is too low, the ball will immediately drop back into the opening unless held up by holding the trip handle. If the new ball doesn't stop the flow of escaping water in the bowl trap, check the intake valve. First, pull up the float rod. If this stops the leak, all you have to do is bend the float rod as in Fig. 20, to put more pressure on the valve. If this does not stop the leak, the trouble is probably in the valve itself. Remove the valve core, float

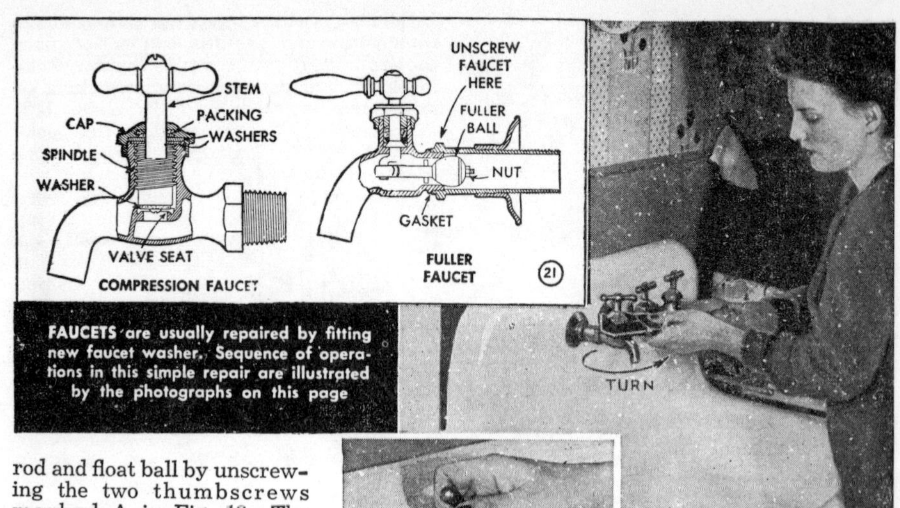

FAUCETS are usually repaired by fitting new faucet washer. Sequence of operations in this simple repair are illustrated by the photographs on this page

rod and float ball by unscrewing the two thumbscrews marked A in Fig. 18. The mechanism you remove will look like the detail in Fig. 19. Replace the washer at bottom (use a faucet washer of the right size), also inspect and replace, if necessary, the leather stuffing washer at the center of the core. When repairing a flush-tank valve, the water supply must be shut off. If the job is merely a new flush ball you can shut the water off at the tank itself by holding up the float rod.

After the flush-tank mechanism has been put in good condition, oil the trip-lever mechanism occasionally. Check the float ball for leaks by shaking it gently with the tank empty. If desired, the end of the refill tube can be pinched together slightly to conserve water since it supplies more than enough water to fill the bowl trap; the end must not be below water level.

Faucets: These need attention more frequently than any other part of the plumbing system. They differ in external appearance, but the working mechanism is always the same. Chances are your faucets are compression type. If the water comes on full blast with half a turn of the handle, they are quick-compression type. If it takes four or five turns, they are ordinary or slow-compression type. Both work the same way. The fuller-ball type of faucet has been off the market for a number of years, but is still found in actual use. Typical compression and fuller faucets are shown in Fig. 21. The compression type is repaired by replacing the washer at the end of the spindle, the whole operation being as shown in Figs. 22

(22) UNSCREW PACKING CAP WITH MONKEY WRENCH

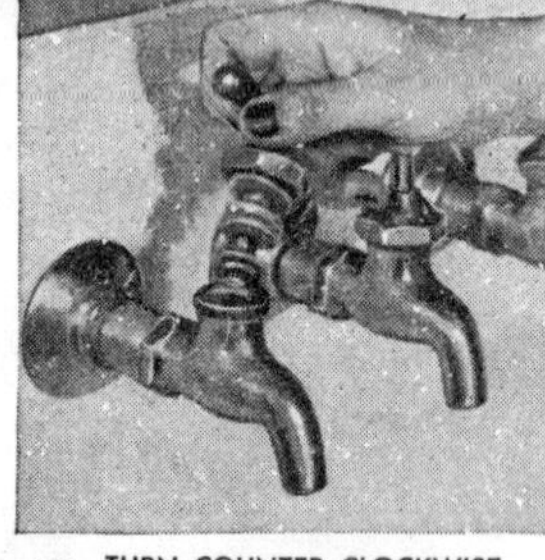

(23) TURN COUNTER-CLOCKWISE AND PULL OUT SPINDLE

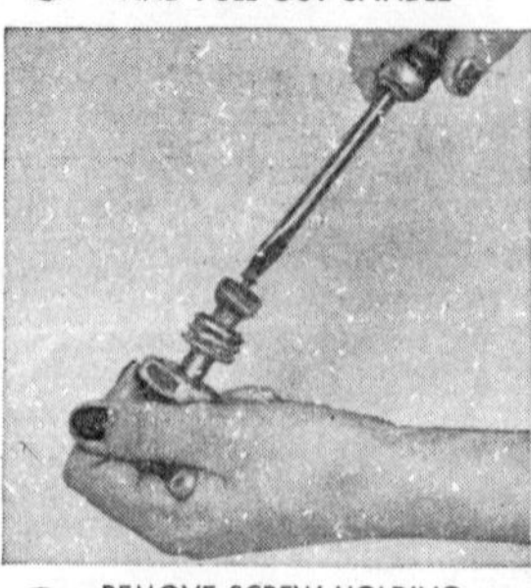

(24) REMOVE SCREW HOLDING WASHER. TAKE OUT WASHER

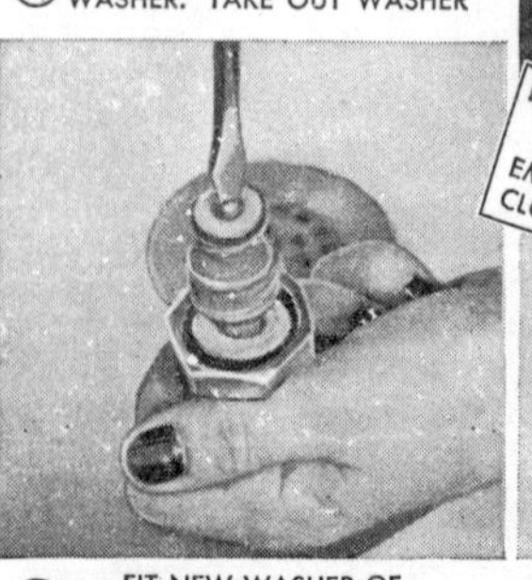

(25) FIT NEW WASHER OF PROPER SIZE. REASSEMBLE

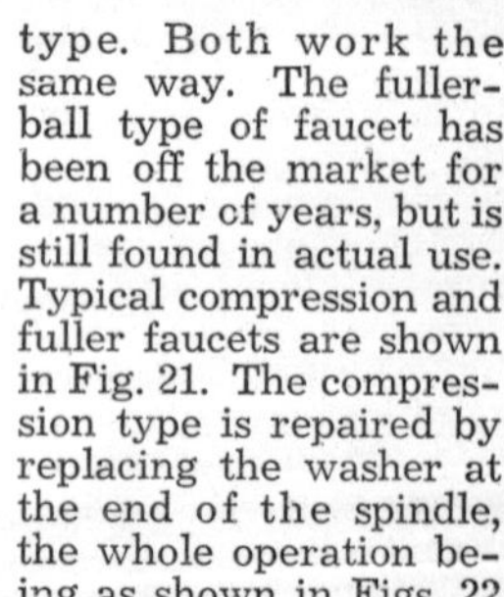

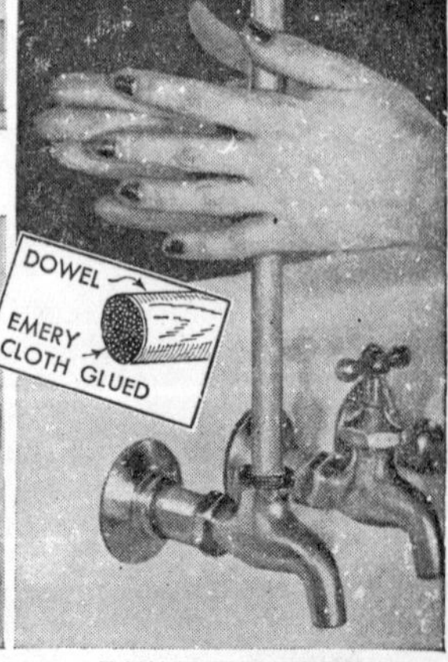

(26) IF VALVE SEAT IS ROUGH, SANDPAPER SMOOTH

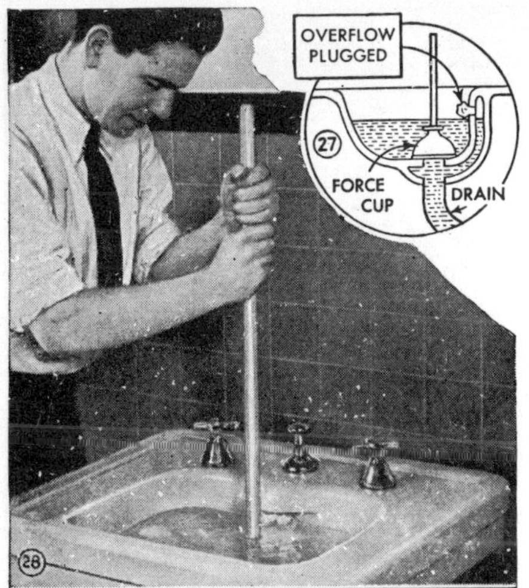

REMOVING OBSTRUCTIONS is less trouble when proper tools such as force cup and coil-spring augers are used. Obstructions treated promptly seldom become serious

to 25 inclusive. Equally simple, the fuller faucet is repaired by unscrewing the portion shown in Fig. 21 and fitting a new rubber fuller ball.

Be sure the main valve is turned off before you fix faucets. Open the faucet to release standing water and back pressure, then go ahead with the repair. While you're at it, inspect the valve seat (compression faucets) since a new washer is of little use if the seat is rough or scratched. If mildly rough, smooth it with a disk of sandpaper on a stick as shown in Fig. 26; if very rough, invest fifty cents in a faucet reamer. Of course, the faucet can leak at other points independent of the washer. If the leak is at the top of the stem, remove the handle and packing cap and replace the packing. If you haven't a regular packing ring, you can use candle wicking or string moistened with oil or soap. If a faucet leaks at the threaded part of packing cap, unscrew the cap and wrap a piece of thread around the threaded portion.

After a faucet valve seat has been smoothed by reaming several times, it may require two washers instead of one to get the necessary contact. If the valve seat is hopelessly worn, you can buy composition insert seats and make the valve as good as new. For a few cents extra you can buy a faucet washer fitted with a ball bearing ring, which reduces abrasion wear to zero and gives good results even on roughened valve seats.

Removing obstructions: Every home owner is familiar with the force cup shown in Figs. 27 and 28. On lavatory and bath connections, you can get more positive results if the waste opening is plugged with a wet cloth as shown in Fig. 27. Obstructions in the toilet bowl usually are easily removed with an inexpensive closet

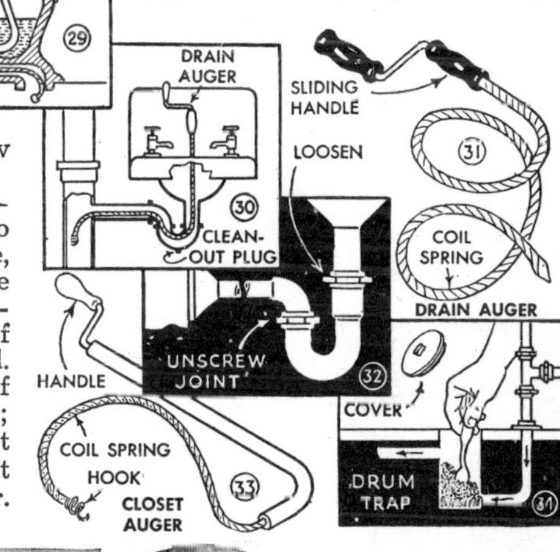

TANK LEAKS can be repaired by using boiler plug. If the tank is not completely rusted out, a repair of this kind will give very good service

auger as in Figs. 29 and 33. A somewhat similar gadget called a drain auger, Figs. 30 and 31, is useful for a wide variety of "stopped-up" conditions. If force cup and auger fail to remove an obstruction in a lavatory or sink, remove the trap by slightly loosening the slip joint and unscrewing the ring at gasket joint, Fig. 32. When replacing trap, inspect gaskets and use new ones if needed. If the trap is the drum type, unscrew the cover and scoop out the dirt and grease with a spoon as shown in Fig. 34.

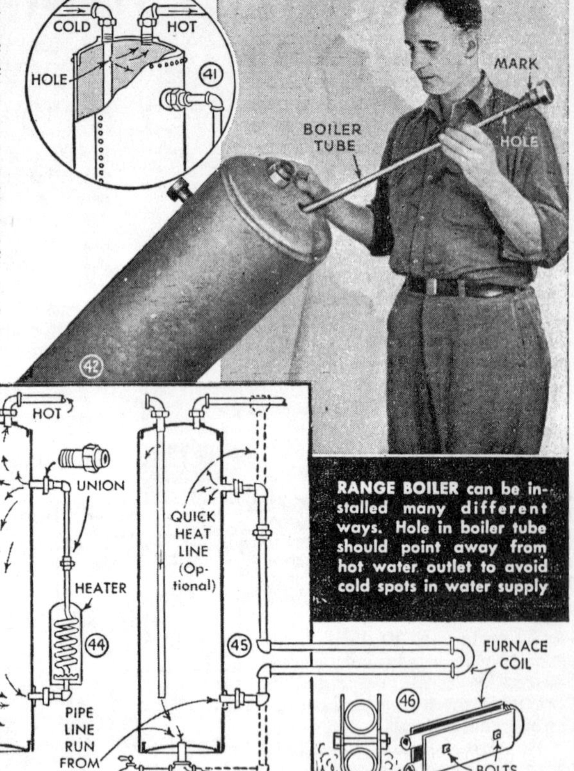

RANGE BOILER can be installed many different ways. Hole in boiler tube should point away from hot water outlet to avoid cold spots in water supply

Tank leaks: The average galvanized water tank has a life of about seven years. When it starts to leak, you might as well get a new one. Leaks can be stopped temporarily by driving in soft wooden plugs, as shown in Fig. 35. More permanent is the regular boiler plug sold for this purpose. To fit the plug, enlarge the hole, Fig. 36, so that the plug can be inserted as in Fig. 37, then fit the rubber washer and draw up tight to complete the job as in Figs. 38 and 39. A similar repair can be done by grinding the head of a bolt, Fig. 40, enlarging the opening to admit it and turning it crosswise, using a rubber disk in the same manner as with the boiler plug.

Installing new range boiler: Any of the installations shown in Figs. 43 to 46 inclusive will give good results at minimum expense for new parts. Simplest of all is the gas ring below the tank, shown in Fig. 43, its only fault being that heat absorption is not efficient due to the small tank area exposed to the gas flame. The side-arm gas heater, Fig. 44, makes a good set-up. A furnace coil is seldom used alone since it works only when the furnace is going. Fig. 9 shows how a furnace coil is combined with a side-arm gas heater or gas ring. The "quick heat" line, Fig. 45, can be installed in any set-up, and has the feature of supplying a small but very hot supply of water almost instantly. In making any installation, remember that hot water always rises to the highest point. Follow the natural flow of hot water in your system and be sure that all lines pitch slightly upward. This insures good circulation, and eliminates air pockets and resultant cracking noises when water is flowing.

The boiler tube must be inserted before the tank is set upright, Fig. 42, since it is too long to be fitted in the average height of a basement. The hole at top of tube prevents water from being siphoned out of the tank when the water is turned off. Its position should be marked so that it can be located facing away from the hot-water outlet, otherwise cold water from the hole mixes with the hot water, Fig. 41.

PLUMBING SYSTEM PLANNING

You can have all the advantages of modern plumbing wherever running water under adequate pressure is available. The first step is careful planning, the second is selecting the right materials and the third is proper installation. The largest portion of a plumbing system is concealed from view and is normally impossible to reach after the walls and partitions are plastered. Fig. 2 shows the extent of the hidden piping of a plumbing system in a small house. Repair or replacement of this piping can be done only at considerable expense. Therefore the pipe, fittings and the workmanship should be of the highest quality.

Basic planning by homeowners: Basic planning in regard to the location of the fixtures, as well as their selection, is a job for the homeowner himself; the details of planning are generally left to an architect, building contractor or plumber. In planning you should consider possible future needs such as an extra bathroom, a basement shower, an outdoor sprinkling system, or in case you live in a rural district, branches to various buildings where water may be required. The installation can be done piecemeal. A layout carefully planned at the beginning makes it possible to do this without discarding, replacing or rearranging previously installed piping and equipment as new parts of the system are added.

Minimum plumbing for houses: Although home plumbing installations differ according to family requirements, it is generally considered that the minimum plumbing needs of the average small home should include a bathroom equipped with a lavatory, water closet, a bathtub having a shower outlet over it, an adequate kitchen sink, a suitable laundry tub and one or two outside hose connections. A combination sink for dishwashing and laundering is recommended only for very low cost homes.

Economy in new-house plumbing: Much greater flexibility in planning is possible when you are building a house than when you are installing plumbing in an existing

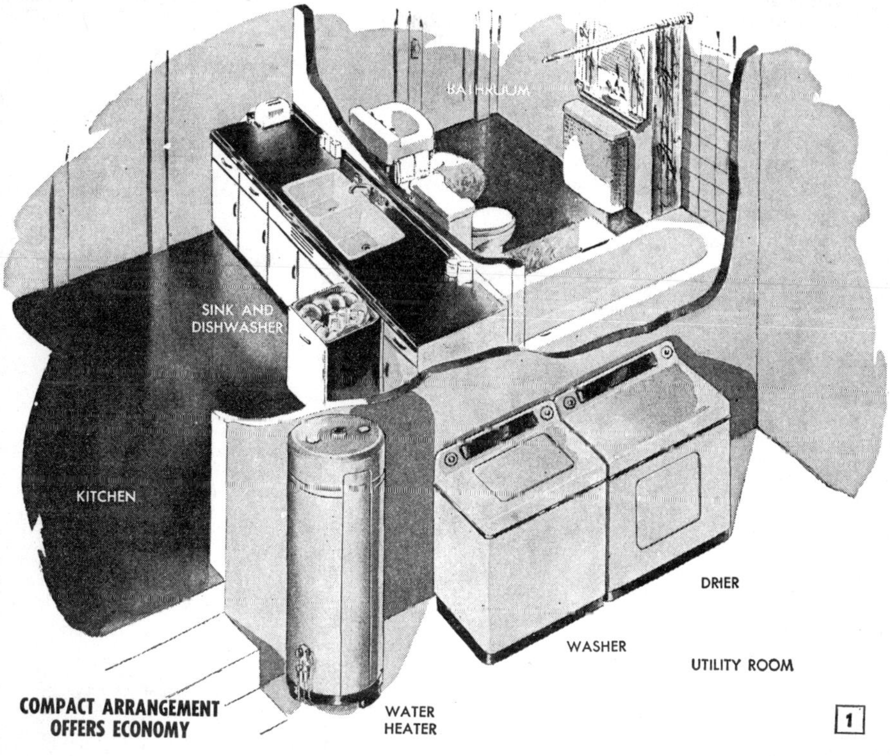

COMPACT ARRANGEMENT OFFERS ECONOMY

1

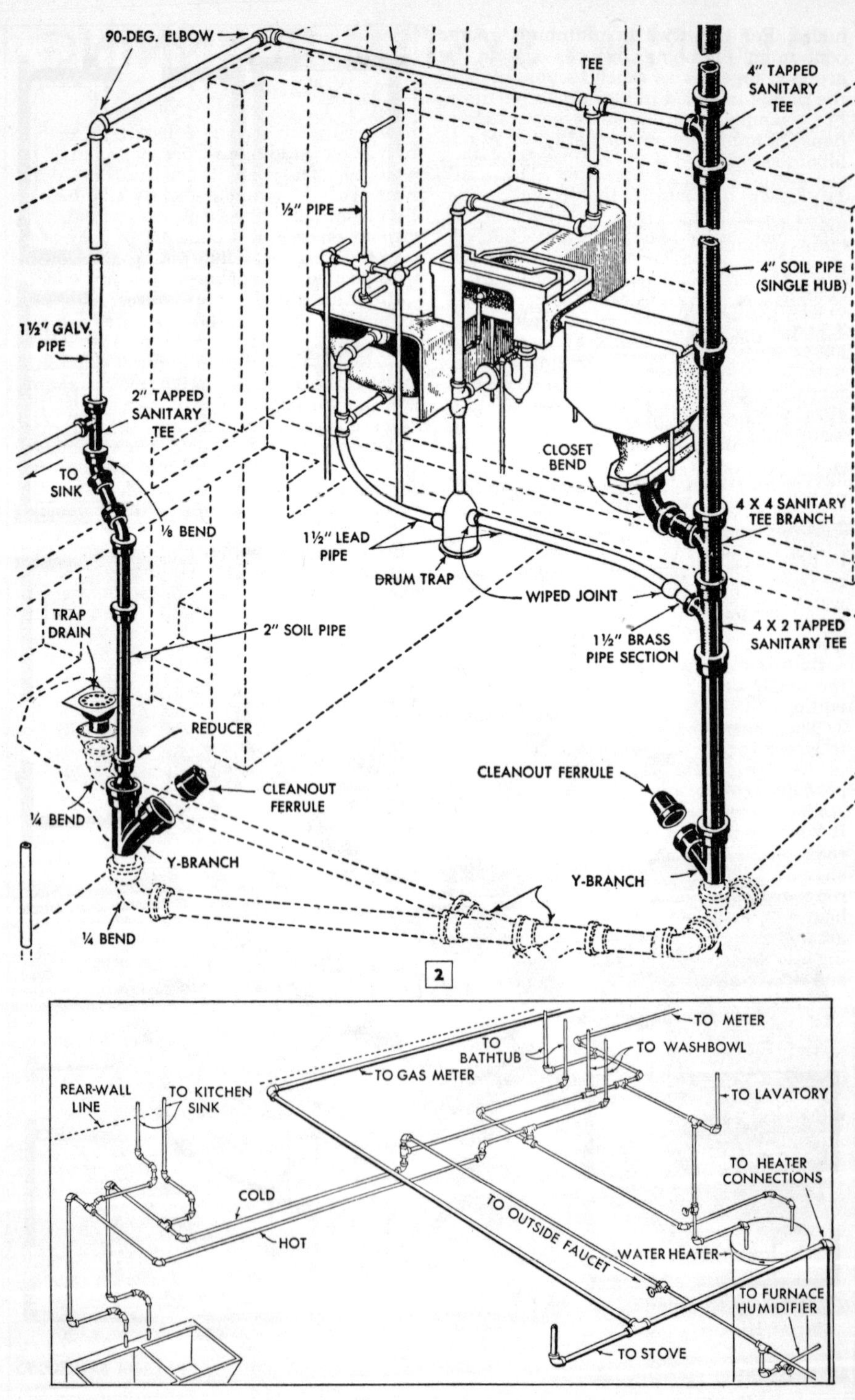

90-DEG. ELBOW
TEE
4" TAPPED SANITARY TEE
½" PIPE
4" SOIL PIPE (SINGLE HUB)
1½" GALV. PIPE
2" TAPPED SANITARY TEE
TO SINK
⅛ BEND
CLOSET BEND
4 X 4 SANITARY TEE BRANCH
1½" LEAD PIPE
DRUM TRAP
WIPED JOINT
1½" BRASS PIPE SECTION
4 X 2 TAPPED SANITARY TEE
TRAP DRAIN
2" SOIL PIPE
REDUCER
CLEANOUT FERRULE
¼ BEND
Y-BRANCH
CLEANOUT FERRULE
Y-BRANCH
¼ BEND
TO METER
TO BATHTUB
TO WASHBOWL
TO GAS METER
REAR-WALL LINE
TO KITCHEN SINK
TO LAVATORY
TO HEATER CONNECTIONS
COLD
HOT
TO OUTSIDE FAUCET
WATER HEATER
TO FURNACE HUMIDIFIER
TO STOVE

2

house. For economy in plumbing, rooms containing plumbing fixtures should be grouped together as much as possible and the piping installed in a common partition. For example, in a one-story basementless house, a minimum amount of material and labor are required if the bathroom fixtures are grouped on one side, and the kitchen sink on the other side of a partition. It is also wise to have this group of fixtures in close proximity to the utility room, as shown in Fig. 1.

Economy can be effected in the plumbing of a two-story house, such as shown in Figs. 3 and 4, by locating a bathroom directly above the first-floor bathroom and kitchen, with a common wall to enclose vertical pipes. In climates where severe freezing occurs, pipes should not be run in outside walls unless absolutely necessary and then only if the pipes are suitably insulated against freezing. Short hot-water lines supplying groups of fixtures not widely separated have an advantage over long lines in that only a small amount of water need be drawn off at the outlets before hot water becomes available. For longer lines the hot-water pipes should be insulated, which prevents water in them from cooling off quickly.

Bathroom suggestions: Six basic layouts for small and medium-size bathrooms equipped with bathtubs are shown in Fig. 3. The same arrangements are adaptable to larger rooms. Surplus space also can be utilized for cabinets, hampers or closets, or perhaps a counter in which a lavatory is installed. Detail A of Fig. 4 shows a 10 by 12-ft. room remodeled into a convenient bathroom equipped with a shower. Detail B shows a 12 by 12-ft. space used for a bathroom and for two closets of an adjacent bedroom, and detail C shows an alternate arrangement with wardrobe closets opening into the bathroom, in which case the tub and water closet are partitioned off from

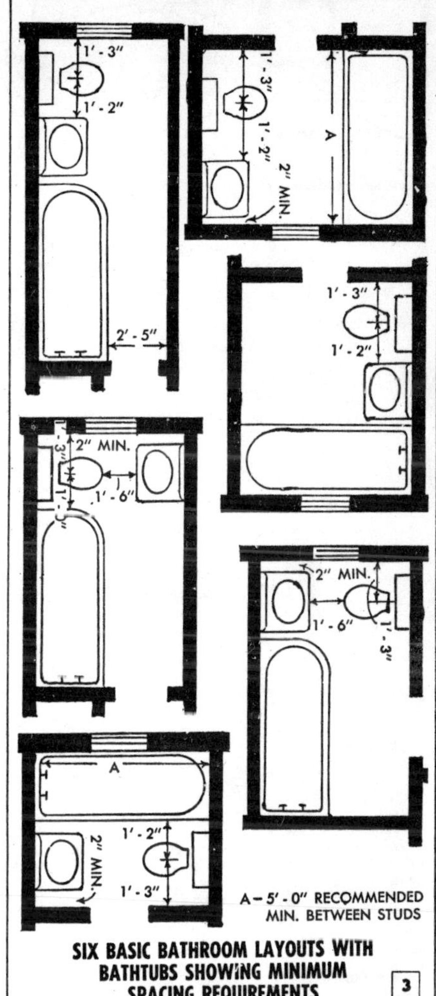

SIX BASIC BATHROOM LAYOUTS WITH BATHTUBS SHOWING MINIMUM SPACING REQUIREMENTS 3

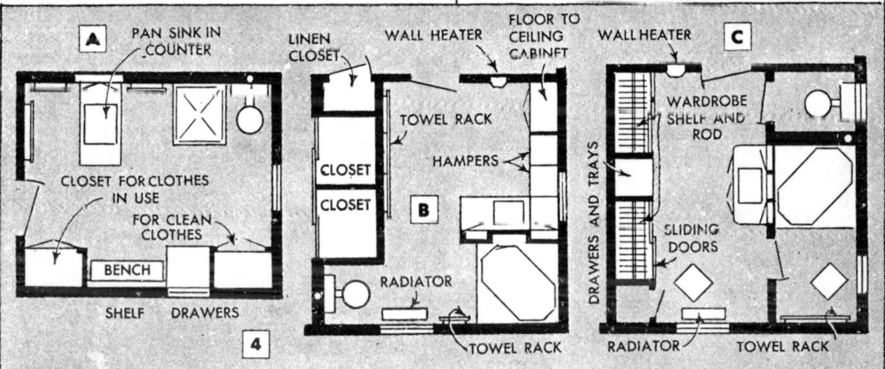

4

ARRANGEMENT OF PLUMBING FIXTURES AND STORAGE SPACE FOR ROOMS REMODELED TO LARGE BATHROOMS

U. S. Dept. of Agriculture illustration

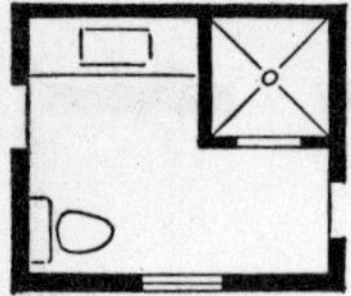

5

SHOWER STALL USED INSTEAD OF TUB IN SMALL BATHROOM PROVIDES MORE FLOOR SPACE, AND IN THIS CASE USE OF A VANITY-TYPE LAVATORY

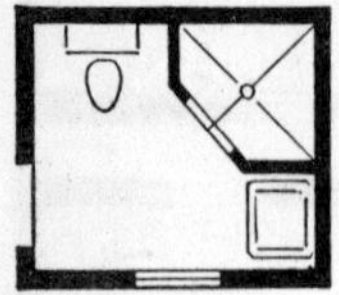

HERE THE USE OF A CORNER SHOWER STALL WITH DOOR AT ANGLE IN CENTER OF ROOM GIVES MOST SPACE AND MAXIMUM CONVENIENCE IN SMALL ROOM

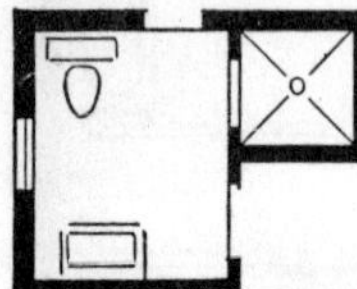

A SMALL BATHROOM CAN BE MADE LARGER BY UTILIZING ADJOINING SPACE SUCH AS A CLOSET FOR THE LOCATION OF A SHOWER STALL

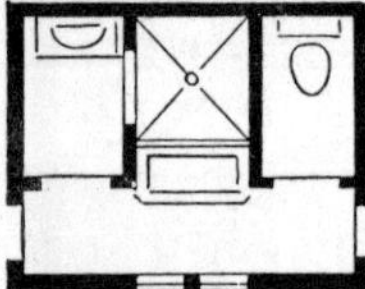

TWO-DOOR ENTRANCE TO THIS BATHROOM GIVES PRIVACY IN THE SHOWER STALL, YET PERMITS SIMULTANEOUS USE OF OTHER FIXTURES

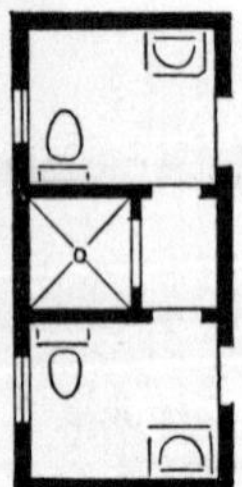

EXAMPLE OF GOOD PLANNING TO GET EQUIVALENT OF TWO BATHROOMS IN SMALL SPACE, A SINGLE SHOWER STALL BEING INSTALLED TO SERVE BOTH

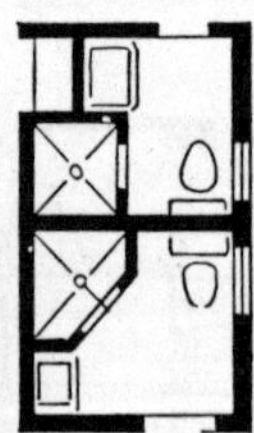

TWO SMALL BATHROOMS REPLACING A SINGLE LARGER BATHROOM WITH TUB, FOR THE GROWING FAMILY. BACK-TO-BACK ARRANGEMENT IS MOST ECONOMICAL

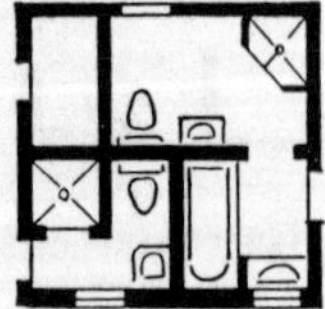

GROUP OF THREE BATHROOMS —A SEPARATE ONE ADJOINING A BEDROOM AND TWO WITH CONNECTING DOOR AND HALL ENTRANCE. INCLUDES TWO SHOWER STALLS AND BATHTUB

Henry Weis Mfg. Co.

6 LARGE BATHROOM DIVIDED BY PARTITION AND FIXTURES REARRANGED

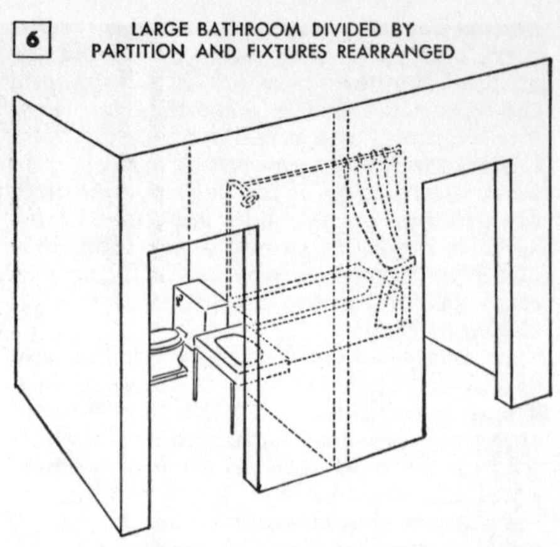

the lavatory. Shower stalls can be substituted for tubs. Seven arrangements for single and grouped bathrooms using shower stalls are shown in Fig. 5. When all the fixtures of a bathroom are arranged along one wall, less piping is needed. However, convenience and comfort should not be sacrificed for a relatively small savings in pipe costs. Fixtures for bathrooms can be obtained in a variety of colors.

If possible, a single bathroom should be located centrally in the house, where it is not necessary to cross another room to enter it. Bath and powder rooms should be located off a passageway where their entrances are not visible. They should not, if possible, open directly into a kitchen, living or dining room.

Adequate ventilation and lighting are essential. Try to arrange a lavatory at right angles to a window for maximum illumination from daylight. A window over a bathtub is not desirable as it is difficult to open and close by reaching over the tub. An extra shower curtain then is necessary to protect the window trim and curtain. A draft also is likely to be felt at times by anyone using the tub. If the window must be located over a fixture, and there is a choice, place it over the water closet so that the sill will come about 4½ or 5 ft. above the floor.

The door may be only 2 ft. wide if necessary. If possible, it should be located so that when opened it will conceal the water closet. The door should swing so that it will not strike anyone at a nearby fixture. If space inside of a bathroom is very limited the door can be swung out instead of in as customary. When fixtures are arranged on one wall, they should be spaced for sufficient elbow room.

A small bathroom is more easily heated than a large one. When a single large bathroom is used frequently by several mem-

Crane Co. photo

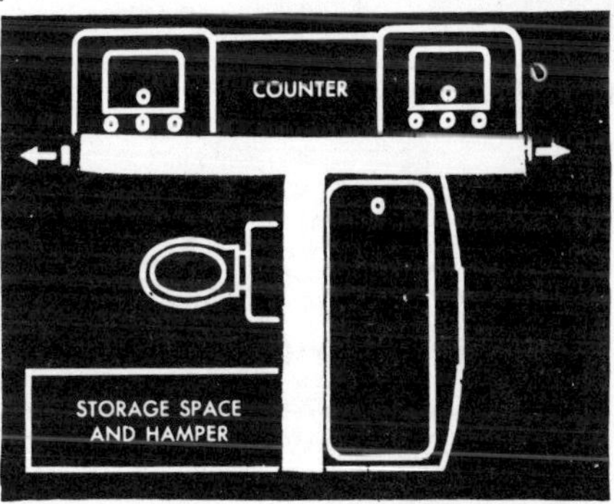

bers of a family, congestion can be relieved by dividing the room by means of a partition as shown in Fig. 6. One part can contain the bathtub or shower; the other the lavatory and water closet. Each is provided with a separate entry. A T-type bathroom, such as shown in Fig. 7, is another practical solution to relieve congestion in a home having only one bathroom. Note that there are two lavatories and a separate shower section. Although ample electric light should be furnished at the lavatory, preferably on either side of the wall cabinet or mirror, above it, no electrical outlets should be located within reach of a person in the bathtub as this involves danger to life.

Detailed planning: When a plumbing system is planned in greater detail than the approximate locations of fixtures, it is necessary to determine the arrangement and positioning of the piping. This is done by taking careful measurements in relation to the building construction. Before doing this, however, you should be thoroughly familiar with the method of assembling pipe, where and how to install vents, traps, etc. Also, the installation must conform to your local plumbing ordinance or "code." In the absence of a local code it is best to plan the installation according to the National Plumbing Code. When making your installation be sure to conform to the code and this will eliminate hazards from improperly installed plumbing. If you hire a building contractor or plumber to do the work, even though you may help, it is his responsibility to plan the job according to your specifications, get a plumbing permit, make the installation meet all code requirements and then obtain local approval.

In case you are building a new house, the location of the plumbing fixtures and pipes should be indicated accurately on the plans, depending on how complete they are. Often however, the plumbing is not planned in detail and is left more or less to the discretion of the plumber. Lack of sufficient planning accounts for the frequent need of making expensive alterations by carpenters to provide space for the plumbing lines; also this negligence accounts for the incorrect installation of some plumbing systems. Therefore, planning the details beforehand often means a considerable saving of time and money.

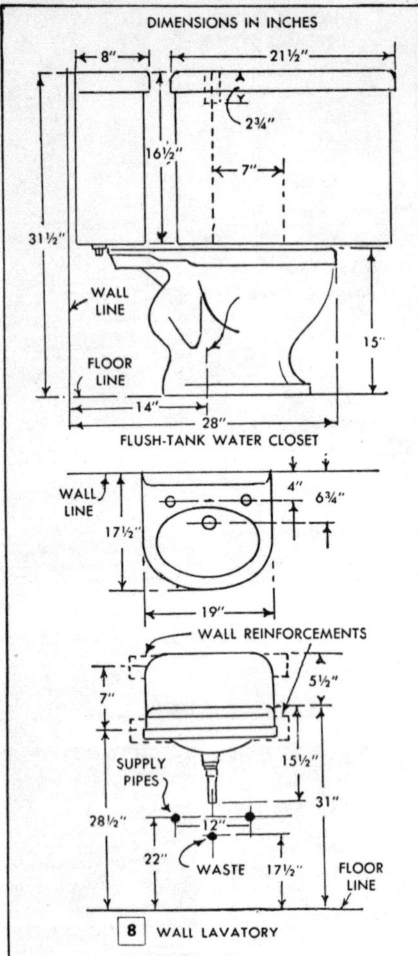

8 WALL LAVATORY

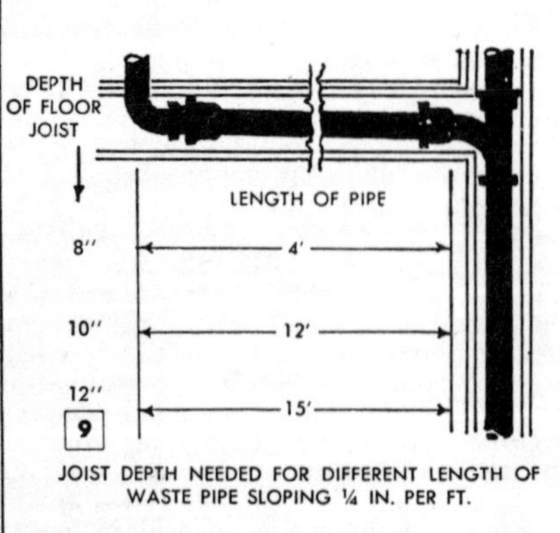

9 JOIST DEPTH NEEDED FOR DIFFERENT LENGTH OF WASTE PIPE SLOPING ¼ IN. PER FT.

U. S. Dept. of Agriculture illustration

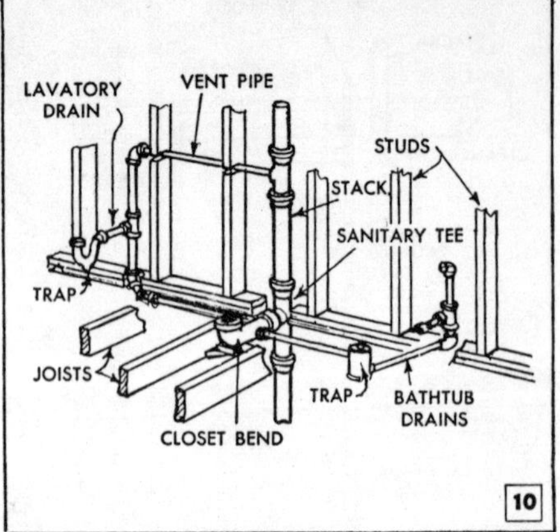

10

Since both water-supply and drainage systems connect to the fixtures, both systems should be planned carefully and coordinated in their relation to each other. You should either have the plumbing fixtures on hand when planning or have all the dimensions pertaining to them. The exact position of the supply and waste pipes, as well as the location of the fixtures, can then be accurately determined. Manufacturer's "roughing-in" sheets that accompany fixtures, and are sometimes available separately, supply this necessary dimensional data. Fig. 8 shows typical drawings and dimensions of roughing-in sheets.

Stack location: Since the soil and vent stack is the least "flexible" part of a plumbing system, and should be installed as close as possible to water closets and also centrally among other fixtures that it serves, its location should be determined first. The soil stack runs vertically and as nearly straight as possible from the house drain into which it discharges, and continues up through the roof for venting. It must be planned to avoid doors, heating ducts or pipes, girders under the first floor, electric-wiring outlets and dormers on the roof. The partition enclosing a stack must be wider than usual to provide sufficient space. Wider studs than usual can be used or regular ones furred out. The added space required varies with the size of the stack. It must be slightly greater than the outside diameter of the pipe at the hubs.

It may be necessary to choose a different location for water closets than originally planned to obtain better stack location. If possible, the horizontal lengths of soil pipe from the stack to the water closets should be run parallel to joists instead of across them. This saves cutting joists and installing extra floor framing. The width of the joists will limit the distance that a soil pipe at proper slope can be concealed between

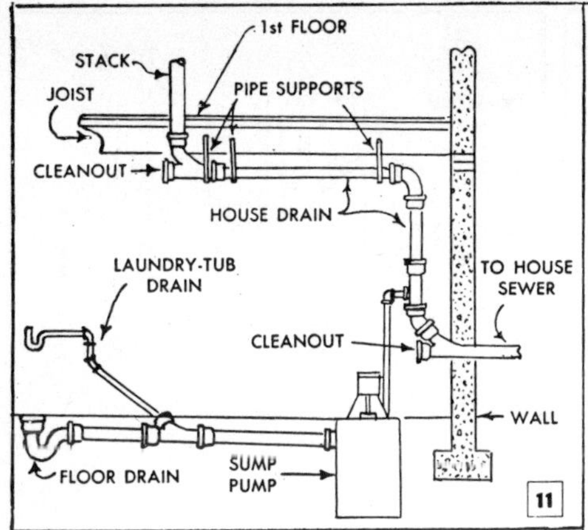

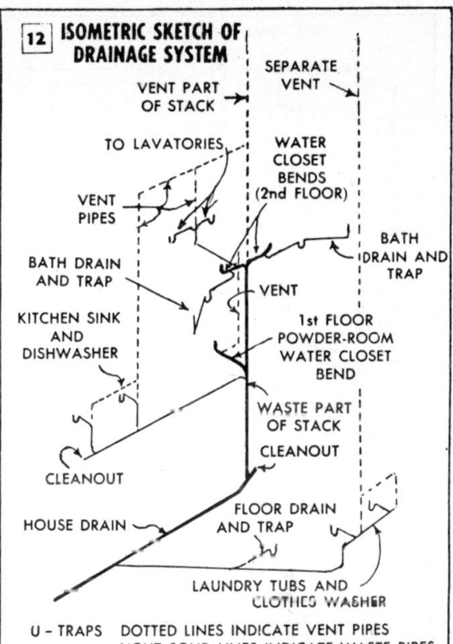

stack and water closet as shown in Fig. 9.

After the stack location has been selected check the house construction, taking measurements if necessary to see whether the stack can be so installed. Also determine the position of the waste pipes, traps and the connections to stack and fixtures. Fig. 10 shows an arrangement which applies to a one-story house or to the second floor of a two-story house. Also determine the location of extra vents or waste stacks if needed.

Position of house drain: The house drain runs horizontally from the stack to the house sewer, generally at a slope of ¼ in. per ft., and connects to the latter about 5 ft. outside of the foundation wall. The house drain may be suspended from the basement ceiling, as in Fig. 11, or it may be run under the basement floor. The latter is usually preferred as it conceals the pipe and provides more headroom in the basement. In basementless houses, it is hung from joists above the crawl space or buried in a trench. In case the outlet of the house drain must be above the basement floor, as for example when a lower level would necessitate burying a septic tank too deep, or when a street sewer is higher than the basement floor, a sump pump is used to raise the waste from the floor drain and laundry tubs up to the house-drain level as in Fig. 11. The house drain should take the shortest straight path to the house sewer, avoiding unnecessary bends. Floor drain and tub waste connections must be carefully determined also. Cleanout plugs are provided to simplify clearing away obstructions if they should occur. These are located at the base of the stack or wherever the house drain changes in direction more than 45 deg. A cleanout should be provided for every 50 ft. of horizontal pipe.

Layout sketches: Next, make an isometric sketch of the drainage system like the

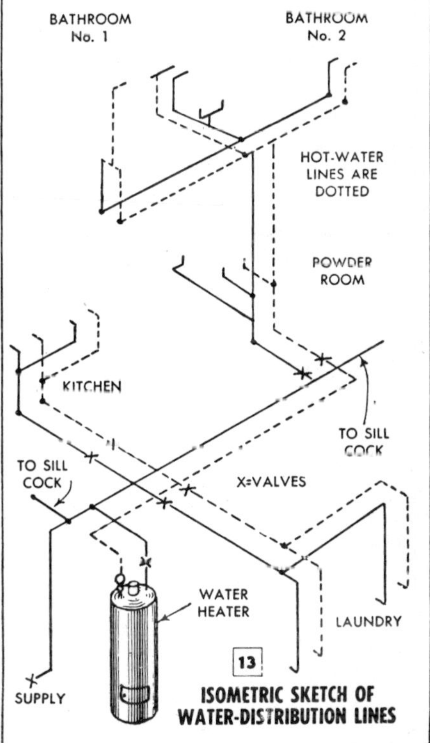

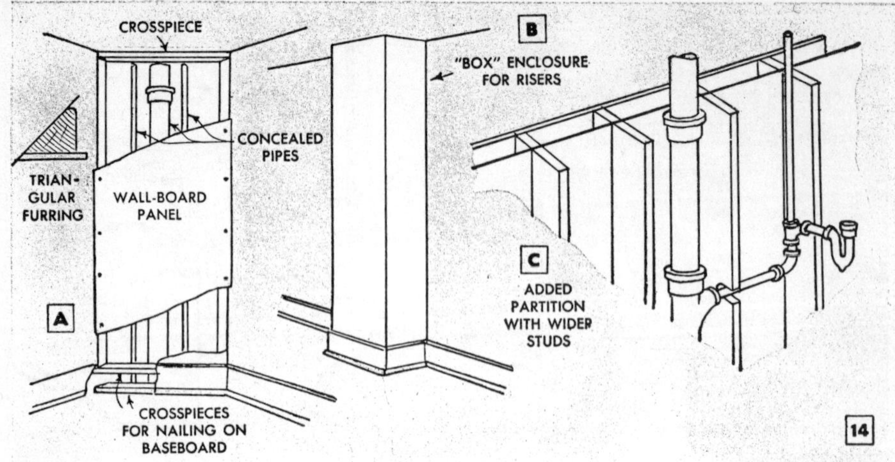

one shown in Fig. 12, entering all the connections and dimensions. This sketch provides a basis for ordering the material needed and also serves as a guide when making the installation. Such a sketch is easily made after ruling a number of light or colored guide lines at two opposite angles of about 30 deg., on which heavy lines to represent horizontal pipes are drawn. The vertical pipes are entered on the sketch by making vertical lines. Only one line is made for each pipe to indicate its center. Upturned "hooks" at waste pipes represent traps. Dotted lines indicate vent pipes.

A similar sketch is made of the water-supply and distribution system, Fig. 13, which you plan next. Because of the smaller size of pipes used, there is more flexibility of installation, although the connections to fixtures must be made at predetermined positions. In general the piping lines are grouped in the same or adjacent partitions if possible. The water-system sketch may have dots to indicate fittings in the pipe lines and X-marks to indicate valves. The sketch enables you to show horizontal pipes extending in any of four directions from vertical pipes and also show which way the openings face.

Before engaging in detailed planning of a plumbing system, it is best to become thoroughly familiar with installation of drainage lines and water-supply lines, some of the requirements covered may influence details of planning. Although you sketch the two systems separately, they should be planned in relation to each other so there will be no trouble of pipe interference.

Adding plumbing to existing houses: Concealed plumbing in existing homes is more difficult to install and also more costly than in homes being built, but it is generally preferred in spite of its added cost. It will be necessary, however, to open floors and remove plaster. The best position of the stack is determined first. Location of bathroom and other plumbing fixtures will be influenced by stack location and vice versa. If a new wall is to be built to enclose the stack and water pipes, be sure to allow sufficient space. You can use 6-in. studs (actually 5½ in. wide) for a partition to enclose 3-in. soil pipe, if this size of stack is permitted in your locality. Sometimes a linen or clothes closet can be used to advantage for concealment of the stack and pipes. Another method is to group the pipes in a corner and conceal them with a panel of wallboard or plasterboard covered with plaster, which is joined to plaster on adjoining walls. Such an arrangement is shown in detail A of Fig. 14. Where pipes cannot be located in a corner they can be boxed in as in detail B. It is also possible to add a wider partition to one that is too narrow in order to accommodate the soil stack as shown in detail C. As plumbing fixtures are heavy, make sure that the floor joists are large enough to take the weight. Extra joists may be required.

Copper tubing used for water lines can be "snaked" through a closed partition, however, after first making sure that there are no obstructions. In such cases the partition is usually opened at the baseboard level of the first and second floors . In cases where minor obstructions in partitions prevent the use of rigid pipe, copper tubing is the best solution as it can readily be bent around such obstructions. However, rigid pipes can sometimes be installed in a partition by lowering them through the roof.

1

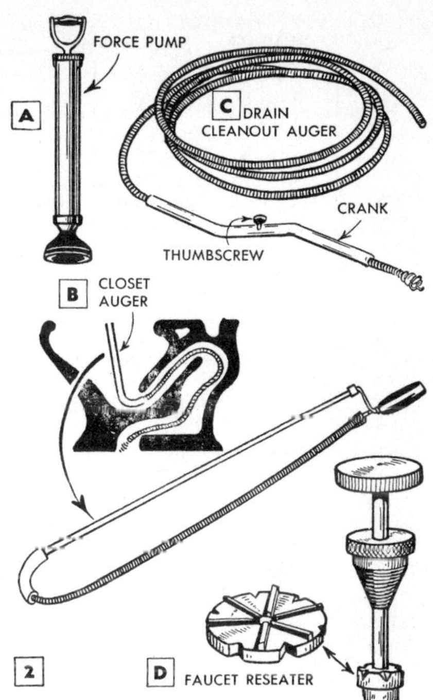

Plumbing Tools and Their Use

BESIDES ORDINARY TOOLS such as pliers, screwdrivers, saws, wrenches, cold chisels, a carpenter's brace and a mason's trowel, there are a few special tools required for plumbing maintenance and pipe installation in the home. Many special tools can be rented or borrowed (some mail-order houses offer this service) as it is rather impractical to buy tools not used often enough to justify their cost.

Tools to clear small drainage lines: A sink plunger or suction cup, Fig. 1, is used mostly for dislodging stoppages in sink traps and water closets. The sink or other fixture where a stoppage exists should be partly filled with water. Then the suction cup is placed over the drain opening and worked up and down vigorously. Air-pressure force pumps, Fig. 2A, produce greater pressure than ordinary suction cups.

Obstructions in drain pipes beyond traps generally require the use of a drain auger. These come in different types, details B and C of Fig. 2. One type, detail B, is particularly designed for use on water closets, but also is handy sometimes for other drains if the obstruction is close to the trap. It consists of a flexible spring-steel coil, from 3 to 6 ft. long, and has a crank at one end with which it is rotated. A similar type auger, detail C, has a tubular handle that slips over the wire so the latter can be advanced into the drain. The handle can be locked on the wire. Such augers are available in lengths from 6 to 100 ft., and in thicknesses of ¼ and ⅜ in. Larger sizes are used in sewers. A screw or hook end is generally provided. After using an auger it should be cleaned thoroughly and oiled to prevent rust.

Faucet and valve-seat dressers: The repair tool shown in Fig. 2D is used to reface faucet and valve seats in order to prolong their usefulness. Refacing seats is necessary when they are rough and leakage persists regardless of any new washers that may be installed. The tool consists of a threaded cone fitted with a spindle having a handwheel at one end and a hardened cutting disk at the other. In use the cone is pressed down into the opening of the faucet body so that the spindle is vertical. Then, while holding the cone, the handwheel is rotated in clockwise direction, using light pressure to avoid corrugating the surface of the seat.

Wrenches: Different types of wrenches are shown in Fig. 3. Most essential for pipe work are pipe wrenches, detail A, which also gives the sizes most suitable for use on pipes of different diameters. Two pipe wrenches, 10 and 18-in. sizes, just about cover the requirements of the average homeowner. Two wrenches are required because it is often necessary to hold pipe from turning with one wrench while the other is used to turn a fitting. If a wrench of still larger size is needed, use a chain wrench. See detail B. A lever-action, jaw-locking pliers, detail C, will serve as a smaller pipe wrench than the 10-in. size.

In placing a pipe wrench on pipe properly, the jaws should fit loosely so that movement of the handle will make the teeth grip the pipe firmly, but without crushing it. Never exert force sideways on a pipe wrench as shown in detail E. This is likely to bend the wrench so that the jaws are out of alignment. A pipe wrench should not be used on brass or plated pipe as it causes marring. The proper tool for such purposes is a strap wrench, detail F. A girth-type pipe wrench, detail G, is used for heavier jobs where pipe must not be marred, or the clearance is too small to permit the use of another type of wrench.

Open-end wrenches, adjustable wrenches and monkey wrenches, details H, I and J respectively of Fig. 3, are used to grip square or hexagon nuts and similarly shaped portions of faucets and valves; a pipe wrench will mar them. Detail K shows a closet-spud wrench which is thin and fits in restricted places. When using an open-end wrench, be sure that it just fits on two parallel flats. If there is excessive play, the corners of a nut or fitting will be marred or rounded. In close quarters, where an open-end wrench cannot be swung far enough to permit slipping it on the next pair of flats, the difficulty is solved by turning the wrench over sideways to present a different angle. An adjustable wrench and also a monkey wrench should always be placed so that most of the pressure is exerted on the stationary jaw. The work is nested as far into the jaws as possible as shown in detail L. A pulling force is safer than a pushing force as it prevents bruised knuckles when the work suddenly "breaks loose." If pushing is necessary, apply pressure to the wrench handle with the palm while holding the hand open. Don't use a wrench as a hammer and don't slip a length of pipe over the handle for extra leverage. Strips of cardboard placed over the flats on plated fittings will keep them from be-

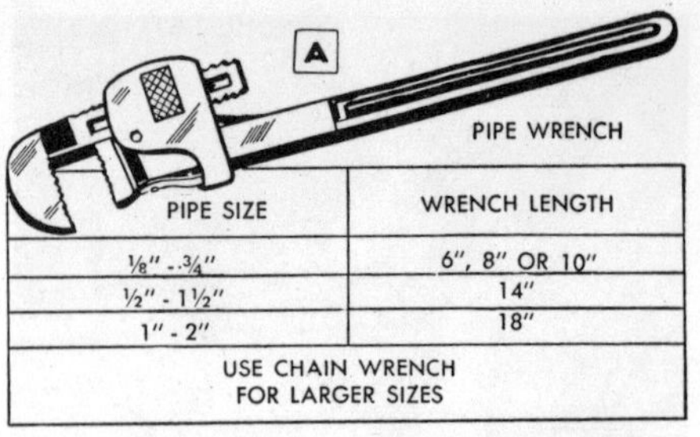

PIPE SIZE	WRENCH LENGTH
1/8" - 3/4"	6", 8" OR 10"
1/2" - 1 1/2"	14"
1" - 2"	18"
USE CHAIN WRENCH FOR LARGER SIZES	

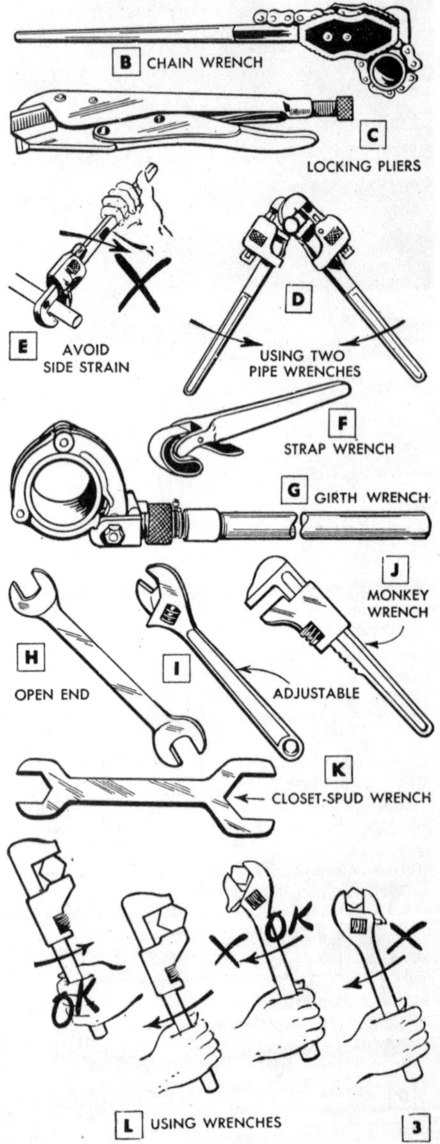

ing marred. Don't use pliers for turning a nut or a plated fitting.

Pipe vises: Holding pipe securely for cutting or threading is almost impossible with an ordinary mechanic's vise. Pipe-vise jaws are serrated like those of a pipe wrench to prevent pipe from turning. The self-locking vise shown in Figs. 4 and 5B can be opened quickly by releasing the upper part, which is pivoted. Less space is required for a chain vise, Fig. 5A. The handle, which swivels on a nut, tightens the pipe placed between the jaw and a length of chain. Another type of pipe vise can be attached to a post. The average homeowner can get a combination pipe and mechanic's vise, detail C, which serves both purposes.

An improvised arrangement that serves as a pipe vise in an emergency, consists of a pipe wrench used in conjunction with a mechanics vise as shown in Fig. 5D. The pipe handle, bearing down on the bench top, takes most of the strain and prevents the pipe from turning in the vise. Detail E shows another improvised arrangement where a pipe wrench is nested between two cleats nailed to the bench. A U-bolt extending through the bench top holds the pipe down.

Plumbers frequently use portable pipe-vise stands as in detail F. When using a pipe vise, a pipe wrench or pliers, avoid gripping hardened rods, sleeves, tubing or other hardened work which is likely to dull the teeth of these tools.

Pipe cutters and reamers: A regular pipe cutter, Fig. 4, cuts pipe accurately at right angles to its axis, and does the job much quicker and easier than possible with a hacksaw. Square cuts, Fig. 7A, are necessary in order to get the threading tool started properly. To use a pipe cutter slip it over the pipe and turn the handle until the pipe is held lightly, with the cutter edge resting on the mark. Don't attempt to cut pipe closer than 1 in. from the end, as this does not leave sufficient support for the cutter. Next, apply some thread-cutting or lard oil to the pipe surface and cutting wheel. Then swing the cutter around to score the pipe, after which the handle is turned a little to advance the cutter each

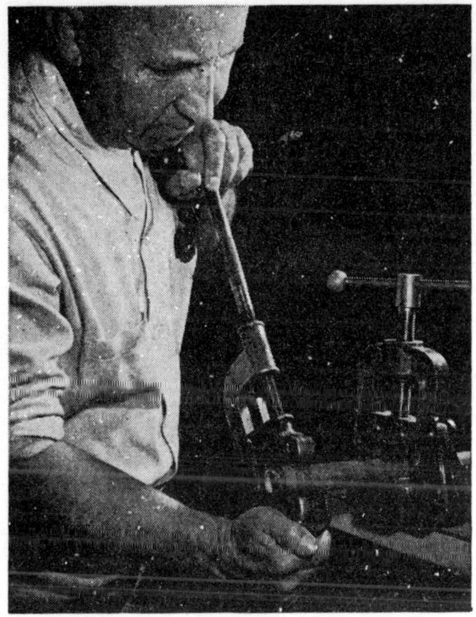

4

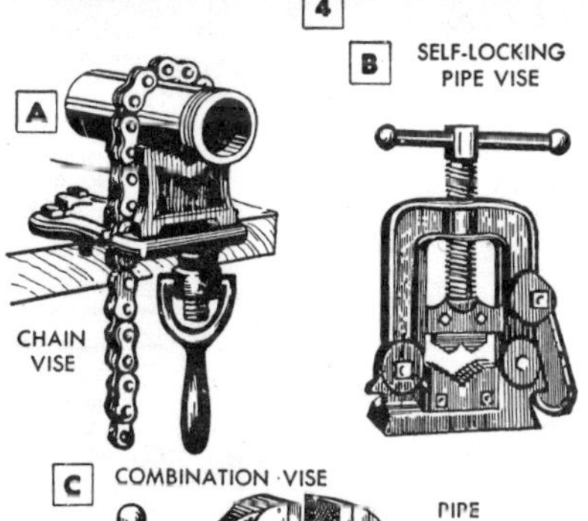

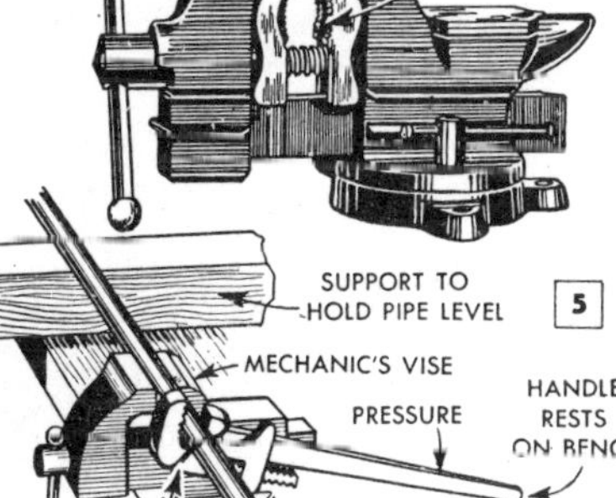

time the tool is brought around the work. Cutting oil is applied from time to time for lubrication and cooling. The cut end of the pipe is reamed, as in Fig. 6, to remove the burr on the inside, Fig. 7A. Three types of pipe reamers are shown in details B, C and D of Fig. 7. Burrs left on the inside of the pipe tend to hold particles that may cause eventual clogging.

Threading tools: External threading at pipe ends, Fig. 8, is done by means of threading dies. There are two types: The solid, nonadjustable dies, detail A of Fig. 9, and the split or adjustable die, detail B, which permits variations of cutting depth. A solid die is best for the average homeowner. A different die is required for each pipe size. Each die is marked with the nominal size of the pipe for which it is designed, and the number of threads per inch. The pipe size is approximate inside diameter.

To use a die you fit it in the head of a stock, together with a guide bushing which is to slip on the pipe first and thus accurately align both pipe and die. As a die cuts a tapered thread, it is necessary that the largest diameter of the threads face the guide bushing. Die stocks may have two handles, Fig. 9C, which shows stocks for solid and split dies, or they may be of the one-handle, ratchet type, detail D. There are also stocks having three die holders so that dies of different sizes are instantly available.

After slipping the guide bushing over the pipe, press the die teeth on the pipe slightly while turning the stock slowly toward the right—clockwise direction. Keep the handle at right angles to the pipe and apply a steady pressure until the die engages. Apply cutting oil liberally; it lubricates and cools both work and tool, preventing ruin of tempered edges. Start cutting the thread by turning the stock forward half a turn, then back again a quarter turn to break the chips, then forward again, etc. Turn the stock slowly to avoid excessive heating and apply cutting oil every two or three turns. Stop threading when the end of the pipe projects about half a thread beyond the small end of the die. This indicates that a thread of approximately standard length has been cut. Good threads are sharp and cleanly cut. Imperfect threads result from using a worn or damaged die, one that is improperly adjusted, clogged with dirt and chips or from not using enough cutting oil while threading.

When it is necessary to screw pipe into a piece of metal, first drill a hole of proper size for a pipe tap. Internal threading is called "tapping." Pipe taps are marked like dies according to the nominal pipe size and number of threads per inch. Some taps are combined with drills of proper size, Fig. 9E.

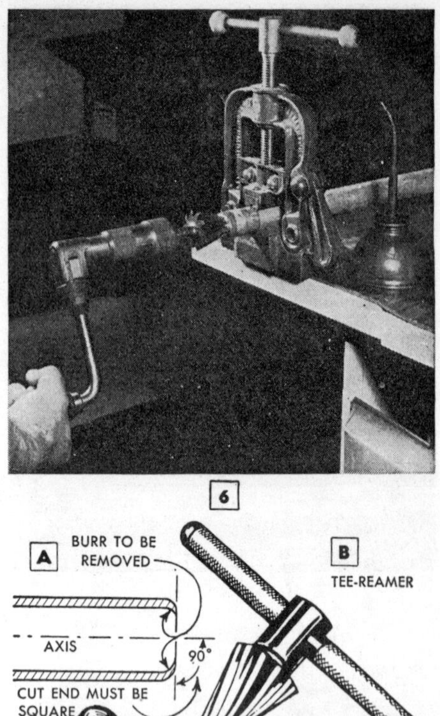

6

7

When a separate drill is used, select one of correct size for the tap according to the information given in table F. Like dies, taps require the application of cutting or lard oil for lubrication and cooling.

Tools for copper tubing: Special tools are needed for copper tubing. A tube cutter, Fig. 10A, is a midget version of a pipe cutter but is not made to cut iron and steel. Both tubing and cutter can be held by hand. Tubing is cut dry, the cutting wheel being advanced ⅛ to ¼ turn per revolution of the tool. Feeding too fast squashes the tubing out of round. Some tube cutters are equipped with a sliding internal reamer. A combination internal and external reamer is shown in detail B. Outside burr can be removed with a file also. Although cutters for large-size tubing are available, a hacksaw fitted with a blade having 32 teeth per in. can be used. For cutting with a hacksaw,

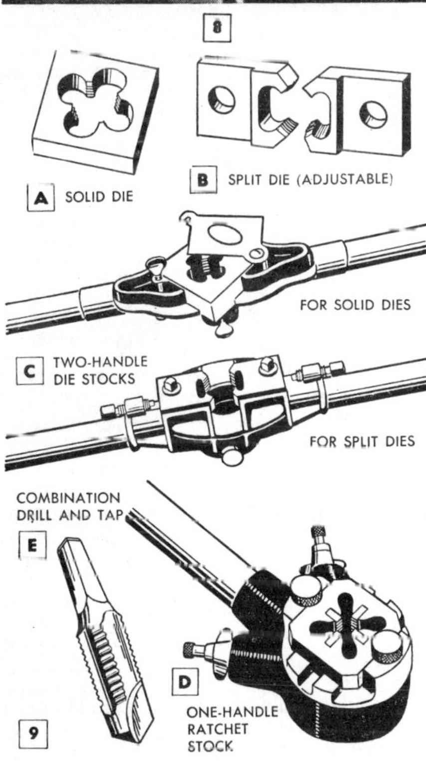

F DRILL SIZES FOR PIPE TAPS			
TAPS	DRILLS	TAPS	DRILLS
1/8"	21/64	1"	1 3/16
1/4"	29/64	1 1/4"	1 15/32
3/8"	19/32	1 1/2"	1 23/32
1/2"	23/32	2"	2 3/16
3/4"	15/16		

the tubing must be held in a jig having a saw guide. See detail C. An improvised jig is shown in detail D.

Where flared-tube fittings are used, accurate flaring of tubing is done after the sleeve nut of a fitting is slipped over it. A flaring tool consists of a flare block and a screw-type punch, detail E. One type has rollers in the spreader cone of the punch that burnish the tubing to assure tighter fitting joints. This will not score the tubing. A drop of oil rubbed on the surface of the flaring cone prevents the tendency of copper from sticking and possibly tearing. Also oil the punch thread. On most of these tools the tube should project 1/16 to 1/8 in. above the flare block—1/8 in. for a 1-in. tube. Most flaring tools accommodate tubing from 1/4 to 5/8 in. in diameter, but they can also be obtained for tubing from 5/8 to 1 1/8 in. A hammer-driven flaring punch is also used for the larger sizes, detail F.

Spring-steel coils shown in detail G, available to fit tubing of various sizes, are slipped over or inside of the tubing in order to prevent kinks when bending. Special bending fixtures, detail H, assure accurate small-radii bends. Some types attach to a bench. Detail I shows the two parts of a sizing tool, used to restore perfect roundness in copper tubing that is slightly bent or dented by handling. There are several sizes. Swedging tools, in sets of several sizes, detail J, are used to enlarge the ends of tubing for a spliced joint. A refacing tool, detail K, with interchangeable cutters, renews damaged seats in flare-type fittings.

Blowtorch: Used for sweat-soldering fittings on copper tubing, for melting out leaded joints such as on soil pipe, and for other purposes, a blowtorch, Fig. 11, generates a flame temperature of as much as 2200 deg. F. Only white gasoline should be used to fill the tank—not leaded gasoline. Do the filling away from combustible material, preferably in open air. The filler plug may be at the bottom or combined with the pump. Fill the tank halfway, then screw the plug in tightly. Operate the pump to build up air pressure. Before starting, let gasoline spilled on the outside evaporate. To start the torch, hold one hand over the nozzle while turning the needle valve to open it. Then the pin stream of gasoline, which is released, will be confined within the combustion chamber and will drip into the priming cup. When doing this, the torch should be placed on a level surface to prevent gasoline from dripping outside of the cup. When the cup is about half full, turn off the valve and ignite the gasoline. The flame heats the vaporizing chamber above the cup.

When nearly all the gasoline has burned, and before the flame dies out, open the

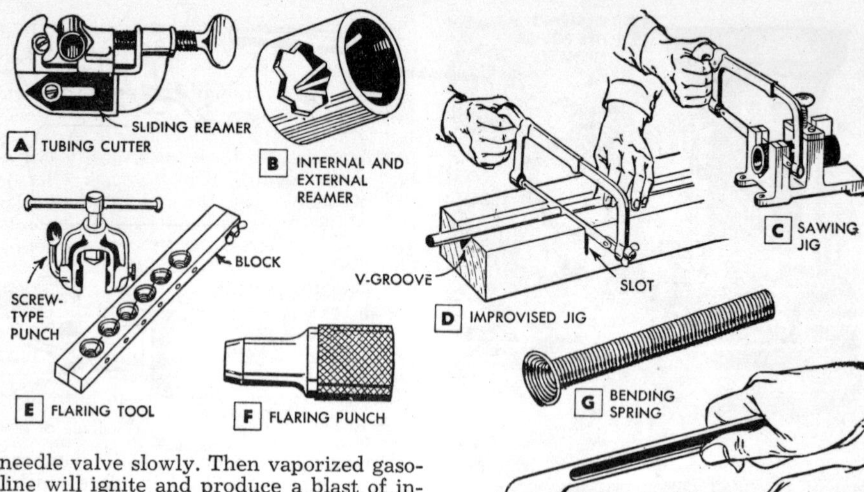

10

needle valve slowly. Then vaporized gasoline will ignite and produce a blast of intense heat. Be sure to open the valve slowly to prevent a stream of fire that results if the vaporizing chamber has not been heated sufficiently. In case of insufficient preheating, the starting process is repeated. After the torch has been started, the size of the flame is controlled with the valve. Occasional pumping is necessary to maintain air pressure in the tank. During its operation the torch keeps the vaporizing chamber hot. Turn the valve shut to extinguish the flame—not too tightly however, as the contraction of the hot metal parts will further tighten the needle in its seat and "freeze" it. Leather pump washers require occasional oiling to keep them pliable.

Use a blowtorch with care. Some fire-insurance policies disclaim liability of payment for fires resulting from a blowtorch used on the premises by the owner or other person not professionally engaged in the work. When working close to combustible material, shield it with a doubled sheet of asbestos or a piece of asbestos-fiber board. As a substitute for a blowtorch on many jobs you can use a special torch that burns liquefied petroleum, which comes in bottled form to fit the torch head. You can also use an acetylene torch. Both kinds produce an instant flame when ignited.

Plumber's furnace: A firepot or small blast furnace, detail A of Fig. 12, is used for melting lead. It operates like a blowtorch and can be used as a substitute for many purposes. The top of a firepot is removable. Keep the pot clean, removing dross and lead oxide with a chisel and wire brush.

P. Wall Mfg. Co. photo

11

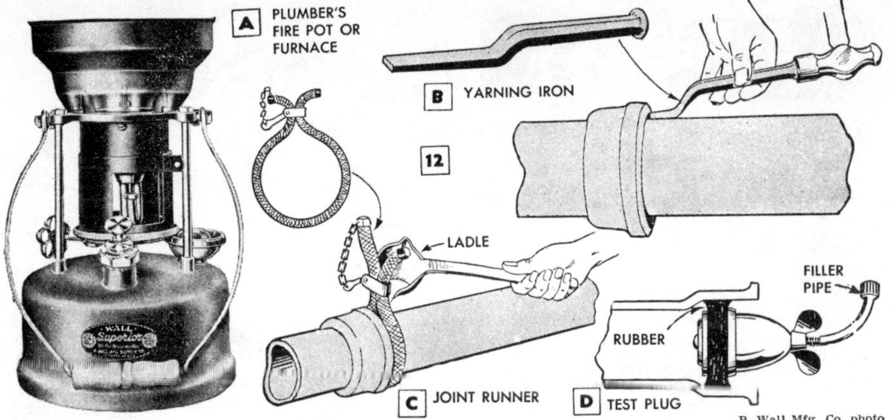

P. Wall Mfg. Co. photo

When melting lead, place the smallest surface of the lead cakes on the bottom to promote rapid melting. Heat the lead to a cherry-red color and don't stir it. This causes oxide to form more rapidly. Preheat the ladle before dipping it into molten lead, and keep it hot when not in use by hanging it over the edge of the pot. Use the ladle bottom to push back dross on the surface so that enough clean lead is exposed to dip out a ladleful without dross.

Precautions when using molten lead: Avoid pouring molten lead on wet or damp surfaces or into joints containing moisture. The quick formation of steam will cause the lead to spatter and with possible injurious results. For this reason it is wise to protect the eyes with goggles and the hands with gloves. Always stand back and hold the ladle at arm's length when pouring.

Calking and leading soil-pipe joints: A yarning iron, Fig. 12B, has a long offset blade for packing down oakum into deep joints such as those on soil pipe. Calking irons are similar except that the blades are shorter. When joints are made in pipe laid horizontally, an asbestos "joint runner," detail C, keeps the lead in place until it hardens. The ends are held with a clip, which may include a pouring spout.

Test plugs: Test plugs, Fig. 12D, are used to seal open ends of a soil-pipe installation when testing for leaks. A test plug consists of a thick rubber ring held between two metal disks. Forcing these together by means of a large wingnut and sleeve expands the diameter of the ring and forces it tightly against the pipe. It has an inlet tube through which the pipe can be filled.

Sewer-cleaning tools: To clear clogged soil pipes and house sewers, large augers or rods and rodding points, Fig. 13, are used. The augers, from ½ to 1 in. in diameter, are rotated by hand. Some are power driven as shown in Fig. 19 of Section 7. Rods, also called "snakes," are worked back and forth. They come in sizes up to ⅛ by 1½ in., in lengths of 25 to 100 ft., and fit into steel frames which make uncoiling and replacing easy. Rods also are made of hickory, ash and steel tubing in 3 and 4-ft. lengths.

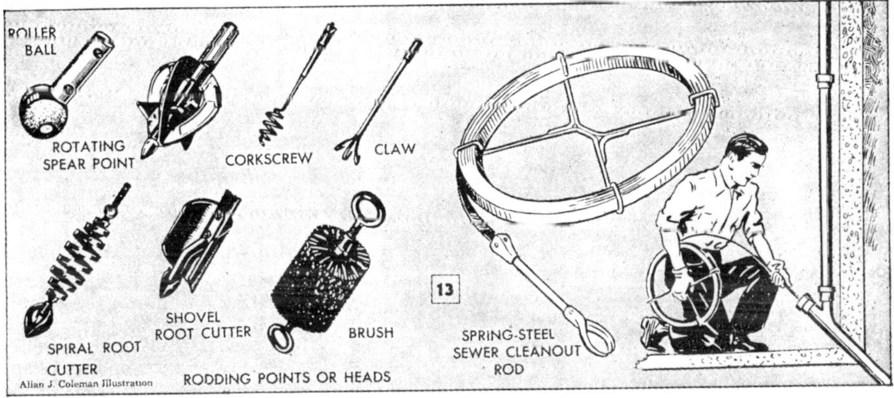

Allan J. Coleman Illustration

PANEL YOUR HOME WITH

ARE YOU INTERESTED in refinishing a room, paneling the attic or basement or completing the interior of a new home? If so, plywood in one of its many textures and finishes can do an excellent job and, best of all, it is easy for the amateur to apply.

Today, plywood is being used extensively on walls and ceilings with striking results—another of the countless applications to which this versatile building material naturally lends itself.

As there is a wide variety of types and price ranges from which to choose, selecting the plywood best suited for your particular purpose becomes but a matter of personal taste and budget. Common fir is the most inexpensive of the plywoods and will make attractive walls and ceilings if finished correctly. At only a slight additional cost, you can have fir plywoods with special surface textures—Plyweave, striated (combed) or sandblasted. Then there are the vertical-grain, or rift, fir panels; fir plywood that is quarter-sawed from logs in the same way as a select board, with tone and grain as rich as many a hardwood. Highly attractive softwood paneling is available in redwood and knotty-pine plywoods. Finally, there are many hardwood plywoods—gum, oak, birch, mahogany, walnut, korina—each distinctive in its grain and coloring, and providing a selection to blend with any interior decorating.

Plywood panels are worked easily with ordinary tools, are exceptionally strong and will provide the most scuffproof and crackproof of dry-wall construction. The major problem with plywood is that it goes

Seven of the many plywoods now available are pictured below. The samples, from left to right, are redwood Plyweave, fir Plyweave, rift-grain fir, rift-grain redwood, walnut, smoky birch and African mahogany

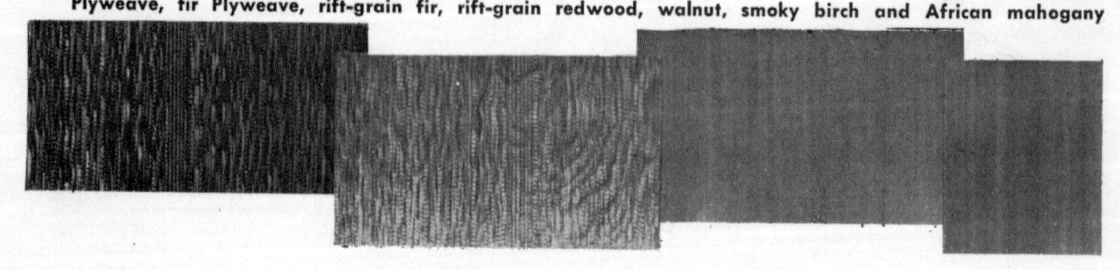

Color photos courtesy M & M Plywood Corp.

PLYWOOD

on the walls so quickly that you are tempted to be careless. However, when you take time to use a good paneling method and finishing procedure, there will be no gaping joints or somber finishes.

The common 4 x 8-ft. panel is the right height for most walls and fits standard studding. Smaller panels also are fairly common, and extra-long panels (up to 12 ft.) are available for covering high walls as well as spanning the width of ceilings. Common fir plywood is available in two types—interior and waterproof exterior. The latter is necessary only around the bathtub and shower. Each type is graded (A, B, C and D) depending on the defects in the panel faces. As only one face is exposed, interior A-D plywood, which has one clear face (A grade) and the other

Wall in living room of *Popular Mechanics* ranch house is of ¼-in. walnut plywood toned with a red-mahogany oil stain

The tasteful use of plywood in cabinets and wall paneling adds warmth to the room and sets off the stone fireplace

Kitchen cabinets are of rift-grain redwood plywood and exposed wall areas are of enameled rift-grain fir plywood

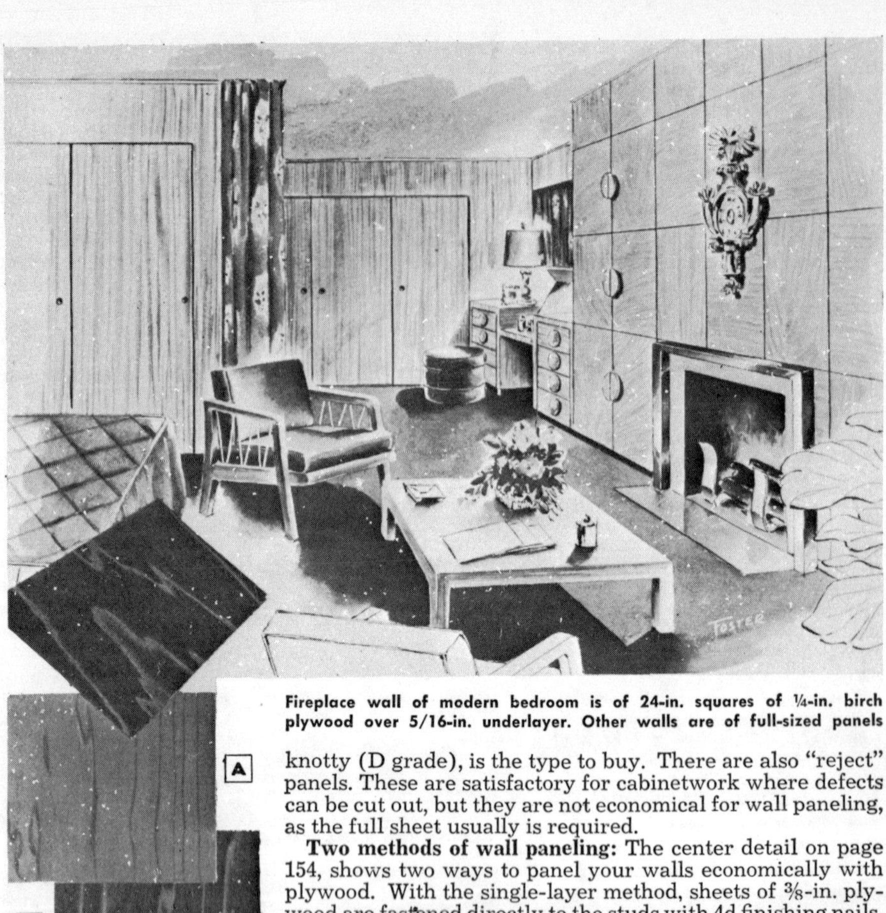

Fireplace wall of modern bedroom is of 24-in. squares of ¼-in. birch plywood over 5/16-in. underlayer. Other walls are of full-sized panels

A

B

C

D

E

knotty (D grade), is the type to buy. There are also "reject" panels. These are satisfactory for cabinetwork where defects can be cut out, but they are not economical for wall paneling, as the full sheet usually is required.

Two methods of wall paneling: The center detail on page 154, shows two ways to panel your walls economically with plywood. With the single-layer method, sheets of ⅜-in. plywood are fastened directly to the studs with 4d finishing nails. It is important to apply a good glue, preferably a plastic resin, liberally along the studs before nailing down the fitted panels. For the sake of economy, ¼-in. plywood can be used, but the panels will have a tendency to "boom" when struck and perhaps to bulge between the studs. This is especially true if the studs are spaced farther apart than the usual 16 in. on centers. The ¼-in. thickness, however, frequently is used under wallpaper and similar coverings.

The double-layer method is the best one to use with the more expensive hardwood plywoods, because it produces an excellent wall with only ¼-in. finish plywood. The underlayer is usually of 5/16-in. Plyscord, which is simply a C-D grade (knotty on both sides) of fir plywood that has been left unsanded. This is the cheapest underlay, but if it is not available, you can substitute ¼-in. fir plywood or good, dry ¾-in. lumber. The underlay is secured to the studs with 6d common nails, without gluing, and is installed crosswise to the direction of the finish panels. The ¼-in. finish layer is nailed to the underlay and studs with 4d finishing nails or ¾-in. brads, with glue under all joints and at spots in between. Try to avoid having joints in both the underlay and finish paneling on the same stud. With both the single and double-layer methods, the nails are spaced 6 in. apart along all edges and are driven at 10-in. intervals to the studs in between. It is recommended practice to leave the paneling unglued but nailed at the room corners to permit expansion in case the wall framing should shift or settle. The double-layer method also should be employed whenever small squares or narrow boards are used for paneling, as the underlay allows the smaller pieces to be nailed and glued securely regardless of whether or not their edges fall on a stud.

On new construction: In the open walls of a new house or unfinished attic, insert short sections of 2 x 4 horizontally between the studs at a height of 4 ft. above the floor. If the panels are applied horizontally, the inserts will provide a backing for the joints; if not, the inserts will form additional bracing and also serve as fire stops. If using single-layer paneling, insert 2 x 4 backing pieces similarly at any spot where a joint will occur.

On old plaster walls: You will find it necessary to apply furring strips over plaster walls before paneling. These can be lengths of 1 x 2 or 2 to 3-in. strips of 1/4 or 3/8-in. plywood. Full-length horizontal strips should be spaced 24 in. apart and short strips nailed vertically over the studs between the horizontal strips. Fasten the paneling to the strips with glue and nails.

On masonry or concrete walls: Use heavier furring strips, 1 x 2 or 2 x 2 stock, on concrete or masonry, spacing the strips as on plaster walls or simply nailing them vertically on 16-in. centers. Use concrete nails or drill the wall, plug the holes with dowels and nail the furring to the plugs.

Masonry or concrete basement walls often are damp, so asphalted building paper should be applied underneath the furring strips. If the wall is definitely damp, it should be given a coat of waterproof cement paint and the backs of the plywood panels coated with aluminum paint. In extreme cases, waterproof plywood should be used.

Paneling layouts: The way in which the paneling is laid out on the walls is entirely a matter of the type of effect you desire. When you intend to accent the panel joints, always panel above and below the openings first, using vertical joints from floor or ceiling to the openings. Then divide remaining wall spaces into the desired pattern.

Joints: When using smooth paneling, the finished wall usually will be most attractive if the joints are accented rather than concealed. Plyweave and striated plywoods present no joint problem, as their texture makes any joint practically invisible. For perfect fitting flush joints, plane the back edge of each panel at the joint to produce a slight bevel. This will assure a tight fit at the front edge, glue filling in the space behind. On painted panels, flush joints may be taped the same as plasterboard. All wall paneling should clear the floor by 1/4 to 1/2 in., the lower joints being covered by the baseboard.

Traditional wall paneling in this room consists of 3/8-in. rift-grain fir plywood glued and nailed to the studs. Panels are outlined by nailing 3/4-in. boards over the plywood and adding stock or picture molding

Recessed shelves and paneling of ¼-in. oak plywood form distinctive entrance to this living room

¼" OR ⅜" PLYWOOD GLUED AND NAILED TO STUD

¼" FINISH PLYWOOD, GLUED AND NAILED

$\frac{5}{16}$" PLYWOOD

SINGLE LAYER

DOUBLE LAYER

Ceilings: Plywood is applied to ceilings in the same way as to walls. However, because ceiling joists usually are lengthy beams with some warp and due to the fact that 2 x 4 blocking between the joists would be required at all panel joints, it usually is easier to apply furring to the ceiling joists in all cases. It is best to install 1 x 3s crosswise to the joists, spacing them 24 in. apart and nailing short lengths of 1 x 3 along alternate joists. Glue and nail the ceiling panels to the furring strips, spacing the nails at 6-in. intervals on the joints and 10 in. between them. Often, ceiling panels are applied in small rectangles or squares to obtain a tiled pattern, but it is easier to simulate tile by scoring full-size panels with a portable electric router or saw. Cut the grooves to the same 24 x 32-in. pattern as the furring so you can nail the panels in the grooves. Ceilings also can be paneled with any of the joints shown for the walls. Always panel the ceiling before the walls, as it is easier to fit the wall panels to the ceiling panels. To handle a large ceiling panel by yourself, build a "horse" like the one detailed on page 156.

Finishing: The finish on any wood-paneled wall is important. On rotary-cut fir plywood and also on rift-grain fir, redwood, gum and birch, a good natural-wood finish is obtained by applying a coat of thinned clear shellac or resin sealer, followed by a coat of white sealer or white paint which is rubbed on with a cloth and wiped off to the desired tone. Third, a finish coat of dull varnish, shellac or lacquer is applied. The white coat softens any orange coloring and

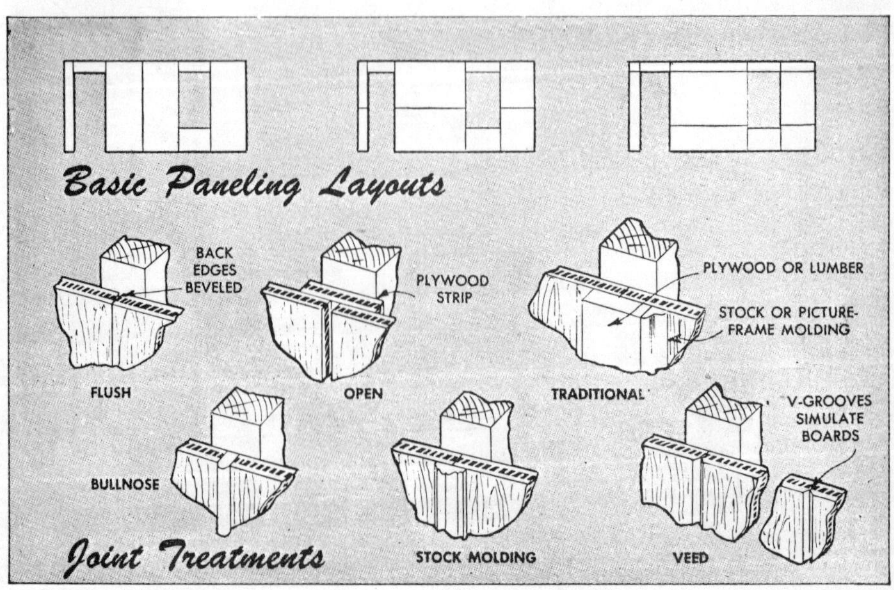

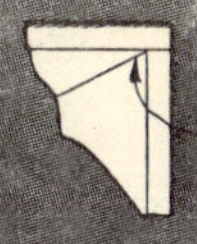
PLANED TO FIT
FLUSH JOINT

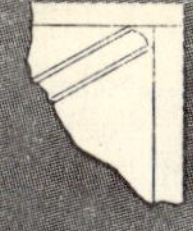
STOCK WOOD MOLDING

ALUMINUM LINOLEUM TRIM

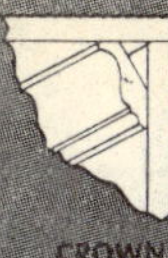
CROWN MOLDING

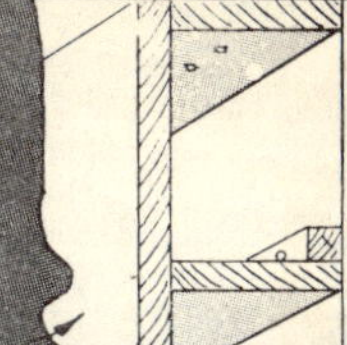
VALANCE BOARD
Ceiling-Wall Trim

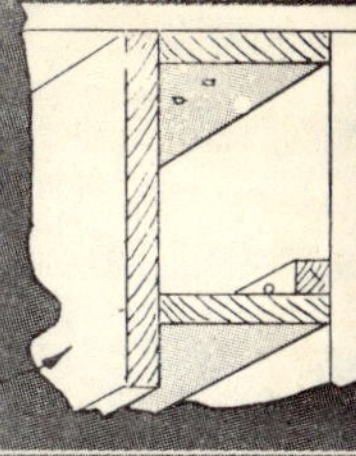

PLANED TO FIT
BUTT JOINT

¼ ROUND OR COVE
STOCK MOLDING

PLAIN OR FLUTED
WIDE MOLDING

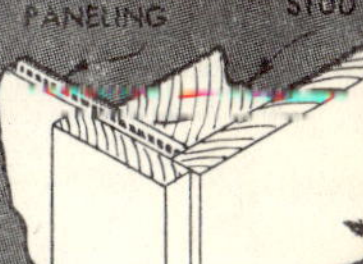
Door and Window Trim
INTERIOR WALL PANELING
STUD
DOOR OR WINDOW FRAME
CONVENTIONAL TRIM

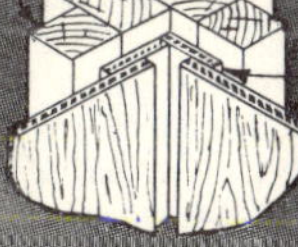
BLOCKING
FLEXIBLE ⅛" CORNER VENEERING
VENEER STRIPS
SAME PLYWOOD
OPEN CORNER

½" SQ. MOLDING
BLOCKED CORNER
Inside Corners

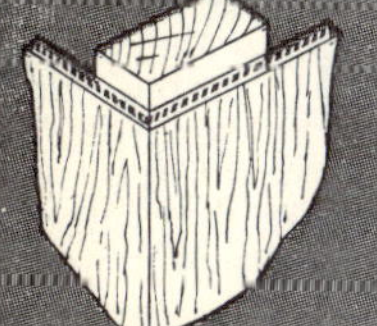
MITER JOINT

WELDWOOD MOLDING

VENEERED ALUMINUM MOLDING
CUT TO THICKNESS OF WALL PANEL
USING OUTSIDE CORNER MOLD

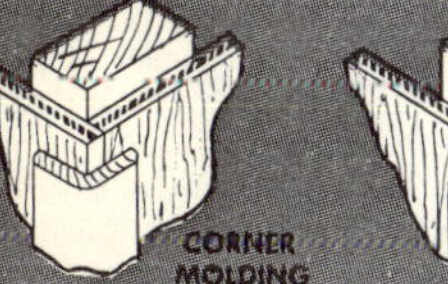
CORNER MOLDING

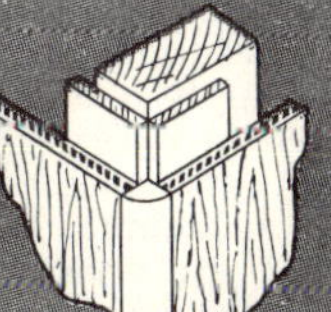
¼ ROUND

OPEN CORNER
Outside Corners

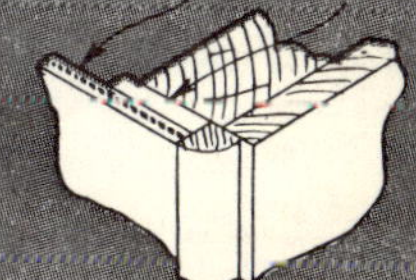
¼" PANELING
¼" STRIP
USING ½" STOCK ¼ ROUND

Wall-Floor Trim
WITH OR WITHOUT SHOE MOLD
"SANITARY" BASEBOARD

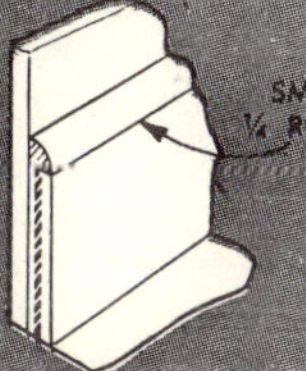
SMALL ¼ ROUND
PLYWOOD TO MATCH PANELING

¼ ROUND OR BEVEL TRIM

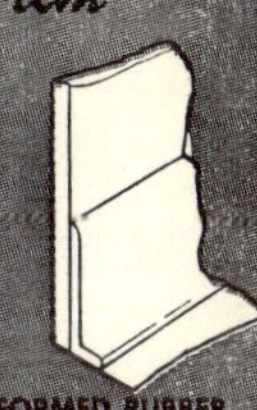
FORMED RUBBER PLASTIC OR ASPHALT BASEBOARD

Note in photo at left how plywood panels are fastened to 1 x 3 furring strips nailed to ceiling joists

neutralizes the tendency of fir to darken. Walls of oak and mahogany can be finished similarly, except that a white filler should be added to the second coat.

For a simple blond finish, brush on a first coat of white resin sealer or thinned undercoat. After a few minutes, rub this down with rags to the tone desired and follow, when dry, with a finish coat of shellac or lacquer. A rich, natural finish on the various hardwood panels is obtained easily by applying one coat of wallpaper lacquer.

An excellent way to stain common fir and any other plywood in a variety of pastel tones is to use ordinary oil paint. Brush on a first coat of any color paint or enamel undercoat, thinned half and half with turpentine. After approximately 15 min., wipe it down to the tone desired and apply a finish coat of varnish, shellac or lacquer. The photos on page 152 show various effects of this method on rotary-cut redwood plywood. The sample at the top is a natural redwood panel; A, stained with dark-yellow paint; B, green; C, gray paint; D, red-mahogany stain; E, light-yellow paint. Various finishes and grain effects are obtained by using different colors and varying the amount of wiping. Another attractive finish is achieved by applying any of the new wax stains and rubbing them to the tone desired. With any staining or toning, experiment first on scraps of plywood. On Plyweave or striated plywood, a soft two-tone finish is produced by applying a white undercoat and then a coat of the color desired. The latter is wiped down to expose the white on the high spots.

For glass-smooth enameled walls, rift-grain fir, gumwood and birch plywoods are best. Apply a first coat of resin sealer to prevent grain rise; next, apply undercoat, 1 part, and enamel, 1 part; then, a finish coat of enamel. For a smooth, enameled surface on rotary-cut fir, first prime the plywood with thin white paint and apply painter's muslin over it, using wallpaper paste. When dry, glue-size the muslin and then apply any conventional enamel finish.

Common fir plywood, with its joints glued, is an excellent base for wallpaper. Apply rough-textured papers directly to the sized panels, and smooth papers to a layer of wallpaper liner or felt. Ceilings can be finished in the same way as walls; however, they usually are preferred in a neutral, plasterlike finish. Here, plastic or resin-base texture paints should be used, applying them with a roller or brushing on and stippling. ★ ★ ★

CEILINGS PANELED WITH 4' X 8' SHEETS

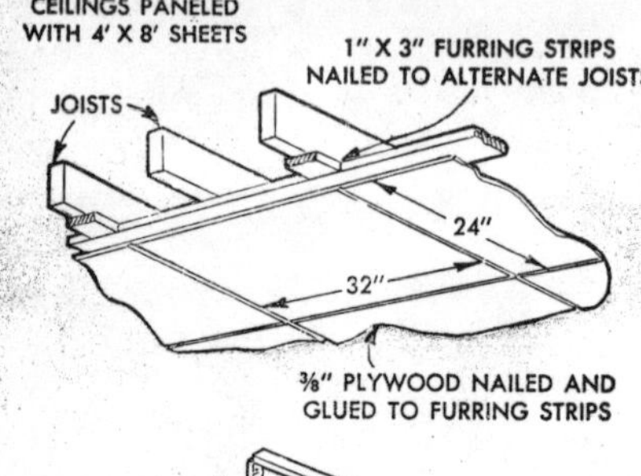

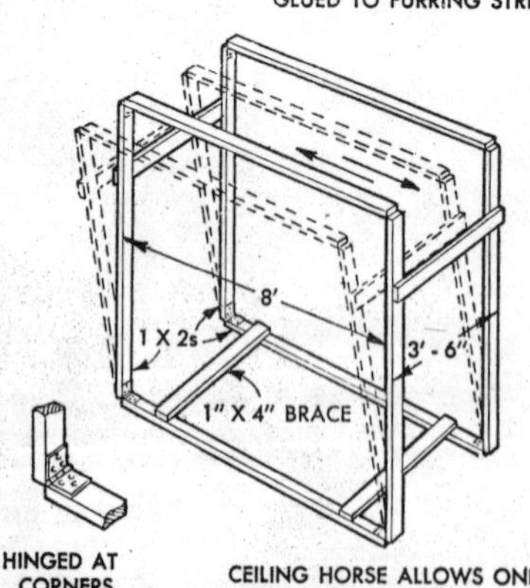

CEILING HORSE ALLOWS ONE MAN TO APPLY LARGE PANELS

To obtain plastered effect, texture paint is brushed on heavily and then surfaced with flat rubber sponge

PLYWOOD BENDING

Here Is Easy Way to Bend Plywood

If you have had difficulty in bending plywood, try the following method: First wet both sides of the wood and then go over it with a hot smoothing iron, preferably an electric one, which is hot enough to convert the moisture to steam. Go over each side of the board twice in this manner. Then, as the wood is being bent, apply the hot iron to the wet surface as the arc is formed. Quarter-inch fir plywood may be bent around a 4-in. radius without cracking.

PLYWOOD CUTTING

Two C-Clamps and Scrap Board Support Plywood When Cutting

Cutting a piece off the overhanging end of a large plywood panel usually is an awkward task. Trying to hold the piece and saw at the same time usually results in the saw binding and the piece cracking off before the cut is completed. To overcome this, Herbert E. Fey of New Braunfels, Tex., supports the work in the manner illustrated. He first saws the panel for a distance of about 12 in. Then, using two C-clamps, he clamps a scrap board across the end of the unsupported piece, attaching one clamp to the plywood at the right side of the line and the other to the outer edge of the piece being cut. This keeps the end from dropping down. The sawing is continued to a point about 12 in. from the rear edge and then the board clamped across the edge is swung down, as indicated by the dotted lines, to give support to the work as the sawing is completed.

PLYWOOD SPLICING

Two Pieces of Plywood Spliced To Make One Large Panel

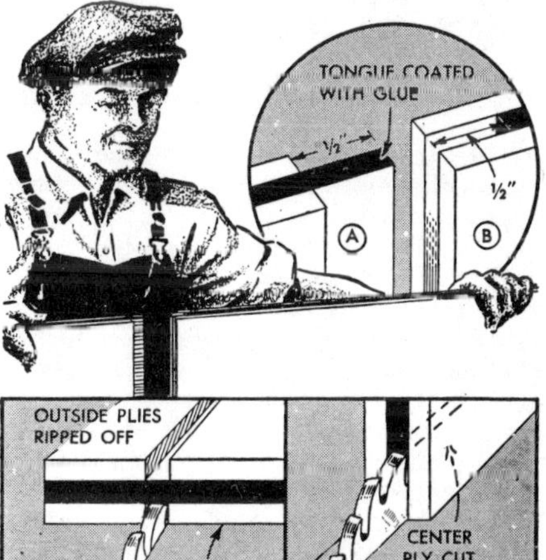

When a plywood panel larger than any available is needed, one can be made by splicing two pieces together. To do this, a tongue is formed on the end of one piece as at A, and the end of the other piece is grooved as at B. On ¼-in. plywood, the groove can be made by cutting out the center ply on a circular saw, and the tongue can be shaped by cutting away the two outside plies. The panel is assembled by coating the tongue with glue and pressing it into the groove. Wood plastic or filler can be used to fill any small cracks at the splice line. After the glue has dried, the joint is sanded smooth and the panel used without any danger of its warping or buckling.-

POLISHING HEAD ATTACHMENT

THIS AUXILIARY polishing head is just the thing for the small shop having one grinder, either of the bench type or pedestal type. It saves the time and inconvenience of changing the grinding wheel when polishing and buffing are to be done. The polishing head is driven from a short spindle mounting two V-pulleys and internally threaded to screw onto the end of the grinder shaft in place of the nut, which normally turns up against the wheel flange. The head, Fig. 2, is supported in a jig clamp attached to the grinder pedestal. A jig clamp for the bench-type grinder is made from a pipe tee and a short length of angle iron as in Fig. 1. The head, Fig. 2, is a machined and welded job mounting ball bearings to carry the high-speed polishing spindle, which is shouldered and threaded at both ends for washers and a castle nut which provides bearing adjustment.

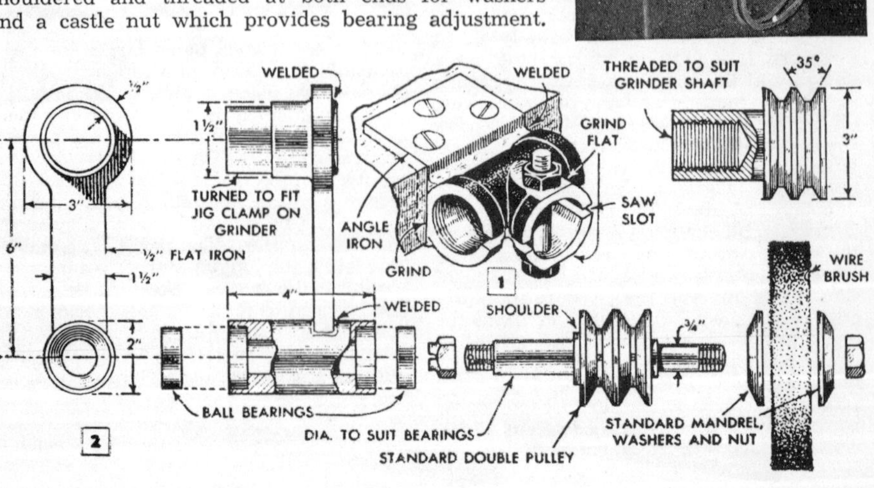

PORCELAIN REPAIRS

ON YOUR SINK, RANGE, REFRIGERATOR

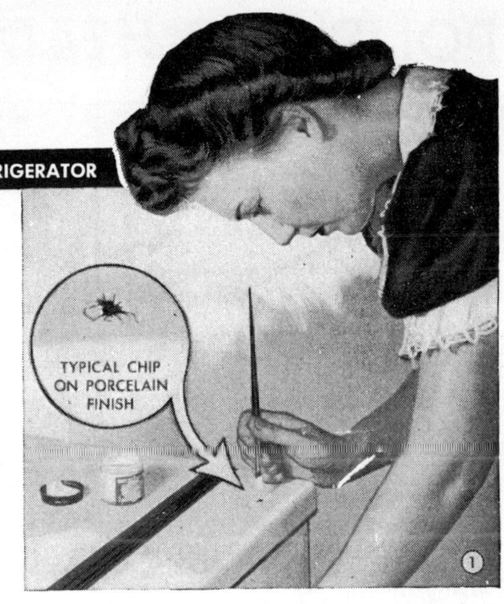

REPAIRING chips and scratches on porcelain or synthetic baked enamel is so simple that no housewife need hesitate to undertake the work. A variety of special patching products is available, usually at dime or hardware stores.

Stick porcelain: As the name implies, this type comes in stick form and is made fluid by heating. Use any thin flexible knife, such as a paring knife, and heat it over a gas or alcohol flame, as shown in Fig. 2, holding the Porcelstix at the end of the knife. Melt off enough to fill the hole and then apply, Fig. 3. Don't worry if you get a little too much on—it dries in five minutes and can be scraped down cleanly and easily with a razor blade. Advantages of this product are speed and a clean, solid patch not easily affected by mild oven heat, cold or fruit juices. Only disadvantage is that white as the stick is, it is not as white as porcelain enamel. For better color matching, you can go over the patch with white enamel or lacquer.

Porcelain putty: Usually a very good

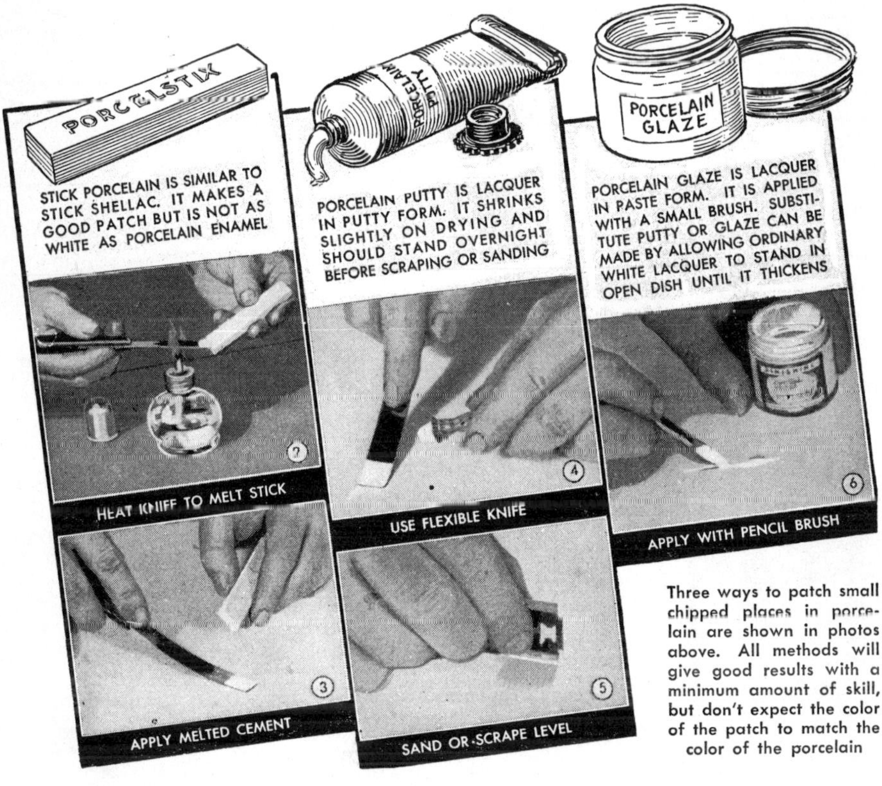

PORCELSTIX

STICK PORCELAIN IS SIMILAR TO STICK SHELLAC. IT MAKES A GOOD PATCH BUT IS NOT AS WHITE AS PORCELAIN ENAMEL

(2) HEAT KNIFF TO MELT STICK

(3) APPLY MELTED CEMENT

PORCELAIN PUTTY

PORCELAIN PUTTY IS LACQUER IN PUTTY FORM. IT SHRINKS SLIGHTLY ON DRYING AND SHOULD STAND OVERNIGHT BEFORE SCRAPING OR SANDING

(4) USE FLEXIBLE KNIFE

(5) SAND OR SCRAPE LEVEL

PORCELAIN GLAZE

PORCELAIN GLAZE IS LACQUER IN PASTE FORM. IT IS APPLIED WITH A SMALL BRUSH. SUBSTITUTE PUTTY OR GLAZE CAN BE MADE BY ALLOWING ORDINARY WHITE LACQUER TO STAND IN OPEN DISH UNTIL IT THICKENS

(6) APPLY WITH PENCIL BRUSH

Three ways to patch small chipped places in porcelain are shown in photos above. All methods will give good results with a minimum amount of skill, but don't expect the color of the patch to match the color of the porcelain

USE 5/0 PAPER FOR SANDING

COMPLETE REFINISHING SCHEDULES

REFRIGERATOR EXTERIORS

1—Wash thoroughly. Let dry. Wipe with alcohol or lacquer thinner on cloth.
2—Sand lightly, 3/0 silicon carbide.
3—(If old surface is badly checked or chipped all over.) Apply coat of white primer-surfacer. Sand thoroughly when dry with 3/0 paper, with water as lubricant. (If old surface is good.) Apply coat of white primer. Do not sand.
4—Apply first coat of white lacquer enamel.
5—Patch all holes with lacquer putty.
6—Sand patches smooth.
7—Apply second coat of white lacquer enamel. Scuff sand.
8—Apply mist coat of straight thinner. Let stand at full gloss.

REFRIGERATOR INTERIORS

1—Wash thoroughly. Let dry. Allow refrigerator to come to room temperature.
2—Spray or brush one coat of white shellac enamel.

KITCHEN RANGES

Follow same schedule as for refrigerator exteriors, but use air-dry-or-bake synthetic undercoats and top coats. Turn the oven on to bake the various finish coats over and around oven; let other parts air dry until fully hard.

white, this product is knifed into the defect, Fig. 4. It should stand a little above the surrounding surface since it will shrink slightly on drying. Allow plenty of drying time, at least overnight, before scraping or sanding smooth. If you sand smooth, use 5/0 paper backed with a felt or cork block, as shown in Fig. 7. With a little practice, you can get a perfectly level patch with a razor blade, used as shown in Fig. 5.

Porcelain glaze: This is thinner than putty—ideal for very small defects. Just take a brushful and apply, as in Figs. 1 and 6, let dry at least overnight, and then sand or scrape. This is usually the best white. Both putty and glaze can be homemade by taking ordinary lacquer or enamel and pouring off a small quantity in a dish. Let it stand in the open air until it thickens to the desired consistency. You can speed the work by adding dry powder color (zinc white or titanium dioxide) to the lacquer.

General rules: Whatever method you use, make a practice patch before starting actual work. Be sure the surface to be patched is clean. If there is an "island" in the chipped place, pry it out. Warm the surface slightly with a warm cloth before patching. Do not expect perfection—it is almost impossible to apply a direct patch and get a perfect color match.

Complete refinishing: This is preferably done by spraying. Follow the schedule shown. Do not attempt to spray lacquer or enamel directly over a porcelain finish—always use a primer or surfacer to get necessary bondage between old and new finish. On kitchen ranges, the best product to use is an air-dry-or-bake synthetic. This will bake hard over the oven at normal oven heat, and will air-dry nicely on other parts. For refrigerator interiors, the best product is white shellac enamel. This sticks fairly well without a primer and has a definite advantage in that it dries without odor. Most other lacquers and synthetics will contaminate milk and butter for several days after application.

Steel Grate Built in Porch Floor Serves as Sanitary Door Mat

A section of steel grating set in an opening in the porch floor in front of the door provides a "mat" that allows dirt scraped from the shoes to fall through to the ground. This helps to keep the porch floor clean, and also it can be used in combination with the regular door mat to automatically dispose of the dust and sand that works through the mat. Furthermore, the grating provides good ventilation if the lower part of the porch is closed in.

PORCH LAMP IN COPPER

ATTACHED to the house wall under a porch roof or a door canopy, this lamp will make the house number easy to read and add individuality to your home. As the lamp is not weatherproof, it is necessary to mount it under a roof to keep out the rain. However, it can be made weatherproof if desired by installing suitable electrical fixtures and sealing the glass panes and metal joints with putty or other waterproof compound. The metal parts are copper, but brass, aluminum or even galvanized sheet iron may be used. If the latter is used, it should be protected with two coats of metal enamel or lacquer. The rear panel of the lamp is of ¾-in. waterproof plywood or solid stock, this thickness being necessary to permit driving screws into the end grain for attaching some of the metal members.

The center detail shows the assembly. As the sheet metal is soft, the various parts can be bent to shape in a vise or between two hardwood strips clamped tightly over the metal. Roundheaded rivets or self-tapping metal screws can be used for assembling the lamp, or the parts may be soldered together. If screws or rivets are used, false rivetheads are soldered along the simulated seam in the top. Patterns for the two-part top section are shown in the lower detail, the parts being bent as indicated by the dotted lines. Sheet-metal strips are used to hold the glass panes in place. The upper and lower strips are mounted inside the panes to form channels between the top and bottom lamp sections, while the center strips are fastened to the upright members on the outside of the panes.

In wiring the original lamp, a candle-type socket from an old ceiling chandelier was used. However, you can use any suitable socket, being sure that it is installed safely to prevent short circuits. Weatherproof fixtures should be purchased at your local electrical store if the lamp cannot be protected from the rain.

METAL PARTS 26-GA. SOFT COPPER

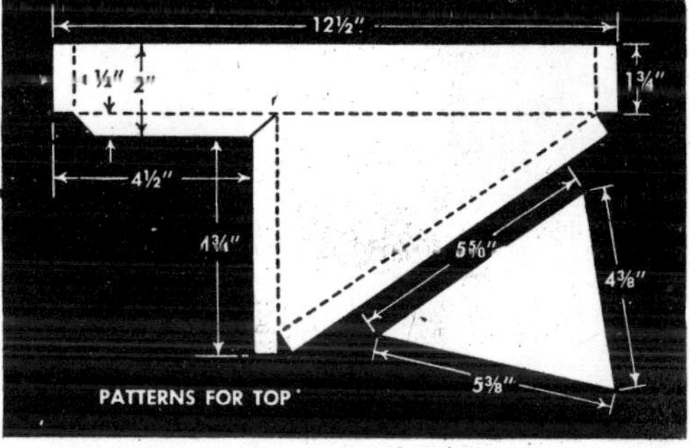

PATTERNS FOR TOP

PORCH LANTERN
in hammered copper

HERE'S a quaint and charming porch lantern that will add a distinctive touch to a colonial entrance. The top and bottom bands are formed to fit the ends of a globe taken from a kerosene lantern. The four staves, which attach to the top band with small machine screws, are bent to spring out at the bottom and permit removal of the globe and bulb. Other parts of the lantern are riveted together where indicated with No. 14 brass escutcheon nails. After a trial fit, all parts are antiqued. To do this, clean with fine steel wool and paint with copper-nitrate solution. Next, apply the flame of a blowtorch and heat the copper until it first turns green and then brown. When cool, burnish the metal with emery paper and then wax.

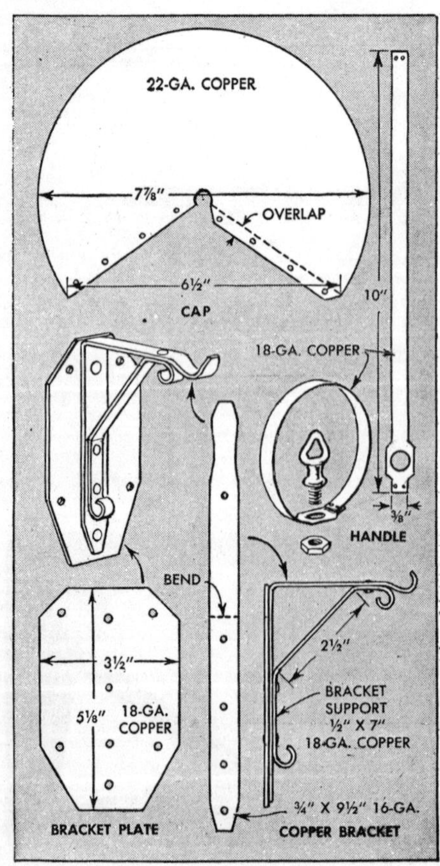

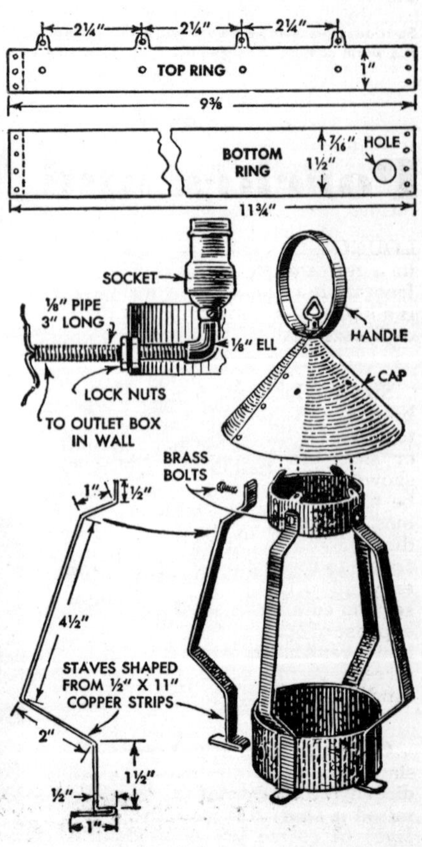

FIG. 1

Spacious breezeway between house an· garage enables you to enjoy all the advantages of outdoor living during the warm summer months—including sleeping and serving meals. It also adds materially to the house value

Porches and Breezeways

LOUNGING COMFORTABLY outdoors in a refreshingly cool breeze, yet shaded from the hot sun and screened from insects, is a luxury you can have by adding a porch or breezeway.

Size and location: A 9 by 12-ft. porch or breezeway is about the minimum satisfactory size for the average small home. Larger sizes are preferred usually, such as shown in Figs. 1 to 3. Where a porch is to be used frequently for serving meals, the most convenient location is alongside both dining room and kitchen. If a separate entrance to the kitchen is impossible, a kitchen window can be fitted with a drop-leaf serving counter as shown in Fig. 4. A full expanse of open sides on a porch gives maximum ventilation, but combination sash and screens permit using a porch during all kinds of weather.

Concrete and flagstone floors: A concrete slab floor, usually 4 in. thick, can be laid directly on compact, well drained earth, or raised a short distance above grade on a layer of coarse gravel or crushed stone. Forms are required at the edges only as shown in Fig. 4. The floor should have a drainage pitch of 1/4 in. per ft., sloping away from the house, or toward one side of a breezeway.

When flagstone is used for porch floors, it should be imbedded in a 4-in. layer of concrete. Laying flagstones directly on the earth allows them to settle unevenly. Earth joints between flagstones also encourage the entrance of ants and burrowing rodents. Flagstone is rough and more difficult to keep clean than smooth concrete.

Where a slab floor must be laid over filled earth, which will settle, the floor should be supported on piers or on foundation walls resting on compact, undisturbed earth as indicated in Fig. 5. You can bore holes for piers with an 8-in. post-hole auger if the earth is firm. In sandy soil you can use sheet-metal furnace pipe for forms.

To prevent such a floor from breaking when a void forms under it because of settling fill, you reinforce it with 3/8 or 1/2-in. steel bars as shown in Fig. 5. These are laid at the center of the floor thickness, in both directions, and are spaced 12 in. apart. Such reinforcement also is required for

FIG. 2

Photo courtesy Andersen Corp.

concrete floors laid several feet above grade, over a crawl space, as shown in Fig. 6. The floor then is cast on horizontal forms adequately supported. An opening must be left in one of the walls to permit the forms to be removed. The foundation for such a raised floor should be of poured concrete.

In locations subject to heaving frosts, foundation walls, and also piers, should extend slightly beyond the depth of frost penetration. They should also rest on suitable footings. A footing 12 in. wide and 6 in. thick is sufficient for a foundation wall of an average-size porch not carrying added weight of a room above it. Where a concrete floor is cast against an existing concrete or brick wall, a non-extruding, asphalt-compound expansion strip, ½ in. thick, is inserted at the joint before laying the floor as indicated in Fig. 4.

Foundation support for wood porches: The underfloor framing of a wood porch, Fig. 7, may rest on wood posts, concrete piers or foundation walls. When set into earth, concrete piers or footings are preferred to wood posts as these are subject to rot and must be renewed periodically.

For wood porches less than 2 or 3 ft. high, concrete piers usually extend up to the underfloor framing. Concrete piers, which often can be obtained ready-made, are 6 or 8 in. square, depending on pier height. Brick piers are 8½ in. or 12¼ in. square according to their height. Those of concrete blocks or hollow tile are 12 in. square.

3

Only hard, well-burned brick or tile should be used, for if the material can absorb moisture it will disintegrate upon freezing.

Footings under piers should be concrete, 12 in. square and 6 in. thick for small porches up to 6 ft. square. For medium-size porches, where the piers are not over 10 ft. apart, the footings should be 18 in. square and 8 in. thick. On large porches, where piers are spaced over 10 ft. apart, footings should be 24 in. square and 10 or 12 in. thick. Piers are located at corners and under the outer ends of one or more cross beams. The roof-supporting columns generally come over the pier positions.

Wood posts are satisfactory for use above grade. They should not be less than 5 in. square, and should rest on concrete footings projecting about 6 in. above grade. A

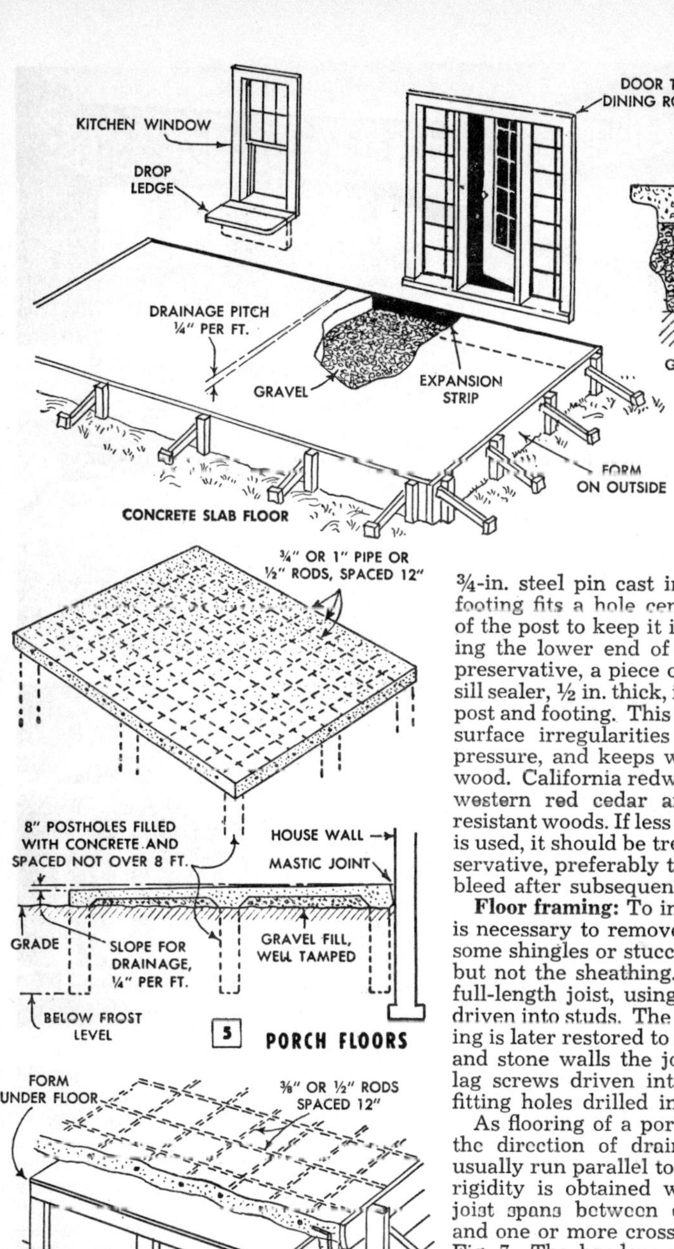

¾-in. steel pin cast in the center of each footing fits a hole centered in the bottom of the post to keep it in place. After treating the lower end of the post with wood preservative, a piece of asphalt-compound, sill sealer, ½ in. thick, is placed between the post and footing. This material conforms to surface irregularities when subjected to pressure, and keeps water away from the wood. California redwood, red cypress and western red cedar are the most decay-resistant woods. If less decay resistant wood is used, it should be treated with wood preservative, preferably the kind that will not bleed after subsequent painting.

Floor framing: To install floor framing it is necessary to remove a section of siding, some shingles or stucco as shown in Fig. 7, but not the sheathing. Then you attach a full-length joist, using nails or lag screws driven into studs. The removed wall covering is later restored to floor level. On brick and stone walls the joist is attached with lag screws driven into expansion sleeves fitting holes drilled in the mortar.

As flooring of a porch should be laid in the direction of drainage, the joists are usually run parallel to the house. Greatest rigidity is obtained with relatively short joist spans between double end headers and one or more cross beams, as shown in Fig. 7. The headers and cross beams are nailed to the joist that is already fastened to the wall. The cross beams may be held to it with iron stirrups. The installation of bridging between floor joists increases their rigidity. After outer framework has been completed, the joists are spaced on 16-in. centers, and end-nailed with 20-d. nails. Joists on either side of the beams are staggered to permit end nailing. For spans

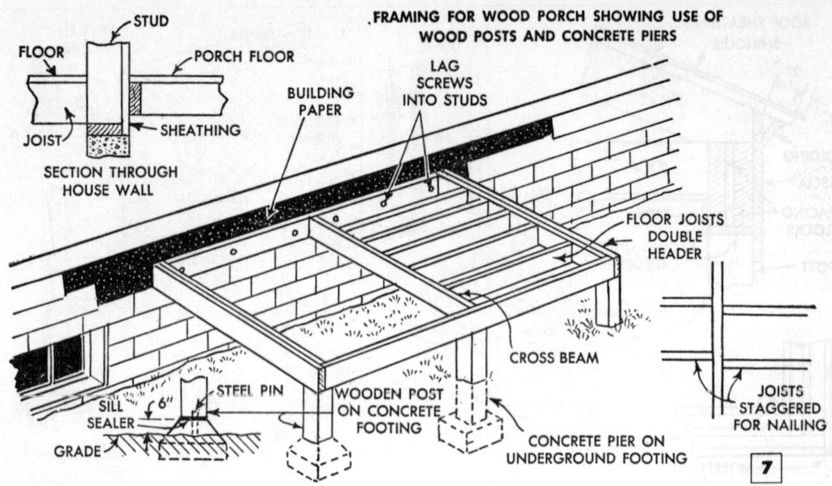

of 8 ft. or less between supports, use 2 by 6-in. framing members. Stock of 2 by 8-in. size is needed for spans from 8 to 12 ft. The framework is given a slight slope of 1/4 in. per ft. away from the house so water will drain readily.

Flooring: Matched tongue-and-groove porch flooring, preferably heartwood, which is most resistant to decay, is nailed across the joists and to each one. To keep water out of the tongue-and-groove joints you seal them with white lead and force the flooring together tightly before nailing it. Aluminum flooring nails do not rust. Drive the nails at a 45-deg. angle at the base of the tongue as in Fig. 8-A, and sink the heads with a nail set. Flooring should extend about 2 in. beyond the framework as in detail B. Let random ends project beyond this distance, then mark and cut off straight, after which the fascia and molding are applied to conceal the framework. The trim is mitered at corners.

Framework for ceiling and roof: Fig. 9 shows how the framework for ceiling and roof can be assembled. Floor-to-ceiling height should not be less than 7 ft. Often a porch roof is built on temporary supports later replaced by permanent posts or columns, after framing is completed. However, the permanent posts may be installed at the start. You start the top framing by attaching a header to the house wall in the same way as the first joist of the floor framework was attached. The girders are temporarily braced while nailing them together and to the header. The underside of girders is covered with a facing piece of equal width. Girders for small porches may consist of two lengths of 2 by 4-in. stock, but 2 by 6-in. stock is preferred generally for medium-size porches. For greatest strength,

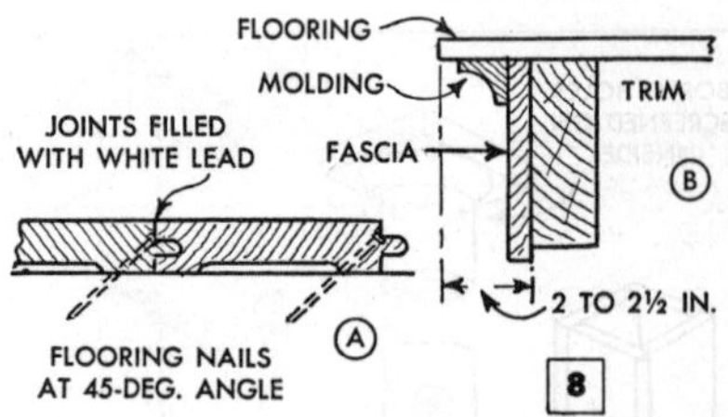

and to prevent any sagging of girders where they span posts, they should be set edgewise. They are nailed together or to spacing strips or blocks between them to make the girder width equal to or greater than that of the post.

After erecting the girders you install the ceiling joists. As these usually carry no weight other than that of the covering material nailed to them, such as wallboard, 2 by 4-in. stock generally is suitable for spans up to 10 ft. The joists can be toenailed to the header and girder, flush with the top edges of these. Ceiling joists, rafters and studs are usually spaced 16 in. on centers, starting from one end.

Roof-supporting posts: Solid wood posts, 4 to 6 in. square, are generally used to support porch roofs. Hollow wood posts may be built up square or round as shown in Fig. 10-A and B, or steel pipe can be used, fitted with floor flanges as in detail C. Hollow wood posts and columns should be ventilated by providing screen-covered holes at the top and bottom as shown in detail B. Here the column base is elevated on nonrusting metal angles to keep the wood dry. Another way to do this is to mount the post on a 1/2-in. asphalt-compound sill sealer as in detail D, which also prevents the post from absorbing water on the floor. For ap-

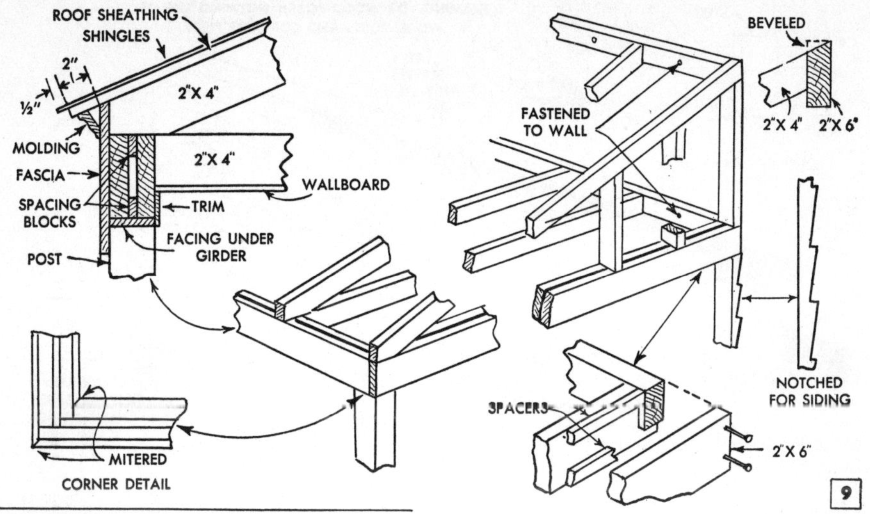

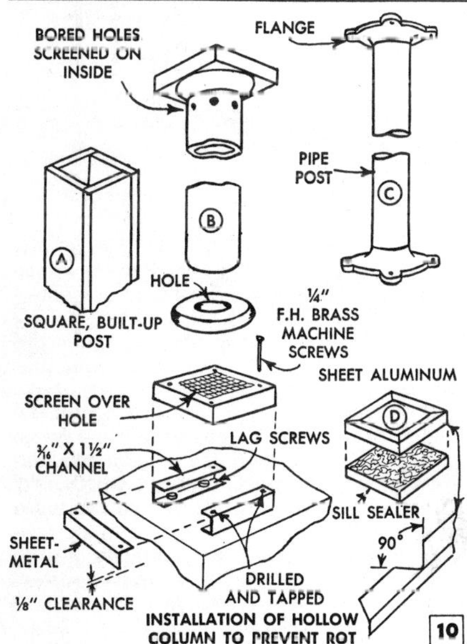

pearance the sill sealer should be covered with sheet-aluminum as indicated. In both cases the lower end of the post or column is first treated with wood preservative for added protection.

If you want to use steel pipe for posts as in Fig. 10-C, the 2-in. size (inside diameter) is adequate for the average 9 by 12-ft. porch where posts are not spaced over 6 ft. apart. The pipe is threaded at both ends for flanges, which are screwed in or out to obtain the exact length desired. The flanges are screwed to wood and are attached to concrete by means of lag screws fitting expansion sleeves in holes that are drilled in the concrete. For porches larger than 9 by 12 ft., and for greater spacing between posts, pipe of larger diameter is used. The posts are arranged to come inside of the screens generally.

Roofing a porch: A shed-type roof, such as shown in Figs. 9, 11 and 12, is easiest to build. It consists of a header attached to the house. Rafters are toenailed to the header and girder after being cut to size and at the correct angles at both ends. If rafters extend beyond the girder, they are notched to fit it. The end rafters are aligned with the side girders.

Nail roof boards and edge strips to the rafters as in Fig. 11. Enclose the wall sections between side girders and end rafters, and apply trim as in Fig. 12. This illustration shows how exterior-type wallboard can be used. In the example shown the fascia closes the opening between the ends of the rafters. In gable and hip-type roofs the rafters next to the house are attached to it.

Start the shingling from the lower edge of the roof, using a double layer for the first course. Let the shingles overlap the roof boards approximately ⅜ inch. You install flashing between the porch roof and the house wall as shown in Fig. 13. Detail A shows flashing under siding and over shingles of a shed-type roof. Detail B shows how flashing is imbedded in mortar between courses of bricks. Where the porch roof has a slope along a brick house wall, double flashing is installed as shown in detail C. An enclosed space between a porch ceiling and roof should be properly vented. Insulation over the ceiling or under rafters will add materially to comfort.

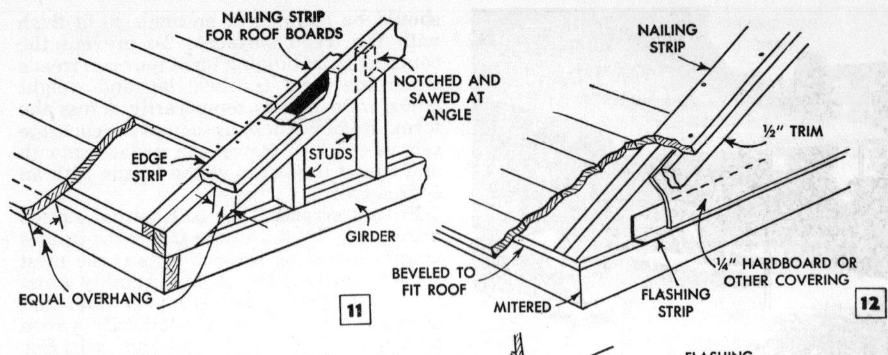

Breezeway framing: On most breezeways the roof is supported by two parallel girders along the sides, which are usually double thickness. One end of the girders often rests on the top plates of the garage wall, for which the garage roof must be opened and altered as necessary to join the roof of the breezeway. At the house end, the wall usually is opened and a header is attached to studs in the same way as is illustrated in Fig. 9. Where the girders are long, the ceiling joists or rafters are installed at right angles to the girders. For short spans, however, the joists can be run parallel to the girders. If the roof is flat, with a slight slope for drainage, the ceiling can be applied directly to the underside of the rafters. If the roof is of the gable type, ceiling joists are required to have a horizontal ceiling.

Canopies: Colorful, waterproof, canvas canopies are fitted on a framework of pipes to which they are lashed, besides being suitably fastened at all edges. Because of constant weather exposure canvas canopies will last much longer if they are taken down and stored during inclement winter weather in northern climates. This entails the semiannual trouble of dismantling and erecting them. As constant exposure to weather deteriorates the fabric, canvas canopies require periodic replacement.

As they are practically indestructible under normal conditions of use, permanent sheet-metal canopies require no further attention, once erected. They are prefabricated in various style and sizes, from small door canopies to large patio roofs. Those made of aluminum, like the one shown in Fig. 14, are lightweight, rustproof and extremely rigid. Designed for easy installation, they come in kit form, which includes the framework and the cover sections, but not pipe or ironwork supports. After assembling the frame, Fig. 15, and attaching it to the house wall and to the supports, the cover sections, which come in baked-enamel finishes, are screwed in place.

Wood steps: Construction of wood steps,

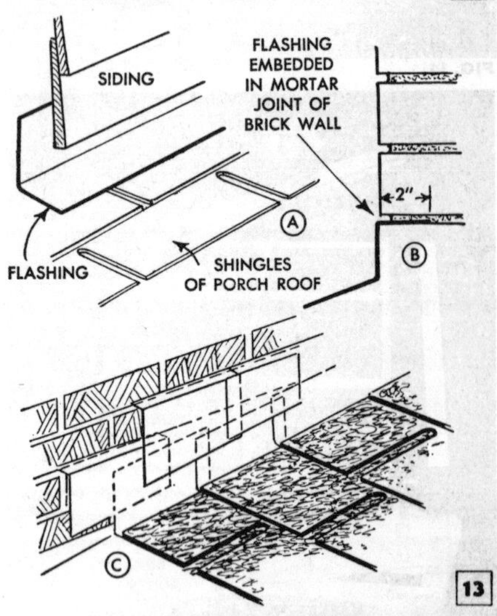

often used on wood porches that are several feet above grade, is shown in Fig. 16. The treads are divided for drainage. Grooved rails that accommodate square balusters are available at most lumber dealers. Balusters are spaced with insert pieces nailed to the railing.

Concrete steps: For permanence, you can build concrete steps as shown in Fig. 17. They will not be subject to settling nor to damage from heaving frosts if they have a 6-in. foundation wall extending just below frost level. In sandy soil a double form is needed for the foundation wall, but where soil is stiff enough to resist caving, an inner form is usually sufficient. After the foundation has hardened, you fill the hole and build the form for the steps. Note from Fig. 17, that tie strips are located well above the edges of the form boards to allow room for finishing the concrete surface with a trowel and edger. Treads should be 10 to 11 in. wide, and the step height should be about 7 in. Slanting the risers inward 1 in. at the bottom provides added toe space. In this case the lower edges of the riser forms

FIG. 14

FIG. 15 Photos courtesy Childers Mfg. Co.

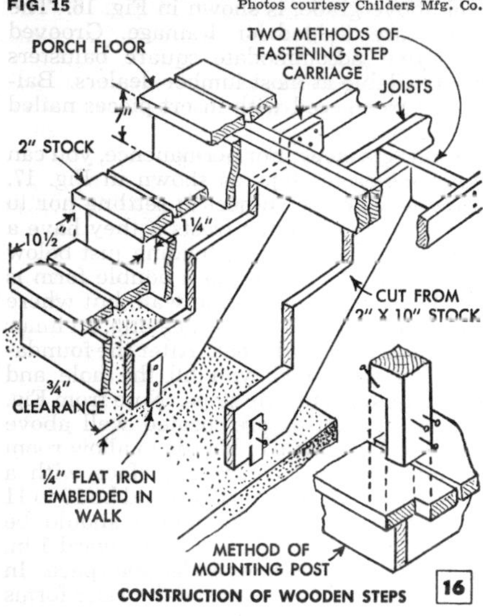

should be planned at an angle to fit flush with the tread surfaces. To prevent the concrete from bulging up at the open treads when the form is filled, lay and weight down wide boards temporarily across the form. Remove these as soon as the concrete sets in order to trowel the surface smooth and round the edges of the treads with an edging tool.

Fitting screens: For substantial screen frames, use 1⅛-in. stock. Cover the frames with non-rusting screen. This is the most economical because of its durability, even though the initial cost is higher than that of usual wire screen. Customarily screen frames are held in place as shown in Fig. 18, using hooks and eyes on one side and stops on the other where frames are joined to square posts. Where the frames are butted together, a strip of molding is used on one side and turnbuttons on the other to hold the frames in alignment. The frames usually rest on the floor or on a sill to which they may be hooked also. When retained in a grooved sill, the frames are subject to constant wetting, which hastens decay.

An arrangement that prevents direct contact of the screen frames with the porch floor, and thus prevents frequent soaking, is shown in Fig. 19. Notice the slot between the members of the top plate into which the frames are pushed before they are let down on the metal sills. These consist of ⅛ by ⅛ by 1 or 1¼-in. angles of brass or aluminum. The sills have drilled holes in which pins on the frames fit. The frames also rest on the angles. To allow for drainage the angles are shimmed up about $1/16$ in. above the floor by means of washers under them and over screws that are used for attachment. Adjoining frames are held together by means of molding strips on the outside and turnbuttons on the inside.

FIG. 17

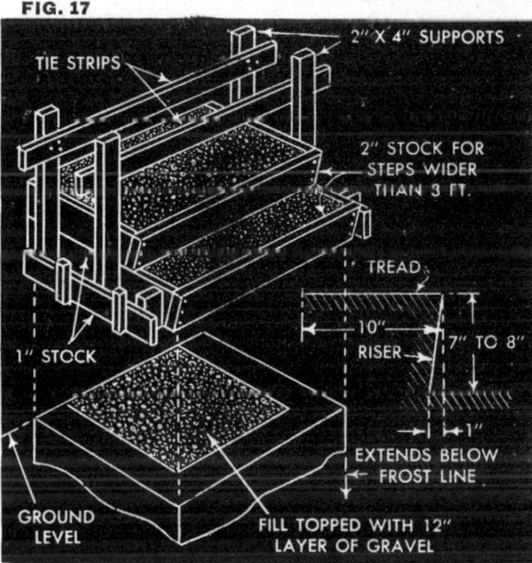

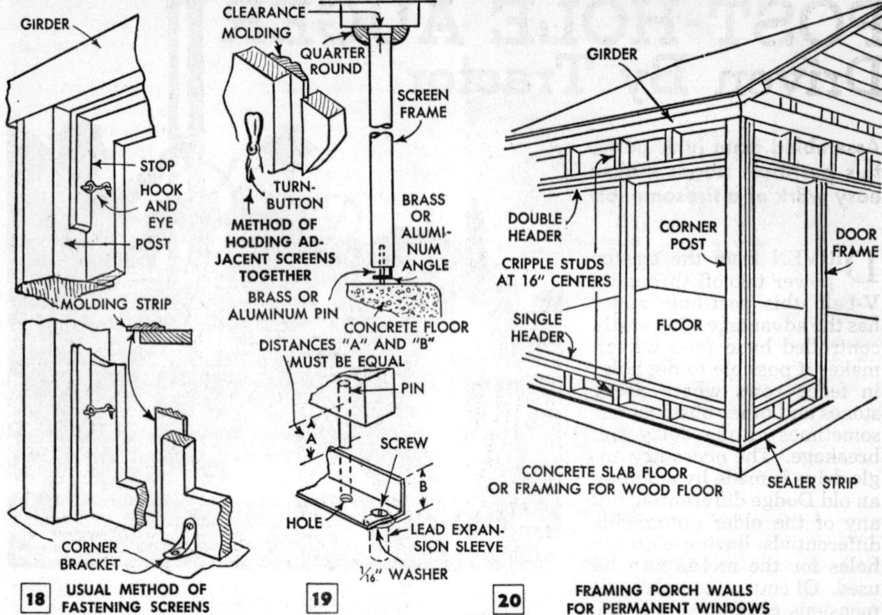

18 USUAL METHOD OF FASTENING SCREENS

19

20 FRAMING PORCH WALLS FOR PERMANENT WINDOWS

Enclosing a porch: You can get year-'round usefulness from a porch by installing permanent windows as shown in Fig. 20. For maximum ventilation use windows of the type that can be fully opened. Ordinary double-hung windows do not provide an unobstructed opening more than 50 percent of the window area. The floor, ceiling and walls should be insulated. Windows should be weatherstripped and provided with storm sash in cold localities, or you can install insulating-type window panes—the kind having two layers of glass hermetically sealed together, with an air space between them.

Steps of procedure: Before you enclose a porch be sure that a wood floor is level and walls plumb. A concrete slab floor in good condition should have adequate support of piers or a foundation wall set below frost level. Perimeter insulation should be installed on the outside of an existing concrete floor, in localities subject to cold weather.

In case of a wooden porch, you first examine the floor and framework underneath it, replacing any unsound or defective portions. Most wooden porches supported by posts or piers not properly installed will settle in course of time. A sagged porch must first be jacked up slightly above level to that it can be let down on new piers set on substantial footings as previously discussed. Termite shields, if necessary, are placed on the piers before the floor framework is let down. Wedges, such as cypress shingles, may be needed for leveling the porch on the piers.

Where a wooden floor is in good condition, it may be left intact; but insulation and a vapor barrier should be provided under the floor as explained in Section 7. An existing floor or a new one should come flush with the outside edges of the floor framing. Next, you temporarily support the roof girders by securely wedging 2 by 6-in. planks between them and the floor. Raise the girders slightly so that the posts or columns can be removed unless they are to become part of the new wall.

To build the wall framework as shown in Fig. 20, you start by installing 2 by 4-in. sole plates laid on ½-in. sill-sealing strips. Fasten the plates to the underfloor framing with 16-d. nails, or to a concrete slab floor with lag screws and expansion sleeves. The corner studs, arranged as detailed in Section 7, are next. Toenail them to the sole plates and girders. Then remove the temporary girder supports and finish the framing, spacing the studs at 16-in. centers. Nailing bases must be provided for the inside wall covering.

POST-HOLE AUGER
Driven By Tractor

Assembled from junk parts, this post-hole auger makes easy work of a tiresome job

DRIVEN from the tractor power takeoff through a V-belt, this post-hole auger has the advantage of an easily controlled hand feed which makes it possible to dig holes in fence rows where roots, stones and other obstructions sometimes cause delay and breakage. The necessary angle drive is made by adapting an old Dodge differential, but any of the older automobile differentials having square holes for the axles can be used. Of course, complete dimensions cannot be given in the detail drawing, nor can the arrangement be followed closely when mounting the auger on the various makes of tractors. Hence the details shown at the right are only suggestions on how to make the assembly of the various parts.

In this case the square drive shaft was taken from a rod weeder, but any square steel shaft of good quality material can be used. The top end of the shaft is carried in a single ball bearing and fitting this properly likely will require some alteration, such as turning down the end of the shaft to fit the inner ball race. On a tractor of a different make than that shown it will be necessary to alter the horizontal driveshaft support so that it will fit the tractor transmission housing. It also will be necessary to change the braces to the tractor drawbar. The details show one way of making these adjustable for length. Other methods of accomplishing this can be used when necessary. The combine header lift makes a handy arrangement for lowering and raising the auger and controlling the rate of feed. Although one man can operate the auger there is less danger of breakage where there are two operators, one to drive the tractor, the other to handle the digger.

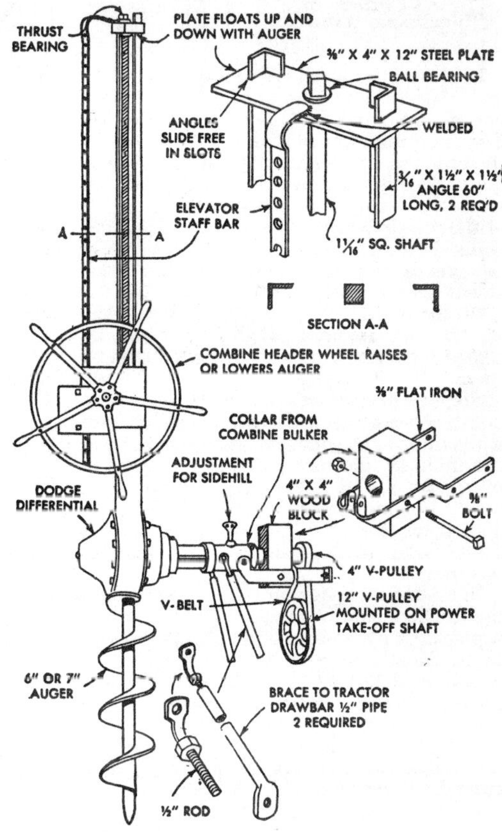

Photo and certain constructional details courtesy of State College of Washington

POULTRY

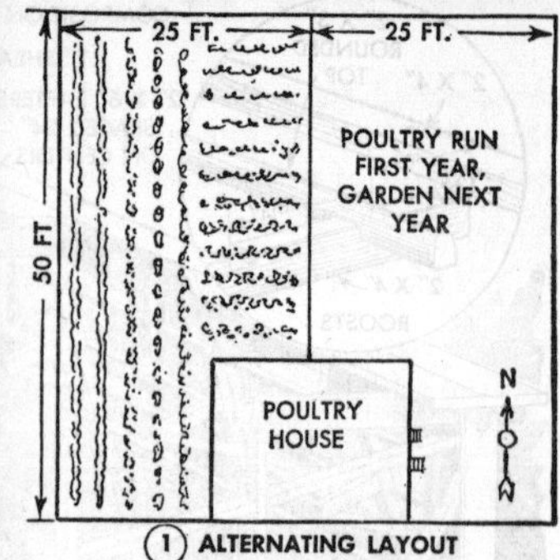

(1) ALTERNATING LAYOUT

SUCCESSFUL poultry raising requires first-class housing, which means ample space, dry floors, plenty of sunshine, good ventilation without drafts, and protection from the elements. About 3 sq. ft. of floor space should be allowed for White Leghorns, and 4 sq. ft. for the heavier meat breeds, such as Rhode Island Reds and Plymouth Rocks. The outdoor pens should allow at least 7 sq. ft. of space per bird. A desirable arrangement for a pen is to have two runs, alternating these for use as a garden in successive years. Fig. 1 illustrates a layout for 100 birds on a 50-ft. plot with one house and two pens. Where space permits, the flock can be doubled or tripled if sections are added to the original house and pens.

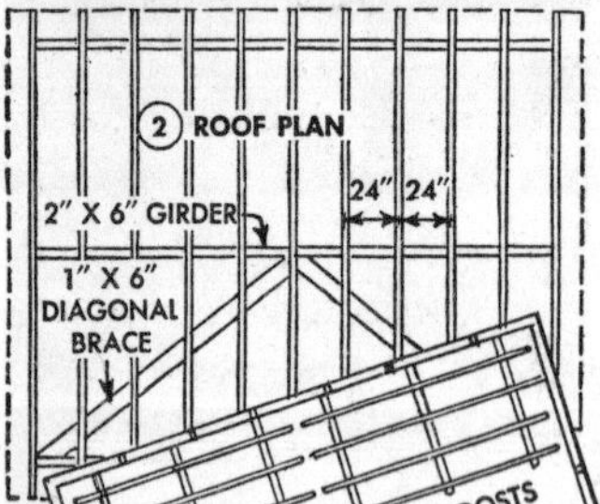

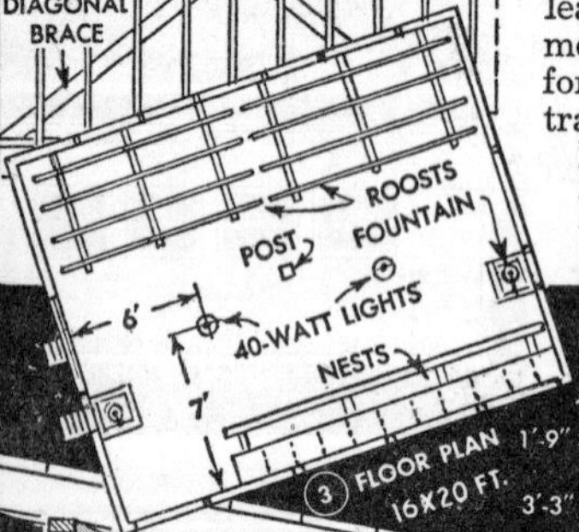

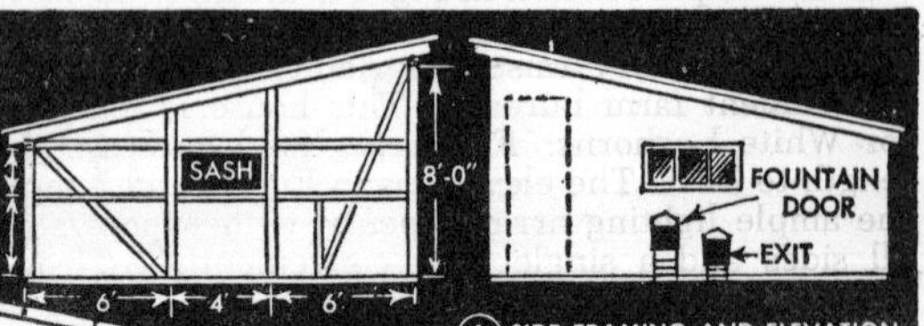

(2) ROOF PLAN

(3) FLOOR PLAN 16 X 20 FT.

(4) SIDE FRAMING AND ELEVATION

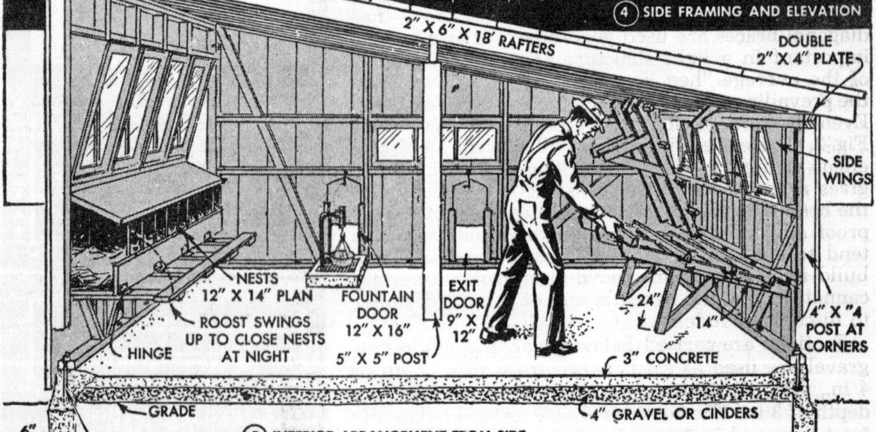

(5) INTERIOR ARRANGEMENT FROM SIDE

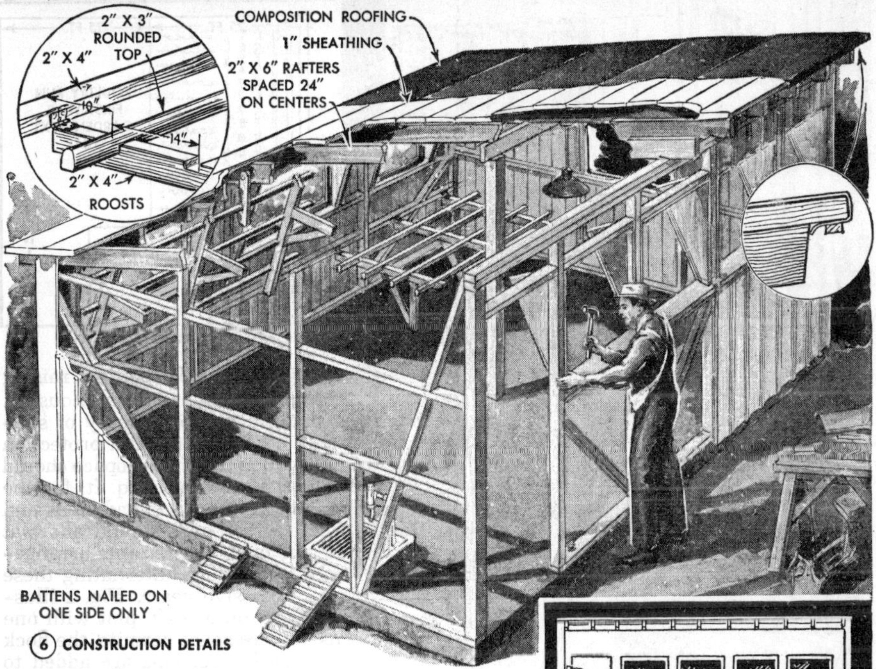

2" X 3"
ROUNDED
TOP
2" X 4"
10"
14"
2" X 4"
ROOSTS
COMPOSITION ROOFING
1" SHEATHING
2" X 6" RAFTERS
SPACED 24"
ON CENTERS
BATTENS NAILED ON
ONE SIDE ONLY

(6) CONSTRUCTION DETAILS

The floor plan shown in Fig. 3 is arranged to combine the best features of those recommended by successful poultry raisers, agricultural schools and government farm bureaus. This house is designed for White Leghorns. For larger fowl, increase the length to 24 ft. The elevations in Figs. 4 and 7 show the ample lighting arrangements, with windows on all sides and a single door conveniently in front. Board-and-batten construction does not require as much framing as horizontal sheathing. Note that diagonal braces are used generously, as this is very important in a light structure. One common fault of the average "hen house" is its slant away from the prevailing wind, due to not having "sway braces." Even the rafters should have diagonal braces as in Fig. 2. These are 1-in. boards and prevent a twisting effect in high winds. The sectional view in Fig. 5 gives a good idea of the construction. Concrete is the best material for a floor as it does not rot, is rat-proof and more easily cleaned than boards, which tend to splinter. If a wooden floor must be used, build it at least 18 in. above grade so that vermin cannot make nests beneath, and dogs can get under to discourage rodents.

Footings are carried below grade and cinders or gravel are used as fill between them to a depth of 4 in., after which concrete is poured over this to a depth of 3 in. The footings should extend below the frost line, and ½-in. anchor bolts spaced 4 ft. apart

FRONT
3' SASH
REAR
FRONT FRAME
SASH
9"
3'-3"
4'
4' 4' 4' 4' 4'
REAR FRAME
1'-9"
2'
6' 8' 6'
3'-3"

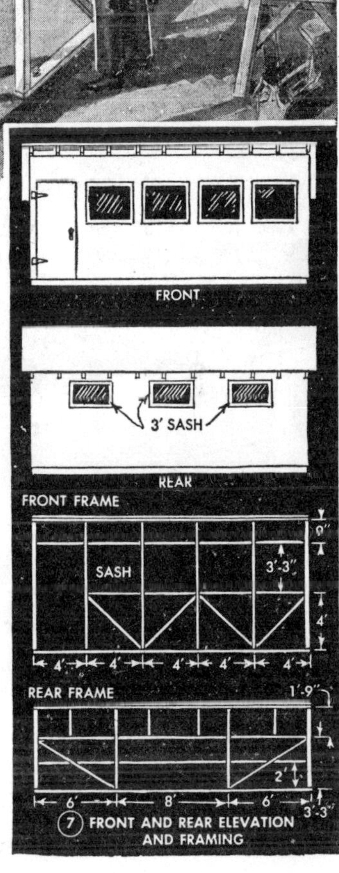

(7) FRONT AND REAR ELEVATION AND FRAMING

should be embedded in the wet concrete to anchor the sills. Studs are toenailed to them and horizontal members and plates are installed as indicated in Figs. 4 and 7. The siding boards then should be nailed on the framing, space being left for window and door openings, before the rafters are installed.

Note in Fig. 5 that the sash are designed to tilt inward and have wings on each side. This forces the ventilation upward, away from nests and roosts, and also affords some protection for the glass-substitute which will last longer than if exposed directly to the force of a heavy downpour. Nests are arranged along the front wall just below the sash, and have a hinged perch which is swung up at night to keep the birds from getting into the nests. Roosts are arranged to swing up out of the way when cleaning the floor. A single center post supports a girder under the rafters. Houses only 12 ft. or less in depth do not require this.

General assembly and arrangement of the structure are shown in Fig. 6. Roosts are built in two units for easy handling. Their construction is shown in the circular detail of Fig. 6. Although not indicated, the framing should be sheathed inside as well as outside where the nests are installed. When putting battens over the siding joints outside, nail each at one side of the joint only, doing this on the side facing prevailing winds. The siding boards will shrink

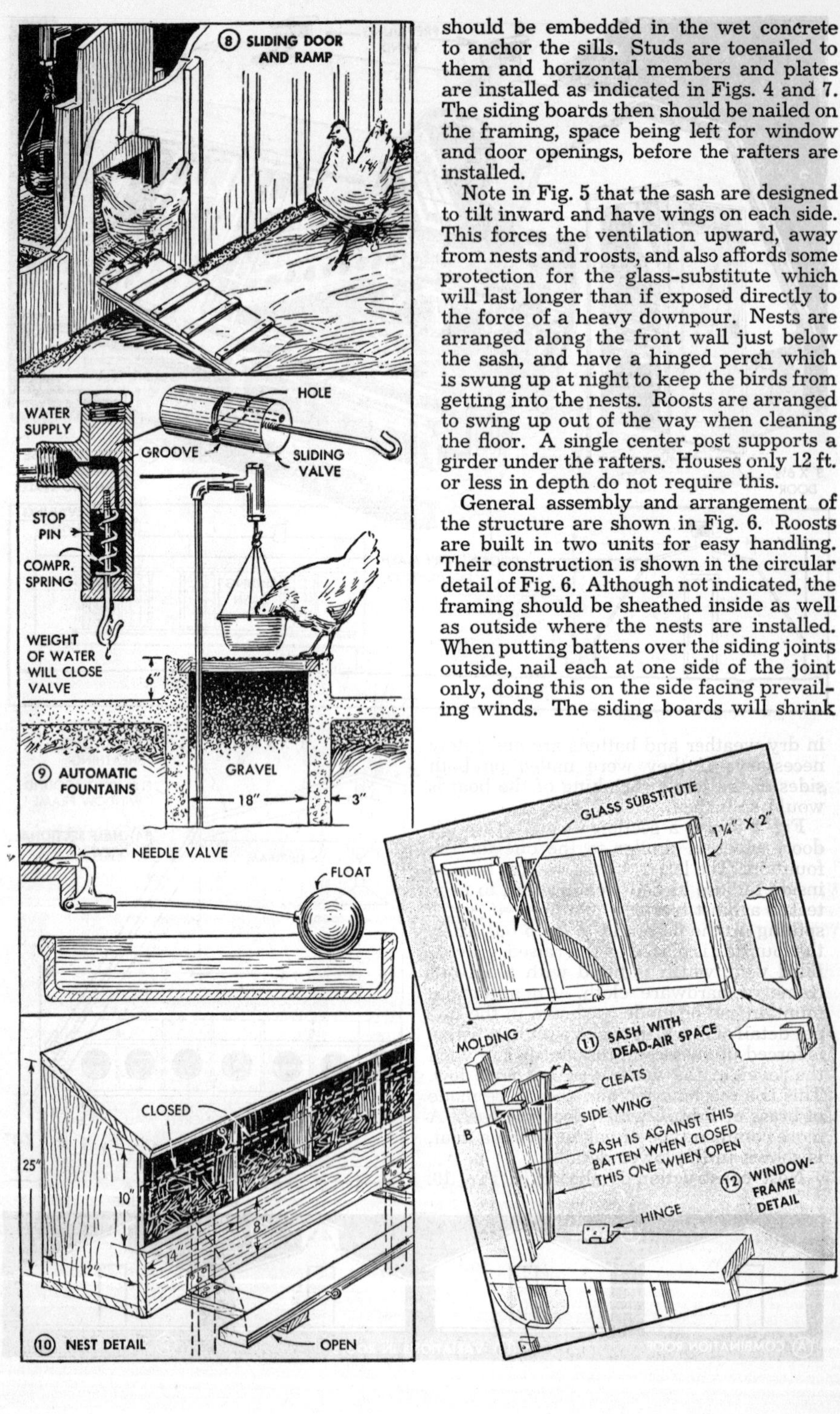

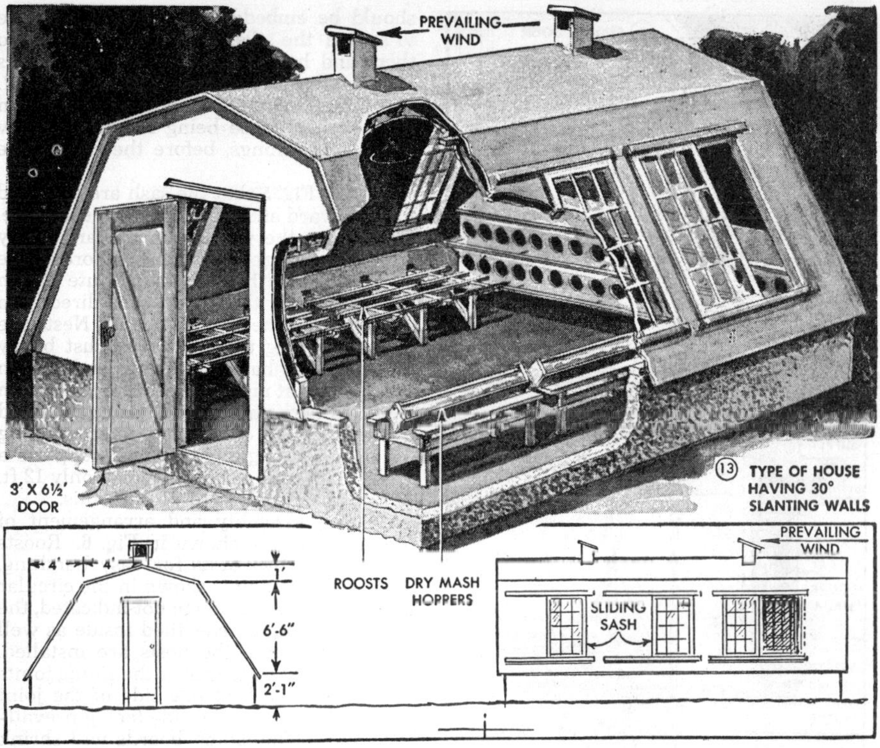

PREVAILING WIND

3' X 6½' DOOR

ROOSTS

DRY MASH HOPPERS

SLIDING SASH

(13) TYPE OF HOUSE HAVING 30° SLANTING WALLS

in dry weather and battens are absolutely necessary. If they were nailed on both sides of the joints shrinking of the boards would split them.

Fig. 8 shows a section through the exit door, which is similar to the one for the fountain. The latter, by the way, is housed inside for use in bad weather and to protect it against freezing. To prevent water spilling on the floor and to keep out litter, the fountain is placed over a raised, gravel-filled well, which is fitted with a lift-out frame of hardware cloth. An automatic fountain can be made as shown in the upper detail of Fig. 9, in which a plunger valve is forced up by a compression spring when the level in the water pan becomes low. This is a machine job and should be made of brass or bronze which does not rust. A more common type of valve having a float, is shown in the lower detail.

Nest construction is shown in Fig. 10.

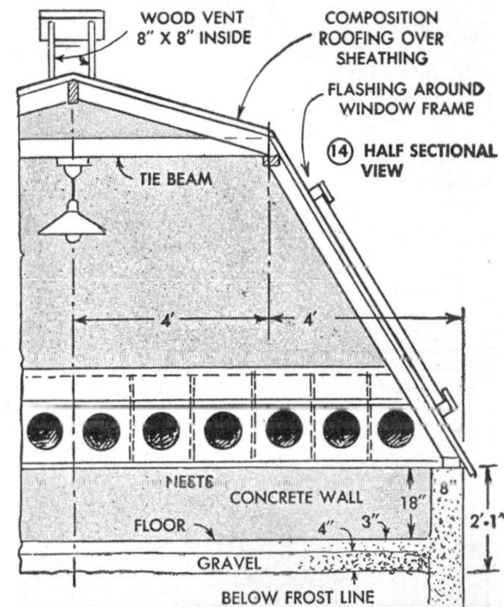

(14) HALF SECTIONAL VIEW

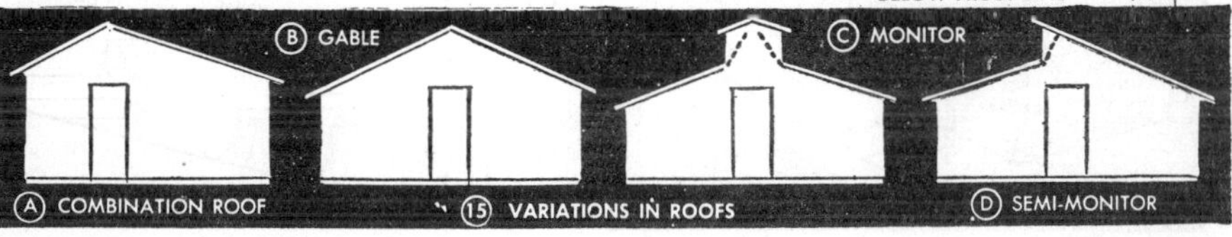

(15) VARIATIONS IN ROOFS

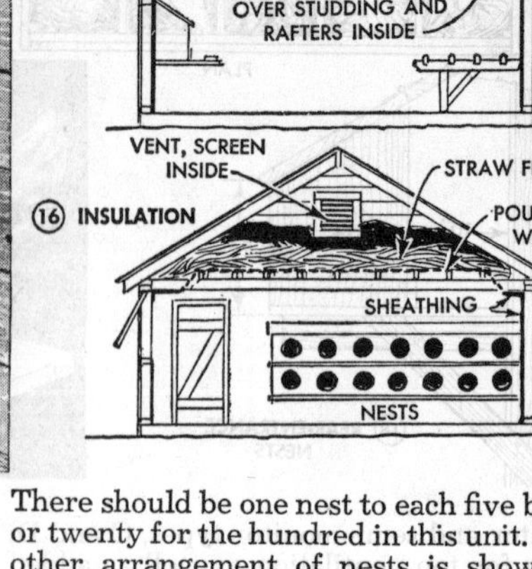

(16) INSULATION

(17) DRY-MASH HOPPERS

There should be one nest to each five birds, or twenty for the hundred in this unit. Another arrangement of nests is shown in Fig. 18 in which the hens enter along a "catwalk" at the rear. The advantage of this arrangement is that the nests are dark, which reduces the possibility of hens eating the eggs.

Side wings for the window sash are shown in Fig. 12. The sash should be hinged at the bottom and fitted with a crescent catch at the top to draw it snugly against the cleat B. When open, they rest against cleat A. The sash are made as in Fig. 11, with mortised corners and a glass substitute on both sides to provide a dead-air space for good insulation without appreciably detracting from the light. Real glass, incidentally, does not retain warmth at night, nor does it pass as much of the health-giving ultra-violet rays as does glass substitute.

Another type of house is illustrated in Figs. 13 and 14, in which the side walls incline at 30 degrees from the vertical, thus permitting light to enter the windows for a longer period than if they were vertical. In this case glass substitute should not be used in the sash, which slide sideways in rails to give more ventilation than afforded by the wooden ventilators on top. Arrangement of the floor plan is similar to that of the preceding design, and construction of the floor is the same except that concrete walls are carried up 18 in. all around. Sides as well as roof are covered with composition roofing, and care must be taken to install flashing around all window frames to render them rainproof. Various types of roofs can be used on poultry houses as shown in Fig. 15. The combination and gable roofs, A and B, are desirable for large structures, but are too deep for the shed roof design described first. The

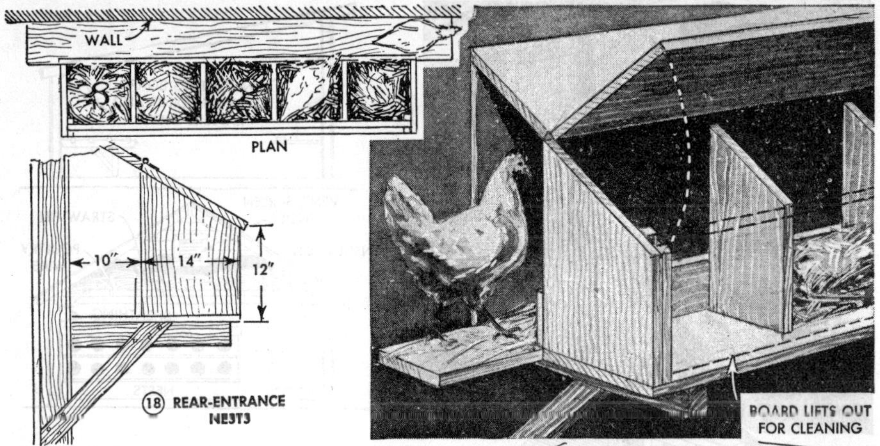

monitor and semi-monitor types, C and D, allow for top ventilation as well as added light through swing-in sash.

Two methods of insulation are illustrated in Fig. 16. Simplest is to line walls and ceiling with insulation board. In cold climates this is important, and in all cases, insulation should be installed behind and above the roosts to prevent chill at night, or moisture condensing on the walls.

Some poultrymen install a droppings board under the roosts, with poultry wire to keep the chickens away from the droppings. The roosts are arranged to swing up as in Fig. 19 to facilitate cleaning. A vent at the eaves is provided by a flap between the rafters and above the plate as indicated in the circular detail of Fig. 19. For growing fowl or young chicks, a "sun room" is made having sides of poultry netting and a hardware-cloth floor just above the ground as in Fig. 20. In the outdoor runs, posts are placed 8 ft. apart and 24 in. deep, with ends creosoted and the wire about 3 in. below grade as in Fig. 21, but deeper if troubled with skunks or other burrowing animals. However, do not put a rail across the tops of the posts as the full grown fowl, especially White Leghorns, will fly up to it. Floor space required for various numbers of hens is given in Fig. 22. Bear in mind that this is about the minimum; allow more if you have the area and the material available.

Dry-mash hopper design is important where a large number of fowl are kept, because when improperly constructed, a considerable waste will result. Two approved types are shown in Fig. 17, each being made of wood. Poultrymen, specializing in egg production, recommend having ample hoppers filled at all times for best results. As much as 24 ft. of hopper length per 100 birds is not too much.

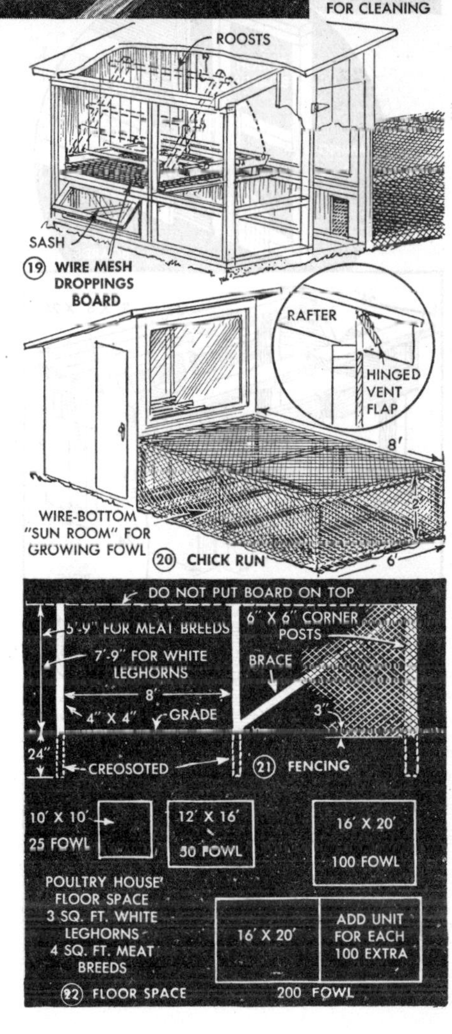

POWER-TOOL

The combination machine is cheaper than the same number of single tools and is much more compact. Drawback is time taken to convert the machines

Machine grouping, as shown by the diagram below, allows as many as four power tools to be operated on a single motor. Only the machine in use is belted to motor. Countershaft-drive setup (shown in the photo lower right) is compact but wastes power

ELECTRIC MOTORS in a range from ¼ to ½ hp. cost as much or more than light-duty power tools. Since the average beginner is short on cash but at the same time obsessed with the idea that he must have at least three power tools, the usual compromise between pocketbook and desires is a setup of two, three or more power tools all operated by one motor.

One system is the combination machine, an example of which is shown at the left. It can be converted into a circular saw, drill press and lathe, plus a few others not available in conventional machines. This unit runs from a single ½-hp. motor, and the combined grouping of tools plus one motor costs less than a similar group of individually motorized tools. Other than low cost, the combination offers a good feature in compactness—you can put your whole shop in a corner. The main fault of the combination is that it takes a little time to change from one machine to another.

System number two is the countershaft drive, as shown below. This is a fairly good setup for certain tools. It is not as compact as the combination and costs a little more, but is somewhat more convenient in operation, providing you can stand the idea and the noise of all machines running at one time. Normally this proves a nuisance to the average worker and the usual procedure is to throw the belts of all machines except the one you are using.

Numerous variations of the countershaft drive are possi-

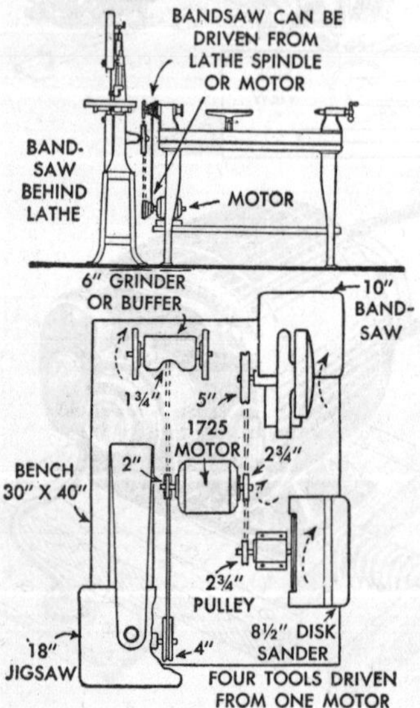

COMBINATIONS

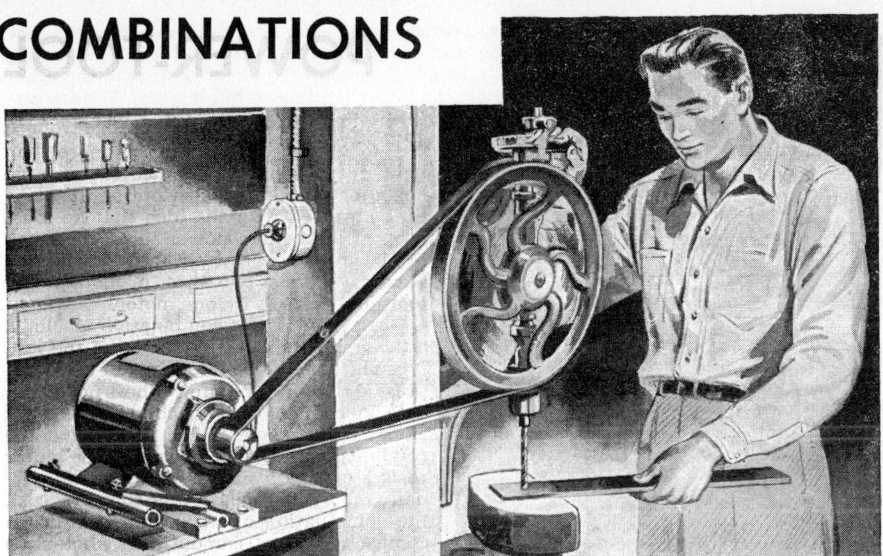

Drawings above and at right show three methods of using portable motor mount on different tools

ble, with the shaft located behind, below or above the tools as desired. The trouble of keeping all belts tight is sometimes solved by using a floating (hinged) countershaft, which automatically tilts back to provide the proper belt tension for the one machine being used at the time.

Grouping of two or more tools to run from one motor is a common practice, the circular saw and jointer combination being the best example. The diagram on the opposite page shows how a bandsaw can run from either spindle or motor of lathe. The lower part of the diagram shows four machines arranged to run from one motor. The jigsaw and disk sander are good machines for grouping with others because they work equally well with either direction of rotation. If any tool grouping requires reversal of the motor, a setup can be made with a motor having a built-in reversing switch.

Perhaps the most popular system of motorizing various tools with one motor is the portable motor setup, three examples of which are shown on this page. The general idea is to use some type of universal base which will fit corresponding mountings located as required at any machine. Unit shown in top photo is simple but effective, consisting only of a length of pipe welded to either side of the motor base. The unit in the center drawing is similar. Both are floating mounts, that is, they use the weight of the motor to provide belt tension. A spring tensioning device is used in the third

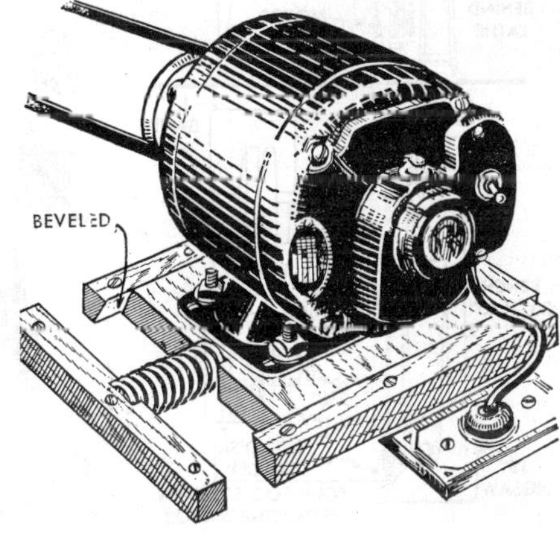

setup, the spring being permanently fastened to the motor base and serving for all installations. This would probably be a little smoother in operation than the floating motor, the latter tending to bounce and vibrate under certain conditions. The installation shown in the top drawing previous pg. is reversible by means of the double mounting legs in combination with a motor having a shaft extension at both ends. All you do here is turn the motor end for end. The other units shown are for one-way only, but could readily be reversed in the same manner.

Changing a motor from one machine to another in the homeshop can be done in less than a minute with the all-position motor mount shown on this page. Some of the many positions in which it can be used are illustrated in Figs. 1 to 4. Only motors built for vertical as well as horizontal mounting should be used as shown in Fig. 3.

Dimensions for the angle-iron frame, Fig. 5, are not given as these will vary according to the type and size of motor used. The corners are cut, bent and welded as detailed in Fig. 5, A, and two holes are drilled to take a ⅜-in. bolt on which the frame hinges. A third hole is drilled and filed to an oval shape for an adjustment screw, which is a ⅜-in. square-headed bolt forged and drilled as shown in Fig. 5, D.

Belt tensioning is accomplished by adjusting a square nut under the angle-iron frame and tightening a wing nut as in

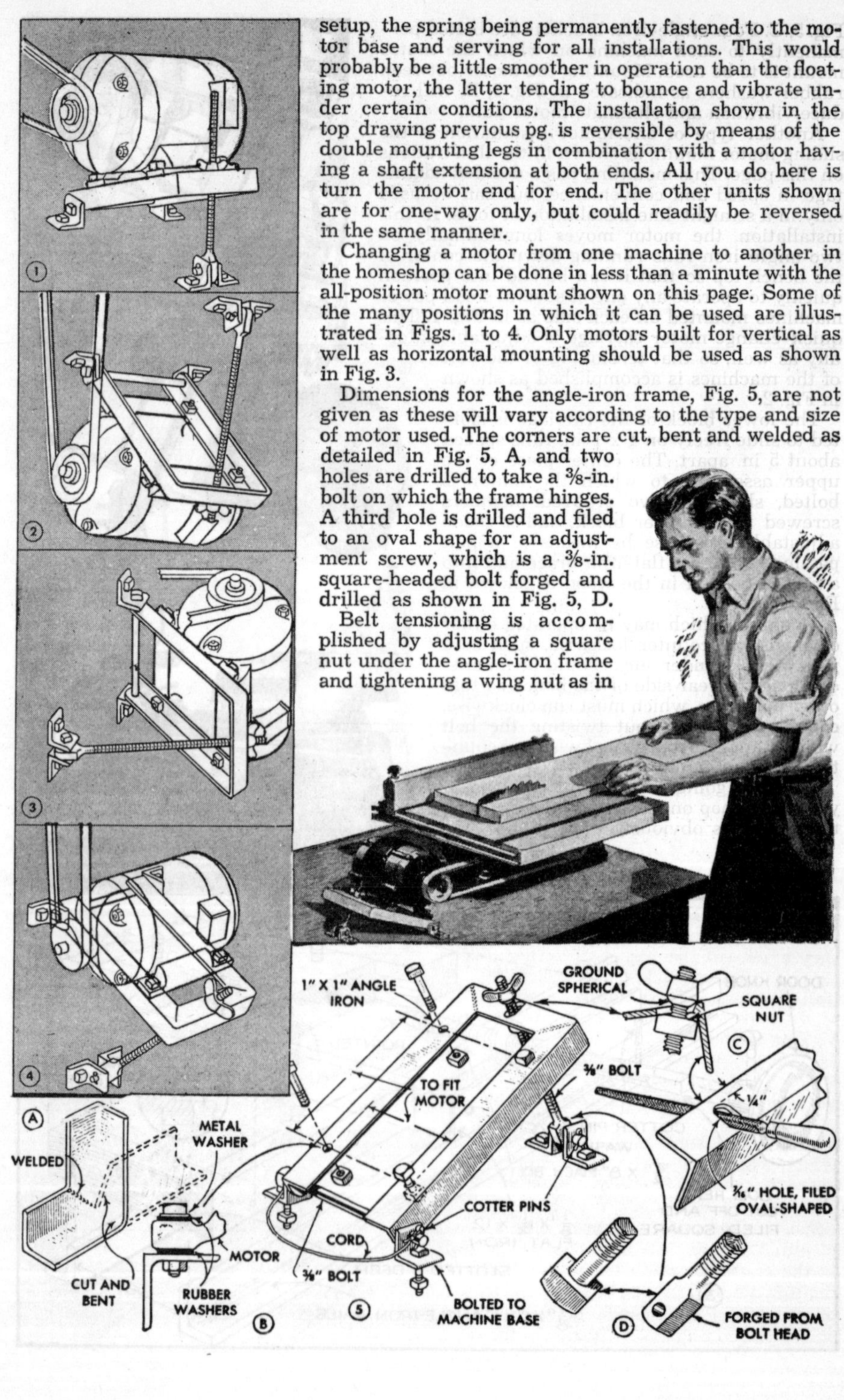

Fig. 5, C. Four angle-iron brackets are bolted permanently to each machine on which the motor mount is to be used. Mounting the motor between rubber washers as indicated in Fig. 5, B, will reduce vibration and eliminate motor hum.

Another type of one-motor installation is the sliding motor mount, as shown in the illustrations on this page. This mounting has a decided advantage in speed and convenience, but can be used only in a straight-line installation of tools. In this installation, the motor moves longitudinally on two angle-iron rails running down the center of the bench top so that it can be slid into position quickly to operate any one of several small power machines mounted on each side as in Fig. 1. This quick-change motor carriage is adjustable laterally as well, so that tensioning of the belt of the machines is accomplished as shown in Fig. 2.

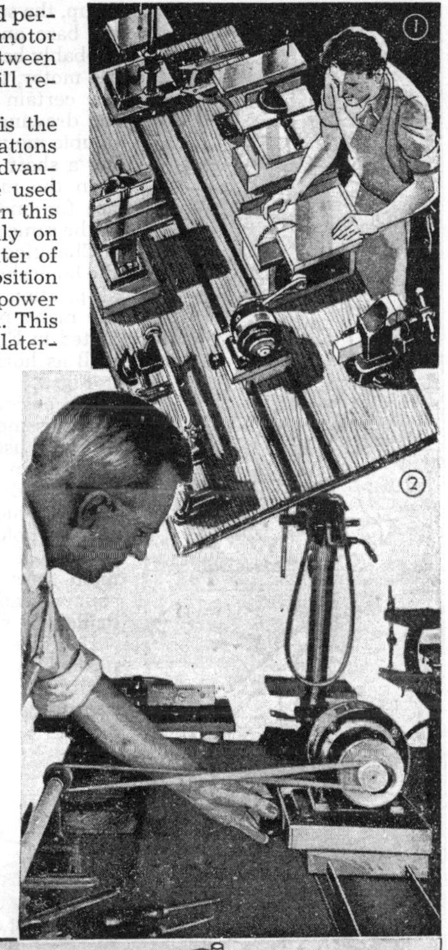

The lower block of the carriage is slotted to slide freely on 1 x 1-in. rails spaced about 5 in. apart. The center piece of the upper assembly, to which the motor is bolted, slides on two grooved members screwed to the lower block, and is made adjustable crosswise by means of a bolt passing through a flat-iron brace and into a nut embedded in the wood as shown in Fig. 3.

Machines which may be operated either clockwise or counterclockwise, such as a jigsaw, disk sander, etc., should be mounted along the rear side of the bench so that other machines, which must run clockwise, can be driven without twisting the belt when changing from a clockwise to a counterclockwise motor.

If you're going to place all the load of your workshop on one motor, the choice of that motor is obviously important.

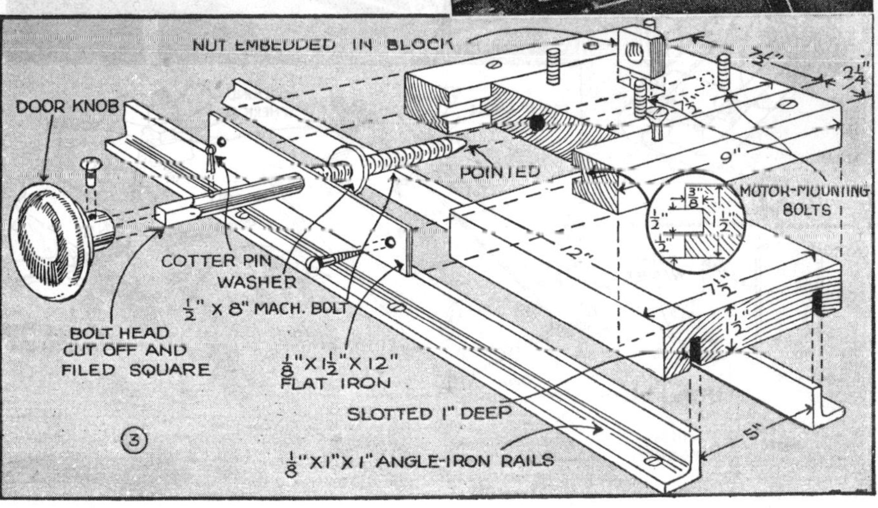

POWER-TOOLS REFINISHING

MASKING TAPE PROTECTS SPINDLE AND NAMEPLATE

NEWSPAPERS OVER WOOD BENCH

Before

After

FRESH paint not only protects your power tools against rust, but also improves their appearance, Figs. 1 and 2, as well as the general appearance of your shop. All tools should be the same color. Machine-tool gray is the most popular color, but if you like blue, buff or green, then use them. Avoid strong colors—a whole shop full of bright red tools gets to be very tiresome. Quite often the old paint will be in good condition and will need only a thorough cleaning and a single coat of enamel. If you are using a spray gun, lacquer enamel is the logical choice. This can be applied successfully over almost any previous finish on metal providing the old finish is aged. If you want to be sure the lacquer will not soften and lift the old finish, use a slow-drying thinner. If you are doing a brush job, the natural choice is a fast-drying synthetic. Any of the popular synthetics sold as 4-hr. enamels will give excellent results. It is, of course, quite practical to use the synthetic finish with spray application.

For a good job, use primer-surfacer on a machine tool. This material is self-leveling and will fill small holes and scratches in the cast iron surface. It provides a good bond to the iron and a good base for the top-coat enamel. Light gray is the proper color to use with any shade of gray-enamel top coat. Primer-surfacer can be obtained in either a lacquer or synthetic product.

The schedule for a complete refinish job with primer-surfacer is given in step-by-step form in Fig. 7. Like all metal-finishing jobs, it starts off with cleaning. It should be noted that sanding does not remove grease and oil—it simply spreads it around. Hence, you get the grease and oil off first. Sanding comes next, Fig. 4, and can be a little or a lot depending on the old finish. Use aluminum-oxide paper, dry. No. 1/0 is a good starting grit and should be

Above, using a backing block of felt or cork to build a level surface when sanding. Below, masking tape or compound will protect polished parts

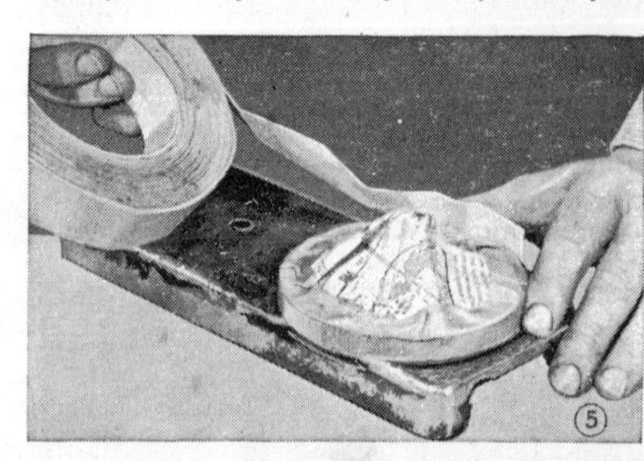

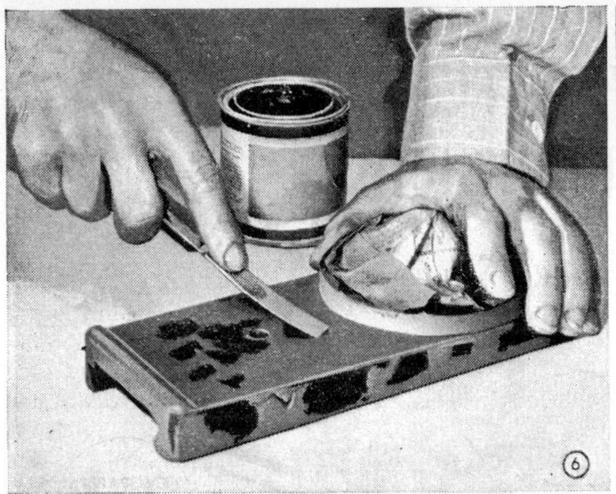

LACQUER PUTTY IS USED TO FILL DEPRESSIONS

followed by 3/0 for finish. Blow or dust the surface clean and wipe with a soft cloth moistened with alcohol. Right here you may find that the existing finish is in fairly good shape, permitting the direct application of top coats to finish the job. However, if you want a smooth, slick job, the next step is to apply a full wet coat of primer-surfacer. The material can be obtained with either a lacquer or synthetic base, and in a variety of colors. Primer-surfacer is almost pastelike in the can and is still quite heavy after reducing (follow the directions on can). However, it sprays smoothly with even light-duty guns. Even with the remarkable "build" of the primer-surfacer, you probably will find a few low spots or holes in the surface being finished. Fill them with lacquer putty. Use this product as it comes in the container, applying and smoothing with a putty knife, Fig. 6.

SMOOTH THE PUTTY WITH A PUTTY KNIFE. A PIECE OF STIFF LEATHER IS USEFUL ON ROUNDED SURFACES

⑦ FOLLOW THIS SCHEDULE

1—Wash with soap and water or household cleanser. Rinse clean and dry.

2—Sand. Use 1/0 for roughing; 3/0 for finish. Wipe clean with alcohol rag.

3—Apply full wet coat of primer-surfacer. Allow 30 minutes dry for lacquer-type material; 1 to 2 hours for synthetic.

4—Sand lightly with 3/0 wet-or-dry paper with water as lubricant.

5—Fill holes or low spots with lacquer putty. Allow 1 hour or more drying time, depending on depth of coating.

6—Wet sand with 3/0 wet-or-dry paper backed with felt block. Wipe clean with soft lintless rag. Inspect. If surface is not smooth, repeat operations 3, 4 and 5.

7—Apply one or more coats of lacquer, enamel or synthetic. Use same type of finishing material throughout—never apply lacquer top coat over synthetic base.

8—If more than one finish coat is applied, scuff-sand between coats with 6/0 paper, dry.

9—If desired, finished surface can be rubbed down with any type of rubbing compound. Many workers use a sprayed-on coat of clear lacquer thinner as a means of obtaining a smooth surface with uniform gloss.

The combined primer-surfacer and putty coat is now ready for sanding. Use wet-or-dry paper with water as a lubricant. Start with 3/0 grit and finish off with 5/0 or 6/0 (180 or 220-grit). Clean off the slush with a soft rag, and then decide whether it is smooth enough for top coats or whether it needs another coat of primer-surfacer. If the machine is a lathe or other tool apt to come in contact with oil, be satisfied with nothing less than a perfectly smooth surface. As many as five coats of surfacer may be needed to smooth up a pebbly or pitted cast-iron surface, sanding each coat until the bare metal shows in the high spots. This is not hard work since the surfacer sands easily and does not clog the paper. If several coats of surfacer are required, it is a good idea to use two different colors. By this method, low spots in the surface are detected instantly. Partial coats directed at a particularly bad spot can be applied and are easily feathered out by sanding. Always use a backing block when sanding; hand backing is useless for building a level surface.

Before applying the finish paint, make certain that there are no breaks to bare metal in the primer-surfacer coat. With a good foundation, one coat of lacquer will do for the finish. If a second coat of lacquer is to be applied, scuff-sand the first coat with 5/0 paper, wet or dry. If you are using synthetic, the first coat should be sanded thoroughly since this product does not "melt" and combine with succeeding coats.

Most tools will require a certain amount of masking if painted with a spray gun, Figs. 3 and 5. The product commonly used for this is masking tape, although old newspapers will do in some places. Large areas of polished metal, such as tables, can be protected by masking compound if desired. However, it is usually quite easy to protect these surfaces by proper manipulation of the gun. Best results are obtained by partially dismantling the tool, removing bright metal where possible, and breaking the paint job into several separate pieces.

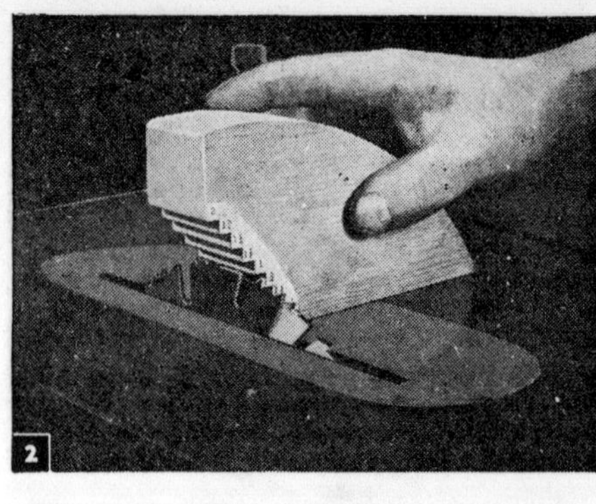

POWER-TOOL

1—When making duplicate angle cuts keep the miter gauge set at 90 deg. and use angle blocks to guide the stock. This saves much time in production work, especially where the angles vary from lot to lot

2—It's easy to get the correct depth of cut when you have a stepped depth gauge. Each step is simply a rabbet cut in the sloping face of a hardwood block

3—If you are making a number of duplicate ripping cuts in thin stock it's a good idea to fit an anti-kick-back pawl on the rip fence. File a serrated edge on a length of ⅛ x ½-in. flat iron and bolt to the fence with a spacer between. Pawl should be free to rise as the end of the work passes underneath it

4—Pattern sawing is easy to do if you clamp a wood guide piece to the saw fence at such a height that the work will slide under it. Outer surface of the blade should be flush with the face of the wood guide

5—Tenoning goes much faster with a jig that rides in the table groove and supports the work in a vertical position. Two saw blades are placed on the arbor with a spacer between equal to the width of the tenon. In this way you can make the cuts in one pass

6—Improvised clamps attached to a crosscut guide enable you to make some unusual cuts on the shaper. Here's a safe way of holding a disk for cutting flutes around the edge. It's a handy jig for making decorative rosettes of the type having a molded edge

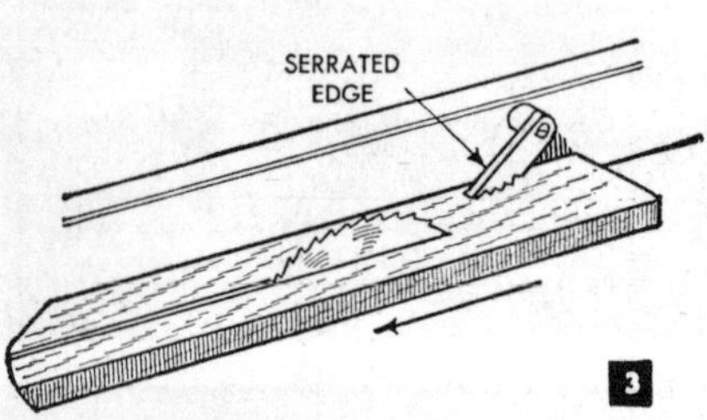

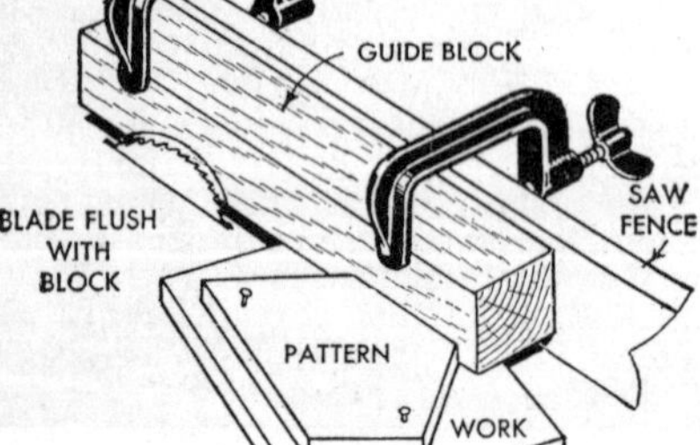

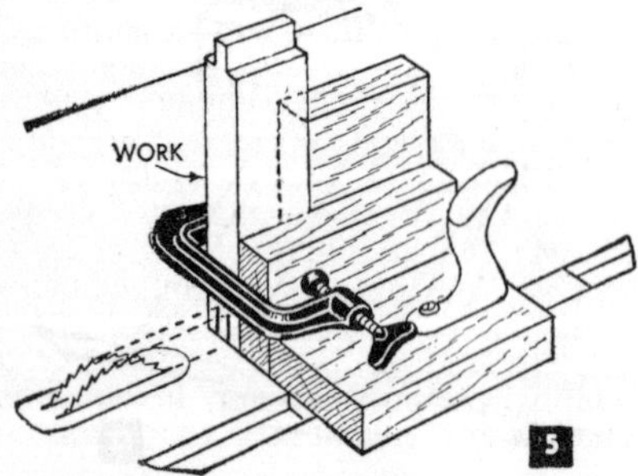

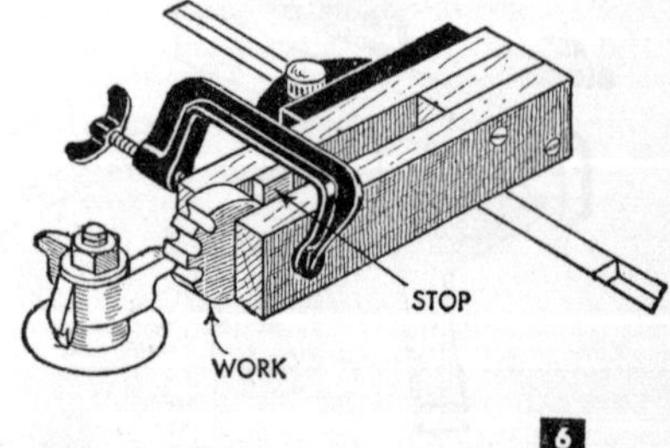

7

8

SHORT CUTS

7—To square large pieces of hard-pressed board on the circular saw, clamp a straightedge to the work so that it projects over one edge and rides against the ripping fence, thus acting as a guide for the squaring cut. Repeat the operation on the four edges

8—A good serviceable hold-down for small pieces can be made from a broken C-clamp. Use the screw part of the clamp as shown and weld a threaded section of rod to it so that it will screw into the crosscut guide in a hole already drilled and tapped for it

9—Another clamp, which is simply a wood cam operated by a handle, can be attached to the crosscut guide by means of a bolt and metal angle. The clamp is handy on shaper when cutting across the grain

10—For sanding small duplicate parts in the lathe make a quick-acting chuck by fitting a length of rubber hose into a turned wood holder. It is not necessary to stop the lathe when changing work

11—A "right-left" miter gauge is a real timesaver for you can miter both ends of a single piece without changing the gauge. The drawing shows how to make it and how it works. Use hardwood for all the parts

12—Ripping duplicate narrow strips on the circular saw is a ticklish business. It can be dangerous, too, unless you take proper precautions. Of course, any careful workman will use a push stick, but another and faster way is to screw a block to the crosscut guide and let it push the strip safely past the saw blade

9

10

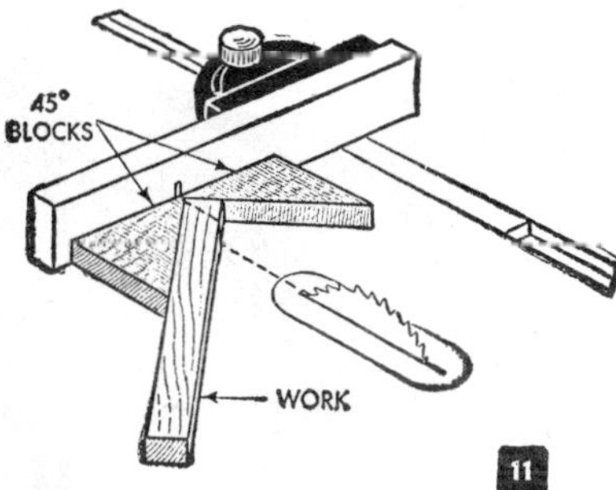

11

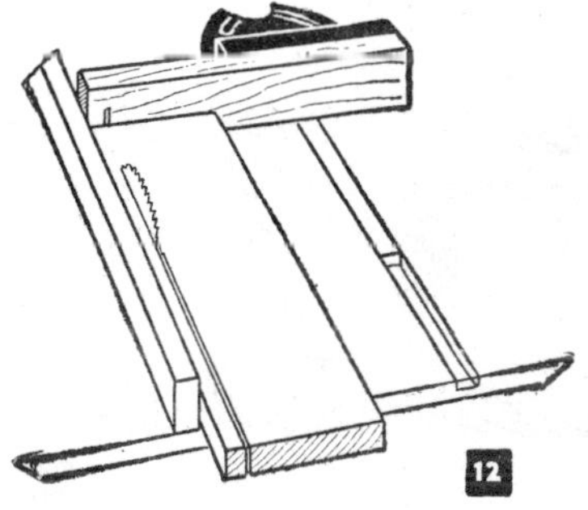

12

13—A screen-door closer of the snap-action "over-center" type makes a good hold-down when cutting thin stock on the circular saw. It prevents the stock being lifted by the blade and thrown forward and also aids in holding material firmly against the fence

14—This same type of door closer also will serve as a hold-down when molding straight work on the shaper. Moreover, it bears right at the point where you ordinarily have to place your fingers when the shaper cutter is working on the lower corner of the stock

15—Mount a sandpaper disk and another of ⅛-in. plywood on the shaper spindle with a spacer between and you have a good setup for rounding corners. As wood disk guides stock it should be smaller than the sandpaper disk. Wear goggles for this operation

16—A high-speed hand grinder clamped to the jigsaw blade guide gives you a router suitable for light routing and veining operations. The guide gives the necessary depth adjustment. On some operations it's better to move the work rather than the router

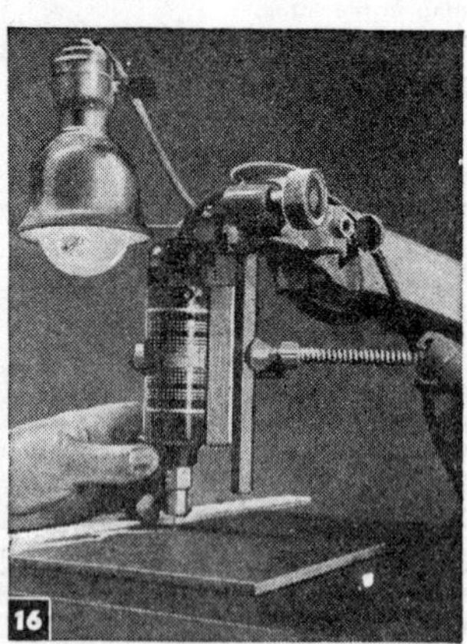

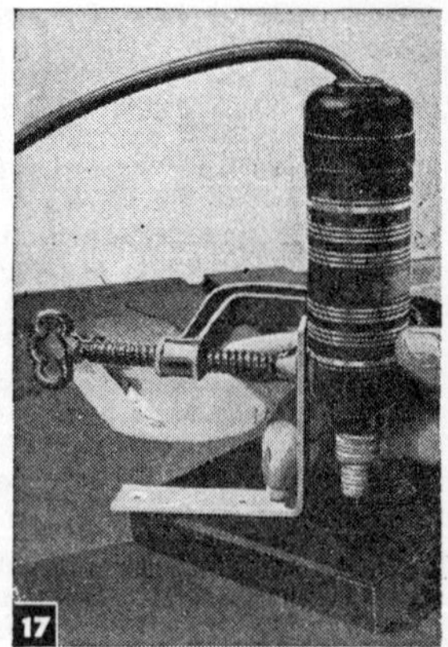

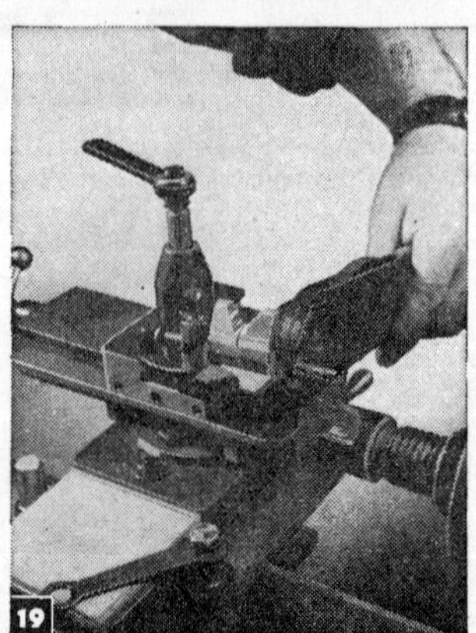

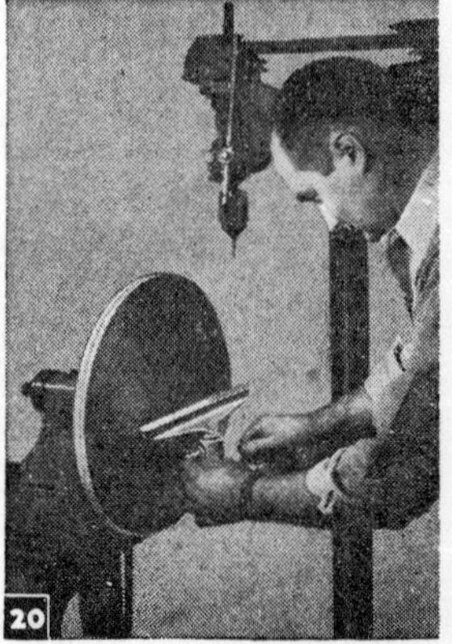

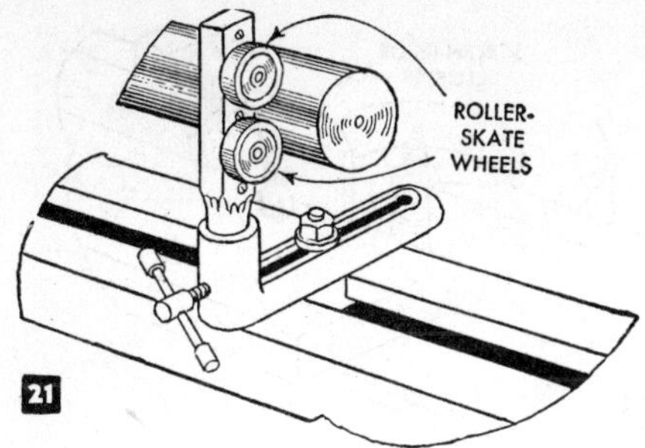

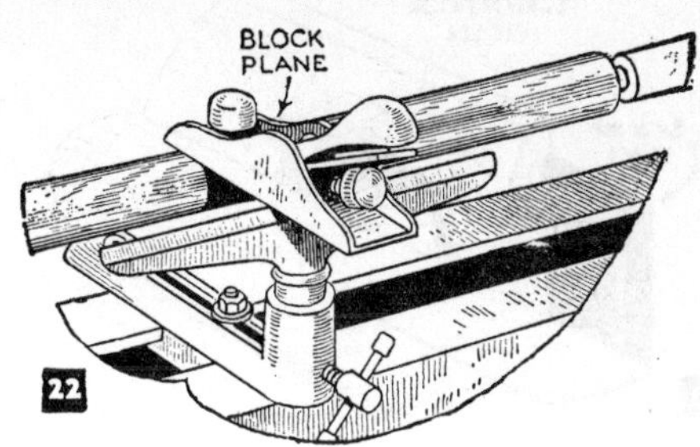

17—Using a metal corner brace, a small C-clamp and a hand grinder you can quickly improvise a high-speed router that can be guided anywhere over the surface of the work. It's especially suitable for cutting shallow recesses for inlay designs of irregular shape

18—The problem of supporting small turning squares in a steady rest is overcome by cutting several plywood disks which slip over the square as shown. Supported in this way the work rides smoothly in the rest. It's easy to make disks for different sized squares

19—A pattern knife, for pattern turning in the lathe, can be made up easily by sliding several shaper cutters over a bolt. Supported in a slide rest, the cutting edges are fed slowly into the work with the cross-feed. Work should be rotated at high speed

20—When you have to turn large-diameter work on the outer end of the lathe spindle, there's no use bothering to construct a makeshift tool rest if you have a floor drill press. Just bolt the lathe tool rest to the drill-press table and you have a solid support for the turning tool with universal adjustments

21—A rolling back rest is usually necessary when turning long spindles in the wood lathe. Two discarded roller-skate wheels bolted to a short length of hardwood will do the trick. Support this improvised rolling rest in the regular tool-rest holder as shown

22—If you require a fine finish on cylindrical turnings, particularly if these are of softwood, try using a block plane as illustrated. Plane should be held at a slight angle with the axis of the work to obtain a shearing cut. It leaves a clear, glass-smooth finish

23—To rough-size a cylindrical turning to a given diameter, clamp two turning gouges between hardwood blocks with both cutting edges projecting the same distance. Then merely slide the block along the tool rest, which has been located parallel with work axis

24—You can check a number of diameters quickly with a single caliper if you first take time to make hardwood gauge blocks for each setting. These act as stops for each predetermined setting. Of course, settings should be carefully checked before using caliper

25—To lay out spiral turnings to almost any pitch an inked "wheel" taken from an ordinary typewriter eraser works fine. The wheel is fitted in a simple holder made from dowel rod. It is held freehand against the work which is supported between centers in the lathe and rotated slowly by hand. Angle of the wheel with the work determines the pitch of the spiral

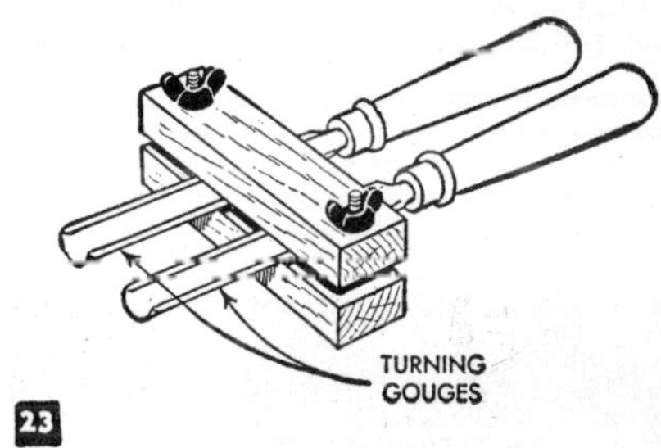

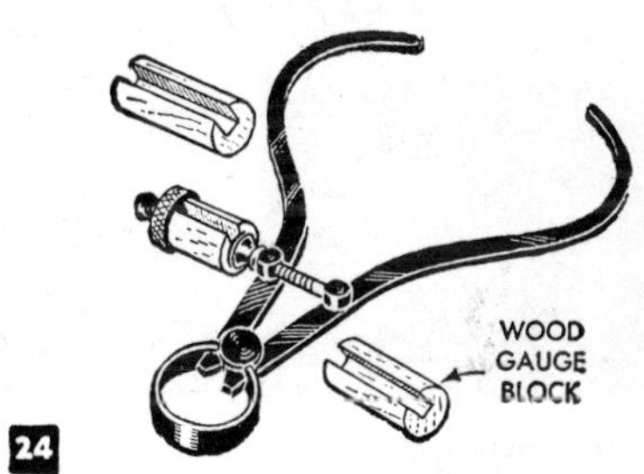

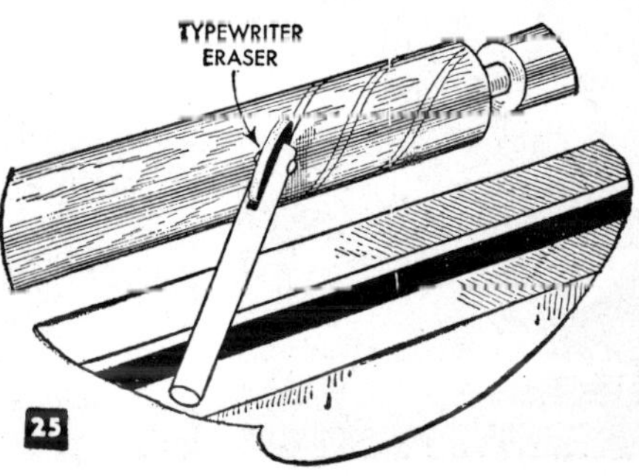